THOSE WHO CAME BEFORE

To the Superintendents of National Park Service installations in the Southwest, who diligently carry out the dictate to protect, preserve, and interpret their cultural resources for the understanding and enjoyment of the public.

THOSE WHO CAME BEFORE

SECOND EDITION

Robert H. Lister and Florence C. Lister

Foreword by Emil W. Haury

*Featuring photographs from the George A. Grant Collection
and a portfolio by David Muench*

SOUTHWEST PARKS & MONUMENTS ASSOCIATION
Tucson, Arizona

Editorial: T. J. Priehs, Sandra Scott
Design: Christina Watkins
Lithographed by Lorraine Press; vegetable ink on acid-free, recycled paper
Photography from the George Grant Collection courtesy
of the National Park Service

The Preservation of Our Cultural Heritage

Each year hundreds of archeological sites in the Southwest are vandalized to the detriment of our cultural heritage; to the detriment of what we might still learn. All prehistoric artifacts are irreplaceable and protected by Federal law. It is also important to understand that potsherds, arrowpoints and other artifacts can only add to our understanding of the past if left completely undisturbed in their original context.

If you discover artifacts, leave them in place and notify National Park Service personnel.

Cover photograph: White House Ruin, Canyon de Chelly National Monument.
DAVID MUENCH.

CONTENTS

Betatakin, Navajo National Monument. GEORGE A. GRANT, NATIONAL PARK SERVICE, 1935.

ILLUSTRATIONS

FOREWORD

The arid American Southwest rightfully boasts of more natural and man-made attractions than any comparable part of the New World. High among its many wondrous features is the treasury of ruins, mute testimony that many people before us found a bountiful haven in the land's embraces.

The spirits lingering in the abandoned hunting camps, and in the villages and towns of the more developed agricultural people, have an eloquence of their own—if we will only listen. How does one recapture the excitement permeating a hunting band that had just succeeded in bringing a mammoth to earth eleven thousand years ago, a feat accomplished with stone-tipped spears and the cunning and bravery of the hunters? That success could only be followed by gorging a hungry gut as long as the protein lasted and by giving thanks to the spirit of the animal whose life had been sacrificed. What of the ceremonied and joyful celebrations at summer's end among town dwellers giving thanks to the ruling spirits for a bountiful harvest and the assurance that hunger will be stayed through the winter? Who those people were, when they were here, and the kinds of lives they led are questions for the archeologist to decipher.

The value of these traces of the past as a part of our national heritage was recognized almost as early as were the incomparable natural wonders of Yellowstone's thermal displays and the glacially sculptured landscape of Yosemite, the former set aside as the world's first national park in 1872, and the latter in 1880. Casa Grande—the Big House—a four-story adobe building erected in the fourteenth century and today rising starkly above the desert brush, was first set aside in 1889, and the notable cliff dwellings of Mesa Verde were brought into the federal system in 1906. That year also saw the passage of the Federal Antiquities Act signaling the concern of Congress for the nation's archeological riches. Soon after, other units were chosen for protection. As a result of these actions, the Southwest boasts more archeological national parks and monuments than the rest of the country. In addition, each of the places set aside for its natural wonders, such as Grand Canyon National Park, has its own wealth of ruins and a human story to tell.

Collectively these places are silent reminders of how Native Americans developed from camp to village to town dwellers, how the arid lands were tamed and made to produce by applying various irrigation and ingenious water-control techniques. Those were largely inspired by the possession of maize, a precious grain that truly "built a hemisphere." All of this spanned many millennia. In the sixteenth century came the *conquistadores* who opened to the western world what had been until then the isolated homeland of the American Indian.

This saga, magnificently preserved in a great variety of ruins, has captivated the popular and the scientific mind for a hundred years. It has been told and retold in fragments and, all too often, in the bewildering and technical prose of the archeologist deemed essential to satisfy the critical eyes of peers.

I have long contended that unless professional archeologists are willing to share the excitement of their findings popularly, they are not fulfilling their potential as discoverers of new truths. The rewards of doing that—or not doing that—are reflected by the often unreceptive or even antagonistic attitudes expressed by laymen or by elected officials. This broader responsibility of the investigator was admirably expressed by nineteenth-century naturalist Elliot Coues (*Elliot Coues: Naturalist and Frontier Historian* by Paul Russell Cutright and Michael Broadhead) when he stated that the popularizer is ". . . an office of not less dignity than that of the systematist or the monographer . . . and one not so easy to fill creditably as those who have never tried to do so might imagine. The increase in knowledge is one thing, and its diffusion another; but the latter is the real measure of the usefulness of the former."

Sensing the need for a book broadly covering the story of Southwest archeology, the Southwest Parks and Monuments Association approached Robert and Florence Lister. One has difficulty imagining a more eminently qualified team to undertake this work. Dr. Robert H. Lister held some of the most prestigious positions in Southwest archeology, including chairman of the Department of Anthropology at the University of Colorado, director of the Archaeological Research Center at Mesa Verde National Park, participant in the University of Utah Glen Canyon Archeological Project, and president of the Society for American Archaeology. His tenures as chief archeologist for the National Park Service and director of the Chaco Center speak to his qualifications for addressing our cultural heritage as preserved in the national parks.

Florence C. Lister has been involved in extensive ceramic research in the Southwest and North Africa, but most recently has specialized in Spanish colonial period maiolica pottery.

Their joint contribution is impressive not only because it has greatly increased our scientific knowledge, but also because they have accepted the responsibility of making that knowledge available to a wide audience. Books such as *Chaco Canyon: Archaeology* and *Archaeologists and Earl Morris & Southwestern Archaeology*, along with this volume, recognize that commitment.

This broad experience has allowed them to expand on the traditional approach of discussing the differences between southwestern prehistoric cultures. Rather, the emphasis is on the similarities of these traditions, on how they interacted and influenced each other. This "pan-southwest interpretation" invites a holistic view of the story.

The old houses and the lands they were built on, the pots and pans, and the myriad tools used by prehistoric peoples are the grist the archeologist must start with in restructuring the life of past societies. Little wonder that the material side of cultures, the artifacts, receive so much attention. They are, after all, the tangible measures of levels of achievements and the substance for working out chronologies and relationships with neighbors. But translating the hardware of culture to the essence of life, the economic, political, and social natures of people, has always confronted the archeologist with a need which has been met with varying degrees of success. I think it is fair to say that this book goes a long way toward breathing life into the dusty record of the past.

It is fitting that this book should address those priceless ruins now protected and interpreted by the National Park Service, steward of the most impressive archeological resources in the Southwest. Lest the reader gain the idea that the inventory of places mentioned encompasses most of the Southwest's ruins, it should be said that for every major site under National Park Service protection, many others exist that are worthy of that care as well. And hundreds more large and significant sites merit state, county, and city protection. Surprisingly, beyond those, there are thousands of vestiges of human activity that together echo the rich, long story of the past here.

It is little wonder then that the Southwest for so long has attracted the world's attention and has become the proving ground for budding archeologists. It was the most fertile and accessible place to go. Whether hired as shovel hands in early expeditions or later as students in numerous university-sponsored field schools, people who have trained here and gone on to gain professional prominence comprise a long list. Their contributions and those of others is the story the Listers have excerpted and condensed for us. It is a story of those who came before, seeking knowledge about man's relationship to this awesome landscape.

This volume is evidence of Bob and Florence Lister's skills in bringing the people and places of the past alive. They favor us by having made a profession of archeology and, in their own way, by making an art out of their profession.

Emil W. Haury, 1904–1992
November 1982

Hohokam pottery plate, Colonial Period. HELGA TEIWES, ARIZONA STATE MUSEUM, UNIVERSITY OF ARIZONA.

PREFACE

Thousands of clues of ancient human activity in the southwestern United States have survived to the present because of a combination of factors. Often left in localities uninviting to modern development, covered deeply by soil and rocks, and residing in a dry climate, the remains have had nature itself as a prime preserver. Also, since President Theodore Roosevelt's administration, credit for the preservation of many of these unique areas goes to a farsighted federal government. Since 1916 the National Park Service has been given this specific responsibility.

Thirty-seven existing or proposed federal areas in Arizona, New Mexico, Utah, and Colorado were devoted to various facets of the archeological record. Where necessary, stabilization programs and continuous maintenance have halted further collapse of the ruins. In addition to making these resources more accessible, continued research has been encouraged in many government parks and monuments to assure an accurate, complete interpretive background for visitors.

Equally, or in some instances more important in documenting the annals of man in prehistoric and early historic times, are the thousands of ruins not included within the national parks. Most of these have been reconnoitered, some have been excavated, and findings from them are as significant as those made within federal preserves. Fortunately, some of the more valuable of these have come under the care and protection of state and local entities and may be examined by the public. This account, however, focuses upon the National Park areas because in them most facets of southwestern archeology are represented in readily accessible localities complete with interpretive personnel, explanatory visitor-center exhibits, and facilities to further the enjoyment and education of hundreds of thousands of people who annually visit the parks.

Circumstances arising from the nature of the archeological remains and their state of preservation, their suitability for exhibition to the public, and events related to their discovery, investigation, and inclusion in the national park system have resulted in an uneven representation of the total spectrum of southwestern prehistory in the parks and monuments. Twenty areas on the Colorado Plateau feature ruins of the Anasazi. Remains of the Hohokam of the Arizona deserts are present in three monuments. Fremont antiquities are found primarily in six facilities. Mogollon materials may be seen in only three facilities in the mountainous region along the south-central Arizona–New Mexico border. Blendings of several cultures are included in twelve installations. A few areas display ruins of two or more cultural developments. Known Paleo-Indian remains are in or near two monuments.

This book is a review of southwestern prehistory, as it is interpreted by archeologists, and a correlation of the regionally designated cultural variants into an interrelated whole. The latter emphasizes the similarities and affinity of all ancient southwestern peoples, shows their dependence upon advanced cultures in Mesoamerica for many basic ingredients, and notes environmentally conditioned regional differences. The account focuses on historical events leading to the exploration, excavation, and interpretation of the antiquities of the public areas. Highlighted are their significance in prehistoric cultural achievement and their particular contributions to a rich panorama of life still partially observable among the modern Tohono O'odham, Mohave, Maricopa, Yavapai, Hualapai, Havasupai, and Pueblo Indians of Arizona and New Mexico. Relations are noted between these southwestern old-timers and the Navajo and Apache newcomers.

In gathering the data for this presentation we have relied upon firsthand knowledge of the Southwest and each of the areas considered. Also, we have drawn upon the works of many scholars who have contributed to our understanding of the archeology of the greater Southwest and particularly their reports upon investigations in National Park Service areas. To those individuals we owe a great deal and acknowledge to them our gratitude and sincere appreciation.

For our brief review of southwestern archeology and our formulation of an integrated scheme of the events of prehistory, we have basically followed the terminology and cultural sequences employed in the Southwest volume of the *Handbook of North American Indians* published by the Smithsonian Institution.

Many of our former associates in the National Park Service made our task easier and enjoyable. The regional directors of the Southwest, Western, and Rocky Mountain regions, and the general superintendents of the Navajo Lands and Southern Arizona groups facilitated our visits to the parks, and members of their staffs assisted us in many ways. We profited from discussions with many Park superintendents and their interpretive personnel. Especially helpful in providing information, unpublished data, or logistical support were Adrienne Anderson, regional archeologist, Rocky Mountain Region; Bruce Anderson, archeologist, Southwest Region; Superintendent Robert Heyder and Archeologist Jack Smith of Mesa Verde National Park; James Truesdale, archeologist, Dinosaur National Monument; Matthew Schmader, archeologist, Rio Grande Consultants; and Archeologists Keith Anderson, George Cattanach, Don Morris, Trinkle Jones, and Adrianne G. Rankin of the Western Archeological and Conservation Center. To all of the above we express our thanks.

Finally, we acknowledge that the concept of this volume was conceived by Earl Jackson, former executive director of the Southwest Parks and Monuments Association, who encouraged us to undertake its preparation. His successor, T. J. Priehs, has provided us stimulation, advice, and constructive criticism throughout our writing, and his staff and consultants have furnished secretarial and editorial assistance and designed the book. The Board of Directors of Southwest Parks and Monuments Association made the book a reality by approving its publication.

The suggested readings following each national park area discussed in no way reflect the many items consulted by the authors but are a list of some accessible works to which inquiring readers may turn for additional discussions and more detailed accounts.

My late husband and senior author of the original text of this book felt a revision was in order because of further research, the addition to the National Park Service system of southwestern monuments containing archeological resources, and the need to include additional facilities in order to expand the prehistoric story. An ardent supporter of the park service goals of preserving, protecting, and interpreting antiquities on federal lands for the benefit of the American public, Robert H. Lister was an occasional member of the team as an employee, collaborator, or advisor. He joined the National Park Service ranks as a ranger-archeologist just out of college in 1938 and retired forty years later after having served as chief archeologist. During that time, he personally was involved with work in seven of the monuments included in this book, in several instances for many years. He was especially proud of receiving the Emil W. Haury Award by Southwest Parks and Monuments Association, given in recognition of his contributions to scientific research in the national parks and monuments of the Southwest.

My efforts to meet Bob's desire for this revision are a small tribute to his enthusiasm, energy, and insight.

To Robert H. Lister, 1915–1990

Florence C. Lister
Mancos, Colorado
October 1992

Robert Lister in the field at Chaco Culture National Historical Park, New Mexico, 1972.

THE SETTING

The American Southwest incorporates notable extremes in contour, climate, and natural resources that have led to its division into four main geographical entities. The Southwest's variable geography inevitably placed limits on human use of each area which necessitated different cultural adaptations.

The northernmost province, the southern Rocky Mountains of central Colorado and north-central New Mexico, was of least importance to the southwestern Indians because of long, frigid winters and lack of arable soil. Only occasional hunting parties roamed through the region in search of game.

South of the Rockies is the Colorado Plateau, encompassing western Colorado, southeast Utah, northern Arizona, and northwest New Mexico. In its lower elevations it is a formidable, though beautiful, landscape of canyons sliced deeply through colorful sandstone, flat mesas rising abruptly above broad valleys, little fertile soil, and only one perennial river system—the Colorado and its northern tributaries. There are cool, moist mountains with pine and fir forests, and uplands with mixed stands of juniper and pinyon. Patches of grass and scrub brush dot the lower mesas. Most of the province has a long, dry, warm summer broken by localized thunderstorms that tear at the thin soil. Winters are cold with considerable snow. Even with so many apparent drawbacks, the Plateau offered a suitable habitat for a dense, aboriginal farming population. In some parts of the region these folk adapted and survived in greater numbers than anywhere else in the Southwest. In others, thoughtless destruction of timber and other resources caused disastrous erosion, stream entrenchment, and their own ultimate downfall.

The Basin and Range province within the United States includes southern Arizona and New Mexico. Here are basins interrupted by steep, jagged mountains of igneous and metamorphic rocks whose higher reaches are temperate and forested. Most streams are intermittent, but the Rio Grande usually flows year-round. The Gila and Salt and some of their tributaries were permanent rivers in the past. Interior drainage basins are common. The extensive desert lands have protracted, withering summers, though punctuated by violent downpours. These slowly yield to mild winters with little rain. Thorny shrubs, cacti, and drought-resistant trees, such as mesquite, are abundant. Surprisingly, man learned to cope with this hostile environment so successfully that he stayed in impressive numbers for centuries.

The southwestern corner of the High Plains province penetrates into eastern New Mexico and west Texas and is bisected by the Pecos River valley. Its broad grasslands once attracted herds of large mammals which, in turn, brought ancient hunters. When the animals disappeared, the hunters left the High Plains, and the region became a buffer zone between the farmers of the Colorado Plateau and the nomads and later villagers of the Plains.

Extremely significant to the prehistoric cultural development of the American Southwest was northern Mexico. The Sierra Madre Occidental, rising from the central

Mexican plateau and the narrow littoral along the Sea of Cortez, includes some of the most rugged terrain in North America. Though potentially a barrier, it has natural north-south corridors through which repeated cultural impulses were transmitted from Mesoamerica north to the distant borderland societies. Had the topography in this intermediate area between central Mexico and the American Southwest been different, cultural attainments of the northerners would surely have been fewer.

THE PREHISTORY

The Paleo-Indian Period

Between about 9500 and 9000 B.C. the Southwest experienced slightly greater moisture and lower temperatures than at present. These environmental factors favored the spread of lush grasslands, which attracted herds of large grazing animals such as mammoths, camels, horses, and bison. In turn, they lured Paleo-Indian hunters, who apparently drifted westward from the mid-continent prairies. Because they roamed over terrain that is now eastern New Mexico, these first southwestern big-game hunters have been named Clovis, after remains found near the town of Clovis.

Clovis culture appeared during a brief time when the mammoth, an extinct elephant, was the preferred prey of the Paleo-Indian. Consistently in archeological finds the remains of one or more mammoths are associated with a group of implements that invariably includes a characteristic fluted point and several kinds of knives fashioned from flakes of stone. The long, leaf-shaped Clovis points, with rudimentary flakes struck from their sides, once tipped spears that were used in dispatching the huge beasts. The knives were then used to butcher them. The inequalities in size and strength between the men and their quarry were partially compensated for by use of a notched throwing stick, known as an atlatl, that provided extra leverage in propelling the spear. Sites yielding Clovis artifacts reveal additional human ingenuity. Generally, they are on formerly boggy pond or lake shores or stream banks where a heavy animal would have been inescapably mired. Skinning the animal, dismembering the carcass, and cutting the flesh from the bones took place at the kill spot. After disposing of the meat, the Clovis drifted on to encounters with other game. Apparently, they gradually established themselves in certain territories to which they returned seasonally year after year. Other than their basic quest for food, their tools, and a presumed informal small band organization, nothing is known about the Clovis people. By approximately 8500 B.C. unfavorable environmental conditions in the western Southwest had doomed the grazing animals, except the bison. Consequently, their pursuers slowly retreated eastward to happier hunting grounds.

As the scope of Pleistocene research widens, it is possible that a pre-Clovis complex of Paleo-Indian hunters may be identified. If so, the arrival of humans in the Southwest will be pushed back thousands of years. A number of suggestive finds of this sort have been made, such as one in a cave near El Paso, Texas. Thus far, lingering questions about stratigraphy, artifact associations, and dating have made cautious researchers slow to accept their authenticity.

Clovis hunters were succeeded by others following the same general mobile life, stalking the surviving bison. These now are identified as Folsom because in 1926 a site near Folsom, New Mexico, was found to have their distinctive fluted points and other stone tools in direct association with bones of bison that had become extinct some time between about 6000 and 5000 B.C. Subsequently, Folsom hunters appear to have specialized

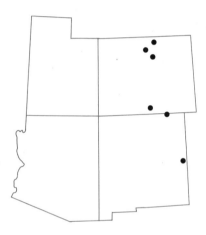

Paleo-Indian sites

in maiming or dispatching the bison in cul-de-sacs or stampeding them over precipices.

After Folsom times, the final era of Paleo-Indian hunters on the southwestern plains is marked by a limited initial occupation by a group called Cody, which substantially expanded in New Mexico and southern Colorado between 6500 and 6000 B.C. Perhaps this was because herds of buffalo and those who hunted them had moved back into the area from the eastern plains in response to a temporary increase in moisture. Most diagnostic of the Cody tools were finely chipped, parallel-edged or lanceolate points. Frequently these had an indented stem.

Triangular knives usually stemmed on one side occur along with other large stone knives, choppers, scrapers, hammerstones, drills, engraving tools, grooved abrading stones, and antler flaking implements. Cody sites usually were located near water and land suitable for the grazing bison. Three kinds of areas have been identified: base camps, where one or more bands gathered periodically; work areas, where groups of hunters apparently flaked projectile points while waiting for game; and processing stations, where slain animals were butchered and hides were processed. The diversity of sites and even greater variety of tools suggest technological advancements to meet the needs of more specialized activities.

The Archaic Period

Beginning about 7000 B.C., perhaps earlier, foraging people that archeologists call Archaic filtered into the Southwest from the west, north, and south to occupy territories abandoned by the hunters. They first appeared in western Arizona and gradually drifted eastward. Although in some areas the foragers and hunters may have been contemporaneous, no evidence exists at present for any direct relationship between them.

The new arrivals exploited such a wide variety of local resources that they were able to utilize regions ranging from broken canyonlands to deserts that had been unimportant to the Paleo-Indians. Although they moved with the seasons to take full advantage of water and certain foods, in some cases the Archaic people sustained themselves long enough in one locality to erect rudimentary shelters. At first these were merely stone-walled "sleeping circles" in work camps. Later, huts or windbreaks may have been erected, and are suggested by shallow circular depressions outlined with postholes. Storage pits for excess foods and cooking pits with fire-cracked rocks occur at a few late Archaic locations.

While stone projectile points had to be continuously manufactured to take small game, fiber snares and nets served to capture birds and rodents. Most important to Archaic survival, however, was an emphasis on simple stone chopping, scraping, cutting, and milling implements used to process fibers, roots, tubers, and seeds. As time passed, the inventory of material goods expanded to include stone, bone, shell, baskets, textiles, cords, and sandals.

The first identified complex of Archaic traits in the Southwest was termed the Cochise by archeologists because of its concentration in and about Cochise County in southeastern Arizona. Its earliest occurrence seems to have centered there, but later

Clovis and Folsom points. TOM MASAMORI, COURTESY OF THE COLORADO HISTORICAL SOCIETY.

followers of this long-lived tradition spread as far afield as northeast Arizona and the Glen Canyon area of the Colorado River, central New Mexico, and southern Chihuahua. Recently, a distinct Archaic pattern called the Oshara has been recognized in parts of the northern Southwest. Still farther north and toward the Great Basin the Archaic horizon is identified as the Desert Culture.

So successful was their adjustment to the varied and often inhospitable environment that the Archaic population swelled over the centuries until hundreds of sites were littered extensively with debris from long occupation. The similarity of cultural remains from different parts of the Southwest testifies to some sort of social intercourse between Archaic bands, likely composed of small groups of related individuals.

Thus, with these beginning steps, by about 2000 B.C. the cultural complexity that was to underlie later developments in the Southwest essentially had been achieved.

Agricultural Beginnings

In the Southwest excavated archeological sites dating between 2000 B.C. and A.D. 500 are spread from northern Chihuahua, Mexico, to southern Colorado and Utah. The small, widely dispersed family groups of nomadic hunters and gatherers were, almost imperceptibly, undergoing a significant modification to an infinitely more complex, sedentary village existence. Such fundamental re-orientation was made possible by the slow diffusing of agriculture, social attitudes, and certain technologies from Mexico. Of these, agriculture was of the most immediate consequence.

The plant that was to become a staple was corn. Corn, or maize, is believed to have evolved from teosinte, a wild grass found in many parts of Mexico. Tiny cobs of an early variety of corn dated approximately 5000 B.C. have been unearthed from dry caves in the Tehuacán valley of central Mexico. But another fifteen hundred years passed before this corn was being purposefully cultivated there. By that time squash, beans, gourds, chili peppers, avocados, and amaranth were to be found in gardens. Through steadily improved growing methods, selective planting, and cross breeding, larger, more nutritional corn was grown at Tehuacán by 1500 B.C. It probably grew in similar, as yet unstudied, ecological pockets tucked away in Mexico's highlands. Corn's importance soon was so great that a mystical regard for its life-sustaining properties made it an object of worship.

Even before improvement of the strain, the vital plant and knowledge of its propagation gradually passed from tribe to tribe up the Mexican northern cordillera into the Southwest. Squash seems to have spread to the north along with early corn. Beans, the third of the domesticated plants that were to become the foundation of southwestern Indian agriculture, did not appear there for many centuries.

Although primitive corn and squash may have reached some parts of the Southwest as early as late Archaic times, they did not appear in any important quantities until after 2000 B.C. Even then and for the next fifteen hundred years, when Mexican cultures began to flourish, these humble domesticated plants had little impact. The possibilities of agriculture were lost upon foragers still in tune with Archaic ways. The introduced plants were casually grown in irregular patches, given little attention while the group engaged in summer hunting and gathering activities; in autumn they were harvested like native crops. Their survival and naturalization were minor miracles. Yields from stunted plants must have been minimal, variable from year to year, and surely insufficient for surplus. As years, even centuries, progressed, the basic diet of wild products remained unaltered though occasionally supplemented by small quantities of homegrown corn, squash, and beans. Nevertheless, the notion of planting and reaping nature's bounty became a fixed, though unexploited, aspect of regional life. Tending the crops would surely follow as agriculture eventually came into its own.

The soil-based revolution occurred in the Southwest after 500 B.C. And revolution it was, because a new cultural intricacy had arrived through converging influences from Mesoamerica, the Great Basin, the California coast, and the Plains. Increased dependence upon agriculture entailed more permanent residences. Pole, brush, and mud habitations soon nestled, partially concealed, in the earth. Communities of such structures arose for distinct purposes such as working, worshipping, sleeping, and hoarding. All the inherent social controls that came with such togetherness were instituted. Leisure time that could be devoted to tasks unrelated to food production or preparation promoted the adoption and perfection of new technologies. Some offered opportunity for aesthetic expression. Pottery making was one of these. Hunting was done by the bow and arrow, which replaced the cumbersome atlatl and spear. There was a heightened appreciation for cooperative, organized labor to increase chances of success. The overriding power of supernatural forces, which seemingly determined the fate of a farmer's crop, was magnified and dramatized. Tomorrow became equally important as today, as times of fallow fields, inclement weather, or natural disaster required stockpiled surpluses. The population expanded or diminished in direct relation to the size of such stores.

What caused the shift from exploitation of environmental diversity to the concentration on a few crop plants? One reason could have been Mexican colonists who had made the transition to village-dwelling irrigation farming farther to the south and had attained an elaborate material and social life. They may have pushed into the Gila and Salt river valleys, absorbing or replacing the local Archaic peoples and influencing others beyond their occupied territory. The hunter-gatherers could have been more gradually transformed by adaptation of southern domestic plants to local environments. Continued introduction of more nutritious strains of corn would have encouraged their greater use. Also, expanding population or a period of deteriorating climate could have pushed some groups into places with such limited wild resources that farming was the only alternative. Whatever the cause, or combination of causes, by A.D. 500 the distinctive Southwest Tradition had emerged in rudimentary form.

The Southwest Tradition

A century of research in what is now regarded as the Southwest Tradition has involved surface examination of thousands of ruins and excavation of hundreds. Material and human residue have been painstakingly identified, diagnosed, measured, compared, and subjected to innumerable physical tests. Living native peoples have been consulted to learn answers about probable social, economic, and religious attributes of their possible ancestors. From all this effort has come the realization that the ancient cultures which arose in the Southwest slightly before or at the beginning of the Christian Era were as varied as their physical settings, even though they shared common Archaic roots. However, the recognition of such dissimilarity and the varying degree of Mexican stimulus partly responsible for it was slow in coming.

Because of their proximity to regions where the earliest, most intense Spanish, Mexican, and American penetration occurred, the large abandoned structures slowly crumbling on the crests and in the faces of the northern mesas were, predictably, the first focus of major archeological interest. The San Juan drainage is the lodestone, and it has thus followed that, for many years, southwestern prehistory was thought to be exclusively the ancient history of Pueblo Indians who lived there. As late as 1927, when a master taxonomic chronology known as the Pecos Classification was accepted by all researchers working in the area, it was rationalized that, despite some puzzling regional differences, what had happened in the northern half of the Southwest also had taken place in the south. To most scholars of the time, ancient southwesterners were ancestral Pueblo Indians regardless of whether they had lived their lives amid the cacti or the pinyons. According to the nomenclature adopted by archeologists meeting at Pecos, New Mexico, in 1927, one could be part of culture stages Basket Maker I through III or Pueblo I through V, depending upon time of existence and level of cultural attainment. Later, one was simply called Anasazi rather than Basket Maker or Pueblo. To the Navajos, the Anasazi were the Old People who had preceded them into the nooks and crannies of the Four Corners region.

Physiographic features divide the Colorado Plateau into four natural provinces to which resident Anasazi made some distinctive adaptations. Archeologically, the San Juan basin is known as the Chaco district. Lands north of the San Juan River from its headwaters westward to the Colorado River comprise the Mesa Verde district. The area south of the San Juan River and west of the present New Mexico–Arizona border to the Colorado River is the Kayenta district. The Arizona Strip north of the Colorado River and southern Utah to Nevada is the Virgin River district, regarded by some researchers as a sub-branch of the Kayenta. While regionalizations of some cultural elements evolved among each of these entities, a basic Anasazi homogeneity remained.

As the ranks of Southwest prehistorians grew and more remains were exposed, it became clear that the Anasazi had had neighbors, some of whom probably could claim to be older. Foremost among the newly recognized people were the desert dwellers of southern Arizona called the Hohokam after a Tohono O'odham word meaning "all used up." Scientists separated this continuum of culture into Pioneer, Colonial, Sedentary, and Classic periods. Within a few years, another grouping was suggested, distinct from the Anasazi and the Hohokam. This complex was named Mogollon, after the rugged highlands along the Continental Divide extending down the New Mexico–Arizona borderlands and into northern Mexico where these antiquities were found. Once the validity of the Mogollon as a distinguishable entity was confirmed, its growth was expressed through a sequence of named or numbered periods.

The Anasazi, Hohokam, and Mogollon retained their identities, though they did not exist in total isolation from each other; some cultural fusion occurred at various times and places. Nor for long were they regarded as the three, sole components of the Southwest Tradition. Following World War II, accelerated research revealed many local deviations. Especially in the zone where the Colorado Plateau breaks down into the Colorado River valley and its adjacent low deserts did the variations become most complex. Among newly recognized groups were Sinagua, around Flagstaff, Arizona, and the upper Verde River; Cohonina, who lived south of the Grand Canyon; Cerbat, who resided along the Colorado River as it emerged from the confines of the Grand Canyon; Prescott, of the verdant elevations west of central Arizona; and Laquish, the riverine dwellers of the lower Colorado. Further studies indicated not only the interdependence and interrelationship of these westernmost peoples, but their coherence as a recognizable unit compatible with, but distinct from, the rest of their southwestern contemporaries. This cluster of regional variations became the Hakataya, a Yuman word for the Colorado River along which they spread. The Hakataya exhibited an unusual blending of traits liberally borrowed from all surrounding contributors.

Another localized development along the modern Arizona-Mexico border has been proposed by some archeologists. They interpret the evidence there as supporting the notion that the indigenous sedentary farmers who shared the simple agriculture and pithouse homes of the arid lowlanders were gradually metamorphosed into a separate group about A.D. 900. This distinction came through an infusion of Mesoamerican traits from the neighboring Hohokam, meagerly reinforced through time by sporadic trade with the south. The name O'otam was bestowed upon this marginal development in the belief that it represented the remote background of the modern Tohono O'odham (Pima-Papago) Indians, whose traditional range this region is.

Another enigmatic group was the Salado. They followed a basically Anasazi lifestyle, but somewhere along the way from the Little Colorado River area, where they may have originated, to the Salt River basin where they settled, the Salado had picked up some Mogollon cultural baggage. In Spanish *salado* means salty, a reference to their place of settlement. Through face-to-face trade, invasion, or more subtle diffusion, the Salado in turn appear to have influenced the nearby Hohokam during their Classic Period, from about A.D. 1300 to 1450.

At the opposite extremity of the Southwest, another regional variant was called the Fremont Culture because of its appearance on the Fremont River drainage of east-central Utah. Its lifeway was seen as another mixture of ideas and traits stemming from an Archaic base, superimposed with elements absorbed from Anasazi, Great Basin, or Plains people.

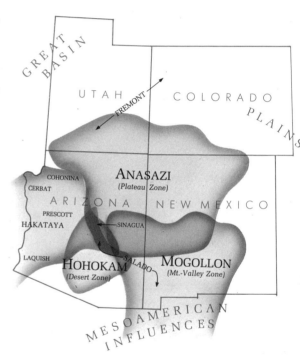

Southwest Tradition:
The overlapping of cultures in central Arizona resulted in various blendings.

THE HOHOKAM

The origins of the Hohokam culture in southern Arizona remain controversial. Perhaps as early as 300 B.C. the original stock from somewhere in the Mexican interior was tempted to migrate northward by the streams that then existed in the deserts and the flat, broad lands suitable for farming. Or over many centuries local Archaic peoples may gradually have adopted certain southern traits, such as farming, communal villages, and hand technologies, which ultimately changed their society completely.

In either case, the Hohokam responded to the challenge of their chosen homeland by evolving into the most skillful desert agriculturalists the aboriginal Southwest ever knew. Through stone implements, organized labor, and sheer human will, the Hohokam created an efficient, lengthy irrigation network from the Salt and Gila river systems to their farmlands that allowed them to survive in an extreme, arid environment against overwhelming odds. Before modern developments obliterated it, the system was so commonly encountered that white settlers in the region dubbed their predecessors the Canal Builders.

As craftsmen, the Hohokam demonstrated an engaging flair. Aided by the simplest tools, their facile hands artistically fashioned utilitarian, religious, and ornamental objects. Their talents were most uniquely revealed in the use of shell obtained by trade from the Gulf of California and the Pacific coast. The Hohokam created an impressive repertory of beads, pendants, rings, and bracelets. Forms were made from blanks by cutting and grinding that demanded a delicate touch because of the fragility of the shell. Geometric or animal shapes were etched or applied as mosaics to their jewelry. The resourceful Hohokam then became entrepreneurs in a thriving trade with their neighbors, the Mogollon and Anasazi.

Hohokam artistry was also displayed in two other, very different materials. Bowls and palettes, rectangular tablets on which paints were prepared, were carefully shaped from hard stone and then decorated with carved replicas of snakes, toads, lizards, birds, and even human stick figures. In clay, comparable skill and uniqueness were apparent. Their coiled pots were finished by use of a paddle to smooth and refine exteriors while an anvil held inside the vessel supported flexible walls. Lively Hohokam creativity expanded into buff utensils decorated with painted red designs, a style that remained characteristic throughout their culture. Figurines of clay, mostly of human females and likely derived from Mexico, probably functioned in fertility rites.

The precise fate of Hohokam culture remains obscure. Quite possibly the present-day Tohono O'odham are linked to that past. An apparent break in the cultural records occurs between the first half of the fifteenth century, when the Hohokam disappear as an archeologically identifiable unit, and the time bridging the sixteenth and seventeenth centuries, when the Spaniards arrived to find a native group of Pima-speaking irrigation farmers.

An idealized Hohokam chronology is divided into four periods. They are not uniform over the entire geographic area inhabited by the Hohokam, and numerous local variations existed.

Pioneer Period (300 B.C. to A.D. 550)

Previously unknown cultural traits appear to have been introduced by the rapid northern extension of a Mexican group that settled along the Salt and Gila rivers. Few, if any, conflicts arose with the native Archaic people because they exploited different zones of the arid landscape. Near their farmlands the newcomers built small, scattered settlements of pole, brush, and mud houses over shallow pits. Corn, beans, squash, and cotton were planted in the fields. Undoubtedly, the extensive canal system helped provide domestic water for the villagers, but wells were dug primarily for that purpose. Despite their expert farming abilities, the Hohokam continued to gather saguaro cactus fruit and mesquite beans that grew wild. They also hunted many desert animals to supplement their domestic foods.

Plain, but well-crafted, early pottery bowls and jars gradually were replaced by buff-colored vessels decorated with red designs. Crude human figurines were produced, along with ground and polished stone bowls, palettes, axes, and several kinds of shell ornaments. Metates and manos for pulverizing corn and beans were the basic tools. Troughed metates were neatly shaped by pecking on porous rock. A mano, or handstone, was pushed back and forth in the trough to grind dry plant foods. Small, chipped projectile points suggest use of the bow and arrow.

To the dismay of those interested in skeletal studies, Hohokam dead were cremated. Their ashes, unconsumed pieces of bone, and the damaged or destroyed funerary offerings of pottery or stone were buried in pits or trenches.

By the end of the Pioneer Period, the Hohokam had spread over a triangular area marked at its corners by present-day Phoenix and Tucson, and the junction of the Verde and Salt rivers.

Colonial Period (A.D. 550 to 900)

Consistent with its name, the Colonial Period was one of expansion. The Hohokam moved into tributaries of the Salt and Gila, up the Verde River valley to the vicinity of Flagstaff, west along the Agua Fria toward Prescott, into the San Pedro and Santa Cruz valleys of southeast Arizona, and east along the Gila to the vicinity of Safford. Many new traits and elaboration of existing artifacts, especially luxury items, suggest strong continuing contact with Mexico. In most respects, the Colonial Period was the climax of Hohokam culture.

Expansion probably was stimulated by improved farming methods, population growth, and increased ties with Mexico and other regions. Villages were larger and settlements more numerous. Among the new traits were notable architectural additions including the platform mound, a hard-surfaced, flat-topped elevation upon which ceremonial structures could be erected or rites performed. Ballcourts, elongated unroofed arenas excavated into the soil, were sites for ritualistic games. Both these constructions were obviously borrowed from Mesoamerica.

Hohokam pottery effigy jar, Sedentary Period. HELGA TEIWES, ARIZONA STATE MUSEUM, UNIVERSITY OF ARIZONA.

Irrigation canal systems were greatly extended, allowing more acres to be cultivated. Canals were cut narrower and deeper so that more water could be accommodated with less surface evaporation.

The designs of the typical red-on-buff pottery were repeated in bands encircling large plates and jars. Especially intriguing were lines of top-knotted quail, rows of dancers holding hands, and figures carrying burden baskets. Ceramic figurines were more lifelike, usually depicting the human female and often emphasizing sexual attributes. Bits of clay or paint representing clothing, headdresses, ornaments, and body tattoos were applied to the figurines.

During the Colonial Period a great deal of attention was paid to carving nonutilitarian objects. Sculptured stone bowls and effigies were decorated with a wide assortment of animal motifs. Archeologists have found buried caches of these objects, deliberately destroyed as if part of some ritual. The appearance of the mosaic plaque or mirror, made of thin, reflective iron pyrites, is further evidence of intercourse with Mesoamerica, where they were manufactured.

Sedentary Period (A.D. 900 to 1100)

During these two hundred years the Hohokam reduced their experimentation and elaboration in arts and crafts. It seems to have been a time of mass production rather than individual craftsmanship. The culture's territorial borders remained fairly stable, with one exception: an extension north and east of Flagstaff occurred about the time of the eruption of Sunset Crater in the A.D. 1060s, believed to have been due to soil improved by volcanic ash and cinders.

The most impressive architectural innovations involved ceremonial structures. Platform mounds were better constructed, and some underwent periodic refurbishing. Generally, settlement patterns changed little, although some houses were arranged around a plaza. Cremations continued, but some burials began during this period.

Large storage jars with the Gila shoulder, a sharp angle formed by the top and bottom parts of the vessel, prevailed. Small, thick-walled vessels, animal effigies, and footed forms also were made. Painted patterns on red-on-buff ceramics displayed complicated geometric panels with fringed lines and interlocking scrolls. Realistically modeled clay heads, with bodies presumably fashioned from perishable materials, represented the only humanlike forms.

Bowls and palettes of stone were less ornate, while mosaic plaques became more elaborate. Most of the Hohokam's creative energy went into working shell. Etching, a technique confined to this period, was introduced. Large concave shells were coated with pitch in geometric or animal designs and then immersed in a mild acid solution probably produced from the fermented fruits of the saguaro cactus. The acid dissolved the uncoated surfaces of the shell, leaving the areas protected by the pitch standing out in relief. Often the shell was then painted. The Hohokam also made trumpets by cutting off the spires of large conch shells.

Small copper bells, perhaps made along the west coast of Mexico, are first found in the Sedentary Period.

Classic Period (A.D. 1100 to 1450)

Once thought to represent the apex of Hohokam culture, researchers now view the Classic Period as one flooded with such great change that its cultural integrity was weakened. The archeological record reveals one major difference from the past: steady territorial contraction. The core area in the middle Gila-Salt valleys remained intact, but most frontier extensions were abandoned.

During this period some Hohokam tended to construct villages farther from rivers, necessitating more and longer canals. In a few areas it appears that dry lands, hillside terraces, and floodwater plains were also being farmed.

Classic communities were larger than Sedentary villages, but fewer sites were occupied. Although the Hohokam continued building houses of wood, brush, and mud over pits, a totally new architectural form appeared. This was a surface structure of contiguous clay-walled rooms, sometimes placed on top of a dirt mound contained by massive walls. Frequently, the walls were surrounded by a stockadelike clay or stone wall up to twenty feet high. Often the enclosures had no entry, so ladders must have been used to climb over the walls. Other compounds had a single portal for access. Within a compound, the randomly scattered houses in pits and the new clay-walled houses created a compact, crowded appearance. Early surface structures were of single stories, but later in the period multistoried buildings, such as the Casa Grande, came into vogue.

The purpose of the compound wall is not known, but defense is certainly suggested. The idea may have been adopted to segregate different segments of the population. It is unknown whether the Great Houses, resembling northern pueblos, represented a fourteenth-century intrusion of Anasazi or Mesoamerican architecture into Hohokam territory. They may have served as priestly houses, ceremonial edifices, observatories, communal storage facilities, or dwellings. Ballcourts continued to be associated with the villages.

In ceramics, the red-on-buff tradition still was followed, but, significantly, white-and-black-on-red wares began to appear. They may have been trade pieces or locally made copies of a ware more typically northern.

The presence of the adz and hoe may indicate some modified agricultural techniques. Luxury items of stone were fewer and less excellent, but those of shell, especially mosaics, increased. Mosaic plaques, stone palettes, and etched shell were no longer used.

Whenever so many innovations—surface houses of adjoining rooms, platform foundations, walled enclosures, burials, polychrome pottery, and farming hillside terraces far from water—surface in cultural waters in such a relatively short time, they generally can be linked to unusual circumstances. These elements may have been dormant for a long time and only developed sufficiently to be recognized during this period. Perhaps this constellation of traits, previously unknown to the Hohokam, resulted from either the generalized Mesoamerican influence or from a meeting with the Anasazi or Anasazi-influenced cultures.

If the first is true, the selective cultural seeding from Mexico at last flowered through increased trade with commercial centers such as Casas Grandes in Chihuahua, Mexico. If the latter is correct, the most likely candidates would be the Salado. This Anasazi group, evolving under Mogollon influence, possibly moved into Hohokam communities from the Tonto basin northeast of Phoenix, bringing their blended lifeway with them.

Meanwhile, the native Hohokam in the low deserts did not experience these dramatic changes but instead clung to their traditional ways by cremating the dead, living in single-room houses just below ground, and finishing their duochrome ceramics with the customary paddle and anvil. This would help explain the fact that two distinct modes seemed to be operating during the Classic Period.

According to this scenario, after a time the restless Salado moved on to the southeast, leaving the Hohokam culture to ultimately disappear or to become so simplified as to be unrecognizable.

Another northerly group possibly responsible for some of the alien elements appearing among the Hohokam was the Sinagua, who lived in the Verde valley. Having absorbed attributes of the Colorado Plateau Anasazi and of the desert Hohokam, they could have served as intermediaries between the two.

Culturally drained by about A.D. 1450, the Hohokam faced obliteration as a viable entity from a probable barrage of troubles. Their irrigation system, parts of which had been in service almost fifteen hundred years, may have fallen into disrepair, its canals silted and in dire need of extensive maintenance that disheartened farmers were not prepared to undertake. Idle farmlands became sterile and choked with salts leached from soils long tilled but not drained or fertilized. Other causes may also have been responsible—disease, skirmishes with neighbors or invading nomads, interruption of contact with Mesoamerica and loss of cultural rejuvenation, or possibly natural disasters. Whatever the reasons, the deserts once again became brown and quiet.

THE MOGOLLON

The group occupying the broken highlands that separate New Mexico and Arizona and the elevated Basin and Range province straddling the Mexican border was the least advanced of the major groups of the Southwest Tradition. Known as the Mogollon, for centuries these people eked out a simple existence. Such limited cultural growth may have been the outcome of a dearth of southern inspiration, surprising considering their juxtaposition to central Mexico. Environmental demands perhaps were too weak to call up those latent human reserves that underlay great achievement elsewhere under less propitious circumstances.

Onto an Archaic hunting and gathering root, successive cultural additions were grafted. These included corn agriculture by about 2000 B.C., bean and squash cultivation somewhat later, use of elementary pithouses around 500 B.C., and pottery making in the centuries between then and A.D. 300. With these traits, several aspects of which had diffused north from Mesoamerica, the Mogollon had sufficiently evolved out of the common background to be reckoned with as a distinct group. But even though they learned to farm the steep slopes and cool valleys and to slightly modify the terrain to bring rain and river waters to their tiny plots, they never abandoned considerable dependence upon their homeland's abundant wild plants and animals. It was this retention of an ageless subsistence pattern that distinguished the Mogollon from their fellow southwesterners.

Between A.D. 900 and 1100 Anasazi cultural dominance virtually swamped the Mogollon. Either their lifestyle was completely submerged by their northern contemporaries, or a merger of Mogollon and Anasazi traits resulted in the formation of a new regional variant called the Western Pueblo. Hohokam ideas also were likely included in this combination. The resultant mixed culture may have contributed heavily to the background out of which the historic Hopi, Zuni, Acoma, and possibly some of the Rio Grande pueblos eventually arose.

Mogollon 1 (200 B.C. to A.D. 650)

Mogollon culture in its formative period was a tenuous transition from nomadism to settled village life made possible by rudimentary farming. Fearful of raids by other foragers, the Mogollon selected easily defensible home sites on promontories near their fields with approaches that could be blocked by rudely constructed walls. Those villages consisted of four to fifty small, identical pithouses, a special chamber now called a Great Kiva, and numerous granary cists.

The tools conceived for this unelaborated life reflect an expectable low standard of manual competence. Ground or pecked stone mortars, pestles, bowls, manos, and metates served as grinding implements. Stone axes, mauls, and hammerstones were construction gear. From chipped or flaked stone there were projectile points, knives, scrapers, and choppers. Small animal and bird bones left from the hunt provided raw material for awls, needles, fleshers, and flakers to be used for making baskets, sandals, and clothing. For the lighter side of life, there were large, stone tubular pipes to which bone or wooden mouthpieces were attached; beads, bracelets, and shell pendants; and bone whistles. Pottery was formed by a coiling technique from a clay heavily impregnated with iron. These vessels fit the term earthenware because they remained a deep earthy brown or reddish color after firing. The moist surfaces of red pots often were compacted and smoothed before firing so that a low sheen was achieved. Brown pots occasionally were gouged, scored, incised, or pinched on the outside.

Mogollon 2 (A.D. 650 to 850)

For the next two centuries the Mogollon remained content with the status quo. Their numbers increased, and they grew complacent enough to forsake the heights and build their larger villages in the valleys near their expanding fields. Modifications in the artifact complex were few. In addition to the usual red and brown types of pottery, Mogollon artisans became sufficiently creative to experiment with banding jar necks with overlapping coils or smudging and polishing bowl interiors to create a two-color, two-texture ware. Most important, they sometimes painted red designs over brown vessel walls. Later they dressed up their customary dark pots with a slip coat of white clay and a poorly executed array of red zigzags, spirals, and serrate lines.

Mogollon 3 (A.D. 850 to 1000)

The population, villages, and cultural complexity continued to grow in direct ratio to the Mogollon farming abilities, although nondomesticated plants and animals augmented their diet. To hold or accumulate tillable soil in their mountainous terrain, the Mogollon erected stone terraces along hillsides or across normally dry stream beds. They laid out lines of stones on slopes to halt erosion and distribute runoff.

Pithouses occasionally were lined with masonry for extra stability. Great Kivas became even greater. Some were up to thirty-five or forty feet on longer sides of a rectangular plan. In pottery, neck bands were pinched into piecrust relief, smudging remained in vogue, and the red-on-white palette was giving way to black-on-white. This color scheme and the introduction of some masonry liners for pithouses are possible evidence for the mounting impact of the northern Anasazi upon their culturally weaker southern neighbors.

Mogollon 4, Anasazi, Western Pueblo (A.D. 1000 to 1450)

The world as the Mogollon had known it came to an end in this period. Perhaps the local people merely resigned themselves quietly to cultural pressures from the north. Perhaps the vigorous Anasazi actually established colonies in traditional Mogollon territory. Or the two groups may have merged to produce a hybrid culture. What is obvious is that the takeover was peaceful.

The most striking change was a great increase in population. Also, an architectural style new to the Mogollon but typical of the Anasazi was adopted. Surface pueblos composed of unworked stones set in mud mortar became common. Early, small units were built in a linear or square plan. Later, larger pueblos, some with several hundred rooms and two stories, were arranged around open courts. In southern New Mexico and northern Chihuahua, small cliff dwellings were placed beneath rock shelters and in caves in canyon walls. A few rectangular and round Great Kivas were in locations suggesting their joint use by several small pueblos. Modest-size kivas in Anasazi style also were included in some communities.

Farming expanded to meet new demands of greater numbers, helped along by the introduction of ditch irrigation.

Burial in pits beneath house floors was practiced. Bodies often were extended and were accompanied by more elaborate offerings, consisting primarily of pottery receptacles that had holes poked in their bases to allow the spirits trapped inside the vessel to accompany that of the deceased.

Common goods were virtually indistinguishable from comparable tools used at the beginning of the Mogollon culture, although ornaments became more commonplace. Imported copper bells from Mexico were popular.

Pottery mirrored the dramatic cultural mixing that had occurred. In addition to the typical Mogollon types, a colorful red-and-black-on-white polychrome was traded into the region and occasionally copied by local potters. Most amazing was the sudden appearance of a stunning, superbly crafted black-on-white ware based on Anasazi methods and artistic leanings but nevertheless distinctive. It came from a restricted area along the Mimbres River of southwestern New Mexico where a throng of settlers poured from all the surrounding regions between A.D. 1050 to 1200. Apparently, in the resulting cultural crosscurrents, an aesthetic spark was ignited. Skillfully controlled brushes precisely executed a typical Anasazi geometric style whose individual elements were bold solids played off against fine line hatchure and parallel lines. But it was a totally original gamut of naturalistic designs depicting humans, animals, and mythical composite figures that made Mimbres earthenware unique. No other southwesterners could claim this fanciful repertory.

The same cloud of defeat that darkened the sky over the Hohokam lengthened over the Mogollon realm at about the same time. Circumstances differed, but the outcome was the same. Depopulation of most of the eastern portion of Mogollon territory, begun in the A.D. 1100s, was complete by A.D. 1250. In the late 1300s in the northwest highlands, people in a few large towns started to leave, but total abandonment did not occur until about A.D. 1450.

THE ANASAZI

The Anasazi, the third major component of prehistoric life in the Southwest, have been the subject of more romanticized, as well as scientific, attention than any other ancient Indian group in the United States. They not only dwelt in the most topographically unusual and starkly beautiful part of North America, but they also left behind thousands of stone houses and piles of discarded goods.

The Anasazi emerged from the same Archaic milieu as the other regional groups, and throughout their history have remained one facet of a larger human mosaic that is the Southwest Tradition. Before the opening of the Christian Era, they had progressed from a hunting-gathering stage to increasing dependence on domesticated corn, squash, and beans. They were, however, more reluctant than the Hohokam or Mogollon to become fully committed to sedentary agricultural life, probably because of their greater distance from Mexican sources of cultural stimulation. However, once certain Mesoamerican elements reached them about A.D. 500, Anasazi culture evolved rapidly.

Anasazi dry farming relied on direct rainfall or manipulation of that moisture.

Anasazi, Basket Maker III, black-on-white bowl. ROBERT H. LISTER, EARL MORRIS MEMORIAL COLLECTION, UNIVERSITY OF COLORADO MUSEUM.

Frequently, garden plots were placed in spots where runoff from summer showers supplemented normal precipitation. Successive lines of stones laid across slopes and terraced arroyos spread surface flows and controlled erosion. In some areas more extensive arrangements were made for funneling runoff water into canals and ditches that led to planted fields. This was not irrigation in the usual sense, but a judicious means for capturing unpredictable rainfall.

A noteworthy Anasazi contribution to prehistoric southwestern culture was their architecture style. Stone masonry, or more rarely adobe, was employed for communal structures of cellular, contiguous, flat-roofed rooms. The edifices ranged in size from several small units sufficient to shelter a few families to immense, many-storied apartment buildings with staggered elevations whose hundreds of living and storage rooms accommodated a swarm of people. Subterranean or semi-subterranean ceremonial rooms, called kivas, were family or clan religious and social centers. Community Great Kivas probably were adopted from the Mogollon.

The craft of pottery making also was borrowed from the Mogollon. Following the introduction of coil and scrape methods of construction, the Anasazi developed a gray ware made into distinctive shapes and often painted with black decorations. As expertise grew, a white slip was applied to the pots over which were drawn geometric motifs. These steadily became more intricate and skillfully executed. Some Anasazi also learned the art of making black-on-red, black-on-orange, red-on-orange, and several combinations of these colors to produce a polychrome product. Likewise, many utility pots were unique. Their interior surfaces were scraped smooth, but exteriors retained the corrugated pattern of unsmoothed, pinched construction coils.

The Anasazi showed a preference for particular styles of axes, milling stones, and tools for cutting, scraping, pounding, piercing, and cultivating. Their individual taste can also be seen in certain kinds of shell, bone, and stone ornaments, particularly those made of turquoise.

Customarily, bodies were flexed when buried in abandoned storage pits, beneath floors of houses, in outside graves, or quite often in a village refuse mound. Funerary offerings were usual.

Trails, roads, and established points from which signals could be sent comprised means of communication. Local and distant trade in utilitarian and luxury goods was extensive. At the cultural climax, a few centers existed where commodities were collected and redistributed. Some had connections to commercial establishments in northern Mexico. Annual ceremonial cycles probably were geared to agricultural activities, and may have been timed by astronomical observations and led by religious specialists.

After about A.D. 1000, when their culture began to peak, Anasazi dominance expanded southward to the Salado and Mogollon regions. Less obvious movements in other directions reached peripheral peoples.

Six hundred years later several reversals had brought severe shrinkage of Anasazi territory. By the early 1600s remaining enclaves existed only around the Hopi mesas in northeastern Arizona; in a scattering around Zuni, Acoma, and Laguna to the southeast;

and along the upper Rio Grande of northern New Mexico. Behind these demographic readjustments may have been climatic changes which affected water supplies and productivity of farmlands and caused erosion and lowering of the water table. Increasing numbers of people in some areas depleted limited resources. Failure in controlling water supply and breakdown in economic, social, or religious customs invited internal conflicts and perhaps raiding by enemies.

Basket Maker II (1500 B.C. to A.D. 400)

Those archeologists who strictly adhere to the Pecos Classification of the initiation of the Anasazi continuum with the partial adoption of maize horticulture place the opening phases of this cultural horizon within the second millennium B.C. Their conclusion is based upon radiocarbon dating of scattered plant remains recovered from a variety of sites with some evidence of early sedentism. While recognizing a prolonged transitional period from nomadic Archaic to more sedentary Anasazi lifestyle, others prefer to begin the sequence closer to the Christian Era, when supporting evidence is greater.

Most known sites of this period of changing subsistence strategies are sparsely scattered in caves and rock shelters throughout the Four Corners region. Because of optimum conditions for preservation, many normally perishable artifacts have been retrieved from dry deposits there. The most important of these are beautifully woven baskets for which this and the succeeding period are named.

Basket Maker II camps or small villages were located where water and soil were adequate for farming but collecting and hunting were also still possible. Corn and squash were cultivated, but wild plants, grass seeds, and pinyon nuts remained important. Also significant was meat from rabbits and other rodents, elk, deer, mountain sheep, and turkeys. Storage pits in the floors of shelters, and surface cists of stone slabs and mud protected stored food supplies from the voracious rodents who claimed the same habitat. Though they are rare, crude dwellings in the open were built of a domelike covering of short logs, poles, brush, and mud over a saucer-shaped depression or circular pit. Most burials were in rock shelters or crevices. The air was so dry that some remains became mummified. Baskets, clothing, and tools frequently accompanied the dead.

Milling stones verify the importance of plant foods. Heavy, rough choppers and hammerstones, large projectile points for spears, knives, and drills, and many simple flake cutting and scraping tools completed the assortment of stone artifacts. Bone awls, fleshers, flakers, and notched scapulas and ribs for combing fibers were used. Gaming pieces and several kinds of ornaments also were crafted from bone. Dried juniper berries and shells were worked into beads and pendants. Tubular pipes were made of stone.

Baskets were made in various forms for specific jobs. Large conical ones held loads carried on the back. Globular containers served for storage, while trays were used for winnowing and parching seeds. Bags, sandals, bands, and bikini-size aprons were finger woven of fibers, particularly yucca. Blankets were prepared from strips of rabbit fur or deerskins.

Anasazi, Pueblo I, gourd-shaped, black-on-white vessel. ROBERT H. LISTER, EARL MORRIS MEMORIAL COLLECTION, UNIVERSITY OF COLORADO MUSEUM.

Hunters used the atlatl for hurling spears, curved sticks to throw at game, large nets into which rabbits were driven, and snares for taking small game and fowl.

Pottery was seldom present. Where found, it resembles Mogollon brown ware and probably was not locally made.

Basket Maker III (A.D. 400 to 700)

The numerous villages with abundant storage facilities and the widespread occurrence of ceramics indicate a full-fledged, settled life in Basket Maker III times. The population increased and moved to valleys and highlands where conditions were suitable for farming. Domesticated plants included beans. Turkeys appear to have been tamed and kept within villages.

Settlements contained two to fifty pithouses, generally deep and circular to rectangular in plan, with pole, brush, and mud above-ground structures. Storage pits were placed within or near dwellings. Many communities had outdoor work areas and Great Kivas. Most frequently the dead were buried with offerings in the communal trash dump.

The abundance of small projectile points suitable for hafting to arrows suggests that the bow and arrow had become popular. Use of turquoise for jewelry increased, and locally made pottery replaced basketry for many uses. Small amounts of Mogollon browns still were imported or copied, but the first gray Anasazi pottery became widespread. Both undecorated bowls and others with geometric black designs were typical. A few crudely modeled female clay figurines, generally unbaked, probably were used in fertility rites.

Pueblo I (A.D. 700 to 900)

Pueblo I villages typically were in localities similar to those of Basket Maker III. Village size varied. Small complexes were common, but a few known ruins had more than one hundred individual dwellings. Rectangular surface structures built in a linear plan were separate or attached. Made of *jacal*, or mud plastered over a pole framework, they may have evolved from the earlier, small surface storage unit. By the end of the period, masonry was substituted for mud and brush in some areas.

Another Pueblo I innovation was the kiva, a subterranean religious or social structure resembling a pithouse. Among its specialized features were an encircling bench, roof support posts, a central firepit, a ventilator shaft for fresh air, and a *sipapu*, a small hole in the floor symbolizing the entrance to the spirit world below. A roof opening allowed smoke to escape and, with the aid of a ladder, it also served as entrance to the kiva. The larger, earlier Great Kiva occurred in some villages.

A typical Pueblo I village often had several dozen jacal living and storage rooms, several old-style pithouses, a few small kivas, perhaps a Great Kiva, and some outside areas for food preparation, cooking, or tool making.

Cotton was added to the list of domesticated plants, presaging the appearance of the true loom. Finger-woven bags and sandals and large carrying baskets and winnowing trays were disappearing. The practice of binding infants to hard cradle boards was instituted. These boards artificially flattened the back of the babies' skulls.

The Pueblo I ceramic assemblage continued to include a few brown wares, some gray wares—including a new utility jar with neck banding—a number of black-on-whites, and regionally important red-on-oranges and black-on-reds. Jars, bowls, and ladles were favorite forms.

Pueblo II (A.D. 900 to 1100)

By the beginning of the Pueblo II period practically all material ingredients of Anasazi culture had been introduced. Thereafter, even though some local differences in agriculture, architecture, and pottery were found, the peoples' movements and trading activities helped preserve a widespread cultural uniformity.

During this period the Anasazi reached their maximum geographic distribution and probably their greatest numbers. Both the dispersed occupation and climate records indicate generally more favorable conditions for elementary agriculture. Also, the refinement of water-control structures was coupled with the introduction of a more productive strain of corn.

Small, compact masonry pueblos of twelve to twenty living and storage rooms, one or more kivas, and a communal trash deposit became ubiquitous. Often they were clustered in larger villages. Kivas normally were circular and masonry-lined. Great Kivas became larger and more elaborate, and they began to exhibit typical features, including stone linings and benches, masonry fireboxes and vaults, ponderous posts or columns to support the heavy, flat roof, and a side entrance. Occasional small rooms, possibly for storing ceremonial paraphernalia or other materials, were built on the surface around the outside of the Great Kivas.

Ornaments of all sorts became more prevalent. Burials and offerings were placed in the refuse and in abandoned houses and storage chambers.

Much experimentation is evident in pottery. Typical products include characteristic gray corrugated jars and numerous types of black-on-whites that are regionally distinct in form, design, clay, pigment, and firing method. Red, black-on-red, and brown with smudged black interiors also were produced. Jars, bowls, pitchers, canteens, ladles, and some effigies were customary objects.

In Chaco Canyon, located in the San Juan basin of northwestern New Mexico, a cultural flowering known as the Chaco Phenomenon occurred. About A.D. 1000 the Chaco Anasazi advanced culturally beyond their contemporaries in numbers, in harnessing runoff waters, and in establishing a sophisticated network of several hundred small- to medium-sized villages and a dozen large towns. Roads and signaling outposts afforded rapid communication within the Chaco territory and with other Anasazi. Contact with the Mexicans brought certain new ideas and materials into Chaco life.

Pueblo III (A.D. 1100 to 1300)

The Anasazi reached their apogee in Pueblo III. At the same time, they occupied fewer but more densely settled localities, many of which were on ledges and in shallow caves in canyons.

Archeological evidence suggests a group of Pueblo III provinces, including Chaco Canyon in the northeast, which was of major importance. Distinct units also were found in Mesa Verde in southwestern Colorado, in the vicinity of Zuni in west-central New Mexico, in the upper Rio Grande in north-central New Mexico, and about Kayenta, the Hopi mesas, and south to the Little Colorado drainage in northern Arizona. Indians in intervening and borderland areas drew on the ideas and products of those principal centers. Thorough Anasazi dominance of former Mogollon territory was achieved.

The Chaco Phenomenon prospered for the first half of Pueblo III, then suffered a rapid decline and final dissolution by about A.D. 1200, if not earlier. To the north, the many spectacular cliff dwellings and large mesa-top and valley towns on or near the Mesa Verde continued to flourish for another century, then were abandoned. Total depopulation of the northern Anasazi provinces saw most people shifting to the south and southeast. Complicated, intertwined reasons were behind the final exodus from most of the San Juan basin. Among them were adverse climate; overpopulation of some of the more favorable places; breakdown of organized agricultural, commercial, social, and religious patterns; and severe competition for lands and resources that ended in internecine raiding.

Architectural achievement was characterized by large, well-planned, multistoried pueblos embracing many plazas. Masonry construction predominated, but techniques varied from province to province. Kivas, by then universal, usually were circular, but some were square. Both circular and square Great Kivas were common, located either within villages or at intermediate spots where they could serve several communities.

There was much local and foreign trading in ceramics, in materials for artifacts and ornaments, and possibly in foodstuffs. Luxury goods, such as raw and worked turquoise, were exchanged with Mexican trading partners for macaws and special objects of shell, stone, and metals.

Water and soil erosion controls were present to some degree in the more populous centers. Artifacts and jewelry did not differ much from Pueblo II. Burials in refuse heaps and in abandoned units of pueblos were the vogue, but puzzlingly few burials are known from such heavily occupied areas as Chaco Canyon.

Regionally distinct black-on-white pottery that was exchanged widely is useful in identifying the important centers of influence. Other black-on-whites of restricted distribution were produced in the outlying zones. Those of the Mimbres region reached an artistic excellence unmatched elsewhere in the Southwest. In several places reds, black-on-reds, black-on-oranges, red-on-browns, and polychromes were of local significance.

Pueblo IV (A.D. 1300 to 1600)

More people continued to concentrate in fewer localities during Pueblo IV, especially around the Hopi mesas, the land of Cíbola around Zuni, and the upper Rio Grande. Cliff dwellings became rare as the canyons were forsaken. While some small settlements existed, large towns of several hundred to more than a thousand rooms were more characteristic.

By A.D. 1450 most of the sites on the Colorado Plateau and in the Mogollon highlands had been deserted. During the next century big urban centers in the settled zones also were vacated. Added to the same factors that prompted earlier Pueblo III withdrawals were the presumed threats from newly arrived nomadic Indians, such as the Ute, Paiute, Apache, and Navajo.

Despite this decline, a lively, colorful pottery industry persisted. Cooking and storage jars had plain or tooled surfaces. Black-on-yellow or -orange and polychromes of red and white added to the designs were favored in Hopi districts. Polychromes in pigments that vitrified upon firing produced a number of wares with glazed decorations in the Zuni and Rio Grande vicinities. Several kinds of black-on-whites and pots with specks of shiny mica also were made by Rio Grande potters.

The ritual side of Anasazi life is strongly substantiated by extensive murals painted on the walls of kivas depicting deities, mythical creatures, masked dancers, and ceremonial objects.

Pueblo V (A.D. 1600 to present)

Pueblo V was the historic period for the Pueblo Indians, the direct descendants of the prehistoric Anasazi. Following the conquest by the Coronado expedition in 1540 and 1541, and the arrival of Spanish settlers, soldiers, and priests, these Indians were subjected to successive, often demoralizing, European influences.

In 1680 the Pueblos, in an unusual alliance, staged a coordinated revolt. Most of the Catholic priests were killed, buildings were sacked, and colonists and soldiers were expelled from New Mexico. Twelve years later Diego de Vargas reconquered the Indians.

Then new troubles descended upon the embattled Pueblos; this time it was other Indians. These were nomads who had converted quickly into raiders after they acquired horses from the Spanish. The Navajos were especially troublesome.

Early in the American era, administrators established some degree of law and order, broke the hold of Hispanic communities on Pueblo lands, reduced the power of the Catholic church, and finally brought an end to Navajo depredations.

The first three hundred years of contact with Europeans meant dramatic changes for the Pueblos. Some groups became extinct; others scattered and disorganized. Still others abandoned and reoccupied their villages or went to live with relatives.

Today there are eighteen pueblos along the Rio Grande. Acoma, Laguna, and Zuni thrive in western New Mexico, as do the Hopi villages in northeastern Arizona. They remain distinct from neighboring Native Americans. However, despite general cultural unity among the Pueblos, differences do exist in language, social institutions, ritual or ceremonial organizations, environments, and resource uses.

THE IN-BETWEENS AND OUTLIERS

Aside from the Mogollon, Hohokam, and Anasazi, local cultures existed in areas where the dominant entities overlapped (the in-betweens) or in border zones where southwesterners met and mingled with non-southwesterners (the outliers). They were variable prehistorically and remain comparatively ill-defined today.

Archeologists do not agree on the names, characteristics, importance, or even existence of all of these groups. The following is one way of identifying these units and outlining their attributes and relationships.

Hakataya

A fourth ingredient of the Southwest Tradition was a loosely knit, heterogeneous grouping called Hakataya. Unlike its contemporaries, it was a composite rather than a clearly defined individual group. The Hakataya assumed an early course of receiving, rather than giving, cultural stimulation.

Two essential factors bound the Hakataya together: their territorial range on the western flanks of the Southwest province and a mutual hunting-gathering background. However, the setting was so varied, extending from the snow-capped San Francisco Peaks to the torrid Colorado Desert, that five regional variants of the Hakataya have been identified. They resulted from contacts with other southwesterners or with people west of the province. Certain cultural hot spots were successively enriched at various times and in different ways, while more isolated peoples languished in a mode of life scarcely advanced beyond the Archaic.

The earliest Hakataya were part-time farmers who, because they relied on limited foraging, needed a certain degree of mobility. Most of them lived in small, transitory camps of jacal or low-walled rock shelters with bedrock milling stones for grinding foods and pits for roasting. None of them erected structures which can be assigned ceremonial usage. They made a few crude stone chopping tools and projectile points and some plain ornaments of stone or shell. Their pottery was a simple brown ware finished by a paddle and anvil technique.

To this shared background, the Laquish of the lower Colorado River valley added a red-on-buff pottery whose methods of manufacture they borrowed from the Hohokam. Meanwhile, in the uplands the Cerbat, Cohonina, and Prescott dipped into a cultural grab bag proffered by the Hohokam, Mogollon, and Anasazi along their borders. From these mixed sources at different times they selected pithouses, surface masonry pueblos, and red- or black-on-gray pottery to augment their usual traits.

The Sinagua are the best known Hakataya regional group. For five hundred years, beginning about the A.D. 500s, these people carved a meager existence from the jagged volcanic field that fanned out east from the San Francisco Mountains near Flagstaff. Pockets of fertile soil and sources of water were so restricted that only a small population could be sustained. The Sinagua followed a usual Hakataya simple life based on corn farming supplemented by whatever nature provided in the way of wild edibles. Some elaboration in lifestyle came with the adoption of pithouse architecture and acquisition of a few items through trade with the Hohokam, Anasazi, and Cohonina.

Contacts with the Hohokam to their south increased as the Sinagua colonized the middle Verde valley. Their influence may have been felt in some modifications to the pit dwelling, but a local sequence of changes on the traditional form was unique. First, the subterranean part of the buildings was lined with timbers, perhaps to seal the living quarters from ground moisture and pervading cold. Then, the same shape structure was erected above ground, with the addition of a side alcove. Apparently reversing older practices, the alcoved surface structure occasionally was placed over a pit. Rarely it was built on a low earthen platform. Examples of these timber-lined and alcove houses have been excavated at Sunset Crater Volcano National Monument.

In the middle of the eleventh century the Sinagua bore the brunt of one of the major physical disturbances of the ancient southwestern world. New, violent volcanic activity fiercely remodeled their homeland with the birth of Sunset Crater. There is no evidence that any of the people were annihilated, but lava flows, ash, and cinders buried their fields and homes and drove them away.

As the earth cooled, astute observers witnessed a rejuvenated soil and a greater volume of both running and retained water. Farming in the area became a more attractive possibility than it had ever been. Shortly, an aboriginal land rush was on, led by returning Sinagua. Other farming peoples quickly followed. Within a century groups of Cohonina and Anasazi from the north, Mogollon from the east, and Hohokam from the south had converged on the Flagstaff area and settled down together. Inevitably, a significant cultural cross-fertilization occurred.

As a direct result, the Sinagua assimilated a bank of alien elements into their traditional mode to reach a peak development between A.D. 1125 and 1215. From the Hohokam they accepted village life and the use of ballcourts. From the Anasazi they adopted masonry communal dwellings in the open, on canyon ledges and in overhangs, as well as certain soil and water conservation practices. And from the Mogollon they learned the manufacture of plain and smudged red wares.

It was at this time that the Sinagua occupied Walnut Canyon, where they erected tiny cliff houses and storage rooms. In the area of Wupatki they came together in pueblos. Some were small, but others were three stories high with one hundred rooms. Crowded out of the Flagstaff environs, other Sinagua moved south into the middle Verde valley where they established large centers such as those at Tuzigoot, Montezuma Castle, and Montezuma Well. Some aspects of their culture may have spread even farther south down the Verde River to the desert country around Phoenix at the beginning of the A.D. 1200s.

Perhaps their most significant role in these times was as strategically placed middlemen in a surging trade between the motley peoples who found themselves thrust together on this western frontier.

By the late thirteenth century the same natural and human dilemmas that brought down the other prehistoric southwesterners confronted the Sinagua. The results were similar: abandonment of settlements and dissolution of a worn cultural pattern.

Some Sinagua may have migrated north to join the ancestral Hopi. According to tradition, others may have trekked southward and mingled with the Tohono O'odham of the desert lowlands. Or perhaps some remained in the vicinity of the San Francisco Mountains, where they reverted to a predominantly hunting and gathering way of life, gradually to evolve into a culture reminiscent of the Yavapai in early historic times.

Salado

The Salado people were first identified as a distinct group living in the Tonto basin of south-central Arizona. They appear to have originated in the upper reaches of the Gila, Salt, and Little Colorado river drainages along the borders between the Anasazi and Mogollon, generally a mountainous evergreen area. For unknown reasons, about A.D. 900 they spread down into the warm arid basin of the middle Salt River. There for the next three centuries they exploited a frost-free climate, fertile soil, and perennial waters to become highly competent farmers. They dug miles of irrigation canals controlled from a series of settlements placed on top of spaced earthen platform mounds, both features perhaps adopted as a result of influence from their Hohokam neighbors further downriver. Numerous granaries and huge earthenware storage jars within house blocks attest to substantial farm yields. At least one recently explored structure suggests a temple where celebrations of the cycles of the sun's movements—so basic to the rhythms of agriculture—could have been part of calendric formulations by a priestly class.

Successful adaptations to a demanding environment afforded the Salado a comfortable life. Their artisans created outstanding polychrome pottery, shell jewelry, and cotton textiles, which were traded for turquoise, obsidian, sea shells, and bird feathers from distant regions. However, around A.D. 1200 trouble seems to have been brewing because the Salado began moving their villages. The selection of isolated, defensible locations suggests pressures from other peoples. The cliff dwellings at Tonto National Monument represent this stage of Salado culture. Finally, after briefly occupying the arid uplands, the Salado again moved. This time they went farther south into the lowlands of the Gila and Salt river valleys where they took up residence among the Hohokam. Most authorities consider them responsible for the appearance among the Hohokam of such foreign elements as multistoried pueblolike structures or Great Houses, compound walls for encircling villages, black-and-white-on-red polychrome pottery, several new types of stone tools, and inhumations. After a brief residency with the Hohokam, the Salado dispersed into southeastern Arizona and southwestern New Mexico, where their presence is traceable through diagnostic pottery types and some ruins dating between A.D. 1300 and

1450. In those are found large, several-storied pueblos that roughly resemble the Great House at Casa Grande. What ultimately became of the Salado is unknown.

Fremont

On its northwestern edge, in southern and eastern Utah and northwestern Colorado, the Southwest Tradition met the cultures of the Great Basin. There, several medleys of the two ways of life evolved. The best known of them is the Fremont Culture, a highly variable response by small groups of people adapting to some of the most diverse ecosystems on the continent. Five regional Fremont variants are recognized, those on the Colorado Plateau exhibiting enough similarities in cultural traits to originally be considered a peripheral branch of the Southwest Tradition. Now all Fremont variants are treated as a development distinct from that of the Anasazi but perhaps influenced in some respects by it. The Fremont remained more rooted in an Archaic-style hunting and gathering subsistence base than the Anasazi, but in favorable microenvironments they practiced some agriculture and enjoyed sedentism. Although many occupations are thought to have been seasonal or short-term, small Fremont villages featured pit dwellings. Houses and granaries of jacal, adobe, or masonry sometimes were included. Kivas were absent. Gray pottery, constructed by coil and scrape method and sometimes embellished with corrugation, incision, applique, or painted decoration, shows some Anasazi influence, as do certain stone implements. Elaborate, well-executed rock art was a typical Fremont attribute. Certain Plains traits, for example bison hunting and use of tipis, moccasins, and shields, also appear in the Fremont complex. Between A.D. 1300 and 1400 the Fremont vanished. Whether the people emerged as the historic Shoshoni, Ute, and Southern Paiute, or straggled south into Pueblo country or east into the High Plains, is uncertain.

Plains Relations

Where southwestern and Plains village farmers met along the east and northeast edges of the Southwest, trading relationships were established and intermediate cultural patterns appeared. The Antelope Creek development of the Texas Panhandle, which drew on Plains agricultural practices and Pueblo architecture, is one such hybrid. Also, within certain Anasazi districts in northern New Mexico the occurrence of pointed bottom pots, effigy vessels, and stockaded settlements suggests some Plains affiliation.

Mesoamerican Relations

Although the Southwest Tradition is distinct, in broad perspective it can be considered a provincial, watered-down version of Mesoamerican cultures. From the south came its first domestic crops and farming methods, its pottery making tradition, and certain architectural details. Ceremonial mounds and ballcourts, intensive irrigation projects, clay figurines, a number of exotic trade goods, and many of its ceremonies,

Yucca sandal from Montezuma Castle. SOUTHWEST PARKS AND MONUMENTS ASSOCIATION.

religious beliefs, and rituals also came from Mexico. Objects, as well as ideas, spread by different routes to the Southwest through diffusion and, in later times, through long-distance traders. Highly important in this Mexican-southwestern association was the establishment of a series of trading centers in northern Mexico by diverse Mesoamerican merchants. Casas Grandes in Chihuahua was one such thriving commercial entrepôt between the late eleventh and the mid-fourteenth centuries. Its merchants and craftsmen assembled raw materials and finished products from distant sources, produced quantities of pottery and luxury items, and distributed many commodities south into central Mexico and north as far as the upper reaches of the Southwest. From the Southwest the Mexican middlemen probably obtained turquoise, peyote, salt, selenite, and perhaps slaves by setting up formal trading channels to various places, including Chaco Canyon. One must credit the Mesoamericans with providing the seeds from which a Southwest Tradition bloomed and for diffusing northward repeated material and spiritual stimulation to keep it thriving. A rippling aftermath of the collapse of the Mesoamerican supportive system may in actuality have hastened the withering of certain southwestern complexes. ▲

Fourteenth-century polychrome olla, Salado culture, Tonto National Monument. GEORGE H. H. HUEY.

Traditional Interpretation

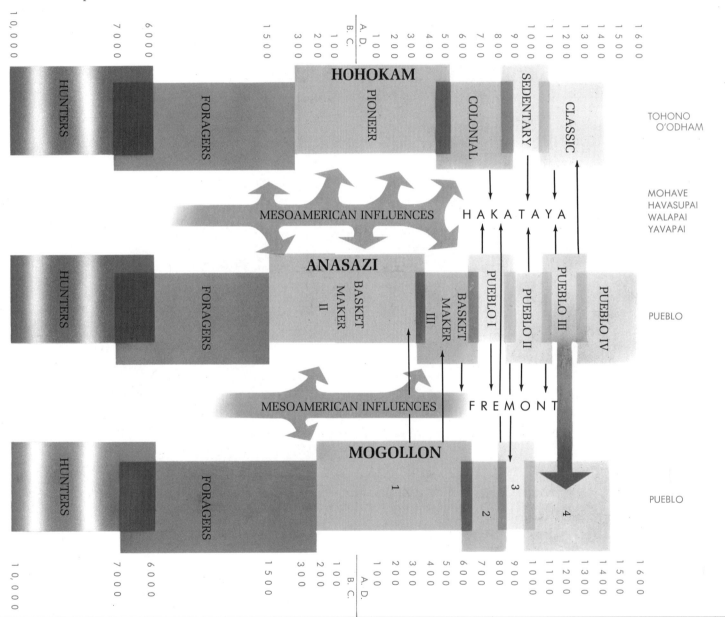

HOHOKAM

ANASAZI

MOGOLLON

MESOAMERICAN INFLUENCES

MESOAMERICAN INFLUENCES

HAKATAYA

FREMONT

HUNTERS

FORAGERS

PIONEER

COLONIAL

SEDENTARY

CLASSIC

BASKET MAKER II

BASKET MAKER III

PUEBLO I

PUEBLO II

PUEBLO III

PUEBLO IV

TOHONO O'ODHAM

MOHAVE
HAVASUPAI
WALAPAI
YAVAPAI

PUEBLO

PUEBLO

1

2

3

4

AN ALL-SOUTHWEST INTERPRETATION

Traditionally, the archeological definition of Southwest prehistory tends to emphasize the differences between cultures. It may foster the impression that the Southwest was so fragmented that each group evolved independently and in isolation.

While this is the conventional approach, an alternate way of explaining the archeological record is to partially attribute regional deviations from the cultural norm to peoples' adjustments to environmental limitations in the Southwest. This interpretation seeks similarities throughout the entire area, shared achievements, and those vital, mutually experienced exchanges that encouraged advancement. In essence, prehistoric human groups appear more as a subtle collage than a distinct mosaic of identifiable pieces. This view paints a picture of interrelated parts that fuse into an orderly whole, given perspective within a time frame.

For the first ten thousand years of human presence in the Southwest, man was a hunter and forager, totally at the mercy of his wits in recognizing and securing life's necessities. First came those who stalked the mammoth and bison, about whom little is known except that they participated in a simple lifestyle that seems to have been centered in the High Plains. When climatic change caused game animals to migrate eastward, those who subsisted upon them trekked out of the Southwest in their wake. They were replaced by others who in distant, less favorable, surroundings already had learned to survive on an astonishing variety of native plants and smaller animals. Both hunters and collectors moved periodically to take advantage of seasonally available foods. Tool kits were meager and portable, containing specialized weapons and tools, including the atlatl and spear. They also made cutting and scraping implements for taking and processing large game. Gatherers created a more general set of milling stones, choppers, baskets and bags for accumulating and preparing plants and small animals. Minimal clothing was made, mainly from skins. The people lived in shelters of brush windbreaks in the open or camps under protective rock overhangs. Small social units, such as extended families, probably ranged together, each member contributing to the well-being of the group. Shamans, medicine men astute in matters of human behavior and wise in the ways of nature, may have arisen through group recognition.

By about 3000 B.C. increasing numbers of Southwest foragers were following much the same lifeway, oriented to an unceasing search for food. While cultural change came slowly, they were understandably receptive to any additional foods that would afford more security. Thus, they were conditioned to accept the growing of corn, a plant evolved from a wild ancestor in central Mexico that had inched northward through the Sierra Madre Occidental to reach the Southwest. Likewise, squash and beans apparently followed shortly thereafter. The Mogollon highlands, with an environment similar to the Mexican interior, appear to have been important in the naturalization of these Mexican domesticates to the Southwest. From there they were dispersed north to the Colorado Plateau. The low deserts of Arizona may not have witnessed this earliest intrusion of domesticated plants because of the necessity for more heat-resistant varieties that presumably evolved later.

No immediate cultural change occurred among the foragers who failed to appreciate the possibilities of becoming full-time food producers. For many centuries the introduced plants were little more than minor dietary supplements. Nevertheless, their initial cultivation, together with improved hunting and gathering techniques and an apparent period of increased moisture, made possible larger groupings of people. More substantial habitations appeared in camps or semi-permanent settlements, accommodating perhaps thirty to fifty individuals and situated in the lee of cliffs or in the open. These were houses made of a light framework of poles, possibly covered with brush, grass, or even hides, placed over a shallow depression and equipped with hearth and storage pits.

The northward flow of cultural stimulation, begun with the diffusion of the fundamental idea of agriculture and its diagnostic plants—corn, squash, and beans—quickened about 500 B.C. A noticeable commitment to food producing was seen. This entailed more sedentary life in permanent villages with sturdier, below-ground homes and more storage chambers for food stockpiling. With this village life, kin groups, formerly made up of mobile social units, possibly were succeeded by organization geared to the new relations of family and community. Leadership likely became necessary to direct occasional group activities. Organized ritualism designed to assure the success of unpredictable dryland farming in the arid Southwest may have arisen.

Pottery making appeared in southern sectors of the Southwest by about 300 B.C. Even the simplest pottery had many advantages over traditional baskets, bags, and skin and gourd containers. Notwithstanding, in the ancient Southwest, pottery never entirely replaced basketry and other types of containers.

Repeated injections of objects and ideas from Mesoamerica continued sporadically for the next millennium. Some of these contributions to Southwest cultures are thought to have been carried unknowingly by peaceful traders, who were more active at some times than others. A few of these merchants had close tribal and economic ties to the central Mexican markets; others were more provincial middlemen with weaker connections to the primary sources of trade goods. The distance from donors, the number and complexity of intervening participants, and the state of cultural advancement of ultimate recipients accounted for uneven acceptance of the cultural adjuncts introduced into the Southwest. For example, pottery did not appear among the emerging northern, culturally disadvantaged farmers of the Colorado Plateau until about A.D. 400, centuries after it was a basic ingredient of more southerly households.

One notable exception to the diffusion-through-trade concept may have been an actual migration of people from the south into the Gila and Salt river valleys of southern Arizona about 300 B.C., bringing in a rich complex of Mesoamerican traits previously unknown in the Southwest. Some of these items greatly influenced people residing elsewhere within the province, while some remained localized but modified to the new cultural context that evolved. The elements introduced were certain pottery techniques and modes, figurines, trough metates, stone bowls, turquoise mosaics, shell ornaments, canal irrigation, and cremations.

The more than one thousand years that prehistoric Southwest culture existed fall naturally into several stages. Each is named for the predominant settlement pattern of the time but ultimately is based on its material inventory of both Southwest and foreign affiliation and its geographical distribution. Three core areas are recognized, coincident with the major environmental zones. The *desert zone* includes the lowland desert expanses about the middle stretches of the Gila and Salt rivers in southern Arizona. A second, the *mountain-valley zone*, encompasses the high mountains and more verdant deep valleys astride the southern New Mexico–Arizona boundary and the northwest Mexican cordillera. The third, the *plateau zone*, is situated along the San Juan, Little Colorado, and a part of the Colorado River drainages of the high pinyon- and juniper-clad Colorado Plateau region of the Four Corners, with an extension eastward into the upper Rio Grande valley. The boundaries of these focal areas expanded and contracted, bringing about different levels of exchange between peoples and, in some instances, complete dominance of one group over another. The basic, sedentary agricultural way of life and the informal regulated contacts between peoples were important factors in maintaining generally uniform culture throughout the region, although growth and regression did occur.

Hamlets (300/100 B.C. to A.D. 500/700)

When food production finally won over dependence upon wild resources, a new subsistence base was established from which issued the dramatic changes that were to distinguish the southwesterners from surrounding peoples. Anthropologists view this shift from nomadism to sedentism as the first great revolution in mankind's history. Though it took centuries, in the Southwest it certainly brought about a new lifeway.

In most parts of the province, the gradual acceptance of corn, squash, and beans, and the development of methods to efficiently grow and utilize them, prompted the slow gathering of previously wandering peoples into small hamlets. In one exception, the agricultural possibilities of the fertile desert river valleys may have attracted a migrant group of Mexicans who were already irrigation farmers and craft specialists. In general, the earliest appearance of these hamlets in the southern deserts, mountains, and valleys of the Southwest was due to their being closer to Mexico. It also took time for various groups to spread from south to north within the Southwest.

Groups lived in simple, family-sized dwellings with walls and roofs built over circular or rectangular pits. Posts were set in the floor or around the pit as a supporting framework for a domelike or sloping-sided superstructure with a flat roof. The roof was made of short sections of logs, poles, brush, and mud. Entrance usually was through a side opening or a short lateral passageway. Firepits or heating pits were located in the middle of hard-packed mud floors, with a smokehole in the roof for ventilation. Storage units either were cut into the floors or were built upon them. Rudimentary as these structures were, they provided shelter and sleeping places during bad weather. Their dimly lighted interiors were used at times for preparing meals, storing foodstuffs, and performing other everyday tasks. Some

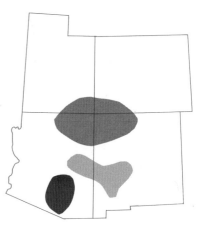

Hamlets

household duties likely took place on the flat roofs of the homes because much time was spent in the outdoors. In some of the eastern and plateau settlements an extra-large pithouse, or Great Kiva, seems to have served as a community meeting place for social and religious affairs.

Social and religious patterning probably was informal and likely did not extend beyond the family or small enclaves of several families. Most of it must have concerned maintaining family harmony and placating the erratic forces of nature. Only the desert hamlets, with their dependence on irrigation systems, might have required some secular leadership in a community.

Depending on several circumstances, the first communities were located in diverse settings. In the desert they were along rivers where nearby farm plots could be irrigated. In the mountains and valleys, selection of steep ridges suggests a concern for defense. On the plateau, large shallow caves or adjoining talus slopes were chosen for the first flimsy structures. Later, after houses became more substantial, open sites were utilized. Often the areas selected not only provided space suitable for gardening, but also were located near sources of game and native plants essential to existence.

The first pottery showed its Mesoamerican ancestry in being well-executed though simple in form and color. It seems to have been part of a ceramic tradition of undecorated brown- and red-slipped utility wares that arose in central Mexico and diffused north through the central Mexican highlands after 1000 B.C., finally to reach the southern border of the Southwest about 300 B.C. A sluggish diffusion, as well as the presence on the plateau of a tradition of fine basketry, forestalled its appearance in the north for nearly seven centuries.

By the end of the hamlet stage, each region had modified ceramic wares into distinctive local schools that continued to flourish. The desert people, the most advanced potters of the period, swung to a convention of buff ware with red designs; the mountain and valley folk continued the plain browns and reds but modified their surfaces with various types of tooling; and the plateau dwellers switched to a gray ware occasionally embellished with black designs. Not only did colors and habitual designs vary from center to center, but manufacturing techniques and firing methods also differed. Jar and bowl forms predominated.

The inhabitants of the Gila and Salt river drainages also excelled in other cultural aspects due to their rapid assimilation of additional traits from Mexico. Paramount to their existence in the arid deserts was irrigation farming. Contemporary southwesterners were less advanced, relying solely upon dry farming. Stone carving and polishing, and turquoise and shell working, were particularly well developed by the desert Indians. They also surpassed their peers in modeling small clay effigies, supposedly of ritualistic significance.

Stone, bone, and wooden artifacts were added to the basic tools. The growing importance of domesticated plant foods is reflected in the increase and improvement of milling implements used in the preparation of vegetal materials and in the presence of pits and cists for storing them. Better cutting, hammering, and piercing tools can also be related to the everyday tasks associated with sedentary life. The plateau people created many baskets, bags, and belts of fiber, but the seemingly greater abundance of such objects in the north may be due to better preservation. Cotton began to spread north from the desert valleys, where it was first cultivated. Clothing and sandals were fashioned from animal hides and various plant fibers. The atlatl and spear were replaced by the bow and arrow. Pipes and gaming pieces attest to lighter sides of life. Cremation was the burial custom in the lowlands; elsewhere inhumation was practiced. Offerings normally accompanied the deceased.

Villages (A.D. 500/700 to 1000/1100)

More people in larger communities, territorial expansion, and more elaborate ceremonialism typify this stage.

Houses built over or in pits continued to be in vogue in the southern deserts and eastern mountains and valleys, but the larger villages of the desert people were frequently placed farther from rivers, necessitating extension of the canal systems. Incorporated into some of their settlements were ballcourts and platform mounds, both Mexican traits associated with religious performances. Colonizing thrusts to the north, west, and east carried the desert variety of life to its maximum distribution. The mountaineers in the east moved their communities down into stream-watered valleys, enlarging them and continuing to include a Great Kiva in most villages.

On the plateau, surface houses gradually made their appearance. First constructed of posts and mud, the rectangular flat-roofed storage and living rooms were built side by side in a line. As stone masonry was introduced, compact pueblos of dozens of rooms placed in an angular plan about a courtyard or plaza became popular. Specialized features were added to the earlier pithouses, creating a kiva for the religious or social activities of small groups. One or more kivas were incorporated into every village. Larger Great Kivas for community functions also came into use. Growth of population and movement into previously unoccupied districts took plateau peoples throughout the Four Corners and southward, bringing them into contact with other Indians scattered through the deserts and mountains.

The dryland farmers became more efficient by setting up simple systems of terraces, rock alignments, and stone-bordered grids to distribute runoff waters and curtail erosion on slopes and in arroyos. However, nowhere did they approach the skills of the desert irrigation agriculturalists. As generations passed, more productive strains of corn evolved in the different ecological zones which, when combined with improved farming technology, resulted in greater yields. The domestication of the turkey in some localities may have provided a more dependable meat supply, as well as feathers for various purposes.

The makers of red-on-buff ceramics of the low country produced quantities of their traditional wares. Many featured designs of repeated naturalistic and geometric motifs. The plateau potters placed white slips on their gray vessels and decorated them with

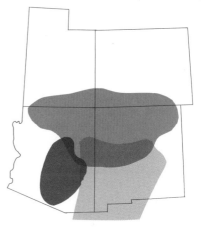

Villages

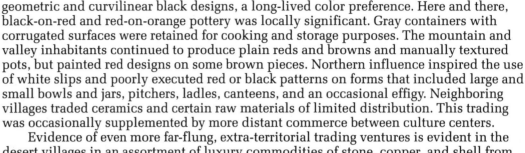

geometric and curvilinear black designs, a long-lived color preference. Here and there, black-on-red and red-on-orange pottery was locally significant. Gray containers with corrugated surfaces were retained for cooking and storage purposes. The mountain and valley inhabitants continued to produce plain reds and browns and manually textured pots, but painted red designs on some brown pieces. Northern influence inspired the use of white slips and poorly executed red or black patterns on forms that included large and small bowls and jars, pitchers, ladles, canteens, and an occasional effigy. Neighboring villages traded ceramics and certain raw materials of limited distribution. This trading was occasionally supplemented by more distant commerce between culture centers.

Evidence of even more far-flung, extra-territorial trading ventures is evident in the desert villages in an assortment of luxury commodities of stone, copper, and shell from Mexico. Throughout the Southwest the use of shell from the Pacific coast and Gulf of California for jewelry making also testifies to the importance of long-distance trade.

The partially sedentary marginal agriculturalists who lived south and east of the Colorado River in Arizona and in the desolation of southeastern California accepted a number of traits from their more settled neighbors. This imparted a superficial southwestern look to some of their material culture. Elsewhere, people from the core areas began to touch less advanced cultures with their pottery, house types, ornaments, and burial customs. Less tangible reciprocal influences in economic, social, and religious aspects of life also can be postulated. As a result, a distinct cultural shatter belt evolved about the San Francisco Mountains and in the Verde valley. On the northern and eastern fringes of the Southwest, intercourse with Great Basin and Plains groups produced comparable cultural fusion. Such relationships between donor and recipient groups continued well into the following cultural stage.

Southwestern villagers did not greatly alter earlier artifacts. Relatively minor changes included greater use of trough metates for pulverizing corn, and the adoption of the true loom, which increased the production of woven fabrics for a variety of objects. The unique process of etching was devised by the desert artisans for embellishing ornaments of shell. Burials generally followed the customs adhered to during the preceding period.

Marked changes in social and religious practices must have occurred throughout the Southwest coincident with the drawing together of large numbers of people into relatively permanent farming villages. Structures for more formalized religious rites, which undoubtedly called for full- or part-time religious leaders, became widespread. Perhaps these same individuals also provided direction for a growing number of social functions and communal projects.

Towns (A.D. 1000/1100 to 1450/1600)

The changes that came in the final stage of the prehistoric Southwest were many, consequential, and often devastating. The eastern mountain and valley cultures were peacefully overwhelmed by stronger northern neighbors. The desert farmers, already past their cultural prime, pulled back from the frontiers into their original homeland, where

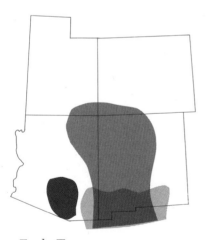

Early Towns

they experienced a cultural regression and dilution of their uniqueness, then final disappearance. The plateau people rose to new cultural heights, aggressively expanding into and dominating new lands. Plagued by misfortunes, they finally withdrew to reassemble in reduced numbers elsewhere. The period also saw the arrival of nomadic peoples, such as the Paiutes, Utes, Apaches, and Navajos, who subjected town dwellers to unaccustomed pressures. Lastly, the Spanish conquerors and settlers appeared, overcame the natives, and initiated rapid changes that eradicated or altered many aboriginal ways.

Architectural advances are the most obvious accomplishments of this period. Construction of great multistoried, many-roomed stone or adobe pueblos occurred on the plateau; erection of large, sometimes walled, communities of single- and several-storied mud buildings took place in the desert. The architecture probably evolved locally but may have received some inspiration from Mexican sources. A peppering of large towns grew up on the flatlands, mesas, and valley bottoms of northern New Mexico and northeastern Arizona. In a more restricted district encircling the Four Corners, similar structures were placed in the shallow caves eroded into canyon walls. Some of these communities had hundreds of storage rooms and living quarters, many kivas, and at least one Great Kiva. When placed in the open, they frequently grew to their final size and shape through an orderly addition of rooms. Rectangles of rooms usually were stepped back from plazas in terraces to heights of four or five stories. Those built in caves were constrained by the caves' outlines, making them appear less systematically arranged.

Where stone masonry was practiced in the north, decided regional variations in style and skill may be observed. The masons of Chaco Canyon excelled, and their pueblos were the grandest in the entire Southwest. At the other extreme, pueblos of the Rio Grande district used irregular blocks set in large amounts of mud mortar, or they depended completely on adobe because suitable building stone was rare. Spacious masonry pueblos (some with kivas and Great Kivas) and small cliff dwellings appeared in the mountains and valleys as the plateau people took over that territory.

In most cases, populous communities along the fertile lands near the southern desert watercourses were incongruous mixtures of the old pole-brush-and-mud-over-pithouses and clay-walled, one-story units of contiguous rooms, plus several Great Houses of adobe built on packed-earth platforms, all surrounded by an earthen wall. Ballcourts were sometimes included. Plateau and/or Mesoamerican influences probably were behind such deviations.

Canal irrigation remained a forte of the desert farmers, but improved systems for collecting and distributing runoff waters appeared among the plateau pueblo dwellers. Knots of population that crowded into some northern districts, such as at Mesa Verde and in Chaco Canyon, depended on being able to gather water from spring thaws and summer rains and direct it to farm plots or storage places by means of diversion dams, reservoirs, canals, and ditches.

In ceramics, the lowland red-on-buff tradition persisted, although plain red increased in popularity and an alien black-and-white-on-red polychrome appeared. On the plateau, black-on-whites were important, but other duochromes and black-and-white-on-red or

Late Towns

-orange polychromes were present in limited distribution. Gray utility wares continued. Plateau-style pottery replaced most of the established red and brown wares of the mountains and valleys when the northerners overran that area. Between about A.D. 1050 and 1200 the most extraordinary black-on-white pottery in the Southwest, featuring excellently executed geometric and naturalistic animal designs, was crafted in pueblos along the Mimbres River in southwestern New Mexico. Along the upper Rio Grande, duochromes and polychromes were painted with pigments that glazed upon firing. Bowls, jars, pitchers, ladles, and some effigies were common forms.

As for other artifacts, most southwesterners relied heavily upon the assemblage that had been in use for many generations. Certain specializations in materials and types are now useful for defining regional and temporal distributions.

In Chaco Canyon on the northern pleateau, a unique cultural brilliance shone for two centuries, beginning about A.D. 1000. There, an integrated political, social, and economic system characterized some sixteen towns and hundreds of smaller communities in and around the now desolate Chaco Wash in northwestern New Mexico. A network of roads and a series of outposts from where signals could be observed and relayed tied together many people from diverse zones. Possibly they functioned in a structured production and redistribution organization whose influences radiated in all directions, probably even as far as northern Mexico. From Mexico came several kinds of special goods in exchange for turquoise and other items valued by the southern traders. Certain Mesoamerican social and religious customs, the practice of making astronomical observations, the means of communication, and economic and architectural principles also seem to have been absorbed by the Chacoans. A high level of control and leadership, perhaps exercised through a stratified society, appears to have been necessary for the complex Chaco development to have prospered. Thus far, their outstanding achievements in so many endeavors appear unique. Architecture, communications, control and distribution of water, production and apportionment of resources, and probably social and ceremonial organization were areas in which the Chacoans excelled. It is likely that town dwellers elsewhere also evolved more complicated social and religious structures and patterns of leadership to cope with enlarged societies and the problems of sustaining them.

The intrusion of plateau people into the mountain and valley country along the southern Arizona–New Mexico border was one example of their urge for expansion during this town stage. Another group apparently moved down into the desert to take up a century-long residence among the southerners. During this time of cohabitation each faction clung to its established patterns of behavior. Two distinct architectural forms, pottery styles, burial modes, and perhaps agricultural techniques were thus brought together.

The long continuum of southwestern culture, which reached a climax among the desert craftsmen and farmers as early as A.D. 700 to 900 but did not attain a comparable elaboration among pueblo builders until several centuries later, began to experience a creeping decay as the town period progressed. Behind such decline was a tangle of physical, social, and moral reasons. Environmental and cultural exhaustion likely were

Contact

fundamental to any of them.

First to feel the adverse effects were groups along the northern plateau. The outstanding, but somewhat exotic, Chaco Phenomenon started to fall apart during the twelfth century, and by A.D. 1200, if not earlier, most Chaco Canyon residents had deserted their customary territory to drift southward. By 1300 the magnificent cliff dwellings and large pueblos of the Mesa Verde area were also abandoned by their residents who likewise moved south to settle among kinfolk. Elsewhere on the plateau, other pockets of farming Indians slowly retreated from former holdings to regroup into three principal locations by about 1450. One was in the vicinity of the Hopi mesas, a second was in the Zuni country, and a third was near the upper Rio Grande. It was in these regions that villages of Pueblo Indians, as they came to be designated by Spanish explorers and colonists, were found in the sixteenth century already on a downward cultural path. Many of them remain in these same regions. Ties between the ancient occupants of the plateau and historic Pueblo people have definitely been established, but no precise correlation between specific prehistoric and contemporary towns can be made. Nevertheless, many aboriginal patterns, especially some concerned with spiritual matters, remain viable ingredients of Pueblo life.

The fate of the desert dwellers is not as clearly discernible. As an archeological entity, their culture dwindled and disappeared by A.D. 1450 for many of the same reasons that underlay the demise of the northern version of Southwest culture. About 1700, when Spanish Jesuit priests first began to write accounts of the natives of southern Arizona, they identified the Tohono O'odham (Pima-Papago) as living along the Salt and Gila rivers and described them as practicing canal irrigation. Although this protohistoric cultural expression little resembles the past glory of the aboriginal occupants of the same area, it is likely that the Tohono O'odham are indeed the inheritors of that tradition.

Ancestors of the tribes along the lower Colorado River temporarily accepted a modicum of southwestern culture but reverted to their simple life once contacts with certain core areas ceased; they include the Mohave, Yavapai, Hualapai, Havasupai, and Maricopa.

Present

ADDITIONAL READINGS

Cordell, Linda S.
    1979 Prehistory: Eastern Anasazi. *Handbook of North American Indians*. Vol. 9.
           Washington, D.C.: Smithsonian Institution. 131–151.
    1984 *Prehistory of the Southwest*. New York: Academic Press.
Eggan, Fred
    1979 Pueblos: Introduction. *Handbook of North American Indians*. Vol. 9.
           Washington, D.C.: Smithsonian Institution. 224–235.
Gumerman, George J., and Emil W. Haury
    1979 Prehistory: Hohokam. *Handbook of North American Indians*. Vol. 9.
           Washington, D.C.: Smithsonian Institution. 75–90.
Irwin-Williams, Cynthia
    1979 Post-Pleistocene Archeology, 7000–2000 B.C. *Handbook of North American*

Indians. Vol. 9. Washington, D.C.: Smithsonian Institution. 31–42.

Jennings, Jesse D.
   1989 *Prehistory of North America*. Third Edition. Mountain View, California:
        Mayfield Publishing Company.

Jones, Dewitt, and Linda S. Cordell
   1985 *Anasazi World*. Portland, Oregon: Graphic Arts Center Publishing Company.

Kelley, J. Charles
   1966 Mesoamerica and the Southwestern United States. *Handbook of North
        American Indians*. Vol. 4. Archaeological Frontiers and External Connections.
        Austin: University of Texas Press. 95–110.

Kidder, Alfred V.
   1962 *An Introduction to the Study of Southwestern Archaeology*. Reprint of 1924.
        New Haven, Connecticut: Yale University Press.

Lipe, William D.
   1983 The Southwest. *Ancient North Americans*. New York: W. H. Freeman. 421–494.

Martin, Paul S.
   1979 Prehistory: Mogollon. *Handbook of North American Indians*. Vol. 9.
        Washington, D.C.: Smithsonian Institution. 61–74.

Noble, David Grant, Editor
   1991 *The Hohokam, Ancient People of the Desert*. Santa Fe, New Mexico: School of
        American Research.

Plog, Fred
   1979 Prehistory: Western Anasazi. *Handbook of North American Indians*. Vol. 9.
        Washington, D.C.: Smithsonian Institution. 108–130.

Schroeder, Albert H.
   1979 History of Archeological Research. *Handbook of North American Indians*. Vol.
        9. Washington, D.C.: Smithsonian Institution. 5–13.
   1979 Prehistory: Hakataya. *Handbook of North American Indians*. Vol. 9.
        Washington, D.C.: Smithsonian Institution. 100–107.

Woodbury, Richard B.
   1979 Prehistory: Introduction. *Handbook of North American Indians*. Vol. 9.
        Washington, D.C.: Smithsonian Institution. 22–30.

Woodbury, Richard B., and Ezra B. W. Zubrow
   1979 Agricultural Beginnings, 2000 B.C. –A.D. 500. *Handbook of North American
        Indians*. Vol. 9. Washington, D.C.: Smithsonian Institution. 43–60.

All-Southwest Overview

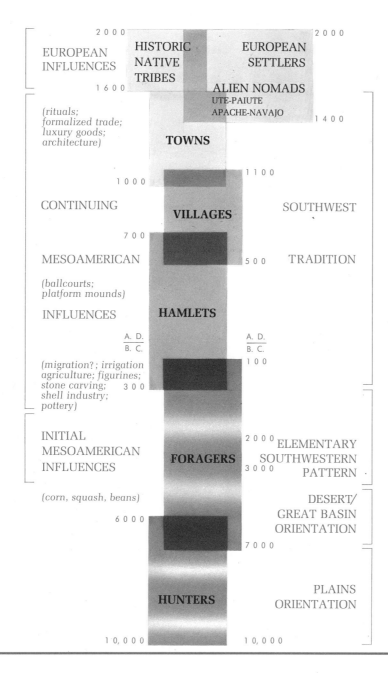

EUROPEAN
INFLUENCES

2000

1600

HISTORIC
NATIVE
TRIBES

EUROPEAN
SETTLERS

2000

ALIEN NOMADS
UTE-PAIUTE
APACHE-NAVAJO

1400

*(rituals;
formalized trade;
luxury goods;
architecture)*

TOWNS

1000

1100

CONTINUING

VILLAGES

SOUTHWEST

700

MESOAMERICAN

500

TRADITION

*(ballcourts;
platform mounds)*

INFLUENCES

HAMLETS

A. D.
⎯⎯
B. C.

A. D.
⎯⎯
B. C.

*(migration?; irrigation
agriculture; figurines;
stone carving;
shell industry;
pottery)*

300

100

INITIAL
MESOAMERICAN
INFLUENCES

FORAGERS

2000

3000

ELEMENTARY
SOUTHWESTERN
PATTERN

(corn, squash, beans)

DESERT/
GREAT BASIN
ORIENTATION

6000

7000

HUNTERS

PLAINS
ORIENTATION

10,000

10,000

Cultural associations represented in the national parks and monuments.

Traditional Archeological Classification	ALL-SOUTHWEST INTERPRETATION		
	HAMLETS	*VILLAGES*	*TOWNS*
HOHOKAM	Montezuma Castle (Well) Organ Pipe Cactus Saguaro	Organ Pipe Cactus	Casa Grande Organ Pipe Cactus
MOGOLLON	Carlsbad El Malpais Gila Cliff Dwellings Guadalupe Mountains Petrified Forest	El Malpais Gila Cliff Dwellings Petrified Forest	Petrified Forest
ANASAZI	Arches Bandelier Canyon de Chelly Canyonlands Chaco El Malpais Glen Canyon Grand Canyon Mesa Verde Natural Bridges Navajo Pecos Petrified Forest Zion	Arches Bandelier Canyon de Chelly Canyonlands Chaco El Malpais Glen Canyon Grand Canyon Mesa Verde Natural Bridges Navajo Pecos Petrified Forest	Aztec Bandelier Canyon de Chelly Chaco El Malpais El Morro Hovenweep Mesa Verde Yucca House Navajo Pecos Petrified Forest Petroglyph Salinas Pueblo Missions
IN-BETWEENS AND OUTLIERS	Bryce (Fremont) Capitol Reef (Fremont) Colorado (Fremont) Dinosaur (Fremont) Glen Canyon (Fremont) Zion (Fremont)	Capitol Reef (Fremont) Glen Canyon (Fremont) Grand Canyon (Hakataya) Montezuma Castle (Hakataya) Petrified Forest (Hakataya) Sunset Crater (Hakataya) Walnut Canyon (Hakataya) Wupatki (Hakataya)	Montezuma Castle (Hakataya) Tonto (Salado) Tuzigoot (Hakataya) Wupatki (Hakataya)

Petroglyphs, Salt Creek, Arches National Park. DAVID MUENCH.

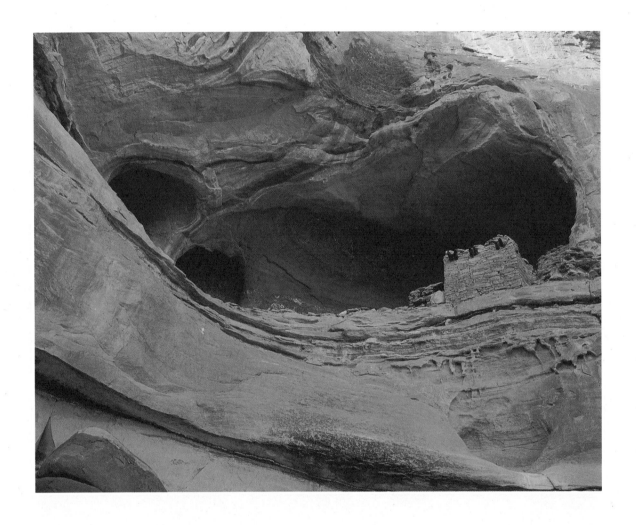

Horse Canyon, Canyonlands National Park. DAVID MUENCH.

White House Ruin, Canyon de Chelly National Monument. DAVID MUENCH.

Tyuonyi Ruin, Bandelier National Monument. DAVID MUENCH.

Pueblo Bonito, Chaco Culture National Historical Park. DAVID MUENCH.

Atsinna Ruin, El Morro National Monument. DAVID MUENCH.

Square Tower House, Mesa Verde National Park. DAVID MUENCH.

Spruce Tree House, Mesa Verde National Park. DAVID MUENCH.

Stronghold Ruin, Hovenweep National Monument. DAVID MUENCH.

Inscription House, Navajo National Monument. DAVID MUENCH.

Montezuma Castle National Monument. DAVID MUENCH.

Kiva and mission, Pecos National Historical Park. DAVID MUENCH.

Mission and pueblo ruins, Gran Quivira, Salinas Pueblo Missions National Monument. DAVID MUENCH.

Wupatki Ruin, Wupatki National Monument. DAVID MUENCH.

Fremont pictographs, Courthouse Wash, Arches National Park. DAVID MUENCH.

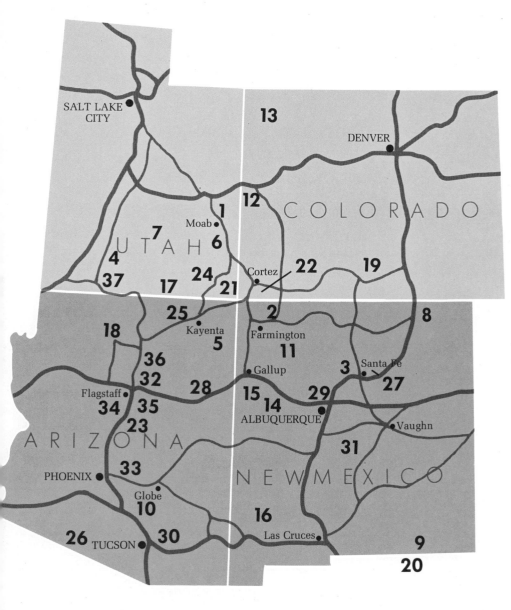

(1) Arches National Park
(2) Aztec Ruins National Monument
(3) Bandelier National Monument
(4) Bryce Canyon National Park
(5) Canyon de Chelly National Monument
(6) Canyonlands National Park
(7) Capitol Reef National Park
(8) Capulin Volcano National Monument
(9) Carlsbad Caverns National Park
(10) Casa Grande Ruins National Monument
(11) Chaco Culture National Historical Park
(12) Colorado National Monument
(13) Dinosaur National Monument
(14) El Malpais National Monument
(15) El Morro National Monument
(16) Gila Cliff Dwellings National Monument
(17) Glen Canyon National Recreation Area
(18) Grand Canyon National Park
(19) Great Sand Dunes National Monument

(20) Guadalupe Mountains National Park
(21) Hovenweep National Monument
(22) Mesa Verde National Park
(23) Montezuma Castle National Monument
(24) Natural Bridges National Monument
(25) Navajo National Monument
(26) Organ Pipe Cactus National Monument
(27) Pecos National Historical Park
(28) Petrified Forest National Park
(29) Petroglyph National Monument
(30) Saguaro National Monument
(31) Salinas Pueblo Missions National Monument
(32) Sunset Crater Volcano National Monument
(33) Tonto National Monument
(34) Tuzigoot National Monument
(35) Walnut Canyon National Monument
(36) Wupatki National Monument
(37) Zion National Park

SOUTHWESTERN ARCHEOLOGY IN THE NATIONAL PARKS AND MONUMENTS

A large measure of the allure that the opening of the West held for most nineteenth-century Americans was that it was not merely the highest mountains, deepest canyons, wildest rivers, and serest deserts that were being proclaimed as common property, but also an intriguing lost world of a vanquished race. Or so it seemed. Within a period of about fifty years such antiquities had been encountered from the Rockies to the Gulf of California, the portion of the nation to become known as the Southwest. Their discovery aroused a healthy curiosity about the human parade that had passed that way before the arrival of Europeans, but it also produced a less admirable treasure hunting fever that threatened to wipe out in a few decades what had lain undisturbed for centuries.

It was the public's good fortune that many of the significant finds were first made known by people with scientific interests who appreciated the inherent intellectual value of their discoveries and embarked on serious research. As a result, the discipline of southwestern archeology was born in the minds of those stalwart few. It was of more enduring consequence that the federal government adopted a policy of protecting this irreplaceable heritage from the casual offender to preserve it for all. Although such action came too late in some areas, the creation of national preserves of Southwest antiquities provided archeologists a chance to study what otherwise might have been lost forever. It also provided citizens an opportunity to learn in pleasant surroundings, which also were often spectacularly scenic. Education never has been made so easy because in no other nation in the world has such an archeological alliance between government, science, and the general public been formed.

Because each National Park Service installation in the Southwest is an independent unit, a visitor may come away with the misconception that each spotlighted site or group of sites was a simple aboriginal world unto itself. In actuality, all the federally maintained southwestern sites once were meshed cogs in a greater Indian universe. The accounts to follow assign each to its proper niche (or niches) as defined in the general reconstruction of the regional prehistory of sedentary peoples; they consider the modern discovery of each and the archeological and preservation activities that have taken place within it, and offer suggested readings for greater detail. ▲

Anasazi granary, Lake Powell side canyon, Glen Canyon National Recreation Area. GEORGE H. H. HUEY.

ARCHES, CANYONLANDS, AND CAPITOL REEF NATIONAL PARKS/NATURAL BRIDGES NATIONAL MONUMENT/GLEN CANYON NATIONAL RECREATION AREA, UTAH

Cultural Significance and Archeological Classification

The region in which these National Park Service areas are located was important in the pioneering days of southwestern archeology, especially in defining the early stages of Anasazi culture. Subsequent research has extended the record of human occupation back to the period of the earliest Archaic hunters and gatherers. Fiber and charcoal samples have dated these Archaic remains from ca. 7000 B.C. to A.D. 400. Both Basket Makers and Fremont peoples making the transition to a subsistence pattern sustained by horticulture evolved out of this cultural base. Anasazi affiliated with the Kayenta tradition moved northwest of the Colorado River gorge in Pueblo II and early Pueblo III times, while others following Mesa Verdean modes settled in the canyons and mesas north of the San Juan and east of the Colorado rivers.

Outstanding examples of rock art may be examined in many places, particularly in Canyonlands and Capitol Reef. Prior to the creation of Lake Powell, Glen Canyon and its tributaries were subjected to a comprehensive survey and excavation program to recover specimens and data from ruins now covered by waters of the lake.

Archaic: Desert Culture
Anasazi: Basket Maker II, III; Pueblo I, II, III
In-betweens and Outliers: Fremont culture (San Rafael)
All-Southwest: Hamlets and Villages, plateau zone

Explorations and Investigations

These five areas in southwestern Utah are noted primarily for a breathtaking landscape eroded from the extensive, red sandstone formations of the Colorado Plateau by millions of years of the action of water, wind, frost, and sun. But it was an agonized terrain that did not attract early penetration or settlement by Spaniards or Mexicans, who considered it a formidable barrier better skirted than crossed. The broken country along the Colorado River above Lees Ferry remained terra incognita to Spaniards. Not until 1776, while seeking a passage connecting the Spanish provinces of New Mexico and California, did Franciscan priests Francisco Atansio Domínguez and Silvestre Vélez de Escalante ride through parts of this wilderness to cross the Green and Colorado rivers. The so-called Crossing of the Fathers in Glen Canyon soon became an important ford for traders and trappers, who by 1840 had become acquainted with much of the forbidding land sliced by the upper Colorado and its tributaries.

After the United States assumed control of the region in 1848, the Colorado River was considered a possible water route from the Rocky Mountains to the west coast, where growth had been accelerated by the discovery of gold. In the 1850s several government explorations looking into the navigability of the Colorado were led by Captain Lorenzo Sitgreaves, Lieutenant Joseph Ives, and Captain J. N. Macomb. The first accurate description of the canyons of the Green and Colorado rivers and much of the adjacent

Sherd of corrugated pottery showing finger prints on the construction coils. FRED MANG, JR., NATIONAL PARK SERVICE

territory, along the more than one thousand winding miles from Green River, Wyoming, to the lower end of the Grand Canyon in Arizona, was provided by John Wesley Powell as a result of his two exploratory trips in 1869 and 1871–72. His writings mentioned prehistoric remains encountered along the route, which bisected Canyonlands National Park and traversed the length of Glen Canyon National Recreation Area. The Colorado River from Arches National Park to its confluence with the Green River in Canyonlands National Park was first described after it was explored by a railroad survey party in 1889.

Accumulation of accurate archeological knowledge of the region commenced with the work of several Hayden Survey parties of the U.S. Geological and Geographical Survey of the Territories in 1873–76. William H. Holmes, artist, geologist, and later chief of the Bureau of American Ethnology, and William H. Jackson, famous for his photographs of the West, participated in some of the reconnaissances and described and depicted Indian remains.

Public awareness of the archeological wealth of the Four Corners area developed in the late 1880s after the discovery and popularization by the Wetherill brothers of Indian structures tucked in the cliffs of the Mesa Verde. Their haul of "relics" from the sites was displayed at museums and fairs and was sold to antiquarians. As a result, during the late nineteenth and early twentieth centuries the Colorado Plateau emerged as a favored spot for a growing number of archeologists. They crisscrossed the mesas and gorges hoping to locate important aboriginal remains and obtain materials from them for institutions in the East. Rivaling their exploits and fortitude were numerous local collectors bent upon lucrative sales to the highest bidder of items removed from the ruins. In some instances wealthy patrons and resident enthusiasts joined forces in scouring what commonly was regarded as the public domain. To their credit, sometimes they were spurred on by the altruistic goal of giving their finds to a reputable museum. One such arrangement led to work in Butler Wash, Cottonwood Wash, and Grand Gulch, all side canyons of the San Juan River that proved to be of great significance in the developing discipline of southwestern archeology.

In 1893 Richard Wetherill and his brothers had completed their explorations and excavations in the cliff houses of Mesa Verde and were eager to examine new territory. Richard had heard stories and seen pictures of abandoned sites in Grand Gulch which reminded him of those at Mesa Verde. He had also seen a large assortment of fine Cliff Dweller artifacts from the sites. He determined to see Grand Gulch and sought financial backing from two young, wealthy brothers from New York, Frederick and Talbot Hyde. He had first met them when they came to the Wetherill ranch in Mancos, Colorado, on their way to visit Mesa Verde. A partnership was formed in which Richard would lead a party, the Hyde Exploring Expedition, into Grand Gulch, and the Hydes would finance the effort. Whatever was recovered would be given to the American Museum of Natural History in New York. Richard realized that he was undertaking something for which he lacked training or education. Because of his former experiences with scientists at Mesa Verde, he knew that the value of any possible Grand Gulch collection would depend entirely upon documentation of his excavations and all specimens recovered. He prepared forms so he could note the location, depth, and catalog number of every object. A permanent catalog number was to be placed on each article. Plans were to be drawn of every ruin investigated, each room in a site was to be numbered, and important features would be photographed before and after excavation.

With his brothers Al and John and several others, Richard left the Wetherill Alamo Ranch in November on horseback. Supplies were lashed into two-hundred-pound packs on mules. Fortunately, the winter of 1893–94 was mild, allowing the party to work steadily for four months in the sand and rubble of more than one hundred caves in Grand Gulch, Cottonwood Wash, Butler Wash, and a few localities south of the San Juan River. At the end of this time, a collection weighing well over a ton and numbering 1,216 specimens had been amassed. It was packed out to Bluff City, Utah, transferred to wagons, and taken back to the ranch. There, Richard worked over the collection, studying and cataloging specimens before crating them for shipment to the New York museum.

Pictographs at Peekaboo Springs, Canyonlands National Park.
GEORGE H. H. HUEY.

Not only were the Hyde brothers and the American Museum of Natural History pleased with the Wetherill collection, but during the course of the expedition an incident took place that had a long-lasting effect upon southwestern archeology. Richard was aware that Charles McLoyd and C. C. Graham of Durango, Colorado, after making the first exploration of Grand Gulch in 1890–91 and bringing out a number of ancient artifacts, had noted that some of the mummies and specimens seemed different from those of the Cliff Dwellers. They speculated that they may have belonged to another, more primitive "race." Richard's party was digging in caves in Cottonwood Wash when he, too, began to find evidence that a people with a distinct culture had used the caves before the Cliff Dwellers. These remains, which he routinely found in deposits below those left by the Cliff Dwellers, were unlike anything he had seen before. The earlier people had long, narrow, undeformed skulls and buried their dead in pits or abandoned storage cists dug into cave floors. They made excellent baskets, had no pottery, used spears propelled by an atlatl, and wore unique sandals. The later Cliff Dwellers had skulls that had been flattened in childhood through use of a hard cradle board. In addition, they had pottery, used the bow and arrow, and wore a style of sandal different from that of their predecessors. Upon these few tatters from the hazy past was based the reconstruction of a long, pulsating pageant of human endeavor.

Richard Wetherill was convinced that he had made a significant discovery. From his field camp in Cottonwood Wash he wrote to the Hydes with news of this and other finds. In reply to Talbot Hyde's request for more specific information, Richard referred to the "Basket People" to distinguish the older folk from the Cliff Dwellers. Later, Hyde wrote that it might be better to call them "Basket Makers," although notes accompanying Al Wetherill's autobiography imply that the Wetherill brothers may have used that term from their first recognition of the pre–Cliff Dweller culture.

Thus, the early stage of what archeologists later were to call the Anasazi culture was recognized and labeled Basket Maker. However, many archeologists were prejudiced against Richard Wetherill's claims and interpretations because to them he was only an untrained cowboy with a reputation for collecting and selling antiquities. It was not until

Anasazi corrugated jar. TOM
MASAMORI, COURTESY OF COLORADO
HISTORICAL SOCIETY.

several years later, after similar finds had been made and reported upon by professionals, that Wetherill's keen deductions were verified and his term Basket Maker, for the first sedentary farmers of the Colorado Plateau, was generally adopted by the academic community. Successive and more advanced stages of what came to be recognized as an Anasazi cultural progression subsequently were designated Pueblo to replace the original, more limited term, Cliff Dweller.

Other Wetherill brothers played leading roles in ruin hunting in southeastern Utah. At Richard's urging, Clayton Wetherill explored Moqui Canyon, a tributary of Glen Canyon, seeking Basket Maker remains. Sometimes accompanied by Al, he also spent many summers guiding T. Mitchell Prudden, an eastern physician turned archeologist, who enjoyed traveling and examining Indian ruins of the San Juan basin. From 1906 until his death in 1944 John Wetherill served as guide, packer, and advisor for nearly every scientific party that entered the Kayenta area.

Beginning about the turn of the century, Byron Cummings and his students began a long exploration program into the basins of the upper Colorado and lower San Juan rivers. Known as the "Dean." because he served for a time as a dean at the University of Utah, his reports upon the country's archeological and geological resources were instrumental in the establishment of several national monuments. One was Natural Bridges National Monument, set aside in 1908 to protect the weathered arches in White Canyon and the prehistoric ruins in the vicinity. Another was Rainbow Bridge National Monument, established in 1910, after he had played an important part in discovering that natural wonder. After he left the University of Utah for the University of Arizona, where he nurtured an active archeology department, he continued his researches in the Navajo country and was one of the first to publicize its grandeur and archeological richness. He also left records of his work in Canyonlands, Natural Bridges, and Glen Canyon.

Cummings's contemporaries likewise were attracted to southeastern Utah and neighboring states to delve into the region's mysteries. Their remarkable work filled gaps in the accumulating information about the ancient people who had dwelt there. One relationship between a prominent New York cottonbroker with an avid passion for exploration and a group of archeologists and veteran southwestern guides eventuated in a series of organized treks much like the earlier Hyde expedition. In fact, the work was similarly undertaken on behalf of the American Museum of Natural History, which received all notes and artifacts.

For more than a decade, beginning in 1920, New Yorker Charles L. Bernheimer made fourteen pack trips through the remote canyons, plateaus, and deserts of the Four Corners. To his advantage, at various times he secured the archeological services of Earl Morris, an eager young researcher, and was guided by John Wetherill and Ezekiel "Zeke" Johnson. A resident of Blanding, Utah, Johnson rivaled Wetherill in his familiarity with the lower San Juan country. In later years he was appointed the first custodian of Natural Bridges National Monument. Bernheimer's wanderings covered much of the area's most inhospitable and little-known corners, including portions of Natural Bridges and Glen Canyon. And even though he successfully charted a southern approach to Rainbow Bridge, scientifically the results of his work were minimal. Several popular magazine articles and a book were published.

By the late 1920s archeologists realized that some areas north of the Colorado River in Utah, the northern periphery of the Southwest, possessed prehistoric remains that differed somewhat from the better-known cultural manifestations of the San Juan drainage. At the suggestion of Alfred V. Kidder, considered by many to have been the foremost early figure in southwestern archeology, the Peabody Museum of Harvard University placed four expeditions in that country between 1927 and 1930 to learn more of its antiquities. Their widespread surveys and excavations took them into districts of Canyonlands National Park, Capitol Reef National Park, and Glen Canyon National Recreation Area. Called the Claflin-Emerson Expedition after its Boston sponsors, its field staff included Donald Scott, Noel Morss, and Henry Roberts. Although the complete results of the expedition's fieldwork were not made available, Morss promptly reported his efforts in the Fremont and Dirty Devil drainages in which he defined the Fremont Culture. This he considered an aberrant form of the more common southwestern mode. His key sites now lie within the boundaries of Capitol Reef National Park. Years later, in 1969, James H. Gunnerson prepared a lengthy monograph synthesizing all available data on the Fremont Culture and the northern frontier, including a belated report of the accomplishments of the Claflin-Emerson Expedition. Shortly after, in her paper on the rock art of Utah, Polly Schaafsma included information gathered during those field trips by Donald Scott.

The possibility of further exciting archeological finds in a setting of such harsh magnificence continued to lure both scholars and adventurers throughout the 1930s. The Rainbow Bridge–Monument Valley Expedition spent six summers conducting extensive scientific investigations, some of which were published.

The next important archeological undertaking was a statewide survey initiated in 1949 by the University of Utah. Various participants in this continuing program have inventoried ancient remains in parts of southeastern Utah, among them sections of Canyonlands, Capitol Reef, and Arches. Investigations in Beef Basin revealed an area of high site density with scientific promise.

Congressional authorization in 1956 for construction of Glen Canyon Dam and several other dams in the upper Colorado River basin set in motion one of the most comprehensive emergency archeology programs ever attempted up to that time in this country. Through research contracts administered by the National Park Service, work on the Glen Canyon Project of the Upper Colorado River Basin Archeological Salvage Program was shared by the University of Utah and the Museum of Northern Arizona. It was anticipated that the flooding of some 153,000 acres in Glen and San Juan canyons would seriously threaten archeological resources. Therefore, farsighted research projects were launched in order to salvage materials and data pertinent not only to prehistory but also to ethnohistory, geology, history, climatology, paleontology, and biology. The ultimate goal was to prepare a natural history of the Glen Canyon region showing how human behavior is tied to and modifies other resources of a land.

With the closing of the gates of Glen Canyon Dam in 1963, the program's fieldwork ended. Behind the dam, Lake Powell extends 183 miles with 1,800 miles of shoreline confined between majestic sandstone cliffs and buttes. The canyon bottoms, where teams of researchers toiled in heat, sand, rain, and hardship, are completely obscured. The Glen Canyon Project amassed a solid body of new data from a vast area, making Glen Canyon one of the best-known archeological areas of comparable size in the West.

Survey teams working from boats, on foot, with saddle horses and pack animals, and in four-wheel-drive vehicles, along with excavation crews isolated for weeks at a time in remote places, charted the precise location and attributes of more than two thousand sites and exposed several dozen representative ruins. The majority of the archeological resources identified in Glen Canyon and its tributaries are now submerged beneath Lake Powell. Some prehistoric trails and steps, rock art panels, and remnants of storage and habitation structures were not flooded and are still visible to boaters and hikers.

As soon as the waters of Lake Powell began rising behind the dam, the lake and environs became an increasingly popular recreation spot. The dam is operated by the Bureau of Reclamation, but in 1971 administration of the recreation facilities was assigned to the National Park Service. Since then National Park Service archeologists and interpreters have labored to protect and preserve accessible examples of rock art and ruins and to develop an interpretive program, including floating wayside exhibits.

The most intensive work was carried out between 1984 and 1987 by researchers from Northern Arizona University under the direction of Phil R. Geib. This latest archeological effort covered almost 19,000 acres to record 489 sites, of which 20 were tested. Without the time constraints associated with the preinundation surveys and with the advancement during the intervening twenty years of techniques and dating methods, it was learned that the Glen Canyon region had supported an Archaic population for an estimated eight thousand years. About A.D. 200 a Fremont culture slowly emerged from this background. Seven hundred years later, Anasazi expansion out of northern Arizona and southwestern Colorado dominated the area.

After its establishment in 1964, one of the first steps in the development of Canyonlands National Park was to appraise the park's archeological holdings. University of Utah archeologists inventoried a portion of the park, concentrating on the Needles District. That area, which is east and southeast of the Colorado River, and Island-in-the-Sky, between the Colorado and Green rivers, were surveyed again in 1989 to record 477 sites. Late Archaic, Pueblo II, and Pueblo III occupation are most commonly represented but, because of the rugged dry terrain, appear to have been seasonal and small-scale.

Spectacular rock art features colossal human figures with elongated or trapezoidal bodies, various animals, and geometric designs. Fine examples occur in the Maze and Needles components of Canyonlands, but more outstanding are those on massive, vertical sandstone cliffs deep in Horseshoe Canyon, a detached unit west of the park.

Capitol Reef became a national monument in 1937. Its boundaries were later adjusted, and in 1971 it was designated a national park. In geologic terms, a reef is a ridge of rock that forms a barrier. The reef for which the park is named has a prominent dome, Capitol Dome, resembling the United States Capitol—hence, Capitol Reef. The first aboriginal

Anasazi structure at Kachina Bridge, Natural Bridges National Monument. GEORGE H. H. HUEY.

works in Capitol Reef to attract scrutiny were the distinctive pictographs and petroglyphs of the Fremont River gorge and vicinity. The most striking characteristic of the typical rock art is a large anthropomorphic figure with headdress, facial decoration, necklaces, and ear ornaments. A figure carrying a shield also is depicted frequently. The rock art, together with other diagnostic elements found at sites in that region, led Noel Morss in 1931 to define the Fremont Culture.

The first archeological program directed specifically at Capitol Reef National Park was a thorough inventory of areas assumed suitable for past human occupancy along or near water sources. Through the work of University of Utah archeologists in the 1960s, fifty-eight sites were identified. More recently, emergency surveys along the right-of-way of the road paralleling the Waterpocket Fold and following the line of a proposed irrigation system found additional localities. All the surveys have revealed nearly ninety sites in the park. It is probable that all the major sites along primary drainages are known, but undoubtedly smaller, more remote sites remain to be found.

Arches is another National Park Service installation that progressed from monument to park status. Although its geologic and scenic wonders earned it national monument status in 1929, its commonplace aboriginal remains did not entice early professionals and amateurs. The park contains no evidence of long habitation; there is no evidence that the essential combination of arable land and reliable water supply existed. Most spots of aboriginal use are camps either in the open or beneath rock shelters, quarries that furnished raw materials for stone tools, and rock art panels. The Barrier Canyon style of the latter, often including front-facing, long, tapering torsos without appendages, is considered to be of Archaic age. While Arches was still a monument, National Park Service personnel recorded some sites in the backcountry. After Arches National Park was created in 1971, the National Park Service contracted with the Office of the Utah State Archeologist for a systematic examination of the northeastern portion of the reserve. These two endeavors have resulted in a list of eighty-eight sites.

From the earliest white settlement in southeastern Utah in the 1880s, the region's numerous antiquities attracted the curious and the acquisitive. It was in the great chasms sharply knifed through evergreen Cedar Mesa where wonderfully preserved masonry houses of the Cliff Dwellers were found to override burial cists of an earlier folk whom the diggers named the Basket Makers. Consequently in 1908, when the government sought to protect three nearby majestic spans of sandstone (now known as Sipapu, Kachina, and Owachomo bridges) through the establishment of Natural Bridges National Monument, concern was expressed for comparable protection of whatever prehistoric remains might be present in that particular part of Cedar Mesa. William B. Douglass, U.S. Examiner of Surveys, was instructed to document evidence of prehistoric occupation within the monument boundaries. Prior explorations anticipated his success in certifying ancient life in the vicinity of the stone arches.

Fifteen years passed before Ezekiel Johnson was named the first custodian of Natural Bridges National Monument. During Johnson's tenure from 1923 to 1941, he thoroughly explored this wild, remote, northern corner of the Colorado Plateau. One old house he found in White Canyon was named Horsecollar Ruin because of an associated pair of intact surface granaries whose open mouths suggested that gear. In 1937 Charlie Steen, National Park Service archeologist who carried out some excavations there, was more interested in a well-preserved rectangular kiva complete with entrance ladder.

For the past thirty years a series of intensive reconnaissances of the canyons and mesa tops within the monument have confirmed the presence of such aboriginal features as hearths, middens, rock foundations and walls, rock art panels, and modest houses and granaries. After a substantial Basket Maker II and Basket Maker III use of the area, an unexplained hiatus occurred until about A.D. 900. At that time Anasazi farmers returned and stayed until the middle of the thirteenth century. Their numbers never were great, probably because of limited arable land.

Artifact collections from the numerous archeological programs in and about these five federal holdings are housed mainly in the institutions that performed the fieldwork. Major assemblages of specimens are to be found in the Peabody Museum of Harvard, the American Museum of Natural History, the University of Utah, the National Park Service Midwestern Archeological Center, and the Museum of Northern Arizona. Minor collections are displayed or stored in the visitor centers of the respective areas.

A large number of comprehensive reports covering various aspects of the research of the University of Utah's Glen Canyon Project have been issued. For brevity, only several of general nature are included in the following suggested readings. ▲

ADDITIONAL READINGS, Arches, Canyonlands, and Capitol Reef National Parks/Natural
    Bridges National Monument/Glen Canyon National Recreation Area
Crampton, C. Gregory
    1959 *Outline History of the Glen Canyon Region, 1776–1922.* Anthropological Papers
        No. 42. Salt Lake City: University of Utah.
    1973 *Standing Up Country: The Canyon Lands of Utah and Arizona.* New York:
        Alfred A. Knopf.
Gunnerson, James H.
    1969 *The Fremont Culture: A Study in Cultural Dynamics of the Anasazi Frontier.*
        Papers, Peabody Museum of American Archaeology and Ethnology, Vol. 59,
        No. 2. Cambridge, Massachusetts: Harvard University.
Jennings, Jesse D.
    1966 *Glen Canyon: A Summary.* Anthropological Papers, No. 81. Salt Lake City:
        University of Utah.
McNitt, Frank
    1966 *Richard Wetherill: Anasazi.* Reprint of 1957. Albuquerque: University of New
        Mexico Press.
Petersen, David
    1990 *Of Wind, Water, and Sand: The Natural Bridges Story.* Moab, Utah: Canyonlands
        Natural History Association.

Schaafsma, Polly
 1971 *The Rock Art of Utah; from the Donald Scott Collection.* Papers, Peabody
       Museum of American Archaeology and Ethnology, Vol. 65. Cambridge,
       Massachusetts: Harvard University.
Sharrock, Floyd W.
 1966 *An Archaeological Survey of Canyonlands National Park.* Anthropological
       Papers, No. 83. Salt Lake City: University of Utah. 49–84.

*Pictographs at Horseshoe
Canyon, The Great Gallery,
Canyonlands National Park.*
GEORGE H. H. HUEY.

West Ruin at Aztec Ruins National Monument, with reconstructed kiva. The roof is now dismantled. GEORGE A. GRANT, NATIONAL PARK SERVICE, 1946.

AZTEC RUINS NATIONAL MONUMENT, NEW MEXICO

Cultural Significance and Archeological Classification

The excavated Aztec West Ruin and its adjacent unexcavated East Ruin are prime examples of the town building of classic Anasazi times. Additonally, they represent a pair of outliers created in the twelfth century to support the Chaco Phenomenon, probably with foodstuffs grown in a fertile valley coursed by perennial waters. A roadway separating the settlements and connecting them to indigenous, smaller cobblestone villages on the adjacent river terrace is suspected. After being abandoned, both sandstone-masonry house blocks were remodeled and reoccupied by Mesa Verdeans, thereby affording an unusual exhibit of extensive interaction between Anasazi in neighboring areas. The restored Great Kiva, the only one of its kind in existence, shows how these massive chambers for communal social, religious, and perhaps economic activities may have been finished inside and out, how they were roofed, and how skilled and industrious their builders were.

Explorations and Investigations

In the first half of the nineteenth century the Spanish defeat of the Aztec Indians of central Mexico had received exhaustive popular treatment (*The Conquest of Mexico* by William H. Prescott) which kindled widespread fascination with American Indian remains. As Americans became familiar with their new western lands, a number of the antiquities encountered there were attributed to the Aztecs. This opinion was fortified by the knowledge that the Aztecs themselves considered their origin to have been in "the north." Such was the case when, in the 1870s, white settlers moved into the Animas valley in what is now northwestern New Mexico. The largest group of stone ruins found heaped on terraces of the Animas River became known as Aztec Ruins. However, the Aztec Indians' roots were no farther north than the north-central Mexican plateau. In fact, as a recognizable entity, they postdated the Animas ruins by several centuries. The builders of the Aztec Ruins were the same predecessors of the modern Pueblo Indians responsible for hundreds of other contemporary settlements scattered over the Colorado Plateau.

The earliest known reference to ruins in the region appears on a map of the route of the Escalante and Domínguez expedition from Santa Fe, New Mexico, into Colorado and Utah, 1776–77. On that simply drawn document is written a notation near the Animas and Florida rivers that their waters were sufficient to have supplied the many ancient towns in the vicinity. The Escalante-Domínguez party probably never actually visited the Aztec Ruins. Considering discrepancies in the map and interpretation of the written account, it appears that they traveled well to the north of Aztec.

After the United States acquired the New Mexico Territory in the mid-nineteenth century, a trickle of scientists visited the Aztec Ruins during the next fifty years and left descriptions of them. John S. Newberry, a geologist, came in 1859 as part of the exploratory expedition from Santa Fe to the junction of the Colorado and Green rivers. He was

Anasazi: *Pueblo III*
All-Southwest: *Towns, plateau zone*

Anasazi, Pueblo III, black-on-white-pottery fragments. FRED MANG, JR., NATIONAL PARK SERVICE.

followed sixteen years later by another geologist, Frederic M. Endlich, a member of the Hayden Survey. Lewis H. Morgan, a prominent anthropologist, toured the mounds in 1878 while on an extensive southwestern trip. Warren K. Moorehead, a teacher at Phillips Academy in Andover, Massachusetts, on a mission of collecting data for an exhibit at the 1892 Chicago World's Fair, camped for two weeks at the largest cluster of ruins. Each of these men added a few details to the growing body of knowledge of the Animas antiquities.

Meanwhile, white settlers moving down out of the Rockies encountered numerous remains of former occupation along the entire Animas valley. Schoolboys on an outing broke into the largest of these, now called West Ruin, and found undisturbed rooms containing burials with clothing, baskets, pottery, ornaments, tools, and weapons. They and older members of the community indiscriminately looted many intact chambers, fortunately breaching only those that required little digging. However, shaped building stones and roof timbers were hauled away for construction purposes. After the property on which the largest mounds stood was acquired in 1890 by John A. Koontz and later was sold to Henry D. Abrams, this practice was stopped.

In 1915 Nels C. Nelson of the American Museum of Natural History traveled to Aztec to inspect the ancient remains. Recognizing their potential for further investigation, he soon convinced his institution that the largest unit of the Aztec group, the West Ruin, should be the scene of a major excavation program. Owner Abrams gave the American Museum of Natural History excavation rights, with the provision that he be allowed to retain some of the recovered specimens. Philanthropist Archer M. Huntington, owner of the Southern Pacific Railroad, agreed to fund what was anticipated to be a long-term undertaking. A budding young archeologist, Earl H. Morris, who had grown up in the Animas valley, been educated at the University of Colorado, and who was well versed in the antiquities of the region, was chosen to head the project. From 1916 through 1922 Morris devoted his energies to excavating the major portion of the West Ruin.

At the outset the museum intended to completely clear the prehistoric settlement and to strengthen or stabilize all walls or other features in need of repair. However, interrupted by World War I and shortage of funds, excavation of only about two-thirds of the rectangular, multistoried town was completed. As revealed by the excavations and surface evidence, the building originally had at least 220 ground-floor rooms, 119 second-story rooms, and probably more than 12 third-story rooms. There were twenty-nine kivas and one Great Kiva. Foundations for a second Great Kiva underlying the cleared example suggest an earlier aborted effort.

In addition to the principal mound of the site, Morris tested some of the associated ruins. Since his time, the National Park Service has opened a few additional units in the West Ruin and sections of other sites in conjunction with preservation and stabilization measures. In 1934, under National Park Service sponsorship, Morris directed the complicated project of refurbishing the Great Kiva which he had dug years earlier.

The Hubbard Site, a small but significant ruin at the northwest corner of the monument, was cleared by National Park Service archeologists in 1953 to learn more about a particular type of archeological feature peculiar to the region along the upper San Juan River. Its primary element is a triple-walled complex encircling a kiva, which is believed to have been employed in religious activities.

The American Museum of Natural History purchased the small tract of land on which the West Ruin is situated in 1920 and subsequently donated it to the government. On January 23, 1923, Aztec Ruins National Monument was established by proclamation of President Warren G. Harding. Morris was its first custodian. Later additions to the monument brought it to a total of twenty-seven acres within which are six major archeological complexes and seven or eight smaller mounds, some of which may merely be refuse dumps from the settlements.

In 1966 the Aztec Ruins National Monument was placed on the National Register of Historic Places. Additional recognition came in 1987 when the United Nations Educational, Scientific, and Cultural Organization included Aztec Ruins with the Chaco Culture National Historical Park as a World Heritage Center. Finally, in 1988 the size of the monument was increased to 319 acres to incorporate adjacent farmlands in order to halt damage from irrigation waters to the fragile cultural resources and uncultivated terraces to the west and north where many Anasazi ruins have been threatened by vandalism. Included in long-term plans is the conversion of a portion of the present visitor center, originally a house Morris built with materials from West Ruin, into a museum devoted to pioneer southwestern archeologists and additional exhibit space.

Most of the artifacts obtained by the American Museum of National History excavations still are deposited in that institution in New York. National Park Service collections include specimens from all sites in the monument, particularly the West Ruin and the Hubbard Site, and in addition contain items from surrounding locations donated by local residents. The Abrams family collections remain in private hands. ▲

ADDITIONAL READINGS, Aztec Ruins National Monument
Corbett, John M.
    1963 *Aztec Ruins National Monument, New Mexico.* Historical Handbook Series, No.
            36. Washington, D.C.: National Park Service.
Lister, Florence C., and Robert H. Lister
    1977 *Earl Morris and Southwestern Archaeology.* Reprint of 1968. Albuquerque:
            University of New Mexico Press.
    1993 *Earl Morris and Southwestern Archaeology.* Reprint of 1977. Tucson, Arizona:
            Southwest Parks and Monuments Association.
Lister, Robert H., and Florence C. Lister
    1987 *Aztec Ruins on the Animas: Excavated, Preserved, and Interpreted.*
            Albuquerque: University of New Mexico Press.
    1990 *Aztec Ruins National Monument: Administrative History of an Archeological
            Preserve.* Professional Papers, No. 24. Santa Fe, New Mexico: Southwest
            Cultural Resource Center, National Park Service.

Morris, Earl H.
    1919 *The Aztec Ruin.* Anthropological Papers, Vol. 26, Pt. 1. New York: American Museum of Natural History.
    1921 *The House of the Great Kiva at the Aztec Ruin.* Anthropological Papers, Vol. 26, Pt. 2. New York: American Museum of Natural History.
Vivian, R. Gordon
    1959 *The Hubbard Site and Other Tri-walled Structures in New Mexico and Colorado.* Archeological Research Series, No. 5. Washington, D.C.: National Park Service.

Custodian Faris and workmen Tatman and Howe at Aztec during 1933–34 repairs. Funded by Civil Works Administration.
NATIONAL PARK SERVICE.

Interior of reconstructed Great Kiva, Aztec Ruins National Monument. GEORGE A. GRANT, NATIONAL PARK SERVICE, 1940.

Partially reconstructed talus village, Bandelier National Monument. GEORGE A. GRANT, NATIONAL PARK SERVICE, 1934.

BANDELIER NATIONAL MONUMENT, NEW MEXICO

Cultural Significance and Archeological Classification

After a limited Archaic presence followed by a long hiatus, a major Anasazi occupation of the verdant Pajarito Plateau began in the eleventh century and reached peak expansion in the thirteenth and fourteenth centuries. Remains consisted of tiny fieldhouses, pueblos with more than a hundred rooms, rooms in alcoves, rock shelters, and lesser features such as cists, hearths, rock art, trails, and check dams.

The large and small talus communities for which Bandelier National Monument is best known demonstrate the adaptation of pueblo architecture to the Pajarito Plateau, where the soft volcanic deposits provided poor building material for stonemasons but whose cliffs were such that cavities could easily be quarried into them. Communities with walls of irregularly shaped building blocks set in large amounts of mud mortar were built against the bases of cliffs, into which additional connecting rooms were carved. Some large pueblos, such as Tyuonyi and Tsankawi, dating from about A.D. 1400–1550, were placed away from the cliffs in canyon-bottom or mesa-top locations.

The coalescence of Pueblo population along the Rio Grande in late prehistoric times is exemplified by these and many other ruins in the vicinity. Reading Adolph Bandelier's *The Delight Makers*, an ethnohistoric novel set in Frijoles Canyon, gives an insight into fifteenth-century Pueblo life and the peoples' struggle against nomadic newcomers.

Archaic: *Oshara*
Anasazi: *Pueblo III, IV*
All-Southwest: *Hamlets, Villages, Towns, plateau zone*

Explorations and Investigations

Adolph F. Bandelier was born in 1840 in Berne, Switzerland. When he was eight, the Bandeliers moved to Highland, a small Illinois town. His father became a partner in a local bank and was prominent in civic affairs. Young Adolph apparently received his primary education in Highland, but from childhood was stimulated by his family's social connections, wide-ranging scientific inquiry, and mastery of foreign languages. Nevertheless, to prepare him for a career similar to his father's, he was sent back to Berne to study law at the university. As a young married man, he assisted at the bank, became active in community matters, and was headed toward a successful business career.

However, Bandelier's latent fascination with natural history and ancient societies, and the influence of newly acquired scientific associates, prompted him at age forty to embark vigorously in the disciplines of southwestern anthropology and history.

Bandelier arrived in Santa Fe in the summer of 1880 and started immediately upon his first fieldwork, which took him to the ruins of Pecos pueblo, the modern pueblos of Santo Domingo and Cochiti, and finally to the canyon of El Rito de los Frijoles. His journal entry for October 23, 1880, describes this initial foot and horseback trip with a group of Cochiti Indians across a series of deep, lava-strewn canyons and sharp mesas to the Rio Grande and then into Frijoles Canyon. Bandelier's enthusiasm for the area was immediate; El Rito de los Frijoles that cut into the Pajarito Plateau and wound through thick pines, oaks, and cottonwoods was always one of his favorite places. The region and its antiquities were described in seven of his scientific reports. It was the setting for his only novel, written first in German as *Die Koshare* but published in 1890 in English as *The Delight Makers*.

The name El Rito de los Frijoles, or Bean Creek, was applied to the stream and its canyon long before Bandelier knew it. Today, it is commonly called simply Frijoles Canyon. By 1800 the canyon had been designated El Rito de los Frijoles, and plots of it were under cultivation periodically, especially in beans, hay, and grain. Archives of a few years later state that cattle thieves banded together to occupy caves in the canyon like those used by the "barbarians." Apparently this was the earliest reference to the aboriginal lodges of the area.

Edgar L. Hewett, first director of the School of American Research and the Museum of New Mexico, both in Santa Fe, followed Bandelier's circuitous trails on the Pajarito Plateau. Beginning in 1896 and continuing for several years, he and his Indian guides tramped over the country exploring, mapping, and making preliminary archeological inquiries. In 1907 Hewett began digging at some of the region's larger, more promising sites, first Puyé, on the Santa Clara Indian Reservation, and then in Frijoles Canyon. There he and his colleagues and students worked for many seasons.

At Frijoles Canyon Hewett's summer field camps served as training grounds for aspiring students of archeology and as a study and conference center for scholars, writers, artists, and others. Tyuonyi, one of the four canyon-bottom community houses, was excavated, and others were tested. Tyuonyi proved to be a large, oval-shaped pueblo, built about a central plaza, completely enclosed except for a narrow entryway. It had more than 250 ground-floor, cell-like rooms made of blocks of the volcanic tuff that forms the crust of the Pajarito Plateau, and may have stood three stories high in places. Three kivas were sunk into its plaza.

Several talus villages in Frijoles Canyon also were cleared. These are ruins of small terraced masonry pueblos set against the base of a vertical cliff where the talus slope meets the wall of the canyon. The floor and ceiling beams of the rear rooms rested in holes cut into the tuff. Sometimes additional interior rooms were created by cutting doorways in the rear rock walls and then expanding the excavation into room-shaped cavities. The volcanic tuff was easily removed with stone or even wooden tools. These ruins are not cliff dwellings in the usual sense, but are more correctly pueblos built into the cliff.

Hewett's crews also dug in Ceremonial Cave situated high on the canyon escarpment, which contains a well-preserved kiva and a few associated rooms. Outside Frijoles Canyon they made limited tests in some of the larger pueblo ruins, such as Otowi, Tsankawi, and Tshirege.

Bandelier's research called attention to the need to protect the fragile ruins of the Pajarito Plateau. In 1902 legislation was introduced in the U.S. Congress to create a Cliff Dwellers National Park, but objections from loggers and ranchers prevented passage of the bill. It was not until Hewett's archeological program further demonstrated the cultural significance of the region, and he had committed himself to a dogged campaign to have the area set aside as a preserve, that the national holding was proclaimed in 1916. President Wilson fittingly named it Bandelier National Monument.

Under National Park Service administration, some minor excavations, such as in Rainbow House, have been completed. Beginning in the 1930s, emphasis was placed on cleaning up the ruins and preserving those in disrepair.

A series of archeological surveys and salvage excavations in the Rio Grande canyon along the monument's southeastern border was initiated in the mid-1960s in conjunction with the construction of the Cochiti Dam by the U.S. Army Corps of Engineers. The reservoir waters have impacted many archeological sites in and south of the monument. These investigations, handled by the University of New Mexico, the Museum of New Mexico, and the National Park Service, have enhanced the understanding of the monument's prehistory.

In 1977 a disastrous wildfire broke out in Bandelier that raged out of control ten days despite the efforts of more than fifteen hundred firefighters. Before it was finally extinguished, fifteen thousand acres of dense forest in and around part of the monument had been consumed. A unique role was played by archeologists during the firefighting, as they accompanied bulldozers clearing fire lanes through trees and scrub growth. The archeologists ranged on foot ahead of the bulldozers, identifying unexcavated ruins and relaying their locations so they would not be obliterated. Once the fire was out, the archeologists returned to the ash-covered, charred landscape to record the many small ruins that previously had been hidden by the thick forest cover. They also tested their contents to determine what effects the fire had had upon the ruins and artifacts. The most obvious damage was to the volcanic tuff used both as unshaped and shaped blocks by Anasazi masons as their basic wall-construction material. Heat caused the soft tuff to spall and disintegrate.

A positive result of the La Mesa conflagration was that it made administrators aware of their lack of knowledge of the volume or exact kind of cultural resources existent within the monument. Therefore, ten years later government funding was obtained to conduct the area's first systematic archeological reconnaissance. Nearly two thousand sites were tabulated, many of them previously unknown.

Most of the collections resulting from the early excavations in the monument by the School of American Research and the Museum of New Mexico are in those institutions in Santa Fe. The National Park Service's Southwest Cultural Resoures Center, also in Santa Fe, the University of New Mexico, and the Museum of New Mexico have materials from survey and salvage projects. A small assortment of artifacts remains in the monument's visitor center. ⏁

ADDITIONAL READINGS, Bandelier National Monument
Bandelier, Adolph F.
    1976 *The Delight Makers*. Reprint of 1890. New York: Harcourt Brace Jovanovich.
Barey, Patricia
    1990 *Bandelier National Monument*. Tucson, Arizona: Southwest Parks and

Ceremonial Cave, Bandelier National Monument. GEORGE H. H. HUEY.

Monuments Association.

Bousman, C. Britt, Paul Larson, and Frances Levine
1974 *Archaeological Assessment of Bandelier National Monument.* Archaeology Research Program. Dallas, Texas: Southern Methodist University.

Hendron, J. W.
1940 *Prehistory of El Rito de los Frijoles, Bandelier National Monument.* Technical Series, No. 1. Coolidge, Arizona: Southwestern Monuments Association.

Hewett, Edgar L.
1938 *Pajarito Plateau and its Ancient People.* Albuquerque: University of New Mexico Press.

Hubbell, Lyndi, and Diane Traylor, Editors
1982 *Bandelier: Excavations in the Flood Pool of Cochiti Lake, New Mexico.* Denver, Colorado: Interagency Archeological Services Division, National Park Service.

Lange, Charles H., and Carroll L. Riley
1966 *The Southwestern Journals of Adolph F. Bandelier, 1880–1882.* Albuquerque: University of New Mexico Press.

Noble, David G., Editor
1980 *Bandelier National Monument, Geology, History, Prehistory.* Santa Fe, New Mexico: Exploration, Annual Bulletin of the School of American Research.

Wing, Kittridge A.
1955 *Bandelier National Monument, New Mexico.* Historical Handbook Series, No. 23. Washington, D.C.: National Park Service.

Tyuonyi, large canyon-bottom community, Bandelier National Monument. GEORGE A. GRANT, NATIONAL PARK SERVICE, 1934.

White House Ruin, Canyon de Chelly National Monument. GEORGE A. GRANT, NATIONAL PARK SERVICE, 1940.

CANYON DE CHELLY NATIONAL MONUMENT, ARIZONA

Cultural Significance and Archeological Classification

Although overshadowed by an awe-inspiring natural setting, its extraordinarily long record of human occupation and abundance of perishable artifacts make Canyon de Chelly National Monument a unique archeological experience. Plentiful Basket Maker remains, numerous late Pueblo II and Pueblo III structures, protohistoric Hopi and Navajo shelters and goods, and a rich array of rock art of all ages confirm the importance of these canyons to the Anasazi and later Native American peoples. The many unexcavated sites available for future study enhance the value of the monument.

Explorations and Investigations

Located on the high plateau of northeastern Arizona near the center of the Navajo Reservation, Canyon de Chelly National Monument encompasses three of the Southwest's most spectacular red-walled canyons—Canyon de Chelly, Canyon del Muerto, and Monument Canyon. The area that became a national monument in 1931 is named for its main declivity, Canyon de Chelly, thought to be a corruption of the Navajo word "tsegi," meaning rocky canyon. It is administered by the National Park Service as a joint-use area with the Navajo Nation.

Scattered on the evergreen canyon rims, in bottom lands, in shallow alcoves, and on high ledges along the canyon walls are remains of some fifteen hundred years of human occupation. These range from early pithouses to silent cliff dwellings marooned high on slick rock, to the hogans of the Navajos who farm the canyon bottom in summer. Exactly when this remnant of civilization became known to the Europeans occupying the Rio Grande valley is uncertain, but a 1776 Spanish map clearly indicates the location of Canyon de Chelly. Certainly within a quarter-century Spanish troops had entered the region, but any observation of antiquities was secondary to their task of bringing the Navajos to justice.

The Navajo Indians are thought to have filtered into the de Chelly area in the mid-1700s from north-central New Mexico, where contact with Hispanic settlers had introduced them to horses, sheep, and goats and gradually changed their way of life. Formerly the Navajos existed by hunting small game, gathering wild plants, and raising a few patches of corn or beans. The acquisition of livestock converted them into full-time pastoral herdsmen who found it easier to raid neighboring farmers than to grow their own crops. Anglo towns along the Rio Grande and the Pueblo Indian villages especially tempted them, with the result that the century between the 1770s and the 1860s saw almost continual friction.

The Spanish method of trying to cope with the Navajos was to offer them bribes and, if that failed, to send punitive expeditions against them. One such foray occurred in 1805, when a military column entered the Canyon de Chelly country bent upon engaging fleeing

Anasazi: *Basket Maker II, III; Pueblo I, II, III, IV (?)*
All-Southwest: *Hamlets, Villages, Towns, plateau zone*

Mescalero Apache pictographs in backcountry cave, Carlsbad Caverns National Park. GEORGE H. H. HUEY.

Casa Grande, Casa Grande Ruins National Monument. GEORGE A. GRANT, NATIONAL PARK SERVICE, 1934.

CASA GRANDE RUINS NATIONAL MONUMENT, ARIZONA

Cultural Significance and Archeological Classification

Archeological features of Casa Grande Ruins National Monument played an important role in defining one of the three major components of the ancient sedentary culture of the Southwest. In addition, the monument preserves the only remaining example of a Great House, a feature common in the once numerous Classic Hohokam towns along the river oases of southern Arizona. Casa Grande tells the story of adaptation to an arid environment which permitted a large population of irrigation farmers to prosper for many centuries.

Hohokam: *Pioneer, Colonial, Sedentary (Snaketown), Classic (Casa Grande)*
All-Southwest: *Hamlets, Villages (Snaketown), Towns (Casa Grande), desert zone*

Explorations and Investigations

Seventeenth-century Jesuit missionary Fray Eusebio Kino was the first European to visit the site and refer to it as the Casa Grande, or Great House. While visiting Indian villages on the northern border of his sweeping territory, called the Pimería or land of the Pima Indians, Kino heard tales of a "casa grande" on the banks of the Gila River. Aided by Indian guides, he reached the ruin in 1694, said mass within its towering crumbling walls, and wrote an account in his journal. He saw it as a four-story building as large as a castle or any church then in Sonora. He also noted thirteen smaller ruined houses in the immediate vicinity.

Kino returned to the Casa Grande several other times. In 1697 he was accompanied by Captain Cristóbal Martín Bernal and a detachment of soldiers. Bernal's narrative provides a few more details about the Casa Grande and notes the existence there of an ancient canal estimated to be ten yards wide and four yards deep.

During the eighteenth and first half of the nineteenth centuries, the Casa Grande became a landmark for other Spanish and American travelers following the Gila River across the desolate stretches of southern Arizona. Some of them wrote accounts that recorded in word and sketch what they saw and how they felt about the unusual structure.

At the time of the war between the United States and Mexico, General Stephen Kearny commanded the Army of the West, which explored and established a string of fortifications across the Southwest to California. The army moved down the Gila and camped at a group of Tohono O'odham (Pima) villages near the Casa Grande in November 1846. Two of Kearny's officers, Lieutenant William H. Emory, a topographical engineer, and Captain A. R. Johnston, examined the ruin, drew ground plans and elevation sketches, and entered notes in their journals. Johnston observed that the massive earthen structure contained plastered walls four feet thick at their bases that curved inward as the upper levels were reached. The first of the four stories was filled with rubbish. He saw wooden joists for the other levels still in place, although at some time floors and roof had been burned. Their charred ends lacked any evidence of having been cut with metal tools.

By the 1880s references to the Casa Grande began to indicate that vandalism, such as removal of wood and wall material and the scratching of graffiti on the plastered walls, was increasing. It was stimulated in part by the completion of the Southern Pacific Railroad through the area, which placed the ruin only twenty miles by a well-traveled road from Casa Grande station. Fortunately, a growing national consciousness of archeology and serious efforts to protect aboriginal sites prevented further destruction of the site and brought professional archeologists to the scene. Staff members of two research institutions founded in 1879, the Archaeological Institute of America and the Bureau of Ethnology, became involved with the Casa Grande.

During an extensive survey in June 1883, Adolph F. Bandelier, under auspices of the Archaeological Institute of America, spent several hot days measuring and mapping the Casa Grande and contiguous structures, examining artifacts from the ruins in the vicinity, and interviewing local Indians about their way of life and their ideas about the ruin. His journal and later reports suggested that the Casa Grande proper could have functioned either as a domestic edifice or as a fortress.

The next scholar to concern himself with the Casa Grande was Frank H. Cushing, leader of the Hemenway Southwestern Archaeological Expedition. This group conducted systematic excavations in the Gila-Salt basin during 1887 and 1888. The expedition, privately sponsored by Mrs. Mary Hemenway, accomplished the first organized archeological work in the Southwest, not only in southern Arizona but later in ruins near Zuni, New Mexico. After examining the Casa Grande and no doubt having been influenced by his earlier study of Zuni, Cushing decided that it had been the assembly place of the priesthood of a highly organized, stratified society.

Agitation for the protection of the Casa Grande began in 1887, along with a proposal to establish an archeological society in Arizona. Congress was petitioned to preserve antiquities on federal lands, but the legislation met with numerous setbacks and delays in Washington. Finally, in 1889 congressional approval for the preservation of the Casa Grande was obtained, together with funds for a stabilization project. Jesse W. Fewkes, who succeeded Cushing as head of the Hemenway party, went to the Casa Grande in 1891 to document the extent of destruction. He observed the damage caused by curious travelers but understood that erosion undercutting construction joints was the principal cause of past destruction and, if allowed to continue, might lead to collapse of the structure.

Cosmos Mindeleff was dispatched in late 1891 by the Bureau of Ethnology to study the Casa Grande before the stabilization was initiated. He made the first accurate topographical maps of the site, drew a scaled ground plan of the building, and wrote one of the most perceptive descriptions of its architecture. Preservation followed. These efforts included clearing debris from within the ruin and underpinning a number of badly weathered wall sections with cement and bricks. Two-by-fours were placed over the doorways, and the south wall was braced with metal tie rods and a wooden beam. The next year 480 acres encompassing the Casa Grande and several other archeological units were made the first federal reservation for a prehistoric site in the United States. When Congress appropriated additional funds for the Casa Grande, Fewkes returned from 1906 to 1908 to prepare it for exhibition to the American public. He excavated the remaining ruins in Compound A, the enclosed complex that included the Casa Grande, as well as several other mounds in the environs.

An important name in the history of the Casa Grande as a public educational attraction is that of Frank H. Pinkley. As a youth in 1901, he was named caretaker of the Casa Grande Ruins shortly after it was placed under the authority of the General Land Office. He served as its manager, protector, and interpreter the rest of his life, during which time the status of the area changed to a national park and finally in 1918 to a national monument. With meager funds he strove to maintain the ruins and improve their accessibility to visitors. Also in 1918 he initiated the first trenching of a depression near the Casa Grande that later was identified as a ballcourt, and he tested several other structures in nearby sites.

Frank Pinkley was not only in charge of the Casa Grande, but he assumed responsibility for other monuments as they began to be set aside. Ultimately in 1924 the National Park Service named him superintendent of all southwestern national monuments. Under his leadership, custodians, rangers, and scientists set about to protect, preserve, and interpret the ruins and missions and to develop visitor and staff facilities. Among the new improvements was a modern roof, erected in 1930–31, to protect the Casa Grande from rain. "The Boss," as Pinkley was warmly known to his men, maintained his headquarters at the Casa Grande.

Continuing studies of the role of the Casa Grande in regional prehistory have involved surveys of the monument, and test excavations in Compound A and several other villages by the Southwest Museum, the Los Angeles County Museum, and the National Park Service. Of narrower focus were observations made in 1969 by John Molloy, a University of Arizona graduate student, in an attempt to demonstrate that some of the openings in the high walls of the principal structure had been used to observe certain celestial events, such as solstices and equinoxes. That information would have been essential to setting up a calendrical system for regulating ceremonial cycles and agricultural routines. It is known that the Pueblo Indian priesthoods, as well as some among Mexican Indians, make such observations.

Even in dry environments, buildings made of sun-dried mud are vulnerable to the elements, making continual care of the Casa Grande imperative. Ways to arrest further erosion and also to reinforce its walls so that they could survive a severe earthquake have been investigated by soil scientists, chemists, and civil engineers. One proposal involves placing a steel grid framework bonded with epoxy in the walls so the building could withstand earth tremors.

In light of this or other potential protective procedures and their resulting disturbance of archeological deposits, the National Park Service called for a definitive architectural study of the Casa Grande. The research was done in 1975 and 1976 by David R. Wilcox and Lynette O. Shenk of the Arizona State Museum of the University of Arizona. Their reports address many questions about the Casa Grande and contain the most detailed analysis ever made of the multistoried house. In an effort to resolve conflicting ideas about such aspects of the site as its time of occupation, method of construction, original height, and purpose, Wilcox and Shenk reached certain conclusions and presented recommendations. Lacking

The original protective roof over Casa Grande. GEORGE A. GRANT, NATIONAL PARK SERVICE, 1925.

tree-ring dates, but using chronological data from archeological materials at the site and making comparisons with better-dated antiquities in the vicinity, they believe it likely that the Casa Grande was built and occupied between A.D. 1300 and 1450. The entire edifice was built at one time using local soil with beams of juniper, ponderosa pine, fir, and mesquite, some of which were obtained at great distance.

Walls were made of lenses of stiff mud piled up in courses lacking internal reinforcing members. The present height of the house closely approximates the original height of four stories. The first story was purposefully filled in during construction; the second and third stories each had five rooms; a single room or tower comprised the fourth story; and a low parapet may have surrounded the uppermost roof levels. The function of the Casa Grande remains unclear, although it may have been a communal dwelling similar to other structures in Compound A. The "observation holes" in some rooms suggest a more special, but undetermined, use.

Within twenty-five miles northwest of the Casa Grande is a large archeological zone called Snaketown. From a scientific point of view, it completely overshadows its neighbor. Because it does not have a dominant, easily recognizable feature such as a Great House, it was of little interest during early explorations and settlement. Once comprehensive archeological investigations got under way in southern Arizona, however, its potential for fruitful research became obvious. As a result, two periods of excavation there have contributed as much to understanding the ancient sedentary peoples of the low desert as the cumulative efforts of all other research in the Southwest.

When Harold S. Gladwin opened his research facility at Gila Pueblo in 1928, he already was on the track of the people responsible for the prehistoric remains of the Gila-Salt basin. The sprawling, unvandalized ruins at Snaketown, covering more than half of a square mile, became known to him years before while he was working through trash mounds at the Casa Grande. Because he was dealing with a new and little-known culture, he postponed digging there until he had better defined its characteristics. Not until he had dug several small ruins and visited and collected from more than twelve thousand prehistoric sites throughout the greater Southwest did he tackle Snaketown.

Aided chiefly by Emil W. Haury and E. B. Sayles of his Gila Pueblo staff, Gladwin excavated portions of Snaketown during 1934 and 1936. Rounded trash mounds, some ten feet high, were conspicuous in the flat desert. Stratigraphic trenches, carefully dug into three of the approximately sixty mounds dotting the site, yielded enormous quantities of potsherds and other artifacts. These were chronologically arranged to help refine and expand upon the generally accepted stages of cultural evolution. Forty single-roomed habitations, obscured by trash and soil, were located and excavated. All had been built in shallow circular to rectangular pits having inclined or vertical walls. They had flat roofs supported and framed with timbers, covered with smaller timbers and earth. Variations of this basic plan distinguished the house types of different periods. Another major find at Snaketown was two ballcourts, a feature commonly found at sites in Mexico and Central America where a game with religious connotations was played. Also present were sections of a canal that had delivered water from the Gila River to garden plots. Development of an irrigation system obviously had been fundamental to the survival of these desert farmers. Ashy remains from cremation of the dead, together with funerary offerings, were found in areas that appeared to have been used only for burial.

Analyses of new findings provided insight into the regional prehistory but left some basic problems unanswered. One nagging question was the time of occupation. Tree-ring dates were not available because they could not be determined from the charred timbers. Hence a chronology was devised based upon trade pottery from cultures which had been dated by tree-rings. A lifetime of some fourteen hundred years was postulated for the village, beginning about 300 B.C. If that date were correct, the initial stage of the Hohokam predated that of other known southwestern cultures.

Gladwin theorized that the regional culture, as exemplified by Snaketown, evolved from an indigenous hunting and gathering group. Over a period of several centuries, epecially from about A.D. 500 to 900, the adaptation of local traditions and the absorption of traits from outside sources stimulated cultural advances. Notable among these were agricultural techniques, arts and crafts, and religious practices. According to the Gladwin reconstruction, after about A.D. 1300, in a stage not represented at Snaketown, people with a somewhat divergent lifestyle moved from the Tonto basin down into the Gila basin and merged with the original inhabitants. The two peoples occupied the same villages. The newcomers built multistoried communal houses such as at the Casa Grande, made a different kind of pottery, and buried rather than cremated their dead. After about a century of coexistence, the immigrants seem to have moved on, leaving the territory to its first occupants, who probably evolved into the modern Tohono O'odham. Other members of the Gila Pueblo staff identified Mexico as the main source of alien traits that enriched the native culture of southern Arizona.

After the initial research at Snaketown, Gladwin re-evaluated his original interpretations and, in 1942 and 1948, he revised the chronology upward in time, pictured the early stage at Snaketown as not ancestral to the more complex culture of southern Arizona, and set the beginning of the Hohokam presence at about A.D. 700. He believed this date better coincided with the infusion of new elements from Mexico. Other concepts had the local peoples being invaded by the Hohokam from Mexico sometime between A.D. 500 and 900. Emil Haury, who had left Gila Pueblo after the Snaketown excavations to become chairman of the Department of Anthropology at the University of Arizona, held to the chronology and general scheme of interpretation as it had been outlined in 1937. Thus, there were sharp differences of opinion among the experts as to the identity of the first farmers of the desert Southwest, and a variation of about one thousand years in estimates for the age of the early stages of Hohokam culture.

In an attempt to resolve the problems, Haury decided to reinvestigate Snaketown and returned in 1964 and 1965 to explore the points of contention. Haury and his crew employed some excavation and dating procedures developed after Gila Pueblo's original work at the site. These included use of mechanical earth-moving equipment and radioactive carbon and archeomagnetic methods for dating certain kinds of remains. Haury also was able to draw on a large body of archeological data of the greater Southwest which had accrued since 1937. Particular attention was paid to a review of the Snaketown chronology, the questions of Hohokam origins and Mexican influences, and the history of irrigation agriculture. Extensive probing in previously undisturbed areas was undertaken in more than one hundred sixty houses, several large trash mounds and rubbish-filled pits, portions of canals, cremation areas, wells, and caches. After more than a decade of laboratory analysis and report preparation, in 1976 the results of Haury's reexamination of Snaketown and the Hohokam appeared.

Haury concluded that the original chronology for Snaketown, a stretch of time from about 300 B.C. to A.D. 1100, could be substantiated. He determined that irrigation agriculture had been practiced at Snaketown from the time it was founded. In a dramatic turn of mind, he decided that the Hohokam themselves had been a migrant group from Mexico. According to this theory, while searching for a new home, the Hohokam had arrived in the Gila basin bearing a diluted version of central Mexican culture dependent upon irrigation agriculture. Once settled in the new surroundings, in effect they were an aberrant Mexican society acting as a donor culture to other southwesterners.

Together Snaketown and the Casa Grande present a rich record of Hohokam cultural evolution. A slow cultural ripening from beginning to climax is scattered over and beneath the sands of Snaketown. Its later stages, when foreigners or influences from elsewhere in the Southwest engulfed the Hohokam, are present at the Casa Grande.

A number of Hohokam artifacts are exhibited at Casa Grande Ruins National Monument. Others have been deposited in the Western Archeological and Conservation Center in Tucson. The Arizona State Museum, University of Arizona, has the large collections from Snaketown. ▲

ADDITIONAL READINGS, Casa Grande Ruins National Monument
Gladwin, Harold S., Emil W. Haury, Edwin B. Sayles, and Nora Gladwin
    1965 *Excavations at Snaketown: Material Culture.* Reprint of 1937. Tucson: University of Arizona Press.
Haury, Emil W.
    1976 *The Hohokam: Desert Farmers and Craftsmen. Excavations at Snaketown, 1964–1965.* Tucson: University of Arizona Press.
Noble, David Grant
    1991 *The Hohokam, Ancient People of the Desert.* Santa Fe, New Mexico: School of American Research.
Wilcox, David R., and Lynette O. Shenk
    1977 *The Architecture of the Casa Grande and its Interpretations.* Archaeological Series, No. 115. Tucson: Arizona State Museum.

Emil W. Haury at Snaketown during excavation. HELGA TEIWES, ARIZONA STATE MUSEUM, UNIVERSITY OF ARIZONA.

North wall of Pueblo Bonito, Chaco Culture National Historical Park after repairs of damages from the 1880s. GEORGE A. GRANT, NATIONAL PARK SERVICE, 1929.

CHACO CULTURE NATIONAL HISTORICAL PARK, NEW MEXICO

Cultural Significance and Archeological Classification

Chaco Canyon includes the largest and some of the most significant and thoroughly studied prehistoric communities in the Southwest. In their desolate surroundings, these remains record a cultural evolution that parallels that of other plateau people until about A.D. 1000. At that time an amazing fecundity resulted in complex economic development and advancement of certain skills unique in the ancient Southwest. One interpretation is that the Chaco Phenomenon that evolved was an integrated system of perhaps as many as seventy-five cooperating communities which produced and assembled goods for local consumption and for widespread distribution over an area of thirty thousand square miles. Another is that there was a politico-religious basis for the obvious regional linkage of eastern Anasazi under the domination of those at Chaco Canyon. Particularly noteworthy in Chaco are the outstanding architectural and construction accomplishments of the builders of the great towns, the networks of roads and visual signaling stations that linked the Chaco world, and the means for harnessing and distributing runoff waters. A hierarchical social system undetected in other contemporary Anasazi societies is implied in these communal endeavors. Physical, social, economic, and moral factors combined to bring the decline and fall of this unusual divergence from the normal Anasazi pattern.

Explorations and Investigations

A presidential proclamation of March 11, 1907, included Chaco Canyon National Monument among a group of eighteen areas reserved during Theodore Roosevelt's tenure. By that time the great ruins of Chaco Canyon had been popularized in fact and fantasy, probed for years by an organized archeological expedition, and subjected to heated debate between those who wished to continue unrestrained digging and those who opposed it.

On December 19, 1980, the U.S. Congress enlarged the monument by 12,500 acres and changed its name to Chaco Culture National Historical Park. An additional system to preserve and protect thirty-three outlying Chacoan sites was proposed. The canyon and its satellite territories are a diamond in the rough compared to other well-manicured national properties, mainly because they are accessible only over rutted dirt roads that at times are impassable. At this writing, improvements are being made.

The ruins of Chaco Canyon likely were known in the seventeenth century to Spanish occupants of northern New Mexico. Military forays already had sallied forth against the Navajos who, long after the first dwellers had deserted their arid canyon lands, had settled in and near the Chaco. Few archival records exist for the years before 1680, when most such documents fell victim to an Indian uprising. In the middle of the next century knowledge of Chaco is confirmed by requests of several men for land near there and by

Archaic: *Oshara*
Anasazi: *Basket Maker III; Pueblo I, II, III*
All-Southwest: *Hamlets, Villages, Towns, plateau zone*

Anasazi, Pueblo III, black-on-white effigy vessel. ROBERT H. LISTER, EARL MORRIS MEMORIAL COLLECTION, UNIVERSITY OF COLORADO MUSEUM.

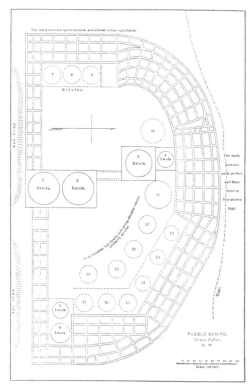

William H. Jackson's map of Pueblo Bonito prepared during his visit to Chaco Canyon in 1877. FROM THE TENTH ANNUAL REPORT OF THE UNITED STATES GEOLOGICAL AND GEOGRAPHICAL SURVEY OF THE TERRITORIES.

the name "Chaca" inscribed on a 1774 Spanish map of the canyon's vicinity.

Military action against the Navajos was responsible for additional knowledge about Chaco Canyon in the early nineteenth century. Soldiers departing from Santa Fe and its vicinity for the Navajo domain usually traveled most of the length of Chaco Canyon.

The first substantive report on the ruins in Chaco came in 1849 shortly after the opening of the American era. Lieutenant James H. Simpson, a member of a U.S. Army outfit pursuing marauding Navajos, spent several days in the canyon. He carefully described seven of the larger ruins, gave them names used by his Indian and Mexican guides, had drawings and measurements made of them, and noted their bleak surroundings. The massiveness of the sites, the excellent engineering skills evident in their construction, and the immense effort involved in erecting and occupying such sizable communities in the demanding environment greatly impressed him.

Slightly more than a quarter-century later the U.S. Geological and Geographical Survey of the Territories sent a field party into northwestern New Mexico. In May 1877, led by photographer William H. Jackson, the group entered Chaco Canyon. Jackson devoted about five days to reconnoitering, mapping, sketching, photographing, and taking notes. Unfortunately, none of the more than four hundred exposures he tediously made with a cumbersome eight-by-ten camera turned out. Jackson re-examined the ruins that Simpson had identified and found and named several others. He was the first to recognize the existence of stairways, which the Chacoans had cut into the cliffs so they could move in and out of the canyon. And he was also the first to comment on the appreciable amount of sedimentation and erosion that had taken place on the canyon floor after the towns were vacated.

The next chapter in the voluminous saga of investigations into Chaco Canyon's prehistory was dominated by a preeminent figure in the opening of this part of the Southwest, Richard Wetherill. Following the pioneering archeological work he and his brothers accomplished at Mesa Verde and Grand Gulch, he brought the Hyde Exploring Expedition to Chaco Canyon in 1896, where it conducted excavations for four years.

Nominally, the Hyde party was directed by Professor F. W. Putnam of the American Museum of Natural History and Harvard University; he actually visited the canyon only twice during the undertaking. The field supervisor was George H. Pepper, one of Putnam's students. With Wetherill as foreman, work commenced at the prominent ruin of Pueblo Bonito. At the end of the fourth and final season, 190 rooms, kivas, and other features had been cleared, and 10,000 pieces of pottery, 5,000 stone implements, 1,000 bone and wooden objects, a few fabrics, a small number of copper bells, and a great mass of turquoise beads, pendants, and mosaic sets had been recovered and shipped to the American Museum of Natural History.

The cost to Talbot and Frederick Hyde had been in the neighborhood of twenty-five thousand dollars, but the materials collected probably exceeded any previous similar effort in this country. On the side, the Hydes set up a string of trading posts across the Navajo Reservation, and marketed Indian rugs and jewelry in the East.

While working at Pueblo Bonito, Wetherill filed a homestead claim on land in Chaco

Canyon. When the expedition concluded, he and his family remained there as ranchers and trading post operators. In June 1910, Wetherill was shot to death by a Navajo after an argument over a horse. He was buried in a small windswept cemetery within sight of Pueblo Bonito.

After the years of activity resulting from the Hydes' scientific and business operations and the excitement engendered by Wetherill's murder, Chaco Canyon fell into its characteristic solitude despite its designation as a national monument. Archeological investigations resumed in 1921, when the National Geographic Society chose Chaco Canyon for an intensive program. Neil M. Judd of the U.S. National Museum was named director of the expedition. For seven summers he and his staff again considered Chaco's prehistory. They cleared the remaining half of Pueblo Bonito, excavated about fifty rooms and kivas of Pueblo del Arroyo, and tested numerous small ruins and isolated remains in the vicinity. Biological and geological studies were correlated with archeological findings to reconstruct the past environment and man's relationship with it. In seeking reasons behind the rise and fall of Chaco culture, special attention was paid to the vegetation patterns and arroyo cutting associated with the time of the aboriginal presence.

In 1929 Frank H. H. Roberts, Jr., formerly a member of Judd's staff, returned to Chaco Canyon on behalf of the Smithsonian Institution to examine what appeared to be a concentration of pithouses on the south rim of the canyon nine miles east of Pueblo Bonito. He uncovered evidence of numerous small habitations that had consisted of a shallow pit over which had been built walls and a roof of poles, brush, and mud. Called Shabik'eshchee Village (Navajo for a large petroglyph near the site), it was a fine example of a community of late Basket Makers, predecessors of the later Pueblos who had erected the villages and towns in Chaco.

Several New Mexico institutions became interested in Chaco Canyon archeology during the 1930s through the efforts of Edgar L. Hewett. He brought students from the University of New Mexico, the Museum of New Mexico, and the School of American Research in Santa Fe to excavate Chetro Ketl. This was an imposing derelict town of jagged wall stubs, filled kivas, and mounded refuse just east of Pueblo Bonito. The situation at Chetro Ketl proved complex. Much of the present ground-level structure was found to have been superimposed over earlier, sometimes deeply buried, phases of the community. In eight seasons of digging, Hewett and his crews covered less than half of Chetro Ketl, or 130 rooms in all, eleven kivas, and two Great Kivas. Trenches were dug in the large trash heap so that its potsherds and bits of charcoal could be used to tell more about the habitation of Chaco.

In addition, various lesser ruins were excavated or tested, sections of the park were surveyed, and smaller archeology or ecology projects were accomplished. Certain architectural features were suggested to have parallels in ancient sites in Mexico and Central America. The excavation and repair of Casa Rinconada, the largest Great Kiva in Chaco directly across the canyon from Pueblo Bonito, was handled by Gordon Vivian under Hewett's direction.

In the late 1930s and 1940s the University of New Mexico's anthropology department conducted well-attended summer research and student training programs, whose staff and trainees cleared a group of small ruins just east of Casa Rinconada. Some of these small rural sites are included in the general chronology used by the National Park Service in interpreting the evolution of Chaco culture. They are pivotal in demonstrating their contemporaneity and interaction with the urbanized Pueblo Bonito and Chetro Ketl.

The appearance and condition of most of the park's exposed ruins and those unexcavated sites with standing walls are due to an intensive stabilization program begun by the National Park Service in 1933. Concurrent with his excavations, Judd had completed some preservation and reconstruction at Pueblo Bonito. Hewett had done likewise in Chetro Ketl. Though the methods they employed were common at the time, they did not prove satisfactory and in some instances actually were detrimental. To remedy this situation, the National Park Service sought other preservation procedures which would not alter the appearance of the edifices but would secure them for the future. Gordon Vivian and a trained crew of Navajos undertook the task of stabilizing and strengthening the masonry walls and wooden elements of the old buildings. They tried to erase all signs of previous preservation endeavors and to realign the natural drainages around the ruins so that moisture damage would be minimal. After many years of work, initial stabilization was realized. Still, maintenance and perfection of methods continue.

Natural forces proved more than a match for the stabilizers on one occasion. National Park Service engineers fruitlessly attempted to arrest the movement of Threatening Rock, a huge, thirty-thousand-ton wedge of sandstone that had towered precariously behind Pueblo Bonito from the time it was built. After centuries of almost undetectable shifting, the enormous monolith finally fell on January 22, 1941, crushing the finest part of the north wall of the town and all or parts of sixty-five rooms. The Pueblo Bonito trail is built over and around the great jumble of boulders and rubble left after that catastrophe.

Nature was met more evenly with the halt of the rapid erosion of the banks of Chaco Wash. Some one hundred thousand trees were planted along the watercourse, eliminating one threat to archeological evidence.

The close scrutiny of Chaco Canyon antiquities by these many representatives of highly respected institutions had resulted in a reasonably full accounting of the area's prehistory. Information concerning probable cultural evolution and the physical environment had been painstakingly gathered. But many questions, some dating from the earliest fieldwork, remained to be answered. Meanwhile, research in surrounding sectors was pushing ahead. As American archeology matured, new theoretical and technical methods had come into use which had not been applied to Chaco. In 1971 the National Park Service, in cooperation with the University of New Mexico, launched a campaign to take a modern, in-depth look at human achievements in Chaco. Robert H. Lister directed the resulting research facility, the Chaco Center, for six years. He was succeeded by W. James Judge.

The first order of the Chaco Center's business was a thorough, three-season reconnaissance of the park to determine the exact number of sites present, their location, characteristics, and cultural affiliation. The surveyors walked the forty-three square miles within and immediately adjoining National Park Service lands. More than two thousand sites were recorded, ranging from camps of the earliest nomadic foragers, through the pithouse to pueblo sequence of the sedentary farmers, to historic Navajo remains. Numerous other traces of past human activity included rock-cut stairways, small circular basins cut into bedrock, water-control devices, and examples of rock art.

The survey results indicated shifting settlement patterns that could be related to climatic fluctuations and changing cultural attributes. A network of line-of-sight signaling stations linking the entire population was defined. Data were also obtained on conditions of sites, their presumed age, their geographic setting, and their promise for further investigation. This information was essential in selecting representative sites for future testing or excavation.

Although the park proper represents the nuclear area of Chaco culture, later surveys encountered a number of comparable Chacoan house blocks a considerable distance away. Three notable such structures on government lands in Colorado are as many as 150 miles from Chaco Canyon. These are Chimney Rock near Pagosa Springs, the Escalante-Domínguez ruins near Dolores, and the Lowry Ruin west of Pleasant View.

The Chaco Center used remote sensing, a specialized analysis of various types of aerial photography, which proved of utmost importance in charting an elaborate, far-flung pattern of prehistoric roads that connected the principal Chaco centers and tied them to nearby small settlements or areas with resources unavailable in the canyon. It also aided in locating canals, reservoirs, and garden plots that had been part of an ingenious form of irrigation agriculture. Site plans and profiles and area maps prepared from aerial photos proved to be accurate, faster to produce, and cheaper than by conventional survey. Archeomagnetic dating, a technique based upon alignment of iron particles in relation to the magnetic north pole, helped date hearths or old conflagrations and thus, by extension, periods of occupation. A concerted effort to collect cores from all original wood construction elements will provide tree-ring dates to help establish building episodes within each structure. Various electronic machines were used for subsurface exploration to determine the presence and extent of buried features.

The Center's major effort was excavation of a series of sites representing each ancient cultural stage at Chaco Canyon. Efforts focused on horizons for which there had been little or no previous information. Most ruins were dug for data only and were backfilled after clearing. A few, such as the large north-rim structure of Pueblo Alto and a group of small houses in Marcia's Rincon, were opened with the intention that they be used as interpretive exhibits. More than twenty-five individual ruins or ruin complexes, including one Navajo homesite, ultimately were excavated. Additionally, minor investigations of some isolated elements and nonhabitation items were carried out. Consideration of these data and preparation of reports continue.

Astronomers and archeologists have become increasingly interested in a widely held theory that ancient southwesterners, possibly those who called Chaco Canyon home, made observations of the sun and other celestial bodies to formulate calendars and regulate ritual and farming cycles. In Chaco such efforts have been devoted to locating what may have been solstice observation stations and to identifying rock art depictions of heavenly bodies and means of reckoning time. One pictograph in a protected overhang at the west end of the canyon is believed to record the supernova of July 4, 1054.

The American Museum of Natural History in New York retains most of the huge Hyde Exploring Expedition collection. In Washington, D.C. the U.S. National Museum has most of the specimens recovered by Neil Judd, although the National Geographic Society kept some of the finer objects. The Museum of New Mexico, Santa Fe, and the Maxwell Museum of Anthropology, University of New Mexico, Albuquerque, have collections resulting from their Chaco investigations. Most artifacts and records assembled by various National Park Service endeavors are housed in the Chaco Center, also in Albuquerque. ▲

ADDITIONAL READINGS, Chaco Culture National Historical Park
Frazier, Kendrick
    1986 *People of Chaco, a Canyon and Its Culture*. New York: W. W. Norton.
Hayes, Alden C., David M. Brugge, and W. James Judge
    1981 *Archeological Surveys of Chaco Canyon, New Mexico*. Publications in
        Archeology, No. 18A. Washington, D.C.: National Park Service.
Judd, Neil M.
    1954 *The Material Culture of Pueblo Bonito*. Smithsonian Miscellaneous Collections,
        Vol. 124. Washington, D.C.
    1964 *The Architecture of Pueblo Bonito*. Smithsonian Miscellaneous Collections,
        Vol. 147. No. 1. Washington, D.C.
Lekson, Stephen H.
    1984 *Great Pueblo Architecture of Chaco Canyon, New Mexico*. Publications in
        Archeology, No. 18B. Albuquerque, New Mexico: National Park Service.
Lister, Robert H., and Florence C. Lister
    1981 *Chaco Canyon, Archaeology and Archaeologists*. Albuquerque: University of
        New Mexico Press.
McNitt, Frank
    1966 *Richard Wetherill: Anasazi*. Reprint of 1957. Albuquerque: University of New
        Mexico Press.
Mathien, Frances Joan
    1985 *Environment and Subsistence of Chaco Canyon, New Mexico*. Publications in
        Archeology, No. 18E. Albuquerque, New Mexico: National Park Service.
Noble, David G., Editor
    1984 *New Light on Chaco Canyon*. Santa Fe, New Mexico: Exploration, Annual
        Bulletin of the School of American Research.
Powers, Robert P., William B. Gillespie, and Stephen H. Lekson
    1983 *The Outlier Survey: A Regional View of Settlement in the San Juan Basin*.
        Reports of the Chaco Center, No. 3. Albuquerque, New Mexico: National Park
        Service.

Vivian, Gordon, and Paul Reiter
1960 *The Great Kivas of Chaco Canyon and Their Relationships.* Monograph, No. 22. Santa Fe, New Mexico: School of American Research.
Vivian, R. Gwinn
1990 *The Chacoan Prehistory of the San Juan Basin.* New York: Academic.
Windes, Thomas C.
1987 *Investigations at the Pueblo Alto Complex, Chaco Canyon, New Mexico; Vol. I, Summary of Tests and Excavations.* Publications in Archeology, No. 18F. Santa Fe, New Mexico: National Park Service.

Cluster of kivas in eastern portion of Pueblo Bonito, Chaco Culture National Historical Park. GEORGE A. GRANT, NATIONAL PARK SERVICE, 1929.

Archaic: *Desert Culture*
In-betweens and Outliers:
Fremont (San Rafael)
All-Southwest: *Hamlets,*
plateau zone

COLORADO NATIONAL MONUMENT, COLORADO

Cultural Significance and Archeological Classification

Enigmatic, undated Archaic/Fremont remains comprise the limited prehistoric resources of Colorado National Monument. They represent the easternmost distribution of the latter culture.

Explorations and Investigations

The broad valley at the northern base of the ruddy spired cliffs of Colorado National Monument through which the Colorado River flows attracted white settlers as soon as the Utes were removed to a more distant reservation in the early 1800s. They created farms and canals, and set about building the town of Grand Junction. The rugged canyon country and whatever human secrets it held were of little concern to most of them.

An exception was John Otto, a 1906 arrival who was enthralled with the area, built trails into it, and ceaselessly lobbied to have it federally protected. Success was his in 1911 when more than twenty thousand acres became a national monument. For the ensuing sixteen years he served as official custodian. However, there is no record of Otto having been more than casually interested in trace evidence of previous Indian presence. This situation prevailed until 1963 when the National Park Service contracted with the University of Colorado for the first archeological survey.

Meanwhile, as interest in southwestern archeology grew in the 1930s, local avocational archeologists identified a number of sites in Glade Park, a ranching area along the Colorado-Utah state line, southwest of the monument. Several test trenches in the fill of two promising caves were dug in 1940 by C. T. Hurst, a professor at Western State College in Gunnison. In the belief that information about the prehistory of the surrounding region might be forthcoming, this initial work was followed up in 1951 by University of Colorado staff members Robert H. Lister, who further excavated Luster and Roth caves, and Herbert W. Dick, who examined three nearby sites exposed by arroyo cutting. The cultural deposits turned out to be relatively thin, with a restricted artifact yield from which it was determined that the occupation probably had been Fremont. The presence of cobs and kernels of corn indicated some farming economy, but no habitations were found. Gray pottery was present, as was a variety of stone, bone, leather, and fiber materials. A large petroglyph panel in Sieber Canyon conforms to others identified as Fremont. Based upon tool typology and stratigraphy, suggested dating of the sites ranges from about sixteen hundred to seven hundred years ago.

The archeological survey of Colorado National Monument, carried out in 1963 by graduate students from the University of Colorado, produced much the same kind of materials as those from Glade Park. Seventy-five aboriginal sites were noted within the monument, none large or with extant dwelling structures. These were twenty-four rock shelters in the canyons or along escarpments and on the mesa top, forty-one open camp sites near intermittent stream beds or large rocks that would have provided shelter, two caves, eight chipping areas lacking habitations or hearths, isolated storage cists, and three petroglyph panels. Limited testing was done at two localities. Surface collections included projectile points, blades, scrapers, manos, metates, cordage, potsherds, basketry, and corncobs. The surveys suggested an Archaic into Fremont occupation with a hunting-gathering lifestyle dominating throughout.

Artifacts and notes are housed at the University of Colorado and with the National Park Service. ▲

ADDITIONAL READINGS, Colorado National Monument
Madsen, David E.
    1989 *Exploring the Fremont*. Salt Lake City: Utah Museum of Natural History.
Lister, Robert H., and Herbert W. Dick
    1952 Archaeology of the Glade Park Area, a Progress Report. *Southwestern Lore*, Vol.
       17, No. 4. Boulder: Colorado Archaeological Society. 69–92.
Wormington, H. M., and Robert H. Lister
    1956 *Archaeological Investigations on the Uncompahgre Plateau*. Proceedings,
       No. 2. Denver, Colorado: Denver Museum of Natural History.

Fremont petroglyph, Colorado National Monument. NATIONAL PARK SERVICE.

Petroglyphs at McKee Springs, Dinosaur National Monument. NATIONAL PARK SERVICE.

DINOSAUR NATIONAL MONUMENT, COLORADO-UTAH

Cultural Significance and Archeological Classification

Caves, terraces, and parks along the Green and Yampa rivers in the corners of northeastern Utah and northwestern Colorado were utilized for approximately six or seven thousand years. Archaic remains are of a generalized Desert Culture, which was being replaced as early as A.D. 100 by a Uinta Basin variant of the Fremont. While adhering to a basic hunting-foraging subsistence pattern, the latter practiced some horticulture, built rudimentary storage chambers and pithouses, and made simple, gray, utilitarian pottery. Their rock art was particularly notable. By about A.D. 1150 these Fremont may have been absorbed into the ancestral Shoshonean (Paiute, Ute, Shoshone) stock later to dominate the Great Basin and northern Colorado Plateau. Today the Northern Ute Indian Reservation shares the Uinta Basin.

Archaic: *Desert Culture*
In-betweens and Outliers: *Fremont (Uinta Basin)*
All-Southwest: *Hamlets, plateau zone*

Explorations and Investigations

Dinosaur National Monument was established in 1915 by proclamation of President Woodrow Wilson to protect a remarkable dinosaur boneyard discovered six years earlier by paleontologist Earl Douglass of the Carnegie Museum in Pittsburgh. The spectacular dinosaur quarry and the unspoiled wild beauty of the monument overshadow the area's prehistory. However, for many centuries its varied topography and wealth of plant and animal resources provided a favorable environment for small bands of people. The limited traces they left behind went unnoticed by the early explorers.

The Spanish Escalante-Domínguez expedition dispatched in 1776 from Santa Fe to find a westward route to San Francisco forded the Green River near the modern quarry site without noting any evidence of ancient people. In 1825 mountain man William H. Ashley and six trappers floated the Green River and through the dangerous Lodore Canyon, as did John Wesley Powell and his party in 1869 and again in 1871. That sheer-walled gorge always had been too difficult for human occupation. At the end of the nineteenth century a handful of white settlers took up holdings in the tiny meadows locked within the canyon fastness. They may have seen Indian remains but were not as interested as Charley Mantle.

Mantle was a pioneer rancher who arrived in Castle Park on the Yampa River in 1919 and soon became aware of artifacts weathering out of the blanket of earth in various caves or along the ridges. He later shared this information with scientists, who in the 1920s and 1930s took note of the antiquities of Dinosaur National Monument. J. A. Jeancon, Colorado State Historical Society; F. Martin Brown, Colorado Biological Survey; Hugo Rodeck and Charles R. Scoggin, University of Colorado Museum; Earl H. Morris, Carnegie Institution of Washington; and a party of National Park Service administrators were among those who visited the canyons during this period in order to appraise the possibilities of future archeological research there. Finally, in 1940 Scoggin and Edison P. Lohr conducted the first excavations in Castle Park, but their studies were halted by World War II.

Following the war, teams from the University of Colorado, headed by Robert F. Burgh, Robert H. Lister, and Herbert W. Dick, returned to Castle Park to complete work on the deposits of Mantle, Marigold, and a half-dozen unnamed caves, and to trench a deeply stratified refuse dump called Hells Midden, where lower levels were pre-agricultural and pre-ceramic. From 1963 through 1965 David A. Breternitz and students from the same institution undertook an intensive archeological survey of the monument and dug in twenty-two sites of various kinds in the Cub Creek area. Twenty years later a National Park Service archeologist was stationed at the monument. His work both substantiated and refined earlier findings and added new information. An especially significant excavation at Juniper Ledge Shelter in the archeologically rich Jones Hole/Ely Creek district yielded evidence of nearly a millennium of human presence.

Archeological specimens from Dinosaur National Monument are housed at the University of Colorado Museum, Boulder, and with the National Park Service. ⬔

ADDITIONAL READINGS, Dinosaur National Monument
Breternitz, David A.
    1970 *Archaeological Excavations in Dinosaur National Monument, Colorado-Utah, 1964–1965*. University of Colorado Studies, Series in Anthropology No. 17. Boulder: University of Colorado.
Burgh, Robert F., and Charles R. Scoggin
    1948 *The Archaeology of Castle Park, Dinosaur National Monument*. University of Colorado Studies, Series in Anthropology No. 2. Boulder: University of Colorado.
Lister, Robert H.
    1951 *Excavations at Hells Midden, Dinosaur National Monument*. University of Colorado Studies, Series in Anthropology No. 3. Boulder: University of Colorado.
    1955 The Ancients of the Canyons. *This is Dinosaur*, edited by Wallace Stegner. New York: Alfred A. Knopf. 48–57.
Madsen, David B.
    1989 *Exploring the Fremont*. Salt Lake City: Utah Museum of Natural History.
Truesdale, James A.
    1990 Archaeological Investigations of the "Uinta Basin" Fremont in Dinosaur National Monument (1988–1990). Paper presented at Plains Anthropological Society Conference, Norman, Oklahoma, November 1–2, 1990.

EL MALPAIS NATIONAL MONUMENT, NEW MEXICO

Cultural Significance and Archeological Classification

Prehistoric occupation within El Malpais National Monument extends from the Archaic through Pueblo III periods. Pueblo II sites are the most numerous. Candelaria, formerly Las Ventanas Ruin, at the Sandstone Bluff Overlook on the east side of the monument is the most southeasterly Chaco outlier thus far identified. Although the structures at this location are unexcavated, eventually they will be made accessible to the public and the Chaco Phenomenon will be an interpretive theme.

Explorations and Investigations

Five craggy lava flows that engulfed the San Jose valley of central New Mexico, and now form the heart of El Malpais National Monument, made travel between two important prehistoric centers of population difficult but not impossible. The Anasazi in the Acoma area to the east of the badlands, and those in the Zuni area to the west, beat an east-west trail across a tongue of all five flows. When a deep break in the layers interrupted their preferred route, resourceful men threw chunks of the rock into the opening to create a bridge. Further, because it was easy to get lost amidst the sea of black lava, they stacked up cairns of rock as markers.

The earliest recorded reference to the lava fields, *malpais* as the Spaniards called them, was made in 1582 by a scribe with the Rodríguez-Chamuscado expedition. Since he did not mention the ancient trail, it is assumed he never saw it. However, the parade of Hispanics who later traveled west from the Rio Grande and paused to note their passage on the cliff at El Morro probably made use of the Indian shortcut. Neither they nor the American soldiers and surveyors who explored along the thirty-fifth parallel during most of the second half of the nineteenth century commented on any regional antiquities.

It remained for Adolph Bandelier, while traversing the Acoma-Zuni trail in 1882, to first document the large Candelaria ruin and mention remains of twenty to thirty small houses in the environs. Together they form a substantial concentration of Anasazi habitations but were given little professional attention until the next century.

During the 1970s the possibility of a federal preserve and nearby highway improvements stimulated the first serious archeological surveys by the School of American Research, the Bureau of Indian Affairs, and the Museum of New Mexico. No substantial excavations resulted. Meanwhile, because the scattering of antiquities had become common knowledge among residents of districts peripheral to the badlands, pothunting took place. Candelaria suffered the most severe damage. With the establishment in 1987 of El Malpais National Monument, administered by the National Park Service, and the surrounding National Conservation Area, under control of the Bureau of Land Management, this destructive activity has ceased.

Archeological surveys confirmed a sequence of Archaic-Pueblo development similar

Archaic: *Oshara*
Anasazi: *Basket Maker III; Pueblo I, II, III*
Mogollon: *1, 2, 3*
All-Southwest: *Hamlets, Villages, Towns, intermediate between plateau and mountain-valley zones*

to that found elsewhere on the eastern Colorado Plateau. Researchers noted a pattern of increased concern with agriculture, shifting residence through time to take advantage of favorable ecological situations, and progression from single-unit pithouses, to small surface dwellings, to multiroomed masonry structures. Whenever excavations are undertaken, it is anticipated that the architectural details and material culture will resemble contemporary occupation on Cebolleta Mesa and east of the monument conservation lands. There, at some periods (especially early Pueblo II) an important interaction with Mogollon peoples to the south has been detected. Judging from surface indications, the malpais was abandoned by the Anasazi during Pueblo III times. They may have migrated eastward to Cebolleta Mesa and other highlands, where they congregated into large, defensible communities such as Acoma pueblo. A significant Pueblo IV presence in this area was in place when the Spaniards arrived.

The most outstanding of the malpais habitations is Candelaria. It sits on a sandstone bluff overlooking the forbidding McCarty flow to the west. Its placement on a prominence within an indigenous settlement is typical of Chaco outliers. Other Chacoan diagnostic features include two house blocks built with core and veneer masonry walls. Although the structure remains in mounded condition, its two units are estimated to contain about eighty-nine rooms. One unit was two stories in height and incorporated a tower kiva. Nearby is the depression of a Great Kiva with four surface alcoves. At the time of Bandelier's visit, six circular sandstone disks that had been used as seating for the kiva roof supports were present. They have since disappeared. A segment of a prehistoric road with some stone curbing runs along the east base of the McCarty flow before coming to an end at the Candelaria mound.

Geological opinion is that the McCarty flow occurred from seven hundred to one thousand years ago. If the former age is correct, the Anasazi had left the region. However, archeological evidence suggests they occupied the Candelaria bluff after that episode of vulcanism. The lava spread in such a way as to block drainages flowing west off Cebolleta Mesa, thereby creating catchments that subsequently filled with alluvium. Some researchers believe these formations became desirable garden plots which made the Candelaria community possible. Some of the stone used in the lower levels of the Chacoan structure is vesicular basalt. Since the customary sandstone was readily available, the choice of basalt must mean that it also was near at hand. Moreover, the road obviously was laid out along the foot of the lava escarpment. Many of the southern Chaco outliers date to the second half of the eleventh century, preceding construction of the road network.

Specimens recovered in the various surveys are housed at the sponsoring institutions.

ADDITIONAL READINGS, El Malpais National Monument
Ireland, Arthur K.
    1988 Cultural Prehistory of the El Malpais National Monument and National Conservation Area. Draft Manuscript. Santa Fe, New Mexico: Southwest Regional Office, National Park Service.

Mangum, Neil C.
1990 *A History of Occupation in El Malpais Country.* Southwest Cultural Resources
Center, Professional Papers No. 32. Santa Fe, New Mexico: Cultural Resources
Center, National Park Service.
Marshall, Michael P., John R. Stein, Richard W. Loose, and Judith E. Novotny
1979 *Anasazi Communities of the San Juan Basin.* Joint Publication of the Public
Service Company of New Mexico and the Historic Preservation Bureau,
Planning Division. Santa Fe: State of New Mexico.
Ruppe, R. J. Jr., and A. E. Dittert
1952 The Archaeology of Cebolleta Mesa and Acoma Pueblo; a Preliminary Report
Based on Further Investigation. *El Palacio*, Vol. 59, No. 7. Santa Fe: Museum of
New Mexico. 191–217.

Inscription Rock, El Morro National Monument. GEORGE A. GRANT, NATIONAL PARK SERVICE, 1940.

EL MORRO NATIONAL MONUMENT, NEW MEXICO

Cultural Significance and Archeological Classification

Although only partially excavated, the large ruin on top of Inscription Rock in El Morro National Monument shows the characteristics of many others in the vicinity. These towns were densely populated while most parts of the northern Southwest were being abandoned beginning in the twelfth century. Hawikuh is one of these towns.

Anasazi: *Basket Maker III; Pueblo I, II, III, IV*
All-Southwest: *Hamlets, Villages, Towns, plateau zone*

Explorations and Investigations

This message is scratched at the base of the jutting promontory of yellowish tan sandstone that is the heart of El Morro National Monument. The Spanish name means headland or knob. The cliff is known as Inscription Rock because from at least 1605 it provided a convenient register for many who paused there to enjoy a natural reservoir of cool water. The Simpson-Kern entry represents the first recording of the 250-year-old roster.

Legible Spanish inscriptions date from that of Juan de Oñate, the first governor of New Mexico, cut on the soft massif in April 1605 or 1606, followed by many other records of visits by soldiers, priests, and administrators.

Inscriber Simpson found no English words on the rock, but after his time, travel past El Morro seems to have become popular. Names of many American emigrants, ranchers, soldiers, engineers, and prospectors were left on the smooth cliffs. Simpson also observed the presence of aboriginal petroglyphs on the rock surfaces and the existence of two ruined pueblo structures on top of the prominence.

Once publicized, this unusual historical catalogue attracted the curious, even though they found getting there difficult. Writer Charles Lummis returned many times after his first visit in 1885. Calling it the "stone autograph album," he made copies of many of the inscriptions and tried to verify their authenticity. Shortly after his first visit, he wrote a preliminary report, never published, in which he discussed the Oñate recording. He felt that its date should be interpreted as April 16, 1605. An earlier inscription that Lummis observed, possibly from the year 1580, is no longer discernible.

The area was made a national monument in December 1906. In 1912 representatives of the Bureau of American Ethnology, headed by Frederick W. Hodge, made photographs and paper molds of all inscriptions of historical interest. Plaster casts secured from the molds were placed in the U.S. National Museum.

In prehistoric times, the region around El Morro was occupied by Zuni ancestors. The ruins atop Inscription Rock are just two of a great number of villages and towns used by a dense, shifting population scattered along the Continental Divide in western New Mexico. At first contact with the Europeans in 1539, the Zunis were living in six major communities on the Zuni River. Following the Pueblo Revolt of 1680, fearful of Spanish reprisals, the Zuni took refuge on defensible mesa tops, especially Dowa Yalanne, or Corn Mountain. Once the Vargas reconquest of New Mexico had taken place in 1692, the Zunis consolidated into a single town, the modern Zuni pueblo about forty miles west of El Morro. Abundant ruins in the area, existence of detailed historical accounts of European contacts with the Zuni, and the fact that the Zuni people have maintained their ceremonialism and world view have stimulated a century of archeological and ethnographical studies among them.

In the 1880s Victor Mindeleff prepared a plan of Zuni pueblo and mapped other sites in the area. The Hemenway Southwestern Archaeological Expedition of 1888–89 did some digging in Halona, the prehistoric and historic town that is now Zuni, and also at the pre-Hispanic town of Heshotauthla. Systematic archeological research began with Alfred Kroeber's 1916 study of the potsherds at ruins near Zuni. Expanding on these findings, Leslie Spier demonstrated that all styles of pottery decoration had begun in small frequency, increased to maximum frequency, and gone out of use. He believed that Zuni's geographical isolation gave a specific "Zunian character" to the locally made pottery.

The most ambitious archeological program attempted in the area was that of the Hendricks-Hodge Expedition under auspices of the Museum of the American Indian, Heye Foundation. From 1917 to 1923 work was carried on at the historic site of Hawikuh, which had been a thriving Zuni pueblo in 1539. In that year Fray Marcos de Niza led a reconnaissance north from Mexico to verify rumors of the existence of "Seven Cities of Cíbola," a group of walled cities reputed to be extremely wealthy. When a few members of Fray Marcos's advance party entered Hawikuh, apparently ostentatiously, a Negro companion of Niza, Estéban, was killed by the inhabitants. The frightened Spaniards decided to view the town from a safe distance before retracing their steps to Mexico. Marcos de Niza exaggerated about seeing "seven fair-looking settlements in the distance," which were said to contain gold and jewels. He also allegedly stated that the city of Cíbola

(Hawikuh) was twice the size of Seville and contained fine four-story houses.

Because of Niza's overblown stories, an expedition was organized on behalf of the Spanish crown to thoroughly explore the borderlands believed to offer such brilliant prospects. Aristocratic young Francisco Vásquez de Coronado, governor of Nueva Galicia, was selected to head the expedition. Setting out from Culiacán, Sinaloa, in February 1540 with a small army of three hundred soldiers and eight hundred friendly Indians and Indian servants, the straggling assembly made its way slowly north, surely one of the most exotic contingents ever to penetrate the United States.

In July Coronado, with an advance force, finally reached Hawikuh. Although tired and hungry, they defeated the natives in a fierce battle. Coronado and his followers then assigned names to many native groups, gave them their first knowledge of certain domestic animals and material goods, and acquainted some of them with Christianity and European mores.

Coronado's disappointment was great when he learned that the Zuni pueblos were not golden cities. Instead, he had conquered humble farming communities. Undaunted, he sent out several exploratory parties, which found the Hopi villages, the Grand Canyon, Acoma, and the Rio Grande pueblos where the expedition spent the winter of 1540–41. In the spring a force was dispatched east to the impressive pueblo of Pecos and to the plains beyond on an ill-fated search for Quivira, another place of supposed riches. Nowhere did Coronado find the gold and treasure the Spaniards so avidly sought. Nevertheless, the Zuni pueblos and the region around them became known as Cíbola. Beset with increasing hardships and disappointments and faced with insurrection among his command, Coronado retreated to Mexico in the spring of 1542.

Nearly forty years later authorities in Mexico City sent another force into New Mexico. The 1581 route through Chihuahua and up the Rio Grande blazed by the Rodríguez-Chamuscado Expedition became the *camino real*, or royal road, for later soldiers, priests, colonists, and supply and commercial caravans.

After the 1600s, Zuni was not on the main caravan route between Mexico and the northern frontier of Spanish civilization. Nevertheless, travelers from Santa Fe to the Hopi villages and farther west usually passed by Acoma, El Morro, and Zuni. Many records of those trips are carved into Inscription Rock. The populous Zuni villages attracted the Spaniards for two reasons: productive farmland at Cíbola and natives available for religious conversion. Missionary labors began in June 1629, when a house in Hawikuh was purchased for use as a mission. Construction of the permanent church, La Purísima Concepción, was started the same year. Another church was built at Halona. Missionary activities and administrative dealings with the Zunis followed the same pattern as elsewhere in New Mexico.

The residents of Hawikuh, like those in the other Zuni pueblos, went through a half-century of sparring with Spanish civil authorities and resident priests. On at least one occasion the populace revolted, killed the attendant priests, burned the church, and left their homes for the mesa-top stronghold of Dowa Yalanne as they had done in Coronado's time. They were persuaded to return to their valley town by promises of better treatment from their oppressors, and the church was refurbished. The final destruction of the Hawikuh church was caused either by an Apache raid in 1672 or by the local inhabitants at the time of the Pueblo Revolt of 1680. Hawikuh never was reoccupied. Thereafter, the Zunis came together at Zuni pueblo.

It was Hawikuh to which Frederick Hodge turned his attention in 1917 in one of the main archeological activities of the first quarter of this century. Even though Pueblos had lived there for centuries before the arrival of the Spanish, Hodge restricted his research to the town as it existed from the time of its discovery by the Iberians until it was vacated. Evidence of occupancy beneath the historic remains was not investigated. When the project terminated six years later, 370 rooms had been cleared, the large mission church and its friary almost completely excavated, at least 1600 whole or restored pottery vessels recovered, about 1000 burials exhumed, and large quantities of potsherds and artifacts of native and Spanish derivation collected.

This inscription was supposedly done by Governor Eulate. It translates:

"I am the Captain General of the Province of New Mexico for the King our Lord, passed by here on the return from the pueblo of Zuni on the 29th of July the year of 1620, and put them at peace at their humble petition, they asking favor as vassals of his Majesty and promising anew their obedience, all of which he did, with clemency, zeal, and prudence as a most Christianlike (gentleman) extraordinary and gallant soldier of enduring and praised memory."

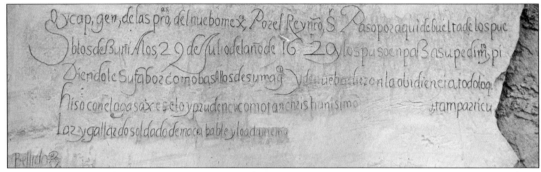

Although Hodge never wrote a general report on the archeology of Hawikuh, he did author several articles and produced an important volume on its history based primarily upon archival research. After Hodge's death, Watson Smith and Richard and Nathalie Woodbury utilized his notes and the materials recovered to put together a thoughtful report on Hawikuh exclusive of certain objects of Spanish or Mexican origin.

For the past decade Zuni pueblo has been sponsoring its own archeological and ethnohistorical programs in the vicinity of the town, as well as farther afield. A crew of professional scientists and Zuni workmen is studying the total range of local culture. In time, the history of ancient life in this sector of the Colorado Plateau, culminating in the modern community, will be known in greater detail than that of any of the contemporary pueblos.

Details of the prehistory of the wider Zuni region, including El Morro, began to emerge with a series of excavations between 1931 and 1940 by Frank H. H. Roberts, Jr. of the Smithsonian Institution. He noted an uninterrupted cultural growth from small, eighth-century pithouse villages to large, many-storied complexes of the contact period. He postulated a link between the Zuni and Chaco Canyon cultures. Roberts dug the Village of the Great Kivas, twenty-two miles northwest of El Morro, a large settlement of three masonry room blocks, seven ordinary kivas, and two Great Kivas. This profusion of ceremonial chambers suggests than an unusually large number of ritual performances may have taken place there.

Archeological investigations in El Morro National Monument took place in 1954 and 1955 when Richard Woodbury cleaned out part of one of the ruins on top of Inscription Rock. Known as Atsinna, Zuni for "writing on the rock," it is typical of many thirteenth- and fourteenth-century Zuni villages in that it is situated on a crest with commanding views in all directions. Atsinna was a large rectangular building of masonry with nearly one thousand rooms, arranged in ascending tiers from the central plaza to three stories around the exterior walls. Its occupants probably got their water from the same pool at the base of Inscription Rock that attracted so many travelers in colonial times. Rooms and kivas in one wing of the site have been stabilized by the National Park Service and may be examined by park visitors. Several other ruins near El Morro, some partially excavated, exhibit similarities to Atsinna and probably are the same age.

Some artifacts from Atsinna are displayed in the monument visitor center, but most are housed in the Western Archeological and Conservation Center in Tucson. Specimens obtained from the Village of the Great Kivas are at the Smithsonian Institution. Those from Hawikuh are at the Museum of the American Indian, New York. Zuni pueblo retains materials from its excavations. ⏶

ADDITIONAL READINGS, El Morro National Monument
Noble, David G.
    1983   *Zuni and El Morro, Past and Present.* Santa Fe, New Mexico: Exploration,
           Annual Bulletin of the School of American Research.
Roberts, Frank H. H., Jr.
    1932   *The Village of the Great Kivas on the Zuni Reservation, New Mexico.* Bulletin,
           No. 111. Washington, D.C.: Bureau of American Ethnology.
Smith, Watson, Richard B. Woodbury, and Nathalie F. S. Woodbury
    1966   *The Excavation of Hawikuh by Frederick Webb Hodge: Report of the Hendricks-
           Hodge Expedition, 1917–1923.* Contributions, No. 20. New York: Heye
           Foundation, Museum of the American Indian.
Woodbury, Richard B.
    1979   *Zuni Prehistory and History to 1850.* In *Handbook of North American Indians.*
           Vol. 9. Washington, D.C.: Smithsonian Institution. 467–473.

Cliff dwellings, Gila Cliff Dwellings National Monument. NATIONAL PARK SERVICE.

GILA CLIFF DWELLINGS NATIONAL MONUMENT, NEW MEXICO

Cultural Significance and Archeological Classification

Gila Cliff Dwellings National Monument has the only Mogollon ruins on exhibit in the National Park Service system. However, the small cliff dwellings, wedged into caves high on the wall of a verdant narrow canyon, were built after the Anasazi had expanded into Mogollon territory along the mountains and valleys of the Arizona–New Mexico border region and implanted many of their traditions. One of these introduced traits was the erection of structures in shallow caves. In addition to other examples of this Anasazi-dominated period, the monument contains some unexcavated ruins of earlier, unadulterated Mogollon pithouse villages.

Mogollon: *1, 2, 3 (pithouses), 4 (cliff dwellings)*
All-Southwest: *Hamlets, Villages, mountain-valley zone*

Explorations and Investigations

In late 1883 Adolph Bandelier made a twelve-day round trip by foot, horseback, and wagon from the mining camp at Mimbres in southern New Mexico to the headwaters of the Gila River to view some cliff dwellings. To reach his destination, he endured sub-freezing weather, a sore foot that made walking painful, and rough mountainous trails. But his goal was reached, and his visit produced an early description of the Gila cliff dwellings.

These were small, roofless cells almost hidden in four irregular overhangs on a cliff high above a confined canyon. Wooden lintels were still in place over doorways. Domestic trash, such as bits of pottery, corncobs, and a discarded sandal, lay scattered about. The style of architecture impressed Bandelier because it was the same he had seen in ruins around Mimbres, but the Gila settlement housed fewer people because of the lack of arable land in the mountain valley.

The upper Gila region was Apache territory during Spanish colonial and early American times, and local white settlers claimed that the Indians had damaged the cliff dwellings. It is unlikely that they were the sole culprits because white cattlemen, soldiers, and drifters are known to have climbed to the ruins also. One casual visitor claimed to have removed stone axes, turquoise beads, red and gray pottery jars, and the desiccated corpse of a child from one house. In 1885 Lieutenant G. H. Sands, from Fort Bayard near Silver City, found a few specimens by grubbing with his hunting knife. Undoubtedly more startling was the mountain lion that jumped over him as he crouched, intent upon his finds.

Nomadic Apaches moved into the Gila headwaters region several centuries after the prehistoric village dwellers had withdrawn. The river's name likely is a Spanish corruption of the Apache word for mountain; one early Spanish document referred to the local inhabitants as "Apache de Xila."

Apache bands, striking out from their camps in the rough mountains along the Continental Divide, grew increasingly warlike under pressure of white colonization. They took to terrorizing and raiding as a means of survival. When pursued, they vanished into the knot of hidden canyons and high plateaus that later became the Gila Wilderness Area.

With American occupation of the Territory of New Mexico in 1846, the United States government soon learned that it had inherited a serious problem in dealing with these natives. For forty years military forces and civil agents fought against, made treaties with, set up reservations for, and encouraged agriculture among the Apache. The federal forces also were guilty of mismanagement, which worsened relationships.

Geronimo, for a decade the feared leader of a small band of the most rebellious Apaches, had been raised on the upper Gila. He frequently crossed the international boundary to avoid capture by Mexican or American forces. These troops had to have official permission to cross the border in either direction. Geronimo, of course, sought no such permission. At last, time ran out for the Apaches. In 1886 a truce and terms of surrender for Geronimo and his renegades were agreed upon, but at the last moment the band fled again to the Sierra Madres in Mexico. It took another six months before General Miles succeeded in rounding them up and forcing them to capitulate, thus putting an end to several centuries of bloodshed. Geronimo and his entire band of about 340 were deported as prisoners of war first to Florida, then to Alabama, and finally to Fort Sill, Oklahoma, where Geronimo died in 1909.

The cliff dwellings of the Gila River were made a national monument in 1907. Because of their location deep in the broken country of the Gila National Forest, they remained relatively unknown. Progress at last brought in a paved road in 1966. Inevitably, increased visitation to both the antiquities and the surrounding Gila Wilderness Area made it necessary to name a full-time superintendent. Gila Cliff Dwellings National Monument was transferred from the National Park Service to the Forest Service in 1975.

One thousand years of widespread cultural development that archeologists now call Mogollon is represented at Gila Cliff Dwellings. Earliest in the sequence are several pithouse villages. One such village, whose material objects were diagnostic of the Mogollon from about A.D. 400 to 600, was excavated because a proposed road would have cut through the site. Another threatened ruin proved to be a complex of fourteen pithouses dated about A.D. 900 to 1000. Both these semi-subterranean villages had been covered by later surface houses erected from A.D. 1000 to 1100, when influence from the Pueblo world to the north had drifted into the region. As masonry architecture then became common, larger towns of many rooms and several stories were erected either within shallow caves or on bottomland terraces. The cliff dwellings for which the monument is named yielded roof beams dated in the A.D. 1280s. The houses continued to be occupied into the middle of the next century. An unexcavated contemporaneous site, the T. J. Ruin, spreads over several acres a short distance behind the visitor center. It is estimated to contain about two hundred rooms in five house blocks, in part erected over earlier pithouses. The cultural stratification represents some nine hundred years of occupation.

Since 1942 the National Park Service has repaired damage to the cliff dwellings engendered by nature and humans. In the course of these efforts some potsherds, and artifacts of stone, bone, wood, fiber, and shell have been reclaimed.

Artifacts from Gila Cliff Dwellings are kept at the Western Archeological and Conservation Center of the National Park Service in Tucson. ▲

ADDITIONAL READINGS, Gila Cliff Dwellings National Monument
McFarland, Elizabeth
 1967 *Forever Frontier: The Gila Cliff Dwellings.* Albuquerque: University of New Mexico Press.
McKenna, Peter J., and James E. Bradford
 1989 *The TJ Ruin, Gila Cliff Dwellings National Monument.* Southwest Cultural Resource Center, Professional Papers, No. 21. Santa Fe: New Mexico: Southwest Cultural Resources Center, National Park Service.
Martin, Paul S.
 1979 Prehistory: Mogollon. In *Handbook of North American Indians*, Vol. 9. Washington, D.C.: Smithsonian Institution. 61–74.

Animals were needed to pack materials into the caves when the Gila cliff dwellings were repaired.
NATIONAL PARK SERVICE.

The ruins at Nankoweap, Grand Canyon National Park. JOHN RICHARDSON.

GRAND CANYON NATIONAL PARK, ARIZONA

Cultural Significance and Archeological Classification

Grand Canyon National Park was a meeting ground of several southwestern cultures, some of which occupied various sections of the canyon at the same time. Anasazi village ruins have been noted on the north and south rims and in the depths of the canyon. South of the canyon two aspects of the widely dispersed Hakataya culture, Cohonina and Cerbat, have been identified. The Grand Canyon Anasazi possessed characteristic southwestern culture, but the Hakataya were marginal groups. They integrated enough traits, such as house types, pottery, and elementary farming, to acquire a similarity to Anasazi lifestyle. Determining the cultural continuum between specific Hakataya groups and historic tribes of the Colorado River is another significant aspect of Grand Canyon prehistory.

Explorations and Investigations

Indians are not usually the primary interest of visitors to Grand Canyon National Park. Most come to see the stupendous, multihued chasm that has been deeply scoured into the Colorado Plateau by eons of uplift and the unceasing charge of the Colorado River. Nevertheless, the canyon and its environs contain many signs of prehistoric inhabitants, and several tribes still live there.

The first Europeans to gaze into the shadowy depths of the Grand Canyon were members of the 1540 Coronado expedition. At the Hopi villages they learned of a great river farther west. A secondary force, commanded by García López de Cárdenas, promptly was ordered to locate and explore it. Securing Hopi guides, Cárdenas and his men traveled twenty days before reaching the brink of the Grand Canyon late in September. The Cárdenas party worked along the south rim of the canyon for some distance, estimated its width to be eight to ten miles, but failed to find a route to the river. The men deduced correctly that the river was the Colorado, known then as the Tizón, or Firebrand.

In the first half of the eighteenth century the Spanish militia made sporadic attempts to bring the Hopi and recalcitrant Rio Grande Pueblos back into their fold. None succeeded. In 1776 Fray Francisco Tomás Garcés, a Franciscan missionary who had explored the Colorado River, was rejected by the Hopi. However, Garcés found the Hualapai, in the western section of the Grand Canyon, and the Havasupai, of Cataract or Havasu Creek, much more hospitable. They served him as guides, provided him with food and shelter, and otherwise contributed to a successful trip that generated a second eyewitness description of the Grand Canyon.

A few months later while returning from an unsuccessful attempt to find a route from Santa Fe to California, Fray Silvestre Vélez de Escalante met a group of Southern Paiute Indians north of the canyon. As a consequence, he compiled the first account of these hunters and gatherers who roamed the plateaus along the north rim.

Although surveys were made of the Grand Canyon region following American

Archaic: *Pinto*
Anasazi: *Pueblo I, II, III*
In-betweens and Outliers: *Hakataya culture (Cohonina, Cerbat)*
All-Southwest: *Villages, plateau zone, western periphery*

acquisiton of Arizona, it was not until John Wesley Powell and his crew made two exploratory boat trips down the Colorado River, first in 1869 and again in 1871–72, that archeological materials were reported there. Powell recorded eight small canyon-bottom ruins, of which only foundations and a tumble of building stones remained.

During the 1870s Powell and his associates in the newly formed Geographical and Geological Survey of the Rocky Mountain Region continued explorations and geological investigations in the Colorado River basin. More attention was given to the conditions, customs, languages, and history of the Indians of the region, prompting the founding in 1879 of the Smithsonian Institution's Bureau of Ethnology dedicated to studying all facets of American Indian culture. Powell was named the first director, and a few years later he also assumed leadership of the new U.S. Geological Survey.

After Powell had demonstrated that the river was navigable, others worked their way through the canyon, finding limited evidence of prehistoric occupation in the inner canyon and on the north and south plateaus. In 1882 Frank Cushing visited the Havasupai, whom he found to occupy and farm Havasu Canyon only in the summer, spending their winters hunting and gathering on the plateau.

During the first half of the twentieth century, systematic description of archeological remains in Grand Canyon National Park and the gathering of more ethnological information about the four native groups who utilized the region—the Havasupai, Southern Paiute, Hopi, and Navajo—began to fill out the previously sketchy picture of regional cultural history. With a program that got under way in 1915, Neil M. Judd, then of the Bureau of American Ethnology, was the first professional archeologist to work within the present boundaries of the park. After several years of survey and excavations north of the Colorado River, he suggested that the sites there were related to those of the prehistoric Pueblo culture, reiterating an idea that Powell put forth fifty years earlier. Both men had no clear perception of the age of the remains.

The necessary ordering of Grand Canyon archeology within a time frame and a better comprehension of its ties to other Puebloan centers came about in the 1930s. Tusayan Ruin on the south rim was studied by Emil Haury, then of the Gila Pueblo, and Walhalla Glades on the north rim was surveyed by E.T. Hall, Jr. The Judd and Hall surveys disclosed nearly five hundred sites, from single-room houses to complicated multiroomed units, and a number of check dams and terraces associated with agricultural plots. Utilizing tree-ring dating and rapidly accumulating information about prehistoric pottery types, these surveys suggested two sources of Puebloan culture in the Grand Canyon. One was the San Juan country to the east, and the other was the Virgin River region to the north and west. An occupation from about A.D. 500 to 1200 was postulated.

Additional archeological investigations were conducted in ruins along the south rim and toward the San Francisco Peaks, primarily by Harold S. Colton and Lyndon L. Hargrave of the Museum of Northern Arizona. These revealed such a distinctive set of architectural styles, pottery, and stone artifact types that a second prehistoric culture, called the Cohonina and believed to have been to some extent contemporaneous with the Anasazi, was suggested. Although there is no evidence of conflict between these two peoples, some constructions of dry-laid masonry on free-standing pinnacles or isolated cliff projections suggest defensive needs.

After excavation of another sixteen sites south of the Grand Canyon by John C. McGregor of the University of Illinois, and further analyses of artifacts, the Cohonina people were judged to be part of a larger cultural component, the Hakataya. They were thought to have occupied an expansive range on both sides of the Colorado River as far north as the Grand Canyon. Although recognized as having an identifiable culture, the Cohoninas adopted many traits of others with whom they came in contact. Some see the Cohoninas as ancestral to the Havasupai. Others disagree, pointing out that they disappear from the cultural record about A.D. 1150. Perhaps it was still another group, the Cerbat, that drifted into the territory from the west after A.D. 1300 and slowly evolved into the modern Havasupai and probably the Hualapai. Meanwhile, Southern Paiute bands claimed the north rim.

Accumulating details about prehistoric use of the inner recesses of the canyon have been contributed by several archeologists, most importantly Douglas W. Schwartz of the School of American Research and Robert C. Euler, formerly of the National Park Service. They have made painstaking surveys of portions of the canyon bottom, some of the river terraces, and many overhangs and caves in the canyon walls to find hundreds of small dwellings and granaries tucked onto ledges, large pits where mescal was roasted, and numerous trails crisscrossing the cliff escarpments. Excavations have been conducted in house and village ruins on Unkar Delta and elsewhere. To date, some fifteen hundred sites have been recorded, with peak occupation in the century between A.D. 1050 and 1150. These projects have convincingly demonstrated that the inner recesses of the canyon offered the Anasazi advantages in the way of wild plants and animals and a floodwater farming opportunity not available on the rims. Seasonal use of lower and higher elevations is likely. Schwartz also has researched Havasupai prehistory and has located and cleared many ancient habitations on Walhalla Glades.

One of the most fascinating developments in Grand Canyon archeology goes back to 1933 when three members of a Civilian Conservation Corps crew found three miniature animal effigies in a cave in the canyon. Each figurine had been made by bending and folding a single split-willow twig. They were thought possibly to have been fashioned by Indians and hence were placed in the collections of the park. More than three hundred similar specimens made of willow and cottonwood have since been collected from several almost inaccessible caves in the Grand Canyon. Additional examples are known from other localities in Arizona, Utah, Nevada, and California. These cleverly contrived representations of deer and desert bighorn sheep, possibly of elk and antelope, have become known as split-twig figurines and are believed to have been created by ancient hunters as magic or religious objects. The caves in which they were placed were shrines for imitative magic rites to assure success in the hunt. Split-twig figurines from the Grand Canyon have been meticulously studied and dated by radiocarbon means at three thousand to four thousand years old. These, some unusual rock art, and Pinto complex projectile points are interpreted as Archaic.

Split-twig figurine, four-thousand-year-old remnant of early Grand Canyon hunters.
COURTESY GRAND CANYON NATURAL HISTORY ASSOCIATION.

Studies are under way to determine the erosional effects on canyon-bottom sites of regulated water release from the Glen Canyon Dam. The Western Archeological and Conservation Center in Tucson is the repository for the large array of specimens resulting from the excavations and surveys by both the School of American Research and the National Park Service. ◥

ADDITIONAL READINGS, Grand Canyon National Park
Euler, Robert C.
    1967 The Canyon Dwellers. *The American West*, Vol. 4, No. 2. Palo Alto, California: American West Publishing Company. 22–27, 67–71.
    1988 Demography and Cultural Dynamics on the Colorado Plateau. In *The Anasazi in a Changing Environment*, edited by George J. Gumerman. Cambridge: Cambridge University Press. 198–200.
Fowler, Don D., Robert C. Euler, and Catherine S. Fowler
    1969 *John Wesley Powell and the Anthropology of the Canyon Country*. Geological Survey Professional Paper, No. 670. Washington, D.C.: U.S. Geological Survey.
Hughes, J. Donald
    1978 *In the House of Stone and Light, A Human History of the Grand Canyon*. Grand Canyon, Arizona: Grand Canyon Natural History Association.
Jones, Anne T., and Robert C. Euler
    1979 *A Sketch of Grand Canyon Prehistory*. Grand Canyon, Arizona: Grand Canyon Natural History Association.
Schwartz, Douglas W., Michael Marshall, and Jane Kepp
    1979 *Archaeology of the Grand Canyon: The Bright Angel Site*. Santa Fe, New Mexico: School of American Research Press.
Schwartz, Douglas W., Richard C. Chapman, and Jane Kepp
    1980 *Archaeology of the Grand Canyon: Unkar Delta*. Santa Fe, New Mexico: School of American Research Press.
    1981 *Archaeology of the Grand Canyon: The Walhalla Plateau*. Santa Fe, New Mexico: School of American Research Press.

GREAT SAND DUNES NATIONAL MONUMENT, COLORADO

Cultural Significance and Archeological Classification

The San Luis valley of southern Colorado is a broad, flat expanse that periodically was wet and grassy. Along its eastern flank are approximately fifty-five square miles of the tallest sand dunes in North America. The valley was an especially favorable, discretely defined environment for Paleo-Indian and Archaic populations. During sufficiently mesic periods, at least three distinct, successive groupings of the former were present in some numbers. Although not yet studied in depth, the latter are thought to have found the valley satisfactory for their hunting and gathering mode of life.

Explorations and Investigations

Their unusual geological history in a mountain-valley setting and their grandeur were the reasons for declaring the Great Sand Dunes a national monument in 1932. There was no thought given to their possible role in southwestern prehistory. The explorers, trappers, soldiers, miners, and engineers who trudged by them in the course of several centuries were unconcerned about what might have transpired there in former times. All these observers knew was that in their time the dunes and the valley beyond was Ute territory, and the Utes were not always friendly. Nor were the dunes.

Only when American homesteaders and cattlemen began inching their way over the surrounding mountain passes and spreading out into the basin below did an awareness begin to grow of former occupation. Collecting a variety of archeological debris became a local pastime. Some of the material was recovered during development of farms, some from open ranges, and some from dunes banked against the base of the Sangre de Cristo Mountains, where shifting sands had a tantalizing way of revealing and then concealing artifacts. Since there were no surface ruins in the valley to suggest settled farmers, this physical evidence of man's passage was variously attributed by the collectors to some amorphous ancient band of wanderers or perhaps to Pueblo or Plains Indians. They did not contemplate any connection between those transients and the dunes.

Until recently, professional interest in the prehistory of the valley has been sporadic and relatively unproductive. E. B. Renaud, professor at the University of Denver, visited the region in the 1930s without doing more than viewing private collections. Just before World War II, C. T. Hurst of Western State College at Gunnison, Colorado, engaged in a small excavation on a ranch near Great Sand Dunes which produced some fossil bison bones and the characteristically channel-fluted Folsom points. Similar finds at another site in the vicinity were made in the 1950s by Adams State University teacher F. C. V. Worman. Also in that decade Frank Swancara, a student at the University of Colorado, conducted a brief reconnaissance of the monument on behalf of the National Park Service.

Finally, in 1977 a team from the Smithsonian Institution, under leadership of Dennis Stanford, launched a long-term ongoing project in the northern end of the valley not far

Paleo-Indian: *Clovis, Folsom, Cody*
Archaic: *Oshara*

from the monument boundaries. To date this project has examined four Paleo-Indian sites with significant results concerning a Folsom occupation. Three of the sites are near shallow ponds or bogs thought to have been more numerous throughout the valley in the past. One is in a blowout on a ranch just to the south of the monument, where subsurface deposits have been partially exposed by wind deflation. Two related activity areas are apparent at these sites. One is where Folsom hunters actually killed both extinct bison and modern species such as antelope, wolves, and rabbits. The other is where they camped nearby just long enough to butcher and process the meat, crack bones for marrow, cure hides, and retouch or make new weapons or implements. Almost two thousand chipped stone artifacts came from one camp. These include fifty-five fluted and unfluted Folsom points, scrapers, flake knives, and discarded stone left from making these objects. Cobbles used as hammerstones, anvils, and abraders for pulverizing pigments round out the recovered tool inventory. The stone resources seem to have originated in a number of sources, some hundreds of miles distant. Bone projectile points, needles, and beads also have been found. There is evidence at the camps for hearths but no shelters.

Although all the studied sites are in the open, the researchers theorize that in the moist conditions believed to have prevailed in the San Luis valley during the Folsom period, estimated to have ended there about 8500 B.C., some ponds of water probably were trapped among the dunes. Men could have hidden in the security of the dunes to ambush animals coming to drink. The heavy bones left from butchering and stone spear points would have sunk into the sand in a short time and now would be exposed only at a chance blowout. The dunes also could have afforded some protection from inclement weather and been used as seasonal campsites.

From observations made of numerous private collections gathered in the valley over years of searching, Stanford believes Clovis hunters wandered the region for several millennia before the Folsom, only to be driven away by drought that affected vegetation and the mammoths that fed upon it. One site yielding mammoth bones but no in situ points has been tested. Folsom bands also eventually were forced to leave the area because of another climatic shift toward aridity. When that xeric cycle ended about 7000 B.C., a new breed of hunters called the Cody moved in. Like their predecessors, they had to leave when the water sources once again dried up. Around 4000 B.C. the pendulum moved back toward a wetter climate. Then the Archaic foragers found the valley a good place to stay during warmer months.

Although the Rio Grande lifeline begins in the San Juan Mountains to the east and flows through the southern portion of the basin, thus far there is no evidence for any Pueblo residence in the San Luis valley. If the San Luis Archaic groups slowly disappeared into the Anasazi mainstream, they did so in some other place. It appears the valley was essentially uninhabited except by occasional Pueblo hunting parties coming north from New Mexico until about the 1600s, when the Moache Utes laid more formal claim to it as their traditional territory.

Specimens recovered from the Smithsonian Institution excavations are at that facility in Washington. Those from the monument are held by the National Park Service. ▲

ADDITIONAL READINGS, Great Sand Dunes National Monument
Hurst, C. T.
    1943 A Folsom Site in a Mountain Valley of Colorado. *American Antiquity*, Vol. 8,
          No. 3. Menasha, Wisconsin: Society for American Archaeology. 250–253.
Jodry, M. A.
    1987 Stewart's Cattle Guard Site: a Folsom Site in Southern Colorado. A Report of the
          1981 and 1983 Field Seasons. Master of Arts Thesis, Department of
          Anthropology. Austin: University of Texas.
Stanford, Dennis J.
    1990 A History of Archaeological Research in the San Luis Valley, Colorado. In *Great
          Sand Dunes National Monument, Stories of the Past*. Alamosa, Colorado: San
          Luis Valley Historical Society. 33–39.
Standord, Dennis J., and Jane S. Day, Editors
    1992 *Ice Age Hunters of the Rockies*. Niwot, Colorado: Denver Museum of Natural
          History and University Press of Colorado.
Swancara, Frank
    1955 The Archaeology of the Great Sand Dunes National Monument, a Preliminary
          Survey. *Southwestern Lore*, Vol. 20, No. 4. Boulder: Colorado Archaeological
          Society. 53–58.

Cliff Palace, Mesa Verde National Park. GEORGE A. GRANT, NATIONAL PARK SERVICE, 1929.

MESA VERDE NATIONAL PARK, COLORADO/HOVENWEEP NATIONAL MONUMENT, COLORADO-UTAH

Cultural Significance and Archeological Classification

Its long, rich record of occupation, striking natural setting, and well-developed visitor facilities and interpretive programs make Mesa Verde National Park the nation's most outstanding preserve devoted to the works of ancient man. Its unique cultural value was recognized by the United Nations Educational, Scientific, and Cultural Organization, which in 1978 chose it and Yellowstone National Park as the first American designees for its prestigious World Heritage List.

Discovery and exploration of the Mesa Verde cliff dwellings played a significant part in promoting early scholarly interest in southwestern prehistory. Its presence was also instrumental in the establishment of federal regulations and reserves to protect these and other antiquities. Many of the material aspects of the evolution of Anasazi culture are present. They illustrate man's adaptability to and modification of the environment and ultimately the disastrous consequences of overpopulation and overutilization of available resources. Mesa Verde culture existed well beyond the limits of the Mesa Verde plateau, for example, the complex of pueblos and towers at Hovenweep where the ancient farmers grouped at strategic points near permanent sources of water.

Explorations and Investigations

Mesa Verde is an expansive, elevated, verdant tableland that from a distance suggests a towering green table, hence its Spanish name. The mesa tilts gently southward, cut into ribbons by a labyrinth of deep canyons. Because of its ruggedness, dense vegetation, and distance from areas early settled by whites, it was a region bypassed in the opening of the Southwest. Between 1765 and 1848 Spanish and Mexican explorers and travelers acknowledged it as a landmark on a route running west from the Rio Grande valley that became known as the Old Spanish Trail; they skirted its perimeters but felt no need to penetrate its interior. Finally, in 1859 the first published record of a visit to the heart of the region came when J. S. Newberry, a geologist accompanying an American party trying to chart feasible wagon and rail routes across northern New Mexico and southern Colorado, wrote that he had clambered to the top of the mesa to enjoy the spectacular panoramic view. Little did he realize the quiet testimony to the past concealed all about him.

William H. Jackson, head of the Photographic Division of the U.S. Geological and Geographical Survey of the Territories, usually is credited with being the first person to photograph and describe in print a Mesa Verde cliff dwelling. It was a relatively insignificant structure, not accessible to the modern tourist, that Jackson named Two Story House. He encountered it during the summer of 1874 when his seven-man party was surveying and photographing mountains in southwest Colorado. While he was camped

Anasazi: Basket Maker III; Pueblo I, II, III (Mesa Verde); Pueblo III (Hovenweep, Yucca House) All-Southwest: Hamlets, Villages, Towns (Mesa Verde); Towns (Hovenweep, Yucca House), plateau zone

Anasazi, Pueblo II, black-on-white dipper. ROBERT H. LISTER.

near Silverton, local folks told Jackson of the Mesa Verde and the Indian ruins rumored to fill some caves there. He promptly secured the guide services of Captain John Moss, a miner working in the La Platas who was familiar with the area and friendly with the local Ute Indians. In early September the group packed into Mancos Canyon, just east of the Mesa Verde, and started its journey through the defile. Almost immediately one of the cliffside houses was spotted. Jackson's official report, with a description and picture of the site, appeared in 1876. Another man in the party, Ernest Ingersoll, actually scooped Jackson's description by two years, when his letter narrating the discovery of Two Story House was published in the *New York Tribune* on November 3, 1874.

In the next few years William H. Holmes, also of the Survey of the Territories, and a few others worked around the craggy flanks of the Mesa Verde. It was the Wetherill family of nearby Mancos who found the antiquities that would make the peaceful plateau into a world-famous archeological zone. With permission from the Utes, whose traditional lands encompassed the Mesa Verde, Benjamin K. Wetherill and his sons ranged their stock there in the 1880s. While riding the promontory looking for water holes and stray cattle, Richard Wetherill and his brother-in-law, Charlie Mason, emerged from the pinyons and cedars covering a mesa top to find themselves staring down the opposite cliff face upon a great masonry shell of an empty house that had once surely quartered many families.

Thrilling though this chance discovery was, it came as no great surprise. Signs of earlier occupation were common throughout the region, and the Wetherills had poked into many of them, randomly searching for artifacts. But the size of this particular ruin, its configuration to the rocky overhang, its degree of preservation, and the promise of discarded materials made it special. Richard grandly named it Cliff Palace. Richard's brother, Al, actually had viewed the site from a distance some time earlier but had not climbed into it because he was too tired.

On the first entry Cliff Palace seemed a house temporarily empty while the residents were away on an errand. Complete clay pots and stone tools sat where last used. But the ashes in ancient fire pits were very cold, and roofs had rotted and collapsed.

By 1890 the Wetherills and their associates had examined 180 Pueblo dwellings perched on the walls of Mesa Verde's canyons, giving the most prominent ones names that are still used. They dug in many of them and accumulated three major collections of specimens and some pertinent data. The artifacts were exhibited at fairs, then sold to private collectors and scientific institutions far from their original sources. Richard sought in vain to interest the Smithsonian Institution and Peabody Museum of Harvard in sponsoring further explorations. Even so, the Wetherill brothers continued their association with Mesa Verde, since scientists and laymen needed guides to the legendary ruins. The Wetherill Alamo Ranch became their headquarters.

One who sought field assistance from the Wetherills was Gustaf Nordenskiöld, a young man from a distinguished Swedish family. With their help in 1891 he excavated in Kodak House, Long House, and Step House on one of the fingerlike projections of Mesa Verde which came to bear the Wetherill family name. He also probed further in Cliff Palace and Spruce Tree House, situated below the rim rock of Chapin Mesa. Nordenskiöld's collection was small, however, because fill in all the sites previously had been turned over by cowboys trying to duplicate the Wetherill haul. The collection was shipped to an unlikely home in the National Museum in Helsinki, Finland. After Nordenskiöld's fieldwork, he wrote the first scientific descriptions of the ancient remains.

Meanwhile, people shocked by what they regarded as blantant vandalism at Mesa Verde began agitating vigorously to have the ruins immediately placed under government custody. Led by archeologists such as Edgar L. Hewett, citizen activists like Virginia McClurg of Colorado Springs, and members of the Colorado State Federation of Women's Clubs and the Colorado Cliff Dwellings Association, their untiring efforts finally succeeded on two fronts in 1906. The Federal Antiquities Act protecting archeological resources on government lands became law that year, and Mesa Verde National Park was established.

Earnest scientific work began at Mesa Verde in 1908 and continues. Intermittently between 1908 and 1922, Jesse Walter Fewkes, of the Smithsonian Bureau of American Ethnology, excavated in Spruce Tree House and fifteen other dwellings on the mesa and in the cliffs. His work included the intriguing Sun Temple structure and a group of ruins at Far View, where some stabilization was undertaken.

Although the first park administrators were necessarily occupied with building roads, developing facilities, and establishing means to display and guard the ruins, Superintendent Jesse L. Nusbaum found time in 1910 to clear and stabilize Balcony House, which represents the classic period of Mesa Verde culture. In the 1920s he cleared several pithouses, including those in Step House. How these sites fit in the local chronology still was based primarily upon the types of artifacts recovered.

During the late 1920s and early 1930s well-preserved timbers in Mesa Verde houses proved important in an electrifying new approach to one of archeology's key questions: when was a given site in use?

University of Arizona astronomer A. E. Douglass theorized that by charting the pattern of annual growth rings in a tree's cross-section, the date at which it was felled could be determined. From a long series of such cross-sections, it might be possible to work out a calendric chart, progressing from the present back in time as far as that particular wood or charcoal had endured. Using hundreds of wood samples from ruins throughout the Colorado Plateau, including those at Mesa Verde, his theory was proved so dramatically that numerous villages are now firmly dated. Cliff Palace, for example, was found to have been occupied between the late twelfth and late thirteenth centuries. The Step House pithouses appeared about the beginning of the seventh century.

Although by 1935 considerable information had been collected about the cliff dwellers, little was known about earlier human occupation of these caves or the mesa tops. To attempt to gauge the size and scope of this horizon, a systematic survey of the park's prehistoric resources was initiated. Locating and recording sites was tedious, and the project extended over forty years. By then, National Park Service and University of Colorado archeologists had found some four thousand sites within Mesa Verde National Park.

Needing more information about Mesa Verde culture before the cliff-dweller period, a

Jesse W. Fewkes conducted research in Mesa Verde for the Smithsonian Institution from 1908 to 1922. NATIONAL PARK SERVICE.

series of excavations in mesa-top and talus-slope village sites was accomplished between 1941 and 1955 by Gila Pueblo, the University of Colorado, and the National Park Service.

Concurrent with accelerated archeological research were activities to preserve additional important Mesa Verde ruins. In 1934 Earl Morris completed repairs and stabilization work at Cliff Palace, Spruce Tree House, Balcony House, and Far View. He was assisted by Al Lancaster, who later managed a maintenance plan for many of the cliff dwellings and more important ruins on the open mesas. This program continues to assure that future generations will see the outstanding accomplishments of the Mesa Verdeans.

By the 1950s the annual number of visitors to Mesa Verde had grown to such proportions that the available ruins were seriously overcrowded and threatened. To alleviate the congestion, the National Park Service decided to prepare for public visitation a series of sites comparable to the Chapin Mesa landmarks of Cliff Palace, Spruce Tree House, and Balcony House. Of equal concern was the desire to conduct a multidisciplinary research program while preparing new exhibits-in-place, to expand those facets of Mesa Verde culture that previously had been only superficially developed, and to pass that information on to scientists and the public. A team of National Park Service archeologists and laboratory specialists, led by Douglas Osborne, was assembled to execute the program.

The area selected for work was Wetherill Mesa, a long narrow tongue of land along the park's western boundary. Sheltered along its cliffs on both sides were several interesting cave sites. Numerous lesser villages were scattered over the top of the mesa. When the Wetherill Mesa Project got under way in 1958, a thorough survey of all archeological remains of the mesa was begun by Alden C. Hayes. Once completed, the survey's findings made it possible to select a representative sequence of sites on the mesa for excavation, stabilization, and display. Three important cliff dwellings to be cleared and prepared for inclusion in the park's interpretive program were Long House by George S. Cattanach, Mug House by Arthur H. Rohn, and Step House by Robert Nichols. Early in the effort the National Geographic Society made possible many auxiliary studies in paleoecology, human osteology and pathology, ethnography among contemporary Pueblo Indians, and analyses of collections of artifacts removed from Mesa Verde during the period of discovery and early exploration.

As anticipated, the Wetherill Mesa Project appreciably added to knowledge of Mesa Verde prehistory. Particularly significant was paleoecological research which, when coupled with archeological findings, provides a more complete perception of prehistoric subsistence techniques, settlement patterns, and living conditions. Dietary habits of the Mesa Verdeans, their illnesses and injuries and likely causes, and certain vital statistics were revealed with analyses of human remains by physical anthropologists. Social organization, internal and external relationships, and ceremonialism were more fully explained after consideration of material attributes, architectural complexes, burial customs, affinity between settlements, and practices of historic Pueblo Indians. And, for the first time, what is left of some of the Mesa Verde cliff dwellings was scientifically excavated and studied. Previously, it had been ranchers and other untrained individuals who had removed most of the artifacts from the caves, generally with total disregard for vital information about origin, condition, or context.

Archeological research at Mesa Verde continued after the Wetherill Mesa Project concluded. Through an agreement with the U.S. Department of the Interior, the University of Colorado established an archeological research center in the park. Working from facilities provided by the National Park Service, students from the university engaged in various studies, directed first by Robert H. Lister and then by David A. Breternitz, for well over a decade. Their activities were not limited to the park but were extended to surrounding areas where Mesa Verde culture also appears. This group completed the archeological survey of Mesa Verde proper and expanded the inventory to include sizable regions adjacent to the park. Numerous sites marked for destruction by road construction, reclamation demands, and other development were salvaged, especially on Wetherill Mesa while it was being prepared for visitor use. In lower Morefield Canyon, a complex of Great Kivas, associated villages, and a water collecting system and reservoir were dug, as was an isolated, above-ground kiva and another village near the Morefield campground. A thirty-five-room mesa-top pueblo, Mummy Lake, and irrigation ditches were cleared in the Far View group. Another extensive survey led by Jack E. Smith during summers 1971–77 covered lands within the park boundaries where no previous work had been done. An additional eighteen hundred prehistoric sites were tabulated, which indicated shifting settlement patterns through time and space. Mesa Verde's Division of Research and Cultural Resource Management continues studies and maintenance of ruins as part of overall park administration.

Beyond the western boundaries of Mesa Verde sprawls the expansive Montezuma valley, which in various sectors experienced a dense Anasazi occupation for at least six centuries. Jackson and Holmes, both of whom traversed the area on their trips during the 1870s, wrote brief accounts of the ruins in McElmo and Yellowjacket canyons. Jackson was the first to apply the Ute word Hovenweep, meaning deserted valley, to the region. Starting about 1890, the Wetherills guided some of their more interested and ambitious visitors to the impressive group of sites in Ruin Canyon. T. Mitchell Prudden accomplished a long reconnaissance and excavation program in parts of this area in the early 1900s. In the same period two young, inexperienced Harvard graduate students, Alfred V. Kidder and Sylvanus G. Morley, struggled through their first archeological survey among sites scattered in the sage plain on the region's western periphery. In succeeding years Kidder and Morley returned as professionals to the region—Kidder to survey and evaluate the principal sites of the Four Corners, including those on Mesa Verde, and Morley to dig in the Cannonball Ruin. To this date that site is the only canyonhead village-tower complex to be excavated.

During the fourteen years that Jesse W. Fewkes worked at Mesa Verde, he periodically diverted his attention to other areas. In 1917 and 1918 he visited, mapped, studied, and named most of the large ruins of the Cajon Mesa. He concluded that the canyonhead towns were contemporaneous with the Mesa Verde cliff dwellings and recommended that they be protected as a national monument. Already the ravages of relic hunters were

Mug House, before excavation and stabilization, Mesa Verde National Park. GEORGE A. GRANT, NATIONAL PARK SERVICE, 1929.

threatening partial elimination of the ruins.

Hovenweep National Monument, under the administration of Mesa Verde National Park, finally was established in 1923 to incorporate six units of the most visible structures on western flanks of the territory. The Cajon Ruin group and the Square Tower Ruin group are in Utah. The Holly, Hackberry, Cutthroat Castle, and Goodman Point ruins groups are in Colorado. Present in these complexes are many-roomed pueblos in the open or clustered around canyon heads, tiny cliff houses, and an unusually large number of well-preserved masonry towers. The towers may have had some purpose in making astronomical observations essential for establishing a calendar by which agricultural routines could be maintained.

Goodman Point Ruin is the only settlement in Hovenweep National Monument not in the Upper Sonoran Desert but instead is at a higher elevation and is surrounded by modern farmlands. It is one of the largest Anasazi communities north of the San Juan River, perhaps as much as twice the size of Cliff Palace at Mesa Verde. In addition to many room blocks and plazas, there are an estimated one hundred ceremonial chambers including two Great Kivas. In recognition of its potential importance, the Public Land Office already had withdrawn the site from homesteading in 1889. Still unexcavated, the pueblo will have value in future research dealing with the final stages of Anasazi presence on the northern Colorado Plateau.

National Park Service experts have strengthened the high-standing walls typical of many Hovenweep ruins. Thorough surveys of the monument and surrounding lands have been performed by government archeologists and university groups from the University of Colorado, Brigham Young University, and San Jose State University. No major excavations have taken place in the monument.

A second detached ruin administered by Mesa Verde National Park is Yucca House, situated near the active Aztec Springs at the base of Sleeping Ute Mountain. Still in mounded condition, it nevertheless is an imposing pair of multistoried house blocks by a courtyard containing a Great Kiva and is one of at least four Chaco outliers in the Montezuma valley environs. A prehistoric road connecting the settlements of the valley to those south of the San Juan likely passed nearby.

During their explorations in the late 1800s Jackson and Holmes visited the site and included descriptions in their reports. It remained for Fewkes to persuade the site's owner, Henry Van Kleeck, to donate the nearly ten acres it covered to the government. Van Kleeck did this with the assurance the ruin would be excavated. However, although Yucca House became a national monument in 1919, no money for its development was appropriated and no public access to it was provided.

Yucca House remains an essentially untapped, relatively pristine archeological reserve. Only limited trenching was done by National Park Service personnel in 1964 in order to better define the structures and obtain wood samples for tree-ring dating. A classic Pueblo period of construction and occupation was confirmed.

Since the 1970s, a burst of archeological activity has gone on in the general Mesa Verde district as a result of possible damaging impact on the antiquities due to exploitation

Anasazi corrugated jar. FRED MANG, JR., NATIONAL PARK SERVICE.

A responsibility of specialized Mesa Verde personnel is to protect and preserve the many habitation remains scattered over the park. Some of the more significant ruins accessible to visitors have been excavated and stabilized. Thus, their features have been exposed, and weakened portions of the structures strengthened.

National Park Service policy is not to rebuild the ruins, but to stabilize them as they are found. Architectural features are secured by reapplying mortar to wall joints, replacing missing or unsteady stone and wooden construction elements, repairing foundations, and protecting the ruins from water.

Cliff Palace was the first ruin to receive such attention. Views on this page show its condition prior to excavation in 1908 and its appearance in 1946 after several preservation programs had been completed.

Photographs on the opposite page illustrate how stabilization was accomplished concurrent with the 1958–1962 excavations at Long House. One view shows the cliff dwelling during the work. Note the hose that brought water from above for the preparation of mortar, the piles of rubble from the ruins from which stones were selected to repair poorly preserved or leaning walls, and the scaffolding erected to facilitate repairs. The other two photographs depict Long House after stabilization and details of its Great Kiva.

PHOTOGRAPHS FROM THE MESA VERDE NATIONAL PARK COLLECTION.

of natural resources and the initiation of long-term educational and research programs. In 1989 several government agencies evaluated proposals for establishment of an Anasazi National Monument in southwestern Colorado. Such a facility would function as an umbrella organization for management of twenty-one major archeological resources with nationally significant attributes. Yucca House and the Goodman Point Ruin were among those considered. No plan of this sort has yet been implemented.

Early commerical exploitation of articles taken from Mesa Verde cliff dwellings led to wide dispersal of a great number of specimens. Fortunately, four Wetherill collections found their way to public institutions. The first was acquired by the State Historical and Natural History Society in Denver. The second eventually was donated to the University of Pennsylvania Museum. The third, the Nordenskiöld Collection, was taken to Sweden and later moved to the National Museum of Finland in Helsinki. The fourth was joined with the first and placed in the Colorado State Museum. The Mesa Verde Museum and Research Center display extensive assortments of artifacts and records from Mesa Verde and Hovenweep, including those from the Wetherill Mesa Project. Housed in the museum are some of the finer specimens from the Mesa Verde and adjacent localities. Also featured in the museum are the excellently crafted dioramas that faithfully reconstruct stages in the evolutionary process of cultural development in and adjacent to Mesa Verde. ▲

ADDITIONAL READINGS, Mesa Verde National Park/Hovenweep National Monument
Arrhenius, Olof W.
  1984 *Stones Speak and Waters Sing, the Life and Works of Gustaf Nordenskiöld.* Edited and annotated by Robert H. Lister and Florence C. Lister. Mesa Verde, Colorado: Mesa Verde Museum Association.
Breternitz, David A., and Jack E. Smith
  1972 Mesa Verde, "The Green Table," *National Parkways*, Vols. 3/4. Casper, Wyoming: World-Wide Research and Publishing Co. 49–88.
Hayes, Alden C.
  1964 *The Archeological Survey of Wetherill Mesa.* Archeological Research Series, No. 7A. Washington, D.C.: National Park Service.
Lister, Robert H., and Florence C. Lister
  1987 *Mesa Verde National Park, Preserving the Past.* Santa Barbara, California: ARA Mesa Verde Company, Sequoia Communications.
McNitt, Frank
  1966 *Richard Wetherill: Anasazi.* Reprint of 1957. Albuquerque: University of New Mexico Press.
Noble, David G.
  1985 *Understanding the Anasazi of Mesa Verde and Hovenweep.* Santa Fe, New Mexico: Exploration, Annual Bulletin of the School of American Research.
Nordenskiöld, Gustaf
  1979 *The Cliff Dwellers of the Mesa Verde, Southwestern Colorado, Their Pottery and Implements.* Reprint of 1893. Glorieta, New Mexico: Rio Grande Press.

Smith, Jack E.
  1987 *Mesas, Cliffs, and Canyons, The University of Colorado Survey of Mesa Verde National Park, 1971–1977*. Mesa Verde Research Series, Paper No. 3. Mesa Verde National Park, Colorado: Mesa Verde Museum Association.
Thompson, Ian
  1993 *The Towers of Hovenweep*. Mesa Verde National Park, Colorado: Mesa Verde Museum Association.
Wetherill, Benjamin A.
  1977 *The Wetherills of the Mesa Verde, Autobiography of Benjamin Alfred Wetherill*, edited by Maurine S. Fletcher. Cranbury, New Jersey: Associated University Presses.
Williamson, Ray A.
  1984 *Living the Sky, the Cosmos of the American Indian*. Norman, Oklahoma: University of Oklahoma Press.

Montezuma Castle, Montezuma Castle National Monument. GEORGE A. GRANT, NATIONAL PARK SERVICE, 1929.

MONTEZUMA CASTLE NATIONAL MONUMENT/ TUZIGOOT NATIONAL MONUMENT, ARIZONA

Cultural Significance and Archeological Classification

The Verde valley in central Arizona provided a natural corridor between the desert dwellers to the south and plateau people to the north, and both groups occupied the valley at different periods. One semi-subterranean dwelling that was part of a small community at Montezuma Well is the only typical Hohokam house on display in the National Park Service system. It apparently was used when desert colonists were migrating northward through the valley to settle in the Flagstaff region. Later, after a cultural fusion from all three core areas had taken place about Flagstaff, people from the north and south moved into the upper Verde valley. Although they built plateaulike villages and towns, their diverse ancestry showed in other material traits. The imposing structures of Montezuma Castle and Tuzigoot stem from this occupation, assigned to the Sinagua version of Hakataya culture.

Hohokam: *Colonial (Montezuma Well)*
In-betweens and Outliers: *Hakataya (Sinagua culture)*
All-Southwest: *Villages, Towns, intermediate between desert, plateau, and mountain-valley zones*

Explorations and Investigations

Montezuma Castle and Tuzigoot national monuments, twenty-five miles apart in the Verde River basin in central Arizona, contain the most extensive archeological remains of one phase of what appears to have been a longer, complicated prehistoric evolution elsewhere in the region. Though these sites and many smaller villages spread across the middle Verde valley have been known for years, relatively little scientific notice has been given them.

A Spaniard, Antonio de Espejo, journeying from Santa Fe to Acoma, Zuni, the Hopi towns, and farther west to investigate reports of rich mines, seems to have been the first white man to have reached the Verde valley and mention its antiquities. Mexican and American trappers and traders followed, who probably saw the stones from old houses or the walls of rooms sheltered by rocky cliffs but who typically kept no written accounts. In the mid-1800s a railroad survey party reconnoitering the area specifically noted abandoned Indian villages on the Verde, which pioneer farmers already were taking for granted. Finally, in 1884 an initial exploration of some of these remains was made by Edgar A. Mearns, a doctor at Fort Verde. Mearns succeeded in mapping and digging pits in several sites, including Montezuma Castle.

Scientific studies of Verde valley antiquities were initiated in 1892 when Cosmos Mindeleff, of the Bureau of American Ethnology, conducted a survey of the entire valley. He made notes, maps, and photographs of the most obvious ruins. Comparing the ancient remains there to those of the plateau and the Salt River valley, he concluded that the old cultural ties had been northerly. Mindeleff further noted the presence of prehistoric irrigation ditches near some ruins. Fortunately his records survive, because most of the aboriginal attempts at water control were destroyed by later land uses.

Three years later another Bureau of American Ethnology scientist, Jesse W. Fewkes, made his way to the Verde valley. He had become an authority on the Hopi Indians of northern Arizona and, like other colleagues, used mythology and so-called migration legends as a basis for formulating ideas about societies and their origins. The purpose of Fewkes's sojourn in the upper and middle Verde basin was to gather archeological data pertinent to Hopi traditions and, coincidentally, to collect specimens for the U.S. National Museum. Specifically, he was seeking data to support the claim of some Hopi that the ancestors of a particular clan came from an area far to the south. Fewkes thought the locale referred to might be the Verde valley and tried to prove his point by systematically comparing the architectural styles of the two regions. To asemble his data for the Verde, he took photographs and drew schematic plans of the more notable pueblos and cliff dwellings. Although Fewkes found the Verde ruins similar to some near the Hopi villages, he was not completely convinced that this resemblance supported the Hopi origin myth. Unsatisfied, he returned to the Verde in 1906 but still reached no conclusions. After that time scientists ignored the area for almost a quarter of a century.

The Verde valley and the surrounding mountainous terrain were part of the Gila Pueblo Foundation's thorough survey of the Southwest. By 1930, 185 sites had been identified. Pottery analysis indicated that in addition to a Pueblo occupation, responsible for many of the multiroomed masonry communities erected in the open and in cliff alcoves, at least three other groups of people had entered the basin, settled, and inevitably interacted. To the Gila Pueblo researchers, the Verde valley represented an aboriginal melting pot.

During the 1920s and 1930s uncontrolled pothunting, which damaged or destroyed much archeological evidence in the middle Verde valley, roused a few professionals to take to the field to recover materials and background information for scientific interpretation before they fell to the picks and shovels of untrained collectors. A leader among them was Byron Cummings. He and his University of Arizona students searched the Verde for ruins and trenched some of them, including Tuzigoot pueblo and a few pithouse structures, which yielded artifacts similar to those found in sites to the south on the middle Gila.

Since the 1940s a number of investigators have spent short periods of time in the Verde valley doing surveys, test excavations, a few major digs, and several salvage projects. Surveys filled the gaps between areas previously worked, identified many more prehistoric irrigation works, and designated sites and areas where additional excavations promised a solution to problems of Verde valley prehistory. An underwater exploration of Montezuma Well was done by a team of National Park Service divers but produced few results. Small-scale excavations cleared ballcourts, meager cave deposits, isolated burials, scatters of stone artifacts, and salvaged the remains being destroyed by nature, vandals, or road construction. More substantial excavations in pueblos, pithouse villages, and cave litter attempted to outline and refine the tentative cultural evolution and confirm external connections enjoyed by the region's aborigines.

The research shows that the Verde valley was for a long time a corridor between major cultural developments, a zone where slightly dissimilar groups intermingled. Complete understanding awaits more detailed study of some of the contributors to this cultural blend. Meanwhile, the federal areas preserve and interpret the most outstanding examples of the period of greatest population concentration in the valley.

One of these is Montezuma Castle. Early white settlers named the site, erroneously believing that the Aztec ruler or his people had migrated through the region. Part of the structure, an earthen and stone house seemingly glued to a hollow in the face of a high limestone cliff, was in danger of disintegration when first observed. To prevent collapse, the Arizona Antiquarian Association performed some emergency repairs on a few walls between 1896 and 1900. Little further attention was given the building until President Theodore Roosevelt proclaimed it a national monument in 1906. Although it came under National Park Service jurisdiction ten years later, the first permanent custodian was not named until 1927. Despite earlier preservation efforts, the National Park Service found that ravages of the elements and nearly a century of wanton destruction by treasure seekers necessitated a complete stabilization of the terraced, twenty-room cliff dwelling. Ceilings of the lower front rooms had to be repaired, and the joints of many outer masonry walls had to be retouched with mud. Even with this work, more than 90 percent of the building is original construction, attesting to the dry climate and the builders' skills.

There are no absolute dates for the occupation of Montezuma Castle. The sequence of settlement patterns, types of locally made pottery and tools, dated trade items introduced into the valley, and comparison with dated sites indicate that the habitation gradually evolved to its maximum size, declined, and finally was abandoned between about A.D. 1100 and 1400.

Many habitations and storage units are in caves and on ledges in Beaver Creek Canyon, a tributary of the Verde River. One poorly preserved community, of at least forty rooms originally, had been fashioned in tiers on recesses eroded in the cliff west of Montezuma Castle. Called Castle A, it was cleared in 1933–34 by Earl Jackson, working for the National Park Service with funds provided by the Civil Works Administration. Some rooms were erected in terraces against the cliff face, while others were created by simply walling up the fronts of small natural caves eroded in the soft whitish limestone. A fire razed the entire building, presumably some time after its builders abandoned it. The conflagration caused the upper tiers of rooms to collapse. Only a few floor remnants and the cliff rooms were left at those levels. Of the lower stories, archeologists found only wall fragments and floors of nine rooms built against the cliff or within small cavities in the rock. A limited assortment of artifacts was recovered during the digging. The most important items were textiles removed from the upper chambers. Castle A contained no datable timbers, but archeological evidence indicates that it is the same age as Montezuma Castle.

A few miles northeast of Montezuma Castle in the national monument is Montezuma Well, a large limestone sink partly filled with water from a constantly flowing spring. Water escaping from the well's outlet was used to irrigate the Indians' gardens. It remains

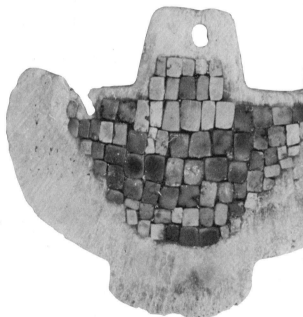

Eagle-shaped shell pendant set with turquoise. SOUTHWEST PARKS AND MONUMENTS ASSOCIATION.

a valuable resource for local farmers. Ruins of a few ancient settlements, including some small masonry houses perched on sheltered outcrops just below the rim of the sinkhole, may be seen. Although none is located in as picturesque a setting as the Castle, as a group they more clearly illustrate various aspects of the cultural history of the Verde valley. Near the well is an excavated pithouse, one of a group cleared by David A. Breternitz in the 1950s for the Museum of Northern Arizona. It represents an early intrusion into the Verde basin of people from the south whose way of life typified those groups dwelling along the middle Gila and Salt rivers of southern Arizona. Closer to the well are the partially cleared remains of two small pueblos more recent than the pithouses, built by people from the north who brought a certain new cultural orientation into the Verde.

A second important aboriginal complex situated in the Verde valley is Tuzigoot. Taking the Apache name for crooked water because of a crescent-shaped lake near the site, this ruin stands on top of a limestone and sandstone ridge that juts above the flood plain on the north side of the Verde River. It is all that remains of one of several early fourteenth-century towns in the vicinity. After white settlement of the region, farmers and ranchers, then prospectors and miners, took to pothunting the site for pleasure. Because Tuzigoot was on land belonging to the United Verde Company, a mining concern, the looting was not as extensive as it might have been.

With local and federal support, the clearing of Tuzigoot was started in 1933 by Louis R. Caywood and Edward H. Spicer, two of Bryon Cummings's graduate students. By 1935 the main block of rooms and four small isolated units had been exposed, amounting to 86 rooms of an estimated 110. Refuse deposits around the main pueblo were tested. Several hundred burials were encountered within the pueblo and in its trash piles. Once the excavations were terminated, floors and masonry walls were preserved and certain rooms of the pueblo were restored for public display. The excavators postulated that originally a few families lived in several small groups of rooms, followed by two periods of growth and expansion that resulted in a pueblo which in its heyday had seventy-seven ground-floor rooms. Several of these had second and possibly third stories. The scientists' deductions were based on superposition of structures, relation of rooms and trash, sizes and types of units, and ceramic analysis. Reliable tree-ring dates were not available at the time the work was done. A museum to house and display the collections from the ruin was built nearby with additional federal relief funds. Finally, through the interest of public-spirited local residents, the entire ridge with the site of Tuzigoot, the museum, and its collections were donated to the federal government. It was proclaimed a national monument in 1939.

A few small archeological investigations have been undertaken at Tuzigoot by National Park Service workers. Some have sought to provide a better chronology and trait list for the site. Others have examined areas before development of monument lands took place. Most significantly, tree-ring dates for the ruin were obtained in 1961, when Caywood submitted some additional wood specimens from the 1933–34 excavations to the Laboratory of Tree-Ring Research. Now, twenty-eight tree-ring dates are available for Tuzigoot. The earliest phase of Caywood and Spicer's architectural history remains undated, but it likely falls in the twelfth century. The two expansion periods of the site occurred about A.D. 1200 and in the late 1300s.

Stabilization and maintenance of the relatively poorly constructed stone and mud walls of the aboriginal building have been a constant problem for the National Park Service.

Most of the collections from Montezuma Castle and Tuzigoot are housed in the National Park Service Western Archeological and Conservation Center in Tucson. Some specimens are displayed or stored in the respective visitor centers. ▲

ADDITIONAL READINGS, Montezuma Castle National Monument/Tuzigoot National Monument
Colton, Harold S.
    1946 *The Sinagua. A Summary of the Archaeology of the Region of Flagstaff, Arizona.* Bulletin, No. 22. Flagstaff: Museum of Northern Arizona.
Fish, Paul R., and Suzanne K. Fish
    1977 *Verde Valley Archaeology: Review and Perspective.* Research Paper, No. 8. Flagstaff: Museum of Northern Arizona.
Hartman, Dana
    1976 *Tuzigoot, An Archeological Overview.* Research Paper, No. 4. Flagstaff: Museum of Northern Arizona.
Jackson, Earl, and Sallie P. Van Valkenburgh
    1954 *Montezuma Castle Archeology, Part I: Excavations.* Technical Series, Vol. 3, No. 1. Globe, Arizona: Southwestern Monuments Association.
Schroeder, Albert H., and Homer F. Hastings
    1958 *Montezuma Castle.* Historical Handbook Series, No. 27. Washington, D.C.: National Park Service.

Keet Seel, Navajo National Monument. GEORGE A. GRANT, NATIONAL PARK SERVICE, 1935.

NAVAJO NATIONAL MONUMENT, ARIZONA

Cultural Significance and Archeological Classification

Anasazi: *Pueblo I, II, III*
All-Southwest: *Hamlets, Villages, Towns, plateau zone*

The three major cliff dwellings of Navajo National Monument are illustrative of that particular time when some Anasazi of the Four Corners preferred to settle in arched caves or on narrow ledges cut into vertical canyon walls. The obvious cost in time and energy to build homes in such unlikely places is made more poignant by their ultimate failure.

Explorations and Investigations

In the winter of 1895 Richard and Al Wetherill and Charlie Mason outfitted themselves in Bluff City, Utah, and for four months packed into Monument Valley, Marsh Pass, and Tsegi Canyon in northeastern Arizona. Many fine ruins were encountered, and quantities of specimens were taken from them. Among them were four hundred pieces of pottery removed from one burial ground, a major Wetherill collection that has not been traced. One site they discovered is the largest cliff dwelling in Arizona. The Wetherills called the 160-room structure Long House, but the Navajo name, Keet Seel, which means broken pottery, became its accepted designation. Although the present building dates to a forty-year period between A.D. 1240 and 1280, excavations in trash deposits suggest utilization of the alcove beginning as early as Pueblo I.

Two years after the discovery of Keet Seel, Richard Wetherill returned to the great ruin in a lofty arched cave worn into a sheer, red sandstone cliff. This time he was guiding an expedition financed by a rich eastern family for their son and his tutor. Richard measured and photographed the cliff house, diagrammed its plan, catalogued everything he found, and kept notes about the site and his diggings. These were practices he followed at all the ruins they examined. After three months of collecting, they loaded pack animals with nearly a ton of specimens to be carried into Bluff City, Utah. From there they were hauled by wagon back to the Wetherill ranch in Colorado. A year later the collection was purchased for the American Museum of Natural History in New York for three thousand dollars.

Betatakin, Navajo for ledge house, was discovered fourteen years later in the summer of 1909. This find was made by Byron Cummings and his party who, with guide-interpreter John Wetherill, were returning from archeological explorations in upper Tsegi Canyon for the University of Utah. The 135-room structure was built on the steep floor of a beautifully vaulted alcove at the head of a forested canyon. It is the only one of the three cliff dwellings in the monument which was not built over remains of an earlier occupation. Cummings worked at Betatakin in the winter of 1909. Neil Judd, a student assistant to Cummings when the site was found, returned there in 1917 to direct a program of preservation and repair. A large portion of the cave roof fell after Betatakin was abandoned by the Anasazi and knocked many room walls into the canyon below.

A few days before Betatakin was discovered, John Wetherill had led the Cummings party to Inscription House, the third important cliff house in the area. Located in a shallow shelter near the base of a sandstone dome in Nitsin Canyon, it contains seventy-four rooms and granaries and one kiva. While the ruin was being examined, the Wetherill and Cummings children found the dim inscription carved in the plaster of a wall. At one time the date accompanying the almost illegible inscription was believed to be 1661 and was thought to have been left by an unknown Spanish traveler. Now most observers agree the date of 1861 may have been scratched into the wall plaster by members of a Mormon party who traversed the region at that time, but no accounts are known of that visit. Cummings returned to Inscription House on several occasions to excavate in the ruin, where blocks of adobe were common building materials. He never reported in any detail upon his findings there or on other investigations at Betatakin.

In 1910 John Wetherill and his partner, Clyde Colville, moved their trading enterprise from Oljeto down the valley some thirty miles to a desert basin in the red sand hills known since as Kayenta. There Wetherill and his wife, Louisa, built a new trading post and a permanent home. For years he and Colville boasted that the store—post office was farther from a railroad than any other in the United States. John was an expert trader to the Navajos, but his love of exploring had never been quelled. While at Kayenta, he became well known as a competent guide, equipper, and expedition organizer for many who came to his part of the Southwest. John Wetherill was also the first custodian of Navajo National Monument, established in 1909 to include Betatakin, Keet Seel, and Inscription House.

Under National Park Service administration, protection and preservation of the ruins has continued. Keet Seel was stabilized in the 1930s by a crew directed by John Wetherill. In the 1970s archeologists from the University of Colorado repaired Inscription House and a nearby nineteen-room cliff village called Snake House.

Archeological research in and around the monument during the last two decades has added to an understanding of the aboriginal cultures. Interest in them was stimulated in the late 1950s and early 1960s by the explorations and research done in connection with the construction of the Glen Canyon Dam. Meticulous studies by the Laboratory of Tree-Ring Research at the University of Arizona of timbers incorporated in the cliff dwellings of the Tsegi Canyon area have provided dates for the sites and demonstrated their relationship with neighboring centers. The Museum of Northern Arizona undertook excavations at Inscription House. Limited archeological materials have been secured from other cliff dwellings concurrent with stabilization. A long-term effort by Southern Illinois University on Black Mesa south of the monument rounded out the regional prehistorical record prior to the time of the cliff dwellings.

Collections from Navajo National Monument are housed at the American Museum of Natural History, New York; Arizona State Museum, Tucson; Museum of Northern Arizona, Flagstaff; Peabody Museum of Archaeology and Ethnology, Harvard University, Cambridge; University of Colorado Museum, Boulder; University of Utah, Salt Lake City; and the Western Archeological and Conservation Center, Tucson. ▲

ADDITIONAL READINGS, Navajo National Monument

Ambler, J. Richard
> 1985 *Archeological Assessment, Navajo National Monument.* Southwest Cultural Resources Center, Professional Papers, No. 9. Santa Fe, New Mexico: Southwest Cultural Resources Center, National Park Service.

Judd, Neil M.
> 1930 *The Excavation and Repair of Betatakin.* Proceedings, Vol. 77. Washington, D.C.: U.S. National Museum.

> 1968 *Men Met Along the Trail, Adventures in Archaeology.* Norman, Oklahoma: University of Oklahoma Press.

McNitt, Frank
> 1966 *Richard Wetherill: Anasazi.* Reprint of 1957. Albuquerque: University of New Mexico Press.

Viele, Catherine W.
> 1980 *Voices in the Canyon.* Globe, Arizona: Southwest Parks and Monuments Association.

Ward, Albert E.
> 1975 *Inscription House.* Technical Series, No. 16. Flagstaff: Museum of Northern Arizona.

Pictographs on the eastern wall of Betatakin, Navajo National Monument (Milton Wetherill in foreground). GEORGE A. GRANT, NATIONAL PARK SERVICE, 1935.

Prehistoric trade routes passed through the Organ Pipe Cactus National Monument area. GEORGE H. H. HUEY.

ORGAN PIPE CACTUS NATIONAL MONUMENT, ARIZONA

Cultural Significance and Archeological Classification

The cactus-studded Papaguería area encompassed within Organ Pipe Cactus National Monument was a prehistoric crossroads for trade or communication routes coming into the desert from all directions. California traditions of the Paleo-Indian and Archaic periods reached their most easterly extent here contemporaneous with local traditions. A later peripheral Hohokam occupation traded with peoples in northern Mexico, the lower Colorado River valley, and the Tonto basin of central Arizona. These Hohokam likely served as middlemen in shell and salt distribution from the Gulf of California to other Hohokam of the Gila and Salt river areas.

Archaic: *Cochise, Amargosa*
Hohokam: *Colonial, Sedentary, Classic*
All-Southwest: *Hamlets, Villages, Towns, desert zone*

Explorations and Investigations

For nearly four centuries Spanish explorers and missionaries, Anglo parties bound for or returning from the California gold fields, Mexican Boundary and Southern Pacific Railroad surveyors, naturalists, prospectors, travel writers, and assorted desert rats made their way along the treacherous Camino del Diablo on the southern periphery of what is now Organ Pipe Cactus National Monument. Except for noting occasional bedrock mortars left by some unknowns, they were oblivious to any antiquities. Ageless geologic upheavals had molded an eerie, forbidding landscape, and the desert flora that sparsely covered it commanded sufficient attention to lead ultimately to the setting aside in 1937 of 516 square miles north of the international border as a natural preserve.

In 1929, as part of a comprehensive archeological survey throughout the Southwest launched by Gila Pueblo, Frank Midvale reconnoitered the Ajo valley in the northern sector of the later monument and recorded a Hohokam village with trash mounds and what appeared to be a diagnostic ballcourt. The same site was visited eight years later by Emil W. Haury following his work at the Gila River Hohokam community of Snaketown. In 1951 on behalf of the National Park Service, Paul Ezell conducted a more wide-ranging reconnaissance of the monument which included this village and a number of others in the vicinity. Although a considerable human presence representing several cultures was indicated, no excavations were done.

In the belief that earlier surveys had been limited, from the 1989 through 1991 seasons a National Park Service archeological team led by Adrianne G. Rankin took to the field. Eight thousand acres were covered to record 188 archeological sites, some of which related to the protohistoric and historic Tohono O'odham (Pima-Papago) and Hia C-ed O'odham (Sand Papago) occupation of the region. No excavations have resulted yet from these preliminaries, but a notable cultural history pointing up needed further research has been outlined.

Beginning in the 1930s a California archeologist, Malcolm Rogers, devoted much of his career to study of the Paleo-Indian period as encountered in the deserts of southern

California, Arizona, and Sonora, Mexico. His student, Julian Hayden, subsequently focused upon the same horizon in the Pinacate Mountains and rocky slopes of the Sonoran Desert to the west of Organ Pipe Cactus National Monument. Sharing data but sometimes disagreeing in interpretation, the men identified two groups of Paleo-Indians who presumably met along both sides of the Mexico–United States border east of the Colorado River. Formerly, the San Dieguito people were thought restricted to the southern California Mohave Desert, while the Cochise territory was the sweep of lands across southern Arizona. The hunters had slightly differing stone-tool technologies, as evidenced by rare scatters of implements and the residue from their manufacture. Elusive traces of rock alignments, still undisturbed on the empty desert floors, perhaps were created by these nomads to serve as windbreaks. Although no specific Paleo-Indian sites have been located within the monument, further investigation likely will show it to have been part of this zone of contact.

The two Paleo-Indian traditions generally are dated from about 10,000 B.C. to 5,000 B.C. Hayden prefers to regard some San Dieguito points bearing coatings of desert varnish as older. His hypothesis of people in the Southwest by 30,000 B.C. may be supported by recent finds near El Paso of points associated with mammals which became extinct many millennia before the mammoth, the usual target of the earliest recognized Paleo-Indian predators.

Using styles of projectile points as a criterion, the same intermixing of western (Amargosa) and eastern (Cochise) Archaic occupations appears to have occurred within the monument. When explored, potentially fruitful open sites and stratified deposits in caves and rock shelters will help define relationships or hybridization of these peoples and their adaptations to a microenvironment that may or may not have been more hospitable than at present.

Most of the sites noted by all surveys within the monument are of Hohokam affiliation. An important concentration of these remains is in the Ajo valley, where loam and ephemeral waters were attractive to farmers. On the basis of surface sherd collections, occupation is thought to have lasted from A.D. 500 to 1450.

Especially worthy of future attention is the large community first documented in the initial 1929 work. Now it is estimated to extend over some two hundred acres. It contains a ballcourt and numerous pithouse and activity clusters, and is densely sprinkled with artifacts such as pottery, shell, and obsidian from a number of far-flung sources. Researchers postulate that this town was on strategic trails running north-south and east-west, and was a major link in an extensive prehistoric trade network that in some cases reached northward into the Anasazi domain. Four small satellite villages, perhaps for seasonal use only, are nearby. A canal segment at one village reveals attempts to capture runoff waters for agricultural purposes.

Organ Pipe Cactus National Monument presently is the only National Park Service facility with an untapped archeological reserve of Hohokam culture extending over at least nine hundred years. Should excavation and study of these remains take place, the importance of this holding will increase enormously.

Artifacts and notes resulting from archeological surveys of Organ Pipe Cactus National Monument are at the Arizona State Museum and the Western Archeological and Conservation Center, both in Tucson. ▲

ADDITIONAL READINGS, Organ Pipe Cactus National Monument
Hartmann, William K.
    1989 *Desert Heart, Chronicles of the Sonoran Desert.* Tucson, Arizona: Fisher Books.
Rankin, Adrianne G.
    1991 *Archeological Survey in Organ Pipe Cactus National Monument: 1991 Progress
        Report.* Tucson, Arizona: Western Archeological and Conservation Center,
        National Park Service.

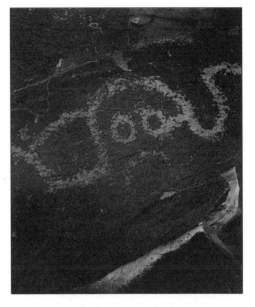

Hohokam petroglyph, Organ Pipe Cactus National Monument.
GEORGE H. H. HUEY.

PECOS NATIONAL HISTORICAL PARK, NEW MEXICO

Anasazi: *Pueblo I, IV, V*
All-Southwest: *Hamlets,
Villages, Towns, plateau
zone*

Cultural Significance and Archeological Classification

The story presented at Pecos National Historical Park encapsulates the human history of this part of the Southwest, encompassing a thousand years that witnessed Indian, Spanish, Mexican, and Anglo-American presence. This chapter focuses upon the two earliest occupations, which, in fact, consumed a giant portion of that time.

*Adolph F. Bandelier at Pecos in
1880.* GEORGE C. BENNETT, MUSEUM OF
NEW MEXICO.

The prehistoric saga began with a few small familial groups of people influenced by the Colorado Plateau Anasazi who occupied simple one-roomed shelters sunk into the ground and ended with two elaborate multistoried, mulitroomed surface structures that accommodated several thousand inhabitants. Particularly well represented at Pecos is the period of turmoil caused by the late prehistoric coalescence along the upper Rio Grande of scores of uprooted Pueblo groups to abandonment of the pueblo in the early nineteenth century. Artifacts and tipi rings confirm extensive contacts between Pecos and Apache and other tribes who roamed the grasslands to the east. A bulky shell of an adobe church and some Europeanization of material culture afford evidence of acculturation during the Spanish colonial period.

Explorations and Investigations

One of the largest and most easterly of the pueblos encountered by sixteenth-century Spanish conquistadors, Pecos was important in the exploration, colonization, and missionization of New Mexico. An archeologically and historically documented story of Pecos and its environs from the middle of the ninth century to the third decade of the nineteenth century has been achieved through a synthesis of data from various sources. Knowledge of the first several centuries of its existence came through the picks and shovels of archeologists. The three hundred years from 1540, when the first Spaniards arrived, to 1838, date of the abandonment of the town, have been fleshed out by accounts written by explorers, missionaries, soldiers, historians, and ethnologists.

Chroniclers of the Coronado expedition of 1540–41 recorded the name of the settlement as Cicuye, which probably was the natives' own designation for their village. Other Pueblo Indians, speaking different languages, called it by a term that Spanish soldiers interpreted as "Pecos."

Pecos was a populous community from the time of first contact with Europeans until the Indians drove the Spaniards from the country during the Pueblo Revolt of 1680. Its inhabitants, who had a reputation for being warlike, are thought to have numbered between one thousand and two thousand. After Santa Fe became the capital of New Spain in 1610, Pecos assumed great importance for the Spanish military, secular, and religious authorities. Strategically located on a natural route from the northern Rio Grande valley around the southern end of the Rockies to the Great Plains, Pecos was seen as a friendly Pueblo community that could provide a buffer against Apache and Comanche raiders. At the same time it could serve as an intermediary in a profitable trade between its inhabitants and the Spaniards.

Fragment of seventeenth-century saucer, found in Pecos Convento.
ROBERT H. LISTER.

The Pecos Indians, however, were unpredictable in their attitudes toward the Europeans. At times they actively resisted intrusion by Spanish military and administrative groups and rejected attempts by dedicated friars to convert them to Christianity. On other occasions they acquiesced to the invaders and adopted use of many of their tools, food, and livestock. They accepted the Spanish god and built structures for his worship. They professed allegiance to a distant king and even joined forces with Spaniards against other pueblos and marauding Indians from the plains. Underlying the pattern of wavering alliance between the conquerors and the conquered was a fierce internal church-state struggle among the colonists. Friars and governors, at cross-purposes, created conflicting regulations and policies concerning the Indians, adding little strength to already uneasy relationships.

Eventually the New Mexico Pueblos had enough of Spanish imposition. Exasperated by unstable affairs, demands for goods and services, and religious persecution, they went to war. During the summer of 1680 Pecos warriors united with those from all the Pueblo villages in a successful revolt, although it is said that a pro-Spanish faction at Pecos warned of the impending rebellion several days before it was launched.

With the Palace of the Governors in Santa Fe under siege for ten days of bloody ambush, raids, and plundering, the Spaniards began their painful withdrawal from New Mexico. Led by Governor Otermín, some one thousand surviving Spaniards and sympathetic Indians made their way south down the Rio Grande to the tenuous security of El Paso. During the hostilities four hundred colonists had been murdered, twenty-one Franciscans martyred, and an unknown number of Indians killed or executed after having been taken prisoner. During and shortly after the uprising, many symbols of Spanish dominance, such as public buildings, homes, farms, and especially religious structures, were put to the torch by the rebels. The church at Pecos did not escape the flames.

In 1692, shortly after he had become governor of the lost province of New Mexico, Captain General Diego de Vargas marched a small army back up the Rio Grande valley. Within four months he had succeeded in a bloodless reconquest of the territory. The village of Santa Fe was re-established as the seat of authority.

When Vargas first approached Pecos, he found the town deserted. Hearing of his coming, the residents had fled. Although the governor contemplated punishing them by burning their homes and cornfields, instead he withdrew from the pueblo and left its fields unharmed. Releasing the few Indians he had captured, he admonished them to tell the others of his kind treatment of them. By these acts of good faith, Vargas hoped to gain the confidence and respect of the Pecos people. In this, he was successful. When he returned several weeks later, Pecos again was thriving, and a welcoming mob awaited him at the entrance to the plaza.

After a rebellious spell in 1696, the Pueblos resigned themselves to dealing with Spanish officials and new residents of the borderlands. Most of their towns, vacated during the rebellion, were eventually reoccupied. Secular officials were selected according to Spanish dictates. A legal code protected the Indians' lands from white encroachment. Inevitably, however, as the Hispanic population expanded the natives were increasingly squeezed into tighter enclaves. In time, the Pecos valley transformed into a predominantly Spanish community. Franciscan padres resumed their duties, which necessitated refurbishing many desecrated missions and building new ones. Old quarrels between the religious and the secular branches were renewed, to the detriment of effective government. Somehow the Indians suffered through these various problems, but they were unprotected against white men's diseases. Smallpox virtually wiped out some villages.

Added to their troubles were mounting incursions by nomadic tribes who, upon acquiring the use of horses, heavily preyed upon them and then galloped to safety. Pecos was particularly vulnerable to such attacks from the Apache and Comanche because of its proximity to the plains where they traditionally roamed. Although small units of Spanish troops sometimes were quartered there to help protect the village and the important communication trail that passed nearby, the constant skirmishes, added to the other difficulties, made inevitable the ultimate abandonment of this easternmost toehold of the Pueblo Indians.

Sixty years after the Vargas re-entry, the once booming town of Pecos had shrunk to half its size. A 1750 census listed only 449 residents, 255 of whom were adults. By 1821, when Mexico became an independent nation with New Mexico its most northern territory, eight or ten Indian families amounting to possibly about fifty people were left. From their crumbling citadel, these doomed survivors glumly witnessed the swell of caravans passing along the Santa Fe Trail to engage in a trade in which they would have no share.

In 1838 the hard decision to move out of Pecos pueblo was made by the last seventeen residents. They packed up their ceremonial gear, gathered their few personal belongings and available crops, arranged with local Spaniards to care for their church, and took the eighty-mile trail northwest to Jemez, the only other pueblo that spoke their language. The people of Jemez had given them permission to come, assisted in the move, and provided houses and fields. But neither the people nor the village of Pecos really died. At Jemez, the Pecos refugees steadfastly clung to their own heritage, although they comfortably settled into their new surroundings. From time to time they made pilgrimages to their ancestral home. Their descendants, who still live in Jemez, retain pride in their old ties to Pecos and annually return in August on the Pecos saint's day for moving services held within the massive adobe ramparts of the church nave.

Pothunters, scavengers, and transients hastened ruination of what had become a lifeless clutter of roofless, cell-like rooms and a wrecked church. Their callous vandalism was softened by a compendium of romantic impressions left by antiquarians, artists, and travelers drawn to the silent site by its enormous size and glowing reputation as one of the most outstanding Rio Grande pueblos.

Sketches in 1846 of both mission church and pueblo ruins by artist John Mix Stanley, who accompanied the Army of the West, depict the pueblo in ruins but still standing, two and three stories in places with a great many beams, lintels, and other wooden elements in place. In these renderings, the church appears relatively intact. By 1858 a painting by German artist Heinrich B. Möllhausen illustrated the rapid deterioration of the town and church, many of whose walls are shown protruding from enveloping masses of rubble and dirt. In 1880 Adolph F. Bandelier began his exhaustive investigations of southwestern Indians by examining the remains of Pecos. He spent a week amid the tumbled walls, photographing them, accumulating artifacts, and interviewing local residents about their recollections of the village and its former occupants. He saw the church gone to ruin because unknown persons had ripped out ornamented beams, scarred the walls, and even disinterred the dead in the cemetery. Bandelier's report on Pecos was the first of a scientific nature and also was the first publication of the Archaeological Institute of America, his sponsor.

It remained for archeologists to pry the truth about Pecos from the blanket of soil and legend which in time surrounded it. Early in the twentieth century Phillips Academy of Andover, Massachusetts, decided to excavate Pecos pueblo. Alfred V. Kidder was placed in charge. Excavations began in 1915 and continued intermittently for ten summer field seasons. The financial crash of 1929 brought an abrupt end to the undertaking, but not before a great volume of data and many artifacts had been gathered.

Kidder's work at Pecos came at a time when southwestern archeology was maturing from the sentimental accumulation of crates of Indian objects for museum display to systematic research, controlled excavations, and detailed analyses. Prior investigations a

Abandoned "Catholic Church," Pecos, 1846. JOHN MIX STANLEY, EMORY, *NOTES.*

short distance to the south conducted by Nels C. Nelson, of the American Museum of Natural History, had proved that stratigraphic excavations of refuse deposits and analytical studies of potsherds from them could produce information about sequences of pottery types. These in turn would permit recognition of contacts and information about occupation of those ruins. This significant step in southwestern archeology set the pattern for later research throughout the area, particularly at Pecos.

Kidder focused on ceramic analysis at Pecos as a means of charting a sequence of pottery types for the entire northern Rio Grande region. The strategic position of Pecos on the main passageway between the interior of the Pueblo domain and the buffalo plains gave hope that excavations would uncover artifacts to link a chronology of local culture with cultures west and east. Wide archeological ties were urgently needed for placing southwestern prehistory in proper perspective. It was hoped that pottery would provide such information. To a considerable extent this expectation was realized.

Situated on a narrow, red stone mesa in the midst of pinyon- and juniper-clad hills, Pecos consisted of two large mounds of house remains, enormous drifts of trash, and the wreckage of its last mission and convent. Aided by a team of highly competent associates, Kidder concentrated on stratigraphic excavations in the trash along the east slope of the mesa and elsewhere. He recovered masses of potsherds, other artifacts, and many burials. Digging into a portion of the north mound, he outlined the final compact, four-sided, multistoried pueblo surrounding a wide plaza, built in the vestiges of an earlier, sprawling one-story community. The south mound was only tested. Uncovering the pueblo ruins proved to be demanding because of the instability of the walls once they were freed from their enveloping dirt and rubble. It became necessary to promptly backfill excavated units to preserve the architecture and avoid danger to the crew and staff.

A notable event took place at the Pecos field camp in August 1927 when, upon an invitation from Kidder, leading regional archeologists met to discuss the status of southwestern archeology and to postulate eight prehistoric periods based on the stratigraphic record. These were Basket Maker I through III and Pueblo I through V.

At the conclusion of his studies Kidder believed that Pecos probably reached its greatest size sometime between A.D. 1500 and 1600, when it had a population of approximately one thousand persons. He thought that the two room blocks, the larger northern four-story unit, and the smaller southern complex likely contained 1,020 rooms. Not all of them were in use contemporaneously. It was obvious that even at its heyday Pecos had continually undergone additions, alterations, and rebuilding. In its later stages, as population declined many sections were deserted, fell into disrepair, and were filled with trash.

While Phillips Academy interested itself in the Pecos ruins, the Museum of New Mexico, under the guidance of Jesse L. Nusbaum, began clearing and repairing the hulking, mud-brick remains of its eighteenth-century church. After Pecos became a New Mexico State Monument, the museum also excavated a portion of the church's convent and a section of the south pueblo. The dilapidated rock walls of the cleared pueblo rooms and the large, adobe religious enclosure were stabilized for display purposes.

For years historians and archivists could not agree on the number and characteristics of the Spanish churches at Pecos. Details given in various eyewitness accounts did not correlate with physical evidence at the site. Following the acquisition of Pecos pueblo as a national monument in 1965, additional digging and stabilization of the last church and convent by a National Park Service archeological team, directed by Jean M. Pinkley, uncovered the buried foundations of an older, much larger church beneath the footings of the one standing at the time. Archeological findings showed that the earlier church had burned and that the existing building had gone up almost entirely within its nave. The edifice that had been consumed by fire turns out to have been the second church at Pecos. Now the evidence in the ground has been neatly meshed with contemporary documents of the seventeenth and eighteenth centuries by Alden C. Hayes to show that Pecos had a succession of four churches, two of which left little trace.

The first was a small isolated church or chapel, erected at the instigation of an unknown friar probably in the late 1590s or early 1600s, several hundred yards northeast of the north quadrangle of the pueblo. It seems to have been in use for only a few years. Between 1622 and 1625 the second house of worship was built by Fray Andrés Juárez at the southern end of the mesa a short distance from the south pueblo. This was a spacious structure embodying three hundred thousand adobe bricks in its eight- to ten-feet-thick walls which enclosed a nave about 40 by 133 feet. There were closely spaced, ground-to-roof buttresses along the exterior walls which may have stood forty-five feet high. Six towers rose above its roof line. Overall, it was the most impressive of the churches erected at the pueblo. A convent with rooms, corrals, and a cloister area was joined to the south wall. It was this edifice which rebellious Indians completely destroyed in 1680.

The third church was little more than a temporary chapel. It was erected after the reconquest in 1694 by Fray Diego de la Casa Zeinas by leveling off the rubble of the south wall of the razed church and building three walls against the north side of the convent wall. A permanent structure placed upon the debris of the pre-revolt church in 1705 by Fray José de Arranegui was the fourth place of Christian worship at Pecos. It was neither as large nor as imposing as the church from whose ruins it grew, but it served until the village was deserted. Today its roofless walls stand as a reminder of the Christianization of Pecos.

Within the past decade, National Park Service archeological survey and testing around the principal settlement have revealed two large partially subterranean pithouses lined with logs which contained a scattering of smashed pottery and other nonperishable specimens attributable to a generalized Pueblo I horizon. Tree rings produced a cutting date of A.D. 850. These are the first such structures found in the upper Pecos area and may have been used only seasonally. At present it appears that the region did not attract many settlers until fourteenth-century population pressures in the Rio Grande valley forced outmigration eastward and were responsible for what became Pecos pueblo. Contemporary small house sites are scattered through the Pecos valley, showing that town and village occupation occurred simultaneously.

In 1990 what had been Pecos National Monument, set aside in 1965 to preserve and interpret for the public the Indian and early Hispanic remains, became Pecos National

Historical Park due to three important additions to the federal holdings that brought the history of the Pecos area up to the twentieth century. One was the 5,500-acre adjacent Forked Lightning Ranch acquired from the estate of Colonel E. E. Fogelson and his widow, Greer Garson Fogelson, long-time benefactors of the monument. Indian and nineteenth-century Hispanic sites on the property offer numerous future research opportunities, as do a riparian environment along the Pecos River and the still-observable ruts of the old Santa Fe Trail that for sixty years in the nineteenth century served as a lifeline between the central United States and this remote corner of the continent. However, historical and ecological value does not stop there.

On August 17, 1846, American forces under orders from President James Polk and led by Brigadier General Stephen Watts Kearny camped near Forked Lightning Ranch lands or Pecos pueblo on their way to seize California. The next day, after Mexicans who were to halt their progress at the narrow defile of Apache Canyon to the west, had fled, Kearny triumphantly raised the Stars and Stripes over the plaza in Santa Fe. Much of the Southwest thereafter belonged to the United States.

A few years later, eccentric Captain Napoleon Kozlowski, a Polish immigrant who had served in Kearny's Army of the West, built a stagecoach stop on what became part of the modern ranch using handy materials salvaged from Pecos pueblo and its mission. This structure later was incorporated into the Forked Lightning Ranch house.

Two other detached parcels of land added to former Pecos National Monument, each in excess of three hundred acres, were where decisive battles of the Civil War took place. One is the former Johnson's Ranch at the west entrance to Apache Canyon. There on March 26, 1862, a Confederate army contingent known as the Texas Rangers and its supply train were routed by Union troops. Although the site itself is historically significant, little other than some ceiling beams still remains of the original ranch buildings.

Two days later a second Civil War engagement was fought at Pigeon's Ranch, located six miles to the east on the old Santa Fe Trail between Apache Canyon and Pecos pueblo. It now also is included in the Pecos National Historical Park. A stage stop at this locality was converted into a hospital for wounded on both sides of the battle that was fought across the surrounding valley. During the 1980s the remains of thirty-one Confederate soldiers were uncovered on these grounds during construction of a residence, three of which were later identified either by uniforms or diaries. The First Colorado Volunteers, the New Mexico Volunteers, and regular army units made up the victorious Grand Army of the Republic, which for a time used the springs behind the Forked Lightning Ranch buildings as its headquarters. The Battle of Glorieta culminating at Pigeon's Ranch effectively ended Southern dreams of creating a new nation reaching from Dixie to the Pacific.

Most of the specimens, photographs, and notes resulting from Kidder's many years of work at Pecos pueblo now are housed at the monument visitor center. Others are in the custody of Phillips Academy. Recovered aboriginal skeletal remains and records derived from their study by E. A. Hooton are curated at the Peabody Museum, Harvard University. The Museum of New Mexico cares for the recently discovered unclaimed remains of some of those who fell at the Battle of Glorieta.

ADDITIONAL READINGS, Pecos National Historical Park

Bezy, John V., and Joseph P. Sanchez, Editors
    1988 *Pecos, Gateway to Pueblos and Plains, The Anthology.* Tucson, Arizona:
        Southwest Parks and Monuments Association.
Hayes, Alden C.
    1974 *The Four Churches of Pecos.* Albuquerque: University of New Mexico Press.
Kessell, John L.
    1979 *Kiva, Cross, and Crown: The Pecos Indians and New Mexico, 1540–1840.*
        Washington, D.C.: National Park Service.
Kidder, Alfred V.
    1932 *The Artifacts of Pecos.* New Haven, Connecticut: Yale University Press.
    1958 *Pecos, New Mexico: Archaeological Notes.* Andover, Massachusetts: Phillips
        Academy.
    1962 *An Introduction to the Study of Southwestern Archaeology with a Preliminary
        Account of the Excavations at Pecos.* Revised edition of 1924. New Haven,
        Connecticut: Yale University Press.
Noble, David G., Editor
    1981 *Pecos Ruins: Geology, Archaeology, History, Prehistory.* Santa Fe, New Mexico:
        Exploration, Annual Bulletin of the School of American Research.
Whitford, William C.
    1989 *Colorado Volunteers in the Civil War, the New Mexico Campaign of 1862.*
        Reprint of 1906 edition. Glorieta, New Mexico: Rio Grande Press.

Jean Pinkley overseeing National Park Service excavations at Pecos Mission. NATIONAL PARK SERVICE.

Puerco Ruins, Petrified Forest National Park, Arizona. FRED HIRSCHMANN.

PETRIFIED FOREST NATIONAL PARK, ARIZONA

Cultural Significance and Archeological Classification

The archeological sequence in Petrified Forest National Park encompasses a cultural continuum extending from an ephemeral Paleo-Indian presence to that of the Pueblo Indians living during the latter half of the fourteenth century. Situated between the Anasazi plateau and Mogollon mountain and valley core areas and bordering the Hakataya territory, the region was subject to different sets of influences from surrounding cultures. The southern impact appeared early in the transitional period between the nomadic Archaic and semi-nomadic Basket Maker II periods, dated here between A.D. 1 and 200, when a brown pottery made by the paddle and anvil method appeared. It is the oldest ceramic material known in the Little Colorado River area. At the final occupation as represented by the Puerco Ruin (A.D. 1250–1380), trade from Zuni to the east and Hopi and Homol'ovi to the northwest is evident. Rock art of this period reflects the introduction from the Jornada Mogollon of the kachina cult. Surprisingly, although petrified wood was used locally for lithics, no substantial trade in this abundant natural resource seems to have occurred.

Archaic: *Oshara*
Anasazi: *Basket Maker II, III; Pueblo I, II, III, IV*
Mogollon: *1, 2, 3*
In-betweens and Outliers: *Hakataya (Sinagua culture)*
All-Southwest: *Hamlets, Villages, Towns, intermediate between plateau and mountain-valley zones*

Explorations and Investigations

Some archeological reconnaisssance had been undertaken in the region of Petrified Forest National Park prior to 1906 when it was set aside as an area of outstanding geological importance by President Theodore Roosevelt. At the end of the nineteenth century Jesse W. Fewkes, of the Bureau of American Ethnology, and Walter Hough, of the U.S. National Museum, located and partially exposed many of the larger ruins in the vicinity and collected more than five thousand specimens. The two also attempted to correlate archeological data with ethnological information to substantiate oral traditions of early Hopi migrations. Hough dug in several ruins now included in the park, some of which have been further cleared.

Harry P. Mera and C. B. Cosgrove, from the Laboratory of Anthropology in Santa Fe, headed a Civil Works Administration archeological project in the 1930s that conducted the first systematic archeological survey of part of the park and probed some of the ruins. One hundred nine ancient features were recorded within and immediately adjacent to the park. An eight-room pueblo, known as Agate House because it was constructed of chunks of colorful agatized wood, was cleared and partially restored. Several rooms were opened in the Puerco Ruin, a 125-room pueblo site on a bluff near the Puerco River, which was added to the federal holding in 1930. Two units of the Flattop Site, a pithouse village, were cleaned out. Mera worked out a chronology of regional pottery development which is used to the present time. National Park Service personnel expanded the survey of the park in 1941 and 1942, bringing the total number of recorded sites to 339. Following World War II Fred Wendorf excavated eight of twenty-five pithouses at the Flattop Site and two others at

Mountain lion petroglyph, Petrified Forest National Park.
GEORGE A. GRANT, NATIONAL PARK SERVICE, 1934.

Twin Buttes Site.

The most comprehensive examination of the antiquities of Petrified Forest National Park occurred during the late 1980s. At that time National Park Service researchers and volunteers undertook an archeological survey along the park boundary, recorded rock art at Mountain Lion Mesa, cleared additional parts of Puerco Ruin, tested an adjacent lithic scatter, and mapped and partially excavated the Basket Maker II hamlet of Sivu'ovi.

Collections and notes from the various enterprises in Petrified Forest are to be found at the Museum of Northern Arizona in Flagstaff, the Smithsonian Institution in Washington, at the National Park Service Western Archeological and Conservation Center in Tucson, and in the park's visitor center. ⛰

ADDITIONAL READINGS, Petrified Forest National Park
Burton, Jeffery F.
　1990　*Archeological Investigations at Puerco Ruin, Petrified Forest National Park, Arizona.* Publications in Anthropology, No. 54. Tucson, Arizona: Western Archeological and Conservation Center, National Park Service.
　1991　*The Archeology of Sivu'ovi, the Archaic to Basketmaker Transition at Petrified Forest National Park.* Publications in Anthropology, No. 55. Tucson, Arizona: Western Archeological and Conservation Center, National Park Service.
Schroeder, Albert H.
　1961　Puerco Ruins Excavations, Petrified Forest National Monument, Arizona. *Plateau*, Vol. 33, No. 4. Flagstaff: Museum of Northern Arizona.
Stewart, Yvonne G.
　1980　*An Archeological Overview of Petrified Forest National Park.* Publications in Anthropology, No. 10. Tucson, Arizona: Western Archeological Center, National Park Service.
Wells, Susan J.
　1989　*Petrified Forest National Park Boundary Survey, 1988: The Final Season.* Publications in Anthropology, No. 51. Tucson, Arizona: Western Archeological and Conservation Center, National Park Service.
Wendorf, Fred
　1953　*Archaeological Studies in the Petrified Forest National Monument.* Bulletin, No. 27. Flagstaff: Museum of Northern Arizona.

Different pottery styles found in Petrified Forest attest to its trade route status. Clockwise from top, Tularosa black-on-white, Walnut black-on-white, St. Johns polychrome. GEORGE H. H. HUEY.

PETROGLYPH NATIONAL MONUMENT, NEW MEXICO

Cultural Significance and Archeological Classification

Archaic: *Oshara*
Anasazi: *Basket Maker II;*
Pueblo IV, V
All-Southwest: *Towns,*
plateau zone

This alfresco art gallery, seventeen miles long and shaped like a shoelace along the west side of the valley in which Albuquerque is situated, contains the most extensive display of prehistoric iconography in the United States. Although some representations pecked into the face and fallen blocks of an ancient lava flow may date to a millennium before Christ and others seem to have been made in the early Christian Era when hunters and gatherers were being transformed into sedentary farmers, the majority of the figures were executed over a 350-year period (A.D. 1300–1650) centered on the opening of the historic era in New Mexico. Their style reflects an important cultural elaboration probably resulting from pervasive influence from the south and an intensification of religious biases attributable to stresses stemming from the abandonment of the Colorado Plateau by the end of the thirteenth century. Some of the visible manifestations of the ideology continue to the present. Nearby is the sole remaining, relatively untouched Pueblo IV–Pueblo V community in this part of the Rio Grande drainage which, if excavated, would provide invaluable insight into the world view of the society responsible for the rock art.

Explorations and Investigations

Geologists estimate that about 190,000 years ago a thin, flat sheet of molten lava poured eastward from a weak spot in the earth's crust and spread across a tableland lying between the drainages of the Rio Puerco and the Rio Grande in what is now the heart of New Mexico. The last phase of this vulcanism saw the formation of five low cinder cones along a north-south fissure, today still visible on Albuquerque's west horizon. The lava stream either stopped abruptly several miles before pouring into the Rio Grande channel or subsequently has been eroded back to form a low, but comparatively abrupt, cliff face on the west flank of the river valley from which thousands of blocky chunks have cascaded downward. This cliff face and its detritus afforded native peoples inviting surfaces for artistic and religious expression.

Archeological surveys and limited excavations in lands to the west of the escarpment and down into the Rio Grande flood plain have revealed an extensive prehistoric occupation covering an estimated twelve thousand years. The beginning and end of this impressive record of human activity are most strongly represented in microenvironments within the tract suitable to the particular subsistence economies practiced at the time.

Judging from scattered finds of stone projectile points which archeologists place into a half-dozen temporal categories, Paleo-Indians stalked large game animals as they came to drink in ponds existing in Pleistocene times in what now are dry basins and arroyos in the western portion of the monument and broken terrain approaching the Rio Puerco. They were succeeded by Archaic hunters and foragers of the Oshara development stage, who adapted to changed ecological circumstances by seeking smaller modern species of

Petroglyphs in Rinconada Canyon, Petroglyph National Monument. GEORGE H. H. HUEY.

animals and processing a variety of vegetal materials. They also congregated near the Rio Puerco until drier weather and an increasing reliance upon horticulture forced movement elsewhere.

One spot that housed those who were making the slow transition to agriculturally based sedentism, defined in southwestern archeological terms as the Basket Makers, was Boca Negra Cave on the side of Bond Volcano.

Although few, if any, of the early groups who were in the general region up to about A.D. 400 or 500 are known to have lived in the immediate proximity of the basalt precipice forming the east face of the West Mesa, stylistic analyses of the petroglyphs placed there suggest that Archaic or Basket Maker bands left behind such pecked motifs as circles, meandering lines, rakes, outlined crosses, sandal tracks, handprints, human stick figures, lizards, and squirrels. Rock art specialist Polly Schaafsma, in relating some of the petroglyph designs to those appearing on pottery, considers them to be Pueblo I in age. However, little evidence of Pueblo I through Pueblo II occupation has yet been noted in this portion of the middle Rio Grande.

About A.D. 1300, or Pueblo IV, throngs of eastern Anasazi migrated into the Rio Grande tributary system because of perennial water, fertile soil, and a reasonably favorable climate for horticulture. They merged with a resident population into large communities on both sides of the main stem of the river. Bottomlands were farmed, but numerous constructions along the base or top of the sinuous petroglyph escarpment show that it too was used. These were lines of rocks set up to form terraces for gardening, others placed to divert runoff waters onto such plots, temporary shelters or windbreaks of stones, and worn rock surfaces where seeds or corn kernels were ground with hand stones.

The regrouping of a large part of the eastern Pueblo population in what seems to have been a more benign environment, and perhaps some influences from the south, brought about a cultural rejuvenation that was expressed in a notable social and artistic enrichment. Much of the West Mesa rock art represents a decided break from the past, both in style and content, due to an infusion of new ideas. One of these appears to have been the kachina cult. Kachinas are interpreted as the physical embodiments of certain deities. They must have been a significant religious expression among the Tiwa of the middle Rio Grande. Many of the human and animal masked figures displayed in West Mesa petroglyphs can be identified with known figures. However, many other representations cannot be placed so definitely in the Pueblo pantheon. These are large animals, reptiles, birds, human hands, star faces, stepped clouds, and kokopellis. Although their symbolic meanings are not totally understood, they confirm a basic cultural continuity dating back to the earliest Anasazi. Perhaps when the thousand-room adobe pueblo of Piedras Marcadas (marked rocks) in a detached area just a mile east of the escarpment is cleared, it will be found to contain a kiva with painted wall murals such as in several other Pueblo IV ruins in the vicinity. Then the underlying symbolism of the petroglyphs executed by the same artisan base will be more fully comprehended.

There is no indication that there was common knowledge among Europeans of the Indian rock art along the West Mesa bluffs until the early eighteenth century. Even though the very first Spanish entrada into the central Rio Grande valley in 1540 must have passed nearby, surviving records fail to note it. Scribes indicated seventeen to twenty native towns along that stretch of the river, two of which the Spaniards destroyed and one in which they wintered. But if the figures pecked into rocks were observed, they were not considered important enough to mention. Nor were the motifs worked into stone documented during the entire seventeenth century, a time when the associated indigenous towns were threatened with extinction because of Spanish oppression, raiding by nomadic Indians, disease, and disillusionment. Those settlements that were not temporarily vacated during the years of the Pueblo Revolt (1680–1692) were emptied soon thereafter and left to melt down into mounds of hardened mud.

In the next century as the Indians moved out, Hispanics moved in. The Villa of Albuquerque was established in 1706 on lowlands east of the Rio Grande, and a number of neighboring haciendas on both sides of the river followed. Sheepherders at the Atrisco Land Grant, encompassing the southern end of the petroglyph panel, grazed their flocks in the protection of the western lava cliffs and the volcanoes. Probably for the first time they became aware of the jumble of strange designs pecked into the patina-blackened stones, and, being superstitious, they hammered Christian crosses alongside some of the them to ward off what they considered evil pagan spirits. Meantime, two pueblos, Sandia to the north and Isleta to the south, were reoccupied. Apparently through the ensuing years, little other attention was given by any group to the aboriginal etched symbols blistering on the bleak terraces west of settlement.

Two hundred years later, after World War II, Albuquerque real estate developers cast covetous eyes on the benches lining the west bank of the Rio Grande. Inevitably, vandalism of the age-old resource resulted. Recognizing the rock art's intrinsic value in understanding the socio-esoteric aspects of the native cultures and its irreplaceable nature, concerned citizens were instrumental in getting the state to take part of the lands on which the petroglyphs are present into its park network. The entire escarpment, designated Las Imagenes National Archeological District, was accepted for a place on the National Register of Historic Places. Later efforts on a higher level resulted in the setting aside in 1990 of 7,060 acres of the West Mesa as Petroglyph National Monument. It is the only such facility in the federal system focused exclusively upon aboriginal artistic works applied to rocks. In addition to the decorated cliff face, the five volcanoes and two geomorphic features called windows were included. The monument is administered by the National Park Service, the state of New Mexico, and the city of Albuquerque. Interpretations and developments designed to enhance tourism are just under way at this writing.

In connection with the founding of Petroglyph National Monument, Congress also authorized a Rock Art Research Center to undertake studies of the Rio Grande and other styles of work within the monument and in more removed sectors of the northern Southwest. Scholarly publications, as well as dissemination of less technical information, will add to the public appreciation of this unique patrimony.

ADDITIONAL READINGS, Petroglyph National Monument

Ireland, Arthur K.
    1987 *The Cultural Resources of the West Mesa Petroglyphs Study Area and Immediate Environs.* Santa Fe, New Mexico: Southwest Cultural Resources Center, National Park Service.

Irwin-Williams, Cynthia
    1973 *The Oshara Tradition: Origins of Anasazi Culture.* Contributions in Anthropology, Vol. 5, No. 1. Portales: Eastern New Mexico University.

Schaafsma, Polly
    1980 *Indian Rock Art of the Southwest.* School of American Research, Southwest Indian Arts Series. Albuquerque: University of New Mexico Press.
    1992 *Rock Art in New Mexico.* Santa Fe: Museum of New Mexico Press.

Schmader, Matthew F.
    1987 *The Archeology of the West Mesa Area, a Summary.* Santa Fe, New Mexico: Southwest Regional Office, National Park Service.

Weaver, Donald E.
    1984 Images on Stone: The Prehistoric Rock Art of the Colorado Plateau. *Plateau.* Vol. 55, No. 2. Flagstaff: Museum of Northern Arizona.

Star Being petroglyph,
Petroglyph National Monument.
GEORGE H. H. HUEY.

SAGUARO NATIONAL MONUMENT, ARIZONA

Archaic: *Cochise*
Hohokam: *Sedentary, early Classic*
All-Southwest: *Hamlets, desert zone*

Cultural Significance and Archeological Classification

Although a secondary resource of Saguaro National Monument, the prehistoric remains cover a long period of time. They represent certain Archaic and Hohokam culture phases and their basic adaptation to the harsh realities of the Tucson basin. Bordered by lands where farming, urban sprawl, and industrial development are rapidly destroying evidences of the past, the monument holds a valuable future reserve of archeological material and data.

Explorations and Investigations

In 1933 Saguaro National Monument was established as an outstanding saguaro cactus ecological zone. Before that time limited archeological surveys and two minor excavations had been conducted in the area by Byron Cummings and Emil Haury. Their projects permitted tentative identification of the local cultural sequence and an idea of how it fit into the prehistory of the larger Tucson basin.

Several kinds of prehistoric sites have been recognized in the two sections of the monument, which are located east and west of Tucson. Temporary campsites where food was gathered and processed are located near arroyos where water would have been available periodically. Bedrock mortars, hearths, scatters of stone chips, and an occasional stone cutting or scraping tool are found at such places. In temporary shelters in shallow dry caves or under rock overhangs can be found preserved cordage, wooden items, and plant materials. Habitation sites, concentrated in the eastern section of the monument, tend to be small, meager remnants of a few brush and mud dwellings. Some larger accumulations of similar houses are situated near major washes where more water allowed larger groups of people to live. The nonperishable discards of village life, such as potsherds, ash, broken stone and bone implements, and the debris from making such artifacts, are scattered over the surface of the dwelling sites. Panels of easily identifiable rock art can be seen at several places.

In both sections of the monument most campsites were left by Archaic foragers, who for thousands of years visited the region in seasons when edible materials were available. Most of the cave and shelter sites and the habitation remains were left by later Hohokam farmers during their Sedentary and early Classic stages from about A.D. 900 to 1300. The rock art seems to have been made during this occupation.

The monument also contains evidence of some historic camps that the Papago Indians used while gathering saguaro cactus fruit.

Outside the monument three main sites excavated by University of Arizona students have confirmed the findings within the monument. These are the Hodges Site on the Santa Cruz River northwest of Tucson, the Tanque Verde Ruin near the headquarters section, and the University Indian Ruin west of the headquarters section.

Small collections of artifacts from Saguaro National Monument are deposited in the park and in the Arizona State Museum, University of Arizona. ▲

ADDITIONAL READINGS, Saguaro National Monument
Gregonis, Linda M., and Karl J. Reinhard
    1979 *The Hohokam Indians of the Tucson Basin.* Tucson: University of Arizona
        Press.
Stacy, V. K. Pheriba, and Julian Hayden
    1975 *Saguaro National Monument, An Archeological Overview.* Tucson: Arizona
        Archeological Center, National Park Service.

*Petroglyphs, Saguaro National
Monument (west section).*
KENNETH ROZEN.

Gran Quivira, Salinas Pueblo Missions National Monument. CHARLES F. LUMMIS, 1894. SOUTHWEST MUSEUM COLLECTION.

SALINAS PUEBLO MISSIONS NATIONAL MONUMENT, NEW MEXICO

Cultural Significance and Archeological Classification

Anasazi: *Pueblo IV, V*
All-Southwest: *Towns, plateau zone*

The three large groups of ruins at Gran Quivira, Abó, and Quarai were populous communities at the time of the Spanish entrada and soon came under the powerful influences of European military, secular, and religious pressures. They did not survive foreign dominance for long, and all had entered the realm of archeology before the Pueblos revolted against the Spanish in 1680. As a part of the population expansion in northern New Mexico during Pueblo IV, these many-roomed, several-storied towns thrived in a marginal area for Pueblo farmers. The ability of Spanish priests to draw on the skills of native craftsmen in building missions in which the newly implanted doctrine was practiced is evidence of the zeal of the Spaniards, many of whom suffered martyrdom in pursuit of their duties.

Explorations and Investigations

Salinas National Monument was established on December 19, 1980, when President Jimmy Carter signed a bill abolishing Gran Quivira National Monument, which had been a National Park Service area since 1909. Subsequently the facility was renamed Salinas Pueblo Missions National Monument. Gran Quivira was combined administratively with the New Mexico state monuments of Abó and Quarai after their formal transfer to the federal government. Now all three sites, including their Indian ruins and impressive remnants of seventeenth-century Franciscan missions, are included in the new installation with headquarters in Mountainair, New Mexico. Salinas is a Spanish word meaning saline or salt lagoons. It is the former name of the Estancia valley, a narrow, interior drainage basin in central New Mexico where the runoff flows into several desolate playas, which are ephemeral lakes ringed with salt, alkali, and other mineral deposits.

The Salinas country supported a large Pueblo Indian population at the time of Francisco Vásquez de Coronado's first exploring party into New Mexico in 1540–41. Though its members managed to visit most other settlements in the Southwest, it is doubtful that they entered the Salinas basin. Forty years later in 1581 and 1583 the expeditions under command of Francisco Chamuscado and Antonio Espejo did visit some of these Indian towns, but the first significant contact between Europeans and Salinas natives came with actual Spanish settlement in the province of New Spain at the end of the sixteenth century. At the urging of the first governor, Juan de Oñate, several hundred Salinas Indians voluntarily took oaths of allegiance to the Spanish crown, although they undoubtedly did not understand the meaning of becoming royal subjects. Within a few months they belligerently rebuffed an attempt by one of Oñate's agents to collect tribute of blankets and provisions. Oñate personally returned to punish the recalcitrants but only succeeded in triggering confrontations in which villages were burned and Indians and soldiers were killed.

By 1600 exchange between natives of Salinas Province and Spanish authorities had formed a pattern that was to cause the indigenes many hardships. In order to exist, the early Spaniards imposed countless levies of food and clothing against all the Pueblos. Those demands were particularly deleterious to the Salinas people because theirs was an unusually harsh land, where survival was difficult even under the best circumstances. Spanish requirements, added to recurring droughts, crop failures, and epidemics, contributed more to population reduction than did the sword. Within three-quarters of a century, they had abandoned their homes and scattered to other parts.

The Spaniards, finding New Mexico less wealthy and productive than they had anticipated, decided to change the nature of their venture there. The abundance of Pueblo souls available for conversion from heathenism kindled the missionary zeal. With greater support from the royal treasury, the church grew in power and number of clergymen. Conflicts with civil governors, *encomenderos* (citizen-soldiers), and private landholders intensified, while all parties vied for control of the Indians, who provided most of the food, clothing, and labor necessary for survival.

Accelerated missionary activities in the Salinas Province began with a 1609 order from the viceroy to concentrate the Indian population into fewer settlements to facilitate their administration. Under the guidance of resident Franciscan friars, by 1630 missions had been erected in six of the larger towns, among them Abó, Quarai, and Gran Quivira. Indian laborers were directed in cutting timbers, quarrying rock, making adobe bricks, carrying water for construction materials, and actually erecting the buildings. A memorial delivered to the Pope at that time related that about ten thousand Indians of the region had been converted to Christianity, most of them having been baptized.

Once established, the missions were virtually self supporting and drew upon their parishioners for help in preparing and tending gardens, maintaining buildings and grounds, tending livestock, and otherwise serving the priests. To varying degrees, priests carried out an edict to eliminate all traces of native religion. Some went so far as to destroy ceremonial paraphernalia and buildings. In many instances those measures caused aboriginal rites to become secretive, evidence that most Pueblos tolerated but did not fully accept Christianity.

Civil authorities and encomenderos, who had been granted land near pueblos and who were allowed to collect tribute, increasingly exploited the Indians for personal gain. Their labor and products, such as corn, beans, pinyon nuts, cotton and woolen cloth, dressed deer and buffalo skins, firewood, jackets, skirts, stockings, and salt, were demanded by government officials. Encomenderos expected labor for operating their ranches and a portion of the food produced by Indians living on their granted lands.

Before Spanish occupation, the Salinas pueblos had a friendly trading relationship with Apache Indians to the south; but when Spanish militia and encomenderos began trading Apache slaves, peace between the two Indian groups broke down. From the 1630s onward, Apaches, made extremely mobile by acquisition of the horse, turned to bloody

Tabira black-on-white pottery canteen, Gran Quivira, Salinas Pueblo Missions National Monument. GEORGE H. H. HUEY.

retaliation against all settlements, Spanish and Christian Indian alike.

The deepening problems faced by the Pueblo residents of the land of the salt lakes took their toll. Several years before the general uprising of all the Pueblos, the southeastern border of Pueblo territory already had been depopulated. The survivors moved west and south, some to join their kin in towns along the Rio Grande in central New Mexico, others to mingle with compatible groups around El Paso.

Though each of the three sections of Salinas Pueblo Missions National Monument is dominated by a large, decayed church complex, all have ruins of former habitations that extend far backwards in time before Europeans entered the scene. It was, after all, the populous communities that had attracted the missionaries.

Several early writers of modern times made references to the antiquities of the Salinas basin. Although Josiah Gregg in his 1844 *Commerce of the Prairies* described Gran Quivira, it is doubtful that he had ever seen it. Major James H. Carleton and his command marched by the ruins during a blizzard in December 1853. Even under such adverse conditions, his descriptions and measurements were accurate, first-hand reporting. Two well-known students of the Southwest, Charles F. Lummis and Adolph Bandelier, provided accounts of Quarai, Abó, and Gran Quivira after each had visited them in the late 1800s. Lummis called the old Salinas towns "The Cities that Were Forgotten," saying that if the mission of Quarai had been on the Rhine, it would be famous, and that Quarai, Abó, and Gran Quivira were smaller versions of Montezuma's capital. Bandelier wrote more from a scientist's point of view. His academic writings did not reach as wide an audience as those of Lummis, but they more often separated truth from fiction.

The main Indian ruins at Quarai are adjacent to the high, reddish stone walls of the church. The oval mound and outlying segments of the former pueblo were partially trenched in 1913 and 1920 by the School of American Archaeology while more extensive excavations were under way at the church and convent. No reports of the work are available, but it is known that the excavators recovered a number of fine pottery vessels and artifacts indicating a long pre-Hispanic occupation. It was believed that the community house had risen in tiers back from the central plazas into which kivas were sunk, to a height of at least three stories, and that a protective wall had surrounded the buildings. The School of American Research completed clearing and repair of the mission units in the 1930s. Wesley R. Hurt directed a Works Projects Administration program in 1939–40, which further excavated the convent, outlined walls of the cemetery in front of the church, and traced the outside walls of the nearby pueblo mounds. After becoming a state monument, the buildings were further stabilized by the Museum of New Mexico.

The conversion of the residents of Quarai and erection of the church of La Purísima Concepción are ascribed to Fray Estévan de Perea about 1628, but earlier missionary efforts are suggested by the presence of ruins of a smaller, earlier chapel that may have preceded the church by several years.

At Abó, the unexcavated Indian ruins and remarkably intact walls of the mission are located on a hill near a steadily flowing spring. The Indian stone houses there had once been three stories high. Erection of the church of San Gregorio de Abó and its attached convent probably began about 1626.

Gran Quivira was the largest pueblo in the Salinas Province. A Spanish chronicler of 1627 estimated that it housed three thousand Indians. Of the Salinas ruins it is the one most frequently studied archeologically and historically. Gran Quivira has come to be the widely used term for the site, though its pre-Spanish name is recorded as Cueloze. After Oñate's era, it was known as Zumanas, Jumanos, or Humanas. During the colonial period until its abandonment, Las Humanas seems to have been the common name, by which it is still known to some scholars. How the place came to be identified as Gran Quivira is not completely clear. Some attribute it to an erroneous association of the site with Quivira, a fabled city of gold and riches which Coronado sought in 1541 during a trek to present Kansas. Others believe it evolved out of persistent rumors that the Spaniards buried valuable bells or a treasure there. Over the years these tales lured a small army of treasure seekers to dig many unproductive shafts throughout the pueblo and mission remains. The last was sunk in 1933.

Archeological excavations at Gran Quivira, with its seventeen significant house mounds and vestiges of two missions, were concentrated first on the only structure whose walls stood well above the ground. That was the large church and convent of San Buenaventura which was cleared by a team from the Museum of New Mexico and the School of American Research, directed by Edgar L. Hewett, from 1923 to 1925. In addition, some digging was done in a burial zone and in rooms and kivas fronting a plaza of the pueblo.

The National Park Service has sponsored two excavation and stabilization efforts at Gran Quivira. The first, led by Gordon Vivian in 1951, exposed thirty-seven rooms of a pueblo unit known as Mound 10, uncovered a kiva, and cleaned out the badly vandalized remains of the small mission of San Isidro, which was filled with the detritus of treasure hunting operations. The second was in the field during the summers from 1965 to 1968. Directed by Alden C. Hayes, it excavated Mound 7, a high, rubble-covered hummock.

Hayes uncovered three superimposed structures in Mound 7. Earliest was a circular, single-story community, whose 150 to 200 rooms were arranged in concentric arcs around a small plaza with one kiva. It is believed to have been occupied from about A.D. 1300 to 1400. Next, a small linear block of rooms and three kivas, in use from approximately A.D. 1400 to the early 1500s, were attached to the original complex. During that time many unoccupied rooms of the first unit were partially razed for building materials needed elsewhere in the village and used as dumping places. For a brief period the entire structure was almost totally abandoned. During that time additional destruction and filling of rooms with rubbish took place. Finally, about 1545, construction of a linear, one-story house block was started on top of the earlier, somewhat demolished, trash-covered habitations. By 1600 the edifice had grown to some two hundred rooms arranged in an F-shape with five associated kivas. This is one of the buildings that was left standing when Gran Quivira was deserted in 1672.

The mission chapel of San Isidro was erected in 1629 by Fray Juan Letrado to minister to Gran Quivira and two other towns in the neighborhood. The first missionary effort did

Mission church at Quarai, Salinas Pueblo Missions National Monument. GEORGE H. H. HUEY.

not last long. Within two decades the building was vacated and possibly wrecked by Apache raiders. When missionary activities were resumed, a new, much larger church with an attached convent was built in 1659. It was dedicated to San Buenaventura by Fray Diego de Santander.

Cultivation of the usual southwestern crops, combined with considerable gathering of wild plants and with hunting, was how most of the region's people lived. The absence of running water at Gran Quivira may have made farming more difficult than at the other Salinas villages. It is possible the Quivirans may have exploited their strategic position between the Pueblos along the Rio Grande and the Apaches to the east and south to act as middlemen in trade of hides and meat from the plains, corn and cotton from the riverine villages, and salt and pinyon nuts from local sources. Domestic water for the town seems to have been supplied by wells and cisterns.

Included among finds at Mound 7 were portions of murals painted on plastered room walls, a collection of faunal remains, and many human skeletons. Artifacts from all three sites included Spanish metal tools and tin-glazed, wheel-turned ceramics. Further Spanish influence on native culture was apparent in vessel forms and burial practices.

Most of the collections resulting from the National Park Service investigations are stored at the Western Archeological and Conservation Center in Tucson. The Laboratory of Anthropology in Santa Fe curates specimens resulting from the Museum of New Mexico work. A small display of artifacts can be seen at the monument visitor center. ◭

ADDITIONAL READINGS, Salinas Pueblo Missions National Monument
Hayes, Alden C., Jon N. Young, and A. H. Warren
    1981 *Excavation of Mound 7, Gran Quivira National Monument, New Mexico.* Publications in Archeology, No. 16. Washington, D.C.: National Park Service.
Hayes, Alden C., et al.
    1981 *Contributions to Gran Quivira Archeology, Gran Quivira National Monument, New Mexico.* Publications in Archeology, No. 17. Washington, D.C.: National Park Service.
Hewett, Edgar L., and Reginald G. Fisher
    1943 *Mission Monuments of New Mexico.* Albuquerque: School of American Research and University of New Mexico Press.
Hurt, Wesley R.
    1990 *The 1939–1940 Excavation Project at Quarai Pueblo and Mission Building, Salinas Pueblo Missions National Monument, New Mexico.* Professional Paper, No. 29. Santa Fe, New Mexico: Southwest Cultural Resources Center, National Park Service.
Kubler, George
    1972 *The Religious Architecture of New Mexico in the Colonial Period and Since the American Occupation,* 4th edition. Albuquerque: University of New Mexico Press.

Murphy, Dan
  1993 *Salinas Pueblo Missions National Monument.* Tucson, Arizona: Southwest
        Parks and Monuments Association.
Noble, David G., Editor
  1982 *Salinas National Monument, Archaeology, History, Prehistory.* Santa Fe, New
        Mexico: Exploration, Annual Bulletin of the School of American Research.
Toulouse, Joseph H., Jr.
  1949 *The Mission of San Gregorio de Abó.* Monograph, No. 13. Santa Fe, New
        Mexico: School of American Research.
Vivian, Gordon
  1964 *Excavations in a 17th Century Jumano Pueblo, Gran Quivira.* Publications in
        Archeology, No. 8. Washington, D.C.: National Park Service.
Wilson, John P.
  1977 *Quarai State Monument.* Santa Fe: Museum of New Mexico Press.

Lower Ruin, Tonto National Monument. GORDON VIVIAN, NATIONAL PARK SERVICE, 1957.

TONTO NATIONAL MONUMENT, ARIZONA

Cultural Significance and Archeological Classification

This amalgam of cultures is another that sprang up in central Arizona due to the overlapping of materials and influences from at least two core areas. Pueblolike habitations and pottery bearing black-and-white designs on a red base were characteristic of the Salado, which gave them an Anasazi resemblance, but canal irrigation farming and earthen platform mounds were borrowed Hohokam traits. Toward the end of their known cultural history, the Salado relocated among the Hohokam. From there, the telltale track of their distinctive pottery indicates that they pushed on to the southeast. Raising and weaving cotton were specialties of the Salado.

Explorations and Investigations

The Tonto basin of central Arizona derived its name from a band of Apache who once ranged there, though in the nineteenth century the term Tonto was loosely applied to many other Apache and some Yavapai Indians living west of the White Mountains. The cliff dwellings situated in caves high above the Salt River valley were identified by the same name by the first whites to observe them. Most likely these were members of military or other parties passing through the region during the 1870s. Certainly the ruins were familiar to the ranchers who moved in during the next decade, who commonly distinguished two separate remains as the Lower and Upper Ruins. These names have continued in use.

The earliest known description of the ruins was that of Adolph Bandelier, who arrived on May 24, 1883. He observed old dwellings in two caves, one at the base of a cliff and the other higher up and more difficult to reach. They were constructed of large, irregularly broken stones set in a gravel mortar. Many roof beams and the cactus ribs, reeds, and mud that topped them were still in place. Local whites told him that Apaches had burned out both houses. Bandelier found a sandal, fragments of basketry, rope and twine, many corncobs, some cane arrow shafts, and several types of potsherds.

In 1907 the ruins and a small amount of land around them were designated Tonto National Monument to protect them from increased visitation and vandalism stimulated by the construction of Roosevelt Dam nearby, at the confluence of the Salt River and Tonto Creek. The installation remained under Forest Service control until 1933, when it was transferred to the National Park Service. Like most other accessible, easily seen ruins in the Southwest, the Tonto cliff dwellings suffered from many years of illicit digging by treasure seekers and collectors of Indian relics until the National Park Service finally could guard them full-time. One of the first orders of business was to stabilize the major ruins, the lower one in 1937 and the upper in 1940.

Concurrent with stabilization of the Upper Ruin, some excavation was necessary to expose portions of walls that required strengthening. Seven rooms were completely

In-betweens and Outliers: Salado culture
All-Southwest: *Towns, intermediate between plateau and mountain-valley zones*

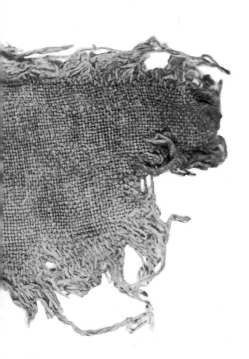

cleared. National Park Service archeologist Charlie Steen, the excavator, estimated that the dwelling originally had about forty rooms, whose walls had been poorly fashioned of native rock set in mud mortar. Thirty ground-floor rooms were outlined, and eight or ten second-story chambers were believed to have existed. Even though the ruins had been subjected to many years of pothunting, archeologists were fortunate to recover a few artifacts of wood, fiber, pottery, stone, bone, antler, shell, plant material, and one burial. Most important was an assortment of well-preserved cotton textiles that furnished information about the processing of fibers, weaving techniques, and types of clothing worn by those who lived in the cave during the fourteenth century.

Because it was more reachable than the Upper Ruin, the Lower Ruin endured greater plundering. At the time of its stabilization in 1937, it was reported that all rooms except one had been gutted. Debris that had been sifted through by pothunters was scattered and heaped in most of the chambers. While cleaning the rooms, the preservation crew found some objects overlooked by those who had thoughtlessly damaged the building and its contents. Retaining walls and sections of rooms were rebuilt and some of the roofs were strengthened. After being opened to the public, the Lower Ruin became the featured attraction of the monument and drew heavy visitation. In 1950 it was further excavated. An adjacent smaller house, called the Lower Ruin Annex, was dug simultaneously. This project tested subfloor deposits of the principal structure and removed the fill from the poorly preserved rooms of the annex. The former had consisted of sixteen ground-floor rooms and a few second-story units built like those of the Upper Ruin. Stubs of twelve rooms were outlined in the annex. Three burials were exhumed in the two caves.

Many perishable items that had been protected by the caves' dry environment are of special interest. The preserved plant material allowed Vorsila L. Bohrer to accurately identify cultivated and wild plants used for food, medicine, clothing, tools, weapons, containers, and religious objects. Kate P. Kent studied the cotton textiles, many having been worked into items of clothing, such as aprons, wrap-around dresses, shoulder blankets, and belts for females; and breechclouts, kilts, shirts, shoulder blankets, and belts for males.

An intensive archeological project, being carried out by Arizona State University on lands to be flooded by raising the water level behind the Roosevelt Dam on the Salt River, is expected to provide much new information about the Salado culture, of which the Tonto cliff dwellings were a late manifestation.

Most items recovered from National Park Service investigations at Tonto National Monument are stored at the Western Archeological and Conservation Center in Tucson.

Many cotton textiles were found in the dry caves at Tonto.
SOUTHWEST PARKS AND MONUMENTS ASSOCIATION.

ADDITIONAL READINGS, Tonto National Monument
Steen, Charlie R., Lloyd M. Pierson, Vorsila L. Bohrer, and Kate P. Kent
    1962 *Archeological Studies at Tonto National Monument, Arizona.* Technical Series,
        Vol. 2. Globe, Arizona: Southwestern Monuments Association.

WALNUT CANYON NATIONAL MONUMENT, ARIZONA

Cultural Significance and Archeological Classification

Among the sheltered ledges of Walnut Canyon are many evidences of tiny cliff houses built by the Sinagua, a Hakataya group that once spread extensively over western Arizona. The archeological remains in the monument were a result of the intermingling in central Arizona of people from all southwestern culture centers and the turmoil and population movements that followed the eleventh-century eruption of Sunset Crater. A strong influx of Anasazi traits from the north is evident.

In-betweens and Outliers: Hakataya (Sinagua culture) All-Southwest: Villages, intermediate between desert, plateau, and mountain-valley zones

Explorations and Investigations

The antiquities of Walnut Canyon, named for the stand of Arizona walnut trees that grow in the canyon bottom, have been known since the 1880s when Smithsonian Institution expeditions combed the area about Flagstaff. James Stephenson was the first to carefully examine the Walnut Canyon cliff dwellings and to collect objects from them to take back to the Smithsonian. At the turn of the century Jesse W. Fewkes searched for archeological evidence throughout the region.

These expeditions had two purposes. One was to record the sites in maps, photographs, and written notes. The other was to gather artifacts for museum display. Their work recognized regional cultural distinctions and exchange between cultures. Although recent research has changed their basic conclusions only slightly, modern advances in theory and methods have made possible more detailed, accurate observations.

Unfortunately, soon after the ruins of Walnut Canyon became public knowledge, they were disturbed or destroyed for personal or commercial reasons. This continued until the area was placed under National Park Service care in 1933. So much of the material left by the Indians was removed, and the dwellings themselves so defaced or damaged, that our perception of what took place at Walnut Canyon has been derived almost entirely from work at other sites in the vicinity.

Harold S. Colton commenced serious archeological studies in the canyon in 1921, when he surveyed its steep slopes and rims. He devoted most of his time to the large, more obvious sites, recording 120 occupation areas. These included pueblos of one to five rooms, cliff dwellings, "forts," and several pithouses. His description of the cliff dwellings was the first of scientific value.

Colton had begun visiting northeastern Arizona in 1910. In the following years he and his wife, Mary Russell F. Colton, crisscrossed the Navajo and Hopi country on foot and by horseback, wagon, and Model T Ford. Greatly impressed by what they saw, both desired to delve more deeply into the natural and cultural history of the region. In 1926 Colton left the University of Pennsylvania, where he was a professor of zoology, and moved permanently to Flagstaff. His personal interest was archeology; those of his wife were ethnology and art.

Stimulated by Colton's enthusiasm, an organizing committee founded the Northern Arizona Society of Science and Art in 1929, setting up a small museum at the local women's club. Within a year the Museum of Northern Arizona was in operation with Colton as its director. In 1934 the museum began to build permanent storage units, exhibition halls, a library, and research laboratories on land three miles north of town. From these attractive, well-equipped facilities the museum has continued research and educational programs in geology, biology, anthropology, and art of the Colorado Plateau.

Colton is best known for his analytical studies of ancient potsherds, identifying types, their relationships, and distribution. His scheme of pottery classification proved useful when combined with other archeological evidence. Utilizing such ceramic information and other data gleaned by a team of experts, Colton's reconstruction of aboriginal life in the Flagstaff area affords a broad understanding of remains at Walnut Canyon, Wupatki, Tuzigoot, and Montezuma Castle national monuments. Colton died in 1970, leaving the Museum of Northern Arizona as a permanent memorial.

Lyndon Hargrave, a Museum of Northern Arizona staff member, was the first archeologist to dig in the cliff dwellings of Walnut Canyon. In 1932 he cleared part of a nine-room unit beneath a rock overhang on what is now the Island Trail and later stabilized it. Since then, archeology within the monument has been performed by National Park Service personnel in conjunction with programs to care for the cliff dwellings.

Aside from those on Island Trail, approximately thirty other small cliff dwellings in the monument have been stabilized. In the process of the preservation work, some artifacts have been recovered from sites that had not been completely gutted by pothunters. A few whole pottery vessels, several thousand potsherds, fragments of textiles, basketry, sandals, and cordage, as well as tools of stone, bone, and wood, were reclaimed. Also recovered were remnants of vegetable and animal foodstuffs. One cave, thought to have been used for ceremonial purposes, yielded wooden prayer sticks similar to those used in the rituals of modern Pueblo Indians. These prayer sticks (pahos) probably will be deposited with the Hopi and the cave closed to the public.

On the north and south rims a 1985 survey identified 241 sites, including small pueblos, boulder outlines that may be remains of farming plots or terraces, and rock shelters. Examination and evaluation of known sites in Walnut Canyon National Monument for inclusion on the List of Classified Structures resulted in the listing of fifty-six sites in the monument, all but two of which are cliff dwellings. The list is an inventory of the nation's historic or prehistoric structures considered important enough for permanent preservation by the federal government. Expansion that would double the present size of the monument has been proposed.

Archeological specimens collected from Walnut Canyon after the era of pothunting are stored in several locations. These include the Western Archeological and Conservation Center, Tucson; the Museum of Northern Arizona and Northern Arizona University, Flagstaff; the U.S. National Museum, Washington, D.C.; and Walnut Canyon National Monument. ▲

ADDITIONAL READINGS, Walnut Canyon National Monument

Baldwin, Anne R., and J. Michael Bremer
  1986 *Walnut Canyon National Monument: An Archeological Survey.* Publications in
       Anthropology, No. 39. Tucson, Arizona: Western Archeological and
       Conservation Center, National Park Service.

Colton, Harold S.
  1946 *The Sinagua: A Summary of the Archaeology of the Region of Flagstaff,
       Arizona.* Bulletin, No. 22. Flagstaff: Museum of Northern Arizona.
  1960 *Black Sand: Prehistory in Northern Arizona.* Albuquerque: University of New
       Mexico Press.

Gilman, Patricia A.
  1976 *Walnut Canyon National Monument: An Archeological Overview.* Tucson,
       Arizona: Western Archeological Center, National Park Service.

Schroeder, Albert H.
  1977 *Of Men and Volcanoes: The Sinagua of Northern Arizona.* Globe, Arizona:
       Southwest Parks and Monuments Association.

*Walnut Canyon cliff dwellings,
Walnut Canyon National Monument.*
NATT DODGE, NATIONAL PARK SERVICE.

Wupatki communal house, Wupatki National Monument. GEORGE A. GRANT, NATIONAL PARK SERVICE, 1935.

About the Authors

Kerry Ferris is Assistant Professor of Sociology at Northern Illinois University. She uses ethnographic methods to study fame as a system of social power. Currently, she is researching the lives of professional celebrity impersonators and analyzing the emotions communicated by celebrities in red-carpet interviews.

Jill Stein is Associate Professor of Sociology and Chair of the Department of Sociology and Anthropology at Santa Barbara City College. In addition to teaching introduction to sociology every semester, she has studied narrative processes in twelve-step programs, the role of popular culture in higher learning, and group culture among professional rock musicians.

Contents

CHAPTER 3: Studying Social Life: Sociological Research Methods 64

Chapter 7: Deviance 178

Part III: Understanding Inequality 205

CHAPTER 8: Social Class: The Structure of Inequality 208

CHAPTER 9: Race and Ethnicity as Lived Experience 242

Chapter 10: Constructing Gender and Sexuality 266

PART IV: Examining Social Institutions as Sites of Everyday Life 299

CHAPTER 11: The Macro-Micro Link in Social Institutions: Politics, Education, and Religion 302

CHAPTER 12:   The Economy, Work, and Working   340

PART V: Creating Social Change and Envisioning the Future 425

CHAPTER 15: City and Country: The Social World and the Natural World 428

Preface

It's time for a new Introductory Sociology textbook that is really new.

After years of experience in college and university classrooms, teaching Introductory Sociology to thousands of students from all backgrounds and walks of life, we had learned a lot about what works and what doesn't when it comes to making sociology exciting and effective. As seasoned instructors, we had developed an approach to teaching and learning that reflected our passion for the subject and our concern with pedagogy. But we were having trouble finding a textbook that encompassed all the elements we had discovered and that made such a difference in our experience. We were tired of the same old formulas found in almost every textbook. And we figured we were not alone. Other students and instructors were probably equally frustrated with repetitive formats, stodgy styles, and seemingly irrelevant materials. That is a great misfortune, for sociology, at its best, is a discipline that is both intellectually stimulating and personally resonant. While the impetus to write this textbook began as a way of answering our own needs, our goal became to create a textbook of even greater benefit to others who might also be looking for something new.

We wrote those words when we embarked on the first edition of *The Real World*, and they are equally true as we roll out the newly revised second edition. We are gratified by the response the textbook has received from instructors and students alike, so we are preserving many of the features that made the first edition a success. At the same time we have made sure to update material and add new examples so that the book remains as current and cutting-edge as possible. For students and instructors, we have maintained a writing style that we hope is accessible and interesting as well as scholarly. One of the basic pedagogical strengths of this textbook is its focus on everyday life, the mass media, and popular culture. In the second edition, we have also included numerous examples in each chapter that deal with the increasingly important role of technology in postmodern society. We know that the combination of these themes is inherently appealing to students. And since the new generation of sociology instructors is looking for something different, another of this book's strengths is an integrated emphasis on critical thinking and analytic skills. Rather than merely presenting or reviewing major concepts in sociology, which can often seem dry and remote, we seek to make the abstract more concrete through real-world applications.

In this text we take a fresh theoretical approach appropriate to our contemporary world. While we emphasize the interactionist perspective, we cover a range of theoretical thought, including postmodernism. We also build innovative methodological exercises into each chapter. We present material that is familiar and relevant to students in a way that allows them to make profound analytic connections between their individual lives and the structure of their society. We provide instructors with ways to reenergize their teaching, and we give even General Education students a reason to be fascinated by and engrossed in their sociology courses. We do this by throwing out the old formulas and bringing our insight, experience, and intellectual rigor to bear on a new way of teaching Introductory Sociology.

Whether you are a student or an instructor, you have probably seen a lot of textbooks. As authors, we have thought very carefully about how to write this textbook and how to make it more meaningful and effective for you. We think it is important to point out the unique features of this textbook and to tell you why they are included and what we hope you will get out of them.

Part Introductions and Original Research

The 16 chapters in this text are grouped into five Parts, and each Part has its own introductory essay. Each Part Introduction focuses on a piece of original sociological research highlighting the major themes that group the chapters together. The in-depth discussion of the featured book shows what the real work of academic sociologists consists of and reveals how sociological research frequently unites topics covered in separate chapters in introductory textbooks.

Opening Vignettes

Each chapter begins with an opening vignette which gives students an idea about the topics or themes they will encounter in the chapter. The vignettes are drawn from everyday life, the media, arts, and popular culture, and they are designed to grab your attention and stimulate your desire to learn more by reading the chapter that follows.

How to Read This Chapter

After the vignette, you will find a section that provides you with some goals and strategies that we believe will be useful in reading that particular chapter. We know from our experience in teaching Introductory Sociology that it is often worthwhile to let students know what to expect in advance so that they can better make their way through the material. Not all chapters require the same approach; we want to bring to your attention what we think is the best approach to each one.

SocIndex

This list of "factoids" at the beginning of each chapter is divided into three categories: "Then and Now," which makes historical comparisons; "Here and There," which makes cross-cultural comparisons; and "This and That," which makes more general comparisons or contrasts. The SocIndex is the one place in this book where we will not be explaining the significance of an example for you. This tactic

is meant as a challenge—to make students think about the variety of human social experience and to connect the statistics or stories presented in the SocIndex with the topics, theories, and themes of each chapter. You may want to refer back to the SocIndex when you reach the end of a chapter—by that time, the links will certainly be clear.

Theory in Everyday Life

Although we provide thorough coverage in Chapter 2, we find that students often need additional help with understanding the mechanics of social theory and how to apply it to various real-world phenomena. These boxes in every chapter break down the major theoretical approaches and illustrate how each perspective might be used to analyze a particular real-world case study. This serves as a simple, practical model for students to then make their own applications and analyses.

Bolded In-Text Terms

As a student of sociology, you will be learning many new concepts and terms. Throughout each chapter, you will see a number of words or phrases in bold type. You may already recognize some of these from their more common vernacular use. But it is important to pay special attention to the way that they are used sociologically. For this reason you will find definitions in the margins of each page, where you can refer to them as you read. You should consider these bolded words and phrases your "tools" for doing sociology. As you progress through the chapters in this textbook, you will be collecting the contents of a toolkit that you can use to better understand yourself and the world around you. The bolded terms can also be found in the Glossary at the back of the book.

Relevance Boxes

In each chapter you will find Relevance Boxes with three different themes: "On the Job," "In Relationships," and "Changing the World." Relevance Boxes allow students to see the practical implications of sociology in their lives. "On the Job" explores the ways different people use sociological insights in a variety of work settings. "In Relationships" looks at how sociology can help us to better understand our friendships, intimate partnerships, and family relations. "Changing the World" focuses on the role sociology and its insights play in bringing about social change. We include these boxes to show how taking this course could bear fruit in your life beyond just fulfilling your college requirements.

Data Workshops

Each chapter features two Data Workshops, one on "Analyzing Everyday Life" and one on "Analyzing Mass Media and Popular Culture." Data Workshops are designed to give students the opportunity to gain hands-on experience in the practice of sociology while they are learning. We think this is one of the fun parts of being a sociologist. Students will use one of the research methods covered in Chapter 3 to deal with actual data from the real world—whether they are data they collect themselves or raw data provided from another source. The Data Workshops lead students through the process of analyzing data using the conceptual tools they have just acquired in the chapter. Each Data Workshop offers two options for completion from which instructors can choose. The Data Workshops can serve as a homework assignment, small-group activity, in-class discussion, or material for an essay. The Data Workshops can also be found on the Study Space website for the textbook, where students can submit completed work online.

Global Perspective Boxes

While this textbook focuses primarily on contemporary American society, we believe that in this time of increasing globalization, it is also important to look at other societies around the world. Each chapter includes a Global Perspective Box that highlights some of the differences and similarities between the United States and other cultures. This feature will help students develop the ability to see comparative and analogous patterns across cultures, which is one of the key functions of a sociological perspective.

Images and Graphics

We think that it is important to include not only written information but also images and graphics in the textbook. This kind of presentation helps students absorb a variety of materials and learn in different ways. We also know that students share our interest in mass media and popular culture, and we want to show the connections between real life and sociological thinking. For these reasons, you will find many kinds of visual images and graphics in each chapter. These are not just decorations; they are an integral part of the text, so please study these as carefully as you would the rest of the printed page.

Closing Comments

Each chapter ends with a set of closing comments that wrap up the discussion and give some final thoughts about the important themes that have been covered. This gives us a chance not so much to summarize or reiterate but to reflect, in a slightly different way, on what we have discussed, as well as to point to the future. We hope that the closing comments will give you something to think about, or even talk about with others, long after you've finished reading the chapter.

End-of-Chapter Materials

The end of each chapter contains a variety of materials that will enhance the learning process. The Chapter Summary provides a succinct review of the chapter's main theories and concepts. The Questions for Review not only helps you prepare for exams but also encourages you to extrapolate and apply what you have learned to other relevant examples. The Suggestions for Further Exploration provides a list of additional readings (fiction, nonfiction, and scholarly research), movies, music, websites, video games, and even field trips that are relevant to the topics of the chapter. Pursuing these suggestions will deepen your understanding of each chapter's themes and should be enjoyable too.

In our experience, the most important thing for students to take away from an introductory sociology class is a sociological perspective—not just a storehouse of facts, which will inevitably fade over time. Sociology promises a new way of looking at and thinking about the social world, which can serve students in good stead no matter what they find themselves doing in the future. We hope that this textbook delivers on that promise, making introductory sociology an intellectually stimulating and personally relevant enterprise for professors and students, in the classroom as well as outside it.

Resources for Students

The practical study aids and exciting new media that accompany *The Real World* are designed to extend the themes of the book and inspire students to connect what they learn in the classroom with the social worlds around them.

The Real World ebook
Available at NortonEbooks.com

"Same great book, half the price"

The Real World is also available in the Norton ebook format. An affordable and convenient alternative, the ebook retains the content of the print book and allows students to highlight and take notes with ease.

Everyday Sociology Blog
www.everydaysociologyblog.com

Designed for a general audience, this exciting and unique online forum encourages visitors to actively explore sociology's relevance to popular culture, mass media, and everyday life. Karen Sternheimer of the University of Southern California moderates the blog, and four other sociologist contributors write biweekly postings on topical subjects. the Everyday Sociology Blog is organized around such categories as Popular Culture and Consumption; Social Problems, Politics and Social Change; Crime and Deviance; Behind the Headlines; Relationships, Marriage and Family; Theory; and Video: Everyday Sociology Talk.

StudySpace
www.wwnorton.com/studyspace

Based on proven learning strategies, the StudySpace website contains assignments that will help you *organize* your study, *learn* essential course material, and *connect* your knowledge across chapters and concepts. *The Real World*'s StudySpace contains free and open study tools and links to premium content.

ORGANIZE

- Chapter Reviews
- Chapter Outline
- Printable Study Sheet

LEARN

- Diagnostic Quizzes offer diagnostic feedback to students over the text content
- Vocabulary Flashcards
- Learning Objectives

CONNECT

- Data Exercises challenge students to apply concepts with recent real-world data
- Everyday Sociology Blog RSS feed
- Everyday Exercises (based on Everyday Sociology Blog postings)
- The Norton Slideshow Maker with Visual Sociology Exercises allows students to use their own photographs and captions to respond to questions
- Video Clip Quizzes focus on the Instructor DVD content
- Sociology in the News RSS feed

Resources for Instructors

Sociology in Practice Documentary DVDs

These DVDs contain over four hours of video clips drawn from documentaries by independent filmmakers. The *Sociology in Practice* DVD series has been expanded to include a new DVD of 21 documentary clips on inequality. The DVDs are ideal for initiating classroom discussion and encouraging students to apply sociological concepts to popular and real-world issues. The clips are also offered in streaming versions on StudySpace. Each streamed clip is accompanied by a DVD quiz.

Instructor's Website
wwnorton.com/instructors

The Instructor's Website features instructional content for use in lecture and distance education, including coursepacks, test-item files, PowerPoint lecture slides, images, figures, and more.

The Instructor's Website features

- FREE, customizable Blackboard, WebCT, Angel, and D2L coursepacks
- Instructor's Manual
- Discussion Boards for smaller, more focused discussions about the Everyday Sociology Blog
- Lecture PowerPoints with Clicker Questions
- Art from book in PowerPoint and JPEG formats
- Glossary
- Test Bank in ExamView, WebCT, Blackboard, and RTF formats
- Website quizzes in Blackboard and WebCT formats

New Online Course-specific Blackboard Coursepack Content

Written by Christina Partin of University of South Florida and Pasco-Hernandez Community College. Each chapter contains 20 multiple-choice questions unique to the coursepack as well as a WebQuest activity and rationale. WebQuests encourage students to explore sociological topics using preselected online resources. Each WebQuest introduces a topic, gives students a task to complete, and provides the resources necessary to complete the task.

New Online Instructor's Forum

This new instructor website allows instructors to submit questions and other teaching materials and browse an evolving bank of materials submitted by other faculty. For more information, please visit wwnorton.com/instructors

Expanded Instructor's Manual

Written by Natasha Chen Christensen of Monroe Community College. *New* materials include:
- One service learning project per chapter
- Everyday Sociology Blog exercises
- Handouts for Data Workshops and estimated completion times
- Suggested documentary clips from the *Sociology in Practice* DVD (divided by chapter) including a description of how to incorporate them in the classroom

Expanded materials include longer recommended film, reading, and web reference lists. In addition, there will be a section on teaching in the online classroom by Christina Partin of University of South Florida and Pasco-Hernandez Community College. Available in print and PDF.

Expanded Test Bank

Written by Neil Dryden of University of California, Santa Barbara and Jill Stein. Each chapter includes a new concept map and 30 new multiple-choice questions bringing the total to approximately 20 True/False, 75 multiple-choice, and 10 essay questions per chapter. *New* features include graphs and tables from the text that are reproduced in the test bank and followed by a series of new questions regarding the material covered in the image. This test bank will include concept maps as well as labels for concept, question type, and difficulty for the multiple-choice questions. Available in print, Word, ExamView, and Blackboard, and WebCT formats.

DVD Library

Integrate engaging examples from television and film with the Norton DVD Library (1 per 50 new copies ordered).

Netflix Offer

Create your own video list! With orders of 100 or more new copies, Norton will provide a four-month subscription to Netflix. During the term of subscription, instructors may rent up to three DVDs at a time from Netflix's library of over 50,000 titles. The Instructor's Manual provides advice on incorporating many selections from the Netflix library into lectures.

Transparencies

Lecture-ready transparencies of all figures and selected maps from the text.

Acknowledgments

The authors would like to thank the many people who helped make this textbook possible. To everyone at W. W. Norton, we believe you are absolutely the best publishers in the business and that we are fortunate to get to work with you. Thank you, Roby Harrington, for signing us. Our deep appreciation goes out to Steve Dunn for believing in us and playing such a critical role in shaping the original vision of this project. Thank you for showing us we could do this and for your substantial support throughout. We would like to acknowledge Melea Seward for her efforts during the early drafts of the book. Her innovative approach and enthusiasm were much appreciated. We owe much gratitude to Karl Bakeman for his tremendous talent, work, and dedication as our editor. He was instrumental in seeing this project through to completion and central to the success it has had. Thanks for your continued faith, boundless energy, and great ideas, which have made this next edition of the book all the better.

We have many others to thank as well. We are especially grateful to our project editors, Rebecca Homiski and Sarah Mann; production manager Jane Searle; and editorial assistants Kate Feighery, Sarah Johnson, and Becky Charney, for managing the countless details involved in creating this book. Copy editor Ellen Lohman did a marvelous job suggesting improvements to the manuscript that have contributed in important ways to the book's final form. Stephanie Romeo and Julie Tesser showed wonderful creativity in the photo research that they did for *The Real World*. Electronic media editor Eileen Connell and ancillary editor Rachel Comerford developed the best textbook support materials in sociology. Finally, art director Rubina Yeh, along with Alex Meyer, Gia-Bao Tran, John McAusland, and Hope Goodell deserve special thanks for creating the beautiful design and art for the book. And we are very appreciative of the exceptional Norton "travelers"; it is through their efforts that this book has gotten out into the world.

In the course of our creating the second edition, many instructors offered advice and comments on particular chapters, or in some cases, large sections of the text. We are deeply indebted to them.

Paul Becker, University of Dayton
Donna Bird, University of Southern Maine
Elizabeth Borland, The College of New Jersey
Allison Camelot, Saddleback College
Linda Cornwell, Bowling Green State University
Lynda Dickson, versity of Colorado, Colorado Springs
Lori Fowler, Tarrant County College
Tina Magouris, San Jacinto College-Central
Karen Mundy, Lee University
Tim O'Brien, Indiana University
Gabrielle Raley, University of California, Los Angeles
Patricia Gibbs Stayte, Foothills College
Jenny Stuber, University of North Florida
James Ulinski, La Salle University
Nicole Vadino, Community College of Philadelphia
Jill Waity, Indiana University
Glenda Walden, University of Colorado
Lisa Warner, Indiana University
Mike Weissbuch, Xavier University
Lee Williams, Edinboro University

We would also like to thank the research assistants who worked with us on this project: Neil Dryden, Kate Grimaldi, Mary Ingram, Ja'Nean Palacios, Whitney Bush, and Karl Thulin. Very special thanks, also, to Natasha Chen Christensen, whose timely and thoughtful contributions to the text proved invaluable.

We wish to especially thank Al Ferris for his wise and generous counsel in helping us to establish our corporate identity and at every juncture along the way. Thanks to Kevin Ebenhoch for his friendly and efficient services. We would like to thank our families and friends whose encouragement and support helped to sustain us through the length of this project and beyond. It is also with great pleasure that we thank Greg Wennerdahl and David Unger, respectively—your presence in our lives feels like our "bonus" for completing the first edition, and we look forward to sharing many happy returns (and future editions) with you.

We are grateful to colleagues who have served as mentors in our intellectual development and as inspiration to a life of writing. And finally, we offer our thanks to all of the students we have had the privilege to work with over the years. Getting to share the sociological imagination with you makes it all worthwhile.

Kerry Ferris
Jill Stein

PART 1

Thinking Sociologically and Doing Sociology

David came from a well-heeled Philadelphia family, attended Harvard Law School, spent his summers sailing yachts, and clerked for a Supreme Court Justice.

Pepper went to Yale when the school had just begun to admit female students, and some campus buildings didn't even have women's restrooms. She wrote the sex advice column for *Glamour* magazine for nine years.

Andrew is an outspoken Roman Catholic priest and the author of over 50 best-selling mystery novels.

Joe endured the Great Depression and violent anti-Semitism as a child. He worked as a supermarket clerk and served in the Army during World War II, but it was a series of trips to India that made the biggest impact on his life.

Jessie was a "corsetless coed," a term for young women in the 1920s who rejected the restrictive undergarments of their mothers' era and instead rolled their stockings down below their knees.

What do these people have in common? They are all prominent American sociology professors. You may not have heard of them (yet), but they have each made an exceptional impact on their profession:

David Riesman made sociology a household word with his influential study of American character and culture, *The Lonely Crowd*. He earned a JD (but never a PhD) and was a professor at the University of Chicago and Harvard. Pepper Schwartz, sociology professor at the University of Washington, is a leading researcher on sex and intimate relationships. Andrew Greeley, now at the University of Arizona, ran the National Opinion Research Center at the University of Chicago for many years and continues to research the sociology of religion as an associate there. Joseph Gusfield, a pioneering sociologist in the area of alcohol use and abuse, is Professor Emeritus in the department of sociology at the University of California–San Diego. And Jessie Bernard, the "grande dame" of American sociology, was a professor at Pennsylvania State University for most of her career, studying women, marriage, and the family. The American Sociological Association gives an annual award in her name to a scholar whose career in the study of gender is as distinguished as Bernard's.

Their stories are compiled in *Authors of Their Own Lives: Intellectual Autobiographies of Twenty American Sociologists*. Edited by University of California–Berkeley professor Bennett Berger, it's a collection of autobiographical essays by well-known contemporary sociologists in a variety of fields. Each sociologist tells the story of entering the discipline and navigating a career path in academia—the obstacles he encountered, the triumphs he experienced, and the relationships between his personal life and his professional career.

SOCIAL SCIENTIST DAVID RIESMAN
What is the American character?

Their paths to sociology were very different, and they each taught and researched different topics. But despite these differences, they share a way of looking at the world. Sociologists have a unique perspective called the "sociological imagination." In fact, we hope that you will acquire your own version of the sociological imagination over the course of this term. Then you will share something in common with the professors who tell their stories in Berger's book.

David Riesman, Andrew Greeley, Pepper Schwartz, and the others also hold in common their commitment to sociological theories and concepts. This means that their ideas, and the questions they ask and answer, are guided by the established traditions of sociological thought. They may build on those traditions or criticize them, but every sociologist engages in a theoretical dialogue that links centuries and generations. You will

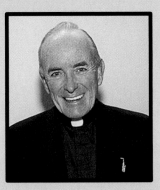

Andrew Greeley

become part of this dialogue as you learn more about sociological theory.

Finally, Riesman, Greeley, Schwartz, and the rest conduct their research using specific sociological methods. Whether quantitative or qualitative, these means of gathering and analyzing data are distinctive to sociology, and every sociologist develops research projects using the methods best suited to the questions she wants to answer.

Pepper Schwartz

In the introduction to *Authors of Their Own Lives*, Berger states that he wants to reveal "the presence of the person in the work, the author in the authored" (p. xv)—in other words, he wants to show how a sociologist's personal journey affects her professional legacy. Berger also believes that knowing something about an author's life helps students understand her work—and we agree with him. A person's values, experiences, and family context all shape her interests and objectives—and this is as true of eminent sociologists like Jessie Bernard as it will be for you.

In the following section, we will introduce you to the discipline of sociology and the sociological imagination (Chapter 1), to sociology's theoretical traditions (Chapter 2), and to its research methodologies (Chapter 3). This section is your first opportunity to get to know sociology—its topics, theories, and research practices.

Perhaps someday your intellectual autobiography will be added to those of Riesman, Greeley, Schwartz, and the rest—and your story will start by opening this book . . .

CHAPTER 1

Sociology and the Real World

auren continues to feud with newly engaged Heidi, accusing her of spreading nasty rumors. Whitney struggles at *Teen Vogue*, and after a trip to Paris, decides to quit. She finds a new job at a public relations firm where Lauren is also offered a position. Lauren and childhood friend Lo buy a house together in the Hollywood hills; despite some friction with Audrina, they invite her to live with them. Lauren finds out that Brody has been seeing someone else, so she hooks up with former boyfriend Stephen. Heidi and Spencer take a "relationship vacation" but later reunite. . . .

Eleven two-person teams—including married ministers, dating Goths, best friends, a grandfather and grandson, and two sets of siblings—race 30,000 miles through 10 countries on four continents in just 21 days, competing for various prizes along the way, until the winners ultimately claim $1,000,000 in the final leg. The contestants are required to perform tasks as they encounter "roadblocks" or "detours" before getting to their next destination. One team must milk a camel and then drink it, while another must learn a traditional dance and perform it in front of a crowd of locals. One team has to don protective gear and run through a barrage of fireworks, while another jumps into the hold of a boat containing 500 live crabs to find the one painted with race colors. . . .

On the very same day that Renee Giunta gives birth to her third child, her husband Paul is in a devastating car accident that requires months of arduous rehabilitation. It's been over two years and he still has not returned home, because the Giunta home cannot accommodate his wheelchair. But the family is about to receive a miracle of sorts. They are sent away on a vacation to Disney World, while a team of hundreds of workers steps in to tear down and rebuild their home—a project that would ordinarily take months to complete—all in just one week. The Giuntas return to a cheering crowd of neighbors and tour their newly remodeled, redecorated, and landscaped home, where they can live together again all under one roof. . . .

Is any of this real? Yes . . . kind of. It's "reality television"—specifically MTV's *The Hills*, CBS's *The Amazing Race*, and ABC's *Extreme Makeover: Home Edition*. And there's a lot more where that came from. The spring 2008 weekly television lineup featured no fewer than 40 reality shows among the major networks and cable stations, with countless more programs in the works for the future. *The Real World*, *American Idol*, *LA Ink*, *Survivor*, *Big Brother*, *Top Chef*, *The Biggest Loser*, *Wife Swap*, *America's Next*

SocIndex

Then and Now

1968: The percentage of college undergraduates who say they discuss social issues with friends or family: over 30%

2000: The percentage of college undergraduates who say they discuss social issues with friends or family: less than 16%

Here and There

United States: A 2002 survey reveals that 51% of the "DotNet" generation (15-to-25-year-olds) use their purchasing power as the primary vehicle for expressing their political and social views

Sweden: In a 2005 survey, 28% of all Swedes between the ages of 16 and 29 say that they boycotted products for political or social reasons

This and That

In 2004, over 12 million, or roughly 44%, of 18-to-24-year-old American citizens have no college experience

A 2004 survey reveals that 18-to-24-year-olds with no college experience are significantly less likely to feel they can make a difference in their communities than their college-attending counterparts

Top Model, and *Deadliest Catch* are just a few of the entries from that time period. Some of the shows claim to follow real people through their everyday lives or on the job, while others impose bizarre conditions on participants (like stranding them on a desert island), subject them to stylized competitions and gross-out stunts, or make their dreams come true. Millions tune in every week to see real people eat bugs, get fired, suffer romantic rejection, reveal their poor parenting, get branded as fat or ugly, cry over their misfortunes, or get voted out of the house or off the island—mortifying themselves on camera for the possibility of success, money, or fame.

Why are we so interested in these people? Because people are interesting! Because we are people too—no matter how different we are from the folks on reality TV, we are part of the same society, and for that reason we are curious about how they live. We compare their lives with ours, wonder how common or unusual they or we are, and marvel at the fact that we are all part of the same, real world. We too may want to win competitions, date an attractive guy or girl, find a high-profile job, feel pretty or handsome, be part of an exclusive group, have a lovely home and family. We may even want to get on a reality show ourselves.

Reality television is interesting because of the social dynamics it reveals. However contrived or formulaic the set-ups are, the issues that each show deals with—interpersonal disputes, family and work issues, racial and regional identities, class, wealth, and poverty, sexuality and gender conflicts, disabilities, body images and standards of beauty, the role of the individual in a larger group—are all sociological issues. Sociology as an academic discipline can help us explain the things that happen on-screen in reality television and the things that happen off-screen in real life.

Sociology allows us to peer into the lives and worlds of many different kinds of people, in many different settings—and we don't have to wait for TV producers to make it happen. Sociology offers us insights into our own lives as well as the lives of others and presents systematic, scientific ways of understanding those lives. Sociology gives us tools to wield as we navigate our everyday social worlds, and it shows us ways of understanding the forces that shape and constrain us in those worlds. Sociology helps us understand both *The Real World* and the real world.

HOW TO READ THIS CHAPTER

With this first chapter, you are embarking on a fascinating journey as you learn to see, think, and analyze yourself and the world around you from a sociological perspective. It is critical that you try to gain the fundamental tools for understanding presented here. They will be the foundation on which you will build new knowledge and insights into social life.

As authors and teachers, we also want to encourage you to develop some basic study techniques that will assist in your success as a new student to sociology (and perhaps beyond). You may want to highlight portions of the text or take notes while you are reading. Mark passages you don't understand, or keep a list of questions you might have about any aspect of the chapter. Don't hesitate to discuss those questions with your instructor or fellow students; sometimes such dialogues can be one of the most gratifying parts of the learning process. Finally, we recommend that you attend class regularly, as there is really no substitute for the shared experience that happens when you do sociology with others.

We are excited to take this journey of discovery with you. Though you may know a lot about social life already, we hope to introduce you to even more—about yourself and the world around you—and to provide you valuable tools for the future. We wouldn't want you to miss a thing. So now here is where we start. . . .

What Does Society Look Like?

Can you see **society**? Really see it? If you can, can you describe it? What does it look like, sound like, smell, taste, or feel like? These are difficult questions to answer. Despite the fact that we talk about, operate in, and make reference to "society" constantly, we are challenged when it comes to describing it—we realize we are talking about something we can't actually see.

Introductory sociology texts often present society to students as *sui generis*—as an object in itself. This is useful in convincing students that the study of society is a worthwhile enterprise. If society is an object, then it can be scrutinized and analyzed like any other object. Introductory texts also often advise students that what a sociologist does to society is much like what a geologist does to a rock, or what a biologist does to a living organism. Society becomes something to be scientifically weighed, measured, and dissected.

But what we find as we begin to dissect this object is that it is made up of countless other components—that things like "culture," "race," or the "working class" appear to be *sui generis* as well, more phenomena to examine by themselves. And these components can be broken down even further into seemingly endless bits and pieces. It seems daunting, even impossible, to imagine that we could analyze something so big, with so many parts, that we can't actually see its shape or boundaries. The question arises: is society a concrete object after all?

Here's a more useful question: if we can't see the whole of society, what *can* we see? We can see people living their lives, interacting with each other, working, playing, eating, dancing, fighting, grieving, gardening, bowling, driving in their cars. There are limitless observable phenomena for us to analyze sociologically, and they're happening all around us. In fact, we participate in them every moment of every day. What we will be investigating in this text are the most familiar things of all—the things we do together, every day.

People actively and collectively shape their lives, organizing their social interactions and relationships to produce a real and meaningful world; and they do this in patterned ways that we as social scientists can analyze. In this text, we will be concerned with the social processes that everyone experiences and how those social processes create the larger society of which we are all a part.

If we can't necessarily see society as a whole, we can at least observe it in its parts, and we can see how those parts are created, changed, and maintained, how they link together, how they shape and influence one another—and what our roles are in those processes. This is what society looks like.

> **society** a group of people who shape their lives in aggregated and patterned ways that distinguish their group from other groups

Asking the Big Questions

People have been pondering the meaning of life for as long as they have been conscious. It is this ancient fascination with why we are here, how things work, and what is going to happen next that is the impetus for modern scientific discovery. Early explanations about the nature of the world and of social life in particular were based in tradition, superstition, and myth. Our ancestors accepted these understandings, which were rarely doubted. But with the rise of modern science in the seventeenth and eighteenth centuries, new forms of knowledge and practices of discovery and verification were established, and during the nineteenth century the concept of "social science" began to emerge.

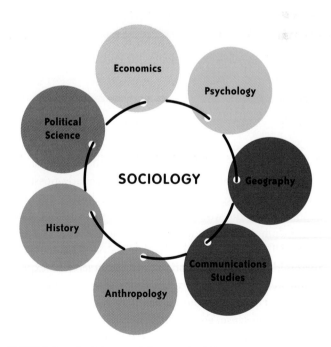

FIGURE 1.1 Sociology and the Social Sciences Sociology overlaps with other social sciences, but much of the territory it covers is unique.

Food and Eating

The need for food is instinctive—we need to eat in order to survive. But when we eat, especially in an affluent country like the United States, are we responding to instinctive drives or socially elaborated requirements? It may be instinctive to seek nourishment, but what, when, where, and with whom we eat, and how we feel about eating—all these are socially constructed, not instinctive.

Take the example of a restaurant meal, whether at Spago in Beverly Hills or at the McDonald's drive-thru down the street from your campus. Neither your cardboard platter of Chicken McNuggets nor your honey-lacquered duck breast with grilled foie gras is in any way naturally occurring. Nor is their meaning intrinsic: Spago is not upscale *sui generis*, nor is McDonald's necessarily vulgar or common. As a society, we create these ways of responding to our instinctual drives—we elaborate on our need for food, shaping a basic drive into something socially, culturally, and historically specific.

Perhaps most important, eating is often done in the company of others, whether the group is large (as in a college dorm's dining room or a military mess hall) or small (a couple on a date, or a family at the breakfast table). Food thus plays a role in many of our social relationships. Indeed, the word *companion* contains the Latin root for bread, *pan*, and literally means "someone to break bread with." In other words, our language explicitly links friendship with food.

Until recently, it was expected that women, as wives and mothers, would take on the responsibility of feeding their family members. Women still do most of the mealtime work—planning, shopping, cooking, and serving (DeVault 1991)—and are expected to show their love for and commitment to their families by doing this work. Think of your own mother or grandmother or aunt: unless your family is somewhat unusual, these women probably spent a good deal of time in the kitchen, and they may even have made an explicit connection between meal preparation and their love for you. How many times were you urged to eat—or eat more—to prove you loved Grandma rather than to satisfy your own hunger?

Although most people have no special training, almost everyone is what you might call a natural sociologist. By virtue of our membership in society, we already possess a great deal of background knowledge to help us form ideas about the way the world works. Every culture passes along to its members conventional wisdom that is taken as fact, and we are all casual observers of and active participants in our surroundings. Thus we tend to think of ourselves as experts in the area of life in society, but this is true only on a small scale. Most of what we know is based on personal experience and common sense. For example, we often assign characteristics to an entire group of people (women, police officers, only children, Germans) based on our experience with one member of that group. We formulate our opinions using conventional wisdom, background knowledge, and personal experience, sometimes combining them with guesswork, intuition, or blind faith.

There are certainly times when we will need to draw from this personal knowledge. At other times, though, it may present a stumbling block to deeper understanding. This is why, in some regards, doing sociology is a radical undertaking. It requires of us a willingness to suspend our own preconceptions, assumptions, and beliefs about the way things are. As sociologists, we need to learn to question everything, especially our own taken-for-granted notions about others and ourselves. Once these have been set aside, even temporarily, we gain a fresh perspective with which to uncover and discover aspects of social life we hadn't noticed before. We are

Ceremonial meals are especially important in forging and maintaining strong bonds. Wedding banquets celebrate the newly married couple as well as the new "in-law" ties created by their marriage. Holiday meals help families express their ethnic and religious ties (Pleck 2000); for example, in the Passover seder ritual, parsley, saltwater, and matzoh crackers have symbolic meanings related to the historic liberation of the Jewish people from slavery in Egypt. And it's no accident that many first dates involve a meal along with whatever other activity is planned—dinner and a movie, dinner and dancing, dinner and a show. Researchers at University College London found that a meal, especially an extravagant one, is the most effective way to woo a love interest (Sozou and Seymour 2005).

Society didn't create our need for nourishment. But society surely shapes the way we eat and the relationships that food helps us form and sustain. Societies produce different cooking styles and preparation techniques, utilize different ingredients, consider different foodstuffs to be delicacies, and allow only certain people to indulge in the most prized culinary pleasures while others must be content with more mundane morsels. The values, hierarchies, and institutions of our society have all intervened in our drive to seek nourishment—to the point where we may no longer be responding to instinct at all but to other, clearly social imperatives: the need for a quick meal that fits into a busy day; the urge to be adventurous and taste an exotic cuisine; the desire to display the status implied by dining in elegant surroundings; or just the need to connect with other people. Food satisfies our social hungers as well as our physical appetite.

"Family" Meals Food and eating help us forge and maintain strong social bonds.

then able to reinterpret our previous understanding of the world, perhaps challenging, or possibly confirming, what we thought we already knew.

What Is Sociology?

Even among those working in the field, there is some debate about how **sociology** is defined. A look at the term's root parts, *socius* and *logos*, suggests that sociology means the study of society, which is a good place to start. A slightly more elaborate definition might say that sociology is the systematic or scientific study of human society and social behavior. This could include almost any level within the structure of society, from large-scale institutions and mass culture to small groups and relationships between individuals.

Another definition comes from Howard Becker, who suggests that sociology can best be understood as the study of people "doing things together" (Becker 1986). This definition reminds us that neither society nor the individual exists in isolation but that each is dependent on and intertwined with the other. It brings to mind the fundamental premise that humans are essentially social beings. Not only is our survival

sociology the systematic or scientific study of human society and social behavior, from large-scale institutions and mass culture to small groups and individual interactions

Famous Sociology Majors

Sociology continues to be a popular major at colleges and universities in the United States and in other countries such as Canada, the United Kingdom, and Australia. According to the American Sociological Association, over 265,000 Bachelor of Arts degrees in sociology were awarded in the United States between 1995 and 2006. Clearly there are many reasons why students who have discovered sociology are enthusiastic about the subject. What may be less clear to new undergraduates, however, is how to turn their passion into a paycheck. Students thinking about majoring in the subject often ask, "What can I do with a degree in sociology?" Their parents may be asking the same question. Some students interested in academic careers will pursue graduate degrees in order to become professors and researchers—real practicing sociologists. But the vast majority of students with degrees in sociology will not necessarily become sociologists with a capital S. Their studies will have prepared them to be valuable, accomplished participants in a variety of different fields, including law and government, business administration, social welfare, public health, education, counseling and human resources, advertising and marketing, public relations and the media, and work in nonprofit organizations.

A major in sociology, in other words, can lead almost anywhere. And while the roster of previous sociology majors contains names both well known and unsung, from former president Ronald Reagan and civil rights leader Martin Luther King Jr. to the public defender giving legal aid to low-income clients and the health care professional bringing wellness programs into large corporations, we would like to

focus here on three important figures in American life you may not have associated with sociology.

The first individual may be the least likely to be identified as a sociology major, since his career was centered in the arts. Saul Bellow (1915–2005) was one of the most acclaimed American writers of the twentieth century; his numerous literary awards included the National Book Award (three times), the Pulitzer Prize, and the Nobel Prize in Literature. In addition to writing novels, he was also a successful playwright and journalist, and taught at several universities. Bellow was born in Montreal to Jewish parents, Russian émigrés who later settled in the slums of Chicago while he was still a child. He began his undergraduate studies in English at the University of Chicago, but left within two years after being told by the chair of the department that no Jew could really grasp English literature. He then enrolled at Northwestern University, graduating in 1937 with honors in sociology. Literary critics have noted that Bellow's background in sociology, as well as his own personal history, may have influenced both the style and subject of his work. Many of the great themes of American social life appear in his novels: culture, power, wealth and poverty, war, religion, the city, gender relations, and above all, the social contract that keeps us together in the face of forces that threaten to tear us apart.

Our next profile is of Maxine Waters (b. 1938), a nine-term member of the U.S. House of Representatives. Waters is considered by many to be one of the most powerful women in American politics and has gained a reputation as an outspoken advocate for women, children, people of color, and the poor. Born in St. Louis, Missouri, one of thirteen

contingent on the fact that we live in various kinds of groups (families, neighborhoods, dorms), but our very sense of self derives from our membership in society. In turn the accumulated activities of people doing things together create the patterns and structures we call society. So sociologists want to understand how humans affect society, as well as how society affects humans.

Broader definitions of the discipline are more readily accepted by a majority of sociologists, whereas more precise

definitions are sometimes disputed. Disagreements arise, in part, because of the fact that sociology encompasses such a large terrain of possible subject matter. In later chapters, as we explore the field's development and some of its substantive areas, we will be able to clarify the myriad possibilities for defining sociology. For now, one way to better understand what sociology does is to contrast it with other social sciences. The **social sciences** are those disciplines that examine the human or social world, much as the natural sciences

children raised by a single mother, she began working at age thirteen in factories and segregated restaurants. After moving to Los Angeles, where she completed high school, she was hired as an assistant teacher and volunteered to be a coordinator in the newly formed Head Start program in Watts. She attended California State University, Los Angeles, and in 1970 earned a Bachelor of Arts degree in sociology. Since 1976, Waters has served in public office, first in the California State Assembly and then in the U.S. House of Representatives, from the district that includes South Central Los Angeles. Throughout her years of public service, Waters has not shied away from tackling difficult and sometimes controversial issues, often the same issues that are of interest to sociologists. Some of her areas of concern have included affirmative action, community economic development, youth-training programs, affordable health care and housing, drug-abuse prevention and treatment, welfare reform, and equal justice under the law.

Our last sociology major is Ahmad Rashad (b. 1940), a former professional football player and award-winning sportscaster. Born Bobby Moore in Tacoma, Washington, he chose his current name (which means "admirable one led to truth") after being inspired by his mentor, Rashad Khalifa, an Egyptian émigré and Muslim religious leader. Rashad attended the University of Oregon, where he played wide receiver and was twice selected for the All-America team. Upon graduating in

Saul Bellow   **Maxine Waters**   **Ahmad Rashad**

1972 with a Bachelor of Arts degree in sociology, he played for three National Football League teams: the St. Louis Cardinals, the Buffalo Bills, and most notably, the Minnesota Vikings, where he was selected for four Pro Bowl games. After his professional football career ended, Rashad began work as a sportscaster for NBC, where his duties included reporting, commentary, and analysis. He won an Emmy Award for writing about the 1988 Olympic Games in Seoul, Korea. The next year, he wrote a bestselling memoir, *Rashad: Vikes, Mikes and Something on the Backside*, in which he discussed not only his sports career but also the media, power, and race in America. Did sociology help Rashad make the transition from football player to sportscaster or better understand the dynamics of the sports world and its wider place in society? We'd like to think it was of some value to him along the way. In 1995, the University of Oregon acknowledged his extraordinary success by presenting him its Pioneer Award, the highest honor given to any alumnus.

examine the natural or physical world. Included in a list of the social sciences are such fields as anthropology, psychology, economics, political science, and sometimes history, geography, and communication studies. Each has its own particular focus on the social world. In some ways, sociology's territory overlaps with that of the other social sciences, even while maintaining its own unique approach.

Like history, sociology compares the past and the present in order to understand both; unlike history, sociology is more likely to focus on contemporary society. Sociology is interested in societies at all levels of development, while anthropology is more likely to concentrate on traditional or primitive cultures. Sociology looks at a range of social institutions, unlike economics or political science, each of which is focused on a single one. Like geography, sociology considers

social sciences the disciplines that use the scientific method to examine the social world; in contrast to the natural sciences, which examine the physical world

microsociology the level of analysis that studies face-to-face and small-group interactions in order to understand how those interactions affect the larger patterns and institutions of society

macrosociology the level of analysis that studies large-scale social structures in order to determine how they affect the lives of groups and individuals

the relationship of people to places, though geography is more concerned with the places themselves. And like communication studies, sociology examines human communication—at both the social and the interpersonal levels, rather than one or the other. Finally, sociology looks at the individual in relationship to external social forces, whereas psychology specializes in internal states of mind. As you can begin to see, sociology covers a huge intellectual territory, making it exceptional among the social sciences in taking a comprehensive, integrative approach to understanding human life.

Levels of Analysis

Micro- and Macrosociology

There are different ways to approach the study of sociology. Consider a photographer with state-of-the-art equipment. She could view her subject through either a zoom lens or a wide-angle lens. Through the zoom lens she sees intricate details about the subject's appearance; through the wide-angle lens,

she gets the "big picture" and a sense of the broader context in which the subject is located. Both views are valuable in understanding the subject, and both result in photographs of the same thing.

The different sociological perspectives are like the photographer's lenses, allowing us different ways of looking at a common subject (Newman 2000). Sociologists can take a **microsociological** (zoom lens) perspective or a **macrosociological** (wide-angle lens) perspective or any number of perspectives located on the continuum between the two.

Microsociology concentrates on the interactions between individuals and the ways in which those interactions construct the larger patterns, processes, and institutions of society. As the word indicates (*micro* means "small"), microsociology looks at the smallest building blocks of society in order to understand its large-scale structure. A classic example of research that takes a micro approach is Pam Fishman's article "Interaction: The Work Women Do" (1978). Like many scholars who had observed the feminist movements of the 1960s and 70s, Fishman was concerned with issues of power and domination in male-female relationships: Are men more powerful than women in our society? If so, how is this power created and maintained in everyday interactions? In her research, Fishman tape-recorded and analyzed heterosexual couples' everyday conversations in their homes. What she found were some real differences in the conversational strategies of men and women, as the transcript in Figure 1.2 illustrates.

Microsociology and Macrosociology Sociologists bring different levels of analysis to the study of people and groups. Microsociology zooms in to focus on individuals and their interactions in order to understand larger social structures. In contrast, macrosociology pulls back to study large-scale social processes and their effects on individuals and groups.

TRANSCRIPT

1
F: I didn't know that. (=)   Um you know that ((garbage disposal on)) that organizational

M: Hmmm? (=)

2
F: stuff about Frederick Taylor and Bishopsgate and all that stuff? (=)   ⌐ in the early

M: UmHm ((yes)) ⌐

3
F: 1900's people were trying to fight favoritism to the schools (4)

M: That's what we needed. (18) |

4
F:

M: never did get my smoked oysters, I'm going to look for ((inaudible)) (14) Should we try the

5
F: OK. That's a change. (72) Hmm. That's very interesting. Did

M: Riviera French Dressing? (=)

6
F: you know that teachers used to be men until about the 1840's when it became a female occupa-

M:

7
F: tion? (2)   Because they needed more teachers because of the increased enroll-

M: Nhhmm ((no)) (=)

8
F: ment. (5)   Yeah relatively and the status (7)

M: And the the salaries started going down probably. (=)

9
F: ⌐ There's two bottles I think ⌐

M: Um, it's weird. We're out of oil again. └ Now we have to buy that. ┘ ((whistling)) (8) Dressing

10
F: It does yeah. (76) That's really interesting. They didn't start

M: looks good. See? (2) See babe? (1)

11
F: using the test to measure and find the you know categorize and track people in American

M:

12
F: schools until like the early 1900's after the army y'know introduced their array alpha things

M:

13
F: to the draftees (?) And then it caught on with the schools and there was a lot of opposition right

M:

14
F: at the beginning to that, which was as sophisticated as today's arguments. The same argu-

M:

15
F: ments y'know (=)   But it didn't work and they came (4)   ⌐ heh

M: Yeah (=)   Leslie White is probably right. ⌐

FIGURE 1.2 Gender and Conversational Patterns Conversation analysis allows us to see patterns like who interrupts more (men) and who asks more questions (women).

SOURCE: Fishman 1978

"The Work Women Do" For her famous microsociological article, Pam Fishman tape-recorded conversations between husbands and wives to learn about their different conversational strategies. She found that women ask three times as many questions.

As you can see, the woman is having a difficult time getting her husband to join her in the topic she proposes, the history of education. He frequently interrupts, changes the subject, fails to respond for long stretches, and even flips on the garbage disposal while she is trying to speak. She perseveres, trying to gain control of the conversation in order to be able to talk about education. Fishman recorded many such conversations and found a variety of patterns. One of her findings was that women ask nearly three times as many questions as men do. While other researchers have proposed that women's psychological insecurities are the reason for this finding, Fishman notes that women are in fact following a firmly held rule of conversational structure: when the speaker cannot guarantee that she will get a response, she is more likely to ask a question. Questions provoke answers; this makes them a useful conversational tool for those who may have less power in interpersonal relationships and in society at large. And women are more likely to be in this position than men. Thus, in her micro-level analysis of conversation, Fishman was able to see how macro-level (*macro* means "large") phenomena like gender and power are manifested in everyday interactions.

Macrosociology approaches the study of society from the opposite direction, by looking at large-scale social structure in order to determine how it affects the lives of groups and individuals. If we wanted to stick to the same topic of gender inequality, we could find plenty of examples of research projects that take a macro approach; many deal with the workplace. Despite the gains made in recent years, the U.S. labor market is still predominantly sex segregated—that

is, men and women are concentrated in different occupations. For example, in 2007 some 99.3 percent of auto mechanics were male, whereas some 96.7 percent of secretaries and administrative assistants were female (U.S. Department of Labor, "Employed Persons," 2007). This feature of social structure, some argue, has a direct effect on the experiences of individual workers, male and female.

A related example comes from the work of Christine Williams (1995). She found that while women in male-dominated fields experience limits on their advancement (dubbed the "glass ceiling" effect), men in female-dominated occupations ride a "glass escalator": they experience unusually rapid rates of upward mobility. Here, then, we see a macro approach to the topic of gender and power: large-scale features of social structure (patterns of occupational sex segregation) create the constraints within which individuals and groups (women and men in the workplace) experience successes or failures in their everyday lives.

As you can see, these two perspectives make different assumptions about how society works: the micro perspective assumes that society's larger structures are shaped through individual interactions, while the macro perspective assumes that society's larger structures shape those individual interactions. It is useful to think of these perspectives as being on a continuum with each other; while some sociologists adhere to radically micro or exclusively macro perspectives, most are somewhere in between. In Chapter 2 we will explore some specific theoretical traditions within sociology, and you will be able to see where each falls along this continuum.

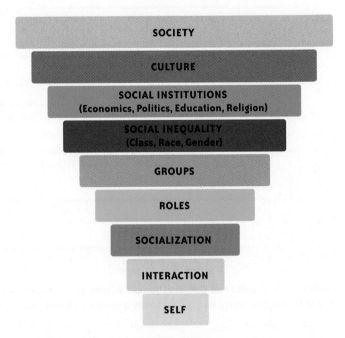

FIGURE 1.3 The Macro-Micro Continuum Sociology covers a wide range of topics at different levels of analysis.

Glass Ceilings and Glass Escalators Christine Williams's comparison of the occupational status of men in a female-dominated industry and women in a male-dominated industry is a good example of macrosociology.

Quantitative and Qualitative Methods

Another way that the discipline of sociology commonly divides up the study of society is by methodological approach. (Methodology involves gathering and analyzing data in order to establish certain facts, support certain theories, or disprove certain hypotheses about the social world.) Again, because of sociology's broad range and flexibility, there is room for a variety of different methods for studying society. As with the micro-macro divide, there is a similar polarization in the area of methodology, this time along a quantitative-qualitative divide (with many sociologists in between).

Sociologists who do **quantitative research** work with numerical data—that is, they translate the social world into numbers that can then be manipulated mathematically. Any type of social statistic is an example of quantitative data: you may have read in the newspaper, for instance, that in 2006 some 38 percent of male teenage drivers involved in fatal motor vehicle crashes had alcohol in their blood, compared with 22 percent of female teenage drivers (Insurance Institute for Highway Safety 2006). Quantitative methodologies distill large amounts of information into numbers that are more easily communicated to others.

Sociologists who do **qualitative research** work with non-numerical data such as texts, written fieldnotes, interview transcripts, photographs, and tape recordings. Rather than condensing lived experience into a number, chart, or graph, qualitative researchers preserve the details of the cases they study. They may engage in participant observation, in which they enter the social world they wish to study; they may do in-depth interviews, analyze transcripts of conversations, glean data from historical books, letters, or diaries, or even use photos or videos in their investigations. Sociologist Gary Fine, for example, has observed a variety of different social worlds, including those of fantasy game players (1983), professional restaurant chefs (1996), and people who harvest wild mushrooms in the woods (1998)! Fine was able to discover important sociological insights through immersion in each of the subcultures he studied. Qualitative researchers like Fine preserve detail and diversity in their data by using interpretive rather than statistical analysis. In Chapter 3 we will explore some specific methodological traditions, and you will be able to see where each falls along the qualitative-quantitative continuum.

No matter what approach is taken, all sociologists seek to illuminate the connection between the individual and society. The great thing about our discipline is that whatever your interests may be, you can take a sociological approach to understanding them. For example, Dr. Stein does research on the careers of rock musicians (1997), the importance of popular music to college students (Stein, Rabow, and El Mouchi 1994; Rabow and Stein 1996), teaching about stigmatization and social justice (Rabow, Stein, and Conley 1999, 2001), and the use of narrative and humor in twelve-step programs (Pollner and Stein 1996, 2001). Dr. Ferris does research on *Star Trek* and soap opera fans (2001, 2004a), celebrity stalking (2005), talk-radio advice shows (2004b), and celebrity impersonators (forthcoming). While most of our research is done from microsociological and qualitative perspectives, we also use macrosociology and quantitative data when appropriate. Our friends and colleagues do work in a wide range of interesting areas as well: participating in feminist movements (Roth 2003), creating racial identity in cyberspace (Burkhalter 1999), changing culture through popular art (Sherwood 2006), experiencing and resisting gender harassment in the military (Miller 1997), feeling scared or angry about having sex offenders as neighbors (Burchfield and Mingus 2008), shaping news interviews through the use of language (Roth 2002), sexualizing the workplace (Van Leuven 1998, 2001), dressing to look like a gang member at school (Katz and Garot 2003), and planning a wedding (Sniezek 2005). Whatever inspires, interests, or confounds us, we can study it sociologically.

quantitative research research that translates the social world into numbers that can be treated mathematically; this type of research often tries to find cause-and-effect relationships

qualitative research research that works with nonnumerical data such as texts, fieldnotes, interview transcripts, photographs, and tape recordings; this type of research more often tries to understand how people make sense of their world

The Sociological Perspective

How do sociologists go about understanding human life in society? The first step is to develop what we call the *sociological perspective*. This can alternately be referred to as taking a sociological approach or thinking sociologically. In any case, it means looking at the world in a unique way and seeing it in a whole new light. This directive will remain our most important task throughout the course. It is what we hope you will acquire from reading this book: the ability to think sociologically.

The Sociological Imagination

One of the classic statements about the sociological perspective comes from sociologist C. Wright Mills (1959), who describes the one quality of mind that all the great social analysts seem to possess in common as the **sociological imagination**. By this he means the ability to understand "the intersection between biography and history," or the interplay of self and the world; this is sociology's task and its "promise."

Mills claims that most of us are "seldom aware of the intricate connection between the patterns of our own lives and the course of world history." As individuals we may suffer and struggle without recognizing how our "troubles of milieu" (of our particular place or situation in life) are connected to the "issues of public social structure" (of what is happening at the level of society as a whole). We normally think of our own problems as being a private matter of character, chance, or circumstance, and we overlook the fact that these may be caused in part by, or are at least occurring within, a specific cultural and historical context. For example, if you can't find a job, you may feel that this is because you don't have the right skills, educational background, or experience. But it may also be the result of problems in the larger economy like outsourcing, downsizing, restrictive policies, changing technologies, or migration patterns. In other words, your individual unemployment may be part of a larger social and historical phenomenon, which means that no matter how skilled you are, there may be no job for you to find.

Most of the time we use psychological rather than sociological arguments to explain the way things are. For instance, we might look at someone who's carrying a large amount of credit card debt and, using psychological reasoning, focus on his lack of self-control or inability to delay gratification when it comes to buying

C. Wright Mills (1916–1962)

things. Sociological reasoning, however, might focus on the impact of cultural norms that promote a lifestyle beyond most people's means, or on the changing economy that requires more Americans to rely on credit cards because their wages have not kept up with inflation.

The sociological imagination requires that we search for the link between the micro and macro levels of analysis. We must look for how larger social forces such as race, class, gender, religion, economics, or politics are involved in creating the context of a person's life. Also, Mills's characterization of sociology as the intersection between biography and history reminds us that the process works in both directions: while larger social forces influence individual lives, there are many ways in which our individual lives can affect society as well. The sociological imagination thus helps us to better understand society, other people, and ourselves.

SCHOOL SHOOTINGS One of the most important things a sociological imagination can do for us is give us a way of looking at the world beyond our own immediate personal experience. It can take us into different worlds, to discover other people who may have radically different ways of experiencing life and interpreting reality. The sociological imagination helps us appreciate different viewpoints and understand how they may have come about. In turn, it helps us to understand better how we developed our own values, beliefs, and attitudes.

How might we apply the sociological imagination to a particular type of event? Let's take as our example the disturbing phenomenon of school shootings. They seem to have become more common in recent years, with the worst incident being the killing of 32 people at Virginia Tech (VT) on April 17, 2007, and more recently the February 14, 2008, shootings at Northern Illinois University (NIU), which left 5 students dead.

Most of us are familiar with the facts: Cho Seung-Hui was a 23-year-old English major at Virginia Tech. Using two handguns that he had purchased, he murdered 2 people at a dorm and 30 people in an academic building before killing himself (CNN 2007). Less than a year later Steven Kazmierczak walked into a classroom at Northern Illinois University with a shotgun in his guitar case and three more guns hidden under his jacket. He wounded 22 people and killed 5 before ending his own life (Bourdreau and Zamost 2008). Most of

> **sociological imagination** a quality of the mind that allows us to understand the relationship between our particular situation in life and what is happening at a social level

Cho Seung-Hui An image that NBC News received from Cho Seung-Hui, the gunman who murdered 32 people at Virginia Tech in 2007.

us were shocked and appalled by these tragedies and left to ask ourselves how they could have happened. Each time we waited to hear more details, to get some kind of explanation. Much of the information centered on the young men themselves. Both struggled with mental illness. Cho had been ordered to seek psychiatric treatment by a Virginia judge and Kazmierczak had been hospitalized for mental illness in the past. They also were both described as men who were quiet and not very outgoing. However, they were different in many ways. Cho mailed a video manifesto to NBC News, while Kazmierczak deliberately destroyed any materials that might have provided a hint or explanation about the violence he planned to commit. Cho was a loner who referred to himself as a "question mark" and wrote menacing plays for his creative writing class. Kazmierczak was a successful student who wrote about his commitment to helping others. Given their biographies, people want to assume that Cho and Kazmierczak were sick, twisted individuals, intent on destruction, who eventually went on a killing rampage. But questions about why continue to nag us.

The sociological perspective suggests that we look at Cho and Kazmierczak as individuals who were shaped by their social circumstances. This does *not* mean that we wish to relieve them of responsibility for their actions. But there are other factors to consider. The two men lived in a particular time and place, within a cultural and historical context, all of which helped create an environment in which this tragedy happened. They were products of family structure and child-rearing practices common to the late twentieth century. They were average in many ways, with the same kinds of interests and background that a lot of other college students have. In part that meant that they were having trouble with adolescence: they felt shy and awkward, alienated and ostracized, and were bullied by other teenagers in high school.

They were exposed to a great deal of violence in the form of entertainment, from movies to video games to the nightly news. Guns were readily available to them, both at home and through friends and gun dealers. Cho and Kazmierczak responded to their environment, and their own internal impulses, by becoming outcasts and rebels.

That all of this erupted into a homicidal and suicidal rage is not unique to them. There have been other school shootings, as well as lesser incidents of hostility, which would indicate that these are not isolated events. Perhaps it is just another example of a more widespread trend toward youthful despair and violence in our society.

What is important to remember is that the sociological perspective does not deny individual responsibility; it does not offer a rationalization or justification. What it does do is give us a broader context for understanding people and situations.

Culture Shock

Many of us may naturally be inclined toward thinking sociologically. In his book *Invitation to Sociology* (1963), Peter Berger describes what kind of person it takes to become a sociologist: someone with a passionate interest in the world of human affairs, someone who is intense, curious, and daring in the pursuit of knowledge. "People who like to avoid shocking discoveries . . . should stay away from sociology," he warns (p. 24). The sociologist will care about the issues of ultimate importance to humanity, as well as the most mundane occurrences of everyday existence. This impulse will lead her to investigate every walk of life, from the sacred to the profane, the popular to the obscure, the fascinating to the commonplace. From the sociological perspective, she will glimpse the richness and variety of human experience.

One way to gain a sociological perspective is to attempt to create in ourselves a sense of **culture shock**. Anthropologists use the term to describe the experience of visiting an exotic foreign culture. The first encounters with the local natives and their way of life can seem so strange to us that they produce a kind of disorientation and doubt about our ability to make sense of things. Putting all judgment aside for the moment, this state of mind can be very useful. For it is at this point, when we so completely lack an understanding of our surroundings, that we are truly able to perceive what is right in front of our eyes.

As sociologists we try to create this effect without necessarily displacing ourselves geographically: we become curious and eager visitors to

culture shock a sense of disorientation that occurs when you enter a radically new social or cultural environment

Changing the World

Kiva.org and Microloans

When you picture the winner of the Nobel Peace Prize it's probably a diplomat or world leader you have in mind, not a banker or an economist, but in 2006 that's exactly who the Nobel Committee selected. Muhammad Yunus and the Grameen Bank, which he founded, were awarded the prize for their "efforts to create economic and social development from below" by making microcredit available to people who couldn't hope to receive a loan from a traditional bank or financial institution (Nobel Foundation 2006).

The roots of the Grameen Bank stretch back several decades, to when Yunus, then a professor of economics at the Chittagong University in Bangladesh, made a personal loan of $27 to a number of poor people in a nearby village. He quickly realized that such a gesture benefited not only the borrowers but also the community and himself. After failing to convince local banks to make credit available to more of the area's poor, he founded the Grameen Bank in 1983. Unlike traditional banks its express mission was to make loans to the poor. Since then literally hundreds of similar new organizations have sprung up to provide microcredit for entrepreneurs in the developing world.

One of the most exciting new organizations is Kiva, from the Swahili for "unity," founded in 2005 by Matthew and Jessica Flannery. Jessica heard Muhammad Yunus speak at Stanford and decided that her career needed to involve microfinance. She and her husband then visited Kenya, Tanzania, and Uganda while working for another microfinance institution, the Village Enterprise Fund (VEF). They saw the power of microfinance to change lives but also the limitations of using local banks as a source of capital. The Grameen Bank had become mostly self-sustaining, but many other smaller microfinance organizations still borrowed money from local banks, and the relatively high interest rates and fees meant that borrowers were still paying an average interest rate of 35 percent on their microloan (Narang 2006). Matthew and Jessica felt that the interest charged by banks to microfinance institutions can make it more difficult for microfinance institutions to become self-sustainable.

Kiva's solution was to create an organization that looked more like a social networking website than a bank. Unlike other microfinance groups, Kiva.org is a person-to-person microlending website, which allows lenders to select the particular project they want to fund by looking at profiles posted to the site. Once an individual has selected a project they can loan as little as $25 or as much as the borrower has requested. Most loans are made by a variety of individuals, each investing a part of the total sum. For example, at this particular moment Muhammad Hanif, a farmer and teacher in Jalalabad, Afghanistan, is seeking about a thousand dollars to buy livestock, and Chin Seun, a widow in Cambodia is trying to borrow $300 to hire a tractor to plow her farmland.

Kiva works by finding local partners who identify and vet potential loan candidates. Their first seven loans all went to start businesses in Tororo, Uganda, and the borrowers were screened by the VEF and a man named Moses Onyango, whom they had met while visiting East Africa. Since then Kiva has partnered with more than 100 institutions all over the world, but the biggest challenge is matching the growth of our lending opportunities with the funds that lenders want to lend. After the website was featured on Oprah, Kiva was forced to change (temporarily) from a minimum loan of $25 to a fixed loan of $25 just to accommodate all the people who wanted to invest.

Within a year of going online, Matthew Flannery had quit his job at TiVo to devote himself full-time to Kiva. As of August 2008 they have facilitated more than 270,000 lenders in loaning over $37 millions dollars to more than 40,000 borrowers in 42 different countries (Kiva). The overall default rate is a tiny 1.47 percent. Microcredit is somewhat like those traditional charities that allow Americans to sponsor children in the developing world and whose only pay-off is emotional, but there are several important differences. First, digital cameras and the internet allow lenders to easily track the projects in which they have invested. Second, the money is a loan, and almost all the loans are paid back. After a loan is repaid lenders are free to do whatever they want with their money, but many lenders choose to reinvest it with a new entrepreneur.

One of the most popular features of the Kiva.org website is the journal feature, posting entries kept by the entrepreneurs who have borrowed money. Kiva is unique among all such organizations in the way it combines microlending with an online community. Way back in 2005 founder Matthew Flannery posted a blog entry explaining that "one of the main reasons I started Kiva" was that "I love the stories and I desire the information" (Flannery 2008). The emotional gratification that comes from seeing exactly how an individual donation makes a difference is what makes investing this way so attractive, but it also serves as a potent reminder of how individual action can change the world, one loan at a time. What is important about Kiva.org, and what is of interest from a sociological perspective, is the fact that it allows individuals to take action. When thousands of individuals help a little, large-scale change can happen.

Microloans Make a Difference
Manuel Acevedo (on the right) loaned money through Kiva.org to Mirtha Ortega (middle) and her daughter Mirella (left) in Peru. When they met in Lima, Mirtha described how the loan from Manuel, her "guardian angel," transformed her family's life.

Culture Shock In the television show *Lost*, six of the characters return from a deserted island to discover that ordinary experiences that they previously took for granted seem strikingly different or unfamiliar.

our own lives. We often find that what is familiar to us, if seen as if from an outsider's perspective, is just as exotic as some foreign culture, only we've forgotten this is true because it's our own and we know it so well. To better understand this state of mind, you might imagine what it would be like to return home from a desert island. For example, consider how the characters in the television series *Lost* dealt with returning home in the fourth season (2008) of the show. As castaways from a plane wreck, they all had to learn to survive the extraordinary conditions on a desert island. After living there for many months, they felt a sense of culture shock when they returned to civilization. Although life back home was instantly familiar, it also seemed strikingly new. In fact, some among the group (referred to as the "Oceanic Six"), including Dr. Jack Shephard and Hugo "Hurley" Reyes, encountered exceptional difficulties adjusting to the life they had known before the island. Of course you don't need to be shipwrecked to see your own everyday life in a new way.

beginner's mind approaching the world without preconceptions in order to see things in a new way

Beginner's Mind

Another possible way of gaining a sociological perspective comes from Bernard McGrane (1994), who promotes a kind of shift in thinking that's borrowed from the Zen Buddhist tradition. McGrane suggests that we practice what is called **beginner's mind**—the opposite of expert's mind, which is so filled with facts, projections, assumptions, opinions, and explanations that it can't learn anything new. If we would like to better understand the world around us, then we must defamiliarize ourselves with it, or unlearn what we already know. Beginner's mind approaches the world without knowing in advance what it will find; it is open and receptive to experience.

Perhaps our greatest obstacle to making new discoveries is precisely our old ideas, or our habitual ways of thinking. "Discovery," McGrane says, "is not the seeing of a new thing—but rather a new way of seeing things" (1994, p. 3). One way to achieve this kind of awareness is to practice being present in the moment. Even when we think we are present, we are all too often preoccupied with thoughts and feelings

as supporters. Despite the controversy it is widely acknowledged that Freud was among the most important social thinkers of the twentieth century. Many of his ideas, from the "Freudian slip" to the "ego trip," have become part of the common vernacular.

Given that Freud is the founder of psychoanalysis, it is especially interesting to consider how the features of his personal life may have influenced his work. He was born in Vienna, Austria, to an impoverished Jewish family. The first boy in his family, he was favored by his parents, who expected great things from him. After graduating from the University of Vienna in 1873, Freud drifted from one subject to the next until he finally discovered neurology (the study of the brain and nervous system), a field that would satisfy his abiding curiosity about the mysteries of the human psyche. In 1881, he received a degree in medicine and set up in a medical practice. Freud was both a medical practitioner and a clinical researcher, and his patients provided him with a wealth of scientific data. In *The Interpretation of Dreams* (1900), Freud outlined the principles of psychoanalysis, and helped to establish his own reputation and that of the emerging discipline.

Freud was interested not only in individual minds but also in the way that mental processes have influenced the whole of history and culture. In his book *Civilization and Its Discontents* (1930), he proposes that there are two primary forces in human nature: the life instinct (**Eros**, or libido) and the death instinct (**Thanatos**, or aggression). Because many of our instincts in their most primitive forms are selfish or inappropriate, they must be turned inward and either repressed or sublimated into other purposes. **Repression** can lead to various neuroses. But **sublimation** can mean that instinctual desires are redirected into more socially acceptable expressions. Thanatos, the death instinct, can result in violence and destruction in its negative expression (repression), but in its positive expression (sublimation) is transformed into competition and protection. Eros can lead to lust and gluttony in its negative expression, but in its positive expression is transformed into social bonding and creativity. Freud believed that all the greatest accomplishments of modern civilization—from scientific discoveries to forms of government and exquisite works of art—were a result of the sublimation of both instincts. Of course, he contends, this is also why we are all somewhat discontented and why living in society is such an uneasy bargain. We can never fully satisfy our deepest desires, so we trade them for a safer, more constructive existence together in a community.

Freud is more often associated with other famous psychologists of his time, such as Alfred Adler and Carl Jung, than with other famous sociologists, such as Marx, Weber, and Durkheim. But like these classical sociologists Freud was concerned with the large-scale social changes of the Industrial Revolution and their effect on the individual. When he discussed discontent he was describing some of the same problems of modern life that were referred to by Marx as alienation, by Weber as disenchantment, and by Durkheim as anomie. Freud was also interested in the development of the self and, much like later social psychologists, saw this as the result of social processes.

During the span of his career Freud became an internationally known figure. His work, in many ways, was threatening to the existing political, social, and moral climate of his times. He had emerged from a Victorian period when references to human sexuality were not a subject for public discussion, and he lived and worked under totalitarian and fascist regimes in which independent thinking was not always encouraged. In 1938, during the Nazi invasion, he was forced to leave Austria. His sisters were even more unfortunate; they perished in the German death camps. Freud emigrated to London, where he died the next year, leaving a legacy that continues to inspire and infuriate.

Eros in Freudian psychology, the drive or instinct that desires productivity and construction

Thanatos in Freudian psychology, the drive or instinct toward aggression or destruction

repression the process that causes unwanted or taboo desires to return via tics, dreams, slips of the tongue, and neuroses, according to Freud

sublimation the process in which socially unacceptable desires are healthily channeled into socially acceptable expressions, according to Freud

paradigm a set of assumptions, theories, and perspectives that make up a way of understanding social reality

Modern Schools of Thought

As the twentieth century dawned and the careers of theorists like Weber and Freud matured, political, cultural, and academic power began to shift from Europe to America. As manifested by the waves of emigrants leaving the Old World for the New, America was seen as the land of opportunity, both material and intellectual. So it was in the twentieth century, and increasingly in the United States, that the discipline of sociology matured and began to coalesce into distinctive schools of thought.

Three major theoretical **paradigms** dominated twentieth-century sociology: structural functionalism, social conflict theory, and symbolic interactionism. These paradigms are like theoretical umbrellas: their explanatory powers are meant to be quite broad. Although none can satisfactorily explain the full range of social phenomena, each one does give us some answers we can't find in the other two. Since these paradigms are so important to the discipline of sociology, we will be covering them in depth in this chapter,

structural functionalism a paradigm that begins with the assumption that society is a unified whole that functions because of the contributions of its separate structures

structure a social institution that is relatively stable over time and that meets the needs of society by performing functions necessary to maintain social order and stability

dysfunction a disturbance to or undesirable consequence of some aspect of the social system

manifest functions the obvious, intended functions of a social structure for the social system

latent functions the less obvious, perhaps unintended functions of a social structure

and a table that summarizes the major paradigms and gives examples of their application is included on page 60. Then, beginning with Chapter 4 each additional chapter in this text includes a "Theory in the Real World" table. These tables provide quick reference for theoretical applications and offer examples of how each of the three major sociological paradigms relates to the chapter's specific topics.

Structural Functionalism

Structural functionalism, or functionalist theory, has been very influential in the history of sociology and at times has been the dominant theoretical perspective in the discipline.

ORIGINS The origins of structural functionalism lie in the thinking of three early sociologists—Auguste Comte, Herbert Spencer, and Emile Durkheim—each of whom conceived of society as a unified whole that functioned because of the contributions of its separate parts. Comte originally proposed that society could and should be studied as a whole. Spencer agreed—and added that society was an organism much like the human body; as there was a discipline of biology to study living organisms, so should there be a discipline of sociology to study social organisms. Durkheim concurred with Spencer and Comte, arguing for the study of society *sui generis*—as an object in and of itself. These ideas, which seem simple from our contemporary perspective, were in many ways revolutionary—crucial steps toward viewing society itself as something worthy of scientific study.

TENETS The main principles of the functionalist paradigm are these:

1. Society is a stable, ordered system of interrelated parts or structures.

2. Each structure has a function that contributes to the continued stability or equilibrium of the whole.
   Structures are identified as social institutions like the family, the educational system, politics, and the economy; Durkheim, for example, was especially interested in religion as a social structure. Structures meet the needs of society by

performing different functions, and every function is necessary to maintain social order and stability. Any disorganization or **dysfunction** in a structure must lead to change and to a new equilibrium, because if one structure is transformed, the others must adjust. For example, if families fail to discipline their children, schools, churches, and the courts must take up the slack.

It may seem contradictory that a theory so concerned with order and stability would emerge in a discipline that itself arose in the nineteenth century, a period of rapid social change. But it is important to remember that these early theorists lived in a world in which change had previously occurred much more slowly and that one response to rapid social change is to try to understand what had come before—stability, order, and equilibrium. It is absolutely appropriate, then, for a discipline that claims to study society to focus on stability and order as well as change and disorder.

OFFSHOOTS Functionalism's strong appeal lies in its ability to bring order to a potentially disorderly social world. This made it a dominant theoretical perspective for much of the nineteenth century and updated by such modern American functionalists as Talcott Parsons and Neil Smelser well into the twentieth. Parsons, for example, specified the types of functions that social structures might fulfill:

1. adaptation to the environment—the socialization of children, for example, by family, schools, and other social institutions

2. realization of goals—the opportunity for success, for example, provided by schools

3. social cohesion—people coming together through, for example, shared morals or religious values

4. the maintenance of cultural patterns—the passing along of traditions, norms, and values in families, schools, and religious communities

Another modern American functionalist, Robert Merton, delineated the theory even further, identifying "manifest" and "latent" functions for different social structures: **manifest functions** are the obvious, intended functions of a social structure, while **latent functions** are the less obvious, perhaps unintended functions. For example, the manifest functions of education are to prepare future members of society by teaching them how to read and write and by instructing them on society's system of norms, values, and laws. However, education has a latent function as well, which is to keep kids busy and out of trouble eight hours a day, five days a week, for twelve years (or longer). Do not doubt that this is also an important contribution to social order!

Gender, Parenting, and Theory

How can seemingly abstract sociological theories apply to our everyday experiences in personal relationships? There are, in fact, many ways. Take, for instance, the work of Nancy Chodorow, who was trained in Freudian theory as well as feminist social science. Her book *The Reproduction of Mothering* (1978) applies Freud's insights to the problem of gender inequality in parenting.

In the Freudian psychoanalytic account of gender, girls develop female identities by seeing themselves as similar to their primary caregiver: their mother. Boys develop male identities through their forced separation from the mother. In other words, girls learn how to be women by emulating the person with whom they form their primary caregiving bond; boys learn how to be men by detaching from and rejecting that person. Hence, boys (and men) tend to reject all the qualities associated with femaleness—including those linked to mothering. This makes it difficult for men to become involved, active parents to their own babies, whether they are boys or girls. As Chodorow states, "Women come to mother because they have been mothered by women. By contrast, that men are mothered by women reduces their parenting capacities" (p. 211). Chodorow's work can help explain the difficulties many couples have sharing parental duties equally. She argues that, according to psychoanalytic theory, men will not be able to parent properly until boys have been properly parented by men. Once men become active, involved parents, both boys and girls will benefit. Furthermore, she believes that eventually society will become less sexist overall, allowing boys and girls, men and women to explore their interests and potential without the constraints of traditional sex-role expectations.

But how will this transformation occur? By preparing for and demanding the active involvement of fathers as well as mothers in their babies' lives. Yes, that means you, male readers! Many of you will someday be fathers, and perhaps some of you already are. You can and should plan to be an active, involved nurturer and caregiver for your baby—on a daily basis, not just on weekends or when "Mom needs a day off." Take responsibility for every aspect of your child's daily needs. Plan your schedule and negotiate with your employer so that you can take the necessary time off. Challenge those who, when they see you pushing the stroller all by yourself, say, "Babysitting today, eh?" As a father, your role should not be to "help" the baby's mother; you should be an equal partner. Not only will you reap great personal rewards, but—according to psychoanalytic theory—you will make your baby's life better as well. And you will contribute to social change while you're at it. What could be more enticing?

Talcott Parsons (1902–1979)   **Robert Merton (1910–2003)**

While the influence of functionalism waned in the late twentieth century, it did not die out. A "neofunctionalist" movement, begun in the 1980s and 1990s, attempts to "reconstruct" functionalist theories so that the connection to classical sociological theory (and Comte, Spencer, and Durkheim) remains relevant in a rapidly changing world. Theorists such as Neal Smelser (1985) and Jeffrey Alexander (1988) (Alexander and Smelser 1998) have attempted to modify functionalist theory to better incorporate problems like racial and ethnic identity in a diverse society.

CRITIQUES Functionalism, generally preoccupied with stability, takes the position that only dysfunction can create social change. This conservative bias is part of a larger problem with functionalism, in that it provides no insight into any social processes; it is a static rather than a dynamic model of society. It seems to have no interest in explaining human action—no apparent interest in the individual at all, except as she is integrated into society by social institutions.

Functionalism's explanations of social inequality are especially unsatisfying. The theory argues that if things like poverty, racism, and sexism exist, then they must serve a function for society; they must be necessary and inevitable. This view is problematic for many social scientists and social actors alike. Sociologist Herbert Gans, in a critical essay, reviews the functions of poverty for society. The poor, for example, do our "dirty work," filling the menial, low-wage jobs that are necessary to keep society running smoothly but that the nonpoor refuse to do. The poor provide a market for used and off-price goods and keep thrift stores and social welfare agencies in business. They have symbolic value as well, allowing the nonpoor to feel compassion toward the "deserving" poor as well as feeling threatened by the "undeserving" poor, who are often seen as dangerous

> **conflict theory** a paradigm that sees social conflict as the basis of society and social change and emphasizes a materialist view of society, a critical view of the status quo, and a dynamic model of historical change

social deviants (1971). Ultimately, the circular reasoning that characterizes functionalist thought turns out to be its biggest problem: the mere persistence of an institution should not be seen as an adequate explanation for its existence.

ADVANTAGES In a more positive vein, the advantages of functionalism include its broad reach and inclusion of all social institutions. Functionalism attempts to provide a universal social theory—a way of explaining everything in society in one comprehensive model. Were it not for some of the volcanic social upheavals of recent history (such as the civil rights, antiwar, and women's liberation movements, not easily explained using this model), functionalist theory might still reign supreme in American sociology.

Conflict Theory

Conflict theory, a catch-all phrase encompassing several theoretical strands that all emphasize social conflict as the basis of society, answers some of the critiques of structural functionalism. Its roots are in the mid-nineteenth-century European intellectual scene, specifically in the ideas of Karl Marx. Sometimes, therefore, the terms *conflict theory* and *Marxism* are used interchangeably in the social sciences.

ORIGINS Karl Marx, the father of conflict theory, wished not only to describe the world but also to change it. In Marx's time, when the Industrial Revolution was bringing sweeping changes, distinct social and economic classes were forming (such as those we are now familiar with: lower, middle, and upper classes) in the new urban society. Marx saw the increasing economic power of industrial capitalism as the primary tool for the oppression of the poor, and he felt passionately about redressing these inequalities of power. He envisioned a kind of classless society, in which each person both contributed to and benefited from the public good. He summed up this idea in an often-quoted remark: "From each according to his ability, to each according to his need." Marx believed that if individuals could be freed from oppressive conditions, they would then be able to pursue higher interests such as art and education. But in order to achieve such a state, the oppressed must first recognize how the current system worked against them, maintaining the status quo, or existing state of affairs.

TENETS Conflict theory proposes that conflict and tension are basic facts of social life and suggests that people have disagreements over goals and values and are involved in struggles over both resources and power. The theory thus focuses on the processes of dominance, competition, upheaval, and social change. The main emphases:

1. a materialist view of society (focused on labor practices and economic reality)

2. a critical stance toward existing social arrangements

3. a dynamic model of historical change (in which the transformation of society is inevitable)

Marx maintained that economic productivity was related to other processes in society, including political and intellectual life. Because the bourgeoisie controlled the financial realm, they could also use their wealth and power to gain control over other parts of society. Many of the other major social institutions served to further reinforce the class structure, so that the state, education, religion, and even the family were organized to represent the interests of those in power.

To Marx, a kind of **ideology**, or belief system, permeated society: "the ruling ideas of each age have . . . been the ideas of the ruling class" (Marx and Engels 1962, p. 52). Thus, the values and beliefs that seemed to be widely held were actually a kind of justification that helped to rationalize and explain the status quo. Most people readily accepted the prevailing ideology, despite the fact that it failed to represent the reality of their lives. Marx referred to this acceptance as **false consciousness**, a condition of naïveté or denial of the truth that allowed for the perpetuation of the inequalities inherent in the class structure. For example, he is often quoted as saying, "Religion is the opiate of the masses." This is not a criticism of religion as much as it is a criticism of the use of religion by the ruling class to create false consciousness in the working class. Encouraged in their religiosity, the proletariat focus on the happiness waiting for them in the afterlife rather than on the deprivations they suffer in this world. Indeed, heaven is seen as a reward for patiently suffering those deprivations. How does this serve the interests of the ruling class? By keeping the working class from demanding better conditions in this life.

Marx argued that the only way to change the status quo was for the masses to attain what he referred to as **class consciousness**, or revolutionary consciousness. This can happen only when people recognize how society works and challenge those in power. He believed that when there was enough tension and conflict, it would eventually lead to social change. He was optimistic in assuming that a system based on economic exploitation essentially sowed the seeds of its own destruction. Marx proposed a **dialectical model** of historical or social change, whereby two extreme positions would eventually necessitate some kind of compromise between them: the resulting "middle ground" would mean that society had actually moved forward. Any existing social arrangement (called the **thesis**) would inevitably generate its opposite (**antithesis**), and the contradictions and conflicts between the two would lead to an altogether new social arrangement (**synthesis**).

OFFSHOOTS Marx's work has been reinterpreted and applied in various ways for more than a hundred years. Some of the most famous examples of Marxism became evident in the communist and socialist systems that developed as a result of his ideas. Some have since fallen (like the former Soviet Union and Eastern bloc countries), others have remained in place (Cuba, North Korea), and new social experiments incorporating aspects of Marxism may be yet to come. Of interest to us as students of sociology is how Marxist ideas have evolved within the greater intellectual community. Many strands of thinking have developed out of Marxism. W.E.B. DuBois, for example, applied Marxist ideas about class consciousness to the experience of racial inequality. African Americans, he argued, possessed what he called a **double consciousness**, meaning that they were entitled to rights and freedoms as Americans that they were denied as people of African heritage. This contradiction caused tension both for African Americans and for the larger society.

ideology a system of beliefs, attitudes, and values that directs a society and reproduces the status quo of the bourgeoisie

false consciousness a denial of the truth on the part of the oppressed when they fail to recognize the interests of the ruling class in their ideology

class consciousness the recognition of social inequality on the part of the oppressed, leading to revolutionary action

dialectical model Marx's model of historical change, whereby two extreme positions come into conflict and create some new third thing between them

thesis the existing social arrangements in a dialectical model

antithesis the opposition to the existing arrangements in a dialectical model

synthesis the new social system created out of the conflict between thesis and antithesis in a dialectical model

double consciousness W.E.B. DuBois's term for the conflict felt by and about African Americans, who were both American (and hence entitled to rights and freedoms) and African (and hence subject to prejudices and discrimination) at the same time

elites those in power in a society

critical theory a contemporary form of conflict theory that criticizes many different systems and ideologies of domination and oppression

Other sociologists inspired by conflict theory included C. Wright Mills, who was interested in the role of **elites** (those in power) in society. Additional conflict-inspired sociological concepts include world-systems theory (Wallerstein 1974/1997), which examines global inequality and the exploitation of poor nations by wealthy nations, and Theda Skocpol's work on political upheaval across different nations (1979).

One of the most widely adopted forms of modern Marxism is called **critical theory** (also sometimes referred to as the Frankfurt School or neo-Marxism). From the 1930s to the 1960s, critical theory was arguably at the cutting edge of social theory. Critical theorists were among the first to see the importance of mass communications and popular

W.E.B. DuBois: Addressing Racial Inequality in Theory and Praxis

William Edward Burghardt (W.E.B. DuBois) was one of the most influential African American leaders of the early twentieth century and a notable pioneer in the sociology of race relations. DuBois was, to his admirers, a brilliant and prolific scholar and a tireless defender of freedom, justice, and equality. After becoming the first African American to earn a PhD from Harvard University, he did groundbreaking research on the history of the slave trade, post–Civil War reconstruction, the problems of urban ghetto life, and the nature of black American society; his most influential ideas are featured in such books as *The Souls of Black Folk* (1903), *The Negro* (1915), *The Gift of Black Folk* (1924), *Black Folk: Then and Now* (1939), and *Dusk of Dawn* (1940).

DuBois was so prolific that it is often said that all subsequent studies of race and racial inequality in America depend to some degree on his work. He was a forerunner in the civil rights, black nationalism, and Pan-African movements; and he was a founding member, in 1909, of the National Association for the Advancement of Colored People (NAACP), an organization committed to the cause of ending racism and injustice. DuBois was recognized by Dr. Martin Luther King Jr., who called him a gifted seeker of social truths and a scholar who aspired to fill the immense void that existed in the study of black people. After a lifetime of groundbreaking scholarship and social activism, though, DuBois finally grew disillusioned with the United States. In 1961, he moved to Ghana, Africa, where he lived and (two years later, at age ninety-five) died, an expatriate in self-imposed exile.

Throughout his life, as a result of his deepening desire to affect social change, DuBois was involved in various forms of social activism. He continued to serve as director of publicity and research for the NAACP and editor of its magazine *Crisis* until 1934. In addition, he wrote weekly columns for a variety of newspapers, delivered thousands of lectures across the country, and took part in the Harlem Renaissance (an artistic movement of the 1920s and 30s) as a poet and playwright. His ideas were widely disseminated, influencing the generations of black Americans who followed. Less than one year after his death, the Civil Rights Act of 1964 made it illegal to discriminate against anyone based on race, color, religion, sex, or national origin.

While it is unlikely that any of us will have the same broad, sweeping impact on our society that DuBois did, it is clear that many of us will follow in his footsteps in some way. If you study race or inequality as part of your major (or in graduate school), you can do so in part because DuBois made it possible. Your participation in any movement for civil rights or social liberation builds on his work as a scholar

W.E.B. DuBois (1868–1963)
DuBois called the United States a country of "magnificent possibilities" but one that was "selling its birthright." He praised America for its noble souls and generous people and was grateful for the education the country provided him, but he also pointed out its ongoing history of injustices, crimes, and mistakes.

and an activist. Whether you join your university's chapter of MEChA (Movimiento Estudiantil Chicano de Aztlan), the Black Student Union, the Asian American Association, the Feminist Society, or the Diversity Club, you are walking on a pathway that was built, in part, by DuBois's efforts. And if you become an activist, working to end discrimination against the disabled or to stop hate crimes against gays and lesbians, you are doing what DuBois hoped we would all do: use our academic knowledge in the fight against inequality, exploitation, and discrimination. According to DuBois, this was the key to a peaceful society. What will your contribution be?

Martin Luther King Jr. at the 1963 March on Washington

culture as powerful ideological tools in capitalist societies. They coined the term *culture industries* to refer to these increasingly important social institutions (Adorno and Horkheimer 1979). They also criticized the growing consumerism associated with the spread of capitalism, believing that this could ultimately lead to a decline in personal freedom and the decay of democracy (Marcuse 1964/1991). Critical theory influenced several generations of radical (leftist) thinkers throughout Europe and the United States, inspiring the cultural studies movement (see Chapter 4) and the postmodernists (see p. 59), who later assumed the cutting edge of social theory in the 1980s and 90s (Habermas 1984, 1987). Two other modern perspectives, feminism and critical race theory, take conflict theory's insights on economic inequality and adapt them to the study of contemporary inequalities of gender and race, respectively (Crenshaw et al. 1996; Matsuda et al. 1993). Thus, despite Marx's single-minded focus on economic exploitation and transformation, his ideas have helped inspire other theorists of inequality in ways he might not have been able to imagine.

CRITIQUES Conflict theory stands in sharp contrast to structural functionalism. Conflict theory argues that just because some social arrangement exists does not mean that it is necessarily beneficial for society; it may merely represent the interests of those in power. The theory challenges the status quo and emphasizes the need for social upheaval and change. In focusing on tension and conflict, however, it can often ignore those parts of society that are truly orderly, stable, and enduring. Although society certainly has its share of disagreements and competition, which threaten to break it apart, there are also shared values and common beliefs that hold it together. Conflict theory can be criticized for overlooking these less controversial dimensions of social reality.

ADVANTAGES One of Marx's great contributions to the social sciences is the principle of **praxis**, or practical action: intellectuals, he felt, should not only theorize about social change, they should act on what they believed. Indeed Marxist ideas have been important in achieving change through many of the social movements of the twentieth century, including the civil rights, antiwar, women's rights, gay rights, animal rights, environmental, and multicultural movements. Without these groups rising up to protest the status quo, we might never have addressed some of the century's social problems. Conflict theory is useful in understanding not only macro-level social issues (like systematic discrimination against minority groups) but also micro-level personal interactions (like those between bosses and employees).

Symbolic Interactionism

Sociology's third major paradigm, **symbolic interactionism**, has proved the most influential of the twentieth century. It is America's unique contribution to the discipline and an answer to many of the criticisms of other paradigms. It helps explain both our individual personalities and the ways in which we are all linked together; it allows us to understand the processes by which social order and social change are constructed. As a theoretical perspective, it is vital, versatile, and evolving.

ORIGINS Symbolic interactionism is derived largely from the teachings of George Herbert Mead, a professor at the University of Chicago in the 1910s and 20s. At that time the burgeoning Sociology Department at Chicago was led by Albion Small, a philosopher by training. There were very few sociology departments in the country then, which meant that Small had to start from scratch. He recruited faculty from various Eastern colleges for the fledgling department, which grew to include such influential sociologists as Robert Park, W. I. Thomas, Charles Horton Cooley, and later Mead and Herbert Blumer. Together they developed one of the most influential branches of sociology in the twentieth century, called the Chicago School. Most of the early appointments that Small made were male professors from theological and philosophical backgrounds. However, the department's development was also profoundly shaped by women sociologists, including Jane Addams, who worked for the rights of the immigrant poor and for women's suffrage, and by pioneering black sociologist W.E.B. DuBois, who saw sociology as a tool to help understand and remedy racial prejudice. Both Addams and DuBois took conflict-inspired ideas about the problem of social inequality and used symbolic interactionist-inspired, street-level approaches to solving it.

Chicago was in many ways a "frontier" city for the twentieth century; transformed rapidly by industrialization, immigration, and ethnic diversity, the city became a laboratory for a new type of sociology. Chicago School sociology is methodologically and theoretically different from what had come before in Europe and America. Instead of doing comparative and historical work, the Chicagoans went

George Herbert Mead (1863–1931)

into the field to perform interviews and collect data. They focused on social action and everyday interactions (such as race relations in urban neighborhoods) as the building blocks of social phenomena.

While the Chicago School is the acknowledged home of symbolic interactionism, the theory's roots can also be traced to Weber's concept of *verstehen* ("empathetic understanding") and to the philosophical perspective called **pragmatism**. One of America's most prominent pragmatists was William James (1842–1910), Harvard professor and "Renaissance man" of the late 1800s and early 1900s. James's interests spanned art, anatomy, medicine, law, education, theology, philosophy, and psychology; he also traveled extensively and was acquainted with some of the most influential scholars of the time. To James pragmatism meant seeking the truth of an idea by evaluating its usefulness in everyday life: in other words, if it works, it's true! He thought that living in the world involved making practical adaptations to whatever we encountered; if those adaptations made our lives run more smoothly, then the ideas behind them must be both useful and true. James's ideas inspired educational psychologist and philosopher John Dewey (1859–1952), who also grappled with pragmatism's main questions: How do we adapt to our environments? How do we acquire the knowledge that allows us to act in our everyday lives? Charles Darwin's theory of natural selection also focused on how organisms adapted to their environments. But while Darwin proposed that this adaptation takes place over generations and generations, pragmatists implied that the process of adaptation was essentially immediate and that it involved conscious thought.

George Herbert Mead pulled these ideas (and others, too) together into a theory meant to address questions about the relationship between thought and action, the individual and society, a theory that focused on micro-level interactions. After his death in 1931, his student Herbert Blumer gave Mead's theory a name: symbolic interactionism.

Mead was born in South Hadley, Massachusetts, in 1863. His father, a professor of theology at Oberlin College, died when George was a teenager, and his widowed mother eventually became president of Mount Holyoke College. Mead attended college at Oberlin and Harvard and did his graduate studies in psychology at the Universities of Leipzig and Berlin in Germany. Before he became a full-time professor of psychology at the University of Michigan and later the University of Chicago, Mead waited tables and did railroad surveying and construction work. He was also a tutor to William James's family in Cambridge, Massachusetts; since his later theories were influenced by James, we can only wonder exactly who was tutoring whom in this arrangement!

Mead was inspired by John Dewey and Charles Darwin, as well as James, to identify a psychology that took the social into account as well as the individual and to explain humans' practical adaptations to their environment. Also, his Protestant upbringing and long association with progressive Oberlin (the first college in the United States to admit women) instilled in him a desire to advance social understanding. As a psychologist, then, he was uniquely positioned to bridge the gap between sociology and psychology and to address the links between the individual and society.

For Mead both human development and the meanings we assign to everyday objects and events are fundamentally social processes—they require the interaction of multiple individuals. And what is crucial to the development of self and society is language, the means by which we communicate with one another. For Mead there is no mind without language, and language itself is a product of social interactions (Mead 1934, pp. 191–92). Here, according to symbolic interactionism, is the essential connection between the individual and the social.

According to Mead the most important human behaviors consist of linguistic "gestures," such as words and facial expressions. People have developed the ability to engage in conversation using these gestures; further, both society and individual selves are constructed through this kind of symbolic communication. Mead argued that we use language to "name ourselves, think about ourselves, talk to ourselves, and feel proud or ashamed of ourselves" and that "we can act toward ourselves in all the ways we can act toward others" (Hewitt 2000, p. 10). He was curious about how the mind developed but did not believe that it developed separately from its social environment. For Mead, then, society and self were created through communicative acts like speech and gestures; the individual personality was shaped by society, and vice versa.

Herbert Blumer's work continued where Mead's had left off. While completing his master's degree Blumer played football for the University of Missouri Tigers, and during the 1920s and 1930s he maintained

> **pragmatism** a theoretical perspective that assumes organisms (including humans) make practical adaptations to their environments. Humans do this through cognition, interpretation, and interaction

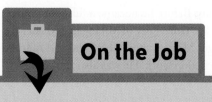

On the Job

In the Footsteps of Jane Addams

Jane Addams was a pioneer in the field of sociology, having studied not only the effects of the Industrial Revolution on the poor and immigrants but also the widely misunderstood role of women in society. She was one of the first proponents of applied sociology, which meant that she did not just theorize about the most pressing problems of her day but addressed them through hands-on activities in the very communities that were the subject of her research. In this way, she brought her training and expertise to the job of establishing and running the community center for which she is best known, Hull House. The idea had come to her on a trip to England, when she had visited a settlement house in the slums of London that was helping to ease the suffering of women, children, and immigrants. She was struck by the need to establish a similar house in the United States that would provide for the needs of the poor.

Hull House opened in Chicago in 1889. It offered medical care, legal advice, and child care to the poor and new immigrants, as well as classes in English, vocational skills, and the arts. A mere two years later, it was serving over two thousand people every week. This was one of the first, and most successful, models of social reform, bringing support and resources into the communities where they were most needed. It became an important meeting place for intellectuals, many of them from the University of Chicago. Addams published several books on the subject, including *Hull-House Maps and Papers* (1895) and her popular autobiography, *Twenty Years at Hull House* (1910). Hull House developed into an internationally renowned institution, as Addams also gained in public reputation.

Because she is so readily identified with her role as a social worker at Hull House, many of Jane Addams's other accomplishments are often overlooked. She sought social reforms in such areas as housing, sanitation, workers' unions and wages, industrial safety, child labor laws, schooling, and juvenile justice. She was an early American feminist, fighting for women's suffrage and against gender discrimination, and was a founder of the American Civil Liberties Union

Jane Addams (1860–1935)
"I do not believe that women are better than men. We have not wrecked railroads, nor corrupted legislature, nor done many unholy things that men have done; but then we must remember that we have not had the chance."

(ACLU) and, along with W.E.B. DuBois, the NAACP. Addams believed that many social problems could be solved by allowing women and ethnic minorities to participate more freely in all spheres of social life, and she proved this by her own example. As an active member of the Sociology Department at the University of Chicago, she was one of a handful of women there who made important intellectual contributions to the Chicago School. And for her work as an antiwar activist and founding president of the Women's International League for Peace and Freedom, she became the first American woman to receive the Nobel Peace Prize.

Hull House is still in operation today—as a museum and event center on the University of Illinois, Chicago campus—and hosts Tuesday lunch discussions that feature free soup for all and open debate about current social and political issues. Addams's ideals have inspired activists all over the world, in community centers, antipoverty workshops, and mutual-aid societies. One excellent example is the Hmong Cultural Center in St. Paul, Minnesota. The Hmong, a Southeast Asian ethnic group, were forced to flee the deadly Communist regimes in Cambodia and Laos in the aftermath of the Vietnam War (1974), having assisted the United States as anticommunist guerrilla fighters. Many came to the United States and settled in the upper Midwest with no proficiency in English, employment qualifications, or other practical skills necessary for life in the industrialized First World. This led to poverty, isolation, and serious cultural conflicts between Hmong immigrants and their neighbors. The Hmong Cultural Center in St. Paul provides the services families need to adjust to life in the United States (language lessons, job skills, and citizenship classes) and teaches Hmong history, culture, and religious practices to people (like doctors and police officers) who work in predominantly Hmong neighborhoods. Under the leadership of executive director Txong Pao Lee, the center's goals are to promote the personal development of Hmong immigrants and to enhance cross-cultural understanding in support of a multicultural society.

When it comes to taking sociological insights into the real world and making them work, Jane Addams set high standards for us to follow. People like the staff and volunteers at the Hmong Cultural Center are living up to these standards. And many of the careers that sociology majors tend to enter also embody the spirit of Addams's legacy. Sociology majors often find themselves drawn to work in social welfare, education, counseling, community organizing, the judicial system, and other "helping" professions. If you become a teacher, a social worker, a juvenile probation officer, a peace activist, a doctor at a free clinic, or a lawyer with a public interest group, you will be putting sociology to work in the tradition of Addams and the women and men of Hull House. Indeed, it is possible that you are doing such work right now, either as a paid employee or as a volunteer at a place like the Hmong Cultural Center. You may never win a Nobel Prize, but your efforts will link you to someone who did. Doing applied sociology, as Jane Addams proved, means that your job can make a difference.

Hmong Cultural Center in St. Paul, Minnesota The center provides essential services for Minneapolis's large Hmong community and offers educational opportunities for non-Hmong to learn about the culture of their Hmong friends and neighbors. These dolls from the center (above) are dressed in traditional Hmong clothing.

dramaturgy a theoretical paradigm that uses the metaphor of the theater to understand how individuals present themselves to others

ethnomethodology the study of "folk methods," or everyday interactions, that must be uncovered rather than studied directly

conversation analysis a sociological approach that looks at how we create meaning in naturally occurring conversation, often by taping conversations and examining them

dual careers as a sociology professor and a professional football player for the former Chicago Cardinals. On Mondays he would often come to class wrapped in bandages after a tough Sunday game. What he did off the gridiron, however, was provide a compelling exposition of Mead's ideas and a clear statement of the fundamentals of symbolic interactionism. Blumer also made a Chicago School appeal for researchers to get "down and dirty" with the dynamics of social life.

Mead and Blumer became the somewhat unwitting founders of a much larger theoretical perspective than they had ever imagined. Mead's death made Blumer into symbolic interactionism's official spokesperson, and his long career at the University of Chicago and later at UC Berkeley meant that many graduate students, among them Erving Goffman and Harvey Sacks, were trained in the "Blumerian" version of symbolic interactionism. When Blumer died in 1986, innovators were able to extend the field in a variety of ways, allowing new perspectives to come under the umbrella of symbolic interactionism.

TENETS For symbolic interactionists society is produced and reproduced through our interactions with each other by means of language and our interpretations of that language. Symbolic interactionism sees face-to-face interaction as the building block of everything else in society, because it is through interaction that we create a meaningful social reality. Here are the three basic tenets of symbolic interactionism, as laid out by Blumer in 1969 (p. 2):

1. We act toward things on the basis of their meanings. For example, a tree can provide a shady place to rest, or it can be an obstacle to building a road or home; each of these meanings suggests a different set of actions, and this is as true for physical objects like trees as it is for people (like mothers or cops), institutions (church or school), beliefs (honesty or equality), or any social activity.

2. Meanings are not inherent; rather, they are negotiated through interaction with others. That is, whether the tree is an obstacle or an oasis is not an intrinsic quality of the tree itself but rather something that people must hash out themselves. The same tree can mean one thing to one person and something else to another.

3. Meanings can change or be modified through interaction. For example, the contractor who sees the tree as an obstacle might be persuaded to spare it by the neighbor. Now the tree is something to build around rather than bulldoze.

Although symbolic interactionism is focused on how self and society develop through interaction with others, it is useful in explaining and analyzing a wide variety of specific social issues, from inequalities of race and gender to the group dynamics of families or coworkers.

OFFSHOOTS Symbolic interactionism opened the door for innovative sociologies that focus on social acts (like face-to-face interaction) rather than social facts (like vast bureaucratic institutions). For example, Marjorie DeVault studied cooking and serving meals (1991/1994), and Sharon Zukin analyzed shopping (2004); both studies show how large-scale social structures like the family and the economy are produced at the ground level by the social interactions of family cooks and mall shoppers.

Erving Goffman carried symbolic interactionist conceptions of the self forward in a seemingly radical way, indicating that the self is essentially "on loan" to us from society; it is created through interaction with others and hence ever-changing. For example, you may want to make a different kind of impression on a first date than you do on a job interview or when you face an opponent in a game of poker. Goffman used the theatrical metaphor of **dramaturgy** to describe the ways in which we engage in presenting ourselves to others; in this way he elaborated on Mead's ideas in a specific fashion, utilizing a wide range of data to help support what for Mead had been a purely theoretical construct.

Harold Garfinkel, the founder of **ethnomethodology** (the study of "folk methods," or everyday analysis of interaction), maintains that as members of society we must acquire the necessary knowledge and skills to act practically in our everyday lives. He argues that much of this knowledge remains in the background, "seen but unnoticed," and that we assume others to have the same knowledge we do as we interact with them. These assumptions allow us to make meaning out of even seemingly troublesome events; but they also can be quite precarious, and there is a good deal of work required to maintain them, even as we are unaware that we are doing so.

Conversation analysis, pioneered by sociologists at UCLA, is also related to symbolic interactionism. It is based on the ethnomethodological idea that as everyday actors we are constantly analyzing and giving meaning to our social world (Schegloff 1986, 1999; Clayman 2002). Conversation analysts are convinced that the best place to look for the social processes of meaning-production is in naturally occurring conversation and that the best way to get at the meanings an everyday actor gives to the things others say and do is to look closely at what he says and does next. Conversation analysts therefore use highly technical methods to scrutinize each conversational turn closely, operating on the assumption that any larger social phenomenon is constructed step-by-step through interaction.

During the second half of the twentieth century, the scope of symbolic interactionism widened, its topics multiplied, and its theoretical linkages became more varied. In fact, Gary Fine argues that "symbolic interactionism . . . has a diversity that may vitiate [eliminate] its center" (1993, p. 65). In other words symbolic interactionism is expanding so fast that it may soon erupt into something else entirely.

DATA WORKSHOP
ANALYZING MASS MEDIA AND POPULAR CULTURE
Theories of Celebrity Gossip

Perezhilton.com is consistently rated as one of the most frequently visited websites among college students. Written and operated by blogger Mario Lavandeira, Perezhilton.com has been exposing the real and rumored doings of celebrities since 2005, posting several brief blurbs each day that chronicle celebrity activities. These entries are accompanied by paparazzi photos and snide commentary by both Lavandeira himself and throngs of readers who post their own observations and criticisms, humorous and serious.

Lavandeira's website is part of a new breed of celebrity gossip outlets, including TMZ.com and WWTDD.com, among others. These sites can almost instantly consolidate and present information that used to take at least a week to appear in printed gossip magazines like *People* or *Us*. They can also provide more explicit editorial commentary than the print magazines can. For example, while *People* might print a picture of Madonna without her husband and speculate that they are breaking up, WWTDD.com

Blogger Mario Lavandeira, a.k.a. Perez Hilton

can print the same picture with the following remarks (on July 28, 2008):

> Madonna left the Kabala center in New York this weekend with her daughter Lourdes, and I think we're close enough by now for me to admit she scares the ever living [****] out of me. From the neck up she looks like the puppet from Saw. Is it any wonder Guy Richie wants to move on? There's no way she's even healthy enough to have sex . . .

It gets worse, but we can't print the rest in a "family" textbook! Finally, these sites allow for almost immediate feedback from and discussion among far-flung readers, something not possible in the pre-internet gossip magazine days.

Other staple entries on celebrity gossip sites include photos of celebrities combined with evaluative commentary about their bodies, outfits, mates, children, and other aspects of their beings and behaviors. While many criticize such information as mean, stupid, and shallow, one doesn't have to enjoy celebrity gossip to see its sociological relevance. And items from celebrity gossip blogs often end up in the mainstream news—in the summer of 2007 Lavandeira "broke a story" on the death of Cuban president Fidel Castro that was picked up by the conventional media and broadcast widely. The story turned out to be untrue—but the incident speaks to the influence of such blogs on our understanding of what constitutes news. And this reinforces the fact that just about every social phenomenon, including celebrity gossip blogs, is worthy of sociological analysis and theoretical application.

In this Data Workshop we'd like you to immerse yourself in the celebrity gossip blog of your choice. Pick five entries—scrutinize the pictures, read the headlines and text carefully, and review the reader comments as well. Now ask yourself the following questions from each of sociology's three major theoretical perspectives:

1. Structural Functionalist Theory
What is the function (or functions) of celebrity gossip blogs for society? What purpose(s) do they serve, and how do they help society maintain stability and order? Are there manifest and latent functions of celebrity gossip blogs? And are there any dysfunctions built into such publications?

2. Social Conflict Theory
What forms of inequality are revealed in celebrity gossip blogs? In particular, what do celebrity gossip blogs have to say about gender, race, and class inequalities? Who suffers and who benefits from the publication of celebrity gossip blogs?

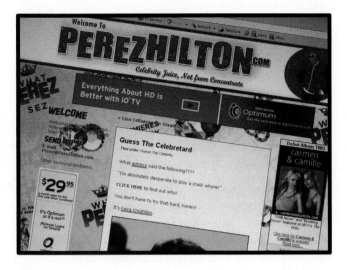

Gary Fine sums up the critiques in this way: symbolic interactionism is "apolitical (and hence, supportive of the status quo), unscientific (hence, little more than tenured journalism), hostile to the classical questions of macrosociology (hence, limited to social psychology), and astructural (hence, fundamentally nonsociological)" (1993, p. 65). These critiques argue that the scope of symbolic interactionism is limited, that it cannot properly address the most important sociological issues, and that its authority is restricted to the study of face-to-face interaction. Each of these critiques has been answered by defenders of symbolic interactionism over the years; ultimately, though, some of the critics have begun to see the usefulness of an interactionist perspective and have even begun incorporating it into more macro work.

3. Symbolic Interactionist Theory
What do celebrity gossip blogs mean to society as a whole? What do they mean to individual members of society? Can they have different meanings for different individuals or groups of individuals? How do those meanings get constructed in interaction? And how do celebrity gossip blogs shape and influence our everyday lives?

Make sure you can explain your answers to each of these questions, and complete one of the following two options, as directed by your instructor.

- *Option 1 (informal)*: Answer each of the three sets of questions above, and prepare some written notes that you can refer to in class. Discuss your answers with other students in small groups.

- *Option 2 (formal)*: Answer each of the three sets of questions above in a three-page essay explaining your positions. You may want to include snippets from your chosen celebrity gossip blog to illustrate your points.

CRITIQUES As a relative newcomer to the field of social theory, symbolic interactionism was dubbed "the loyal opposition" (Mullins 1973) by those who saw it solely as a reaction to the more dominant macrosociological theories (functionalism and conflict theory) that preceded it. Criticisms of symbolic interactionism proceed from this standpoint: that it must remain merely a supplement, rather than a competitor, to the more macrosocial theories because it doesn't take up the same questions that those more traditional perspectives do.

ADVANTAGES Symbolic interactionism has been integrated relatively seamlessly into sociology, and its fundamental precepts are widely accepted. Symbolic interactionism proposes that social facts exist only because we create and re-create them through our interactions; this gives it wide explanatory power and a versatility that allows it to address any sociological issue.

One of the critiques of symbolic interactionism noted above is that it may be "astructural"; but interactionism does not refute the power of social structure to shape an actor's interpretive choices (see Chin and Phillips [2004] on social class and children's summer-school experiences, or Stacy Burns [2004] on judges' decision-making processes in cases involving uninsured defendants and the "deep pockets" of wealthy insurance companies). Another critique is that it is unscientific, without a systematic method for examining the social world—this could not be further from the truth; sociological methods in the interactionist tradition such as ethnography and conversation analysis are data rich, technically complex, and empirically well grounded (Schegloff 1999; J. Katz 1997). Interactionism sees the social world as subject to empirical description and analysis just as other scientific paradigms do. Even in the hotly contested micro-versus-macro debate, a kind of détente has been established, recognizing that all levels of analysis are necessary for sociological understanding and that interactionist theories and methods are critical for a full picture of social life to arise.

As society changes, so must the discipline that studies it, and symbolic interactionism has invigorated sociology in ways that are linked to the past and looking toward the future. It is "the only perspective that assumes an active, expressive model of the human actor and that treats the individual and the social at the same level of analysis" (O'Brien and Kollock 1997, p. 39). Therein lie its power and its appeal.

DATA WORKSHOP

ANALYZING EVERYDAY LIFE

Shopping for Theoretical Perspectives at Wal-Mart

In this Data Workshop, you will be asking and answering theoretically driven questions about a familiar social institution: Wal-Mart. Wal-Mart, the highest-grossing company in the United States (*Fortune* 2008a), is part of a widespread retail phenomenon called the "big box." Big-box stores are huge, warehouse-like buildings that feature just about every imaginable commodity under one roof. The Wal-Mart Super Center in East Peoria, Illinois, is an excellent example: in its vast, cavernous interior, you can buy groceries, guns, gardening equipment, books, clothes, appliances, furniture, pharmaceuticals, and greeting cards, all while waiting for your photos to be developed and your tires to be rotated. Wal-Mart seeks to be all things to all people—and judging by its position at the top of the Fortune 500 list, it seems to have succeeded.

Wal-Mart's success, though, has driven out of business thousands of local "mom and pop" stores, which just can't compete with the low prices and huge selection of the big box. When Wal-Mart moves into a town, independently owned businesses soon go under. Also, the company has been accused of underpaying and exploiting its low-wage workers (Ehrenreich 2001), union busting, and engaging in sex discrimination in hiring and promoting. There are at any given time multiple lawsuits pending against this corporate giant for its labor practices.

Think about your own shopping experiences (if not at Wal-Mart then at another big-box retailer). You might even want to visit your local store (you're bound to have one!). Walk up and down the aisles and observe the other shoppers. Note how and where the goods are displayed. How do the shoppers and staffers interact with the products and with each other? If you get a chance, try to view several of Wal-Mart's television commercials as well. Then sit down with the following questions and write out your answers. They should help you see how making different theoretical assumptions can allow us to analyze the same object but come up with different interpretations.

1. *Functionalist questions*

   What are the functions of Wal-Mart for society?

   Are they the same or different from the functions of Wal-Mart in our individual lives? How do the two types of functions connect?

Analyzing Wal-Mart How do different theoretical assumptions lead to different interpretations of a single research subject, such as Wal-Mart?

   Does Wal-Mart have both manifest and latent functions? What are they?

   Are there any dysfunctions of Wal-Mart for society? If so, what are they? How might these dysfunctions serve as incentives or catalysts for social change?

2. *Conflict questions*

   Does Wal-Mart affect every group in society in the same way?

   If not, what are the differences?

   How does Wal-Mart perpetuate the inequalities (of gender, race, class, religion, age, sexual orientation, etc.) in our society?

   How does Wal-Mart contribute to conflict between unequal groups in our society?

   How might Wal-Mart contribute to social change or the amelioration of inequalities in society?

3. *Interactionist questions*

   What kind of symbolic world are you likely to encounter inside a Wal-Mart store, and how does that affect the shopper's experience?

   How does Wal-Mart influence our interpersonal interactions?

   How do interpersonal interactions shape the Wal-Mart experience for shoppers? For workers?

How does Wal-Mart contribute to our socially constructed reality?

There are two options for completing this Data Workshop.

- *Option 1 (informal)*: Prepare written notes that you can refer to in class. Discuss your observations and responses to the above questions with other students in small groups. Listen for any differences or variations in each other's insights.

- *Option 2 (formal)*: Write a three- to four-page essay describing your observations and answering the questions posed above. Make sure to refer to specific observations made during your Wal-Mart visit to support your analysis.

The creative application of each of these perspectives to the same social phenomenon can result in very different meanings—remember the blind men and the elephant? Whatever you think about Wal-Mart personally, you can use sociological theories as tools to help you see it differently and understand its position in the larger society.

New Theoretical Approaches

Because the three major paradigms all have weaknesses as well as strengths, they will probably never fully explain the totality of social phenomena, even when taken together. And because society itself is always changing, there are always new phenomena to explain. So new perspectives will, and indeed must, continue to arise. In this section we will consider three contemporary approaches: feminist theory, queer theory, and postmodern theory. Each is linked to a major area of contemporary social transformation: changing ideas about gender roles, changing notions of sexual identity, and the changes associated with a postindustrial, technologically based society.

feminist theory a theoretical approach that looks at gender inequities in society and the way that gender structures the social world

queer theory a paradigm that proposes that categories of sexual identity are social constructs and that no sexual category is fundamentally either deviant or normal

postmodernism a paradigm that suggests that social reality is diverse, pluralistic, and constantly in flux

Feminist Theory

Feminist theory has developed in the last 30 years in a way that revolutionized society, the social sciences, and the humanities. Feminism began as a social and political movement dedicated to securing the same rights for both women and men. It developed into a way of looking at the world that focuses on enhancing scholarly understanding of gender inequities in society. By applying its assumptions about gender inequality to various social institutions—the family, the economy, the mass media—feminist theory allows for a new way of understanding each of those institutions.

There is a link between feminist theory and conflict theory in that both deal with stratification and inequality in society, and both seek not only to understand that inequality but also to provide remedies for it. So feminist theory asks us to think and act differently when it comes to gender relations. Theorists such as Judith Butler (1999), bell hooks (2003), and Catharine MacKinnon (2005) link gender inequality with other social hierarchies—racial and ethnic inequality, class inequality, and inequality based on sexual orientation—and argue that gender and power are inextricably intertwined in our society.

Queer Theory

The gay and lesbian civil rights movement gained momentum in the 1970s and 80s, advocating changes in society's definitions of "normative" and "deviant" sexual identities. Again, this social and political movement gave rise to a new set of theoretical and conceptual tools for social scientists: **queer theory**. Queer theory, which arose in the late 1980s and early 90s, proposes that categories of sexuality—homo, hetero, bi, trans—are social constructs (Seidman 2003). In other words no sexual category is fundamentally deviant or normal; we create these meanings socially (which means that we can change those meanings as well). Indeed some theorists, such as Marjorie Garber (1997), argue that strict categories themselves are no longer relevant and that more fluid notions of identity should replace conventional dichotomies like gay/straight. In this way queer theory is related to the final theoretical perspective we'll be examining here: postmodernism.

Postmodern Theory

In the late twentieth century, some social thinkers looked at the proliferation of theories and data and began to question whether we could ever know society or ourselves with any certainty. What is truth, and who has the right to claim it? Or for that matter what is reality, and how can it be known? In an era of increasing doubt and cynicism, has meaning become meaningless? **Postmodernism**, a theory that encompasses a wide range of areas—from art and architecture, music and film, to communications and technology—addresses these questions.

Jacques Derrida (1930–2004), Jean Baudrillard (1929–2007), and Michel Foucault (1926–84) While many commentators and critics identify these French intellectuals as "postmodernists," each one distanced himself from the label.

The postmodern perspective developed primarily out of the French intellectual scene in the second half of the twentieth century and is still associated with three of its most important proponents. It's probably worth noting that postmodernists themselves don't really like that label, but nonetheless Jacques Derrida (1967), Jean Baudrillard (1981/1994), and Michel Foucault (1980) are the major figures most often included in the group.

In order to understand postmodernism, we first need to juxtapose it with **modernism**, the movement against which it was a reaction. Modernism is both a historical period and an ideological stance that began with the eighteenth-century Enlightenment, or Age of Reason. Modernist thought values scientific knowledge, a linear (or timeline-like) view of history, and a belief in the universality of human nature. In postmodernism, on the other hand, there are no absolutes—no claims to truth, reason, right, order, or stability. Everything is therefore relative—fragmented, temporary, and contingent. Postmodernists believe that certainty is illusory and prefer to play with the possibilities created by fluidity, complexity, multidimensionality, and even nonsense. They propose that there are no universal human truths from which we can interpret the meaning of existence. On one hand postmodernism can be celebrated as a liberating influence that can rescue us from the stifling effects of rationality and tradition. On the other it can be condemned as a detrimental influence that can imprison us in a world of relativity, nihilism, and chaos.

Postmodernists are also critical of what they call "grand narratives," the overarching stories and theories that justify dominant beliefs and give a sense of order and coherence to the world. Postmodernists are interested in "deconstructing," or taking apart and examining, these stories and theories. For example they claim that "factual" accounts of history are no more accurate than those that might be found in fiction. They prefer the notion of mininarratives, or small-scale stories, that describe individual or group practices rather than narratives that attempt to be universal or global.

These mininarratives can then be combined in a variety of ways, creating a collage of meaning.

One way of understanding what postmodernism looks like is to examine how it has crept into our popular culture. Hip-hop music is an example of a postmodern art form. It is a hybrid music that borrows from other established genres, from rhythm and blues to rock and reggae. Hip-hop also takes samples from existing songs, mixes these with new musical tracks, and overlays it all with rap lyrics, resulting in a unique new sound. A film like *Moulin Rouge* also exemplifies the postmodern perspective: although ostensibly set in 1900 Paris, the film includes popular culture references from across many different time periods and cultures, so that characters can be dancing the can-can and singing "Diamonds Are a Girl's Best Friend" and Nirvana's "Smells Like Teen Spirit" while dressed in classic Indian garb.

Many resist the postmodern turn and its position against essential meaning or truth; the rise in all types of religious fundamentalism may be a reaction to the postmodern view, an expression of the desire to return to absolute truths and steadfast traditions. Sociologists are quick to criticize postmodernism for having discarded the scientific method and the valid knowledge they believe it has generated. Social leaders with a conservative agenda have been suspicious of the postmodern impulse to dismiss moral standards. While it is clear that many people are critical of postmodernism, probably a much larger number are simply oblivious to it, which in itself may be more damning than any other type of response.

Nevertheless, although it is neither a well-known nor widely practiced perspective, postmodernism *has* gained supporters. Those who challenge the status quo, whether in the arts or politics or the academy, have found postmodernism attractive because of its ability to embrace a multiplicity of powerful and promising alternatives. At the

> **modernism** a paradigm that places trust in the power of science and technology to create progress, solve problems, and improve life

very least postmodernism allows us to question our scientific ideals about clarity and coherence, revealing the inherent shortcomings and weaknesses in our current arguments and thus providing a way toward a deeper, more nuanced understanding of social life. As the most contemporary of the theoretical perspectives, postmodernism corresponds to the current Information Age and feels natural and intuitive for students whose lives are immersed in this world. By putting the focus back on individuals and small-scale activities in which change happens on a local, limited basis but in which it may ultimately be more successful, postmodernism seems to offer an alternative to such cultural trends as increasing consumerism and globalization. However unwelcome the theory

might be to some of its critics, it is likely that the postmodern shifts we have already seen in society (in music and films for example) will continue.

Closing Comments

As a discipline sociology possesses the same qualities as the society it seeks to understand: it is complex, ever-changing, and deeply fascinating. It is also, however, somewhat unwieldy, and both classroom teachers and textbook authors often use a particular strategy to bring order to their

TABLE 2.1	Theory in Everyday Life		
Perspective	**Level of Analysis**	**Focus of Analysis**	**Case Study:** **College Admissions in the United States**
STRUCTURAL-FUNCTIONALISM	Macrosociology	Assumes that society is a unified whole that functions because of the contributions of its separate structures.	Those who are admitted are worthy and well-qualified, while those who are not admitted do not deserve to be. There are other places in society for them besides the university.
CONFLICT THEORY	Macrosociology	Sees social conflict as the basis of society and social change and emphasizes a materialist view of society, a critical view of the status quo, and a dynamic model of historical change.	Admissions decisions may be made on the basis of criteria other than grades and scores. For example, some applicants may get in because their father is a major university donor, while others may get in because of their talents in sports or music. Some may be denied admission based on criteria like race or gender.
SYMBOLIC INTERACTIONISM	Microsociology	Asserts that interaction and meaning are central to society and assumes that meanings are not inherent but are created through interaction.	University admissions processes are all about self-presentation and meaning-making in interaction. How does an applicant present himself or herself in a way that will impress the admissions committee? How does the admissions committee develop an understanding of what kind of applicant it is looking for? How do applicants interpret their acceptances and rejections?
FEMINIST THEORY	Macro- or microsociology	Looks at gender inequities in society and the way that gender structures the social world.	Gender differences in admissions statistics reveal gender-based decision-making criteria and portend gendered differences in future college experiences. Female and male students receive different treatment in and out of the classroom.
QUEER THEORY	Macro- or microsociology	Questions the basis of all social categories, including but not limited to those involving sexuality.	Social categories (like sexuality, gender, race, etc.) shape university admissions decisions and the treatment of students once enrolled.
POSTMODERNIST THEORY	Macro- or microsociology	Suggests that social reality is diverse, pluralistic, and constantly in flux.	An acceptance doesn't mean you are smart, and a rejection doesn't mean you are stupid; be careful of any "facts" you may be presented with, as they are illusory and contingent.

presentation of sociology: they narrow their focus to a limited set of theoretical perspectives. It is our view, however, that an introductory sociology text should prepare students for the current state of the discipline. Though a historical perspective is indeed important, it is our feeling that you need to know what's happening in sociology *now*.

Despite the claims of some theorists, there is no acknowledged universal social theory that satisfactorily explains all sociological phenomena. And as you have learned in this chapter, this means that new social theories are always being developed, with the hope of explaining and predicting the patterns of social life even more comprehensively. For example each of the major theoretical perspectives discussed earlier has continued to develop since its inception: there are now neofunctionalist and neo-Marxist theories, as well as interactions between various classical theoretical perspectives that their originators could not have foreseen (one example is Marxist psychoanalytic theory!). Also, symbolic interactionist theories arose as distinctive critiques of the macro-level

theories that had come before, so symbolic interactionism can be seen as a new theory in itself.

Social theory is a way of trying to explain what we observe in the world around us. For every new social phenomenon there will be attempts by theorists to explain it, understand it, analyze it, and predict its future. Trends, events, and transformations all beg for explanations, and social theories, classical and contemporary, attempt those explanations. Functionalism and feminism, for example, as different as they may seem on their respective faces, are really trying to accomplish similar goals: to explain why society is the way it is and to predict how it may change.

Ultimately, what is important to remember is that in every case, the contemporary grows out of the classical: older theories inspire and provoke newer ones. Theorists past and present engage in a dialogue with each other through scholarly responses to each other's ideas. That elephant called society has yet to be fully described, and until it is, the branches of sociology's family tree continue to grow and flower.

 Find more review materials online at
www.wwnorton.com/studyspace

CHAPTER SUMMARY

- **Theory and Sociology's Family Tree** Pioneers of early social theory like Auguste Comte, Harriet Martineau, and Herbert Spencer lived at the beginning of an era of radical political and economic change, bringing unprecedented social problems. It was also an era when the scientific method began to be applied to the social world.

- **Classical Sociological Theory** Emile Durkheim, Karl Marx, and Max Weber took for granted the effectiveness of the scientific method. In their theories, they tried to explain social order, social change, and social inequality as they watched the Industrial Revolution change their world. Durkheim examined the way changes to the economic system changed the type of social solidarity holding society together. Marx, troubled by the effects of capitalism, emphasized the importance of change and social conflict. He believed that scientific study required looking below the surface of society to the material and

economic processes that created the social world. Weber saw rationalization and bureaucracy as dehumanizing forces but focused less on large-scale social structures and more on the process by which individuals interpret the social world.

- Sigmund Freud's ideas help explain how early childhood experiences (which are social) lead to the formation of the self. Nancy Chodorow, for example, has used Freudian psychology to help explain how gender differences in parenting styles can affect gender roles.

- **Modern Schools of Thought** Structural functionalism assumes that society is a stable, well-ordered system of related structures and that each structure contributes to the stability of the whole. It has been criticized for a conservative bias toward the status quo and for its failure to explain change. Conflict theory, in contrast, focuses on the material processes by which society sustains itself, largely struggles over resources and power. It has been criticized for ignoring elements of society that are stable and free of conflict. Symbolic interactionism focuses on the creation of meaning through individual interaction; offshoots include dramaturgy, ethnomethodology, and conversation analysis. It is sometimes criticized for ignoring social structure.

- **New Theoretical Approaches** Though partially inspired by conflict theory, feminist theory has explored gender inequality and the ways gender structures our social lives. More recently, queer theory has questioned the categories of sexual identity, and postmodern theory has questioned the very existence of *any* essential meaning or truth.

QUESTIONS FOR REVIEW

1. Think back to the biographical information about Marx, Durkheim, and Weber. Are there particular events that may have influenced their theories?

2. The sociological theorists dealt with in this chapter are all from Europe or the United States, evidence of a Eurocentric bias in sociology. Are your other classes also Eurocentric?

3. Make a list of all the people you rely on to provide for your daily needs. How many of them do you think are similar to you? Does this support Durkheim's conclusion that we rely more on organic solidarity today?

4. Marx argued that the proletariat suffer from alienation as a result of losing control over the products of their labor. Make a list of all the jobs you can think of where you would have control over your own work. Do you think this control would make a difference in your own happiness?

5. Weber saw the proliferation of bureaucracies as one of the key features of the modern age. Think about the bureaucracies that are relevant to you. Do they allow you to make decisions based on your own personal desires? For example, what criteria does your university or college use to determine what classes you will take?

6. Pick a social structure other than education, and describe it in terms of its manifest and latent functions. For example, what is the manifest function of religion in your community? Can you think of any latent functions, ones that were not intended by the people in charge?

7. Marx described the way religion can be used by the ruling class to create false consciousness in the working class. Can you think of other types of ideologies that serve the interests of the ruling class?

8. Symbolic interactionism argues that meanings are not inherent in things or gestures but are socially derived and negotiated through interaction with others. Think of some recent fashion trend. Can you describe this trend in terms of what it means to those who embrace it? What sorts of interactions produce and maintain this meaning?

9. Because society is always changing, there are always new social phenomena that need a theory to make sense of them. If postmodernism rejects the belief that experience is structured or linear, what sort of changes in society do you think necessitated this insight?

SUGGESTIONS FOR FURTHER EXPLORATION

Berman, Marshall. 2001. *Adventures in Marxism*. New York: Verso. Describes the changes in Marxism that followed the publication of *The Economic and Philosophical Manuscripts of 1844*, which revealed a Marx full of "sensual warmth and spiritual depth."

Dialectics for Kids (dialectics4kids.com). This website was created by Jack Fleck, the father of movie director Ryan Fleck, and uses examples, songs, and essays to explain how social change happens.

Douglas, Mary. 2002. *Purity and Danger*. London: Routledge. Extends Durkheim's insights into the way that religion creates social solidarity and "religious ritual makes manifest to men their social selves."

Half Nelson. 2006. Dir. Ryan Fleck. THINKFilm. An idealistic young teacher teaches his eighth graders dialectics, illustrated with arm wrestling.

Hofstadter, Richard. 1992. *Social Darwinism in American Thought*. Boston: Beacon Press. Discusses the way early sociologists approached the insights of Charles Darwin and the very different conclusions drawn by pragmatist philosophers like William James.

The Magnetic Fields. 1999. "The Death of Ferdinand de Saussure." *69 Love Songs*. Merge. A tongue-in-cheek pop song about the indeterminacy associated with postmodernism.

Pfohl, Stephen. 1992. *Death at the Parasite Cafe: Social Science (Fictions) and the Postmodern*. Basingstroke, UK: Palgrave Macmillan. A hard-to-classify piece of postmodern theory in which the author flirts with fiction and adopts a series of different personae including Rada Rada, Jack O. Lantern, and Black Madonna Durkheim.

What the #$! Do We Know?*! 2005. Dir. Betsy Chasse, William Arntz, and Mark Vicente. 20th Century Fox. This movie—part documentary, part drama—asks some very postmodern questions about reality and how we know it.

Zaretsky, Eli. 2004. *Secrets of the Soul*. New York: Vintage. A social history of the reception of psychoanalysis.

Žižek. 2006. Dir. Astra Taylor. Zeitgeist Films. A documentary film on the Slovenian cultural theorist Slavoj Žižek, whose postmodern synthesis of Marx and Freud has made him as famous as a rock star in Europe.

CHAPTER 3

Studying Social Life: Sociological Research Methods

umorist Dave Barry, the Pulitzer Prize–winning columnist and author, has written many entertaining articles as a reporter and social commentator. Some of his thoughts on college, however, seem particularly appropriate for this chapter. In one of his most popular essays, Barry advises students not to choose a major that involves "known facts" and "right answers" but rather a subject in which "nobody really understands what anybody else is talking about, and which involves virtually no actual facts" (Barry 1994). For example, sociology:

> For sheer lack of intelligibility, sociology is far and away the number one subject. I sat through hundreds of hours of sociology courses, and read gobs of sociology writing, and I never once heard or read a coherent statement. This is because sociologists want to be considered scientists, so they spend most of their time translating simple, obvious observations into scientific-sounding code. If you plan to major in sociology, you'll have to learn to do the same thing. For example, suppose you have observed that children cry when they fall down. You should write: "Methodological observation of the sociometrical behavior tendencies of prematurated isolates indicates that a causal relationship exists between groundward tropism and lachrimatory, or 'crying' behavior forms." If you can keep this up for fifty or sixty pages, you will get a large government grant.

Although Barry exaggerates a bit, if there weren't some truth to what he is saying, his joke would be meaningless. While sociologists draw much of their inspiration from the natural (or "hard") sciences (such as chemistry and biology) and try to study society in a scientific way, many people still think of sociology as "unscientific" or a "soft" science. In response some sociologists may try too hard to sound scientific and incorporate complicated terminology in their writing.

It is possible, of course, to conduct research and write about it in a clear, straightforward, and even elegant way, as the best sociologists have demonstrated. Contrary to Barry's humorous claims, sociology can be both scientific *and* comprehensible. So let's turn now to a discussion of how sociologists conduct their research, which

SocIndex

Then and Now

1824: The first known example of an opinion poll, a local straw vote conducted by *The Harrisburg Pennsylvanian*, predicts that Andrew Jackson will be elected president

2001: Approximately 49% of people interviewed in a Roper poll agree or somewhat agree that polls are based on sound scientific practice

Here and There

United States: Conversational analysis emerges in the 1960s and 70s as a radical new qualitative research method, focusing on micro-level talk in interaction

China: Sociology as a discipline, abolished by the government in 1952 and reintroduced in the 1980s, largely emphasizes macro-level, quantitative methods like survey research

This and That

27% of sociologists with PhDs are employed in noneducation fields

34% of the work done by sociologists in noneducation institutions is applied research, such as surveys and ethnographies

includes the methods of gathering information and conveying that information to others. For the record, Dave Barry went to Haverford College near Philadelphia, where he majored in English.

HOW TO READ THIS CHAPTER

Much like Chapter 2, this chapter on sociological methods seeks to provide you with a set of tools that will help you develop a particular perspective on the social world. They will also help you in the Data Workshops throughout the book, which are designed to give you the experience of conducting the same type of research that professional sociologists do. For this reason, we recommend that you look at this chapter as a sort of "how-to" guide: read through all the "directions" first, recognizing that you will soon be putting each method into practice. Then remember that you have this chapter as a resource for future reference. These methods are your tools for real-world research—it's important that you understand them, but even more important that you get a chance to use them.

An Overview of Research Methods

While theories make hypothetical claims, methods produce data that will support, disprove, or modify those claims. You are already familiar with some methods sociologists use. When you pick up a newspaper or watch the news on TV, you might learn about an opinion poll on the president's popularity, new census figures, or the results of a market research project. These types of surveys usually produce **quantitative** data (numbers), which are easy to transmit to the public: "40 percent of Americans approve of the job being done by President Bush," or "28 percent of Americans use credit cards to pay for regular expenses such as rent or groceries," for example.

You are also familiar with some **qualitative** methods, the focus of this book. Qualitative methods include observation and informal interviews. For example, when you are a new member in a group (such as a sorority or fraternity, a dance class, or a neighbor's party), you often spend part of your time observing the other members closely. What are they saying and doing?

quantitative a type of data that can be converted into numbers, usually for statistical comparison

qualitative a type of data that can't be converted into numbers, usually because they relate to meaning

scientific method a procedure for acquiring knowledge that emphasizes collecting concrete data through observation and experiment

What seems important to them? How can I best fit in? Do I even want to fit in? Such a situation is a practical version of what sociologists do in ethnographic research. They observe a group in order to determine the members' norms, values, rules, and meanings. Like sociologists, we also use a qualitative method when we "interview" new friends or potential romantic partners in order to discover their important qualities and beliefs. Although our questions are unsystematic and nonscientific—we don't usually take a list of interview questions with us on a date—they are related to the methods we will consider in this chapter.

The Scientific Approach

The **scientific method** is the standard procedure for acquiring and verifying empirical (concrete, scientific) knowledge. The scientific method provides researchers with a series of basic steps to follow; over the years, sociologists have updated and modified this model so that it better fits the study of human behaviors. While not every sociologist adheres to

Sociological Methods Take Many Forms They can be quantitative, but they can also include interviews, surveys, and participant observation.

Does Watching Violence on Television Cause Children to Behave Violently? In his famous 1965 study, Albert Bandura supported his hypothesis by observing children who had watched a video of an adult beating a doll behaving similarly toward the doll afterward.

each of the steps in order, the scientific method provides a general plan for conducting research in a systematic way.

1. In the first step the researcher identifies a problem or asks a general question like "Does violent TV lead to violent behavior?" and begins to think about a specific research plan designed to answer that question.

2. Before proceeding, however, a researcher usually does a **literature review** to become thoroughly familiar with all other research done previously on a given topic. This will prevent a researcher from duplicating work that has already been done and may also provide the background upon which to conduct new research.

3. Next the researcher forms a **hypothesis**, a theoretical statement that she thinks will explain the relationship between two phenomena, which are known as **variables**. In the hypothesis "Watching violence on TV causes children to act violently in real life," the two variables are "watching violence on TV" and "acting violently." In short the researcher is saying one variable causes the other. The researcher can use the hypothesis to predict possible outcomes: "If watching violence on TV causes children to act violently in real life, then exposing five-year-olds to violent TV shows will make them more likely to hit the inflatable clown doll placed in the room with them." The researcher must clearly give an **operational definition** to the variables so that she can observe and measure them accurately. For example, there is a wide range of violence on television and in real life. Does "violence" include words as well as actions, a slap as well as murder?

4. In this step the researcher chooses a research design or method. A classic example is to perform an experiment meant to isolate the variables in order to best examine their relationship to one another. Other methods are also available and will be discussed later in the chapter.

5. The researcher then collects the data. In this case the researcher would conduct the experiment by first exposing kids to TV violence, then observing their behavior toward the clown doll. Data might be collected by using video equipment as well as by taking notes.

6. Next the researcher must analyze the data, evaluating the accuracy or inaccuracy of the hypothesis in predicting the outcome. In the real-life experiment this example is based on, the children were more likely to hit the clown doll themselves if they saw the TV actors being rewarded for their violent behavior; if the actors were punished for their behavior, the children were less likely to hit the doll (Bandura 1965).

7. Finally the researcher then disseminates the findings of the experiment in the scientific community (often through presentations at professional meetings and/or publications) as well as among the general public, thus completing the last step in the research process.

One limit of the scientific method is that it can't always distinguish between **correlation** and **causation**. If two variables change in conjunction with each other, or if a change in one seems to lead to a change in the other, they are correlated. Even if they are correlated, though, the change in one variable may not be caused by the change in the other variable. Instead there may be some **intervening variable** that causes the changes in both. The classic example of this is the correlation between ice cream sales and rates of violent crime. As ice cream sales increase, so do rates of violent crime like murder and rape. Does ice cream consumption cause people to act violently? Or do violent actions cause people to buy ice cream? Turns out

literature review a thorough search through previously published studies relevant to a particular topic

hypothesis a theoretical statement explaining the relationship between two or more phenomena

variables one of two or more phenomena that a researcher believes are related and hopes to prove are related through research

operational definition a clear and precise definition of a variable that facilitates its measurement

correlation a relationship between variables in which they change together. May or may not be causal

causation a relationship between variables in which a change in one directly produces a change in the other

intervening variable a third variable, sometimes overlooked, that explains the relationship between two other variables

(Adler and Adler 1991). Ethnographic methods excel at telling stories that otherwise might not have been told.

2. Ethnographies can challenge our taken-for-granted notions about groups we thought we knew. For instance, from Stacey's work on what seem like typical working-class families, we learn about the emergence of new family forms and relationships that may come to typify families in the future.

3. The detailed nature of ethnographies can help to reshape the stereotypes we hold about others and on which social policy is often based. A study like Stacey's can have policy consequences because it sheds light on the creative ways that families cope with such demands of everyday life as work, child care, and divorce.

4. Much of the pioneering methodological innovation of the last half-century has come from within the field of ethnography, especially on the issue of reflexivity and researcher roles in the field.

DISADVANTAGES

1. Ethnographies suffer from a lack of **replicability**, the ability of another researcher to repeat or replicate the study. Repeating a study in order to test the validity of its results is an important element of the scientific method, but because of the unique combinations of people, timing, setting, and researcher role, no one can ever undertake the same study twice.

2. A major critique has to do with ethnographies' degree of **representativeness**, whether they apply to anything larger than themselves. What is the value of studying relatively small groups of people if one cannot then say that these groups represent parts of the society at large? Though Stacey's work focused on just the Gamas and Lewisons, her conclusions were supposed to apply to working-class families in general.

3. Ethnographers must also be wary of **bias**. There is always a possibility that prejudice or favor can slip into the research process. Not all researchers are transparent about their own agendas. We need to keep in mind how a researcher's own values and opinions might affect his research and analysis.

replicability research that can be repeated, and thus verified, by other researchers later

representativeness the degree to which a particular studied group is similar to, or represents, any part of the larger society

bias an opinion held by the researcher that might affect the research or analysis

DATA WORKSHOP

ANALYZING EVERYDAY LIFE

Observing and Describing Verbal and Nonverbal Communication

While producing fieldnotes may sound fairly easy (don't we all know how to describe the things we've observed?), it turns out to be one of the most grueling forms of data collection in the social sciences. Why? Because thick description is a much more demanding accomplishment than the description you're used to providing in everyday conversation. It requires a rigorous consciousness of what is going on around you while it is happening and a strenuous effort to recall those goings-on after leaving the field and returning to your computer.

This Data Workshop is a practicum in thick description. To make things a little easier for you, we have separated the verbal and the visual so that you can concentrate on one kind of description at a time. But in your future ethnographic work, you'll be writing fieldnotes that describe both verbal and nonverbal behavior at once.

Observation: First, for 10 to 15 minutes, listen to (eavesdrop on) a conversation whose participants you can't see. They might be sitting behind you on a bus or in a restaurant—you're close enough to hear them but positioned so that you can't see them. Then, for 10 to 15 minutes, observe a conversation you can't hear—one taking place, for example, on the other side of the campus quad. Even though you can't hear what's being said, you can see the interaction as it takes place.

Written Description: Write an extremely detailed description of each conversation. Describe the participants and the setting, and include your ideas about what you think is going on and what you think you know about the participants. Try to describe everything you heard or saw in order to support any conclusions you draw. For each 10- to 15-minute observation period, your written description should be three to four typed pages.

There are two options for completing this Data Workshop.

- *Option 1 (informal)*: Choose a partner from your class and exchange your written descriptions with your partner. As you read through your partner's descriptions, mark with a star (*) the passages where you can see and hear clearly the things your partner describes. Circle the passages that contain evaluative words (like "angry" or "sweet") or summaries of action or conversation rather than detailed description (like "They argued about who would pay the bill"). And place a question mark next to the passages where you are left feeling like you would like to know more. Your partner will do this with your description as well, and you can discuss your responses to each other's work. Finally, as a class, use your discussions to develop a group consensus about what constitutes good descriptive detail. This is the kind of detail ethnographers strive to produce in their fieldnotes every day.

- *Option 2 (formal)*: Turn in your written descriptions to your instructor for individual feedback.

Interviews

Sociologists use **interviews**—face-to-face, information-seeking conversations—to gather information directly from research subjects, or **respondents**. When researchers conduct interviews, they try to do so systematically and with a more scientific approach than is typically seen in more casual television or newspaper interviews.

Sometimes interviews are the only method used in a research project, but sociologists may also combine interviews with other methods such as participant observation or analysis of existing sources. Closely related to interviews are

The Second Shift In her groundbreaking book, Arlie Hochschild interviewed working women and their partners to learn about the time-binds that they face as they balance work, family, and running a household.

surveys, which we will consider in the next section. Interviews, however, are always conducted by the researcher, whereas surveys may also be taken independently by the respondent.

When using interviews to collect data about a particular question or project, sociologists must identify a **target population**, the larger group they wish to generalize about, and then select a **sample**, or smaller group who are representative of the larger group. The number of possible respondents depends on the type of study, the nature of the questions, and the amount of time and staff available. In most research studies, interviews can be administered to a limited number of people, so the scope of such projects is usually smaller than for other methods such as surveys. The researcher must get implied or **informed consent** from those participating—in other words, respondents must know what they are getting into and explicitly agree to participate.

Arlie Hochschild (Hochschild and Machung 1989) used interviews to conduct her landmark study on parents in two-career families, *The Second Shift*. In this book Hochschild looks at how couples handle the pressures of working at a job and then coming home to what she calls "the second shift"—doing housework and taking care of children. Hochschild, who was herself in a two-career family, wanted to find out how couples were dealing with changing family roles in light of the fact that more women had entered the workforce. Were women able to juggle all their responsibilities, and to what extent were men helping their wives in running the household? Hochschild and her assistants interviewed 50 couples in two-career marriages (many were interviewed more than once) and 45 other people who were also a part of the respondents' social arrangements, such as babysitters, day-care providers, and teachers.

When conducting an interview, how do you know what to ask? Composing good questions is one of the most difficult parts of interviewing. Most interviewers use many different questions, covering a range of issues related to the project. Questions may be closed- or open-ended. A **closed-ended question** imposes a limit on the possible response: for example, "Are you for or against couples living together

interviews face-to-face, information-seeking conversation, sometimes defined as a conversation with a purpose

respondent someone from whom a researcher solicits information

target population the entire group about which a researcher would like to be able to generalize

sample the part of the population that will actually be studied

informed consent a safeguard through which the researcher makes sure that respondents are freely participating and understand the nature of the research

closed-ended question a question asked of a respondent that imposes a limit on the possible responses

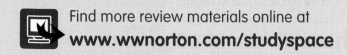
CHAPTER SUMMARY

- **An Overview of Research Methods** Quantitative research produces data that can be converted to numbers. This often means survey research, which tends to answer questions about cause-and-effect relationships. Qualitative research produces data that cannot be meaningfully converted to numbers and is more likely to address questions of meaning.

- **Taking a Scientific Approach** Whether qualitative or quantitative, most sociological research uses the scientific method, which calls for researchers to begin with a hypothesis stating a potential relationship between two or more variables. These variables are carefully defined so they can be measured; data are then collected that allow the hypothesis to be tested.

- **Ethnographic Methods** Ethnography is often a two-part activity: active participation in and observation of a naturally occurring setting, and a written account (fieldnotes) of what goes on there. Research may be overt (open) or covert. Ethnographic studies can't be truly replicated, don't always study groups that are representative of a larger population, and are particularly vulnerable to researcher bias.

- **Interviews** Interviews involve direct, face-to-face contact with respondents and often generate large quantities of qualitative data. The researcher identifies the population about whom she wishes to generalize and carefully selects a sample of people to be interviewed from that population. Like surveys, interviewers must be careful to construct questions that will produce meaningful answers and to avoid leading or double-barreled questions as well as the use of ambiguous or emotional language.

- **Surveys** Survey research is usually quantitative and generates more respondents than any type of qualitative research. In order to generalize about a population, surveys require a representative sample, often a simple random sample in which every member of a population has an equal chance of selection. The lack of a qualitative component lowers the validity of survey work, a risk that is increased by low response rate or self-selected respondents.

- **Existing Sources** Comparative-historical research and content analysis rely on existing sources of data from both the past and the present. This allows access to distant times and places and much larger data sets than any one researcher could gather alone. Digital media provide a wealth of material as data and make it particularly easy for future researchers to replicate analysis.

- **Experiments** Sociological experiments offer great advantages to those trying to construct models or build theories, as they allow control over every aspect of a situation and provide a high degree of replicability. However, by screening out the complexities and messiness of the real world, experiments also lose some of their ability to simulate real social life.

- **Issues in Sociological Research** In the past it was considered desirable to remain objective and value free, but this position is now hotly debated. Issues of reactivity and reflectivity come into play with both positions. All sociologists agree that ethical research is important, and to this end most research now passes before an institutional review board, which exists to protect the rights of research subjects.

QUESTIONS FOR REVIEW

1. Judith Stacey carried out her ethnography of working-class families by means of participant observation, often acting as a full participant within the setting. How do you think this affected what she learned? How would her conclusions have been different if she had simply done interviews?

2. Under what circumstances do you think that covert research is justified? How did Richard Mitchell, who studied militant survivalists, justify hiding his intentions from his subjects? How would you feel if you found out someone was secretly studying you?

3. According to Clifford Geertz, ethnographers should try to write "thick description." Imagine you are in the field, and you see one of your subjects quickly close his right eyelid. What sort of details would you have to record for your readers to know if this action was a wink or a twitch?

4. Does reflexivity sound like a good or bad thing to you? How did it play out for Judith Stacey in her ethnographic work? Can you imagine a field setting where you would be at a disadvantage by the way your presence affected the group? How about a field setting where you would have an advantage?

5. Try to write a survey or interview question that asks about a respondent's political affiliation without being biased or using language that might spark an emotional response.

6. "Did you understand everything in this chapter, and what was your favorite part?" If this was an interview question, what would be wrong with it?

7. Imagine that your teacher asks you to do a simple random sample of your class. How would you select your sample so that you could be sure each member had an equal chance of being included?

8. Researchers are now using social networking websites like Facebook and MySpace to gather a wide variety of data. If researchers read your profile (or those of your friends or family), do you think they would have a valid understanding of who you (or they) are? Is there a weakness of research that relies on existing sources?

9. Do you think you would react differently to an ethnographer from a market research firm than you would to one from a university?

SUGGESTIONS FOR FURTHER EXPLORATION

Becker, Howard. 1998. *Tricks of the Trade: How to Think about Your Research While You're Doing It*. Chicago: University of Chicago Press. Describes a multitude of tricks to make research more successful; includes discussions of qualitative and quantitative research, reactivity, and sampling.

Clifford, James, and George E. Marcus, eds. 1986. *Writing Culture: The Poetics and Politics of Ethnography*. Berkeley, CA: University of California Press. Deals with the problem of treating ethnography as if it were an objective science.

Emerson, Robert M., Rachel I. Fretz, and Linda L. Shaw. 1995. *Writing Ethnographic Fieldnotes*. Chicago: University of Chicago Press. An excellent and hands-on introduction to the oft-neglected art of taking fieldnotes.

Erickson, Kai T. *Wayward Puritans: A Study in the Sociology of Deviance*. New York: Wiley. This study of deviance in seventeenth-century Massachusetts relies on existing data (mainly court records) to present a surprising picture of crime, alcoholism, and premarital sex.

Huff, Darrell. 1993. *How to Lie with Statistics*. New York: W. W. Norton. Although not specifically about the statistical analysis of survey data, the insights expressed will still help any reader become a more skeptical consumer of survey research.

Myerhoff, Barbara. 1976. *Number Our Days*. New York: Touchstone Press. An excellent and moving example of what ethnography can be, providing insight into the process of gaining access.

Number Our Days. 1978. Dir. Lynne Littman. Direct Cinema Limited. This wonderful short film, a record of Barbara Myerhoff's ethnographic work with an elderly Jewish population in Venice Beach, California, won an Oscar for best documentary short.

SurveyMonkey. This website enables anyone to create online surveys quickly and easily. Learn more about writing and administering questionnaires. Of course, such surveys are not necessarily scientific. Available at: http://www.surveymonkey.com/

The *Up* series: *Seven Up* (1964), *7 Plus Seven* (1970), *21 Up* (1977), *28 Up* (1984), *35 Up* (1991), *42 Up* (1998), and *49 Up* (2005). Dir. Michael Apted and Paul Almond. First Run Features. Director Apted began in 1963 by interviewing 14 English seven-year-olds from diverse class backgrounds, and he returned to interview them again every seven years.

How does culture shape our social worlds? How are our personal identities produced by our cultural contexts and social interactions? How does participation in group life shape both individual experience and social structure? How are what is normal and what is deviant defined, and what are the consequences for people who are labeled accordingly? Part II of this text addresses these questions in four chapters on culture (Chapter 4), the self and interaction (Chapter 5), groups (Chapter 6), and deviance (Chapter 7). The ability to examine, describe, analyze, and explain the points of intersection between the individual world and the social world is sociology's special contribution to the larger scholarly endeavor. Over the next four chapters you will encounter many works by sociologists that illustrate the links between the individual and society. Verta Taylor and Leila Rupp's book *Drag Queens at the 801 Cabaret* (2003) is perfect for highlighting these themes.

Drag Queens at the 801 Cabaret is an ethnographic portrait of a Key West drag club, where gay male performers don sexy dresses, lavish wigs, and theatrical makeup and sing and dance for a diverse audience: tourists and locals, men and women, gays and straights. Rupp and Taylor get to know the "801 Girls," their friends, family, and audience members, and the authors even try out their own sort of drag. (That's right—women dressed as men dressed as women!)

Rupp and Taylor recognize that the particular culture of the 801 Cabaret is nestled within multiple contemporary American subcultures. For example, Key West is an island subculture that offers a year-round, touristy, carnivalesque atmosphere as part of its charm. It "remains a flamboyant mix of cultures. . . . [I]t shelters not only vibrant Cuban and

Bahamian enclaves, but also artistic, hippie, and gay communities. . . . The city, [says journalist Charles Kuralt,] is 'full of dreamers, drifters, and dropouts, spongers and idlers and barflies, writers and fishermen, islanders from the Caribbean and gays from the big cities, painters and pensioners, treasure hunters, real estate speculators, smugglers, runaways, old Conchs and young lovers . . . all elaborately tolerant of one another'" (pp. 50–51). For the 801 girls, this means that the subcultures associated with both gay masculinity and drag performance are supported and sustained on the island in ways they might not be on the mainland. Because of the island's unique mix of subcultures, one of the performers asserts that "Key West is the true home of accepted diversity" (p. 55).

In Key West's culture, many kinds of people feel free to be themselves. But what does that really mean? For the drag queens at the 801 Cabaret, their performances are about putting on a different identity than the one they present in their everyday lives. These are men with flashy female alter-egos—Kevin becomes "Kylie"; Roger becomes "Inga"; Dean becomes "Milla." And their process of becoming is elaborate and grueling:

> Some of the girls shave all over their bodies, some their faces, chests, legs, and arms, some just their faces. . . . They powder their faces, necks, and chests, using a thick base to hide their beards. . . . Eyeliner, eye shadow, mascara, false eyelashes, lip liner, and lipstick are painstakingly applied. (pp. 12–13)

So far, this doesn't sound all that different than the ablutions many women perform every morning in front of the mirror. After the makeup, however, things get a little more intricate, as the "girls"

> tuck their penises and testicles between their legs, using a gaff [a special panty], or several, to make sure everything stays out of sight . . . panty hose, sometimes several layers . . . corsets and waist cinchers . . . they all, of course, wear bras . . . [filled with] water balloons (the tied end makes an amazingly realistic nipple), half a Nerf football, lentil beans in a pair of nylons, foam or silicone prostheses. (pp. 20–21)

All this work to look like women—and that's not taking into account the exhausting work of acting the part, onstage and off. While drag queens do not seek to convince their audiences that they are "real" women, they do move, speak, sing, and dance in stereotypically feminine style as part of their performances. And that's the insight that drag queens

Verta Taylor and Leila Rupp

Drag queens and drag shows allow others to cross between groups, to see what life might be like in a world in which gender boundaries are fluid and homosexuality is normal:

> As one of the few ways that straight people encounter gay culture—where, in fact, straight people live for an hour or two in an environment where gay is normal and straight is other—drag shows . . . play an important role for the gay/lesbian movement. Precisely because drag shows are entertaining, they attract people who might never otherwise be exposed to gay politics. As one female audience member put it, they "take something difficult and make it light." (pp. 207–208)

Finally, drag shows also challenge our notions about what is normal and what is deviant, when performers embrace what would otherwise be considered a stigmatized identity and turn it into something to be proud of. Drag queens can be seen as voluntary outsiders, unconcerned about fitting into mainstream society. Rupp and Taylor make the argument that drag is a form of social protest—against a society in which gender and sexual orientation are crammed into limiting, two-category systems; against a society in which identities are seen as immutable; and against a society in which certain forms of cultural expression are marginalized. Their analysis of the social world of one Key West drag club offers sociological insights into the lives of the individual performers who work against social stigma and limitations to provide new ways of looking at culture, self, and society.

provide about our own identities: it's *all* performance! Our male and female selves are the products of interactional accomplishments (see pp. 130–133), and "real" women do many of the same things that drag queens do in order to express femininity.

Because the drag queens perform different identities onstage and off, the 801 Cabaret calls into question some of our most important and taken-for-granted boundaries between social groups: males and females, and gays and straights. In fact, drag queens are living examples of the intersections between these groups. One of the performers says:

> Last night—though this happens almost every night—[this woman] goes, "I'm straight, I'm a woman, I'm not a lesbian, but you're so beautiful, I find you so attractive" . . . [and] a straight guy, has been straight for like fifty years or something like that . . . goes, "You know, I've been straight all my life, and I know you're a man, but you're so beautiful . . . I can't keep my eyes off you." (p. 201)

CHAPTER 4

Cultural Crossroads

On 2000 and 2001 Lieutenant Colonel Martha McSally, the highest-ranking female fighter pilot in the U.S. Air Force, was stationed in Saudi Arabia and was one of the only women to pilot her fighter jet on combat and patrol missions in the "no-fly zone" over Iraq. When on the job, she wore her uniform with pride—it identified her as a pilot, an officer, and a patriot. But whenever she left the Air Force base in Saudi Arabia for any reason, even to conduct official business, she was not allowed to wear her uniform.

At that time the U.S. military required female soldiers in Islamic countries to wear traditional garb when they went off base. In Saudi Arabia, women in the military had to wear head scarves and *abayas* (floor-length black robes). They also had to obey other Saudi laws: they could not drive cars (and had to sit in the back seat, behind the male driver) or go out in public without a male chaperone. The military's rationale was that it was respecting local values (including *sharia*, or Islamic laws) and protecting American servicewomen.

Lt. Col. McSally refused to obey these rules. She wanted to wear her own clothes and would not put on the *abaya* when she left her base. Her insubordination drew threats of court-martial proceedings; in return, in January 2002, McSally filed a lawsuit against the Department of Defense (DOD), arguing that as a non-Muslim, she should not be bound by *sharia*—indeed, she stated that obeying *sharia* made her "deny her own faith" as a Christian. She also claimed that the dress code violated her individual rights as an American and that it undermined military unit cohesion and command structure. In other words, it was confusing for men to take orders from her on base but to chauffeur her in nonmilitary attire off base. As McSally testified, "It's demeaning and humiliating, and affects my authority as a military officer." Many of her colleagues, both male and female, agreed.

As a result of McSally's lawsuit—and her additional appeals to Congress—the military has changed some of its rules. In May 2002, the House of Representatives passed a bill preventing the DOD from requiring or even "strongly advising" traditional Muslim dress for American servicewomen. They are still, however, prevented from driving alone off base. While the new legislation satisfied some of the claims in McSally's suit, she is still considering how to further the cause of women's rights

SocIndex

Then and Now

1915: Gillette markets its first razor made especially for women: Milady Décolletée.

2006: Approximately 80% of professional women in the United States shave their legs and underarms.

Here and There

Connecticut: With 115 samples, memorabilia dealer John Reznikoff owns the largest collection of hair samples, taken from such historical figures as Abraham Lincoln, Albert Einstein, and Marilyn Monroe.

Andhra Pradesh, India: Each year, at the temple of Tirupati, 6.5 million religious pilgrims shave their heads and donate their hair, which is auctioned and generates approximately $2.2 million a year for the temple.

This and That

Approximately 35 million American men and 25 million American women with thinning hair spend more than $1.5 billion a year on hair restoration products, drugs, and surgery.

The number of laser hair removal treatments reached 1.4 million in 2006, making it the second-fastest-growing noninvasive surgical procedure in the United States.

in the military and to secure cultural and religious freedoms for servicepeople. The publicity surrounding her case generated significant interest outside the legal and military communities. Accordingly, a book and movie about McSally's story are currently in development.

McSally has since gone on to become a colonel and the first woman to lead an Air Force fighter squadron into combat, and Saudi Arabia has promised to lift its ban on women drivers by 2009. But this case also brings up many questions related to the study of culture. Why are there such seemingly vast differences between American and Saudi Arabian cultures? Why does each culture have such different ideas about the way women should interact with men and how they should dress? Why was the Air Force so

Then-Lt. Col. Martha McSally in 2002 McSally asked a judge to decide whether military rules governed the attire of American servicewomen traveling off the base in Saudi Arabia. Before her lawsuit, servicewomen were required to wear the *abaya* (right).

adamant about military personnel respecting the culture of their host country? Why were American values such as individualism and gender equality so important to McSally? How do different cultures influence or conflict with one another? Can institutions such as the military or even religious traditions such as Christianity and Islam allow for change? This chapter will provoke you to ponder such cultural issues.

HOW TO READ THIS CHAPTER

Culture is one of the fundamental elements of social life and thus a very important topic in sociology. Many of the concepts presented here will come up again in almost every subsequent chapter. You will need to keep these concepts in mind as you learn about other substantive areas. You will also want to think about how culture is relevant to the things you already know from your own life experience. Try to come up with some of your own examples as you read along. The subject of culture is probably inherently interesting to most people. But although culture is familiar to all of us, you should be seeing it in a new and different way by the time you finish this chapter.

> **culture** the entire way of life of a group of people (including both material and symbolic elements) that acts as a lens through which one views the world and is passed from one generation to the next

What Is Culture?

Culture encompasses practically all of human civilization and touches on almost every aspect of social life. It is so much a part of the world around us that we may not recognize the extent to which it shapes and defines who we are. In the broadest sense, we can say that **culture** is the entire way of life of a group of people. It can include everything from language and gestures to style of dress and standards of beauty, from customs and rituals to tools and artifacts, from music and child-rearing practices to the proper way for customers to line up in a grocery store. It forms basic beliefs and assumptions about the world and the way things work and defines the moral parameters of what is right and wrong, good and bad.

Although culture varies from group to group, all societies develop some form of culture. It is the human equivalent of instinct in animals: although we humans do have some basic instincts, culture actually accounts for our great success as a species. We are totally dependent on it to deal with the demands of life in society. As culture develops, it is shared among members of a group, handed down from generation to generation, and passed along from one group or individual to another.

Although culture may seem to us to be "second nature," it is actually something that is learned, rather than innate. Because we learn it so slowly and incrementally, we are often unaware of the process. For instance, few of us would be conscious of having *learned* all the slang words we currently use or the distance we typically maintain from someone while talking with him. We may not remember exactly when we first felt patriotic or how we formed our opinions about people from the upper class. We all carry culture inside ourselves; it becomes ingrained and internalized into our way of thinking and acting. Culture guides the way we make sense of the world around us and the way we make decisions about what to do and how to do it. We can talk about the culture of a given country, state, or community, of people belonging to an ethnic or religious group, or of those working in the same profession. We can even say that sports enthusiasts, schoolmates, or a clique of friends share in a common culture. We'll discuss some of these cultural variations later in the chapter.

How Has Culture Been Studied?

People study culture in a variety of ways. Theologians and philosophers, for example, might debate the morals and values of an ideal culture. Anthropologists often investigate smaller societies outside the United States. They travel around the world and engage in empirical fieldwork, collecting stories and artifacts that document the realities of the cultures they study (Margaret Mead and Gregory Bateson are two of the most well known). In many cases, though, these cultures are often seen as "other"—interesting because of their distinctive differences from the anthropologist's home culture, which often goes unexamined.

In contrast, sociologists mainly focus on culture closer to home, usually the same societies to which they belong. They do this by using the different theories discussed in Chapter 2—functionalism, conflict theory, symbolic interactionism, and postmodernism—as well as the research methods discussed in Chapter 3. At the same time, however, sociologists may also engage in the process of "othering" by studying the unusual, extraordinary, or deviant in cultural groups. In so doing, they may fail to consider some aspects of the culture that is right in front of them. This is where the sociology of everyday life offers certain benefits. By studying the mundane as well as the exceptional, we can learn about culture in all its interesting permutations. We can learn not only about the differences between cultural groups—"us" and "them"—but also the similarities.

Ethnocentrism and Cultural Relativism

Culture acts as a lens through which we view the world. That lens, however, can either elucidate or obscure what we are looking at. Often we can't clearly see our own culture, precisely because we are so familiar with it. Yet when exposed to another culture, through travel, television, or other means, we can readily see what is different or exotic. Rarely does our perspective allow us to recognize the strangeness in our own culture.

One of the best examples of the challenges in observing culture is presented in a famous article by Horace Miner called "Body Ritual Among the Nacirema" (1956). The article focuses on the beliefs and practices of this North American people concerning the care of their bodies. Miner observes that their fundamental belief appears to be that the human body is ugly and is susceptible to decay and disease, and the only way to counter these conditions is to engage in elaborate ceremonies and rituals. All members of the Nacirema culture conform to a greater or lesser degree to these practices and then pass them along to their children. One passage describes the household shrine where many of the body rituals take place:

> While each family has at least one shrine, the rituals associated with it are not family ceremonies but are private and secret. . . . The focal point of the shrine is a box or chest which is built into a wall. In this chest are kept the many charms and magical potions without which no native believes he could live. . . . Beneath the charm-box is a small font. Each day every member of the family, in succession, enters the shrine room, bows his head before the charm-box, mingles different sorts of holy water in the font, and proceeds with a brief rite of ablution.

> The Nacirema regularly visit medicine men, "holy-mouth men," and other specialized practitioners from whom they procure magical potions.

> The Nacirema have an almost pathological horror of and fascination with the mouth, the condition of which is believed to have a supernatural influence on all social relationships. Were it not for the rituals of the mouth, they believe that their teeth would fall out, their gums bleed, their jaws shrink, their friends desert them, and their lovers reject them. The daily body ritual performed by everyone

includes a mouth-rite. It was reported to me that the ritual consists of inserting a small bundle of hog hairs into the mouth, along with certain magical powders, and then moving the bundle in a highly formalized series of gestures.

Do the Nacirema seem like a strange group of people, or are they somehow familiar? Miner writes as though he were an anthropologist studying some exotic tribe of primitive people. In actuality, the passages above describe the bathroom and personal health-care habits of the average American. (Note that "Nacirema" is "American" spelled backward.) He doesn't embellish or make up anything; he merely approaches the topic as if he knew nothing about its meaning. So the "charm-box" is the standard medicine cabinet, the "holy water" font is a sink, the medicine men and "holy-mouth men" are doctors and dentists, and the exotic "mouth-rite" is the practice of brushing teeth.

One of the reasons that Miner's article has become so popular is that it demonstrates how easy it is to fail to see our own culture, precisely because we take it for granted. The article reminds students who are becoming social analysts how useful culture shock is in helping to see even what is most familiar to us as bizarre or strange. Throughout this chapter, keep in mind that your powers of observation must be applied to looking at both "them" and "us."

Another, related problem arises when trying to understand cultures other than our own. Generally, we think of our own culture as being the "normal" one, a belief known as **ethnocentrism**. We don't realize that culture is something learned and that there is nothing inherently better about ours. Ethnocentrism means that we use our own culture as a kind of measuring stick with which to judge other individuals or societies; anyone outside our group seems "off-center" or abnormal.

As sociologists, we want to have as clear a view of any society as possible; this requires that we suspend, at least temporarily, our ethnocentrism. There are several ways to do this. In Chapter 1, we learned about the sociological imagination, culture shock, and beginner's mind—all ways to see the world anew. We can add to that list **cultural relativism**, which means seeing each different culture as simply that— different. Not better or worse, not right or wrong, but on its own terms. This helps us place different values, beliefs, norms, and practices within their own cultural context. By practicing cultural relativism, or being culturally sensitive, we begin to see others more

ethnocentrism the principle of using one's own culture as a means or standard by which to evaluate another group or individual, leading to the view that cultures other than one's own are abnormal

cultural relativism the principle of understanding other cultures on their own terms, rather than judging or evaluating according to one's own culture

"Body Ritual Among the Nacirema" Horace Miner reminds us how easy it is to overlook aspects of our own culture, precisely because it seems so normal to us.

clearly, and without judgment, and therefore to appreciate their way of life. We can discover viewpoints and interpretations of reality different from our own. Cultural relativism becomes all the more important in our increasingly diverse society. The Data Workshop below will help you see how.

DATA WORKSHOP

ANALYZING EVERYDAY LIFE
A Comparison of Religious Services

Some people argue that religions are cultures within themselves. This is easiest to see in the case of groups such as the FLDS (a fundamentalist Mormon sect whose members practice polygamy and tend to live in isolated rural compounds) and the white-supremacist World Church of the Creator (whose leader, Matt Hale, is currently in prison for conspiring to kill a federal judge), but even your friendly neighborhood congregation has a specific set of beliefs that are particular to itself. This Data Workshop will help you uncover some characteristics of two specific religious cultures and compare them in nonjudgmental ways. This is an ethnographic exercise and is meant to help you identify ethnocentrism and practice cultural relativism. (Refer back to Chapter 3 if you need a refresher on ethnographic methods.)

Step 1: Observing Services
Select two different houses of worship—church, synagogue, temple, mosque, or other place of worship—and attend one service at each. You may want to compare two different

Comparing Religious Cultures Every religion has a culture—its own set of norms, values, beliefs, and practices that differ from those of other congregations, even within the same denomination. As an ethnographic exercise, visit two houses of worship and compare your experiences.

denominations within the same broad religious category (a Catholic mass and a Protestant service, for example, both Christian denominations) or two different religions (a Catholic mass and an Islamic prayer service). Any choice is fine (including one you are familiar with, if any) as long as it is open to the public. You may want to call their offices first, to find out if there are certain dress code requirements or other things you need to know about before you arrive. Remember, when you visit your chosen houses of worship,

you must behave in a respectful manner. If you suspect that you can't maintain a quiet (if that's called for) and respectful demeanor, then choose a different service to attend.

Observe closely all that you encounter. Since it is probably not appropriate for you to jot down notes during a religious service, you should write your fieldnotes as soon as you can afterward. Record in as much detail as possible what was said, done, or sung during your period of observation.

- When do people act in unison?

- When do they act individually?

- What types of different roles do people take on in the ceremony—leaders, helpers, participants?

- Are they all deeply involved at all times?

- Who is staring at the ceiling or whispering to their neighbor?

- How do others respond to such behavior?

Observe the architecture, any decorations, the clothing worn by different participants, and the objects—books, scrolls, musical instruments, statues, paintings, vessels, collection plates—that are part of the service. Pay as much attention as possible to the interactions that are a central part of the ritual, as well as those that occur on the margins (either just before or just after the ceremony).

Step 2: Identifying Similarities and Differences
Read through your fieldnotes and reflect on each experience. Then answer the following questions.

- What similarities and differences did you notice in the material aspects of the two ceremonies—that is, in the arrangement of the space, the use of furniture, statues, or other objects that were part of the service?

- What about the "text" and "script"; the types of words that were uttered (and by whom, and when); their sources (sacred books, hymnals, photocopied programs); the music that was played or sung; the periods of prayer or meditation; the ways in which participants were invited to speak (or to remain silent) or otherwise take part? In addition to noting their differences, consider whether there were any similarities in either form or content.

- What similarities and differences did you notice in the behavior of the participants? Were both children and adults present? Did both men and women participate in the same ways? Did participants engage in similar actions and interactions?

- Can you identify any differences in actual beliefs as a result of your observations? What about similarities?

material culture the objects associated with a cultural group, such as tools, machines, utensils, buildings, and artwork: any physical object which we give social meaning

Beliefs may be similar in form, if not exactly in content—for example, most religions feature beliefs about what happens after we die, but while some believe our souls dwell permanently in either heaven or hell, others believe our souls are reincarnated in new bodies in an unending cycle.

- What did you observe in either service that seemed especially unfamiliar to you? What did you observe that seemed the most familiar, even if it was in an unfamiliar setting?

The key here is to focus on both the differences and the similarities. It often happens when we step into a new cultural milieu that we see only the differences and remain blind to the similarities. But identifying fundamental commonalities can make even the most bizarre practices seem less threatening. For example, according to Durkheim (1912/1995), all religions have a set of beliefs about the relationship between the sacred (holy, godlike, supernatural) and the profane (the ordinary, of this world). Can you identify these beliefs in the communities you observed? In addition, every religion has a set of practices that are designed to connect the holy and the worldly in some way. Think about the different rituals you observed: taking communion, for example, or simply praying or singing in a specially designated space. Aren't these rituals each designed to do just that, connect the sacred and profane?

There are two options for completing this Data Workshop.

- *Option 1 (informal)*: Consider the bulleted questions above, and prepare some written notes that you can refer to during in-class discussions. Compare your notes and experiences with other students in small-group discussions. Take this opportunity to learn more about culture and different religious traditions.

- *Option 2 (formal)*: Write a three- to four-page essay analyzing your field experiences and taking into consideration the bulleted questions above. Make sure to refer to your fieldnotes in the essay, and include them as an attachment to your paper.

Components of Culture

Since culture is such a broad concept, it is more easily grasped if we break it down into its constituent parts. Sociologists conceive of culture as consisting of two major categories: material culture and symbolic culture.

Material Culture

Material culture is any physical object to which we give social meaning: art and artifacts, tools and utensils, machines and weapons, clothing and furniture, buildings and toys—the list is immense. Any physical thing that people create, use, or appreciate might be considered material culture.

Examining material culture can tell us a great deal about a particular group or society. Just look around you, whether in your dorm room, a library, a coffee house, or a park—there should be many items that you can identify as belonging to material culture. Start with your own clothes and accessories and then extend your observations to your surroundings—the room, building, landscaping, street, neighborhood, community, and further outward. For instance, the designer label on a woman's purse might convey that she follows the current fashion trends, or the athletic logo on a man's T-shirt might tell us that he is into skateboarding. Likewise, the carpeting, light fixtures, furniture, and artwork in a building can tell us something about the people who live or work there. And the sports arenas, modes of transportation, historical monuments, and city dumps reveal the characteristics of a community. Perhaps the proliferation of drive-thru fast-food restaurants in practically every corner of the United States says something about American tastes and lifestyle: we spend more time on the road, cook fewer meals at home, and prefer the ease and predictability of knowing what we'll get each time we pull up to our favorite chain. If you were visiting another country, then you might see some very different items of material culture.

Studying the significance of material culture is like going on an archeological dig, but learning about the present rather than the distant past. Let's take as an example a sociological "dig" in Santa Barbara, California, where one of the authors of this book lives. Local leaders there have been active in preserving the image of the city, particularly in its downtown historical area. The original mission, presidio (military post), courthouse, and other landmarks built by early Spanish settlers are all still intact. Although the town has grown up around these buildings, zoning regulations require that new construction fit with the distinctive Mediterranean architecture of the "red tile roof" district. The size and design are restricted as well as the use of signs, lighting, paint, and landscaping. Thus, the newly built grocery store with its textured stucco walls, tile murals, and arched porticos may be difficult to distinguish from the century-old post office a few blocks away. By studying its material culture, we can see how Santa Barbara manages to preserve its history and heritage and successfully resist the pressures of encroaching urban development. The distinctive "old California" look and feel

How Is the Architecture of Santa Barbara an Example of Material Culture? Local leaders in Santa Barbara have preserved its history and resisted the pressures of encroaching urban development by insisting on maintaining the look of "old California."

of the city is perhaps its greatest charm, something that appeals to locals and a steady flock of tourists alike.

Symbolic Culture

Nonmaterial or **symbolic culture** reflects the ideas and beliefs of a group of people. It can be something as specific as a certain rule or custom, like driving on the right side of the road in the United States and on the left side in the United Kingdom. It can also be a broad social system such as democracy or a large-scale social pattern such as marriage. Because symbolic culture is so important to social life, let's look further at some of its main aspects.

FORMS OF COMMUNICATION: SIGNS, GESTURES, AND LANGUAGE One of the most important functions of symbolic culture is to allow us to communicate—through signs, gestures, and language. These form the basis of social interaction, a subject so central to sociology that the entire next chapter is devoted to it.

Signs (or symbols) such as a traffic signal, price tag, sheet of music, or product logo are something designed to meaningfully represent something else. They all convey

information. Numbers and letters are the most common signs, but you are probably familiar with other graphic symbols indicating, for instance, which is the men's or women's bathroom, where the elevator is going, how to eject a DVD from the disk drive, or in what lane you should be driving.

While we can easily take for granted the meaning of most symbols, others we may have to learn—like emoticons, those cute (or devious) little expressions that we can now create on our computers. Some symbols may be nearly universal, while others may be particular to a given culture. It may take some interpretive work to understand what a sign means if you are unfamiliar with the context in which it is displayed.

Gestures are signs that we make with our body—clapping our hands, nodding our head, or smiling. Sometimes these acts are referred to as "body language" or "nonverbal communication," since they don't

> **symbolic culture** the ideas associated with a cultural group, including ways of thinking (beliefs, values, and assumptions) and ways of behaving (norms, interactions, and communication)
>
> **sign** a symbol that stands for or conveys an idea
>
> **gestures** the ways in which people use their bodies to communicate without words; actions that have symbolic meaning

language a system of communication using vocal sounds, gestures, or written symbols; the basis of symbolic culture and the primary means through which we communicate with one another and perpetuate our culture

require any words. Gestures can be as subtle as a knowing glance or as obvious as a raised fist.

Most of the time, we can assume that other people will get what we are trying to say with our gestures. But although gestures might seem natural and universal, just a matter of common sense, few of them besides those that represent basic emotions are innate; most have to be learned. For instance, the "thumbs up" sign, which is associated with praise or approval in the United States, might be interpreted as an obscene or insulting gesture in parts of Asia or South America. Every culture has its own way of expressing praise and insulting others. So before leaving for a country whose culture is unfamiliar, it might be worth finding out whether shaking hands or waving goodbye are appropriate ways to communicate.

Language, probably the most significant component of culture, is what has allowed us to fully develop and express ourselves as human beings and what distinguishes us from all other species on the planet. Although language varies from culture to culture, it is a human universal and present in all societies. It is one of the most complex, fluid, and creative symbol systems: letters are combined to form words, and words combined to form sentences, in an almost infinite number of possible ways.

	:-)	=	Smile
	:-(	=	Frown
	;-)	=	Wink
	:-P	=	Tongue Out
	:-D	=	Laughing
	:-[	=	Embarrassed
	:-\	=	Undecided
	=-O	=	Surprise
	:-*	=	Kiss
	>:o	=	Yell
	8-)	=	Cool
	:-$	=	Money Mouth
	:-!	=	Foot in mouth
	O:-)	=	Innocent
	:'(	=	Cry
	:-X	=	Lips are Sealed

Emoticons Symbolic communication takes many forms. As we communicate more frequently through electronic devices, we develop quick symbolic shortcuts like these emoticons to articulate more complex thoughts and feelings.

Gestures and Body Language
If you travel to a foreign culture, pay special attention to how others interpret your body language. Common friendly gestures in one culture can be offensive or confusing in another.

Language is the basis of symbolic culture and the primary means through which we communicate with one another. It allows us to convey complicated abstract concepts and to pass along a culture from one generation to the next. Language helps us to conceive of the past and to plan for the future; to categorize the people, places, and things around us; and to share our perspectives on reality. In this way, the cumulative experience of a group of people—their culture—can be contained in and presented through language.

Language is so important that many have argued that it shapes not only our communication but our perception—the way that we see things—as well. In the 1930s, two anthropologists, Edward Sapir and Benjamin Lee Whorf, conducted research on the impact of language on the mind. In working with the Hopi in the American Southwest, the anthropologists claimed to have discovered that the Hopi had no words to distinguish the past, present, or future and that therefore they did not "see" or experience time in the same way as those whose language provided such words. The result of this research was what is known as the **Sapir-Whorf hypothesis** (sometimes referred to as the principle of linguistic relativity), which, breaking with traditional understandings about language, asserts that language actually structures thought, that perception not only suggests the need for words with which to express what is perceived but also that the words themselves help create those same perceptions (Sapir 1949; Whorf 1956).

The studies by Sapir and Whorf were not published until the 1950s, when they were met with competing linguistic theories. In particular, the idea that Eskimos (or Inuits, as they are now called) had many more words for snow than people of Western cultures was sharply challenged, as was the notion that Hopi had no words for future or past tense (Martin 1986; Pullum 1991). But although there is still some disagreement about how strongly language influences thought (Edgerton 1992), the ideas behind the Sapir-Whorf hypothesis continue to influence numerous social thinkers. Language does play a significant role in how people construct a sense of reality and how they categorize the people, places, and things around them. For instance, the work of sociologist Eviatar Zerubavel (2003) looks at how different groups (like Jews and Arabs, or Serbs and Croats) use language to construct an understanding of their heritage—through what he calls "social memory." In a country like the United States, where there are approximately 50 million foreign-born people who speak well over 100 different languages, there are bound to be differences in perceptual realities as a result.

Does the Sapir-Whorf hypothesis hold true for your world? Let's take an example closer to home. Perhaps you have seen the 2004 movie *Mean Girls*, loosely based on a pop sociology book by Rosalind Wiseman, *Queen Bees and Wannabes*, about the culture of high school girls (2002). Both book and film present a social map of the cafeteria and school grounds, identifying where different groups of students— the "jocks," "cheerleaders," "goths," "preppies," "skaters," "nerds," "hacky-sack kids," "easy girls," and "partiers"— hang out. The book also includes the "populars" (referred to in the movie as the "plastics") and the popular "wannabes."

You were probably aware of similar categories for distinguishing groups at your school. Do such classification systems influence the way you see other people? Do

Sapir-Whorf hypothesis the idea that language structures thought and that ways of looking at the world are embedded in language

***Mean Girls* and the Cafeteria Classification System** This map from the film *Mean Girls* is an example of how we use different classification schemes to identify and categorize the world around us. Do these classification systems influence the way that you see other people?

they lead you to identify people by type and place them into those categories? If no such labels existed, would you still perceive your former classmates the same way? Probably not. These kinds of questions highlight how important language is to the meanings we give to our everyday world.

Values, Norms, and Sanctions

Values and norms are symbolic culture in action. When we know the values and norms of a group (and see how they are controlled by sanctions), then we can understand their beliefs and ideals and see the evidence of these throughout their everyday lives.

VALUES Values are the set of shared beliefs about what a group of people consider to be worthwhile or desirable in life—what is good or bad, right or wrong, beautiful or ugly. They articulate the essence of everything that a cultural group cherishes in its society. For instance, most Americans value the equality and individual freedoms of democracy. Structural functionalists, like Durkheim, stress the strength of shared values and their role in regulating the behavior of society's members. However, there is not always widespread agreement about which values should represent a society, and values may change or new values may emerge over time. For example, workers' loyalty to their company was once much more important than it currently is. In today's economy, workers realize that they may be "downsized" in times of financial trouble or that they may change careers over the course of their lifetime and hence feel less obligation to an employer.

NORMS Norms are the rules and guidelines regarding what kinds of behavior are acceptable; they develop directly out of a culture's value system. Whether legal regulations or just social expectations, norms are largely agreed upon by most members of a group. Some norms are *formal*, or officially codified. These include **laws** (such as those making it illegal to speed in a school zone or drink before you turn twenty-one), rules for playing basketball or for membership at your local gym, the Amendments to the U.S. Constitution, and the behavioral prescriptions conveyed in the Ten Commandments. Despite the relative authority of formal norms, they are not *always* followed.

Other norms are *informal*, meaning that they are implicit and unspoken. For instance, when we wait in line to buy tickets for a movie, we expect that no one will cut in front of us. Informal norms are so much a part of our assumptions about life that they are embedded in our consciousness; they cover almost every aspect of our social lives, from what we say and do to even how we think and feel. Though we might have difficulty listing all the norms that are a part of everyday life, most of us have learned them quite well. They are simply "the way things are done." Often, it is only when norms are broken (as when someone cuts in line) that we recognize they exist. You learned this firsthand in the "doing nothing" experiment in Chapter 1's Data Workshop.

Norms can be broken down further in three ways. **Folkways** are the ordinary conventions of everyday life and are not strictly enforced. Examples are standards of dress and rules of etiquette: in most places, wearing flip-flops with a tuxedo is just not done! When people do not conform to folkways, they are thought of as peculiar or eccentric but not really dangerous. **Mores** are norms that carry a greater moral significance and are more closely related to the core values of a cultural group. Unlike folkways, mores are norms to which we all are expected to conform. Breaches are treated seriously and often bring severe repercussions. Such mores as the prohibition of theft, rape, and murder are also formalized, so that there is not only public condemnation for such acts but also strict laws against them. **Taboos**, a type of more, are the most powerful of all norms. We sometimes use the word in a casual way to indicate, say, a forbidden subject. But as a sociological term it holds even greater meaning. Taboos are extremely serious. Sociologists say that our sense of what is taboo is so deeply ingrained that the very thought of committing a taboo act, such as cannibalism or incest, evokes strong feelings of disgust or horror.

Norms are specific to a culture, time period, and situation. What would be a folkway to one group might be a more to another. For instance, public nudity is acceptable in many cultures, whereas it is not only frowned upon in American culture but also illegal in most instances. At the same time, Americans do permit nudity in such situations as strip clubs and nudist resorts, allowing for a kind of moral holiday from the strictures of imposed norms. At certain times like Mardi Gras and spring break, mild norm violations are tolerated. Certain places may also lend themselves to the suspension of norms—think Las Vegas (and the slogan: "What happens in Vegas, stays in Vegas").

values ideas about what is desirable or contemptible and right or wrong in a particular group. They articulate the essence of everything that a cultural group cherishes and honors.

norm a rule or guideline regarding what kinds of behavior are acceptable and appropriate within a culture

law a common type of formally defined norm, providing an explicit statement about what is permissible and what is illegal in a given society

folkway a loosely enforced norm involving common customs, practices, or procedures that ensure smooth social interaction and acceptance

more a norm that carries great moral significance, is closely related to the core values of a cultural group, and often involves severe repercussions for violators

taboo a norm ingrained so deeply that even thinking about violating it evokes strong feelings of disgust, horror, or revulsion

Norms Are Specific to a Situation, Culture, and Time Period For example, at Mardi Gras or during spring break trips, mild norm violations are tolerated.

Similarly, what would be considered murder on the city streets might be regarded as valor on the battlefield. And we are probably all aware of how the folkways around proper etiquette and attire can vary greatly from one generation to the next; fifty years ago, girls would never wear jeans to school, for example.

SANCTIONS **Sanctions** are a means of enforcing norms. They include rewards for conformity and punishments for violations. *Positive sanctions* express approval and may come in the form of a handshake or a smile, praise, or perhaps an award. *Negative sanctions* express disapproval and may come in the form of a frown, harsh words, or perhaps a fine or incarceration.

From a functionalist perspective, we can see how sanctions help to establish **social control**, ensuring that people behave to some degree in acceptable ways and thus promoting social cohesion. There are many forms of authority in our culture—from the government and police to school administrators, work supervisors, and even parents. Each has a certain amount of power that they can exercise to get others to follow their rules. So when someone is caught violating a norm, there is usually some prescribed sanction that will then be administered, serving as a deterrent to that behavior.

But equally important in maintaining social order is the process of socialization by which people internalize norms. For instance, in 1983, the U.S. Department of Transportation pioneered the slogan "Friends Don't Let Friends Drive Drunk"; over the years, the slogan has helped change the way we think about our personal responsibility for others, with nearly 80 percent of Americans now claiming that they have taken action to prevent someone from driving while intoxicated. What began as an external statement of a social more quickly became our own personal sense of morality. We are often unaware of the extent to which our own conscience acts to keep us from violating social norms in the first place. If we have internalized norms, then outside sanctions are no longer needed to make us do the right thing. Social control, then, frequently looks like self control.

Variations in Culture

For instance, sociologists who have tried to identify the core values that make up American society (Williams 1965; Bellah et al. 1985) have found that while there do seem to be certain beliefs that most Americans share, such as freedom and democracy, there are also inconsistencies between such beliefs as individualism (in which we do what is best for ourselves) and humanitarianism (in which we do what is best for others), and between equality and group superiority. New values such as self-fulfillment and environmentalism could also be added to the list, having gained popularity in recent years.

It is even difficult to speak of an "American culture." *Cultural diversity* and *multiculturalism* have both become buzzwords in the past few decades, precisely because people are aware of the increasing variety of cultural groups within American society. **Multiculturalism** generally describes a policy that involves honoring the diverse racial, ethnic, national, and linguistic backgrounds of various individuals and

sanction positive or negative reactions to the ways that people follow or disobey norms, including rewards for conformity and punishments for norm violations

social control the formal and informal mechanisms used to increase conformity to values and norms and thus increase social cohesion

multiculturalism a policy that values diverse racial, ethnic, national, and linguistic backgrounds and so encourages the retention of cultural differences within society rather than assimilation

In Relationships

Institutional Values and College Life

As a college student, you may live on campus or make use of the student health services. In doing either of these things, you are in a situation in which someone else's values (in this case, those of the college) can influence your individual choices. For example, even if you get to choose your own roommate, the university has adopted a set of values that narrows your choice for you before you even make it. And if your student health service is operated by an outside contractor (for example, the local Catholic hospital), there may be constraints placed on the type of reproductive health services you can receive there.

Rules like these come from a tradition in which the university acts *in loco parentis*—in place of the parents—to protect and provide moral guidance for its students. The Bradley University Student Handbook for 1952–53, for example, forbids women from entering men's residences at any time and places severe constraints on when and under what conditions men may enter women's residences. This same handbook lists a complicated procedure for female students to follow in order to attend off-campus events in

the evenings, and there are even lists of appropriate attire for the classroom, athletic events, and other university functions.

While most universities have abandoned the strict behavior codes that were once widespread, they still act *in loco parentis* in a variety of ways. One of them is the restrictions they place on different-sex roommates, even in coed dorms. The university has taken on the job of protecting students from the apparently undesirable consequences of living with a romantic partner. And if the student health service limits your access to certain means of birth control, then choices about whom to live with, how to conduct your sex life, and how to include your romantic partner in your domestic life have already been made for you by the university. If you want to live in university housing and use student health services, you must accept the constraints imposed by university values, even if you do not share those values. If you want to live without those constraints then you must choose to live in a private, off-campus setting.

groups. In following chapters, we will explore some of these differences in greater depth.

Dominant Culture

Although *culture* is a term we usually apply to an entire group of people, what we find in reality is that there are often many subgroups within a larger culture, each with its own particular makeup. These subgroups, however, are not all equal. Some, by virtue of size, wealth, or historical happenstance, are able to lay claim to greater power and influence in society than others. The values, norms, and practices of the most powerful groups are referred to as the mainstream

dominant culture the values, norms, and practices of the group within society that is most powerful (in terms of wealth, prestige, status, influence, etc.)

hegemony term developed by Antonio Gramsci to describe the cultural aspects of social control, whereby the ideas of the dominant social group are accepted by all of society

or **dominant culture**, while others are seen as "alternative" or minority views. The power of the dominant culture may mean that other ways of seeing and doing things are relegated to second-class status—in this way, dominant culture can produce cultural **hegemony**, or dominance (Gramsci 1985, 1988).

Let's take popular music as an example. Commercial radio stations often have very limited playlists. No matter what the format (country, pop, hip-hop, metal), the songs you can listen to are determined by station and record company business interests, not your artistic preferences. Truly new artists and alternative sounds can be heard only on public, college, or pirate radio stations or online—and these outlets have significantly fewer financial resources and reach far fewer listeners. The dominant status of commercial radio and the corporate interests of the music industry dictate that musicians outside the mainstream like Firekites, The Tunics, and Ra Ra Riot will never be as big as Beyoncé or Justin Timberlake.

Subcultures

If sociologists focus only on the dominant culture in American society, we risk overlooking the inequalities that structure our society—as well as the influences that even nondominant cultural groups can exert. The United States is filled with thousands of nondominant groups, any of which could be called a **subculture**—a culture within a culture. A subculture is a particular social world that has a distinctive way of life, including its own set of values and norms, practices, and beliefs, but that exists harmoniously within the larger mainstream culture. A subculture can be based on ethnicity, age, interests, or anything else that draws individuals together. Any of the following groups could be considered subcultures within American society: Korean Americans, senior citizens, snowboarders, White Sox fans, greyhound owners, firefighters, Trekkers.

Countercultures

A **counterculture**, another kind of subgroup, differs from a subculture in that its norms and values are often incompatible with or in direct opposition to the mainstream (Zellner 1995). Some countercultures are political or activist groups attempting to bring about social change; others resist mainstream values by living outside society or practicing an alternative lifestyle. In the 1960s, hippies, antiwar protestors, feminists, and others in the so-called political left were collectively known as "the counterculture." But radicals come in many stripes. Any group that opposes the dominant culture, whether they are eco-terrorists, computer hackers, or modern-day polygamists, can be considered a counterculture.

In the mid-1990s, American countercultures of the far right gained prominence with the revelation that the main perpetrator of the April 1995 bombing of the Alfred R. Murrah Federal Building in Oklahoma City, Timothy McVeigh, had ties to "militia" or "patriot" groups. And he wasn't the only one. In 1996, the Southern Poverty Law Center, which tracks such groups, counted 858 active groups in the United States belonging to the "militia movement" (the number was reduced to 171 in 2003). Members of this movement, who trace their heritage to the Minutemen of the American Revolution (an elite fighting force, the first to arrive at a battle), saw themselves as the last line of defense for the liberties provided in the U.S. Constitution. They believed, moreover, that the federal government had become the enemy of those liberties. They held that gun control, environmental protection laws, and other legislation violated individual and states' rights and that events like the FBI's 1993 siege of the Branch Davidian compound in Waco, Texas (resulting in 82 deaths), called for armed grassroots organization.

Since the Oklahoma City bombing, some militia groups have courted recognition as legitimate American institutions rather than radical organizations. Others have remained openly countercultural. While members of such groups consider themselves "patriots" and "true Americans," they believe that the institutions and values of contemporary American society need drastic revision.

> **subculture** a group within society that is differentiated by its distinctive values, norms, and lifestyle
>
> **counterculture** a group within society that openly rejects and/or actively opposes society's values and norms

Old and New Countercultures The Black Panther Party, which was founded by Huey Newton, is an example of a social movement from the 1960s counterculture. New countercultures can include polygamist families like Tom Green and his five wives.

Changing the World

Principles and Practices— Values, Norms, and Laws in Flux

1770: George Washington and Thomas Jefferson grow hemp (*cannabis sativa*, the botanical classification for marijuana) on their Virginia plantations. Hemp was used to make fabric, rope, and paper, including the paper on which Jefferson drafted the Declaration of Independence.

1937: In schools across the United States, students watch a scholastic film called *Reefer Madness*, an antimarijuana propaganda piece that uses images of insanity, rape, and murder to paint a picture of pot as a catastrophic scourge on society. Every state in the country outlaws the use of marijuana as an intoxicant, and hemp farming is effectively eliminated at the federal level by the passage of the prohibitive Marijuana Tax Act.

1992: Arkansas governor and presidential candidate Bill Clinton admits on MTV's *Rock the Vote/Choose or Lose* that he smoked marijuana in college but "didn't inhale" (Schlosser 2003).

He "Didn't Inhale" Bill Clinton appears on MTV with young voters during his first presidential campaign in 1992.

2002: A number of states, including California, Colorado, Illinois, New York, and Ohio, decriminalize marijuana use and possession to varying degrees, including allowing the medical use of marijuana for cancer and AIDS patients. However, other states such as Oklahoma and Indiana punish mere possession of marijuana with long prison sentences, up to and including life without parole. In some cases, selling marijuana can be punished more harshly than rape or murder (Schlosser 2003).

Reefer Madness This cautionary film from 1937 was shown to students to warn them about the dangers of marijuana, including rape, insanity, and murder.

Hemp Can Be Used to Make Fabric, Rope, and Paper This farmer measures crops to see if they are ready for harvesting. Kim Roberts helps a customer at her store, All about Hemp, which sells hemp-based products including shoes, clothing, and shampoo.

2005: The Supreme Court rules that federal antidrug laws can be used to prosecute those involved in cultivating and prescribing marijuana for medical purposes, even in states that have legalized the practice.

2008: Massachusetts representative Barney Frank introduces a federal marijuana decriminalization bill to Congress.

As you can see, American values and norms surrounding the various uses of *cannabis sativa* have shifted over time and sometimes seem downright contradictory. The very first marijuana-related law *required* Virginia colonists to grow hemp in 1619 (Schlosser 2003, p. 19); by 1937, all its uses were outlawed. Today, we confront a kind of cultural schizophrenia about marijuana—our desire to benefit from its helpful properties is matched only by our fear of

its harmful ones. Should we allow hemp farming to stop the clear-cutting of ancient forests by the paper industry? Should we allow restricted marijuana use to relieve the suffering of cancer, AIDS, epilepsy, and glaucoma patients, as medical research suggests? Or should we treat pot as we treat other illegal drugs like crack cocaine and heroin, by severely punishing those who grow, buy, and sell it? Isn't there some middle ground?

The case of changing marijuana laws serves as an example of an important cultural principle: what was once mainstream may later be defined as deviant; what is now seen as deviant may someday be normal and acceptable. Why? Because values change over time and differ across cultures. Changing values lead to changing laws and changing practices in our everyday lives.

Are there any current counterculture values that you think might someday enter the mainstream? No matter how dangerous or threatening they may seem now, it is entirely possible that they will be taken for granted as normal in 10, 25, 50, or 100 years. And what about the mainstream values that we currently take for granted? In a decade or a century, some will be rejected as aberrant. It's hard to imagine right now . . . but history tells us it will most definitely happen.

culture wars clashes within mainstream society over the values and norms that should be upheld

ideal culture the norms, values, and patterns of behavior that members of a society believe should be observed in principle

real culture the norms, values, and patterns of behavior that actually exist within a society (which may or may not correspond to the society's ideals)

At the furthest extreme are militia groups who hold that the present American government is entirely illegitimate and that they are not its subjects but rather "sovereign citizens," "common-law citizens," or "freemen." Members refuse to carry documents such as driver's licenses and social security cards and refuse to pay taxes or observe any government restrictions on their property. They have gone so far as to establish "common-law courts" that oppose local and federal government regulations and seek to prosecute government officials (Diamond 1995). They also often train in "survivalist" tactics, preparing for a more cataclysmic confrontation with the government. And in an interesting example of the influence of countercultural values on the mainstream, many ordinary Americans found themselves adopting "survivalist" attitudes in preparation for the disastrous social breakdowns predicted at the beginning of 2000 (Y2K). Many stocked up on supplies such as freeze-dried foods, electrical generators, and weapons for self-defense, ordering from suppliers who had previously only catered to the countercultures of the far right.

Culture Wars

Although a countercultural group can pose a threat to the larger society, conflict does not always come from the extreme margins of society; it can also emerge from within the mainstream. Culture in any diverse society is characterized by points of tension and division. There is not always uniform agreement about which values and norms ought to be upheld. The term **culture wars** is often used to describe the clashes that arise as a result (Bloom 1987; Garber 1998). The clashes are frequently played out in the media, where social commentators and pundits debate the issues. Culture wars are mainly waged over values and morality and the solutions to social problems, with liberals and conservatives fighting to define culture in America. One notable example of a battle in the culture wars was a speech given by then Vice-President Dan Quayle in 1992, in which he condemned the fictional TV character Murphy Brown for "choosing" single parenthood; another is the scuffle over media and morality that surrounded singer Janet Jackson's breast-baring during the 2004 Super Bowl telecast. Other questions of family values, changing gender roles, frontiers in bioethics, violence in the media, and school prayer have all been recent topics for discussion. Culture wars are bound to continue as we confront the difficult realities that are a part of living in a democratic society.

Ideal vs. Real Culture

Some norms and values are more aspired to than actually practiced. It is useful to draw a distinction between **ideal culture**, the norms and values that members of a society believe should be observed in principle, and **real culture**, the patterns of behavior that actually exist. Whether it is an

Culture Wars Often Play Out on Early-Morning or Late-Night Television George Stephanopoulos (second from left) spends every Sunday morning interviewing politicians on *This Week with George Stephanopoulos*. On weeknights, comedian Jon Stewart (far right) hosts *The Daily Show*, which satirizes the network news and levels comedic criticisms against mainstream media and politics.

organization that falls short of its own mission statement or a person who says one thing and does another (a devout Catholic, for example, who finds himself seeking a divorce), what we believe in and what we do may be two different things.

Let's take, as another example, corporate culture in America. The ideal culture of the workplace usually dictates that raises and promotions be given to employees who have demonstrated exemplary performance or productiveness through skill, dedication, or innovative thinking. In practice, these rewards are also given to less deserving employees who are appreciated for other qualities such as obedience, charisma, or their special relationship with the boss. While most people believe that hard work or initiative should be what determines success, they know that in reality it is not always these qualities that are rewarded and that indeed sometimes employees climb the ladder for more dubious reasons (Hagberg and Heifetz 2002).

Another example of how real and ideal culture may clash in the workplace comes from a management book called *Weird Ideas That Work*, by Stanford professor Robert Sutton (2001), who observes that while corporate executives often claim they value innovation, they usually reward conformity instead. Sutton recommends that instead of hiring comfortable, familiar types of people who know the rules and submit without argument to the authority of their superiors, corporations should hire eccentrics who ignore the rules, enjoy a good fight, and defy authority. For those who claim they value creativity, Sutton argues this is the only way to really achieve their ideals.

High, Low, and Popular Culture

Culture wars can be fought just about anywhere. In the summer of 1998, an exhibit opened at the Guggenheim Museum in New York City that was uniformly panned by the critics. The *New Republic* called the exhibit "a pop nostalgia orgy masquerading as a major artistic statement," and *Salon*'s art critic accused the Guggenheim of "wear[ing] its cultural pants around its ankles" and "sucking down to our lowest impulses." What were they so upset about?

The exhibit was entitled "The Art of the Motorcycle," and the critics were upset because motorcycles weren't, in their opinion, art. The public, on the other hand, loved it— the exhibit broke all previous museum attendance records. People who might never otherwise have set foot in the

museum came to view this colorful collection of motorcycles dating from 1868 to 1998.

The motorcycles at the Guggenheim stirred up a long-standing debate that questioned the very definitions of art and culture. The critics' objections were based on their perception that **popular culture**, or mass culture (motorcycles), had invaded a **high culture** venue (the Guggenheim Museum). In this case, popular culture was seen as unsavory and even dangerous—the implication being that pop culture is a mass phenomenon that somehow threatens the position of the elites by challenging their preferences. As with so many sociological concepts, these terms come originally from the German; in this case, *kultur* (the culture of the elite classes) and *massenkultur* (the culture of the masses). But are these two categories really that separate?

First, there are multiple high cultures and multiple pop cultures, based on differences in taste and aesthetics. Also, each category has its own set of hierarchies. For example,

popular culture usually contrasted with the high culture of elite groups; forms of cultural expression usually associated with the masses, consumer goods, and commercial products

high culture those forms of cultural expression usually associated with the elite or dominant classes

Is This Art? The 1998 show "The Art of the Motorcycle" at the Guggenheim Museum in New York broke attendance records but attracted negative reviews from art critics for "sucking down to our lowest impulses."

rap and hip-hop music are definitely pop culture phenomena. Produced by mostly minority artists for whom "street credibility" is one of the most important qualifications, these musical forms have widespread popular appeal, especially among teenagers and young adults. But rap and hip-hop have their own elites, artists who are at the top of the charts and who have a great deal of influence within and outside their pop culture domain. Examples such as Sean "Diddy" Combs, Queen Latifah, Kanye West, and Jay-Z, the elites of the rap and hip-hop worlds, show that the distinction between mass and elite is a fuzzy one.

There is another way in which this distinction is problematic. In the real world, most cultural products contain elements of both mass and high culture. Why do you think we call certain TV programs soap "operas"? The storylines and intense emotions of *All My Children* parallel and sometimes rival those of Giacomo Puccini's *Madama Butterfly* and Wolfgang Amadeus Mozart's *Don Giovanni*. Led Zeppelin and Van Halen songs, when written out in standard musical notation, show a recognizable symphonic structure. Rap and hip-hop overtly draw on other types of music in the practice of sampling, and Ludwig von Beethoven, Georges Bizet, and

High Art and Pop Art Are Not Mutually Exclusive Even though Warhol's work is now exhibited in high culture venues like esteemed modern art museums, he was perceived as a threat to the "real" art world when he began his work in the 1960s. At bottom is Warhol's subversion of a high art masterpiece, Leonardo da Vinci's *Last Supper* (above).

Béla Bartók have all been sampled by R&B artists. These examples, and many others, indicate that high and pop culture are not mutually exclusive and can coexist within the same product.

The distinctions between high and popular culture are based on the characteristics of their audiences. Differences of class, education, race, and even religion help create these categories. Sociologist Herbert Gans (1999) calls the groups of people who share similar artistic, recreational, and intellectual interests **taste publics**. Taste publics aren't necessarily organized groups, but they do inhabit the same aesthetic worlds, which Gans calls **taste cultures**—that is, people who share the same tastes will also usually move in the same cultural circles as well. For example, sociologist David Halle (1993) found that members of the upper class are more likely to have abstract paintings hanging in their homes, while members of the working class are more likely to display family photographs in their homes.

The music, movies, clothes, foods, art, books, magazines, cars, sports, and television programs you enjoy are influenced at least in part by your position in society. Unknowingly, you belong to a number of taste publics and inhabit a number of taste cultures, in that you share your interests with others who are similar to you sociologically. What you think of as your own unique individual preferences are in some ways predetermined by your age, race, class and education levels, and regional location.

Polysemy, Audiences, and Fans

The saga of the motorcycles at the Guggenheim should help us understand an important concept in the study of culture: polysemy. Sociologists use the term **polysemy** to describe how any cultural product is subject to multiple interpretations and hence has many possible meanings (Hall 1980; Fiske 1989). For instance, a cartoon like *The Simpsons* can be enjoyed on a variety of levels, by children and adults, for its humor alone and for its political commentary. Polysemy helps us understand how one person can absolutely love the same movie (or song, painting, cartoon, necklace, car, meal, or tattoo) that another person absolutely hates. Meaning is not a given, nor is it entirely open—we make meaning individually and together, as audiences and consumers of culture.

Some researchers have been concerned with whether popular culture can cause certain types of behavior (Gerbner and Gross 1976; Gerbner et al. 1980; Malamuth and Donnerstein 1984; Weinstein 1991, 2000). Do TV crime shows increase our propensity to violence? Do pornographic magazines lead to the abuse of women? Does heavy metal music make teenagers suicidal? Such questions suggest that cultural products impose their intrinsic meanings on their audiences in a simplistic, stimulus-and-response fashion. But while it is true that mass media products are potentially powerful transmitters of cultural values and norms, the process is neither immediate nor uncomplicated. As we know, audiences come from different backgrounds, which help define experiences and interpret the cultural products we consume. This makes it more likely, then, that polysemy will come into play: that audience members will interpret the same texts in different ways.

One way we can make meaning together is by being part of an **interpretive community**, a group specifically dedicated to the consumption and interpretation of a particular cultural product. For example, let's say you get together with friends every week to watch *Lost*. You enjoy discussing the intrigue surrounding Jack, Sawyer, Hurley, Kate, and the others while the show is on and at other times during the week (perhaps in e-mails). Indeed, if you have to skip an episode for some reason, you must be brought up to date by one of your comrades. Alternatively, you could visit the network's official website and get caught up there, or visit one of the many fan websites where you can interact with other fans. And there you have it—you're part of an interpretive community! By consuming a cultural product as a group, members make its meaning collective rather than individual and can influence each other's cultural experience.

We may acknowledge that things like watching soap operas, reading comic books, and playing video games are trivial in the larger scheme of things, but if these forms of pop culture give us pleasure and connect us with others, they may not be so trivial after all. Serious sociological insights can be gained from studying what appear to be superficial pursuits (Postman 1987; Schudson 2003). In fact, we will devote an entire chapter to leisure and recreation later in the book. Culture is actually serious business.

taste publics groups of people who share similar artistic, literary, media, recreational, and intellectual interests

taste cultures areas of culture that share similar aesthetics and standards of taste

polysemy having many possible meanings or interpretations

interpretive community a group of people dedicated to the consumption and interpretation of a particular cultural product and who create a collective, social meaning for the product

On the Job

U.S. Military

An e-mail from Afghanistan, May 30, 2003:

> A couple of hours after we landed, we had a convoy to Kabul. It took about two hours, but I will never forget the trip. The scenery was incredible. I knew that there were mountains in Afghanistan, but there are so many that it is an unbelievable sight. . . . The native people are also a sight to see. These people are incredibly resourceful making shelter from clay and mud and using the minimal resources they have to work with. (Carroll 2006, p. 67)

Like most Americans, the writer of this e-mail, Army Sergeant Andrew Simkiewicz, had never been to Afghanistan before. His deployment there was part of Operation Enduring Freedom, America's post–September 11th effort to hunt Al Qaeda terrorists, depose Taliban leaders, and find Osama bin Laden. You might not think a soldier would notice the beauty of the Afghan landscape, but soldiers aren't one-dimensional warriors, and their missions aren't solely combat oriented. Wherever they serve, American military personnel have the opportunity to learn about other cultures and to act as representatives of American culture to the people they encounter.

When "in country," soldiers notice the effects of war on the citizens of places like Iraq. They also notice the differences between Iraqis' experiences and those of ordinary Americans at home. Here Army Captain James R. Sosnicky describes an Iraqi woman he knew who sold cigarettes in the Baghdad Green Zone:

> When she was a young girl, Iranian missiles pounded the street. The Americans have bombed her three times since, in 1991, 1998 and 2003. Mariam . . . knows things women her age in the United States do not. A couple of weeks ago I was in Baghdad, visiting with Mariam. There was an explosion in the distance. "What do you think," I asked, "car bomb or mortar round?" "Definitely a mortar round," she replied. Most girls in the U.S. have a tin ear for such things. (Carroll 2006, p. 130)

Soldiers also come to recognize the deep connections and similarities between the people whose territory they occupy and their friends and family members back in the United States, as does Army First Sergeant August C. Hohl, Jr., writing from Afghanistan:

> [T]heir personal and religious beliefs are not unlike ours in that everyone understands the importance of reaching out to and being charitable towards one another. . . . [W]hile we all might live differently due to environmental, geographical and educational conditions, people are basically the same inside. Learning some of the history, social habits, and religion of this country has left me with a profound sense of hope that we can assist the people here. But we're not so smart that we can't learn from them, too. (Carroll 2006, p. 68)

U.S. service personnel represent U.S. culture anywhere they are posted—often in war zones where they may or may not be welcome. So they engage in humanitarian work in addition to their combat assignments—here, Sergeant Simkiewicz tells of breaking Army rules to help Afghan children:

> We were told not to give any of our food or water to the natives. However, I find it hard to see these cute children starving on the side of the road while I have a case of bottled water next to me in the cab. Needless to say, a half dozen of my waters were hurled from my window along the way. (Carroll 2006, p. 67)

Elsewhere in Afghanistan, soldiers like Army Chief Warrant Officer II Jared S. Jones distribute humanitarian aid, "ranging from personal hygiene to school supplies, shoes and soccer balls. It is always a pleasure to see the difference we are making for these people, even if it is only one small village" (Carroll 2006, p. 70). As Chief Warrant Officer Jones reminds us, "combat is only one facet of the military, a necessary evil" (Carroll, 2006, p. 71). Their other roles will include "cultural emissary" and "cultural observer" as well, roles that are just as important—and perhaps even more important—than the role of warrior.

The Voice of America: Spreading Propaganda or Democratic Values?

The Voice of America (VOA) began in 1942 as a radio news broadcast to parts of Europe and North Africa. Today, it broadcasts in 44 languages, 24 hours a day, around the globe, on radio, TV, and the internet. Whether the broadcasts are in Dari, Amharic, or Macedonian, the VOA claims to provide objective news about the United States and the world, including uncensored news about the host country, whatever its internal politics may be. Some listeners, foreign and domestic, criticize VOA's claims of objectivity, saying that it is American political propaganda; others trust its world news service, even listening in secret in order to find out what is really happening in their own countries and abroad.

Daw Aung San Suu Kyi

VOA broadcasts, whatever their actual content (which can include music, interviews, and variety shows as well as news), also transmit core American values such as freedom of speech and of the press, human rights, and democratic decision making. To some repressive regimes, these values are seen as dangerous and inflammatory and are held up as evidence of America's cultural imperialism. VOA frequencies are sometimes blocked by those who seek to stifle the ideas VOA communicates. And sometimes VOA listeners are punished for the very act of tuning in.

Burmese human rights activist Daw Aung San Suu Kyi has spent almost 15 years under house arrest at the hands of Myanmar's (Burma's) military dictatorship, was separated from her husband and children in London for even longer, and won the Nobel Peace Prize in 1991 for her selfless efforts on behalf of Burmese democracy. In a 2000 message to the U.N. Commission on Human Rights in Geneva, Suu Kyi told the story of a Burmese man persecuted for merely listening to VOA:

> U Than Chaun, the 70-year-old proprietor of a coffee shop in Schwe-goo township, Kachin state, was arrested and his radio, which was tuned to the Voice of America Burmese broadcast, was seized.... [H]e was charged and sentenced to two years' imprisonment. U Than Chaun's wife was suffering from a heart ailment . . . and she passed away while he was in prison. He himself suffers medical problems which have now become life threatening.

> She also asks: "In which country of the world are people so oppressed that listening to a radio deserves two years of imprisonment?" The VOA would like the answer to that question to be "none."

Politics can generate the same anti-American feeling. For example, the United States has recently been involved in attempts to stem the development of nuclear weapons in developing countries like Iran and Pakistan while still maintaining our own nuclear arsenal at home. Other nations may question why American politicians think they should be able to withhold from other countries privileges the United States itself enjoys, such as developing a nuclear weapons program. Much of the resentment against America abroad emerges as a result of this type of phenomenon—our perceived failure to live up to our own political values and ideals or to apply them fairly to others.

Putting American culture in perspective means recognizing that because it is pervasive, it may also be viewed with suspicion and even contempt when the values it expresses clash with those of other cultures. But the nature of anti-Americanism is complex—it's not merely a failure by other nations to understand "good" television shows or accept "superior" political systems. There are meaningful cultural differences between Americans and others, and we should keep those differences in mind as we read about or travel to other cultures. Indeed, there are cultural differences of similar magnitude within the United States as well. The question of the meaning of American culture is a complicated one.

TABLE 4.1 *Theory in Everyday Life*

Perspective	Approach to Culture	Case Study: Religion
STRUCTURAL-FUNCTIONALISM	Cultural elements such as values and norms contribute to social stability by constraining individual desires.	Religious prohibitions against premarital sex encourage people to marry and start families, which is functional for society and contributes to social stability.
CONFLICT THEORY	Values and norms can be different within different subgroups, and norms may be applied to different groups unequally. In addition, norms and values may be imported from one group to another, or used by one group to change or control another.	Iran officially censors non-Islamic media to impede the spread of secular, Western values such as sexual freedom or permissiveness that may be embedded in television shows such as *Grey's Anatomy* or *Sex in the City*.
SYMBOLIC INTERACTIONISM	Values and norms are social constructions, created, maintained, and changed through continuing interaction.	Religious rituals are verbal and gestural—in other words, they are interactional. Reciting the Lord's Prayer, bowing toward Mecca, keeping a kosher home—all of these actions and interactions help create meaning for those who practice religion. Interaction creates religious change as well—in 2003 the Episcopal church ordained Gene Robinson, its first gay bishop, after weeks of heated debate.

Closing Comments

In this chapter, we have seen how seemingly simple elements of material culture (cars and comic books) and symbolic culture (norms and values) create complex links between the individual and her society, as well as between different societies around the globe. American culture in particular, sociologists often argue, is hegemonic (dominant), in that certain interests (such as creating a global market for American products) prevail, while others (such as encouraging local development and self-determination) are subordinated. Within the United States, this can mean that the cultural norms, values, beliefs, and practices of certain subcultures—such as minority ethnic or religious groups—are devalued. Elsewhere, it can mean that America is accused of cultural imperialism by nations whose values and practices are different than ours.

Whose cultural values and practices are "better" or "right"? The sociological perspective avoids these evaluative terms when examining culture, choosing instead to take a relativistic approach. In other words, different cultures should (in most cases) be evaluated not according to outside standards but according to their own sets of values and norms. But we should always recognize that this commitment to cultural relativism is a value in itself—which makes cultural relativism neither right nor wrong but rather a proper subject for intellectual examination.

Find more review materials online at
www.wwnorton.com/studyspace

CHAPTER SUMMARY

- **What Is Culture and How Is It Studied?** Culture, one of the broadest and most fundamental concepts of social life, is the lens through which we view the world. Culture is learned slowly and incrementally, it is internalized, and it is ubiquitous. It is difficult to study, in part because it is all-encompassing and in part because it is hard for sociologists to view cultures (including their own) impartially.

- Unlike anthropologists, who often intentionally seek out foreign cultures, most sociologists focus on their own cultures. However, many sociologists still engage in the process of "othering," selecting areas of culture that seem exotic or bizarre. When studying any group it is important to employ cultural relativism—that is, to see and study any culture in its own right rather than making judgments based on your own culture's norms.

- **Components of Culture** Students of culture may divide the topic into two categories: material culture, which consists of any physical object to which we give meaning (from buildings and architecture to key chains and toys), and nonmaterial or symbolic culture composed of ideas and beliefs. Symbolic culture can then be broken down further into types of communication as well as values and norms.

- Communication is one of the most important functions of symbolic culture. Signs and gestures are the simplest forms of communication. Language, the basis for symbolic culture, is more complicated. Some theorists, like Edward Sapir and Benjamin Lee Whorf, have argued that language goes beyond mere communication and shapes our perceptions. Although some of their findings have been discredited, this idea remains influential.

- Values, shared beliefs about what the group considers worthwhile or desirable, guide the creation of norms, which are formal and informal rules about acceptable behaviors. Types of norms can be distinguished by the strictness with which they are enforced. Folkways, ordinary conventions of everyday life, are loosely enforced norms. Mores are closely related to the culture's core values, so they carry much greater weight and are more likely to be formalized. Taboos, the most strongly enforced norms of all, are felt so deeply that even thinking about a violation is disturbing.

- Positive and negative sanctions help maintain norms and enforce social control. This control may also be enforced by authority figures such as parents and police, but socialization is equally important, since internalized norms become self-enforcing. Additionally, it is important to distinguish between ideal culture, the norms that members of a group believe should be observed, and real culture, which describes actual patterns of behavior.

- **Variations in Culture** Although much research focuses on the differences between cultures, the variation within a culture is just as important. Large cultural groups may contain subcultures whose ideals and goals are distinct from, though generally harmonious with, those of the dominant culture, and countercultures, groups whose ideals and goals are largely incompatible with mainstream norms. Even mainstream culture is often characterized by points of dissension and division, which are sometimes called culture wars.

- **High, Low, and Popular Culture** High culture is distinguished from low culture based on characteristics of their audiences, not characteristics of their cultural objects. In fact, arguments about whether a particular cultural product constitutes high or low culture usually indicate a struggle over values and beliefs, not just aesthetics or taste. Individual cultural consumption is shaped not only by personal preference but also by interpretive communities and a variety of institutions responsible for creating, advertising, and disseminating products.

- **Cultural Change** Though culture usually changes slowly, change can also happen rapidly, as it does in much of the world today. Technological determinism explains recent cultural change by arguing that new technologies, like the microchip, are the determining factors in social life. Because this sort of technology connects people around the world, it also facilitates change through cultural diffusion, cultural leveling, and cultural imperialism.

QUESTIONS FOR REVIEW

1. In this chapter, you read about how Horace Miner described the body rituals of the Nacirema. Choose another aspect of daily life and describe its associated artifacts, practices, and beliefs in similar detail. How might a complete stranger view the bar scene, for instance, or spectators at a sporting event? What does this tell you about ethnocentrism?

2. List five pieces of material culture you have with you right now, and explain what they indicate about the tastes, habits, and lifestyle supported by your cultural group.

3. Describe a norm that used to be a more but has transitioned to folkway status. How did you decide it was a now a folkway?

4. When was the last time you violated a folkway? How were you sanctioned? What sorts of sanctions do we impose on those who go against our accepted mores?

5. Same-sex marriage has been a focal point of recent culture wars, with some states (and nations) taking steps toward legalization of such unions, some directly banning them, and others taking a middle course. What values are in conflict here? Do both sides adhere to values that may be defined as "American"? What tactics are the different sides using in this culture war?

6. In the late 1990s and the early 2000s, a series of protests against the World Trade Organization were launched worldwide. The protesters represented a multitude of organizations and causes coming together to support a loosely defined common goal. In your opinion, would these protesters be more accurately characterized as subcultures or countercultures? Why?

7. Travelers in the United States used to encounter very different customs, traditions, and foods from one region to the next. These days, one may find a McDonald's or Starbucks in almost every American town—and in many countries across the globe. Is this good or bad? Why? Does it truly lessen cultural differences?

8. Make a list of ways in which the media—including advertisements—reach you each day. How many of these media messages represent mainstream Western ideals? What kinds of media messages don't conform to these norms?

SUGGESTIONS FOR FURTHER EXPLORATION

Adorno, Theodor. 1991. *The Culture Industry*. London: Routledge. A sharp critique of the business of culture, arguing that our consciousness is controlled by corporations that manipulate our desires to maximize profits.

Coupland, Douglas. 1995. *Microserfs*. New York: Harper-Collins. A darkly humorous novel about the consequences of living in a world dominated by technological change and electronic media. Although fictional, the story of overworked computer programmers' struggle to "get a life" addresses serious questions about the effects of technology.

Fadiman, Anne. 1998. *The Spirit Catches You and You Fall Down*. New York: Farrar, Straus and Giroux. A true story of clashing values, norms, and beliefs experienced by a Hmong immigrant family in the United States, it depicts the power of cross-cultural communication.

Hebdige, Dick. 1979. *Subculture: The Meaning of Style*. London: Methuen. The classic study of musical subcultures in Great Britain, from teddy boys to mods and rockers to skinheads, punks, and beyond. If you've ever wondered how a subculture maintains its own distinctive identity, Hebdige has an answer.

High Times. A monthly periodical "dedicated to presenting the true independent voice of today's culture through provocative coverage of politics, arts and entertainment, news, fiction, and fashion not found in the mainstream media," with a focus on the cultivation and uses of *cannabis sativa*. Also online at www.hightimes.com.

Kincaid, James R. 1998. *Erotic Innocence: The Culture of Child Molesting*. London: Duke University Press. Examines the social functions of the fascination with one of our culture's strongest taboos. It's obvious why pedophilia is taboo but less obvious why so much attention is paid to it given how rare it is. This book helps to explain how taboos contribute to social control.

Lewin, Ellen, and William L. Leap, eds. 1996. *Out in the Field: Reflections of Lesbian and Gay Anthropologists*. Urbana: University of Illinois Press. A collection of narratives describing the fieldwork of lesbian and gay anthropologists. Many of the entries describe how members of a culture often treated as "other" sometimes can more easily notice cultural differences and similarities.

Liberman, Mark, and Geoffrey K. Pullum. 2006. *Far from the Madding Gerund and Other Dispatches from Language Log*. Wilsonville, OR: William, James & Co. Provides an interesting assessment of the Sapir-Whorf hypothesis and summarizes, often humorously, the research on the "great Eskimo vocabulary hoax."

My Big Fat Greek Wedding. 2002. Dir. Joel Zwick. Warner Bros. A romantic comedy highlighting the differences between mainstream and subcultural groups through the story of two people who meet and fall in love, one from an immigrant Greek family and the other from a typical WASP (White Anglo-Saxon Protestant) family.

Schlosser, Eric. 2004. *Reefer Madness: Sex, Drugs, and Cheap Labor in the American Black Market*. New York: Houghton Mifflin. Discusses the contradictions between America's real and ideal culture, which harshly punishes marijuana dealers and pornographers while allowing migrant workers to toil in horrible conditions.

Žižek, Slavoj. 2002. *Welcome to the Desert of the Real*. London: Verso. A provocative discussion of the limits of multiculturalism.

Want to learn more?

ⓢ Visit StudySpace
(wwnorton.com/studyspace)
to find these additional
resources:

▶ Data Exercises to apply
  concepts to real-world
  data.

▶ "Sociology in the News"
  lets you read the latest
  media coverage about
  sociology.

▶ Watch "Sociology in
  Practice" video clips from
  indie documentaries (by
  using the password in the
  front of your book).

CHAPTER 5

The Self and Interaction

Who are you? Well, it really depends on the situation. In the classroom, you are a student; at home, you are a child, a sibling, a parent, a spouse, or a partner. In your office, you are the boss or the employee; in your studio, you are an artist or a woodworker. These are all facets of who you are, grounded in the real activities of your everyday life—school, work, hobbies, relationships. Online, though, reality need not limit you to such mundane identities. Online, you can be anyone you want!

Below is a sampling of actual online usernames from a variety of internet domains. Since people generally choose their own usernames, we can assume that they are meant to express something about the user's personality—sort of like a personalized license plate. Some names might cause us to modify our opening question a bit: Who do these people *think* they are? Or, perhaps, *wish* they *were*?

angelbabee3	mostwanted
bluechihuahua	motherwitch
crazyaboutjesus	nerd87
heartbreakah	rebelcutie
intensejello	superman22
ladyinpain	viciousvixen
luvsexxy	yummmiest
mauiwowee	

Choosing a username is one of many ways we express ourselves in social interaction. Because our online identities are usually disembodied and removed from the context of our everyday lives, we can say anything we want about who we are (or think we are, or wish to be). Whether or not these folks are actually heartbreakers, rebel cuties, or supermen in real life, they can be those things online. What's your username?

SocIndex

Then and Now

600 B.C.: A Hindu surgeon performs the first rhinoplasty (nose job), reconstructing a patient's nose from a portion of tissue from the cheek

2007: 284,960 nose jobs are performed in the United States alone

Here and There

United States: Almost 50% of American women are on weight-loss diets on any given day

Nigeria: Waikiriki women are confined to a "fattening" hut for five weeks before their wedding

This and That

The top five cosmetic surgery procedures for women are breast augmentation, liposuction, nose reshaping, eyelid surgery, and tummy tuck

The top five cosmetic surgery procedures for men are nose reshaping, eyelid surgery, liposuction, male breast reduction, and hair transplantation

region in the dramaturgical perspective, the context or setting in which the performance takes place

backstage in the dramaturgical perspective, places in which we rehearse and prepare for our performances

frontstage in the dramaturgical perspective, the region in which we deliver our public performances

social construction the process by which a concept or practice is created and maintained by participants who collectively agree that it exists

manner, and style of dress (or "costume"), as well as gender, race, and age—helps establish the definition of the situation as well.

For example, Dr. Ferris is told quite often that she "doesn't look like a professor." This illustrates how we use elements of personal front to make judgments about people: our images of professors usually involve gruff, grizzled, older men in unfashionable clothes, and so someone who is younger, friendlier, and female and who wears hipper jewelry must work harder at convincing others that she is in fact a professor. Similarly, when a student happens to see Dr. Ferris at a restaurant, movie theater, or department store, the student's response is almost always the same: "What are you doing here?"

The social setting, or **region** (which includes the location, scenery, and props), makes a big difference in how we perceive and interact with the people we encounter there. Students and professors recognize one another and know how to interact when on campus or in the classroom. But in other venues, we are out of context, and this can confuse us. We seldom think of our professors as people who have off-campus lives—it's hard to see them as people who dine out, see movies, or buy under-

wear (for that matter, professors rarely think of their students this way either!). So when we encounter one another in unfamiliar regions, we often don't know how to behave because the old classroom scripts don't work.

In addition, there are places known as back regions, or **backstage**, where we prepare for our performances—which take place in front regions, or **frontstage**. We behave differently—and present different selves—frontstage than we do backstage; your professor behaved differently this morning while he showered, shaved, dressed, and made breakfast for his kids than he is behaving now, lecturing and answering questions in his sociology classroom. For Goffman, the key to understanding these nuances in impression management is to recognize that we present different selves in different situations, and the responses of others to those selves continually shape and mold our definitions of situation *and* self. Thus we can say that the self is a **social construction** (Berger and Luckmann 1966). The self is something that is created or invented in interaction with others who also participate in agreeing to the reality or meaning of that self as it is being presented in the situation.

We also make claims about who we are in our interactions. These claims can be either accepted or contradicted by others, which can make things either easier or harder for our self-image. Most of the time, others support the selves we project. For example, when your professor starts lecturing and you begin to take notes, you are supporting the version of self that he is presenting: he is "doing professor," and in response, you are "doing student." Another way that we support the selves that people present is to allow them to save

Front and Back Regions Just like Gene Simmons, pictured on stage with his band, Kiss, and at home, we present ourselves differently depending on the situation. Others' responses to our behavior in those different settings shape our definitions of ourselves.

| TABLE 5.1 | Theory in Everyday Life | |

Perspective	Approach to the Self and Interaction	Case Study: Identity in Childhood
PSYCHOANALYSIS	Freud's theory of the unconscious mind as composed of an interrelated system (id, ego, superego) that underlies human behavior; personality develops through psycho-sexual stages.	Parents instill a conscience (superego) in children through rules that govern their instinctual behavior (id) until children mature and are self-governing (ego).
LOOKING-GLASS SELF	Cooley's theory of the self concept as derived from how we imagine others see us, and the feelings about ourselves based on the perceived judgments of others.	Parents and significant others serve as a reflection to children, who develop a sense of self based on their appraisals, real or imagined.
MIND, SELF, AND SOCIETY	Mead's theory of the self that develops through three stages (preparatory, play, and game); in role taking the particular or generalized other, we learn to see ourselves as others do.	Children gain a sense of self through imitation, play, and games, in which they learn various roles and take on the perspectives of others.
DRAMATURGY	Goffman's theory of the presentation of self; we are like actors on a stage whose performance strategies aid in impression management.	Children learn the arts of impression management and may present a different self to their parents than to other children or teachers.

face—to prevent them from realizing that they've done something embarrassing. Goffman calls this **cooling the mark out**, a phrase borrowed from con games, but it can be used as a tool of civility and tact as well. When the professor mixes up two related concepts in a lecture, for example, you let it pass because you know what she really meant to say. Or, even worse, you overlook the spinach between your professor's teeth until it can be called to his attention privately!

There are also situations in which the selves we project are contested or even destroyed. For example, if you raised your hand in a 200-person lecture hall and told the professor that he had spinach between his teeth, you would be undermining the self he is trying to present. His identity as an expert, an authority figure, a senior mentor, would be publicly damaged once you called attention to his dental gaffe (unless he was able to deflect the situation gracefully). In Goffman's view, then, the presentation of self and impression management are about power as well as about self. If you embarrass your professor in front of an auditorium full of students, he no longer possesses quite as much power as he did a few moments before.

Goffman's view of our interactions can be disturbing to some people, for it suggests that we are always acting, that we are never being honest about who we really are. But Goffman would challenge this interpretation of his work. Yes, some people deliberately deceive others in their presentation of self, but we must all present *some* type of self in social situations. Why wouldn't those selves be presented sincerely? As Goffman-inspired sociologist Josh Meyrowitz says, "While a dishonest judge may pretend to be an honest judge, even an honest judge must play the role of 'honest judge' " (1985, p. 30).

DATA WORKSHOP

ANALYZING EVERYDAY LIFE

Impression Management in Action

This exercise in ethnography is designed to help make your own impression management visible—and to help you see how integral it is to your everyday life. You will observe yourself acting and interacting in two different social situations and will then do a comparative analysis of your presentation of self in each setting. Observing one's own behavior is a variant of the ethnographic method you read about in Chapter 3 known as **autoethnography**.

Step 1: Observation

Choose two different situations that you will encounter this week in everyday life, and commit to observing yourself for 30 minutes as you participate in each. For example, you may observe yourself at work, at a family birthday celebration, at lunch with friends, in your math class, riding on the bus or train, or watching a softball game. The two situations you choose don't need to be extraordinary in any way; in fact, the more mundane, the better. But they should be markedly different from one another.

Step 2: Analysis

After observing yourself in the two situations, consider the following questions.

cooling the mark out behaviors that help others to save face or avoid embarrassment, often referred to as civility or tact

autoethnography ethnographic description that focuses on the feelings and reactions of the ethnographer

Total Institutions The military, prisons, and cults are examples of total institutions where individual's identities are stripped away and reformed.

the last time you were in it—"safe sex," "splitting the check," and other new norms may be hard for older daters to assimilate. Adult socialization often requires the replacement of previously learned norms and values with different ones, what is known as **resocialization**. Facing a serious illness or growing old also often involves intensive resocialization. In order to cope with a new view of what their aging body will permit them to do, people must discard previous behaviors in favor of others (not working out every day, for example).

Another dramatic example of resocialization is found in **total institutions** (Goffman 1961), places such as prisons, cults, and mental hospitals, and in some cases even boarding schools, nursing homes, monasteries, and the military.

In total institutions, residents are severed from their previous relations with society, and their former identity is systematically stripped away and re-formed. There may be different ends toward which total institutions are geared, such as creating good soldiers, punishing criminals, or managing mental illness, but the process

of resocialization is similar: all previous identities are suppressed and an entirely new, disciplined self is created.

Relatively few adults experience resocialization to the degree of the total institution. All, however, continue to learn and synthesize norms and values throughout their life as they move into different roles and social settings that present them once again with the challenges and opportunities of continued socialization.

Statuses and Roles

While agents of socialization play an important role in developing our individual identities, so does the larger scaffolding of society. This happens as we take on (or have imposed upon us) different statuses and roles.

A **status** is a position in a social hierarchy that comes with a set of expectations. Sometimes these positions are formalized—"professor," "president," or even "parent." Parental obligations, for example, are written into laws that prohibit the neglect and abuse of children. Other statuses are more informal—you may be the "class clown," for instance, or the "conscience" of your group of friends. The contours of these informal statuses are less explicit but still widely recognizable. We all occupy a number of statuses,

resocialization the process of replacing previously learned norms and values with new ones as a part of a transition in life

total institution an institution in which individuals are cut off from the rest of society so that their lives can be controlled and regulated for the purpose of systematically stripping away previous roles and identities in order to create new ones

status a position in a social hierarchy that carries a particular set of expectations

NFL vs. Family: Chris and Stefanie Spielman

In 1998, Chris Spielman, a linebacker for the Buffalo (New York) Bills, was getting ready to return to the field after recovering from a major injury. He and his wife, Stefanie, and their two small children were moving from their home state of Ohio to New York, and he'd get back into the game he loved. Stefanie had been Chris's cheerleader—literally and figuratively—for ten years, supporting him as he pursued his football career. "Captain Crunch" was the nickname of this four-time Pro-Bowler, and opponents on the field had no problem understanding why: Spielman was a big, tough guy, and football was his life. Then Stefanie was diagnosed with breast cancer, and their lives changed dramatically. Stefanie now needed to remain in Ohio for chemotherapy treatments, and Chris faced a crisis of decision making: go to New York to play football, or stay home with his wife and kids?

Chris Spielman was experiencing role conflict. His occupational role—professional athlete—required actions that were seemingly incompatible with his familial role, husband and father. The expectations attached to his occupational role included a willingness to move about the country to training camp and away-games and even to be traded to a team in another city. The expectations attached to his familial role included being able to provide hands-on care and nurturing for a sick wife and two small children. These expectations were not only incompatible, they may have created a certain amount of role strain related to his gender: it's still easier to see a big, strong man as a hard-hitting linebacker than as a nurturing husband and father. But Chris said, "I wanted to be the one to hold her hand when she vomited. I wanted to be there when they shaved her head. I wanted to take her to her chemo treatments" (Cabot 1999). None of this would be possible if he was in Dallas one week and Tampa the next. Role conflict was forcing him into a difficult choice: his job or his family?

Chris chose his family. As he said in a 1999 interview, "I wouldn't give my life for football, but I'd give my life for my family. There's no comparison. They're not even in the same stratosphere."

You may not become a professional athlete with a critically ill spouse, but it is absolutely certain that you will find yourself in situations where the demands of your occupational role clash with those of your familial role. Perhaps you already have. How will you resolve those role conflicts? Chris Spielman, now a commentator for ESPN, sums it up this way: "My kids can look back and say, 'When Dad had a tough decision to make, he did the right thing.' I wanted to set a good example for them" (Cabot 1999).

Chris Spielman, His Wife, Stefanie, and Their Two Children

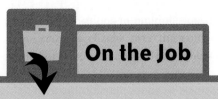

On the Job

The Wages of Emotion Work

According to executives at Nordstrom department stores, keeping the customer happy is what it's all about. Nordstrom, along with a host of other stores, takes a great interest in developing a corporate culture based on customer service (Zemke and Schaaf 1990; Spector and McCarthy 1996). After all, loyal, satisfied customers are the key to profit making. Nordstrom has become so successful at customer service that it ranks as the national standard. The secret to the company's success lies partly in what Hochschild (1983/1985) calls "the commercialization of feeling," or emotion work.

Nordstrom became a leader in this area through a variety of training techniques. Through staff meetings and workshops, managers coached employees in customer service. Using videotapes and role-playing scenarios, workers learned how to act out various emotions convincingly. But their acting techniques went beyond such displays as smiling and showing friendliness. Salespeople were also supposed to take an in-depth interest in their customers by keeping a "client book" with detailed information about customers' likes and dislikes, favorite brands, style preferences, color choices, and anything else that might help salespeople to better anticipate their needs. Some Nordstrom managers

even required their salespeople to perform extra duties while off the clock, like writing thank-you notes to customers and delivering items to their homes.

While these practices were good for Nordstrom's bottom line, the consequences for the workers themselves were a different story. The work of producing emotions takes its toll. Though displays of feeling are actually "sold" to the customer as a kind of commodity, the worker is not necessarily compensated. What was once a private resource has now become a company asset, a new source of labor—emotional labor. But because it is impossible for anyone to be that upbeat all the time, workers must find ways to display or evoke the required emotions. They may do so through surface acting, displaying the emotion by wearing a smile, for example. In contrast, a very dedicated employee may do deep acting by trying to actually feel the emotion that he or she must display. There are consequences for faking or conjuring emotional responses: Workers may experience "emotional exhaustion and burnout" (Grandey 2003) or become estranged from their real feelings (as did Hochschild's flight attendants)—a situation that Marx would refer to as alienation.

Despite a number of employee protests—and a 1991 class-action suit involving off-the-clock work—many of

---

very differently—what makes one person laugh may make another cry. It would seem, then, that our emotions are the one thing about our lives that aren't dictated by society, that can't be explained with reference to sociological concepts or theories.

Well, our emotions aren't fully determined by society, but they are indeed social. We respond individually, but there also are social patterns in our emotional responses. For example, some emotional responses differ

according to the culture—even an emotion as personal as grief, as you will see in the Global Perspective box.

The Social Construction of Emotions

Sometimes our interaction with others affects our emotional responses: we may yell angrily at a political rally along with everyone else, realizing only later that we don't really feel that strongly about the issue at all; we may stifle our tears in front of the coach but shed them freely after the game. **Role-taking emotions**, such as sympathy, embarrassment, and shame, require that we be able to see things from someone else's point of view. When a friend is injured in an accident, you know she is feeling pain, so you feel sympathy for her. **Feeling rules** (Hochschild 1975) are socially

> **role-taking emotions** emotions like sympathy, embarrassment, or shame that require that we assume the perspective of another person or many other people and respond from that person or group's point of view
>
> **feeling rules** socially constructed norms regarding the expression and display of emotions; expectations about the acceptable or desirable feelings in a given situation

Emotion Work In many sales and service jobs, employees must engage in surface or deep acting to display the emotions that their jobs require.

the problems relating to emotion work remain unresolved (Nogaki 1993). Employees at Nordstrom and elsewhere are still trying to figure out how to preserve some sense of authenticity while making the necessary emotional adjustments to perform their job. The risk remains that employees may become burned out, cynical, or numb from the demands of their occupational roles.

Many of you will be dealing with these same issues in your careers. How will you factor in the cost to yourself of emotional labor? Do you think employees should be compensated financially for emotion work, or do you consider it part of being a good employee? What other kind of compensation—extra days off, more frequent breaks—might be appropriate, especially for salespeople?

constructed norms regarding the appropriate feelings and displays of emotion. We are aware of the pressure to conform to feeling rules even when they are unspoken or we don't agree with them (for example, "Boys don't cry," "No laughing at funerals"). Emotions are thus sociological phenomena, and our individual reactions are influenced (if not determined) by our social and cultural surroundings.

Finally, emotions can also be influenced by social institutions, such as workplaces or religious groups. Arlie Hochschild's (1983) study of flight attendants revealed that when airlines required their employees to be cheerful on the job, the employees' authentic emotions were displaced (they weren't necessarily always cheerful). Flight attendants were required to manage their own feelings as a requirement of their job—what Hochschild calls **emotion work**—

maintaining a bright, perky, happy demeanor in-flight, no matter what they actually felt. Because of the structural pressures of emotion work, they became alienated from their own real feelings.

New Interactional Contexts

As we learned in earlier chapters, sociological theories and approaches can change over time—indeed, they must. As the society around them changes,

emotion work (emotional labor) the process of evoking, suppressing, or otherwise managing feelings to create a publicly observable display of emotion

Mediating Interaction Using new technologies like digital video webcams, we can interact with each other outside of physical copresence. How will these new technologies affect our interactions and identities?

sociologists can't always hold on to their tried-and-true ways of looking at the world. New and innovative approaches take the place of traditional paradigms.

Most sociological perspectives on interaction, for example, focus on interactions that occur in **copresence**—that is, when individuals are in one another's physical company. More and more, however, we find ourselves in situations outside physical copresence, aided by rapidly developing technologies. Businesspeople can hold video conferences with colleagues in other cities.

The lovelorn can seek relationship advice and learn the dos and don'ts of sex and dating through late-night radio. Students can instant-message their friends at faraway colleges and carry on real-time text-based conversations. Doctors on the mainland can perform remote surgery on shipboard patients in the middle of the ocean. Do conventional theories have the explanatory power to encompass these new ways of interacting? And since interaction is vital to the development of the self, how do these new ways of interacting create new types of social identities?

Researchers like Josh Meyrowitz (1985), Marc Smith and Peter Kollock (1998), Steve Jones (1997), Philip Howard (Jones and Howard 2003), and Barry Wellman (2004) are among the pioneers in the sociology of technologically mediated interaction. They look at how we interact with each other in cyberspace and via electronic media—and how we interact with the machines

copresence face-to-face interaction or being in the presence of others

themselves. Sherry Turkle, for example, directs the Initiative on Technology and the Self at the Massachusetts Institute of Technology (MIT), where she and others study different ways that technology and identity intersect—through our use of computers, robots, technologically sophisticated toys, and so on (1997, 2005). danah boyd examines how the rapid adoption of social networking sites such as MySpace and Facebook into the lives of teenagers is affecting their sense of self and their relationships with others (2007). These and other researchers seek answers to the following question: Who will we become as we increasingly interact with and through machines? Their work is helping sociology enter the age of interactive media and giving us new ways of looking at interactions and identities.

Postmodern theorists claim that the role of technology in interaction is one of the primary features of postmodern life. They believe that in the Information Age, social thinkers must arrive at new ways to explain the development of the self in light of the electronic and digital media that inundate our social world (Holstein and Gubrium 2000). We are now exposed to more sources and multiple points of view that may shape our sense of self and socialize us in different ways than ever before (Gottschalk 1993). Kenneth Gergen has coined the term the *saturated self* to refer to this phenomenon and further claims that the postmodern individual tends to have a "pastiche personality," one that "borrow[s] bits and pieces of identity from whatever sources are available" (Gergen 1991, p. 150). What this means is that the self is being constructed in new ways that were unforeseen by early symbolic interactionists, who could not have imagined that interaction would one day include so many possible influences from both the real world and the world of virtual reality. In Chapter 14, we'll investigate in greater depth how new technologies are affecting social life.

Closing Comments

By now you may be wondering, are we all just prisoners of socialization? How much freedom do we really have if we are all shaped and influenced to such an extent by others and by society? Are our ideas of ourselves as individuals—unique and independent—just a sorry illusion?

It is true that the process of socialization can be rather homogenizing. And it tends to be conservative, pushing people toward some sort of lowest common denominator, toward the mainstream. But still, not everybody ends up the same. In fact, no two people are ever really alike. Despite all the social forces at play in creating the individual, the process by which we gain a sense of self, or become socialized members of society, is never wholly finished.

agency the ability of the individual to act freely and independently

We are not just passive recipients of all the influences around us. We are active participants. We possess what is called **agency**, meaning that we are spontaneous, intelligent, and creative. We exercise free will. Symbolic interactionism tells us that we are always doing the work of interpreting, defining, making sense of, and responding to our social environment. That gives us a great deal of personal power in every social situation. The process is not unilateral; rather it is reciprocal and multidirectional. Remember that you are shaping society as much as it is shaping you.

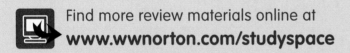

Find more review materials online at
www.wwnorton.com/studyspace

CHAPTER SUMMARY

- **What Is Human Nature?** The nature vs. nurture debate argues about the relative influences of genetics and socialization on human behavior. Of course both nature and nurture contribute to human nature, but sociologists emphasize the many ways in which even the most intimate features of the self have a social basis. Biology dictates that we must do certain things to stay alive, but the ways we do them are entirely a product of our societies.

- **The Process of Socialization** A society or group teaches individuals to become functioning members, and individuals learn and internalize the values and norms of the group. One way to understand the importance of socialization is to study the experiences of children who were deprived of interaction at an early age and consequently fail to develop a normal sense of self.

- **Theories of the Self** Sociology offers several theories of the development of the self. Sigmund Freud's psychoanalytic approach divides the mind into three interrelated systems: the id, the ego, and the superego. Unlike most sociologists, Freud often focused on instincts and biological drives, but his theory also included the superego, which develops as a result of socialization and inhibits these drives.

- Charles Cooley believed that one's sense of self depends on seeing one's self reflected in interactions with others, which he believed revealed the looking-glass self. Influenced by Cooley, George Herbert Mead articulated a developmental process of self that corresponds to the acquisition of language skills and the growth of mental capacities. These theories share the assumption that in the development process, individuals internalize aspects of society. In contrast, Erving Goffman believed that meaning is constructed through interaction. His approach, dramaturgy, compares social interaction to the theater, where individuals take on roles and act them out to present a favorable impression to their "audience." Goffman is less concerned with the internal self and assumes that situations determine what sort of self we choose to act out.

- **Agents of Socialization** The process of socialization is twofold: society teaches us how to participate, and we internalize the society's values and norms. There are four primary agents of socialization in American society: family, school, peers, and the media. Families teach us the basic values and norms that shape our identity and our first interactions with the wider world. Schools, the first agents of socialization outside the family, provide education and socialize us through a hidden curriculum that teaches many of the behaviors that will be important later in life. Peers provide very different social skills and often become more immediately significant than the family. The media have become an important agent of socialization, often overriding the family and other institutions in instilling values and norms. Though socialization is most intensive during our early years, adult socialization often requires replacing previously learned norms and values through the process of resocialization.

- **Statuses and Roles** Statuses and roles help shape our identities by providing behavioral guidelines and influencing the ways others respond to us. Statuses may be ascribed or achieved, and they come with social expectations. The expectations of one status may clash with those of another status held simultaneously (role conflict), and sometimes there are contradictory expectations within a single status or role (role strain).

- **The Social Construction of Emotions** Though we tend to believe that our emotions are highly personal and individual, there are social patterns in our emotional responses. Role-taking emotions like sympathy and embarrassment require that we take the perspective of others; feeling rules influence our emotions and the ways we express them.

- **New Interactional Contexts** Though most sociological perspectives on interaction focus on situations in which individuals are in one another's physical presence (copresence), modern society increasingly encourages us to interact with people far away, including those we may never meet in person. Postmodern theorists like Kenneth Gergen believe that interacting through technology exposes us to more information and diverse perspectives that may shape our sense of self and socialize us in new ways.

QUESTIONS FOR REVIEW

1. Think about a social issue about which you hold a very different opinion from your grandparents or people their age, like drug legalization, sexual mores, or even fashion. How might this difference of opinion be the result of different socialization?

2. What are some of the reasons symbolic interactionism is useful for explaining the development of the self?

3. According to Erving Goffman, we all engage in impression management to control what others think of us. Choose one interaction and list every aspect of the personal front you use to manage the impression you create.

4. In a con game the criminals usually allow the victim or "mark" to win a little, then take him for everything, leaving the victim angry and embarrassed. In order to prevent retaliation, accomplices help the victim redefine the situation to make it bearable, or "cool the mark out." Erving Goffman pointed out that life abounds with situations that people redefine this way. Can you think of a situation where you helped to "cool the mark out"?

5. How do the theories on the development of the self in this chapter differ one from another? Which theory best explains your experience? Why?

6. Are the basic principles your family taught you supported or undermined by your peers? Can you name two or more of your roles that sometimes conflict?

7. Describe a situation in which you were resocialized. Perhaps you met someone from a different culture and abandoned some cultural stereotypes, or you learned to fit into a new work environment. Do you think that your resocialization is permanent, or will you revert to your old ways?

8. Describe yourself in terms of your statuses and roles. Which are master statuses? Which roles are less important? Which statuses have changed over the course of your lifetime? Which roles do you anticipate occupying in the future?

9. What feeling rules do you find yourself obeying? Do you expect the same of others? Have you ever done emotion work? What were the circumstances?

10. Do you agree with Gergen's claim that the postmodern person has a pastiche personality? Why? Do you think the internet provides a unique type of information, or could a well-read person of your grandparents' generation have accessed the same types of knowledge?

SUGGESTIONS FOR FURTHER EXPLORATION

FeralChildren.com A website with extensive information and links about feral children through the ages, both real and fictional.

Goffman, Erving. 1967. *Asylums: Essays on the Social Situation of Mental Patients and Other Inmates*. Chicago: University of Chicago Press. One of the finest discussions of the effects of total institutions like asylums.

Hochschild, Arlie. 2003. *The Managed Heart: Commercialization of Human Feeling*. Berkeley: University of California Press. A classic study of the consequences of emotion work.

Mead, George Herbert. 1934/1967. *Mind, Self, and Society: From the Standpoint of a Social Behaviorist*. Chicago: University of Chicago Press. The foundation for the theory of symbolic interactionism. Mead gives a detailed explanation of how individuals internalize aspects of society.

Nell. 2004. Dir. Michael Apted. Fox Home Entertainment. Jodie Foster portrays a woman who has lived for years without human contact after her speech-impaired mother died. She is discovered by a doctor, played by Liam Neeson, who tries to understand her.

Six Degrees of Separation. 2000. Dir. Fred Schepis. MGM. The film, starring Will Smith, is based on a true story about a young man who deftly uses impression management to convince upper-class New Yorkers that he is one of them.

Spigel, Lynn. 1992. *Make Room for TV: Television and the Family Ideal in Postwar America*. Chicago: University of Chicago Press. A social history of the impact of television on U.S. popular culture and how mass media became a significant agent of socialization.

Swofford, Anthony. 2005. *Jarhead*. New York: Scribner. A fascinating memoir about life in the U.S. Marine Corps during the First Gulf War that illustrates the effect of a total institution.

The Wild Child. 2001. Dir. Francois Truffaut. MGM. This film is based on a real-life, eighteenth-century behavioral scientist's efforts to civilize a feral boy, who was found living like an animal in the woods. Victor, the Wild Boy of Aveyron, is perhaps the best-known case of a feral child.

CHAPTER 6

Separate and Together: Life in Groups

O n November 4, 2000, Robert Burgess woke up in a Los Angeles emergency room with no memory of what had happened to him the night before. How had he broken his collarbone and wrist, and why was there bleeding in his kidney? Burgess couldn't remember because his blood alcohol level had been measured at .19 percent—two and a half times the legal limit in California.

Eventually, he was able to recall the previous evening. He had attended a party at the Sigma Pi fraternity house at UCLA, where, as a pledge, he was being evaluated by the Sigma Pi brothers for full membership. He was told that he could either drink alcohol or a nonalcoholic beverage of unknown origin stirred up by the brothers; if he refused, he would relinquish his bid for membership. Burgess chose the alcohol and handed over his car keys for safety. He was then led, blindfolded, through the frat house and forced to have a drink in each room. Members of the Chi Omega sorority who were at the party scribbled on his drunken body in permanent marker. At some point during the evening, he passed out, but he later apparently woke up, retrieved his car keys, and drove away—only to crash into a wall and end up in the ER.

No doubt you've heard stories like this before. Generally referred to as *hazing*, this process is meant to test newcomers and transform them into group members—if you can endure the abuse, you can be part of the group. Although hazing is usually associated with college fraternities, it has been known to occur in high school clubs, athletic teams, sororities, and even police and fire departments and the military. In fact, according to a study in the medical journal *Contemporary Pediatrics* (2000), 24 percent of high school church group members reported being hazed. Although hazing is against the law in almost every state and is usually prohibited by group charters, it is still a popular—though risky—way of initiating new members. Every year, it results in at least one student death and countless injuries, and alcohol plays a major role in most of these incidents (Nuwer 1999).

In November 2001, with his injuries healed, Robert Burgess filed a civil suit against both the fraternity and the sorority, alleging that he was forced to overindulge in alcohol and that the party hosts had returned his car keys while he was obviously too drunk to drive. Burgess's lawsuit highlights a key question in all hazing cases: Who is

SocIndex

Then and Now

1962: Number of women participating in college sports just before passage of Title IX legislation prohibiting sex discrimination in federally funded educational programs: 62,000

2005: Number of women participating in college sports 33 years after passage of Title IX legislation: 205,492

Here and There

The United Nations: The Universal Declaration of Human Rights provides for freedom of association for all persons in 1948

United States: The U.S. Supreme Court affirms the right to private, consensual intimacy for gays and lesbians in 2003

This and That

Number of confirmed African American members of the top five country clubs in Dallas, Texas, in 2007: Zero

Number of hate crimes committed against African Americans in Texas in 2007: 103

responsible when the consequences of hazing include illegality, injury, or even death? The host group or the individual who submits to hazing?

The relationship between the individual and the group is a complex one. We sometimes do things in groups, both good and bad, that we might never do as individuals. Exploring group dynamics from a sociological perspective can help us understand and even eliminate problems like hazing and maximize the benefits of group life as well.

HOW TO READ THIS CHAPTER

This chapter explores some of the different ways we organize our lives in groups. Here you will gain some of the analytic tools you can use to understand the specific groups we'll be investigating in later chapters. Concepts such as peer pressure, teamwork, bureaucratization, and anomie can be fruitfully applied to analyses of families, work and volunteer organizations, political groups, and religious communities. Consider this chapter an introduction to group dynamics in general—a springboard from which to begin our sociological analysis of particular types of groups. As you read, think about the groups you belong to and how they affect your values and behavior. What is your influence on such groups? Have you ever "gone along" with group rules but later wished you hadn't?

group a collection of people who share some attribute, identify with one another, and interact with each other

crowd a temporary gathering of people in a public place; members might interact but do not identify with each other and will not remain in contact

aggregate a collection of people who share a physical location but do not have lasting social relations

primary groups the people who are most important to our sense of self; members' relationships are typically characterized by face-to-face interaction, high levels of cooperation, and intense feelings of belonging

secondary groups larger and less intimate than primary groups; members' relationships are usually organized around a specific goal and are often temporary

What Is a Group?

We often use the term *group* to refer to any collection of two or more people who have something in common, whether it's their appearance, culture, occupation, or just a physical proximity. When sociologists speak of a **group** or social group, however, they mean a collection of people who not only share some attribute but also identify with one another and have ongoing social relations—like a family, a *Star Trek* fan club, a soccer team, a sorority, or the guys you play poker with every month.

A **crowd**, therefore (such as the throngs of sightseers at a tourist attraction or people who gather to watch a fire), would not usually be considered a group in the sociological sense. While crowd members do interact (Goffman 1971), they don't necessarily have a sense of common identity, and they rarely assemble again once they disperse. Collections of people such as crowds, audiences, and queues are known as **aggregates**—people who happen to find themselves together in a particular physical location. People in aggregates don't form lasting social relations, but people in groups do.

Similarly, people belonging in the same category—everyone 18 years of age or all owners of Chevy trucks, for example—don't regularly interact with one another or have any common sense of connection other than their status in the category.

Primary and Secondary Groups

Groups in which we are intimately associated with the other members, such as families and close friends, are known as **primary groups**. Primary groups typically involve more face-to-face interaction, greater cooperation, and deeper feelings of belonging. Members often associate with each other for no other reason than to spend time together.

Charles Horton Cooley (1909) introduced the term *primary* for this type of group because such groups have the most profound effects on us as individuals. Primary groups provide most of our emotional satisfaction through interaction with other members, are responsible for much of our socialization, and remain central to our identity throughout our lives. We measure who we are, and perhaps how we've changed, by the way we interact with primary group members. To Cooley (as we saw in Chapter 5), primary groups represent the most important "looking glasses" in the formation of our social selves—they constitute our "significant others."

Larger, less intimate groups are known as **secondary groups**: these include coworkers, college classes, athletic organizations, labor unions, and political parties. Interaction here is more formal and impersonal. Secondary groups are

Primary Groups Are Typically Families or Close Friends
Deborah Daniels (front left, in pink) opened her home to four generations of her family after Hurricane Katrina destroyed their New Orleans home in 2005.

usually organized around a specific activity or the accomplishment of a task. Membership is often temporary and usually does not carry the same potential for emotional satisfaction that primary group membership does. Nonetheless, a great deal of what we do involves secondary groups.

Because secondary groups can include larger numbers of people and be geographically diffuse, membership can be almost completely anonymous. At the same time, however, secondary group membership often generates primary group ties as well. Close personal relationships can begin with the more impersonal ties of secondary groups (the friends you make at work, for example) and are sometimes a direct outgrowth of our attempts to counteract the depersonalizing nature of secondary groups. For this reason, it is sometimes difficult to classify a particular group. Your soccer team may indeed be goal oriented, but you've probably also developed personal ties to at least some of your teammates. So is your team a primary or secondary group? It features elements of both, proving that real life can be even more complex than the models sociologists devise to explain it.

Social Networks

You and your family, your friends, peers, colleagues, teachers, and coworkers constitute a **social network**. Sociologists who study networks call the connections between individuals **social ties**. Social ties can be direct, such as the tie between you and your friend, or indirect, such as the tie between you and your friend's cousin, whom you've never met.

To understand how a social network works, think of yourself at the center with lines connecting you to all your friends, family, peers, and so on (see Figure 6.1, p. 159). These lines represent direct ties. Now think about all the family, friends, and peers who belong to each of *these* people. The lines connecting you to this second group must pass through the people in your first network; this second set of lines represents indirect ties. Indirect ties can include business transactions—flows of goods, services, materials, or monies—between organizations or nations. They can even represent flows of ideas. For instance, when you read ancient Greek philosophy, you become part of a network that spans centuries of writing and thinking and educating.

Sociologists who study networks are concerned not only with how networks are constructed but also with how influence moves along a network, and thus which persons or organizations have more influence than others within the network. In his book *Six Degrees: The Science of a Connected Age* (2003), sociologist Duncan Watts examined not only the connections individuals have to one another but also how those connections shape our actions. He found, for example, that we may change our minds about whom to vote for if enough of our friends are voting for the other candidate.

How does the flow of influence work at the level of an international organization? We could take the World Trade Organization (WTO) as an example. Comprising 148 member nations, the WTO monitors the trade rules between countries and resolves international disputes over trade. While all member nations are part of the network, they hold different positions of power within it. We might hypothesize that nations that win the most disputes have the most influence within the network. But Joseph Conti (2003, 2005) finds that while the United States, one of the most powerful members of the WTO, is involved in the vast majority of disputes, it usually loses. The question that remains for the network theorist is whether or not "winning" or "losing" is an effective way to measure influence. What Conti concludes is that America's centrality, a network analysis term that means an actor with

social network the web of direct and indirect ties connecting an individual to other people who may also affect her

social ties connections between individuals

Social Networks This network of friends and lovers from the television show *The L Word* exemplifies how social ties directly and indirectly bind people.

the most ties in a given network, is what gives it powerful influence and not the actual outcomes of the disputes.

Jobs and Networks

Some sociologists look at how personal networks, including both direct and indirect ties, influence a person's life. For example, in the pathbreaking work "The Strength of Weak Ties" (1973), Mark Granovetter measures how a person's distant relatives and acquaintances, attached to different social networks, pass along information about job opportunities. An individual with high socioeconomic status, or SES (taking into account income, education, and occupation), for example, usually has relatives and acquaintances with similarly high SES. Because those relatives and acquaintances belong to different social networks, all with high SES, the job seeker now has indirect connections with a vast array of high-SES contacts who can provide job leads. In other words, if your father, mother, and sister are all actors, you would likely "inherit" a network of acting contacts. The implications of Granovetter's findings are that people tend to form homogeneous social networks—to have direct ties to those who are like themselves, whether through race, class background, national origin, or religion. Further, individuals with low SES are likely to form direct ties to others with low SES and thus indirect ties as well. Information about job opportunities is less likely to travel along those networks.

Gender and Networks

More recent findings about the strength of weak ties, from Matt Hoffman and Lisa Torres (2002), indicate that women who are part of networks that include more men than women are more likely to hear about good job leads. But if their networks include more women than men, then those same women are less likely to hear about quality jobs. The number of men or women within a man's network doesn't seem to matter; men are just as likely to get quality information about job opportunities from both men and women in their social networks. Hoffman and Torres offer two rationales to explain their findings. First, women are simply less likely than men to hear about job leads. Second, women who do hear about them are more likely to pass along that information to men; they may feel threatened by the idea of more women in their places of employment and fear loss of their own jobs.

So it's not just what you know, it's whom you know. And whom they know, and whom *they* know.

Separate from Groups: Anomie

According to Durkheim, all the social groups with which we are connected (families, peer groups, workplaces, and so on) have this particular feature: the norms of the group place certain limits on our individual actions. For example, you may have wanted to backpack through Europe after you graduated from high school, but your parents demanded that you stay home, work, and save money for college. Durkheim argues that we need these limits—otherwise, we would want many things we could never have, and the lengths to which we would go in search of our unattainable desires would be boundless. Think about it: if you were always searching for but never getting the things you wanted, you would be very unhappy and over time might even become suicidal. Durkheim (1893/1964) called such a state of normlessness **anomie** and believed that group membership keeps us from feeling it. So group membership not only anchors us to the social world—it's what keeps us alive.

Durkheim was worried that in our increasingly fragmented modern society, anomie would become more and more common. Other scholars share Durkheim's position, noting that Americans today are less likely than ever to belong to the types of civic organizations and community groups that

can combat anomie and keep us connected to one another. Harvard professor Robert Putnam, in his book *Bowling Alone: The Collapse and Revival of American Community* (2001), argues that we no longer practice the type of "civic engagement" that builds democratic community and keeps anomie at bay: fewer people bowl in leagues than ever before, and people are less likely to participate in organizations like the League of Women Voters, PTA, or Kiwanis or engage in regular activities like monthly bridge games or Sunday picnics. He even offers statistics on how many angry drivers "flip the bird" at other drivers every year—all part of his argument about our disintegrating collective bonds.

Putnam's critics argue that he longs for "good old days" that can never be again (and perhaps never were) and that he disregards the many new ways of staying connected. For example, the internet has made it possible for fans of different books, bands, and films to come together in larger numbers than ever—albeit in cyberspace. Activist networks address social problems via online communications. Support groups form to deal with different personal issues or medical conditions. All of these involve people who might never have otherwise met. It may be true that we don't belong to bridge clubs anymore—but we have a new set of resources to help us connect with others and avoid anomie. If both types of groups can serve as social anchors, then is one necessarily better than the other?

> **anomie** "normlessness," term used to describe the alienation and loss of purpose that result from weaker social bonds and an increased pace of change

The Good Old Days? In *Bowling Alone*, Robert Putnam argues that the decline of group activities, like bingo nights or league bowling, represents a decline in civic engagement. However, technologies like the internet and social networking sites have allowed large numbers of people to gather, connect, and avoid anomie.

Social Networking Sites: Pros and Cons

Who's reading about your life online? More people than you think . . .

In the past several years, the news has been full of stories detailing problems that have emerged as a result of social networking sites such as MySpace and Facebook. College and high school students have been suspended or expelled from their institutions because of what they have posted in their profiles at Facebook. In 2005, Cameron Walker was expelled from Fisher College after joining a controversial online group. In 2007, Hayden Barnes was expelled from Valdosta State College for criticizing the construction of two new parking garages on campus in his Facebook profile. School administrators have officially disciplined numerous college and high school students for posting pictures of underaged drinking or doing illegal drugs. Law enforcement officers and school officials frequently use MySpace and Facebook to target and locate illegal activity. In fact, activity on MySpace has been used to arrest suspects on charges of conspiracy to commit murder, sexual crimes, and assault.

One commonly reported practice is the use of Facebook and MySpace to screen prospective employees' lifestyles. Increasingly, individuals are being denied jobs due to the pictures and information that they have posted on their personal profiles. Usually cited are pictures of drinking, illegal drug use, and smoking as "red flags" about personal integrity and interpersonal skills. With this in mind, many people are choosing to limit access to their profiles. In many cases, people are only allowed to access other's profiles after placing a personal request and being approved.

Limiting access to personal profiles runs counter to the "six degrees of separation" principle, which suggests that everyone in the world is connected to everyone else within six steps: "If you know 100 people, and each of them knows 100 more, then you have 10,000 friends-of-friends. Take that a step further to three degrees and you are connected to one million people. At six degrees, the number increases to nine billion" (Schofield 2004). MySpace and Facebook's profiling technology means that anyone you might be interested in could be vouched for (or against) by a friend or a friend-of-a-friend. Using this same reasoning, some employers are looking to Facebook and MySpace friend lists to find references for prospective employees. Eve Tahmincioglu reports "In many cases, if an HR person shares a job seeker's connection on a networking site, they'll just e-mail that contact to find out the dirt on the applicant without permission from the applicant" (2008). Although many individuals are comfortable with placing a casual acquaintance on their friends list, they may not be as comfortable with having a prospective employer use, for an example, the boyfriend of a classmate as a personal reference.

LinkedIn.com provides a professional networking alternative to more casual sites like MySpace and Facebook. LinkedIn is a business-oriented online social networking site created in 2002 and launched in 2003. As of summer 2008, it had more than 24 million registered users. The purpose of LinkedIn is to allow the user to create a list of people (called "connections") that they know and trust in their business. This original list of connections is then used to generate a

DATA WORKSHOP

ANALYZING MASS MEDIA AND POPULAR CULTURE
Virtual Communities and "Netiquette"

The idea of what constitutes a group has necessarily changed as modern society has evolved through the Industrial Revolution to the current Information Age. Just what do you call a

bunch of people who gather together to share interests, offer advice, provide support, or exchange ideas but who never meet in person and may not even know each other's real names? Such groups have come to be known as **electronic or virtual communities**.

When usage of the internet became more widespread in the early 1990s, there were few rules about how people should communicate. In addition, early electronic communities lacked the sense of organization that we often associate with other kinds of groups. Soon, though, sociologists who

people who attended the same college, came from the same hometown, or liked the same bands weren't very meaningful because there was no way of searching for other users based on their interests, backgrounds, and demographic details. Using a professional networking site such as LinkedIn as a public online social network while setting Facebook and MySpace accounts to privacy mode allows an individual to take advantage of existing social networks without the risk of having their private lives exposed. Even so, users of casual social networking sites such as MySpace and Facebook should think twice about what they post on their personal profiles.

Already, some media outlets are cautioning against collecting too many online references. While LinkedIn provides an initial fulcrum for job seekers, many employers still don't view the use of personal online references as a legitimate professional practice. As Chuck Pappalardo, managing director of Trilogy Search, a retained executive recruitment firm headquartered in the San Francisco Bay Area, says: "At this juncture, Facebook is simply not a serious site for business at the level I place folks. LinkedIn, however, is becoming increasingly more useful as a networking tool and in identifying candidates. But any posted reference can't be taken seriously on any level."

As social networking sites grow more sophisticated, they may play an even greater role in our primary and secondary groups. They also have the potential to affect relationships in both positive and negative ways. By taking advantage of friendship-based and business-based networking sites, individuals are able to use their internet connections to their advantage recreationally and professionally.

network of their direct connections, the connections of their connections (second-degree connections), and the connections of second-degree connections (third-degree connections). This social network can be used both by job seekers and by employers. The details that are listed in a user's profile include educational and professional experience as well as the useful job skills that they possess. Users are asked to identify connections that can serve as professional references.

In sociological terms, social networking sites aim to help people make the most of their primary and secondary groups. For example, they might keep you in touch with family members or friends who have moved out of the neighborhood. But secondary groups can be altered even more profoundly. In the past, such secondary associations as

study the internet (Jones 1997; Smith and Kollock 1998) began to see group traditions, roles, and norms emerging, as online members were socialized into belonging. In fact, it appears that social rules are as important as technical conventions when it comes to using the internet. For example, on eBay, where strangers buy and sell everything from old T-shirts to Old Masters paintings in an environment of mutual trust, participants feel confident that their payments will be received and their merchandise shipped because everyone has agreed to a shared set of rules and regulations.

In addition to the social rules that may govern a specific chat room or bulletin board, most online communications also observe "netiquette"—the standards for communicating. Examples of netiquette include prohibitions against "yelling" (writing in all capital letters) or "flame wars" (virulent online arguments). A special online language has also evolved, which includes new words and phrases (such as "g2g"

electronic or virtual communities
social groups whose interactions are mediated through information technologies, particularly the internet

for "got to go") and emoticons like those on p. 102.

This Data Workshop asks you to conduct a sort of "cyber-ethnography" to examine how group values and norms are expressed in electronic communities. In addition to doing some participant observation in a group, you will also be gathering material from existing sources and doing a content analysis of what you find (see Chapter 3 for a review of these research methods). Choose an active chat room, newsgroup, or bulletin board, preferably one that is not bizarre or extreme. Gather examples of the roles, language, norms, and expectations, either formal or informal, of this online group. One place to look is in the FAQ (Frequently Asked Questions) section of a website, but the elements of cyber-group life are present in all online interactions in one form or another. So immerse yourself in those interactions until you feel you have a sense of the life of this particular group. Here are some guidelines to follow as you do your research.

Roles
Observe the role that a "moderator" or "webmaster" plays in presenting information to "newbies" (those new to the group) or sanctioning those who violate group norms. See if you can identify any other online roles, such as "lurkers" (those who log on to a site but don't participate in the interaction).

Language
What kind of language is used by members? Make a list of commonly used terms, such as "emoticons" and acronyms like LOL ("laugh out loud"), IMHO ("in my humble opinion"), and ^5 ("high five").

Norms and Expectations
What are some of the social rules that apply to members of the electronic community? What happens if someone engages in a "flame war," sends "spam" to the list, or uses too much bandwidth for messages? Document how members sanction each other for violations in behavior.

There are two options for completing this Data Workshop.

- *Option 1 (informal)*: Prepare written notes that you can refer to in class. Share your observations and responses to the above questions with other students in small-group discussions. Listen for any differences in each other's insights.

- *Option 2 (formal)*: Write a three- to four-page essay describing your observations and answering the questions

above. Make sure to refer to specific features of your online group to support your analysis.

By taking part in this cyber-ethnography, you have begun to identify the ways that group life is created, maintained, and changed online by group members who might share many things but never actual physical copresence.

Group Dynamics

Sociologists have always been interested in how groups form, change, disintegrate, achieve great goals, or commit horrendous wrongs—add all these phenomena together, and they constitute **group dynamics**. How do groups affect an individual's sense of self? What forces bind members to a group? How do groups influence their members? When do groups excel at the tasks they undertake? What are the qualities of group leaders? When are groups destructive to the individual? How can relations between groups be improved? We will attempt to answer some of these questions in the next sections.

Dyads, Triads, and More

The size of a group affects how it operates and the types of individual relationships that can occur within it. A **dyad**, the smallest possible social group, consists of only two members—a married couple, two best friends, or two siblings, for example (Simmel 1950). Although relationships in a dyad are usually intense, dyads are also fundamentally unstable, because if one person wants out of the group, it's over. A **triad** is slightly more stable because the addition of a third person means that conflicts between two members can be refereed by the third. As additional people are added to a group, it may no longer be possible for everyone to know or interact with everyone else personally (think of all the residents of a large apartment building), and so policies may have to be established to help with communication and resolve conflicts. The features of dyads and triads point out an important axiom of group dynamics in general: the smaller a group is, the more likely it is to be based on personal ties; larger groups are more likely to be based on rules and regulations (as we'll see later when we examine bureaucracies).

In-Groups and Out-Groups

An **in-group** is a group a member identifies with and feels loyalty toward. This member usually feels a certain distinctness from or even hostility toward other groups, known as

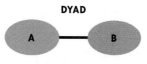

DYAD

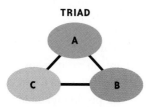

One Relationship

TRIAD

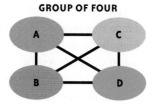

Three Relationships

GROUP OF FOUR

Six Relationships

GROUP OF FIVE

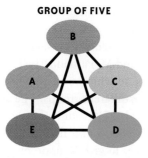

Ten Relationships

FIGURE 6.1 The Effects of Group Size on Relationships
Smaller groups feature fewer and more intimate personal ties; larger groups feature more relationships, but they are also likely to be more impersonal.

out-groups. Most of us are associated with a number of in- and out-groups, stemming from our ethnic, familial, professional, or educational backgrounds, for example. Group loyalty and cohesion intensify when differences are strongly defined between the "us" of an in-group and the "them" of an out-group; we may also feel a sense of superiority toward those who are excluded from our in-group. School sports rivalries make clear in-group and out-group distinctions, as evident in this popular slogan seen on T-shirts and bumper stickers all over Los Angeles: "My favorite teams are UCLA and whoever's playing USC!"

As we might expect, in-group membership can be a source of prejudice and discrimination based on class, race, gender, sexual orientation, religion, or political opinion. The differences attributed to an out-group often become exag-

gerated, if not entirely fabricated to begin with—"All Irishmen are drunks," or "All Mexicans are lazy," for example. Robert Merton (1968) noted the phenomenon that the same qualities or behaviors are viewed positively when they are "ours" and negatively when they are "theirs": the out-group is "lazy," whereas the in-group is "laid-back"; they are "snobbish," we are "classy"; they are "zealots," we are "devout." At their worst, in-group/out-group dynamics create the backdrop for social tragedies such as slavery and genocide.

out-group any group an individual feels opposition, rivalry, or hostility toward

reference group a group that provides a standard of comparison against which we evaluate ourselves

Reference Groups

Our perception of a group and what it takes to be a bona fide member can be crucial to our sense of self. When a group provides standards by which a person evaluates his own personal attributes, it is known as a **reference group**. A common reference group is one's family. We often try to "live up to" the standards of our parents, siblings, and extended family members. If we don't see ourselves as having the qualities of a "true" family member, we may adopt a negative self-image. A reference group may also be one to which we aspire to belong but of which we are not yet members; we saw one example at the beginning of this chapter, the pledge who wanted to belong to the fraternity so much that he was willing to risk his own health and safety.

DATA WORKSHOP

ANALYZING EVERYDAY LIFE

The Twenty Statements Test: Who Am I?

This Data Workshop, combining material from Chapters 5 and 6, asks you to look at how social affiliations with groups help shape our self-concept. You will be using a method that is similar to survey research to complete this Data Workshop (see Chapter 3 for a review). Start your work, however, by completing Step 1 below, without reading any farther than the line of stars!

Step 1: The Twenty Statements Test (TST)
In the spaces provided below, write down twenty different responses to the question "Who am I?" Don't worry about evaluating the logic or importance of your responses—just

write the answers in the order they occur to you. Give your-self five minutes to complete this task.

1. I am _____.
2. I am _____.
3. I am _____.
4. I am _____.
5. I am _____.
6. I am _____.
7. I am _____.
8. I am _____.
9. I am _____.
10. I am _____.
11. I am _____.
12. I am _____.
13. I am _____.
14. I am _____.
15. I am _____.
16. I am _____.
17. I am _____.
18. I am _____.
19. I am _____.
20. I am _____.

* *

Step 2: Analysis
Now it's time to analyze your responses. Rate each one according to the four categories listed below. Evaluate, to the best of your ability, which responses fall into the A-mode, B-mode, C-mode, and D-mode categories.

A-mode responses are the type of physical characteristics found on your driver's license: "I am a blonde"; "I am short"; I am a Wisconsin resident."

B-mode responses describe socially defined statuses usually associated with group membership of some sort: "I am a college student"; "I am a Catholic"; I am an African American."

C-mode responses describe styles of behavior or emotional states: "I am a happy person"; "I am a country music fan"; "I am a fashionable dresser."

D-mode responses are more general than individual: "I am part of the universe"; "I am a human being."

You may have some difficulty deciding how to categorize some of your responses—for example, where does "I am an American" go—in A, B, or D? Use your best judgment. Count the number of each type of response. Now compare the totals—which category got the most responses?

You may want to compare your findings with those of your classmates; where do your fellow students get their sense of self? We predict that, even if you yourself gave more B-mode responses, the predominant mode in your classroom is C. Those with more B-mode responses base their self-concept on group membership and institutional roles. Those with more C-mode responses see themselves as more independent and define themselves according to their individual actions and emotions rather than their connections to others. It is likely that there are few (if any) people whose responses fall predominantly in the A or D mode. Those with more A-mode responses may feel that they have a "skin deep" self-concept, based more on their appearance to others than on their internal qualities. Those with more D-mode responses are harder to categorize and may feel uncertain about the source of their sense of self.

The TST was developed by social psychologist Manfred Kuhn (Kuhn and McPartland 1954) as a way of determining the degree to which we base our self-concepts on our membership in different groups. The test was used later by Louis Zurcher (1977) to study the changing self-images of Americans. Zurcher found that in the 1960s individuals were more likely to give B-mode responses, but in the 1970s and 1980s people were more likely to give C-mode responses. While you might think it better to be an independent actor than to be defined by your group membership, Zurcher and his colleague Ralph Turner became concerned about this trend away from group identification and toward a more radically individualistic sense of self. Why were they so concerned?

The primary characteristics of the C-mode, or "impulsive," self (Turner 1976) are the pursuit of individual satisfaction, an orientation toward the present, and a sense that the individual should not be linked to others and that group obligations inhibit individual expression. The primary characteristics of the B-mode, or "institutional," self are a willingness to adhere to group standards and to accept group obligations as well as an orientation toward the future and a sense that the individual is linked to others. Zurcher and Turner worried that a society full of self-interested (and even selfish), impulsive individuals might no longer care about the common good and would only work to satisfy their own needs.

Group Cohesion "People easily form clubs, fraternal societies, and the like, based on congeniality, which may give rise to real intimacy. . . . Where there is a little common interest and activity, kindness grows like weeds by the roadside."
—Charles Horton Cooley, 1909

Do you do things for your own benefit or for the benefit of the group? What do you think are the consequences for a society overwhelmingly populated by one personality type or the other? Are these two orientations mutually exclusive, or can you combine the best parts of both? If the latter, what can you do in order to bring that about?

There are two options for completing this Data Workshop.

- *Option 1 (informal)*: Make some notes on your findings to share with other students in small-group discussions. How many "institutional" or "impulsive" selves are part of your discussion group? Do Zurcher and Turner's categories satisfactorily describe the way we consider our selves now, in the twenty-first century? Perhaps you can come up with a new category of self that better describes the individuals in your group.

- *Option 2 (formal)*: Find a small sample population of 3 to 5 other people and administer the TST to each of them. Collect, compare, and analyze your findings from the group. Answer the following questions in a three-page essay: If the majority of your fellow Americans fell into the same category, what would this mean for society? How would schools, families, workplaces, sports teams, governments, and charitable organizations operate if almost everyone fell into the same category? Make

sure to refer to your TST in the essay, and include it as an attachment to your paper.

Group Cohesion

A basic concept in the study of group dynamics is **group cohesion**, the sense of solidarity or team spirit that members feel toward their group. Put another way, group cohesion is the force that binds them together. A group is said to be more cohesive when individuals feel strongly tied to membership, so it is likely that a group of fraternity brothers is more cohesive than a random group of classmates. The life of a group depends on at least a minimum level of cohesion. If members begin to lose their strong sense of commitment, the group will gradually disintegrate (Friedkin 2004).

Cohesion is enhanced in a number of ways. It tends to rely heavily on interpersonal factors such as shared values and shared demographic traits like race, age, gender, or class (Cota et al. 1995). We can see this kind of cohesion, for example, in a clique of junior high school girls or members of a church congregation. Cohesion also tends to rely on an attraction to the group as a whole or members' ability to cooperate in achieving goals (Thye and Lawler 2002). This might help explain cohesion among fans of the Green Bay Packers or members of a local Elks lodge.

GROUPTHINK Whereas a high degree of cohesion might seem desirable, it can also lead to the kind of poor decision making seen in fraternity hazings. In a process Irving Janus (1971, 1982) called **groupthink**, highly cohesive groups

group cohesion the sense of solidarity or loyalty that individuals feel toward a group to which they belong

groupthink in very cohesive groups, the tendency to enforce a high degree of conformity among members, creating a demand for unanimous agreement

Group vs. Individual Norms: The Caning of Michael Fay

In March 1994, Michael Fay, an eighteen-year-old American citizen living with his mother in Singapore, was convicted of vandalism in a Singaporean court and sentenced to a $2,200 fine (in U.S. dollars), four months in prison, and six lashes with a rattan cane on his bare buttocks. By contrast, in the United States, Fay would have almost certainly ended up with a punishment no more severe than probation. Although many countries use caning or whipping to punish illegal activity, because Fay was an American, his six lashes quickly became international news. Opinions diverged on whether caning was an appropriate consequence for Fay's offense. Groups like Amnesty International describe caning as torture. The four-foot-long, half-inch-thick bamboo cane used to administer the blows is soaked in saltwater, and a trained prison guard or martial arts expert administers the strokes. The victim is tied to an A- or X-shaped frame to keep him from collapsing or fainting. Each hit with the cane is meant to split the skin, causing bleeding and eventual scarring, and those who have been caned describe not being able to sit down or lie on their back for weeks afterward.

Before the saga ended (with Fay on the receiving end of only four lashes, a reduced sentence), hundreds of articles had been written, 34 members of Congress had signed a petition requesting clemency, and then-president Bill Clinton spoke out on three separate occasions against the caning. Despite the official outcry, however, some Americans expressed support for caning, even going so far as to suggest that such penalties be imported to the United States. In fact, in May 1994, two months after Michael Fay's conviction, three different lawmakers tried to introduce pro-caning bills in three different legislative bodies (Poor 1994).

Singapore is a country with a low incidence of crime. Though it would be tempting to thus view caning as a possible remedy for out-of-control crime in the United States, there are also demographic and societal explanations for Singapore's low crime rate. First, the demographics of the two countries are radically different from each other (Walsh 1994). Singapore, for instance, has a population of around 3 million and is approximately 76 percent ethnic Chinese,

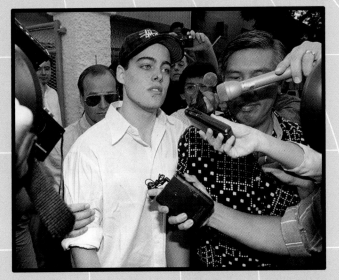

Michael Fay After receiving four strokes from a rattan cane, Fay was released from prison and allowed to return to the United States.

with a relatively cohesive set of mores. The United States, on the other hand, is composed of hundreds of different peoples, and the debate over whether we share a common culture is ongoing.

There is also a fundamental difference in philosophy between the East and the West regarding the importance of the individual. Jon Huntsman Jr., a former U.S. ambassador to Singapore, described the country as "a very traditional, Confucianist society in which the family is still the most important unit . . . a society that believes in the well-being of the whole, not necessarily the individual" (Poor 1994). This means that in Singapore, the group (family, community, society) is seen as more important than the individual—and the idea that the individual should suffer severe punishment for his offense against the group is not as difficult to swallow as it is in the United States. Though some Americans, on learning about Michael Fay's punishment, were keen to achieve lower crime rates by importing similar methods, it is unlikely that they would have been willing to sacrifice their individual freedoms to achieve that goal.

Groupthink According to sociologist Diane Vaughan, the *Challenger* shuttle disaster may have been caused by scientists failing to take seriously weaknesses in the shuttle's design.

may demand absolute conformity and punish those who threaten to undermine the consensus. Although groupthink does help maintain solidarity, it can also short-circuit the decision-making process, letting a desire for unanimity prevail over critical reasoning. When this happens, groups may begin to feel invulnerable and morally superior (White 1989). Members who would otherwise wish to dissent may instead cave in to peer pressure (see the next section).

The problem of groupthink can reach the highest level of industry or government, sometimes with disastrous results. For instance, there are those who believe that the explosion of the space shuttle *Challenger* in 1986 may have been a result of NASA scientists' failing to take seriously those who suspected weaknesses in the shuttle's launch design (Vaughan 1996). More recently, groupthink may have been to blame for the failure of the CIA and the White House to accurately assess the state of Saddam Hussein's programs for weapons of mass destruction; the perceived existence of such weapons was a primary rationale for the 2003 Iraq War. A Senate Intelligence Committee report claims that a groupthink dynamic caused those involved to lose objectivity and to embellish or exaggerate findings that justified the U.S. invasion (Ehrenreich 2004; Isikoff 2004).

Social Influence (Peer Pressure)

While you may not have had any personal experience with groupthink, you are certain to find the next set of sociological concepts all too familiar. When individuals are part of groups, they are necessarily influenced by other members.

Sociologists refer to this as **social influence**, or **peer pressure**. Knowing how social influence works can help you when you need to convince others to act in a certain way (like agreeing on a specific restaurant or movie). In turn it can also help you to recognize when others are trying to influence you (to drink too much or drive too fast, for example).

The idea of social influence is not new—the ancient Greek philosopher Aristotle considered persuasion in his *Rhetoric*. But the more modern studies on social influence date back to World War II, when social scientists were trying to help in the war effort by using motivational films to boost morale among servicemen. Since then, the study of social influence has become an expanding part of the field devoted to discovering the principles that determine our beliefs, create our attitudes, and move us to action (Friedkin and Cook 1990; Cialdini and Trost 1998; Friedkin and Granovetter 1998). Recent research on social influence has revealed that everything from our performance in school (Altermatt and Pomerantz 2005) to the likelihood that we will commit rape (Bohner et al. 2006) can be subject to the influence of others. We will focus here on how social influence functions in everyday situations.

Almost all members of society are susceptible to what is either real or imagined social pressure to conform. In general, we conform because we want to gain acceptance and approval (positive sanctions) and avoid rejection and disapproval (negative sanctions). We follow **prescriptions**, doing the things we're supposed to do, as well as **proscriptions**, avoiding the things we're not supposed to do.

Social psychologists have determined that social influence results in one of three kinds of conformity: compliance, identification, or internalization. **Compliance**, the mildest kind of conformity, means going along with something because you expect to gain rewards or avoid punishments (for example, adhering to a dress code at work or school even if you wish you didn't have to). When people comply, however, they don't actually change their own ideas or beliefs. **Identification**, a somewhat stronger kind of conformity, is induced by a person's desire to establish or maintain a relationship with a person or group (for example, emulating the fashion style of people

social influence (peer pressure) the influence of one's fellow group members on individual attitudes and behaviors

prescriptions behaviors approved of by a particular social group

proscriptions behaviors a particular social group wants its members to avoid

compliance the mildest type of conformity, undertaken to gain rewards or avoid punishments

identification a type of conformity stronger than compliance and weaker than internalization, caused by a desire to establish or maintain a relationship with a person or a group

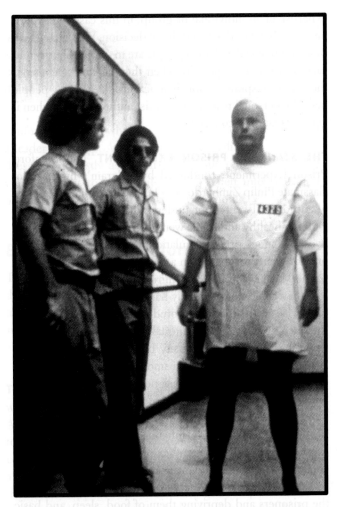

The Stanford Prison Experiment Why do you think the students in Zimbardo's experiment inhabited their roles so completely? What does it reveal about group behavior?

historical and cultural context in which the experiment was conducted seemed to have an effect on how subjects performed (Bond and Sussex 1996). This conclusion echoes some of Ralph Turner's findings about the institutional or impulsive self, discussed in an earlier Data Workshop: namely, he found that patterns of behavior can change over time and that separate generations may respond differently to social pressures.

Yet the power of the group continues to interest sociologists, psychologists, and others who want to understand what drives our powerful impulse to comply (Cialdini 1998). The experiments remain relevant because real-life examples of obedience continue to occur—whether in the case of the prison guards at Abu Ghraib or in a serial telephone hoax perpetrated on fast food workers in which a caller posing as a police officer instructed assistant managers to abuse fellow workers (Wolfson 2005).

social loafing the phenomenon in which as more individuals are added to a task, each individual contributes a little less; a source of inefficacy when working in teams

Teamwork

Are two heads better than one? Or do too many cooks spoil the broth? Early research on groups (Homans 1951) typically assumed that it was always more productive to work in a team rather than alone. However, researchers soon recognized that both the nature of the task and the characteristics of the group have a lot to do with the comparative advantage or disadvantage of working in a group (Goodacre 1953). When we measure productivity, groups almost always outperform single individuals. Things get a bit more complicated, however, when groups are compared with the same number of people working by themselves.

In one of the earliest attempts to systematically study group productivity, experimental social psychologist Ivan Steiner (1972) compared the potential productivity of a group (what they should be able to do) with their actual productivity (what they in fact got done). According to Steiner, actual group productivity can never equal potential productivity because there will always be losses in the team process. Two major sources of inefficiency in particular come with the group process, and both get worse as group size increases. One source is organization: coordinating activities and delegating tasks. For example, if four friends are going to help you move to a new apartment, some time will be lost while you figure out who should pack what, how the furniture will be arranged in the truck, where the boxes should go in the new apartment, and so forth.

Another source of inefficiency is the phenomenon known as **social loafing**, which means that as more individuals are added to a task, each one takes it a little easier (Karau and Williams 1993). Furthermore, as more people become involved, the harder it will be to discern individual effort. If it is impossible for any single person to receive credit or blame, motivation usually suffers. Have you ever asked too many people to help you move to a new apartment? If so, chances are a few did most of the work, some showed up late and helped out a bit, and others did very little but had a good time talking and eating pizza. Having too many "helpers" may contribute to social loafing.

Solutions to the problem of social loafing include recognizing individual effort and finding ways to make a task more interesting or personally rewarding, but such solutions are not always possible. It might be difficult, for instance,

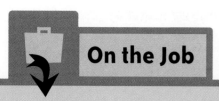

Teamwork and the Tour de France

In 2005, American Lance Armstrong won the Tour de France for the seventh straight time. The cyclist has earned a hero's reputation for his preeminence in a race usually dominated by Europeans and furthermore racked up his wins after surviving advanced testicular cancer. Clearly, Armstrong is a man of unusual perseverance, courage, and physical endurance. In the news media, he is presented as someone whose heroic individual qualities have made his athletic prowess possible—and indeed they have. But the Tour de France is, after all, a team event.

Armstrong's all-important teammates for the 2005 race included eight other men that you have probably never heard of: José Azevedo, Yaroslav Popovych, Benjamin Noval Gonzalez, George Hincapie, Paolo Savoldelli, Manuel Beltran Martinez, Pavel Padrnos, and José L. Rubiera Vigil. In the Tour de France, a race lasting over three weeks and covering more than 2,000 miles, each team member has a particular specialty, and each stage of the race requires a different strategy. Sprinters may be needed to make a "breakaway" early in the race; "super-climbers" are necessary in the mountainous regions; and sometimes the entire team has to protect the team leader, "blocking" and "drafting" in order to save energy. Teamwork is required to organize bathroom and food breaks, as the race stops for no man. Extremely consistent riders (*rouleurs*) are prized, as are those who ride with aggressiveness and bravery (*combativité*). When the individual winner crosses the finish line on the Champs-Elysées in Paris, it is the sacrifices of his altruistic teammates that have made his win possible.

In the years since 2005, the Tour de France has seen its share of scandal—American Floyd Landis's 2006 victory was stripped from him when tests showed he had used banned substances during the race. Other riders, including favorites Jan Ullrich and Ivan Basso, have also been banned from the Tour due to doping allegations. However, the Tour remains an event in which premier athletes compete in complex teamwork relations to push the limits of human achievement.

Which position will you find yourself in when you enter the workplace? Will you be the team leader, whose individual successes depend on the contributions of others? Or will you be the team member, whose special skills support the achievements of the group? It is likely that you will find yourself in both situations over the course of your working life. So remember, when you don the *maillot jaune* (the yellow jersey worn by the Tour de France leader), that in most cases it takes a team effort to get you to the winner's circle.

to make "moving day" more rewarding. Another solution, however, is suggested by **social identity theory**. Having a social identity, as opposed to a personal one, involves thinking and feeling like a representative of a group (R. Turner 1987); you have a real desire to belong to, not simply keep company with, the group. According to this model the most efficient teams are characterized by the greatest social identity among their members; such social identity increases motivation and places the needs of the group above purely personal concerns.

Qualities of Leadership: Power, Authority, and Style

Effective group leaders possess a variety of qualities, some of which are particular to the kind of group they lead. The leader of a therapeutic support group, for example, needs the proper credentials as well as experience and compassion for his patients. The captain of a sports team must display expertise at her game as well as the ability to inspire her teammates. An office manager must be well organized and good at dealing with different kinds of people. A police commander must be in good physical shape, skilled in law enforcement tactics, and quick-thinking in a crisis.

One thing almost all leaders have in common, though, is **power**—the ability to control the actions of others. Whether it is **coercive power** (backed by the threat of force) or merely **influential power** (supported by persuasion), leadership involves getting people to do things they may or may not want to do. For example, a football coach might wield both coercive and influential power over his players. Although the athletes would definitely want to win games, they might not want to run their training drills every day. During a workout,

Qualities of Leadership Leaders like Bill Clinton and Nelson Mandela possess both legal-rational and charismatic authority.

team members might respond to either the threat of being kicked off the team or the encouragement they receive from the coach. Power, in whatever form it takes, is both a privilege and a requirement of leadership.

Since leadership requires the exercise of power, most formal organizations have institutionalized it in some officially recognized form of **authority**. Max Weber (1913/1962) identified three different types of authority that may be found in social organizations. **Traditional authority**, based in custom, birthright, or divine right, is usually associated with monarchies and dynasties. Kings and queens inherit the throne, not only through lineage but also by divine appointment, meaning by higher authority. Their personal qualities don't really matter, and they can't be replaced by legal proceedings. **Legal-rational authority**, on the other hand, is based in laws and rules, not in the lineage of any individual leader. Modern presidencies and parliaments are built on this kind of authority. The third type, **charismatic authority**, is based in the remarkable personal qualities of the leader her- or himself. Neither rules nor traditions are necessary for the establishment of a charismatic leader— indeed, the leader can be a revolutionary, breaking rules and defying traditions. This is perhaps the only place we will ever find Jesus Christ and Adolf Hitler in the same category: both were extremely charismatic leaders.

The three types of authority are not necessarily mutually exclusive—they can coexist within the same leader. Bill Clinton and Ronald Reagan were appealing and charismatic

social identity theory a theory of group formation and maintenance that stresses the need of individual members to feel a sense of belonging

power the ability to control the actions of others

coercive power power that is backed by the threat of force

influential power power that is supported by persuasion

authority the legitimate right to wield power

traditional authority authority based in custom, birthright, or divine right

legal-rational authority authority based in laws, rules, and procedures, not in the heredity or personality of any individual leader

charismatic authority authority based in the perception of remarkable personal qualities in a leader

leaders within the context of the legal-rational authority of the presidency; the Kennedy family is considered an American political dynasty of sorts, following a tradition of leadership within the structure of electoral politics. The late King Hussein of Jordan was revered for his extraordinary charisma and statesmanship despite his traumatic ascent to the throne: as a teenager, he witnessed his grandfather's assassination and, as his heir, was crowned less than a year later. For people like Bill Clinton (a legal-rational ruler) and King Hussein (a traditional ruler), their charisma was not necessarily the root of their authority, but it did play a part in their ability to rule.

In addition to different types of power and authority, group leaders may exhibit different personal leadership styles as well. Some are more **instrumental**—that is, they are task or goal oriented—while others are more **expressive**, or concerned with maintaining harmony within the group (Parsons and Bales 1955). An instrumental leader is less concerned with people's feelings than with getting the job done, whereas an expressive leader conveys interest in group members' emotions as well as their achievements. We often consider leadership styles through the lens of gender, expecting men to be more instrumental and women to be more expressive. In fact, we sometimes feel surprised or upset when these gendered expectations aren't met: a male leader with a more expressive style (like former California gover-

nor Jerry Brown, nicknamed "Moonbeam" for his emotive, touchy-feely style) is sometimes seen as weak, while a female leader with a more instrumental style (such as U.S. Secretary of State Hillary Rodham Clinton, whose ambition and drive earned her criticism both while her husband was in the White House and while she was campaigning herself in 2008) is sometimes seen as pushy.

instrumental leadership leadership that is task or goal oriented

expressive leadership leadership concerned with maintaining emotional and relational harmony within the group

bureaucracy a type of secondary group designed to perform tasks efficiently, characterized by specialization, technical competence, hierarchy, written rules, impersonality, and formal written communication

Bureaucracy

Examples of **bureaucracies**, a specific type of secondary group, are everywhere in your life—your university, employer, internet service provider, fast-food restaurant, and even church are likely to be organized bureaucratically. Bureaucracies are designed to perform tasks efficiently, and they approach their tasks, whatever they are, with calculations designed deliberately to meet their goals.

Bureaucracies Are Everywhere Bureaucratic regulations are supposed to make organizations run smoothly; however, bureaucracy can also be impersonal, inflexible, and hyperrational.

Burning Man Finale Each year thousands of "burners" gather in the Black Rock Desert to celebrate the rejection of values like conformity, bureaucracy, and capitalism.

summer, at a festival called Burning Man (Sonner 2002; Chen 2004). The festival, begun in 1990 on a beach near San Francisco with just 20 participants, now draws almost 40,000 people each year. Burning Man is hard to describe for those who have never attended. It is a freewheeling experiment in temporary community, where there are no rules except to protect the well-being of participants ("burners") and where everyone gathers together to celebrate various forms of self-expression and self-reliance not normally encountered in everyday life.

Burning Man attracts a wide variety of individuals from different backgrounds (though it may be difficult to tell beneath the body paint, mud, or costumes that many wear), most of them in their 20s and 30s. Unlike many places in the real world, participants are encouraged to interact with each other; there are no strangers at "the Burn." Each year is characterized by a different theme—like "Beyond Belief" in 2003, "Psyche" in 2005, and "American Dream" in 2008—and participants are invited to contribute in some meaningful way to its realization, most often artistically.

Much of what is appealing about Burning Man is that it challenges many of the norms and values of mainstream society, especially those that are associated with conformity, bureaucracy, and capitalism. Black Rock resembles a city when the thousands of participants converge there, but one comprised of tents and RVs gathered into neighborhoods with names like "Tic Toc Town" and "Capitalist Pig Camp" (Doherty 2000). The city has its own informal economy as well. Once an admission fee is paid, money is no longer used. Participants must bring enough supplies to support themselves

TABLE 6.1	*Theory in Everyday Life*	
Perspective	**Approach to Groups**	**Case Study: Fraternities**
STRUCTURAL-FUNCTIONALISM	Life in groups helps to regulate and give meaning to individual experience, contributing to social cohesion and stability.	Affiliation groups like fraternities help create social cohesion in the context of a larger, possibly alienating, university system by bringing young men with shared values together.
CONFLICT THEORY	Group membership is often the basis for the distribution of rewards, privileges and opportunities in our society. An individual may be treated preferentially or prejudicially based on his or her group membership .	In-group and out-group dynamics can contribute to stereotyping and conflict as fraternity brothers develop an "us vs. them" perspective regarding other frats and non-Greeks.
SYMBOLIC INTERACTIONISM	Group norms, values, and dynamics are generated situationally, in interaction with other members.	The pressure to conform to group culture (as in the cases of peer pressure and groupthink) can lead individuals to do things they might never do alone, and can have negative consequences, as in the case of fraternity hazing and binge drinking. It can also lead to positive actions, such as when fraternity members volunteer or raise money for charity.

or use alternate forms of currency such as barter, trade, gifts, or services. Corporate sponsorship is strictly avoided, and logos of any kind are banned.

On the last night of the festival, the giant wooden structure known as the Burning Man is lit on fire, and the celebrants discover their own personal epiphanies as they watch it burn. When the festival is over, participants are committed to leaving no trace behind; the desert is returned to its pristine condition. One burner called the festival "authentic life" with the other days of the year "a tasteless mirage, a pacific struggle against the backwardness of middle America—consumer culture, bad politics, *Fear Factor* and fear thy neighbour" (Babiak 2004). So while Burning Man participants don't abandon permanently the web of contemporary bureaucracies that shape their lives, they gain some relief by ditching it all once a year, just for a few days.

Closing Comments

Groups make our lives possible by providing us with the necessities of our existence—food, clothes, cars, homes, and all the other things we use on a daily basis. Groups make our lives enjoyable by providing us with companionship and recreation—from our friends and families to the entertainment conglomerates that produce our favorite music and films. Groups also make our lives problematic—bureaucracies can squelch our individuality, major manufacturers can create social and environmental problems, and some organizations can engender conflict and prejudice between groups. We are at our best in groups, and our worst. We can do great things together, and horrible things. Sociology helps us understand group life at both extremes and everywhere in between.

 Find more review materials online at
www.wwnorton.com/studyspace

CHAPTER SUMMARY

- **What Is a Group?** Unlike crowds, members of a group have something in common, consider this shared attribute meaningful, and interact with each other. We can further classify groups based on the type of interaction they provide. Primary groups provide intimate face-to-face interaction and are most responsible for our emotional satisfaction and socialization. Secondary groups are much larger and more likely to be organized around a specific goal, and so our interactions with them are more likely to be more formal and impersonal.

- **Social Networks** Social network theory provides a vocabulary for understanding how groups form and how they work. Each individual is the center of his or her own social network, a web of direct and indirect links to other social actors. While it may be obvious that who you know is important, research on social networks has shown that indirect ties can be equally important—so it's not just who you know, but who they know.

- **Anomie** Social groups provide the values, norms, and rules that guide our lives. Sociologists like Emile Durkheim and Robert Putnam have worried that in the

modern world we have become increasingly disconnected from our groups and more likely to suffer from anomie, or normlessness. However, some critics believe that these worries are overstated and that new technologies like the internet allow us to connect with others in new ways.

- **Group Dynamics** One reason sociologists study groups is to understand group dynamics, the ways in which groups form and fall apart, and the ways they influence their members. Dyads, triads, and other small groups facilitate intimate, intense interactions, but they are also relatively unstable, as even one person leaving can break them up. As groups grow they become more stable at the cost of intimacy. When groups reach a certain size it may be impossible for everyone to interact. Such groups often develop formal rules and regulations. However, even large, formal groups may command intense loyalty.

- Defining group memberships in terms of in-groups and out-groups may enhance the feeling of belonging that group members enjoy. Distinctions between groups increase group cohesion, which ensures the survival of the group but can also lead to intolerance and groupthink. Reference groups provide a standard against which to measure our performance.

- **Social Influence** Almost everyone is influenced by fellow group members. Generally, we conform to group norms and expectations because we crave acceptance and fear rejection. Social influence can produce different types of conformity depending on the strength of the individual's commitment to the group. Social psychological experiments have shown the power of the group to induce conformity and the extent to which individuals are socialized to obey authority, even when orders conflict with their own sense of morality.

- **Teamwork** Sociologists have studied teamwork to determine whether groups are more efficient than individuals. A group almost always outperforms an individual but rarely performs as well as it could in theory. A group's efficiency usually declines as its size increases, because organizing takes time and social loafing increases with group size. Group leaders can increase efficiency by recognizing individual effort or by increasing members' social identity, the degree to which they identify with the group.

- **Types of Leadership** Leaders can be classified in terms of the type of power they possess (coercive or influential) and according to their leadership style (instrumental or expressive). Alternately, leaders can be understood by looking at the basis for their authority. Max Weber identified three types: traditional, legal-rational, and charismatic. Rational-legal authority is the most common type in modern societies and is associated with bureaucracies: highly efficient secondary groups that operate on the principle of rationalization.

- **Bureaucracy** Max Weber identified six characteristics of bureaucracy: specialization, technical competence, hierarchy, formal regulations, impersonality, and formal written communication. Although bureaucracies often seem heartless and undemocratic, they are extremely efficient and are responsible for providing many basic necessities. However, many sociologists are concerned about the spread of bureaucracy and rationalization throughout society.

QUESTIONS FOR REVIEW

1. Sociologists have found that even indirect ties within our social networks can be very helpful, especially economically. Describe a time when you've gained some material benefit from your social network. Job hunting is the obvious example, but there are many other ways that you might have used indirect ties to your advantage.

2. Many sociologists worry about the anomie that may result from declining membership in groups. Are you a member of any formal organizations, or do you take part in any regular group activities? Alternatively, do you belong to any electronic communities like Friendster, MySpace, Facebook, or others? Which type of group influences you more?

3. Think of at least three groups to which you belong. Which out-groups are associated with these group identities?

4. Which groups serve as your reference groups? Are you a member of all your reference groups? How do these reference groups affect your self-image?

5. The text identifies three different types of conformity: compliance, identification, and internalization. Describe some moments when you've exhibited each type of conformity.

6. One way to decrease the incidence of social loafing is to recruit members with a strong sense of group identity. Do any of your group memberships involve a particularly strong or weak social identity?

7. Legal-rational authority is by far the most common type of authority in modern society, but older forms still exist. Can you think of a contemporary authority figure whose power was granted on the basis of tradition or custom? How about a charismatic authority figure?

8. What are some institutions that you encounter in your everyday life that don't fit Max Weber's description of a bureaucracy?

9. Theorist George Ritzer believes that McDonaldization, the spread of the organizational principles of bureaucracies to all areas of life, is a growing concern. Thinking about Weber's six characteristics of bureaucracies, can you identify areas of your life that have been McDonaldized?

SUGGESTIONS FOR FURTHER EXPLORATION

Doherty, Brian. 2004. *This Is Burning Man*. New York: Little, Brown and Company. A portrait of this annual desert festival from an insider's viewpoint. Into what sort of group would you classify Burning Man participants?

FitzGerald, Frances. 1986. *Cities on a Hill*. New York: Simon & Schuster. A journalistic account of four groups with radically different ideologies and lifestyles: San Francisco's mainly gay Castro neighborhood, Jerry Falwell's Liberty Baptist Church, a Florida retirement community, and an Oregon commune. FitzGerald presents them as quintessentially American examples of the power of group life to stimulate individual and social change.

Groupthink. 1992. CRM Learning. Examines the Space Shuttle *Challenger* prelaunch conference and other historical events in which decisions based on groupthink led to disaster. See www.groupthinkfilm.com for more information.

Hausbeck, Kathryn, and Barbara Brent. 2006. "McDonaldization of the Sex Industries: The Business of Sex" in *McDonaldization: The Reader*. Ed. George Ritzer. Thousand Oaks, CA: Pine Forge Press. This essay shows just how pervasive the process of rationalization has become.

Heller, Joseph. 1955. *Catch-22*. New York: Simon & Schuster. The term "catch-22" has come to mean a no-win situation, especially one in which a bureaucracy has created rules and regulations so complicated that they create self-contradictory situations. Pay attention to how bureaucracies work (or fail) in this satirical novel.

Klaw, Spencer. 1994. *Without Sin: The Life and Death of the Oneida Community*. New York: Penguin. The Oneida colony was a utopian socialist experiment in cooperative living that rejected monogamy and supported itself through the manufacture of silverware. Much like the participants at Burning Man, they attempted to escape the constraints of a bureaucratically regimented life.

Kreuter, Holly. 2002. *Drama in the Desert: The Sights and Sounds of Burning Man*. San Francisco: Raised Barn Press. Captures the spirit of this vibrant community through color photographs and contributions from group members.

Obedience (1962). A documentary film of Milgram's classic experiment on authority, shot at Yale University.

Quadrophenia. 1979. Dir. Franc Roddam. The Who Films. This rock opera was composed, performed, recorded, and translated onto film by The Who. Set in London in 1964, it addresses the role of group subcultures in the lives of working-class youth by examining the clashes between Mods and Rockers. These groups give the young protagonists a sense of belonging and identity—however, group boundaries also drive individuals apart and lead to violence.

Quiet Rage: The Stanford Prison Experiment (1991). A documentary film featuring the college students who participated in the now-famous (and unethical) experiment conducted in the basement of the Stanford psychology building.

"We Do What We're Told (Milgram's 37)." This song, written by Peter Gabriel, was inspired by the Milgram experiment.

Wilson, James Q. 2000. *Bureaucracy: What Government Agencies Do and Why They Do It*. New York: Basic Books. A helpful explanation of bureaucratic behavior, especially the relationship between a government organization's structure and its specific goals.

Zwick, Mark, and Louise Zwick. 2005. *The Catholic Worker Movement: Intellectual and Spiritual Origins*. Mahwah, NJ: Paulist Press. Describes the social and cultural context of the Catholic Workers Movement and the resources that Peter Maurin and Dorothy Day drew upon in order to resist the claims of bureaucracy and modern authority.

Whenever you get the opportunity, even if it's long after you take this class, visit any of the following museums dedicated to different cultural groups in American life—or visit a similar museum in your home town.

National Museum of the American Indian
Washington, DC
www.nmai.si.edu

Simon Weisenthal Center Museum of Tolerance
Los Angeles, CA
www.museumoftolerance.com

The African American Museum
Philadelphia, PA
www.aampmuseum.org

Arab American National Museum
Dearborn, MI
www.arabamericanmuseum.org

American Swedish Institute
Minneapolis, MN
www.americanswedishinst.org

Museo de las Americas
Denver, CO
www.museo.org

Chinese Historical Society of America
San Francisco, CA
www.chsa.org

CHAPTER 7

Deviance

D espite a great deal of confusion on the morning of September 11, 2001, the facts were fairly quickly established. Nineteen men armed with box cutters hijacked four planes, crashing them into both towers of the World Trade Center in New York, the Pentagon in Washington, D.C., and a field in Pennsylvania. The men were part of an organization known as Al Qaeda, headed by exiled Saudi billionaire Osama bin Laden. Despite this quick consensus, the squabble over what *really* had happened was just beginning.

In the United States, among other places, the attack was considered an act of terrorism. In his State of the Union address the following January, President Bush spoke of "truths that we will never question" and declared that "evil is real, and it must be opposed." The rhetoric of good and evil dominated the discussion of these events in the United States: the "evil" of terrorism was perpetrated by "evildoers" who belonged to a "cult of evil which seeks to harm the innocent and thrives on human suffering." As journalist Michael Kinsley (2002) put it, "There has never in our entire history been a proposition from which fewer Americans dissent than 'Osama Bin Laden is evil.' "

However, in other parts of the world, the interpretation was radically different. Although official messages of sympathy and condolence were received from every world government except Iraq, in parts of the Middle East this official attitude did not always reflect the popular mood. Pro–bin Laden demonstrations erupted in many spots around the Islamic world immediately after the attacks. In Sudan and Pakistan, Osama bin Laden T-shirts were selling briskly. Protesters in Egypt chanted, "There is no God but God, and Bush is the enemy of God" (Macfarquhar 2001). To these people, the September 11 hijackers were not "evildoers" but martyrs. An Afghani cleric who had known one of the hijackers described him as "one of the pious men in the [Al Qaeda] organization," who "became a martyr, Allah bless his soul." Bin Laden himself (in a videotaped lecture) explicitly argued that it was the United States and its troops stationed in Saudi Arabia that were evil: "Every Muslim must rise to defend his religion. The wind of faith is blowing and the wind of change is blowing to remove evil from the Peninsula of Mohammed." From this point of view, it was a religious obligation to make war on the West, and the hijackers fulfilled their duties with great success, at the expense of their own lives.

How is it possible that people who are basically in agreement about what happened on September 11 can be in such extreme disagreement over the meaning of these events? To almost all Americans, the hijackers were deviants—terrorists and murderers. However, to the supporters of Al Qaeda, the hijackers were heroes and martyrs. How can this disagreement be explained? The sociological answer is that no behavior, not even one that is intended to kill great numbers of people, is inherently deviant. It is the cultural context, the values and norms of a particular society, that makes it so.

HOW TO READ THIS CHAPTER

Have you ever driven faster than the posted speed limit? Have you ever gotten caught picking your nose in public? Did you have your first taste of beer, wine, or hard liquor before you reached the legal drinking age? Did you pierce something (your lip, eyebrow, or belly button) that your grandmother wouldn't have wanted you to pierce? If you work in an office, did you ever take home a pen, pencil, or packet of Post-it notes?

If you answered yes to any of these questions, you are the embodiment of what we seek to understand in this chapter: you are deviant. Remember this as you read the chapter.

Defining Deviance

Deviance is a behavior, trait, or belief that departs from a norm and generates a negative reaction in a particular group. The norms and the group reactions are necessary for a behavior or characteristic to be defined as deviant (E. Goode 1997). The importance of norms becomes clear when we remember that what is deviant in one culture might be normal in another (see Chapter 4); even within the same culture, what was deviant a century ago might be perfectly acceptable now (and vice versa). The importance of group reactions is clear when we look at the varied reactions that norm violations generate: some violations are seen as only mildly deviant (like chewing with your mouth open), but others are so strongly taboo that they are almost unthinkable (like cannibalism).

Deviant behavior must be sufficiently serious or unusual to spark a negative sanction or punishment. For example, if you were having dinner with friends and used the wrong fork for your salad, you would be violating a minor norm but your friends probably

deviance a behavior, trait, belief, or other characteristic that violates a norm and causes a negative reaction

wouldn't react in a negative fashion; they might not even notice. On the other hand, if you ate an entire steak dinner—meat, mashed potatoes, and salad—with your hands, your friends probably *would* react. They might criticize your behavior strongly ("That's totally disgusting!") and even refuse to eat with you again. This latter example, then, would be considered deviant behavior among your group of friends—and among most groups in American society.

Because definitions of deviance are constructed from cultural, historical, and situational norms, sociologists are interested in a number of topics under the rubric of deviance. First, how are norms and rules created, and how do certain norms and rules become especially important? Second, who is subject to the rules, and how is rule breaking identified? Third, what types of sanctions (punishments or rewards) are dispensed to society's violators? Fourth, how do people who break the rules see themselves, and how do others see them? And finally, how have sociologists attempted to explain rule making, rule breaking, and responses to rule breaking?

Deviance Across Cultures

It is important to remember that when sociologists use the term *deviant*, they are making a social judgment, never a moral one. If a particular behavior is considered deviant, this means that it violates the values and norms of a *particular* group, not that it is inherently wrong or that other groups will make the same judgment.

Much of the literature on deviance focuses on crime, but not only do different cultures define strikingly different behaviors as criminal, they also differ in how those crimes are punished. Most serious crime in the United States today is punished by imprisonment. This method of punishment was rare until the nineteenth century, however, as maintaining a prison requires considerable resources. Buildings must be constructed and maintained, guards and other staff must be paid, and prisoners must be fed and clothed. For groups without these resources, incarceration is not a possibility, even assuming it would be a desirable option. Instead, there are a whole host of other techniques of punishment.

For example, the Amish, a religious community whose members do without modern devices like electricity, cars, and telephones, practice *meidung*, which means shunning those who violate the strict norms of the group (Kephart 2000). A biblical rule instructs them "not to associate with any one who bears the name of brother if he is guilty of immorality or greed, or is an idolater, reviler, drunkard, or robber—not even to eat with such a one" (1 Corinthians 5:11). In other words, the Amish believe they should not associate with lawbreakers even when they come from within their own family. No one does business with, eats with, or even talks to the guilty party. The shunning is temporary, however: after a short period the violator is expected to publicly apologize and make amends, and is then welcomed back into the community.

A much more permanent method of punishment is total banishment from the community. For many Native American people, the social group was so important that banishment was considered a fate worse than death (Champagne 1994). It was one of a variety of practices that were used to maintain social control—along with shaming songs, contests, and challenges of strength—and something of a rarity, as the death penalty is in the United States today, because it completely severed ties between the group and the individual. Banishment has a long history of use in all parts of the world, from the British prisoners who were "transported" to Australia to Russian dissidents exiled to Siberia, and has been one of the most cost-effective methods of punishment ever discovered.

Just as methods of punishment vary between societies and groups, so they also change over time. In Colonial America, for example, corporal punishment was the rule for the majority of crimes (Samuel Walker 1997). These days, the phrase *corporal punishment* conjures up images of elementary school teachers spanking students, probably because spanking was the last vestige of what was once a vast repertoire of penal techniques. Thieves, pickpockets, and others who would today be considered petty criminals were flogged, had their ears cropped, had their noses slit, had their fingers and hands cut off, or were branded. These punishments were designed not only to deliver pain but also to mark the offender, and as such the particular punishment was often designed to fit the crime. A pickpocket might have a hand cut off; a forger might have an "F" branded on his forehead. Brands were also used to mark African American slaves as property during the 1800s.

Body Modification

Branding has long since died out as a method of punishment, but in a perfect illustration of the mutability of deviance, it is making a comeback as a form of body decoration (Parker 1998). What used to be an involuntary mark of shame has been reclaimed as a voluntary mark of pride. Small branding irons of stainless steel are heated with a blowtorch until white hot and held on the skin for a second or two. Some who undergo the procedure burn incense to cover the smell of their own flesh burning. Many African American fraternities have a long tradition of branding, usually in the shape of one of the fraternity's Greek letters. The practice has received a public boost in recent years as several popular athletes have prominently displayed their fraternity brands. Basketball star Michael Jordan sports such a brand, as does former Dallas Cowboy Emmitt Smith. Branding is spreading to other youth subcultures, where it is just another extension of tattoos, Mohawks, and body piercings as an outward manifestation of youthful rebellion.

When it comes to body modification, what Americans might label deviant might be identified as desirable or normal in other cultures and vice versa. Among the Suri of southwest Ethiopia, progressively larger plates are inserted into the lower lip so that it gradually becomes enlarged. The Padaung women of Burma stretch their necks with brass rings. Young girls begin by encircling their necks with just a few rings, then add more as they grow; by the time of maturity, their necks are considerably elongated. Breast augmentation surgery is commonplace in the United States, but in Brazil, where large breasts are considered undesirable, a breast augmentation would be regarded as impairing rather than improving beauty.

Body modification does not always need to be dramatic. In reality, there are a great number of subtle methods of body modification practiced by most Americans that may not seem so obvious if we concentrate on nose rings and biker tattoos. First of all, there have always been body modifications for the middle and upper classes. Corsets, worn by women through the ages until the early twentieth century, are an obvious example. Stomachs were flattened with "stays," long strips of some rigid material like whalebone. A tightly laced corset could achieve a dramatically narrow waistline, but often at a serious cost to the wearer's health. Women sometimes even had ribs removed in order to accommodate them.

These days, we have a rich array of techniques to bring our bodies into line with contemporary standards. Recently the Food and Drug Administration has approved the use of injections of Botox, a strain of botulism toxin that works by freezing facial nerves, for removing fine lines and wrinkles on the forehead. The hair salon is another great unacknowledged

One Culture's Deviant Behavior Might Be Desirable or Normal in Another Padaung women use brass rings to stretch their necks, a Suri woman uses plates to modify her lip, an American man has split and pierced his tongue, and an American woman has a rose tattoo on her hip.

center for body modification. If you get a perm, you are breaking the disulfide bonds in your hair and reshaping them to straighten them or make them curly. Even a simple haircut is a type of body modification—luckily, for those of us who have gotten bad haircuts, they're temporary! Some body modifications seem so "normal" that we practice them as routines without considering how they may seem deviant elsewhere. Other cultures may view Americans' obsession with hair removal—shaving, plucking, tweezing, and waxing—as bizarre. As you can see, whether it's corsets, branding, or shaving your legs, the boundaries between beauty and deviance are fluid across time and place.

Delicious or Disgusting?
Food, Culture, and Deviance

Although as Americans we enjoy a great number of ethnic foods, there are some food boundaries we will not cross. One is the ancient practice of *entomophagy*, the eating of insects. Even though the 1,462 known species of edible insects are very environmentally friendly to raise and have a better feed-to-meat ratio and better protein-to-fat ratio than any other animal, there are few taboos as indestructible in America as that against eating bugs.

People in Algeria traditionally eat desert locusts, aborigines in Australia snack on certain moths and grubs, some Africans sauté termites, and the Japanese sometimes eat fried grasshoppers.

Probably the most notorious of culinary insects is the agave worm found in bottles of the Mexican liquor *mezcal*, usually eaten (if at all) in America as the result of a drunken dare rather than for its nutritional value.

One thing Americans *do* love is bacon cheeseburgers. For billions of people throughout the world, though, this is an abomination. It violates the dietary laws of three major world religions (Judaism, Hinduism, and Islam), and members of those groups may look on you with horror, disgust, or even pity as they watch you eat one. Jewish dietary laws called *kashrut* prohibit eating meat and dairy products at the same meal. The Hindu religion prohibits eating beef, and the Islamic religion regards pork as *haraam*, or forbidden food, and Jewish laws also prohibit eating pork. Sociologists maintain that what is deviant is always socially learned, relative to a particular culture. Certainly with food, standards of deviance vary widely across cultures.

How to Eat Fried Worms A cook at the upscale restaurant Hostería Santo Domingo in Mexico City adds a dollop of guacamole to a plate of deep-fried worms.

Theories of Deviance

In this section, we will learn how three sociological theories we considered in Chapter 2—functionalism, conflict theory, and symbolic interactionism—can be applied to deviance. We will also learn about other, related theories that have been developed specifically to explain particular aspects of deviance.

Functionalism

As you may recall, adherents of functionalism argue that each element of social structure helps maintain the stability of society. What, then, is the function of deviance for society?

Emile Durkheim came up with a couple of functions. First, deviance can help a society clarify its moral boundaries. We are reminded about our shared notions of what is right when we have to address wrongdoings of various sorts. In 2005, Terri Schiavo, a hospital patient from St. Petersburg, Florida, received national attention when a legal battle was fought over her life. Schiavo had been in a persistent vegetative state since 1990 and kept alive through a gastric feeding tube. Her husband, Michael, petitioned the courts in 1998 to end life support—he thought it was the right thing to do and was what Terri would have wanted. Her parents, Mary and Robert Schindler, took legal action against Michael's decision—they thought it was wrong. While most people might have had a vague idea of how they felt about artificially prolonging life, the Schiavo case forced them to think concretely about how such choices affect actual people. After a seven-year process, the courts sided with Michael Schiavo, and on March 18, 2005, his wife's feeding tube was removed. She died 13 days later.

Another function of deviance is to promote social cohesion (one of functionalism's valued ideals); people can be brought together as a community in the face of crime or other violations. For example, while the country was divided over the decision in the Schiavo case, an opinion poll by ABC News on March 21, 2005, reported that 70 percent of Americans believed that Michael Schiavo had the authority to make decisions on behalf of his wife and that the case should not have been a federal matter. In the same poll, 63 percent maintained that the federal government was involved solely for political advantage. Whatever they believed about prolonging life, the majority of Americans thus agreed that the choice was best made by family and not the government.

Conflict Theory

Conflict theorists, who study inequalities of wealth and power, note that inequalities are present in our definitions of deviance as well. In other words, they believe that rules are applied unequally and that punishments for rule violators are unequally distributed: those at the top are subject to different rules and sanctions than those nearer the bottom, and the behaviors of less powerful groups and individuals are more likely to be criminalized than the behaviors of the powerful.

Author Kate Bornstein's "Who's on Top?" (1998) provides a useful way to look at hierarchies of power and privilege in our society. Bornstein uses a pyramid analogy: the bottom represents the masses of people who have little power; the higher on the pyramid we go, fewer people amass more and more power. Bornstein argues that the top of the pyramid is the perfect identity—an imaginary person who represents all the different facets of power in our society. This person would be a white, rich, heterosexual male who is educated, athletic, and handsome, owns a home, has never broken the law, and is married with two children. The more we deviate from this perfect identity (and all of us do in one way or another), the lower we fall in the pyramid.

Sociologist William Chambliss looked at the history of vagrancy laws to demonstrate the relationship between power and deviance. According to Chambliss (1973), vagrancy laws have always been used to target different groups—the

Who's on Top? Kate Bornstein represents power hierarchies with a pyramid. She argues that the top of the pyramid represents the "perfect" identity. The more we deviate from this identity—as we all do—the lower we fall in the pyramid.

homeless, the unemployed, racial minorities—depending on who seemed most threatening to the elites at the time. When preparing for big events like political conventions or televised sports tournaments, for instance, local police officers may sweep "undesirables" from downtown areas so that a city appears to be free from panhandlers, drug users, hookers, or the homeless (at least until the cameras are turned off).

As recently as 2003, some U.S. states still imposed heterosexuality on their citizens through antisodomy laws, which prohibited any sexual acts that did not lead to procreation. While in theory antisodomy laws could include acts like masturbation and heterosexual oral sex, in practice these laws are generally imposed against same-sex partners. Before the Supreme Court repealed all state antisodomy laws in *Lawrence vs. Texas* (2003), sexual acts done in the privacy of your own home could be penalized with fines and jail time in states like Virginia, Michigan, and Texas. From a conflict theorist perspective, antisodomy laws are a way for the heterosexual majority to control homosexuals.

As a final example, in 2006, Rochester, New York, had the highest murder rate per capita in the entire state, including New York City. The mayor, Robert Duffy, proposed a new law that would require all young people age 16 and under living within city limits to be off the streets from 11:00 P.M. to 6:00 A.M. during the summer break from school. Because statistics have shown that more crime occurs during the summer among youth living in the city, Duffy believed that the curfew would reduce violence. Not only does the curfew demonstrate ageism, in that control is wielded by adults over relatively powerless youth, but also classism, as the curfew applies only to kids who live in the city, leaving wealthier teens in the suburbs free to do what they like. Unfortunately, there is a good deal of evidence to support the conflict theorists' argument that rules are applied unequally in our hierarchical society.

Structural Strain Theory

Robert Merton's **structural strain theory** (1938/1976) provides a bridge between functionalist and conflict theories of deviance. Like Durkheim, Merton acknowledges that some deviance is inevitable in society. But like conflict theorists, he argues that an individual's position in the social structure will affect his experience of deviance and conformity. Social inequality can create situations in which people experience tension (or strain) between the goals society says they should be working toward (like financial success) and the means they have available to meet those goals (not everyone is able to work hard at a legitimate job). The rewards of conformity, therefore, are available only to those who can pursue

approved goals through approved means. Any other combination of means and goals is deviant in one way or another. **Innovators**, for example, might seek financial success via unconventional means (such as drug dealing or embezzlement). **Ritualists** go through the conventional motions while abandoning all hope of success, and **retreatists** (like dropouts or hermits) renounce the culture's goals and means entirely and live outside conventional norms altogether. At the far end of the continuum, **rebels** reject the cultural definitions of success and the normative means of achieving it and advocate radical alternatives to the existing social order.

For example, consider the characters in the 1999 film *Office Space*, a comedy that satirizes a large, bureaucracy-laden business. In the film, conformity is represented by Bill Lumbergh, a high-ranking

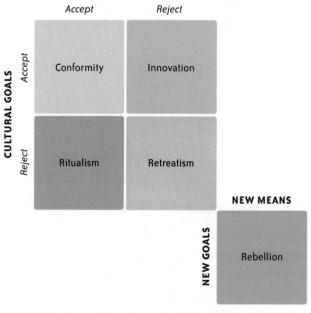

FIGURE 7.1 Merton's Typology of Deviance Different orientations toward society's goals and differential access to the means to achieve those goals combine to create different categories of deviance.

Structural Strain Characters in the comedy *Office Space* exemplify Merton's categories of deviants. Peter Gibbons (right) is an innovator who plans to rob the company and thwart his conformist manager, Bill Lumbergh (left).

boss who has apparently attained his position by following the rules of the organization. The protagonist, Peter Gibbons, is an innovator who spends most of the movie attempting to find meaning and fulfillment in a job that increasingly makes little sense. Rather than adhering to the bizarre and elaborate rules within his organization, Peter comes up with a scheme to rob the company. The most humorous character in the movie, Milton, is a ritualist. Milton shows up to work every day and puts up with a lot of abuse from his superiors even though, as we soon learn, he was fired five years ago and never removed from the payroll. Peter's neighbor Lawrence provides an example of a retreatist: he doesn't work in an office at all. By the end of the movie, Peter realizes that happiness can't be found working in a bureaucratized organization. He rebels by taking a lower-paying job as a construction worker and finds fulfillment in his personal relationships instead.

differential association theory Edwin Sutherland's hypothesis that we learn to be deviant through our associations with deviant peers

labeling theory Howard Becker's idea that deviance is a consequence of external judgments, or labels, which modify the individual's self-concept and change the way others respond to the labeled person

Symbolic Interactionism

While conflict theorists and functionalists focus on inequalities and the social functions of deviance, interactionists consider the way that interpersonal relationships and everyday interactions shape definitions of deviance. One such approach

is Edwin Sutherland's **differential association theory** (Sutherland 1939; Sutherland et al. 1992), which asserts that we learn to be deviant through our interactions with others who break the rules. This is the theory of deviance that your mother subscribed to when you were a teenager: don't hang out with the bad kids!

This theory of deviance seems at first glance to be pretty sensible—interacting often with those who break the rules would seem to socialize an individual into their rule-breaking culture. But as it turns out, not all who hang out with deviants become deviant themselves, and plenty of people who engage in deviant acts have never consorted with other rulebreakers. Also, in cases where deviance is not the result of a willful act (mental illness, for example), a learning theory such as this one is not a useful explanation. While differential association theory seeks to explain "why they do it," it cannot fully explain every case of deviant behavior—nor can any theory of deviance.

LABELING THEORY Howard Becker's **labeling theory** (1963) proposes that deviance is not inherent in any act, belief, or condition; instead, it is determined by the audience. A man who kills an intruder who is attacking his child may be labeled a hero, while a man who kills a cashier in the process of robbing a store may be labeled a villain. Even though the act of murder is the same, the way the person is treated differs greatly depending on the label.

Labeling theory recognizes that labels will vary depending on the culture, time period, and context. David Rosenhan's study "On Being Sane in Insane Places" (1973) provides a striking demonstration of the power of labeling and the importance of context. Rosenhan and seven other researchers gained admission to psychiatric hospitals as patients. Other than falsifying their names and occupations, the eight subjects gave honest answers to all but one of the questions in the entrance examination; they all complained of hearing voices, a symptom often linked to schizophrenia. Nevertheless, the subjects felt certain that once they were hospitalized, they would be quickly exposed as "pseudopatients," not really mentally ill.

In fact, the opposite turned out to be true. Once admitted, the pseudopatients turned immediately to the task of getting themselves discharged—and failed miserably. Although they behaved as normally and pleasantly as possible, doctors and nurses continued to treat them as mentally ill patients in need of treatment. No amount of explanation on the part of the pseudopatients could convince hospital staff of their sanity (though, in an interesting twist, it was usually obvious to the other patients). When they were finally discharged (after one to seven weeks!), it was not because the staff had finally seen through the deception; they were all released with

Fat Actress Kirstie Alley turned a potentially negative label into a positive one by using the media's focus on her weight gain (primary deviation) to leverage a deal for a television show in which she capitalized on her fat identity (secondary deviation). After her show was cancelled, she won a contract as a spokesperson for weight loss (tertiary deviance) with Jenny Craig.

Labeling theory is also concerned with how individuals think of themselves once a deviant label has been applied. Recall Cooley's concept of the "looking-glass self": how we perceive ourselves depends in part on how others see us, so if others react to us as deviant, we are likely to internalize that label (even if we object to it). Applying deviant labels can also lead to further deviance, as a patient moves from **primary deviation** (the thing that gets her labeled in the first place) to **secondary deviation** (a deviant identity or career) (Lemert 1951).

For instance, Kirstie Alley, a popular TV actress in the 1980s and 1990s, gained enough weight in the early 2000s that she received national attention for it. In her case, the primary deviation was gaining weight; she became labeled as a fat person. Alley's response was to create a show called *Fat Actress*, in which she used comedy as a way of demonstrating her secondary deviation (her identity as an overweight American). Because Alley was unable to avoid the media's scrutiny of her weight, she decided to participate in publicizing her label through her show and through numerous interviews on the topic.

Although deviant labels are sticky—they are hard to shake—it is sometimes possible for an individual to turn

primary deviation in labeling theory, the act or attitude that causes one to be labeled deviant

secondary deviation in labeling theory, the deviant identity or career that develops as a result of being labeled deviant

their schizophrenia "in remission." As Rosenhan concludes, "Once labeled schizophrenic, the pseudopatient was stuck with that label" (1973, p. 253). The effects of this "sticky" deviant label on actual patients can follow them through their lives, even after they leave the hospital.

TABLE 7.1	*Theory in Everyday Life*	
Perspective	**Approach to Deviance**	**Case Study: Plagiarism**
STRUCTURAL-FUNCTIONALISM	Deviance clarifies moral boundaries and promotes social cohesion.	Punishing those who plagiarize separates those who should be in college from those who aren't responsible enough.
Structural Strain Theory	An individual's position in society determines whether they have the means to achieve goals or must otherwise turn to deviance.	A student's attitude about plagiarizing depends on whether she has the means to write the paper.
CONFLICT THEORY	Definitions and rules of deviance are applied unequally based on power.	Students with fewer resources are punished more harshly and have fewer options afterward; students with more money or connections can either transfer to another school or rely on parents for help.
SYMBOLIC INTERACTIONISM		
Differential Association Theory	Deviance is learned through interactions with others who break the rules.	Students learn to cheat because they hang out with other students who plagiarize.
Labeling Theory	Deviance is determined by the audience; applying deviant labels to an individual may lead them to further deviance.	Plagiarism may be labeled deviant in U.S. courses but not in Russia or India; a student who is caught plagiarizing may come to believe she is unable to write without cheating.

Tuy Sobil and the Tiny Toones of Phnom Penh

All around the world, from Latin America to South-East Asia and beyond, there is an unusual problem brewing. American-style gang activity is appearing in new areas, complete with turf wars, drug dealing, graffiti, and crime, just like in troubled American cities. What's really unusual about this new gang problem is its source. As you might expect, it came from the United States, but instead of local teenagers imitating gangsters they see in the American media, places like Cambodia and El Salvador are getting an influx of actual gang members, unwilling immigrants deported from the United States.

In 1996, following the first attack on the World Trade Center and with an election to think about, Congress passed the Illegal Immigration Reform and Immigrant Responsibility Act, which dramatically increased the number of offenses for which noncitizens could be deported, sending many into permanent exile for nonviolent misdemeanor offenses, even if they served a their sentence and had a perfect record of good conduct (Human Rights Watch 2007). The law was especially hard on families, as it was made retroactive, so legal immigrants who had committed crimes years ago were suddenly eligible to be deported, with no grounds for appeal.

Although they may seem less sympathetic, some of the most poignant cases involve troubled young people or gang members who have been deported back to countries they had little or no memory of. El Salvador and Cambodia in particular have produced many troublesome cases, because those countries produced a great many refugees who differ from traditional immigrants in a number of ways. While immigrants purposely seek out a new home, refugees are driven by violence and starvation. They often arrive in a new country with physical and psychological scars and little or no support and find themselves living in bewildering new cities.

The children of such refugees are often at-risk as youth and sometimes end up involved in gangs, which now can lead them to be deported back to their "native" country.

The effort to fight gangs like Mara Salvatrucha, which was "founded by Central Americans who fled wars at home in the 1980s, and landed in US ghettos without work or protection from existing gangs," or "the Tiny Little Rascals gang, the main Asian gang on the West Coast," has led to a vast increase in the number of deportations for criminal behavior, including many legal residents who had never applied for citizenship (Lakshmanan 2006). Many of the young men who have been deported this way have only the haziest memories of their "homelands" and had never thought of themselves as anything but American. Most are not fluent in any language but English. Many had moved to the United States as infants, and in the case of some, had been born in refugee camps and had never before lived in the country to which they were "re"-patriated.

This was the situation that Tuy Sobil faced following a conviction for armed robbery at age 18. After spending 10 years in various jails and immigration facilities, Sobil was repatriated to Cambodia, a country he had never set foot in before, having been born in a refugee camp in Thailand after his parents fled the Khmer Rouge. He has not seen any of his family since then, including his son, and deportees are legally barred from ever reentering the United States. His nickname is K.K., gang-style initials for "Crazy Crip," after the gang he had belonged to when he lived in Long Beach, California. But since arriving in Cambodia he has reinvented himself, leaving his gang persona behind. Like many other deportees, he arrived in Phnom Penh with few resources, but he has persevered and even triumphed in his new home. After working as a drug counselor, he founded the Tiny Toones, a break-dancing troupe he hopes can "help save

Tiny Toones Break-Dancing School Tuy Sobil, aka K.K. (far right), started the break-dancing school in Cambodia after being deported from Long Beach, California.

Cambodian street kids from the sort of dead-end detour he took" (Krausz 2007). With little more than a boom box and the skills he learned as a teenage "b-boy" (slang for break dancer) he found a way to organize and teach hundreds of street kids who had nowhere else to turn. Having grown up in a harsh environment, with few hopes for success, Sobil understands the needs of the street children of Cambodia. And he hopes that break dancing can help kids stay out of trouble and build a sense of community based on positive achievements. Learning head spins, "one-hand hops, elbow tracks, flairs, halos, air tracks and windmills" brings a little slice of old-school hip hop flair to the streets of Cambodia and helps provide the hundreds of members

of the troupe with a place to go and a positive focus for their energy.

Sobil has been supported in his efforts by a variety of international nonprofit groups, and at least one group of American students has journeyed to Cambodia to make a film about him and the Tiny Toones. The Tiny Toones performed at a Christmas party for the American embassy in 2007 and were then invited to visit the United States, a trip that Sobil can't make with them, as he is legally barred from ever entering the United States again. But ultimately he has succeeded, and despite the desperate poverty and hardships faced by the children he mentors, he continues to work at changing the world, one b-boy at a time.

Forming Friendships in the Face of Stigma

In her book *Autobiography of a Face* (1994), poet Lucy Grealy tells the story of her struggle with childhood cancer and the disfiguring surgery that resulted. Because of a series of operations that removed one-third of her jaw, she survived Ewing's sarcoma but grew to adulthood looking—and feeling—very different from her peers.

When other kids reacted negatively to her scars, Grealy tried to cover them with turtlenecks, scarves, and hats but couldn't completely conceal her disfigurement. Boys at school yelled at her to "take off that monster mask!" Ironically, the only time she felt perfectly comfortable was on Halloween, when she could wear a mask and feel just like part of the crowd. Her high school years were lonely—she had a hard time making friends and worried that she would never have a boyfriend or never be in love. She felt as though she fit in only when she was with her family—or on the children's ward in a hospital.

At Sarah Lawrence College, a private school just outside New York City, Grealy finally found a group of friends with whom she felt comfortable, who were themselves outsiders:

> To be on the fringe at a school as fringy as Sarah Lawrence was itself an accomplishment, but it was this very quality that I loved most about my friends. They wore their mantles as "outsiders" with pride, whether because of their politics, their sexuality, or anything else that makes a person feel outside of the norm. Their self-definition was the very thing that put me at ease with them. I didn't feel judged. (p. 196)

Grealy finally experienced real friendship when she was able to feel accepted by others, and she felt this only with those who were similarly stigmatized. While they didn't share her specific facial disfigurement, they each felt marginalized or abnormal in some way. They were, in Goffmanian terms, "the own"—those who share the experience of being stigmatized and thus find comfort and safety in each other's presence.

Lucy Grealy

Grealy suffered through several more grueling reconstructive surgeries on her face, which left her in chronic pain. After college, she enrolled in the Iowa Writer's Workshop, where her roommate was another student she had known from Sarah Lawrence, Ann Patchett. The two women became best friends and, as they moved from the Midwest to New York in pursuit of their careers, embarked on a relationship that helped define their lives and work over the next twenty years. Grealy went on to win awards for her poetry and essays and wrote her critically acclaimed and hugely successful memoir. Patchett, too, became successful as an award-winning novelist (Patchett 2001).

Unfortunately, Lucy Grealy's story does not have a happy ending. Ultimately fame, fortune, and friendship were not enough to save her from her own demons. Ann Patchett's book *Truth & Beauty: A Friendship* (2004) details Grealy's decline into depression, drug addiction, and repeated attempts to commit suicide. She died in December 2002 from what was ruled an accidental overdose of heroin.

It would be too simplistic to conclude that Grealy killed herself because of the years of suffering she had endured as a result of her stigmatized identity. There are too many factors involved in her complex life story to assign blame with any assurance. Perhaps she would have become depressed or addicted even if she hadn't been disfigured. Perhaps it was the physical pain rather than the psychic pain that became too much for her. Whatever the reasons, these two books about Lucy Grealy's life and death reveal in gritty and compelling details the desperate desire to fit in and the lengths to which this woman went in order to pass as "normal" in society.

United Against Prejudice Groups like the National Association to Advance Fat Acceptance embrace an in-group orientation and reject the standards that mark them as deviant.

alcoholic might resist taking a typical nine-to-five job, claiming that the stress of corporate work had always made him drink before. Another recovering alcoholic who refuses to attend family gatherings might offer as an excuse that she can't be around family because they drink at every occasion. In such ways, people become voluntary outsiders, finding it preferable to be a deviant in spite of the prevailing norms of mainstream society.

DATA WORKSHOP
ANALYZING EVERYDAY LIFE
Personal Stories of AA Members

In this Data Workshop, you will examine the life history of selected members of Alcoholics Anonymous in order to analyze the process of deviance avowal. You will be doing a content analysis of an existing source (see Chapter 3 for a review of this research method). The stories appear in *Alcoholics Anonymous* (1939/2001), often referred to by members as the "Big Book," which features accounts of thousands of recovered alcoholics as well as AA's basic twelve-step program. The first 164 pages have remained virtually the same since the first printing in 1939, but in each subsequent edition, the personal stories of additional members have been added. These stories are intended to help newcomers to the program to identify with and relate to the lives of other recovering alcoholics.

For this workshop, you will focus on "Women Suffer Too," one of the first stories published in the Big Book. The title refers to the fact that years ago many people believed that only men were alcoholics. The story is told from the perspective of a sober alcoholic looking back on her life and understanding that through the process of deviance avowal (by accepting her alcoholism) she was able to transform a negative past into a positive life.

The text of the story can be found in the Big Book or accessed online at silkworth.net/bbstories/2nd/222_229.html. Read it in its entirety, keeping in mind how the study of life histories or oral histories can reveal important features of societal norms and everyday life. Pay close attention to how the story describes both deviant behavior and the process of deviance avowal, and consider the following questions.

- Identify the instances of deviance described in the writer's story. Why do we consider these behaviors deviant?

- In what ways was she in denial, or actively trying to disavow the deviant behavior?

- At what point did she engage in deviance avowal?

- How did deviance avowal affect her self-concept?

- In what ways did deviance avowal allow her to consider her past in a different light?

- How has her deviant identity become a positive part of her life?

There are two options for completing this Data Workshop.

- *Option 1 (informal)*: Prepare some written notes based on your answers to the questions above that you can refer to during in-class discussions. Share your reactions and conclusions with other students in small-group discussions. Listen for any differences in each other's insights.

- *Option 2 (formal)*: Write a three- to four-page essay answering the questions above. Include your own reactions to the story. Make sure to refer to specific passages that support your analysis.

Studying Deviance

When studying deviance, sociologists have often focused on the most obvious forms of deviant behavior—crime, mental illness, and sexual deviance. This "nuts and sluts" approach (Liazos 1972) tends to focus on the deviance of the poor and powerless, while accepting the values and norms of the powerful in an unacknowledged way. Social scientists tended to apply definitions of deviance uncritically in their research and failed to question the ways in which the definitions themselves may have perpetuated inequalities and untruths.

One sociologist at the University of California–Berkeley, David Matza (1969), set out to remedy this situation. Matza urged social scientists to set aside their preconceived notions in order to understand deviant phenomena on their own terms—to take a "naturalist" perspective. Verta Taylor and Leila Rupp, for example, spent three years with a dozen drag queens in order to gain perspective for their research in *Drag Queens at the 801 Cabaret*—at one point, they even performed onstage. Matza's fundamental admonition to those studying deviance is that they must appreciate the diversity and complexity of a particular social world—the world of street gangs, drug addicts, strippers, fight clubs, outlaw bikers, homeless people, or the transgendered. If such a world is approached as a simple social pathology that needs correcting, the researcher will never fully understand it. A sociological perspective requires that we seek insight without applying judgment—a difficult task indeed.

The Foreground of Deviance: The Emotional Attraction of Doing Bad Deeds

Most sociological perspectives on deviance focus on aspects of a person's background that would dispose him to act in deviant ways. This is the case with both functionalist and conflict perspectives: for example, many sociological studies of crime make the case that youth with limited access to education may be more likely to turn to dealing drugs or theft. Labeling theory also suggests that a person's social location is a crucial determinant: it shapes how others see the person, as well as his or her own self-view, and these perceptions can lead a person from primary to secondary deviance and into a deviant career. One of the main problems with such theories, however, is that they can't explain why some people with backgrounds that should incline them to deviance never actually violate any rules, while others with no defining background factors do become deviant.

Approaches that focus exclusively on background factors neglect one very important element—the deviant's own in-the-moment experience of committing a deviant act, what sociologist Jack Katz refers to as the "foreground" of deviance. In *The Seductions of Crime* (1988), Katz looks at how emotionally seductive crime can be, how shoplifting or even

committing murder might produce a particular kind of rush that becomes the very reason for carrying out the act. For example, what shoplifters often seek is not the DVD or perfume as much as the "sneaky thrill" of stealing it. Initially drawn to stealing by the thought of just how easy it might be, the shoplifter tests her ability to be secretly deviant—in public—while appearing to be perfectly normal. This perspective explains why the vast majority of shoplifters are not from underprivileged backgrounds but are people who could easily afford the stolen items. How else might we explain why a wealthy and famous actress such as Winona Ryder would try to smuggle clothes out of a department store?

Similarly, muggers' and robbers' actions reveal that they get more satisfaction from their crimes than from the things they steal. They are excited by the sense of superiority they gain by setting up and playing tricks on their victims. In fact,

The Seduction of Crime Jack Katz's research on the emotional rush produced by crime might explain why a wealthy actress like Winona Ryder would try to steal clothes from a department store.

they can come to feel morally superior, thinking that their victims deserve their fate because they are less observant and savvy. Even murderous rages can be seen as seductive ways to overcome an overwhelming sense of humiliation. A victim of adultery, for example, may kill instead of simply ending the relationship because murder, or "righteous slaughter," feels like the most appropriate response. In effect, he is seduced by the possibility of becoming a powerful avenger rather than remaining a wounded and impotent victim.

Katz's foreground model of deviance deepens our appreciation for the complexity of deviant behavior and reminds us that social actors are not mere products of their environment but active participants in creating meaningful experiences for themselves even if harmful to others.

Deviance in a New Interactional Context: Cyberbullying

Although parents and schools have been worried about cyberbullying ever since children and teenagers started using the internet, the phenomenon moved to the forefront of national consciousness after the suicide of 13-year-old Megan Meier in October of 2006. Megan had received a MySpace message from a boy named Josh, who said that he lived nearby but that his family didn't have a phone. Over the next several weeks they sent messages back and forth and seemed to have become close very quickly. Then, without warning, Josh started taunting and abusing her. Megan was devastated and hung herself in her closet. Several weeks later the Meiers learned that "Josh" was not a real person and that the MySpace account had been created by their neighbor, Lori Drew, in order to get back at Megan for snubbing her daughter. But regardless of who was sending the messages, Megan was a victim of **cyberbullying**, the use of electronic media (webpages, social networking sites, e-mail, instant messengers, and cell phones) to tease, harass, threaten, or humiliate someone.

Researchers say that between 10 percent and 30 percent of all teenagers have been victims of cyberbullying, with girls and older teens more likely to be at risk. The one thing that seems beyond doubt is that cyberbullying is on the rise. A report from the Centers for Disease Control found 50 percent more teens reported being the victims of electronic harassment in 2005 compared to 2000, and as more schools require laptops, and computers and cell phones become a more important part of the daily life of children and teenagers, this trend will surely continue.

Although cyberbullying is still less common than its offline equivalent, in several ways it's more frightening. Like every phenomenon created by the information revolution, cyberbullying (sometimes called "electronic aggression")

is faster and connects more people than off-line activity. Traditional bullying usually happens at school, while cyberbullying can happen anytime and in the privacy of your own home. Likewise, the effects are longer lasting. One of the most common forms of cyberbullying involves spreading rumors about someone. Traditional bullying relied on word of mouth or the proverbial graffiti on the bathroom wall to do this. But word of mouth is limited, and only so many people can read nasty comments scrawled on the stall in the bathroom before the janitor washes it off. Online there is almost no limit to how many people might see a nasty comment, even if is later taken down.

So far, most research has focused on cyberbullying that is perpetrated by someone who knows the victim in real life, but there have always been internet bullies (or "trolls") who seek to abuse people they've never met or only have encountered

> **cyberbullying** the use of electronic media (web pages, social networking sites, e-mail, instant messengers, and cell phones) to tease, harass, threaten, or humiliate someone

Cyberbullying Tina Meier holds two pictures of her daughter Megan, who committed suicide after receiving cruel messages on MySpace.

online. For example, after Megan Meier's suicide, a blog was created called "Megan Had It Coming" and contained posts from a cast of characters who purported to know Megan, all expressing a distinct lack of remorse. Later it was established that the entire blog was really the work of a 32-year-old computer programmer from Seattle with no connection to anyone involved in the case. As more and more of people's lives play out online, this sort of cyberbullying will only become more common.

DATA WORKSHOP

ANALYZING MASS MEDIA AND POPULAR CULTURE

Norm Breaking on Television

It's clear that deviance is a fascinating subject not only for sociologists but for television viewers as well. In recent years, shows have begun to feature people breaking every kind of social norm from folkways to taboos. Some obvious examples might include MTV's documentary series *Juvies*, which shows what happens when teens get caught breaking the law and end up in juvenile detention, or A&E's reality series *Dog the Bounty Hunter*, whose criminals are attempting to evade justice. But it's not just documentaries and reality shows that feature deviance. Various other types of programs like crime dramas *Law and Order* or *Criminal Minds*, newsmagazine programs *Dateline NBC* or *48 Hours*, and even comedies such as *Nip/Tuck* or *South Park* regularly deal with the pathological or dysfunctional.

Why is there so much deviance on television? Are these shows merely entertainment, or is something more going on here? When we watch them, do we feel morally superior or get some kind of vicarious thrill? Does the experience reinforce our social norms or serve to break them down?

This Data Workshop asks you to do a content analysis of an existing source, in this case a particular TV show (see Chapter 3 for a review of the research method). You will be documenting the ways in which deviant behavior is portrayed in the show you choose. Choose a show that is on DVD or online, or simply record an episode off TV so that you can watch it multiple times.

Consider the following:

• Who is the intended audience for this program? Why did you choose it?

• What kind of deviance is featured? Give specific examples of situations, scenes, dialogue, or characters, and explain why they are examples of deviance.

• Is the deviance celebrated or condemned?

• How does it make you feel to watch the program?

• What effect do you think the show has on other viewers?

• Do you think the program serves to reinforce or challenge prevailing social norms?

There are two options for completing this Data Workshop.

• *Option 1 (informal)*: Prepare some written notes that you can refer to in small-group discussions. Compare

Why Is There So Much Deviance on Television? *Dog the Bounty Hunter* and *South Park* portray pathological and dysfunctional characters. What other television shows feature types of deviance? Do you think the programs serve to reinforce or challenge prevailing social norms?

and contrast the analyses of the different programs in your group. What are the similarities and differences between programs?

- *Option 2 (formal)*: Write a three- to four-page essay answering the questions above and reflecting on your own experience in conducting this content analysis. What do you think these shows tell us about contemporary American society and our attitudes toward deviance?

Crime and Punishment

Crime is a particular type of deviance: it is the violation of a norm that has been codified into law, for which you could be arrested and imprisoned. These official, state-backed sanctions can make laws more powerful than nonlegal norms— for example, if you risked arrest for gossiping about your roommate, you might think twice about doing it. "Might," however, is the key word here, for the risk of arrest and jail time does not always deter people from breaking laws. In fact, as we saw earlier, ordinary people break laws every day without really thinking about it (driving faster than the speed limit, drinking while underage, taking pens or pencils home from work). As we also saw earlier, being bad can feel good, and even murder can feel "righteous" at the time, depending on the circumstances (J. Katz 1988).

In the United States, crime is officially measured by the **Uniform Crime Report (UCR)**, the FBI's tabulation of every crime reported by over 17,000 law enforcement agencies in the country. In particular, the UCR is used to track the "crime index," or the eight offenses considered especially reprehensible in our society: murder, rape, aggravated assault, robbery, burglary (theft inside the home), larceny-theft (of personal property), motor vehicle theft, and arson. The first four are categorized as **violent crime**, while the last four are considered **property crime**. Even though the UCR has been shown to be a flawed system, it is useful in helping to track trends in overall crime as well as particular patterns; it also records the number of arrests made compared with the number of crimes committed, which is the most traditional measure of police effectiveness.

Through the UCR, criminologists are able to make comparisons in crime rates using such variables as year and region. One notable finding is that rates of violent crime declined significantly in the last decade of the twentieth century. The year 1991 saw the highest number of homicides in U.S. history, 24,000. But between 1991 and 2000, there was a dramatic drop of 44 percent in homicide rates, and that number has held steady since then. Other findings include the observation that murder rates peak in the months of July and August. Perhaps related to the influence of heat, they are also higher in the southern states. Murder is committed most frequently by a friend or relative of the victim, seldom by a stranger. Robbery occurs most frequently in urban areas among youth.

Other trends are visible in the UCR as well. Property crimes occur more frequently than violent crime. The most common crime is larceny-theft, with burglary and motor vehicle theft trailing far behind. Although there has also been a decline in rates of property crime over the last decade, it is not as extreme as the drop in violent crime.

crime a violation of a norm that has been codified into law

Uniform Crime Report (UCR) an official measure of crime in the United States, produced by the FBI's official tabulation of every crime reported by over 17,000 law enforcement agencies

violent crime crimes in which violence is either the objective or the means to an end, including murder, rape, aggravated assault, and robbery

property crime crimes that did not involve violence, including burglary, larceny-theft, motor vehicle theft, and arson

Crime and Demographics

When criminologists look at quantitative crime data, which provide information on who is more likely to commit or be a victim of crime, they may learn more about the cause of crime. We should, however, question the assumptions and biases of the data. For example, Robert Merton's theory of the self-fulfilling prophecy prompts us to ask, if society has a tendency to cast certain categories of people as criminal types, will this assumption ensure that they will indeed be labeled and treated like criminals? And, as David Matza warns, will our preconceived notions about a category of people influence our interpretations of numerical data? In this section we will look at the relationship between crime and demographics like class, age, gender, and race and examine alternate explanations for what may seem like clear numerical fact.

CLASS Statistics consistently tell us that crime rates are higher in poor urban areas than in wealthier suburbs, but these higher crime rates may not actually be the result of increased criminal behavior. Rather, police tend to concentrate their efforts in urban areas, which they assume are more prone to crime, and thus make more arrests there. It appears that class is more directly related to how citizens are officially treated by the police, courts, and prisons than to which citizens are likely to commit crime. And even if we do accept

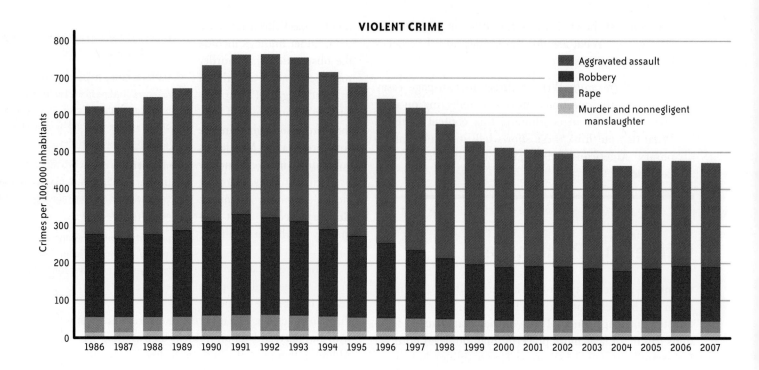

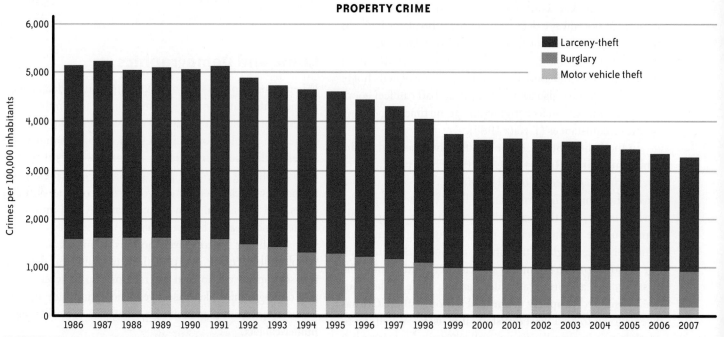

FIGURE 7.2 Crime in the United States, 1986–2007

SOURCE: FBI 2008

these statistics as an accurate representation of crime rates, theorists such as William Julius Wilson and Robert Sampson (2005) argue that the same factors that cause an area to become economically and socially disadvantaged also encourage criminal activity. Lack of jobs, lack of after-school child care, and lack of good schools, for example, are all factors that can lead to economic strain and criminal activity.

On the other end of the social class spectrum, **white-collar crime** has been defined by sociologist Edwin Sutherland as

white-collar crime crime committed by a high-status individual in the course of her or his occupation

Is "Cash Register Honesty" Good Enough?

While we might like to think that most employees wouldn't take money from the cash register or merchandise from the showroom floor, wouldn't walk away with a laptop computer, drive away with the company car, or filter sales receipts to their own bank account, employee theft is still a major problem. The U.S. Chamber of Commerce estimates that it costs businesses somewhere between $20 and $40 billion a year and accounts for about 30 percent of business failures (INC.com 1999). According to research by Michael Cunningham, a professor of psychology at the University of Louisville and a consultant to the security industry, only one in every three potential employees will be completely trustworthy. Of the other two, one may be tempted to steal given the opportunity, while the other will be more or less constantly looking for a chance to get away with taking company property.

Although we may consider ourselves the trustworthy ones, we may not recognize that our own behavior could still be contributing to the billions of dollars lost each year. How? Well, have you ever taken home paper clips, Post-it notes, a pen, or a pad of paper from the office? Made personal copies on the Xerox machine? Used the company computer to surf the net, download MP3s, play solitaire, or send an e-mail message to a friend? Eaten or drunk company products? How about taking a little more time than you're supposed to on your lunch break or leaving work a little early?

It's called pilfering, and it happens on the job tens of thousands of times a day. And it all adds up. Most companies consider these kinds of losses as just another factor in the cost of doing business. But how is it that so many people think nothing of these small infractions in spite of prevailing social norms that discourage stealing and while otherwise being upstanding or even exemplary employees?

You could say that these people are practicing "cash register honesty." That is, they draw the line at actually stealing money (or its equivalent) out of the till but don't hesitate to make off with other odds and ends that might have a less easily calculable value. They might be appalled at the suggestion that they are less than honest, especially since everyone else seems to take something (if only internet time) now and then. But is this kind of honesty really enough? Perhaps more employees should strive to adhere to a higher standard. Not because they are necessarily going to be caught by the boss or that they individually are costing the company a lot, but because of the inherent satisfaction of knowing that they are doing the right thing.

What kind of honesty do you practice in the workplace?

"a crime committed by a person of respectability and high social status in the course of his occupation." White-collar crime can include fraud, embezzlement, or insider trading and most white-collar criminals come from a relatively privileged background (Shover and Wright 2001).

AGE The younger the population, the more likely its members are to commit crimes. Criminologists have shown that this relationship between age and crime has remained stable since 1935, with the peak age for property crime being 16 and the peak age for violent crime 18. In the United States, 13- to 17-year-olds make up about 6 percent of the population yet account for 25 percent of criminal arrests. On the other end of the spectrum, people 65 and older make up more than 12 percent of the population and account for fewer than 1 percent of arrests. We call this trend of aging out of crime **desistance**. Here too, however, we must be careful about what we read into official statistics. Since our stereotypical image of a criminal is youthful, it may be that the

> **desistance** the tendency of individuals to age out of crime over the life course

public and police are more likely to accuse and arrest young people and less likely to target seniors. In addition, youth may commit more visible crimes (like robbery or assault), while older people may commit crimes that are more difficult to detect, like embezzlement or fraud.

GENDER Males are more likely to commit crime. In fact, males comprise 80 percent of all violent crime arrests. Earlier researchers hypothesized that the gender difference in crime rates was based on physical, emotional, and psychological differences between men and women. The logic was that women were too weak, passive, or unintelligent to commit crime. This argument has been replaced by a focus on the social and economic roles of women. Starting in the 1970s, criminologists found that lower crime rates among women could be explained by their lower status in the power hierarchy. Conflict theorists such as James Messerschmidt (1993) argued that once women start gaining power in the labor market through education and income, crime rates among women will rise to more closely match those among men. This hypothesis has been largely supported by recent trends. Between 1992 and 2002, male arrest rates decreased by 4 percent, while female arrest rates increased by almost 18 percent. So while at first glance it may seem logical to argue that women's crime rates are lower because of biology, on closer examination, we see that social structure plays an important role.

RACE The relationship between race and crime is a controversial one. According to the UCR, African Americans make up 12 percent of the U.S. population but account for 37 percent of violent crimes and 31 percent of property crimes. Once again, sociologists caution against making a link between biology and criminal activity. Instead, they maintain that the relationship can be explained by Merton's self-fulfilling prophecy and by class variables. For example, we could hypothesize that African Americans are exposed to higher rates of crime because more of them live in lower-class neighborhoods—and that here, it is class that matters more than race.

deterrence an approach to punishment that relies on the threat of harsh penalties to discourage people from committing crimes

retribution an approach to punishment that emphasizes retaliation or revenge for the crime as the appropriate goal

incapacitation an approach to punishment that seeks to protect society from criminals by imprisoning or executing them

rehabilitation an approach to punishment that attempts to reform criminals as part of their penalty

criminal justice system a collection of social institutions such as legislatures, police, courts, and prisons, which create and enforce laws

capital punishment the death penalty

Deterrence and Punishment

The question of **deterrence** is part of an ongoing debate about our criminal laws. Theorists who maintain that offenders carefully calculate the cost and benefits of each crime argue that punishment has a deterrent effect—that if the punishment seems too severe, people won't commit the crime. That's the logic behind California's controversial "three strikes" law: the punishment for three felonies is an automatic life sentence. While deterrence theory seems practical enough, it is important to note that in matters of sociology, seldom is there such a direct and causal link between two factors—in this case, the cost of punishment vs. the benefit of the crime.

Other justifications for punishment include **retribution**—the notion that society has the right to "get even"—and **incapacitation**, the notion that criminals should be confined or even executed to protect society from further injury. Some argue, though, that society should focus not on deterrence but on **rehabilitation**: the prison system should try to reform the criminal so that once released, he will not commit the same crimes again. Each approach to punishment invokes different ideas about who the criminal is and what his relationship is to the larger society: Is he someone who can plan ahead and curb his illegal behavior so as not to face a possible negative outcome? Is she someone who can work toward personal transformation? Is he someone who must be punished quid pro quo? Or should she just be removed from society permanently?

In the United States, the local, state, and federal government bureaucracies responsible for making laws together with the police, courts, and prison systems make up the **criminal justice system**—a system that, like any other social institution, reflects the society in which it operates. This means that the American criminal justice system, while it provides important benefits such as social control and even employment for its workers, also replicates some of the inequalities of power in our society.

In 2003, for example, 17 inmates on Illinois's death row were found to be innocent of the crimes for which they had been sentenced to die; some cases involved errors made by overworked or underqualified defense attorneys. Further, more than two-thirds of the inmates were African American, many of them convicted by all-white juries (Ryan 2003). As a result, then-governor George Ryan became convinced that **capital punishment** was unfairly and even wrongly applied in some cases, and he suspended the death penalty altogether. When inequities and errors such as these exist in the criminal justice system, we must question the true meaning of the word *justice* in our society.

"Positive" Deviance?

Are there instances in which a rule violation is actually a principled act that should generate a positive rather than negative reaction? The next two examples are cases of what we might call **positive deviance**. Both individuals broke laws; in hindsight, they are now considered heroes.

The first example is the simple act of civil disobedience by Rosa Parks on December 1, 1955, in Montgomery, Alabama, an act often considered pivotal in launching the Civil Rights Movement. In those days, a Montgomery city ordinance required buses to be segregated: whites sat in front and blacks in the back. Rosa Parks defied the law by refusing to give up her front seat to a white man and move to the back. Her arrest galvanized the black community and triggered a bus boycott and subsequent protests that eventually ended segregation in the South. It is worth recognizing that Parks was not an accidental symbol; she was an experienced activist. In her one small, courageous act of defiance, she served as a catalyst that eventually helped advance the fight against racial discrimination all across America. More than 50 years after the day she had taken her seat on the bus, Parks was

awarded the Presidential Medal of Freedom. When she died in 2005, it was front-page news. Her funeral was attended by luminaries of all types and races: mayors, members of Congress, presidents, CEOs, clergy, celebrities, and as many others as could fit into the packed church.

> **positive deviance** actions considered deviant within a given context but which are later reinterpreted as appropriate or even heroic

The second example is the story of three soldiers who put a stop to a massacre during the Vietnam War. On March 16, 1968, the men of Charlie Company, a U.S. battalion under the command of Lieutenant William Calley, stormed into the village of My Lai in South Vietnam on a "search and destroy" mission and opened fire on its civilian inhabitants. The boys and men of the village had gone to tend the fields, leaving only unarmed women, children, and the elderly. Hundreds were killed on that terrible day, in direct violation of military law. Although the soldiers should have ceased fire when they saw that the enemy (members of the Viet Cong) was not present, they obeyed the commands of their leaders and continued ravaging the village. Calley was later convicted in a court-martial; his men, claiming that they were only "following orders," were not held responsible.

The massacre would have continued unchecked had it not been for three other American soldiers—Hugh Thompson, Lawrence Colburn, and Glenn Andreota—who flew their helicopter into the middle of the carnage at My Lai, against the orders of their superiors, and called for back-up help to airlift dozens of survivors to safety. They then turned their guns on their fellow Americans, threatening to shoot if they tried to harm any more villagers. For years, the army tried to cover up the three men's heroism in order to keep the whole ugly truth of My Lai a secret. But finally, in 1998, the men were recognized for their bravery with medals and citations—for having had the courage and skill to perform a perilous rescue and the moral conviction necessary to defy authority as well.

Positive Deviance In his eulogy at Rosa Parks's funeral, Senator Ted Kennedy said, "When Rosa Parks sat down half a century ago, America stood up. Her quiet fight for equality sounded the bells of freedom for millions and awakened the moral conscience of the nation. We will always remember that great December when Rosa Parks sat alone so that others could sit together."

Closing Comments

The sociological study of crime and deviance raises complicated issues of morality and ethics. When we study sensitive topics like rape and alcoholism or vulnerable populations like juvenile delinquents and the mentally ill, we have a responsibility as scholars to recognize the effects our attention may have on the people we study. As David Matza noted, we must try to eschew moral judgments in our work, no matter how difficult that may be. And as our professional code of ethics demonstrates, we must protect the people we study from any negative outcomes. Groups lodged under the rubric of deviance can be disempowered by this label, and policy decisions made on the basis of social science research may further injure an already marginal group. On the other hand, a sociological perspective on deviance and crime provides for the possibility that groups previously labeled and marginalized may someday receive assistance and legitimacy from the larger society as well. The sociological perspective is a powerful tool.

 Find more review materials online at
www.wwnorton.com/studyspace

CHAPTER SUMMARY

- **Defining Deviance** Deviance does not reside in the characteristics of activities, but in the reaction when an activity violates a norm; the term *deviant*, as used by sociologists, is always a social judgment and never a moral one. The definition of deviance varies widely across cultures and times and not just in terms of which acts are considered criminal. The way we modify our bodies, select our foods, and even punish criminals is very different around the world as well as in the past.

- **Theories of Deviance** Several theoretical perspectives attempt to explain deviance. Functionalists argue that deviance serves a positive social function by clarifying moral boundaries and promoting social cohesion. Structural strain theory argues that while each society has normative goals for its members, social inequalities create strain or tension in people who lack socially acceptable means to achieve those goals. This strain can cause individuals to reject socially approved goals, socially approved means of achieving those goals, or both.

- Conflict theorists believe that a society's inequalities are reproduced in its definitions of deviance, so that less powerful groups and individuals are more likely to be criminalized. Symbolic interactionist theories of deviance focus on how interpersonal relations and everyday interactions shape definitions of deviance and influence those who engage in deviant behavior. Differential association theory argues that we learn to be deviant through our interactions with rule-breakers. Labeling theory focuses on the consequences of considering an individual or act deviant, arguing that the act of labeling someone deviant can make

it so. In this way labels serve as self-fulfilling prophecies, as our expectations greatly influence social outcomes.

- **Stigma and Deviant Identity** An individual branded as deviant has been stigmatized; his identity has been "spoiled" by the deviant label, and he or she may be treated poorly. Passing, or concealing stigmatizing information, is one way that some people manage their marginalized status. Some stigmas, however, may be difficult or impossible to conceal. As a result, some stigmatized people embrace their identities while rejecting the notion that those identities are deviant. However, not everyone identified as deviant rejects that label—in fact, some people welcome being characterized as deviant and use that label to align themselves with a particular group or culture.

- **Studying Deviance** Sociologists have often focused on the most obvious forms of deviance—criminals, the mentally handicapped, and sexual deviants—because of deeply rooted social bias in favor of the norms of the powerful. David Matza suggests that researchers overcome this bias through a naturalistic approach in which they set aside preconceptions and focus on the diversity and complexity of the social worlds they study.

- **The Foreground of Deviance** Most sociological perspectives on deviance focus on the aspects of an individual's background that would predispose her to become deviant. In contrast, Jack Katz, who examines the emotional components of crime and deviance, argues that the in-the-moment experience of deviant behavior can be emotionally seductive. Katz argues that researchers can better understand crime by considering how criminals experience their acts of deviance.

- **Crime and Punishment** Crime is the violation of officially codified social norms (laws). In the United States, the Uniform Crime Report, collected by the FBI, allows sociologists to study the relationship between crime and demographics like class, age, gender, and race. While these statistics are valuable, it is also important to remember the ways they may be biased. For example, people often assume a high correlation between poverty and crime because crime rates are higher in poor areas. However, this disparity may have more to do with the way the police and the judicial system enforce the law.

- There is an ongoing debate about the role of punishment in the criminal justice system. Those who believe in deterrence assume that harsh penalties will discourage crime. When crimes occur some favor rehabilitation, to reform the criminal, while others advocate retribution or incapacitation.

- **Positive Deviance** Although most of the acts of deviance discussed in this chapter are generally considered harmful, without some forms of deviance, social change would be next to impossible. Given the rapid pace of change in recent history, it is hard to imagine what our social world would look like without certain acts of deviance that, sometimes after they were committed, were accepted as righteous and heroic.

QUESTIONS FOR REVIEW

1. Years ago, it was considered deviant in the United States for women to wear pants and for men to wear jewelry like earrings. Today, both are common. What did these notions of deviance say about American norms? What does the fact that these "deviant" behaviors are now normal say about the nature of deviance?

2. There are many ways to be mildly deviant without breaking any laws. How do we sanction minor deviant acts?

3. Think of the last act of deviance you committed and describe how the different sociological theories of deviance would explain it. Which theory fits best, and why?

4. Every cultural group maintains different standards for body modification, and in our society these change rapidly. What kinds of body modification that seem normal to you would appear deviant to your parents or grandparents?

5. Symbolic interactionist theories of deviance focus on the way that interpersonal relationships and everyday interactions shape definitions of deviance. Did you ever find yourself doing deviant things because of your friends? What theory describes this pathway to deviance?

6. Howard Becker's labeling theory focuses on how judgments of deviance are made and the consequences of labeling an individual deviant. Have you witnessed people being labeled as deviant? If so, did the label stick?

7. Have you ever known someone to reject the "deviant" label and turn his negative identity into a positive one? What was the deviant identity? What term describes this sort of deviance?

8. What are some of the advantages and disadvantages of passing? Are there ways in which you pass? What effect do you think passing has on those who disguise their stigmatized identities?

9. Under what circumstances might a person choose to label himself or herself as deviant? Discuss some situations in which deviance avowal is a useful strategy.

10. Provide a real-life example of positive deviance (other than the ones described in the chapter). What norms were violated? What was the outcome? Does your belief system affect whether you perceive this deviance as positive? (How might someone else have viewed it as negative?)

SUGGESTIONS FOR FURTHER EXPLORATION

Barthelme, Frederick, and Steven Barthelme. 2001. *Double Down: Reflections on Gambling and Loss*. San Diego, CA: Harvest/HBJ Books. A remarkable memoir of a gambling problem that cost the two brothers $250,000 in just a few years. The book explores the personal appeal of gambling and explains the social changes that allowed riverboat gambling to return to Mississippi.

Becker, Howard S. 1953. "Becoming a Marihuana User." *American Journal of Sociology*, vol. 59 (November): 235–243. Describes the way that deviant behaviors are learned, in terms of both practical technique and learned enjoyment. Becker argues that deviance should not be explained away through preexisting psychological traits but rather should be understood as learned though experience.

Cohen, Rob, and David Wollock. 2001. *Etiquette for Outlaws*. New York: Harper Paperbacks. This book and the website www.etiquetteforoutlaws.com provide a rather racy field guide to contemporary deviance detailing the unspoken rules and proper manners for engaging in numerous deviant behaviors, including gambling, smoking, drinking, stripping, fighting, and other vices.

Foucault, Michel. 1995. *Discipline and Punish: The Birth of the Prison*. New York: Vintage. Analyzes the ways that changing social structures lead to changes in the nature of punishment, which has tended away from public torture and toward private imprisonment. Be warned, though, the first chapter describes an execution in France in 1775 that would be considered horribly deviant today!

Grand Theft Auto. Rockstar Games. A video game series in which the player controls a character in the employ of organized crime. Throughout the game, the player is rewarded for committing deviant and criminal acts. (Warning: Some of these are rated Mature.) What does this game say about societal norms and deviance? How do video games affect players?

Hegi, Ursula. 1995. *Stones from the River*. New York: Simon & Schuster. The story of Trudi Montag, a dwarf living in Germany in the 1930s and 40s. Trudi's village is home to many unusual characters, including her mentally ill mother, her cross-dressing friend, and her Jewish neighbors—but the Nazis see only some of these people as "undesirable." The story addresses views of "deviance" and "normalcy" during a horrific time in German history.

The Human Stain. 2004. Dir. Robert Benton. Miramax. This film is based on Philip Roth's best-selling book of the same title. Anthony Hopkins plays a classics professor who is hiding a deep secret about his racial background and is forced to retire under false charges of racism.

Larsen, Nella, and Thadious M. Davis. 1997. *Passing*. New York: Penguin. A story about a black woman passing for white and living the high life in Chicago and New York in the 1930s, this book shows the perils of losing one's carefully constructed false identity.

Menzel, Peter, and Faith D'Aluisio. 1998. *Man Eating Bugs: The Art and Science of Eating Insects*. Berkeley, CA: Ten Speed Press. A humorous take on the eating habits of diverse cultures that describes such tasty dishes as fried tarantula and Simple Scorpion Soup.

Pileggi, Nicholas. 1985. *Wiseguy*. New York: Pocket Books. An account of the criminal career of Henry Hill, whose life in the mob ended when he entered the witness protection program. This book includes lots of interviews with Hill and helps explain the appeal of criminal acts, as distinct from the appeal of their reward. It later became the basis for the movie *GoodFellas*.

Twitch and Shout. 1995. Dir. Laurel Chiten. Fanlight Productions/New Day Films. A compassionate, disturbing, and even humorous documentary about Tourette's syndrome. Chiten's film examines how Tourette's sufferers deal with a neurological disorder that causes physical and vocal tics: they may jerk, blink, moan, or shout words uncontrollably. In a society that values self-control, Tourette's sufferers are often stigmatized because of these disruptive, involuntary behaviors.

PART III | Understanding Inequality

All societies have systems for grouping, ranking, and categorizing people, and within any social structure, some people occupy superior positions and others hold inferior positions. While such distinctions may appear to be natural, emanating from real differences between people, they are actually social constructions. Society has created and given meaning to concepts such as class, race, and gender, and as such, they have taken on great social significance. The social analyst's job is to understand how these categories are established in the first place, how they are maintained or changed, and ways they affect society and the lives of individuals.

For instance, sociologist Mitchell Duneier's book *Sidewalk* (1999) includes the story of a marginalized group of New York City street-vendors whose lives and social identities are much more complex than the casual passerby might imagine. The story considers the convergence of class (Chapter 8), race (Chapter 9), and gender (Chapter 10) in the social structure of the city and its inhabitants' everyday interactions. In many ways, *Sidewalk* brings together the themes of these next three chapters.

Duneier studied men and women who live on the streets of New York's Greenwich Village, selling used goods—mostly books and magazines—to passersby. Duneier befriended the vendors and became part of their curbside culture for five years, during which he conducted his ethnographic research. By examining the intersecting lives of people who frequent the Village, Duneier shows what social inequality looks like and feels like and what it means to those who live with it every day. On Sixth Avenue, the class differences between the vendors and their customers are obvious. The vendors live from

day to day in a cash-based, informal economy; they are poor and often "unhoused"; most are African American males; some are educated, others are not; and all have stories of how they became part of the sidewalk culture. The passersby, on the other hand, are of all ages, races, and occupations, and they are likely to be both employed and housed. They are often well-educated; some are wealthy. Interactions between these vendors and customers cut across boundaries of both class and race, and sometimes gender—all interrelated forms of social inequality.

A key insight in Duneier's work is that the street vendors are not necessarily what they seem at first glance. It would be easy to characterize these people as lacking any social aspirations, given that so many are homeless and don't fit into conventional social roles. Though they might offend some by their appearance, few are drug addicts, alcoholics, or criminals—and they are pursuing the same kinds of goals as many of the passersby. In this liberal neighborhood, sales of written material are allowed on the streets without permits or fees, thus providing these marginalized citizens an opportunity for entrepreneurial activity and a chance to earn an honest living. Most vendors say they are trying "to live 'better' lives within the framework of their own and society's weaknesses" (p. 172). Most work hard to construct a sense of decency and reputability in their dealings with customers. Although some of them violate social norms, in most ways the vendors adhere to a code of conduct that minimizes any negative impact they might have on the surrounding community.

Many vendors develop friendly, ongoing relations with regular buyers despite their different positions in social status hierarchies. Sometimes, however, the chasm between

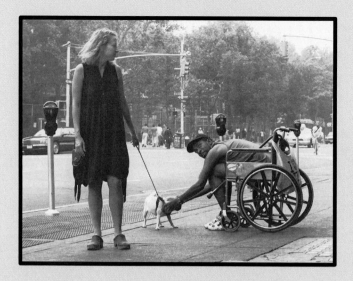

businesses. Yet Duneier believes that expelling these street vendors in an effort to improve the neighborhood would actually be counterproductive. Without the unconventional form of employment that street vending provides to these otherwise destitute people, there would likely be more crime, panhandling, and deviance. Moreover, as law-abiding citizens with a strong desire to conform to social norms, the vendors often serve as mentors to other homeless people, easing them back into mainstream society. Duneier contends that street vendors are an asset to the area and that they contribute to the vibrancy and health of the Village.

While the study is particularly focused on New York's Sixth Avenue vendors, it provides insights into the structure of difference and social inequality in the United States, showing that interactionist perspectives can also be relevant to the study of class, race, and gender, which are more often examined through macrosociological theories. What we come to learn is that the world of sidewalk vending is highly complex and organized, with its own rules and social order.

the vendors and their customers is difficult to bridge. For example, the male vendors in Duneier's study regularly engaged in flirtatious banter with female passersby. Their efforts at engaging the women in interactions brought a fleeting sense of entitlement and power to men who otherwise have few resources. Typically, the vendors were ignored or rebuffed by the women. When asked why this was the case, one of the vendors said, "She wants room and board, clothing, makeup, hairdos, fabulous dinners, and rent" (Duneier 1999, p. 196). In other words, because he is poor, he cannot provide these upper-middle-class amenities. The women, however, may perceive this behavior as sexual harassment, and accordingly may use standard streetwise avoidance techniques. Here social class becomes the great divide in everyday gender relations.

Some people oppose the street vendors' presence in the neighborhood, and they are frequently the target of anti-peddling campaigns by the mayor's office, police, and local

CHAPTER 8

Social Class: The Structure of Inequality

The photographs on the next page show average families from six different countries—the United States, Kuwait, Mali, Bhutan, Argentina, and Albania. They are each pictured outside the family home, with all their worldly goods displayed around them. These pictures, from Peter Menzel's book *Material World: A Global Family Portrait*, clearly illustrate some of the inequalities of wealth and power between societies worldwide.

Compare, for example, the U.S. and Albanian families, the Skeens and the Cakonis. What are the differences between these families as evidenced in their possessions? The two Skeen children have their own bedrooms; the four Cakoni kids sleep together on a couch in the kitchen. The Cakonis own a number of working animals: a donkey for transportation and goats, cows, and chickens to provide milk, meat, and eggs. In contrast, the Skeens have a pet dog and several stuffed deer heads hanging on the wall, trophies of Mr. Skeen's favorite pastime, hunting. Every two weeks, the Cakonis hike seven miles to the nearest town to shop for groceries; Mrs. Skeen drives her minivan to a suburban supermarket to stock up whenever she wants. The Skeens have three radios, three stereos, five telephones, two televisions, a VCR, a computer, and three different vehicles; the Cakonis own one radio and one television, which the family considers its most valued possession.

Similar comparisons may be made between the Natoma family in Mali, the Namgay family in Bhutan, the Carballo family in Argentina, and the Abdulla family in Kuwait. The younger Mrs. Natoma carries water from the village well in a bucket balanced on her head; the Abdullas have a private indoor swimming pool. The Carballos have been robbed several times, and Mr. Carballo loads his gun every night at dusk to protect his family; the Namgays own little and live near a Buddhist monastery where monks chant daily for peace. These photographs reveal stark contrasts between the world's wealthiest citizens in places like the United States and Kuwait and its poorest people in countries like Albania and Bhutan. What are the real meanings of terms like *rich* and *poor*, and how do sociologists define them?

Family Portraits From the top left: the Skeens (Pearland, Texas), the Cakonis (Bei Burrel, Albania), the Natomas [illegible] (Gh-xljhyx,Bhutm), the Carballos (Salta, Argentina), and the Abdullas (Kuwait City, Kuwait).

after he studied poor Hispanics in Mexico and the United States. Lewis suggested that the poor, because they were excluded from the mainstream, developed a way of life that was qualitatively different from that of middle-class societies and allowed them to cope with the dire circumstance of poverty. This way of life includes attitudes of resignation and fatalism, which lead the poor to accept their fate rather than trying to improve their lot. It also emphasizes immediate gratification, making it difficult for the poor to plan or save for the future or to join trade unions or community groups that might help them improve their situation. Once such a culture is formed, Lewis argued, it takes on a life of its own and is passed on from parents to children, leaving them ill-equipped to change.

The culture of poverty theory was later adopted by other social scientists (Banfield 1970) and applied to the American poor, particularly those in inner cities. Not surprisingly, though, the theory has been met with considerable controversy, in part because it suggests that there is little point in trying to eradicate poverty because it's more a problem of culture (attitudes, lifestyle, and behavior) than of economics. By focusing on individual character and personality, the theory tends to blame the victims of poverty for their own misfortunes while overlooking the force of their social conditions.

The tendency to see victims of social injustice as deserving of their fates is explained by what social psychologists call the **just-world hypothesis**. According to this argument, we have a strong need to believe that the world is orderly, predictable, and fair in order to achieve our goals in life. When we encounter situations that contradict this belief, we either act quickly to restore justice and order or persuade ourselves that no injustice has occurred. This can result in assuming that the victim has "asked for it" or deserves whatever has befallen her. This attitude is continually reinforced through the morality tales that are a ubiquitous part of our news and entertainment, which tell us that good is rewarded and evil punished (say, in a news story about a homeless man who returns a lost wallet full of cash to its owner, who then shares the money with him).

The just-world hypothesis, developed by Melvin Lerner (1965, 1980), was tested through a series of experiments that documented how people can convince themselves that others deserve what they get. In these experiments, cash prizes were randomly distributed to students completing the exact same tasks in the exact same way—observers, however, judged the cash recipients as the more deserving, harder workers. Other researchers (Rubin and Peplau 1975) have found that people with strong beliefs in a just world tend to "feel less of a need to engage in activities to change society or to alleviate

the plight of social victims." In the face of poverty, many simply become apathetic. It is important to be aware of our own tendencies to follow such thinking, so that we might avoid becoming blind to others' misfortunes.

Another problem with the culture of poverty theory is that it lacks a certain sociological imagination. It fails to take into account the structural factors that shape culture and are part of the preexisting problem in which poor individuals find themselves. Dalton Conley, a sociologist at New York University, argues that to solve the problem of poverty, we must examine wealth as well (2002). A social system that allows extremes of both wealth and poverty (as ours does) reveals structural reasons why poverty persists, such as laws that protect the inheritances of the wealthy but provide few breaks for working families. Research like Conley's helps us understand that there are alternative explanations for why people are poor and even suggests that extreme wealth ought to be conceptualized as a social problem similar to that of extreme poverty.

The Invisibility of Poverty

Although we are used to seeing televised images of abject poverty from overseas—crying children with bloated bellies and spindly limbs in Asia, Africa, or Latin America—we rarely see similar images from the United States. While it may be true that few Americans are as poor as the starving Somalis or Bangladeshis, some 37.3 million Americans lived below the poverty line in 2007 (U.S. Census Bureau 2008c). That's almost 13 percent of the population of the wealthiest nation in the world. How can such large numbers of people remain hidden to their fellow Americans? What makes poverty invisible?

RESIDENTIAL SEGREGATION One factor is **residential segregation**—the geographical isolation of the poor from the rest of the city (or in the case of the rural poor, from any neighbors at all). Such segregation often occurs along racial as well as socioeconomic lines, further exacerbating class divisions (Massey and Denton 1993). In the phrase "wrong side of the tracks," used to describe poverty-stricken neighborhoods, there is usually a racial connotation as well, since railroad tracks traditionally served as boundaries that kept

> **just-world hypothesis** argues that people have a deep need to see the world as orderly, predictable, and fair, which creates a tendency to view victims of social injustice as deserving of their fates
>
> **residential segregation** the geographical separation of the poor from the rest of the population

Residential Segregation
High-density housing projects frequently isolate the poor from the rest of the city.

black neighborhoods separated from white ones in the nineteenth century (Ananat 2005).

Residential segregation is accomplished most notably through public housing projects, which are typically high-density apartment complexes in urban areas, funded and managed by the Department of Housing and Urban Development (HUD). Living in these apartment complexes, many of which are in low-income, high-crime neighborhoods and are poorly maintained, can be dangerous as well as unpleasant.

Residential segregation is also exacerbated by the practice of "redlining," in which banks and mortgage lenders identify high-risk areas (usually poor or minority neighborhoods) and either refuse mortgages to applicants from those neighborhoods or offer loans at prohibitively high rates. Redlining keeps the poor from acquiring assets (like real estate) that might allow them to rise out of poverty and move to a more affluent neighborhood. Though illegal, redlining is still practiced today: in 2002, a major mortgage company, MidAmerica Bank, settled a redlining case in Chicago by agreeing to open more branches in poor and minority neighborhoods and to include poor and minority consumers in their advertising campaigns, which had previously targeted only buyers at higher income levels.

disenfranchisement the removal of the rights of citizenship through economic, political, or legal means

POLITICAL DISENFRANCHISEMENT The poor may remain invisible to the larger society because of their lack of political power, as well. **Disenfranchisement** is a correlate of poverty: the poor are less likely to vote or otherwise participate in political life (Kerbo and Gonzalez 2003). When everyday life is a struggle to make ends meet, it is difficult to muster the extra energy necessary to work for political change. The poor may also feel that the system has not served them; if the government ignores their interests, why bother to become involved? Because of their lack of involvement, the poor lack political clout and the resources to make their plight a high-profile political priority. Politicians at the local and national levels have little motivation to address their needs, because as a constituency the poor wield less power than such groups as senior citizens, "soccer moms," and small-business owners. When the poor do organize politically, even their successes may not be well known. One group, Mothers of East Los Angeles (whose motto includes the phrase "not economically rich, but culturally wealthy"), has been successfully protecting their neighborhood from environmental degradation and exploitation for 20 years. They have rebuffed plans to build a prison, toxic waste plants, and an oil pipeline near homes and schools in their community. But have you ever heard of them?

HOMELESSNESS In certain situations, the very poor are deliberately removed from public view. Police are sometimes

Marching for Welfare Rights During the Republican National Convention in 2000, the Kensington Welfare Rights Union protested against government poverty policies. The city of Philadelphia denied the group a permit to march, but they demonstrated anyway and attracted the attention of journalists, photographers, and politicians.

ordered to scour the streets, rousting the homeless and herding them out of sight, as they did in 1988 in New York City's Tompkins Square Park (an infamous riot ensued). High-profile occasions such as political conventions and major sporting events put a media spotlight on city streets. In the summer of 2000, for example, on the eve of the Republican National Convention, the city of Philadelphia denied a permit to a group of welfare rights protesters who wanted to demonstrate against government poverty policies. The hope was that in denying the permit, the group would not make an appearance on streets already crawling with politicians, demonstrators, journalists, and photographers. But the protesters marched anyway—with a police escort—and were able to make their voice heard despite the lack of official permission to do so.

Mostly, though, the poor and homeless remain invisible. We don't know exactly how many homeless live in the United States. The Census Bureau focuses its population counts on households, so the homeless living in long-term shelters may get counted, but not those on the streets. The current estimate is that about 1 percent of the U.S. population (over 2.5 million people) will experience homelessness at least once during a given year (Burt and Aron 2000).

Each year the city of New York attempts to measure the number of homeless men and women. Volunteers comb the streets in the overnight hours, making note of all those they find sleeping on park benches or in building stairwells. They do not, however, enter abandoned buildings or subway tunnels, where many of New York's homeless seek shelter. While the 2008 count showed a decrease in the homeless population (down to 3,306 from 3,755 in 2007), it can't be considered scientifically accurate (New York City Dept. of Homeless Services 2008). It does, however, help the city estimate its needs for homeless services in the coming year.

The homeless also remain invisible to most of us because of our own feelings of discomfort and guilt. John Coleman, a former college president and business executive, discovered this when he lived in poverty, if only temporarily, on the streets of Manhattan. Coleman went "undercover" as a homeless man for 10 days and found that the minute he shed his privileged identity, people looked at him differently—or not at all. During his days on the streets, Coleman passed by and made eye contact with his accountant, his landlord, and a coworker—each looked right through him, without recognition. But he was not invisible to everyone. Police officers often shook him awake to get him moving from whatever meager shelter he had found for the night. A waiter at a diner took one look at him and forced him to pay up front for his 99-cent breakfast special. Other homeless men, though, showed him kindness and generosity (Coleman 1983).

Michael Moore's *Roger & Me*

Michael Moore was born in Flint, Michigan. His father worked for General Motors (GM), and his uncle took part in the landmark 1936 sit-down strike at the plant that led to the birth of the United Auto Workers (UAW), a powerful labor union. In the early 1980s, General Motors, Flint's primary source of employment, announced a series of plant closings that would eliminate more than 30,000 jobs. The effect was disastrous: huge swaths of the town were boarded up, crime rates soared, and suicides and alcoholism increased, while at the same time GM posted almost $5 billion in profits.

Moore, originally a print journalist with no experience in film, decided to make a documentary on the economic implosion of a small Midwestern industrial town. Friends gave him some pointers on documentary making, and the rest he learned as he went. The final result, *Roger & Me*, chronicles his far-fetched attempt to obtain an interview with Roger Smith, the CEO of General Motors, and ask him about the human cost of the massive layoffs. Moore tries to get Smith to spend the day with him, driving around Flint in a van, surveying the economically decimated town together. He wanted Smith to get to know some of the locals, like Fred the eviction man and the woman who raises rabbits (either as pets or for meat).

To finance the film's eventual $160,000 budget, Moore sold his house and held weekly Bingo games to raise cash. Political activist Ralph Nader, an old adversary of the auto industry, donated a little money and some office space. When the film was finished in 1989, the impossible happened: Moore sent it off to the film festival circuit, where it was an immediate hit. Critics loved it, and Warner Brothers beat out stiff competition to release it nationally. Even more improbably, the film became a huge success commercially, an almost unheard-of feat for a political documentary.

Roger & Me, more than just good entertainment, is also good sociology. A more traditional documentary might have focused solely on the actions of General Motors and left out the ways that Flint residents tried to cope with their economic problems—but that wouldn't have required much of a sociological imagination. *Roger* isn't just a movie about General Motors or about the way large corporations work, and it isn't just a movie about what life was like in Flint, Michigan, in the 1980s. It's about all these things and, more importantly, about the connections between them. When Moore

Roger and Me Michael Moore, Rhonda Britton (Flint's Bunny Lady), and Fred Ross (a repo man) in front of a Buick ad.

shows a family being evicted on Christmas Eve and then quickly cuts to Roger Smith giving a speech to industry, he is trying to show the connection between "personal troubles" and "social structure."

Moore hoped that if he made people laugh (and the movie is very funny, especially when he is repeatedly kicked out of Smith's office building), the film's images would stick in their minds. He also hoped that if he could show how the very structure of opportunity had collapsed in Flint and similar American towns, then people might be forced to reconsider society's economic and political institutions. In short, he hoped to make a film that would help to explain how poverty is created and in so doing perhaps inspire people to demand that things be done differently.

To whom are the poor visible? Those who work with them: case workers, social service providers, government bureaucrats, volunteers and charity workers, clergy, cops, business owners (including those who may not want to deal with the poor, as well as those who may exploit them). And now, you.

With a sociological perspective, you can now see the effects of social stratification everywhere you turn. And when you recognize the multiple, complex causes of poverty—such as limited educational and job opportunities, stagnating wages, economic downturns, racism, mental illness, and substance abuse—it will no longer be as simple to consider each individual responsible for his or her own plight. Finally, the sociological perspective will give you the ability to imagine possible solutions to the problems associated with poverty—solutions that focus on large-scale social changes as well as individual actions, including your own. Don't let poverty remain invisible.

Inequality and the Ideology of the American Dream

Ask almost anyone about the American Dream and they are likely to mention some of the following: owning your own home; having a good marriage and great kids; finding a good job that you enjoy; being able to afford nice vacations; having a big-screen TV, nice clothes, or season tickets to your team's home games. For most Americans, the dream also means that all people, no matter how humble their beginnings, can succeed in whatever they set out to do if they work hard enough. In other words, a poor boy or girl could grow up to become president of the United States, an astronaut, a professional basketball player, a captain of industry, or a movie star.

One problem with the American Dream, however, is that it doesn't always match reality. It's more of an ideology: a belief system that explains and justifies some sort of social arrangement, in this case America's social class hierarchy. The ideology of the American Dream legitimizes stratification by reinforcing the idea that everyone has the same chance to get ahead and that success or failure depends on the person (Hochschild 1996). Inequality is presented as a system of incentives and rewards for achievement. If we can credit anyone who does succeed, then logically we must also blame anyone who fails. The well-socialized American buys into this belief system, without recognizing its structural flaws. We are caught in what Marx would call false consciousness, the inability to see the ways in which we may be oppressed.

The American Dream? Oprah Winfrey's meteoric rise from poverty to immense wealth is the classic American Dream story. However, her experience is the exception, not the rule. In fact, most Americans will experience much more modest upward mobility, if any at all.

Nevertheless, it's not easy to dismiss the idea of the American Dream, especially when there are so many high-profile examples. Take, for instance, Oprah Winfrey. Born in Mississippi in 1954, Winfrey endured a childhood of abject poverty. Fifty years later, *Forbes* magazine listed her as number 215 of the 400 richest Americans, with a personal wealth of $1.3 billion. Not only is she the highest-paid black female, she is also one of the most highly paid entertainers of all time. She is widely praised for her achievements as talk-show host and philanthropist and viewed as a symbol of the American Dream. The problem is, we tend to think of her as representing the rule rather than the exception. For most Americans, the rags-to-riches upward mobility she has achieved is very unrealistic.

Though popular opinion and rhetoric espouse the American Dream ideology, or that the United States is a **meritocracy** (a system in which rewards are distributed based on merit), sociologists find contrary evidence. In fact, no matter how hard they work or seek a good education, most people will make little movement at all. And the degree of mobility they do achieve can depend on a person's ethnicity, class status, or gender rather than merit. For example, whites are more likely to experience upward mobility than persons of color (T. Davis 1995), and married women are more likely to experience upward mobility than nonmarried women (Li and Singelmann 1998). Immigrant persons of color are the most likely to experience downward social mobility (McCall 2001).

Although the American Dream tends to promote consumerism as a way to achieve "the good life," the fact is that chasing after it has left us feeling less secure and satisfied—not to mention less wealthy—than in previous generations (De Graaf et al. 2002). Some pundits suggest that we have lost focus on the original meaning of the American Dream,

meritocracy a system in which rewards are distributed based on merit

that our increasing obsession with the idea of "more (or newer or bigger) is better" is leading to more debt, less free time, and greater discontent. Americans now carry 200 percent more credit card debt than they did in 1990 (Susan Walker 2004), and an Ohio State University study recently reported that Americans have less free time and feel more rushed than they did 30 years ago (Sayer and Mattingly 2006).

A countervailing trend in American life, however, sometimes referred to as the **simplicity movement**, rejects rampant consumerism and seeks to reverse some of its consequences for the individual, for society, and for the planet. This movement, a backlash against the traditional American Dream, encourages people to "downshift" by working less, earning less, and spending less in order to put their lifestyles in sync with their (nonmaterialistic) values (Schor 1999). What does this mean in practice? Growing your own vegetables, perhaps, or riding your bike to work, recycling and composting, and spending more time with friends and family and less time commuting, spending money, or watching TV.

DATA WORKSHOP

ANALYZING MASS MEDIA AND POPULAR CULTURE

Advertising and the American Dream

We are surrounded by advertising, which aims not only to give us information about products but also to create and stimulate a buying public with demands for an ever-increasing array of goods and services. Advertising shapes our consciousness and tells us what to dream and how to pursue those dreams. It provides us with a concept of the good life and tells us that it's available to everyone. Advertising equates shopping and acquisition with emotional fulfillment, freedom, fun, happiness, security, and self-satisfaction.

And the sales pitch seems to be working. Like no other generation, today's 18- to 34-year-olds have grown up with a culture of debt—a product of easy credit, a booming economy, and expensive lifestyles. They often live from paycheck to paycheck and use credit cards and loans to finance restaurant meals, high-tech toys, and new cars that

they really can't afford. Many are slipping into a troubling downward financial spiral. Policy analysts Tamara Draut and Javier Silva, in their 2004 study called "Generation Broke," found that in 2001 the average credit card debt among adults aged 25 to 34 was $4,088; the average for those aged 18 to 24 was $2,985. Some 15–20 percent of all young adults are in debt hardship, where monthly debt payments reach 40 percent or more of household income, and they have the second-highest rates of bankruptcy of any age group (Draut and Silva 2004).

In this Data Workshop, you will evaluate some advertisements in terms of the ideology of the American Dream. You will use existing sources to do a content analysis of the ads (see Chapter 3 for a review of the research method). To start your research, find three or more ads from magazines, newspapers, websites, or other sources. Look for ads that are of interest to your particular age group or that are selling the idea of the "good life."

Consider the following questions for each ad.

- Whom is the message intended for?

- What product or service is being advertised?

- In addition to a product or service, what else are the advertisers trying to sell?

- How does the message make you feel? Does it play on your emotions or sense of self-worth? If so, in what ways?

- Does the ad "work"? Would you like to buy the product? Why or why not?

More generally:

- How does advertising affect your life and buying habits?

- What ads have a strong effect on you? Why?

- What is the lure of shopping and material possessions?

- What kinds of pressures do you feel to keep up with the material possessions of your friends, neighbors, or coworkers?

There are two options for completing this Data Workshop.

- *Option 1 (informal)*: Bring your ads to class, and discuss your answers to the questions above with other students in small groups. Compare and contrast each other's contributions.

- *Option 2 (formal)*: Write a three- to four-page essay discussing your general thoughts on consumption and the American Dream. Apply these thoughts to your conclusions about the specific ads you chose.

Closing Comments

Social stratification is all about power. Stratification systems, like SES, allocate different types of social power, such as wealth, political influence, and occupational prestige, and do so in fundamentally unequal ways. These inequalities are part of both the larger social structure and our everyday interactions. In the following chapters, we will examine other systems of stratification, namely, race and ethnicity, and sex, gender, and sexual orientation. While we separate these topics for organizational purposes, they are not experienced as separate in our everyday lives. We are women or men, working class or upper class, black or white, gay or straight simultaneously. Our experiences of these social categories are intertwined, as we will see.

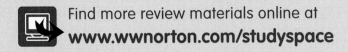

Find more review materials online at
www.wwnorton.com/studyspace

CHAPTER SUMMARY

- **Social Stratification and Inequality** Every society has some form of social stratification dividing the population into groups with differential access to resources and prestige; these groups may be based on different criteria (such as race, class, and gender). This fundamental source of inequality is persistent; social status tends to be passed along by parents to their children, even in systems where status is not formally inherited. Stratification also creates a set of beliefs about the different groups within a society.

- **Systems of Stratification** Historically there have been three major types of social stratification: slavery, caste systems, and social class. Although slavery and caste-related segregation are not officially practiced today, both systems persist. However, social class, the primarily economic system of stratification associated with capitalism, has become increasingly prevalent.

- **Social Classes in the United States** Most Americans claim to be middle class, even when their life experiences and backgrounds suggest otherwise. This helps sociologists understand Americans' class consciousness; more precise definitions allow sociologists to study how class affects our lives. Unlike in a system of slavery or castes, the borders between the classes are not sharply defined, and it is useful to think of class as a continuum rather than strictly divided groups.

- This text uses a six-part model of the U.S. class system: upper (capitalist) class, upper-middle class, middle class, working (lower-middle) class, working poor, and underclass. Many individuals display status inconsistency; that is, they possess characteristics associated with more than one class.

- **Theories of Social Class** Karl Marx believed there were two classes in capitalist societies: the capitalists (or bourgeoisie), who owned the means of production, and the workers (or proletariat), who possessed only their labor, which they were forced to sell for wages. In Marx's model, only economic relationships matter, and he believed social inequality would grow as the workers continued to be exploited. Modified versions of this theory remain popular among sociologists. Max Weber offered a similar model that also accounted for cultural factors. He argued that class status was the product of three components: wealth, power, and prestige.

- More recently, Pierre Bourdieu has attempted to explain social reproduction, the stability of social classes across generations. According to his theory, children inherit not only wealth but also cultural capital: the tastes, habits, expectations, and other cultural dispositions that help them to take on their parents' class status. Symbolic interactionists examine the ways we notice status differences and categorize ourselves and others accordingly. As Erving Goffman pointed out, our clothing, speech, gestures, possessions, friends, and activities all provide information about our socioeconomic status.

- **Socioeconomic Status and Life Chances** Belonging to a certain social class has profound consequences in all areas of life. Members of different social classes set and achieve different educational goals, work at different types of jobs, and receive different levels of quality in their medical care. People tend to marry someone whose social and cultural backgrounds are similar to their own, in part because they are more likely to encounter people like themselves.

• **Defining Poverty** In the United States, the federal poverty line—an absolute measure of annual income—is frequently used to determine who is categorized as poor. However, this measure of poverty is often criticized because it classifies those with only marginally higher incomes as nonpoor and ignores regional variations in the cost of living. In America there are persistent calls to scale back welfare, often under the mistaken assumption that it constitutes a large percentage of the federal budget. Residential segregation, political disenfranchisement, and the use of law enforcement to control the homeless render poverty invisible to many Americans.

• **Inequality and the American Dream** Though we aren't always aware of it, the United States has a distinct ideology that explains and justifies our social system. The American Dream—that anyone can achieve material success if they try hard enough—has been criticized for several reasons. For example, it justifies the class hierarchy by reinforcing the idea that success depends only on effort, suggesting that the poor are simply lazy. It also encourages consumerism and valorizes material wealth, leaving Americans with less free time and more debt, a trend that the simplicity movement has begun to fight.

QUESTIONS FOR REVIEW

1. Think about your own class status. Is it consistent across the criteria that make up socioeconomic status (income, wealth, education, occupation, and power)? Or are you an example of status inconsistency?

2. Max Weber theorized that there is more to class than wealth and advocated classifying socioeconomic status according to power and prestige. Why do we need these additional elements? Can you think of a job that brings more wealth than power? How about one that brings little wealth but lots of prestige?

3. According to Pierre Bourdieu, the cultural tools we inherit from our parents can be very important in trying to gain economic assets. What sort of cultural capital did you inherit? Has it ever helped you materially? Have you ever done something to acquire more cultural capital?

4. Erving Goffman says we "read" other people through social interaction to get a sense of their class status. What sort of clues can tell you about a person's social class within 30 seconds of meeting her?

5. People of lower socioeconomic status are more likely to encounter the criminal justice system, both as perpetrators and as victims of crime. Many people believe this is because the poor are more criminally minded. What are some other explanations?

6. Sociologists know that people are more likely to marry someone with a social and cultural background similar to their own, largely because those are the people we tend to encounter. Add up the people you know on a first-name basis who come from a different class than you according to the six-part definition of U.S. social class.

7. The United States considers itself a meritocracy with an open class system. What kinds of structural factors in American society make vertical social mobility more difficult? Do these factors apply to everyone in society or just certain groups?

8. Are you aware of anyone within your community who suffers from absolute deprivation? If not, do you think you just live in a lucky community, or are there other factors that make the poor invisible?

9. When you picture the good life, what do you see? If you had a choice between making more money or having more free time, which would you pick? How much of your leisure time involves spending money or consuming? What does this tell you about the ideology of the American Dream?

SUGGESTIONS FOR FURTHER EXPLORATION

The Global Rich List (www.globalrichlist.com). Find out how your income compares to earnings worldwide. From the site's authors: "[W]e gauge how rich we are by looking upwards at those who have more than us. This makes us feel poor. We wanted to do something which would help people understand, in real terms, where they stand globally."

Hardt, Michael, and Antonio Negri. 2000. *Empire*. Cambridge, MA: Harvard University Press. A neo-Marxist explanation for the way that inequality is structured globally and how this changes the functioning of power. Interestingly, while Michael Hardt is a professor of literature at Duke University, Antonio Negri is an inmate at Rebibbia Prison in Rome, convicted in the 1970s of trying to overthrow the Italian state, a charge he has always denied.

Harrison, Bennett, and Barry Bluestone. 1988. *The Great U-Turn: Corporate Restructuring and the Polarization of America*. New York: Basic Books. A compelling analysis of the increasing polarization of the American economy and the specific ways that the wealthy protect their assets while the middle class and the poor are increasingly hard-pressed.

The House of Yes. 1997. Dir. Mark Waters. Miramax. A darkly comic peek at cultural capital in a wealthy, dysfunctional family. When Marty Pascal attempts to get married, his jealously possessive twin sister mocks his fiancée for lacking refinement and for being from Pennsylvania, "a state that's in your way when you want to go someplace else."

Katz, Michael B. 1986. *In the Shadow of the Poorhouse: A Social History of Welfare in America*. New York: Basic Books. Explores the ways in which the welfare system has remained in place, despite being consistently unpopular throughout American history.

Krog, Antjie. 1999. *Country of My Skull: Guilt, Sorrow, and the Limits of Forgiveness in the New South Africa*. New York: Times Books. The story of South Africa's Truth and Reconciliation Commission, established to deal with the crimes committed under apartheid. The commission powerfully gives voice to those who suffered in a racially segregated South Africa, while the author, an Afrikaner, also tries to find an honorable way to live in a country still deeply divided along racial lines.

People Like Us: Social Class in America (www.pbs.org/ peoplelikeus). Created by Louis Alvarez and Andrew Kolker. A documentary that uses many individuals' life experiences to explore the American class system, which most of us have trouble talking about.

Pollin, Robert, and Stephanie Luce. 1998. *The Living Wage: Building a Fair Economy*. New York: New Press. As part of the ongoing effort to document the struggles of the working poor, Pollin and Luce document a nationwide movement for economic justice that argues that paying a living wage is good for employers, cities, and employees.

Schor, Juliet B. 1999. *The Overspent American: Why We Want What We Don't Need*. New York: HarperCollins. A breezily written indictment of America's obsession with designer clothes, athletic shoes, luxury cars, and other high-status consumer goods.

Twine, France Winddance. 1998. *Racism in a Racial Democracy: The Maintenance of White Supremacy in Brazil*. New Brunswick, NJ: Rutgers University Press. An ethnographic study of the way that racial segregation in Brazil is disguised by a class-based ideology.

CHAPTER 9

Race and Ethnicity as Lived Experience

iger Woods is often hailed as the person who opened up the field of professional golf to African Americans. But Woods doesn't describe himself as black: he's "Cablinasian," a term he coined to describe his multiracial background (which includes Caucasian, black, American Indian, and Asian American ancestries). In 2002, Halle Berry became the first African American ever to win the Academy Award for best actress. As she tearfully accepted the statuette on stage, the camera cut to her mother sitting in the audience, beaming with pride at her daughter's accomplishment—and unmistakably white. Blonde actress Heather Locklear is a descendant of a group known as the Lumbees: an isolated triracial community in North Carolina that is part Caucasian, part African American, and part Tuscarora Indian.

Despite America's record of racial discrimination and segregation, there have always been multiracial people in its history, beginning with the European settlers who mixed with Native Americans and black slaves alike (Clinton and Gillespie 1997; Brooks 2002). More and more, we are recognizing and celebrating our multiracial heritage. In 2000, the Census Bureau gave Americans the opportunity for the first time to check multiple boxes to identify their race, thus creating 63 different racial categories. Approximately 7 million, or 2.4 percent of the population, took advantage of the new option. And the number identifying themselves as multiracial will only grow, according to the bureau: by 2050, the population of multiracial identities will double to about 14 million. As the United States is a nation of immigrants (some involuntary), it is only logical that the separate lineages of the American population would eventually meld. We might, therefore, wonder: will race continue to be as important in the future as it has been in the past? In this chapter, we will examine the sociological understandings of race, which will provide us with the insights we need to answer this question.

SocIndex

Then and Now

1870: Number of African American senators: 1

1970: Number of African American senators: 1

2008: Number of African American senators: 1

Here and There

United States: Most Native Americans were granted citizenship in 1924

Canada: Most Native Americans were granted citizenship in 1956

This and That

In 2006, the percentage of American youth aged 15–25 who believe that it is their responsibility to get involved to make things better for society:

Hispanic: 45%
African American: 44%
Asian: 43%
White: 35%

HOW TO READ THIS CHAPTER

Our goal in this chapter is for you to acquire a fundamental understanding of race and ethnicity as socially constructed categories. While each is based on traits we may see as biological, such as skin color or facial features, the meanings attached to race and ethnicity are created, maintained, and modified over time through social processes in which we all take part.

When a society categorizes people based on their race and ethnicity (and all societies do), it creates a system of stratification that leads to inequality. Society's resources—wealth, power, privilege, opportunity—are distributed according to these categories, and this perpetuates inequalities that are all too familiar here in the United States. We also hope you will come to understand the importance of race and ethnicity in forming individual identity. Our racial identities have profound effects on our sense of self, and our bonds to other people may be based on shared identities—or may transcend those racial categories entirely.

Defining Race and Ethnicity

Race and *ethnicity* are words we use so often in everyday speech that we might not think we need a definition of either. But people tend to use the words interchangeably, as if they mean essentially the same thing. There is, however, a significant difference between commonsense notions of race and ethnicity and what social scientists have to say about them.

The idea of different races as belonging to distinguishable categories has existed for hundreds of years. In the nineteenth century, biologists came up with a schema that grouped humans into three races: Negroid, Mongoloid, and Caucasoid (corresponding roughly to black, Asian, and white). It was believed that each race was characterized by its own biological makeup, separate and distinct from the others. Modern scientists, however, possess advanced tools for examining race in a much more sophisticated way. What they have found, ironically, is that there are no "pure" races, that the lines between races are blurry rather than fixed. A person who looks white will inevitably have biological material from other races, as will someone who looks black. There is also no such thing as a "superior" race, as race itself is not the reason that different groups might display positive or negative characteristics (such

> **race** a socially defined category based on real or perceived biological differences between groups of people
>
> **ethnicity** a socially defined category based on common language, religion, nationality, history, or another cultural factor

as intelligence, athleticism, or artistic ability). Furthermore, there is greater genetic diversity *within* racial populations than between them. So within the Asian population, members differ more from each other (Koreans from Chinese, for example) than they do from whites. From a biological standpoint, the difference between someone with type O blood and someone with type A blood is much more significant than the differences between a dark-skinned and a light-skinned person. And yet blood types have no correlation to race at all.

New genetic testing technologies seem to hold out the prospect of accurately identifying biological differences between racial groups—some "ancestry testing" services purport to be able to identify clients' genetic and geographic origins down to the region, village or tribe. However precise or imprecise such conclusions may be, they overlook the fact that all humans, whatever racial categories they seem to inhabit, are 99.9 percent genetically identical. And of that remaining 0.1 percent of our genetic material, only 15 percent of its variation occurs between geographically distinct groups. In other words, there's not enough "wiggle room" in the human genome for race to be a genetic trait (*Harvard Magazine*, 2008).

Sociologists, then, have come to understand **race** as a social category, based on real or perceived biological differences between groups of people. Race is more meaningful to us on a social level than it is on a biological level (Montagu 1998). Actress Heather Locklear certainly "looks white," and you have probably perceived her in that way, but in some Southern states in 1925, she could just as easily have been considered black or Native American. Does knowing Locklear's racial background now make you think of her in a different way?

Ethnicity is another social category that is applied to a group with a shared ancestry or cultural heritage. The Amish, for instance, are a distinct ethnic group in American society, linked by a common heritage that includes language, religion, and history; the Amish people, with few exceptions, are also white. The Jewish people, on the other hand, contrary to what the Nazis and other white supremacists may believe, are an ethnic group but not a race. The stereotypical image is challenged when we see a blonde, blue-eyed Jew from Scandinavia or a black Ethiopian Jew.

As an example of the social construction of race and ethnicity, let's look at the evidence documenting the historical changes in the boundaries of the category "white." In the early 1900s, native-born Americans, who were frequently Protestant, did not consider recent Irish, Italian, or Jewish immigrants to be white and restricted where these groups could live and work (Ignatiev 1996; Brodkin 1999). Such housing discrimination forced new immigrants to cluster in urban neighborhoods or ghettos. After World War II, however, as the second generation of Irish, Italian, and Jewish immigrants reached adulthood, the importance of ethnic identity declined and skin color became the main way to differentiate between who was white and who was not. Today, the question is whether people of Middle Eastern descent are white. In the post–9/11 climate, Arabs and Muslims have been identified as racially and ethnically distinct in significant and even harmful ways. While these groups possess a range of skin colors and facial features, it may be their symbolic labeling in these difficult times that makes them "nonwhite."

"Ethnic Options": Symbolic and Situational Ethnicity

How do we display our racial and ethnic group membership? We may do so in a number of ways: through dress, language, food, religious practices, preferences in music, art, or literature, even the projects we find interesting and the topics we pursue at school. Sometimes these practices make our group membership obvious to others; sometimes they don't. White ethnics like Irish Americans and Italian Americans, for example, can actually choose when and how they display their ethnic group membership.

One way group membership is displayed is through **symbolic ethnicity**, enactments of ethnic identity that occur only on special occasions. For example, most Irish Americans have been so fully assimilated for several generations that their Irish ancestry may not matter much to them on a daily basis. But on St. Patrick's Day (especially in cities like Boston and New York), displays of Irish identity can be pretty overwhelming! Parades, hats, "Kiss me, I'm Irish" buttons, green clothing, green beer (and in Chicago, a green river!), corned beef and cabbage—all are elements of symbolic ethnicity. Similar ethnic displays occur on holidays such as Passover, Cinco de Mayo, and Nouruz.

Another way we can show group membership is through **situational ethnicity**, when we deliberately assert our ethnicity in some situations while downplaying it in others. Situational ethnicity involves a kind of cost-benefit analysis that symbolic ethnicity does not: we need to appraise each situation to determine whether or not it favors our ethnicity. For example, Dr. Ferris's Lebanese ancestry never mattered much, outside her own family, when she lived in Southern California. In fact, it was often something she felt she should downplay, given a political climate in which people of Arabic background were sometimes viewed with suspicion. But when she moved to Peoria, Illinois, she discovered that this small city had a relatively large population of Lebanese

> **symbolic ethnicity** an ethnic identity that is only relevant on specific occasions and does not significantly impact everyday life
>
> **situational ethnicity** an ethnic identity that can be either displayed or concealed depending on its usefulness in a given situation

Mulberry Street at the Turn of the Century In the early 1900s, Irish, Italian, and Jewish immigrants were not considered "whites." Because of residential segregation, new immigrants poured into densely populated neighborhoods like this one on New York's Lower East Side where they had little choice but to live in squalid tenements and work in sweatshops.

Heritage Tourism: Getting in Touch with Our Roots

As global travel becomes easier, faster, and more affordable, a phenomenon called heritage tourism has been on the rise. Heritage tourism is related to the idea of the pilgrimage—a journey to a geographical location of significance to one's religion. Examples of traditional pilgrimages include the *hajj*, an excursion to Mecca in Saudi Arabia, which is required of all Muslims once in their lifetime. Catholics may travel to the Vatican or to other important sites such as the grotto and sanctuary at Lourdes in France or the Cathedral of Santiago de Compostela in Spain. But heritage tourism is less about religion and more about the cultural legacies of different racial and ethnic groups. Members of racial and ethnic groups who now live outside the countries of their ancestors (such as African Americans or Irish Americans) are sometimes attracted by the possibility of traveling to the "old country," and tourism ministries worldwide market their countries and cultures as must-see places for members of the diaspora—displaced peoples who may have emigrated generations ago. Here are a few examples of heritage tourism campaigns from around the world:

Ireland

The U.S. Census reports that 10 percent of the American population—or 30 million people—claimed Irish heritage in 2000. That's a lot of potential tourists, and the official Irish tourist bureau caters specifically to those who wish to investigate their Irish ancestry. The tourism industry in Ireland encourages people of Irish descent to take tours that trace their family's heritage. The tourism office, in association with the Irish Genealogical Project, entices travelers to visit Irish Family History Foundation Centres around the country and promises "a personal and emotional journey . . . of discovery" as travelers discover the roots of their family tree.

Israel

For many contemporary Jews, their Jewish identity is as much ethnic as it is religious, and the existence of a Jewish state may have an impact on their travel plans. For example,

Ethnic Options We can display group membership by embracing ethnic identity on special occasions like St. Patrick's Day or Cinco de Mayo (symbolic ethnicity) or in special situations (situational ethnicity).

Israel's Ministry of Tourism encourages American Jewish families to consider traveling to Israel for their children's Bar or Bat Mitzvah celebrations. Ceremonies can be held at any of a number of well-known historical locations such as the Western Wall or the Masada, and Bar or Bat Mitzvah visitors may also tour the important religious, cultural, and political sites of Jerusalem as part of their holiday. Parents and politicians alike hope that vacations such as these will strengthen the children's connection to their Jewish heritage and begin a process of attachment to Israel itself that may ultimately lead to "making *aliyah*," or moving there permanently.

Ghana

Because of the historical brutalities of slavery, it is often difficult for African Americans to pinpoint their cities or countries of ancestral origin—but since most African slaves were taken from West Africa, some countries in that region have begun exploring the touristic implications of slavery's tragic legacy. Ghanaian tourism officials, for example, want the far-flung "diasporan" descendants of American, European, and Caribbean slaves to think of Africa as home and to consider making a pilgrimage to the land of their ancestors. They offer tours that focus on slave-trade sites like the forts in which newly enslaved Africans were imprisoned before being shipped to the New World (which most visitors find both deeply moving and disturbing). But they also entertain visitors and educate them about Ghanaian culture and customs with colorful festivals, dancing, and feasting. Ghanaian officials hope that some visitors will choose to make Ghana their permanent home, offering special visas for diasporans to make it easy to travel to and from the homeland.

descent and that the mayor, a city councilman, the state senator, the congressman, local business, arts, and religious leaders, and prominent families were all Lebanese. This suddenly made Dr. Ferris's ethnicity a valuable asset in a way that it had never been before. She received a good deal of social support and made new friends based on shared revelations of ethnic group membership. In the case of situational ethnicity, we see how larger social forces can govern the identities we choose—if we have a choice.

Neither situational nor symbolic ethnicity is available to those who are visibly nonmainstream, whatever that may look like in a given society. In the United States, this generally means that nonwhites find themselves in fewer situations where they have a choice about whether to display their group membership (although this may eventually change as we become a "majority minority" nation). As sociologist Mary Waters says, "The social and political consequences of being Asian or Hispanic or black are not, for the most part, symbolic, nor are they voluntary. They are real, unavoidable, and sometimes hurtful" (1990, p. 156).

DATA WORKSHOP

ANALYZING EVERYDAY LIFE

Doing Symbolic Ethnicity

Choose a setting where you can watch people "doing" ethnicity. For instance, you can go to a St. Patrick's Day parade, if your city hosts one, or attend an ethnic festival of some sort (such as St. Anthony's Feast Day in Boston's Italian North End or Los Angeles's annual African Marketplace). Or just visit one of your city's ethnic neighborhoods: stroll through an Italian market in South Philadelphia, or shop the streets of Chicago's Ukrainian Village, Greektown, or Pilsen (a Mexican American neighborhood). If you think your town is too tiny to have any ethnic diversity, think again: even minuscule Postville, Iowa (population 1,500), includes a large Hasidic Jewish population, with significant clusters of Mexican, Guatemalan, Ukrainian, Nigerian, Bosnian, and Czech immigrants. You may even find an appropriate setting on your college campus or at one of your own family gatherings.

Once you have chosen a setting, join in the activities around you while at the same time carefully observing how the other participants display their ethnic membership. As part of your observation, consider the following.

- What are participants wearing? Traditional ethnic costumes, contemporary T-shirts, other symbols displaying their ethnic identity?

- What kind of music is being played, and what types of foods or crafts are available?

- Are different languages being spoken? If so, by whom, and in what situations?

- What are the differences in the activities of adults and children? men and women? members and visitors?

- Listen for snatches of conversation in which members explain such traditions as buying a goldfish on the first day of spring (Iranian), wrapping and tying a tamale (Mexican), or wearing the claddagh ring (Irish).

Record your observations, and bring them back into the classroom for discussion and analysis. There are two options for completing this Data Workshop.

- *Option 1 (informal)*: Prepare written notes that you can refer to in class. Discuss your experience with other students in a small group. Consider all the questions and points above.

- *Option 2 (formal)*: Write a three- to four-page essay describing your observations and answering the questions in this workshop. Ask yourself the same questions about your own ethnic identity as you did about the people you observed. Do you have the option to display your ethnicity in some situations and withhold it in others? Why or why not? How do you decide whether/when/how to do this? What kind of cost-benefit analysis do you use? What role do ethnic and racial stereotypes play in this process? And how are these displays received by others?

What Is a Minority?

A minority is commonly thought of as a group that's smaller in numbers than the dominant group. Thus, most

> **minority group** members of a social group that is systematically denied the same access to power and resources available to society's dominant groups but who are not necessarily fewer in number than the dominant groups

Americans would say that in the United States, whites are a majority while African Americans, Asians, Hispanics/Latinos, and Native Americans are minorities, because whites outnumber each of these other groups. In South Africa, however, blacks dramatically outnumber whites by a ratio of 7 to 1, yet before the 1994 election of President Nelson Mandela, whites controlled the country while blacks occupied the lowest status in that society. California provides us with a different kind of example. In 2005 the Census Bureau reported that whites made up less than 45 percent of the state's population, whereas other ethnic groups (Hispanics, African Americans, Asian Americans, Native Americans) when added together constituted a majority of 56 percent (Longley 2005). California, then, is technically a "majority minority" state: whites are less than half the population but still remain the dominant group in terms of power, resources, and representation in social institutions (Texas and New Mexico are also "majority minority" states). Hispanics/Latinos continue to be underrepresented in the University of California system, as both students and faculty, as well as in the state government and as business owners. They are, however, overrepresented in prisons, in poverty counts, and as victims of violent crimes.

As sociologists, then, we must recognize that minority status is not just about numbers—it's about social inequalities. Sociologists define a **minority group** as people who are recognized as belonging to a social category (here either a racial or an ethnic group) and who suffer from unequal treatment as a result of that status. A minority group is denied the access to power and resources generally accorded to others in the dominant groups. Members of a minority group are likely to perceive of themselves as targets of collective discrimination (Wirth 1945).

Membership in a minority group may serve as a kind of "master status," overriding any other status (such as gender or age). Members may be subjected to racist beliefs about the group as a whole and thus suffer from a range of social disadvantages. Unequal and unfair treatment, as well as lack of access to power and resources, typically generates a strong sense of common identity and solidarity among members of minority groups. Perhaps because of this sense of identification, minorities also tend to practice high rates of in-group marriage (endogamy), although the percentage of mixed-race couples in America continues to grow.

Racism, Prejudice, and Discrimination

In order for social inequality to persist, the unequal treatment that minority groups suffer must be supported by the dominant groups. **Racism**, an ideology or set of beliefs about the superiority of one racial or ethnic group over another, provides this support; it is used to justify social arrangements between the dominant and minority groups. Racist beliefs are often rooted in the assumption that differences between groups are innate, or biologically based. They can also arise from a negative view of a group's cultural characteristics. In both cases, racism presumes that one group is better than another.

Prejudice and discrimination are closely related to racism, and though the terms are often used interchangeably, there are important distinctions between them. **Prejudice**, literally a "prejudgment," is an inflexible attitude (usually negative, although it can work in the reverse) about a particular group of people and is rooted in generalizations or stereotypes. Examples of prejudice include opinions like "All Irish are drunks" or "All Mexicans are lazy." Prejudice often, though not always, leads to **discrimination**: an action or behavior that results in the unequal treatment of individuals because of their membership in a certain racial or ethnic group. A person might be said to suffer discrimination if she is turned down for a job promotion or a home loan because she's black or Hispanic.

It is possible, though unlikely, that a person can be prejudiced and still not discriminate against others. For example, a teacher can believe that Asian American students are better at math and science, yet deliberately not let this belief influence his grading of Asian American students. Conversely, a person may not be prejudiced at all but still unknowingly participate in discrimination. For instance, a small child can innocently use the racist terminology she learns from her parents even though she herself holds no racist views. And prejudice and discrimination don't always flow from the dominant group toward minorities. In the 2005 movie *Crash*, for instance, we see depictions of whites who are prejudiced against blacks and blacks who are prejudiced against whites; Middle Easterners and blacks who are both prejudiced against Hispanics; whites defending blacks and Middle Easterners defending Hispanics; blacks who are prejudiced against themselves and whites who are prejudiced against other whites.

Discrimination can also take different forms. **Individual discrimination** occurs when one person treats others unfairly because of their race or ethnicity. A racist teacher might discriminate against a Hispanic student by assigning him a lower grade than he deserves. **Institutional discrimination**, in contrast, usually more systematic and widespread, occurs when institutions (such as governments, schools, or banks) practice discriminatory policies that affect whole groups of individuals.

A rather startling example of institutional discrimination comes from Ira Katznelson (2005) in his book *When Affirmative Action Was White: An Untold History of Racial Inequality in Twentieth Century America*. We usually associate

Discrimination Takes Many Forms The film *Crash* weaves together stories about different families in Los Angeles who each confront different forms of racism.

affirmative action with the advances of the Civil Rights Movement of the 1960s and with benefiting blacks and other minorities. Katznelson, however, examines one instance of government policies benefiting whites. In 1944, Congress passed the G.I. Bill of Rights, which provided funding for college or vocational education and home loans to returning World War II veterans. While this should have supported black and white veterans alike, in practice blacks were largely impeded from taking advantage of the new benefits, while whites more easily climbed into the rapidly expanding American middle class. Typically, loans were granted only to those buying homes in all-white neighborhoods. And blacks were effectively barred from buying homes in those neighborhoods, either through legal restrictions or from hostile actions on the part of loan officers, realtors, and homeowners who were prejudiced against having blacks live next door. To make matters worse, loans were even denied to blacks who wished to buy homes in black neighborhoods; these

racism a set of beliefs about the superiority of one racial or ethnic group; used to justify inequality and often rooted in the assumption that differences between groups are genetic

prejudice an idea about the characteristics of a group that is applied to all members of that group and is unlikely to change regardless of the evidence against it

discrimination unequal treatment of individuals based on their membership in a social group; usually motivated by prejudice

individual discrimination discrimination carried out by one person against another

institutional discrimination discrimination carried out systematically by institutions (political, economic, educational, and others) that affect all members of a group who come into contact with it

were seen as risky investments. Later affirmative action programs were actually modeled after those of the postwar era that ironically benefited whites and created an even greater economic disparity between racial groups.

Another example comes from Lawrence Otis Graham, a Princeton- and Harvard-trained African American lawyer who investigated firsthand institutionalized racism in the upper-crust world of the East Coast elite. He found that, for example, he was not able to join a particular Connecticut country club as a member; however, he was welcome to serve in the capacity of busboy to the club's all-white membership and wait staff (1996). This shocked Graham; he believed his Ivy League credentials would have opened any door but discovered that in a racially stratified society, a black man with privileged socioeconomic status is still a black man in the end.

Some students have difficulty in recognizing just how persistent and pervasive racism is in contemporary American society, while others experience it on a daily basis. We hear claims that it has been erased. But although there have been tremendous strides, especially in the wake of the Civil Rights Movement, racism is not yet a thing of the past. There is still deep skepticism among minorities that negative racial attitudes are changing in America (Bobo, Kluegel, and Smith 1997; Bobo and Smith 1998). A survey conducted by Gallup in 2003 showed that 59 percent of whites believe that race relations in the United States are good and 24 percent believe they are bad, while 48 percent of blacks believe that race relations are good and 37 percent believe they are bad. Another striking result of the survey revealed that more than half of both whites and blacks believe that relations between the two will always be a problem in the United States.

Racism today may not be as blatant as it once was—blacks don't have to use separate bathrooms or drinking fountains—but it has taken other, more subtle forms (such as the high concentration of liquor stores in predominantly black urban areas). If we are to have a truly "color-blind" society, it will take much more education and change in the social conditions that perpetuate inequality.

Theoretical Approaches to Understanding Race in the United States

Sociologists reject the notion that race has an objective or scientific meaning and instead seek to understand why race continues to play such a critical role in society. They have produced a number of different theories about the connections between race, discrimination, and social inequality.

For example, functionalist theory has provided a useful lens for analyzing how certain ethnic groups, mainly European immigrants (like the Irish and Italians) arriving in the early 1900s, eventually became assimilated into the larger society. Functionalism, however, has proven less successful in explaining the persistence of racial divisions and why other races and ethnicities, such as African Americans and Hispanics, have continued to maintain their distinct identities alongside the white majority culture today.

Perhaps what functionalism can best offer is an explanation of how prejudice and discrimination develop, by focusing on social solidarity and group cohesion. Groups have a tendency toward ethnocentrism, or the belief that one's own culture and way of life are right and normal. Functionalists contend that positive feelings about one's group are strong ties that bind people together. At the same time, however, this cohesiveness can lead members to see others, especially those of other races or ethnicities, in an unfavorable light. According to functionalists, these cultural differences and the lack of integration into the larger society on the part of minorities tend to feed fear and hostility.

Conflict theory focuses on the struggle for power and control. Classic Marxist analyses of race, developed by sociologists in the 1960s, looked for the source of racism in capitalist hierarchies. Edna Bonacich, for instance, argues that racism is partly driven by economic competition and the struggle over scarce resources. A "split labor market," in which one group of workers (usually defined by race, ethnicity, or gender) is routinely paid less than other groups, keeps wages low for racial and ethnic minorities, compounding the effects of racism with those of poverty (1980). William Julius Wilson believes that openly racist government policies and individual racist attitudes are the driving forces in the creation of a black underclass but that it is perpetuated by economic factors, not racial ones (1980). But while this link between race and class is useful and important, it doesn't provide a satisfactory explanation for all forms of racial and ethnic stratification.

In recent years, conflict theorists have developed new approaches to understanding race. In his book *Racial Fault Lines: The Historical Origins of White Supremacy in California* (2008), for example, Tomas Almaguer looks at the history of race relations in California during the late nineteenth century. He describes a racial hierarchy that placed whites at the top, followed by Mexicans, blacks, Asians, and Native Americans at the bottom. Rather than focusing exclusively on class, he examines how white supremacist ideology became institutionalized. Racist beliefs became a part of political and economic life during that period. Ideas like "manifest destiny" (the belief that the United States had a mission to expand its territories) helped justify the taking of

TABLE 9.1   *Theory in Everyday Life*

Perspective	Approach to Race and Ethnicity	Case Study: Racial Inequality
STRUCTURAL-FUNCTIONALISM	Racial and ethnic difference is a necessary part of society. Even racial inequality has functions that help maintain social order.	The functions of racial inequality and conflict for society could include the creation of social cohesion within both the dominant and minority groups.
CONFLICT THEORY	Racial and ethnic differences create intergroup conflict—minority and majority groups have different interests and may find themselves at odds as they attempt to secure and protect them.	Some members of majority groups (whites and men in particular) object to affirmative action programs that assist underrepresented groups. This can create conflict between racial groups in society.
SYMBOLIC INTERACTIONISM	Race and ethnicity are part of our presentation of self.	Some individuals—white ethnics and light-skinned nonwhites in particular—have the option to conceal their race or ethnicity in situations where it might be advantageous to do so. This may allow them as individuals to escape the effects of racial inequality but does not erase it from the society at large.

lands, and the notion that Native Americans were "uncivilized heathens" helped justify killing them. Sociologists like Michael Omi and Howard Winant also argue that race isn't just a secondary phenomenon that results from the class system: it permeates both lived experience and larger-scale activity such as the economy and the government (1989).

Still others have sought to understand the meaning of race from the individual's point of view and have begun to analyze the ways that race, class, and gender inequalities intersect. For instance, writers like Patricia Hill Collins (2006), bell hooks (1990), and Gloria Anzaldúa (1987) argue that race must be explained in the terms in which it is experienced, not as overarching general theories. Though some of these writers have been sharply critical of the symbolic interactionist tradition, which they believe does not take into account macro social forces that shape the realities of stratification, they share with interactionism a conviction that race, like all other aspects of social life, is created symbolically in everyday interactions. It is this idea to which we now turn.

Race as an Interactional Accomplishment

Remember Erving Goffman's ideas about how we project our identities in interaction with others? This process is constant and ongoing—there is no "time out." We "read" others through a myriad of cues, and we in turn make ourselves readable to others by our own self-presentations. Our identity is constructed in the negotiation between what we project and what others recognize. Even master statuses like race, gender, and age are negotiated in this way. So how *do* we project our racial or ethnic identities and read the racial or ethnic identities of others? We might think immediately of stereotypes like hip-hoppers with baggy pants, skateboard dudes, sorority girls, "welfare moms," and so on. But in fact there are more subtle ways in which we project and receive our racial and ethnic identities.

Passing

Racial **passing**, or living as if one is a member of a different racial category, has a long history in the United States. Both during and after slavery, some light-skinned African Americans would attempt to live as whites in order to avoid the dire consequences of being black in a racist society. And people of different racial and ethnic backgrounds still pass, intentionally or unintentionally, every day in the contemporary United States. Passing involves manufacturing or maintaining a new identity that is more beneficial than one's real identity. W.E.B. DuBois's concept of "double-consciousness" (see Chapter 2) seems relevant to a discussion of passing—DuBois asks whether one can be black and at the same time claim one's rights as an American. Given the history of oppression and enslavement of African Americans, DuBois is not the only person to wonder if this is possible. There are many social forces that disenfranchise and exclude African Americans, and the phenomenon of passing suggests that, in some places and times, it has been more advantageous to play down the "African" part of "African American" if at all possible.

> **passing** presenting yourself as a member of a different racial or ethnic group than the one you were born into

The Sweeter the Juice Shirlee Taylor Haizlip's grandfather, who abandoned his family to live as a white man, is an example of racial passing.

But whatever its perceived benefits, living as if one is a member of a different racial category takes its toll. Passing is stressful, hard work, and almost entirely interactional: light-skinned blacks can "do white" only if they are skillful at behaving and talking like a white person and keeping their past racial identity a secret from people in their white present.

Shirlee Taylor Haizlip, a Los Angeles journalist, chronicled the passing stories of one half of her family in her book *The Sweeter the Juice* (1994). Haizlip grew up the daughter of a prominent black Baptist minister, attended Wellesley College, and lived a life of privilege and comfort as a member of a small East Coast African American elite in the 1950s. She always knew that she had white relatives (75 percent of all African Americans do) and that these relatives had something to do with her mother's story of being abandoned as a child by her own father. Haizlip decided to use her journalistic skills to find out who these relatives were and how they had disappeared into the white world. She tracked down an aunt (her mother's sister) and learned that her grandfather, who was very light skinned, had apparently not been able to resist the desire to escape the constraints of blackness for the privileges of whiteness. So he fled with his lightest-skinned child (Haizlip's aunt), leaving his other, darker children behind—and lived the rest of his life as a white man, cut off from his black ancestry.

In this story of passing, situational context is important: merely by surrounding himself with white people, Haizlip's grandfather accomplished whiteness rather effectively. In a socially segregated world, whom you hang out with goes a long way toward defining who you are, whether you are passing or not. But there are other requirements as well. Haizlip's aunt, for example, made sure her face was always well powdered, married a white man, and had no children, lest genes

embodied identity those elements of identity that are generated through others' perceptions of our physical traits

give her secret away. Indeed, while some of the white relatives Haizlip contacted knew about the black-white schism in the family, others did not—some were so surprised when Haizlip revealed that they had a former slave as a common great-grandfather, they blurted out, "Do you mean a *black* slave?" Their pasts had been so successfully erased through passing that after only one generation they were completely unaware of their black heritage.

Embodied and Disembodied Identities

When we interact with others online, we're usually not able to see what they look like. This has been touted as one of the democratizing traits of the internet—that aspects of **embodied identity** (the way we are perceived in the physical world), historically used as the basis for discrimination, are not available to those interacting online. But in online communities that are *based* on racial identity, race must still be "done" interactionally (in this case, textually), as sociologist Byron Burkhalter found in his study of an internet community based on African American culture (1999). To sound authentically African American online, for instance, you have to include what Burkhalter calls "racially relevant" content and language—for example, "sister" to refer to other African American women. Responses also help establish racial identity: it's not just what you say, but how others receive it.

In some discussions, the African American identity of participants is accepted, but in other cases, that status is contested, in what Burkhalter calls "identity challenges." Identity challenges are usually accusations that one is not "really" black or not black enough, or that one is a "Tom"[1] or a racist. These challenges are usually made when postings reveal opinions that don't fit into a certain set of socially approved boundaries (such as opinions about the use of "proper" English versus slang).

Burkhalter argues that race is not irrefutably identifiable even in face-to-face interactions (as evidenced by the familiar, if irritating, question "What are you?") and that we must establish it interactionally both on- and offline. Stereotypes come into play in both arenas but in different directions: in face-to-face interaction, seeing racial characteristics leads to stereotyping; online, applying stereotypical templates leads to assumptions about race. The internet is thus not a place where all the problematic distinctions disappear—they just manifest themselves in different ways.

---

[1] "Tom" is a derogatory reference to the main character (a black slave) in Harriet Beecher Stowe's 1852 novel *Uncle Tom's Cabin*, whose servile devotion to his white masters earned him the reputation (some argue, undeserved) of being a traitor to his race.

Racial Identity: "More Than the Sum of Our Parts" President Barack Obama, left, listens to the inauguration ceremony at the U.S. Capitol on January 20, 2009. Behind Obama is his family, including wife Michelle, daughters Malia and Sasha, his sister Maya Soetoro-Ng and her husband Konrad Ng, and Obama's mother-in-law Marian Robinson.

DATA WORKSHOP

ANALYZING MASS MEDIA AND POPULAR CULTURE

The Politics and Poetics of Racial Identity

I am the son of a black man from Kenya and a white woman from Kansas. I was raised with the help of a white grandfather who survived a Depression to serve in Patton's Army during World War II and a white grandmother who worked on a bomber assembly line at Fort Leavenworth while he was overseas. I've gone to some of the best schools in America and lived in one of the world's poorest nations. I am married to a black American who carries within her the blood of slaves and slaveowners—an inheritance we pass on to our two precious daughters. I have brothers, sisters, nieces, nephews, uncles and cousins, of every race and every hue, scattered across three continents, and for as long as I live, I will never forget that in no other country on Earth is my story even possible.

It's a story that hasn't made me the most conventional candidate. But it is a story that has seared into my genetic makeup the idea that this nation is more than the sum of its parts—that out of many, we are truly one.

—FROM BARACK OBAMA'S SPEECH TO THE NATION, MARCH 18, 2008, PHILADELPHIA, PENNSYLVANIA

Barack Obama, the 44th president of the United States, is the first black man to be elected to the office. Issues of race featured prominently in his 2008 campaign, and during a campaign stop in Philadelphia Obama gave one particularly famous speech on race that was discussed, analyzed, scrutinized, and evaluated by pundits and ordinary citizens alike for months afterward. In the speech, Obama ostensibly addressed some controversial comments about race delivered by the pastor of the church his family attended in Chicago. But he also spoke to bigger issues that everyone, regardless of race, has had to grapple with simply as part of being an American. Indeed, he presented the issue of racial prejudice as one of America's defining social problems and challenged all Americans to work toward solving it.

This Data Workshop asks you to do a content analysis of a speech, song, poem, or performance that deals with racial and ethnic identity. Check out text and video of Obama's speech at http://www.barackobama.com/2008/03/18/remarks_of_senator_barack_obam_53.php. You can also look up other important political speeches at the Library of Congress's "American Memory" website, dedicated to providing the public with electronic access to "written and spoken words, sound recordings, still and moving images, prints, maps and sheet music that document the American experience": http://memory.loc.gov/ammem/index.html.

You may also choose a poem from your favorite writer and consider how racial and ethnic identity are socially constructed in poetry. Or you might rent or record an episode of the HBO series *Def Poetry Jam*, which features artists such as Mos Def, Jay-Z, Caroline Kennedy, Rakim, Erykah Badu, Mutaburuka, and Jill Scott. Or analyze the lyrics from your favorite musical artist (in the case of rap or hip-hop artists, some are also Def Jam poets). Consider other kinds of sources as well, such as the stand-up routines of

In Relationships

"Jungle Fever": Interracial Romance, Dating, and Marriage

Forty-one out of the fifty American states prohibited **miscegenation**—romantic, sexual, or marital relationships between people of different races—at some point in their history. In 1958, for example, Mildred and Richard Loving, an African American woman and a white man, married and settled in their native state of Virginia. In July of that year, they were arrested for violating the state's "Act to Preserve Racial Purity" and convicted. The judge sentenced them to a year in prison but suspended the sentence on the condition that the couple leave the state. The Lovings moved to Washington, D.C., where in 1967 the Supreme Court overturned all such laws, ruling that the state of Virginia had denied the Lovings their constitutional rights. While the Loving decision technically cleared the way for interracial marriages nationwide, states were slow to change their laws; Alabama finally overturned its antimiscegenation statute in 2000.

Society at large does seem more accepting of interracial relationships now than it was in 1967. By 2002, almost 20 percent of 18- and 19-year-olds reported being in an interracial relationship (Kao and Joyner 2005). At the same time, though, about 27 percent of Americans still expressed disapproval. Despite all the steps we have taken toward racial equality and integration, American society is not ideally structured to promote interracial contact, let alone romance. Cultural stereotypes and media images, for example, provide serious obstacles to interracial relationships. Several researchers point out that minorities tend to be exoticized or

Mildred and Richard Loving

stereotyped by the general population. Thus, Asian women are seen as subservient, mysterious, seductive, and/or sex objects; conversely, Asian men are portrayed as nonsexual geeks or martial arts pros (Le 2001). Black men are mythologized as having especially strong sex drives, and black

Korean American comic Margaret Cho, the Chicano comedy troupe Culture Clash, the Middle Eastern comics in "Axis of Evil," or the African American Queens of Comedy. Finally, you could also write an original speech or poem about your own experience of your racial or ethnic identity, then discuss it using the principles of content analysis. Whichever option you choose, remember to focus on how the text expresses ideas about race, ethnicity, identity, inequality, and solidarity.

There are two options for completing this Data Workshop.

• *Option 1 (informal)*: Prepare written notes on your chosen text that you can refer to in class. Compare your notes and experiences with other students in small-group discussions.

• *Option 2 (formal)*: Write a three- to four-page essay analyzing your chosen text.

How Do You Feel about Interracial Relationships? The 2006 film *Something New* (with Sanaa Lathan and Simon Baker) confronts some of the stereotypes about interracial relationships.

women are assumed to be unable to control their sexual urges (Foeman and Nance 1999); white women are thought to be accommodating in bed (Shipler 1997). These stereotypes, though they are not borne out in reality, still have the power to influence our attitudes and behavior.

Movies sometimes provide a warning. In both Spike Lee's 1991 movie *Jungle Fever* and the 2001 Julia Stiles movie *Save*

the Last Dance, white women in interracial relationships are criticized by people in the African American community for taking available black men away from black women, a problem that is exacerbated by the higher levels of incarceration and murder among young black men. A young African American woman is quoted in an *Ebony* magazine article as saying, "Every time I turn around and I see a fine Brother dating outside his race, I just feel disgusted. I feel like, what's wrong with us? Why do you choose her over me?" (Hughes 2003).

People who date interracially must deal with in-group pressures to date—and especially marry—someone of their own race. This phenomenon is most commented on in the African American community (though by no means exclusive to it). In fact, although blacks are as likely to date interracially as members of any other group, they are less likely to outmarry than any other nonwhite group. Anita Allen, a professor of law and philosophy at the University of Pennsylvania, has observed that many African Americans view marrying a nonblack as being disloyal to the community (NPR 2003). Commentary on this subject can be found in scores of magazine articles and in movies and even comic strips (see Aaron McGruder's "Boondocks").

How do you feel about interracial relationships? This topic is not just a hot-button issue for you to discuss with friends and family; it provides an opportunity for you to apply your sociological perspective to understand an important area of debate in everyday social life.

Race, Ethnicity, and Life Chances

A law professor decides that it is time to buy a house. After careful research into neighborhoods and land values, she picks one. With her excellent credit history and job as law professor, she easily obtains a mortgage over the phone. When the mortgage forms arrive in the mail, she sees to her

surprise that the phone representative has identified her race as "white." Smiling, she checks another box, "African American," and mails back the form. Suddenly, everything changes. The lending bank wants a bigger down payment and higher interest rates. When she threatens to sue, the bank backs down. She learns that the bank's motivation is falling property values in the proposed neighborhood. She doesn't understand this because those property values were completely stable when she was researching the area.

Then she realizes that *she* is the reason for the plummeting values.

As Patricia Williams's (1997) experience illustrates, membership in socially constructed categories of race and ethnicity can often carry a high price. We now look at other ways this price might be paid, in the areas of health, education, work, family, and criminal justice.

Family

Data from the Census Bureau (2008e) showed that of the white population over 18 years of age, 55.6 percent were married, 9.8 percent divorced, 6.0 percent widowed, and 26.7 percent never married. Of the African American population over 18, 33.8 percent were married, 10.7 percent divorced, 6.1 percent widowed, and 44.8 percent never married. The Hispanic population was more similar to the white population with 49.8 percent over 18 married, 7.3 percent divorced, 3.3 percent widowed, and 36.1 percent never married. Thus, African Americans are more likely than whites and Hispanics to never marry, to be divorced, or to be widowed.

Kathryn Edin (2000) argues that low-income women of all ethnicities see marriage as having few benefits. They feel that the men they are likely to encounter as possible husbands will not offer the advantages (financial stability, respectability, trust) that make the rewards of marriage worth the risks. This doesn't mean, of course, that most low-income women don't love their male companions; it only means that they believe a legal bond would not substantially improve their lot in life.

In 2006, the birth rates for American teenage mothers (ages 15 to 19) varied significantly by race. The birth rate for white teenage moms was 27 per 1,000 births, while the birth rate for African Americans was 64 per 1,000; for Hispanics it was 83 per 1,000 (National Center for Health Statistics 2007b). Social thinkers such as Angela Y. Davis argue that African American teenage girls in particular see fewer opportunities for education and work and choose motherhood instead (2001). Davis believes that social policies aimed at punishing teenage mothers of color will be ineffective; only by attacking the racism inherent in the educational system and the workforce will these teens be at less risk of becoming mothers.

Health

Health care is an area in which we find widespread disparity between racial and ethnic groups. Because there is no universal health care in the United States, consumers must rely on insurance benefits provided through their employer or buy individual policies in order to meet their medical needs. Many Americans, however, cannot afford basic

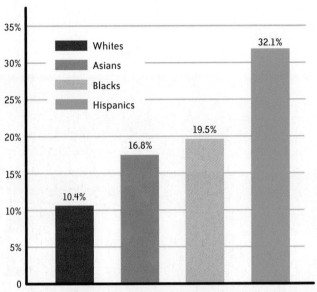

FIGURE 9.1 Americans without Health Insurance by Race, 2007
Disparities in access to health care adversely affect different groups.

SOURCE: U. S. Census Bureau 2008c

health-care coverage. In 2007, some 10.4 percent of whites were without health insurance, along with 16.8 percent of Asian Americans, 19.5 percent of blacks, and 32.1 percent of Hispanics (Figure 9.1).

Disparities in access to health care may help explain the life expectancy rates for men and women of different races. White male children born in 2004 can expect to live to be 75.7, while white females can expect to live to be 80.8. However, African American males' life expectancy is only 69.8 years, and African American females' is 76.5. Hispanic males' life expectancy, on the other hand, is 77.2 years, and Hispanic females' is 83.7. Minorities are also often exposed to other factors that impact lifespan, such as dangers in the workplace, toxins in the environment, or personal behaviors like drinking and poor diet (National Center for Health Statistics 2007a). While life expectancy statistics are only crude indicators of general health, they do reveal continuing race-based discrepancies, including the ongoing mystery of why Hispanics live longer, a question researchers are still trying to answer.

Education

One of America's cultural myths is that everyone has equal access to education, the key to a secure, well-paying job. However, by looking at those who actually receive degrees, we can see that the playing field is not that level. According to the Census Bureau (2008b), in 2006, 95 percent of white students earned a high school diploma, while 92 percent of African American students and 88 percent of Hispanic students did so. The reasons for dropping out are complex,

Race in College Admissions

Affirmative action policies were first put in place in the 1960s to make sure that racial and ethnic minorities had equal access to opportunities that had historically been available only to whites. While in principle these policies were lauded as a way to create a "level playing field" for all Americans, problems began to surface in practice. In 1978, a white student named Alan Bakke sued the University of California for "reverse discrimination": Bakke claimed that his application to UC Davis's medical school had been rejected in favor of lesser-qualified minority applicants because the school had set aside 16 percent of its medical school slots for minority applicants. The case went to the Supreme Court, and while the Court upheld the idea of affirmative action in general, it outlawed the "quota system" that had contributed to Bakke's rejection.

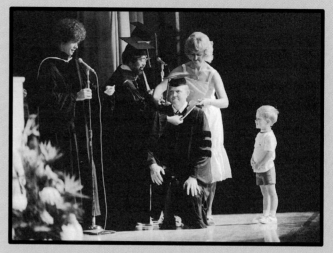

Alan Bakke

Since then, colleges and universities, private employers, and governments at all levels have struggled with the principles of affirmative action. Influential state university systems in California, Washington, Texas, and Michigan have faced additional legal challenges to their admissions criteria and have attempted to craft race-blind policies that produce the same effects as affirmative action. While seeking to avoid "quotas" and "preferential treatment," these schools also wish to increase diversity and create opportunities for historically underrepresented groups. How can these goals be accomplished simultaneously? Not without difficulty, it seems. California's public university system saw a substantial decrease in the number of minority applicants immediately following the policy changes made in 1996 that prohibited using race, sex, or ethnicity as a basis for admission or financial aid (Weiss 2001). Although the admission rates in the University of California system for non-Asian minority students rose in fall 1999 (almost to the levels of 1997, the last year of race-based admissions), they have continued to decline in the years since.

College admissions staff grapple with questions about race every day when they arrive at work. Rachel Toor, a former admissions officer at Duke University, maintains that "Duke was firmly committed to Affirmative Action," but evidently there was much confusion over what its affirmative action policies actually were. In her position on the admissions committee, Toor says, "I tried to discuss larger social and cultural issues relating to race . . . I rolled my eyes when [colleagues] made racist comments." But decisions taking race into account remained difficult and contentious. Toor herself supports affirmative action policies because, she says, "if left in the hands of admissions officers, the way Duke's rating system is set up, there would be very few students of color" (2001).

The problems facing Toor and her committee are not unique to Duke. Until 2003, the University of Michigan had affirmative action programs for both its undergraduate and law school students. The undergraduate admissions procedure was based on a rigid point system, which led white students who had been denied admission to complain that additional points given to minority students solely on the basis of race gave them an unfair advantage. The law school admissions procedure used race as one of several factors to be considered. In 2003, the Supreme Court upheld the law school policy and revised the undergraduate policy. Supporters at the University of Michigan argued that the Court had firmly endorsed the principle of diversity articulated by Justice Powell in the *Bakke* decision. Outgoing Dean Jeffrey Lehman said, "By upholding the University of Michigan Law School's admissions policy, the court has approved a model for how to enroll a student body that is both academically excellent and racially integrated." Further, "The question is no longer whether affirmative action is legal; it is how to hasten the day when affirmative action is no longer needed" (J. Peterson 2003).

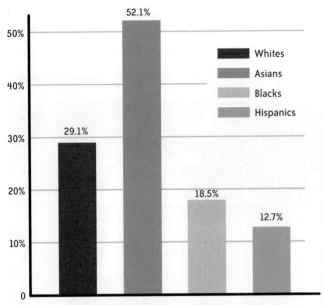

FIGURE 9.2 **U.S. Bachelor's Degree Holders by Race, 2007**

SOURCE: U. S. Census Bureau 2008b

but the highest rates are associated with those from economically disadvantaged and non–English-speaking backgrounds. Only Asian Americans at 98 percent show higher high school graduation rates than whites.

In higher education, the numbers are similar. In 2007, 52.1 percent of Asian Americans, 29.1 percent of whites, 18.5 percent of blacks, and 12.7 percent of Hispanics earned a bachelor's degree (Figure 9.2). Further, in 2005, 15.3 percent of Asian Americans, 8.8 percent of whites, 5.1 percent of African Americans, and 3.3 percent of Hispanics earned advanced degrees (master's, professional degrees, and doctorates). Thus, Asian Americans and whites enjoy more success overall in the U.S. educational system than African Americans and Hispanics. The reasons for the disparity are again complex, involving both economic and cultural factors. Earning an education is extremely important in American society. Not only does it translate to greater success in the workforce, it also confers social status and cultural capital that can prove valuable in other arenas.

Work and Income

African Americans make up 11.3 percent and Hispanics 10.9 percent of the total workforce. If jobs were truly given to people regardless of racial or ethnic identity, we would expect to see these same distributions across occupations. However, that is not the case. For example, in 2007, African Americans constituted 6.3 percent and Hispanics 7.4 percent of all executive and managerial professions (U.S. Bureau of Labor Statistics 2008b). That means that these positions, usually requiring advanced degrees, are primarily held by whites.

In contrast, persons of color carry the burden of some of society's most difficult jobs. In 2007, 33.6 percent of all nurses and home health aids and 24.8 percent of all postal clerks were black, while Hispanics were more likely to be employed in farming (40.4 percent of total) and as private household cleaners (40.4 percent of total). Except for nursing, these jobs are more likely to be semiskilled or unskilled. Thus, people of color, who are less likely to achieve high levels of education, are more likely to swell the bottom rungs of the job market (U.S. Bureau of Labour Statistics 2008b). Interestingly enough, some lower-level jobs have shifted from African Americans to Hispanics over time. For instance, in 1983, African Americans accounted for 42.4 percent and Hispanics for 11.8 percent of all private household cleaners; by 2007, blacks accounted for only 17.6 percent. A similar shift may be seen with other low-wage jobs. This means that persons of color increasingly compete with each other for such jobs.

In 2005, the median income for whites was $48,977, for African Americans $30,134, and for Hispanics $34,241. Asian Americans had the highest median income at $57,518 (U.S. Census Bureau 2008g). The median incomes of Asian Americans and whites thus place them in the middle class, while those of blacks and Hispanics place them in the lower-middle (working) class. African Americans and Hispanics are more disproportionately represented than whites in the income brackets between $0 and $49,999, while whites are more disproportionately represented in income brackets above $50,000. In 2006, 10.3 percent of whites lived below the poverty line, compared with 24.3 percent of African Americans and 20.6 percent of Hispanics (U.S. Census Bureau 2008g). These numbers make it easy to see how race and class intersect to influence life outcomes.

Criminal Justice

Although the majority of the U.S. population is white—about 69 percent, as opposed to about 13 percent black and 13 percent Hispanic—we don't find these same proportions in the prison population. Of all state and federal male prisoners in 2007, 39 percent were African American, while 36 percent were white and 20 percent Hispanic (U.S. Bureau of Justice Statistics 2008). Why are African American men and Hispanic men much more likely to go to prison than white men?

Some laws that don't seem race based still create racially differentiated outcomes. For example, until 2007 federal law handed out tougher sentences to crack users (who are more likely to be black) than to users of powdered cocaine (who are more likely to be white): if you possessed of a small amount of crack (for personal use), you'd get the same stringent sentence

TABLE 9.2	Federal Cocaine Offenders by Race/Ethnicity, 2000			
	POWDER COCAINE		CRACK COCAINE	
Race/Ethnicity	Number	Percent	Number	Percent
White	932	17.8	269	5.6
Black	1,596	30.5	4,069	84.7
Hispanic	2,662	50.8	434	9.0
Other	49	0.9	33	0.7
Total	5,239	100	4,805	100

SOURCE: U.S. Sentencing Commission 2000 Datafile

that you would if you possessed a huge amount of cocaine (enough for hundreds of uses). While this discrepancy was remedied in 2007, it left many convicted of crack possession awaiting official reductions in their sentences. Unemployment rates are higher among minority groups, as are dropout rates, and these may affect incarceration rates. There is also some evidence that there are connections to declining marriage rates and incarceration (Pettit and Western 2004).

It is also clear that African Americans are far more likely than whites to be murdered: In 2007, whites accounted for 46.8 percent of the murder victims nationwide, while African Americans accounted for 49.3 percent (Federal Bureau of Investigation 2008). Again, these percentages don't reflect the racial distribution of the U.S. population as a whole. Finally, over half of the reported hate crimes in 2006 were attributed to racial discrimination, with over two-thirds of those targeting blacks (U.S. Department of Justice 2007b).

Race Relations: Conflict or Cooperation

The relationships between racial and ethnic groups in a society can take different forms. In some instances, groups may be tolerant and respectful of one another, while in other cases there is unending hostility. In this section, we will examine five basic patterns of intergroup relationships, from the most violent to the most tolerant. Keep in mind that some ethnic groups, such as Native Americans, may suffer several different patterns of hardship over a period of time.

Genocide

The first pattern represents the worst possible outcome between a dominant and a subordinate group. Not only has **genocide**, the deliberate and systematic extermination of a racial, ethnic, national, or cultural group, taken place in the

past, it continues today in certain parts of the globe. One of the most horrific and wide-scale examples was the Holocaust of World War II, when more than 6 million European Jews and several million more non-Jewish "undesirables" (including Gypsies, Poles, Slavs, political enemies, Jehovah's Witnesses, Catholic clergy, homosexuals, and people with disabilities) were moved to concentration camps and executed by the German Nazis (Friedman 1995). Since then, genocide, or "ethnic cleansing," has destroyed more millions of lives in Eastern Europe, Southeast Asia, and Africa. It is also possible to consider the violence perpetuated by the early Americans against the Native American tribes who occupied North America as a form of genocide. While Native Americans died from diseases introduced by the settlers, they were also systematically killed by the European colonists. In the few hundred years that it took for the United States to be settled from coast to coast, the Native American population was almost completely decimated. Estimates for the total number killed range anywhere from 15 million up to 100 million (Stannard 1993; Cook 1998).

Population Transfer

The treatment of Native Americans leads us to the next pattern of group relations—**population transfer**, or the forcible removal of a group of people from the territory they have occupied. In the early nineteenth century, Native Americans who had not perished in battles with U.S. soldiers were forced by the U.S. government to move onto Indian reservations (also referred to as tribal lands or American Indian nations) west of the Mississippi River. They were often moved far away from the lands where they had lived for generations (mostly Southern states), as these were desirable territories that the whites wished to acquire for themselves. Between 1838 and 1839, in one of the most well-known examples, the state of Georgia and the federal government forcibly marched 17,000 Cherokees westward over 800 miles, a grueling journey known as the "Trail of Tears." Along the way, over 4,000 people died of hunger, exposure, or disease.

The separate territories established for the Native Americans are an example of a kind of partitioning that we can see happening today in Israel between the Israelis and Palestinians in the West Bank and Gaza Strip. There, the Israeli government restricts the movement of Palestinians and has even built miles of barriers designed to wall them in and keep them separate from the Israeli population. Sometimes population transfer takes a more indirect

genocide the deliberate and systematic extermination of a racial, ethnic, national, or cultural group

population transfer the forcible removal of a group of people from the territory they have occupied

Changing the World

Stories of Genocide

The twentieth century witnessed numerous incidents of genocide. From 1915 to 1923, during and after World War I, the Turkish government massacred 1.5 million Armenians in what is often referred to as the "forgotten genocide." Nazi Germany under Adolf Hitler's rule killed two-thirds of the Jews of Europe. Few paid attention to the Armenian tragedy, and many refused to believe the initial reports of Hitler's death camps as well (Hitler himself recognized this, and is alleged to have asked, "Who remembers the Armenians?" when he embarked on his own genocidal project). In the latter half of the century, such events became all too common. From the atrocities of Darfur to Slobodan Milošević's ethnic cleansing in the Balkans and the Hutu slaughter of Tutsis in Rwanda, genocide has become a familiar feature of the modern landscape.

Faced with such overwhelming horror, it would be easy to give up and assume that there's nothing one person can do to stop it. However, this has not been the attitude of those who lived through these events, some of whom have begun recording their life histories. The documentarians who collect these stories hope to change the world in two different ways. First, they hope the histories will serve as a permanent reminder so that future generations might avert such tragedies. Second, they hope to provide some relief to the survivors, who are often traumatized and guilt ridden.

Around the world, for example, wherever Holocaust survivors have settled, archives have sprung up to record their testimony. The most ambitious of these programs may also be the most recent. In 1994, after filming *Schindler's List*, director Steven Spielberg founded the Survivors of the Shoah Visual History Foundation to document the experiences of Holocaust survivors. Spielberg believed the foundation's mission was particularly pressing because of the advanced age of most of the survivors. To capture their experiences, the foundation videotaped more than 51,000 testimonies in 32 languages by people living in 57 countries. These interviews are available to anyone, not just researchers, and are especially valuable to the communities where they were recorded.

Another project comes from Donald and Lorna Miller, who present a written record of the Armenian tragedy in their book *Survivors: An Oral History of the Armenian Genocide* (1999). After interviewing 100 survivors, the authors chronicled their experiences of brutality, despair, strength, and hope for future generations. And the photography exhibit "I Witness," which toured the United States in 2002, features portraits of aging Armenian survivors taken by photographers and activists Ara Oshagan and Levon Parian.

Telling these stories is immensely painful but also very important to survivors. This is why, even 50 years later, so many come forward to be interviewed. As Miriam Fridman, president of the Holocaust Survivors of South Florida, put it: "Telling our story rips us apart . . . but they will see us, know that we existed and what happened. Then we leave a legacy that history should not repeat" (quoted in Adams 1994). The Armenian ethnographer Verjine Svazlian offered her collection of life histories "as an evidence of the past and a warning for the future" (Svazlian 2000).

This sort of large-scale enterprise is not necessarily available for victims of more recent crises. Atrocities in the Balkans, Sudan, Rwanda, and elsewhere have created a large new refugee population that does not yet have the

form. For instance, it is possible to make life so miserable in a region that a group of people will choose to leave "voluntarily." This was the case with early Mormons, whose religious persecution in the East and Midwest between 1846 and 1869 drove 70,000 to cross the country (taking what is called the Mormon Pioneer Trail) and settle in the Great Salt Lake Valley region of Utah.

internal colonialism the economic and political domination and subjugation of the minority group by the controlling group within a nation

Internal Colonialism and Segregation

The term *colonialism* refers to a policy whereby a stronger nation takes control of a weaker foreign nation (the "colony") in order to extend its territory or to exploit the colony's resources for its own enrichment. The "British Empire," which once included such distant countries as India, Burma (now Myanmar), the West Indies, South Africa, and Australia, as well as America before its independence, is an example of colonialism. **Internal colonialism** describes

Survivors of Genocide Holocaust survivor Ehud Valter, 79, displays the card documenting his transfer between the Auschwitz and Buchenwald concentration camps. Anna Karakian, 101, survived the mass killings of Armenians in 1915 in what was then the Ottoman Empire.

organization or the resources to create something like the Shoah Foundation (though see the creative nonfiction book *What Is the What* [Eggers 2006]). They do, however, have a desperate need to document their experiences.

Does the telling of stories of genocide actually help to prevent such events? Earlier life histories don't seem to have prevented racism and intolerance: after all, ethnic violence and genocide seem to be alive and well in the world today. However, we might argue that changing the world for the better is a process to engage in, not a goal that can be reached. In each generation atrocities will be committed, and each generation must reach out to the survivors and look for the seeds of social change. Telling and preserving stories can change the world—even if only one person at a time.

the exploitation of a minority group within the dominant group's own borders.

Internal colonialism often takes the form of economic exploitation and includes some sort of physical **segregation** of groups by race or ethnicity. For example, in the U.S. South up to the 1960s, not only did blacks live in separate neighborhoods, they were restricted to "coloreds"-only sections of buses, parks, restaurants, and even drinking fountains. If members of the minority group live close by yet in their own part of town (for instance, on the "other side of the tracks"), they are separate, and hence unequal, but still near enough to serve as workers for the dominant group.

Assimilation

With **assimilation**, a minority group is absorbed into the dominant group: this process

segregation the formal and legal separation of groups by race or ethnicity

assimilation a pattern of relations between ethnic or racial groups in which the minority group is absorbed into the mainstream or dominant group, making society more homogenous

racial assimilation the process by which racial minority groups are absorbed into the dominant group through intermarriage

cultural assimilation the process by which racial or ethnic groups are absorbed into the dominant group by adopting the dominant group's culture

pluralism a cultural pattern of intergroup relations that encourages racial and ethnic variation within a society

is the central idea behind America's "melting pot." On the surface, assimilation seems like a reasonable solution to the potential conflicts between different groups. If everyone belongs to the same group, if the society is largely homogenous, then conflict will decrease.

During much of the twentieth century, immigrants to the United States were eager to adopt an American way of life, become citizens, learn English, and lose any trace of their "foreign-ness." The Irish, Italians, and Eastern Europeans were all once considered "ethnics" but eventually assimilated into the larger category of white Americans. Today they are practically unrecognizable as distinct ethnic groups, unless they choose to emphasize characteristics that would so distinguish them. It is likely that this process will continue with the newer wave of immigrants; for instance, some census-type forms no longer distinguish Hispanic or Middle Eastern as separate categories from white.

But although there is something to be gained by assimilation, namely, membership in the dominant population, there is also something to be sacrificed. Minority group members may lose their previous ethnic or racial identity, either through **racial assimilation** (having children with the dominant group until the different races are completely mixed) or through **cultural assimilation**, in which members learn the cultural practices of the dominant group. In some cases, both types of assimilation take place at the same time.

In addition, the process of assimilation is not always entered into voluntarily. Sometimes a minority group may be forced to acquire new behaviors and forbidden to practice their own religion or speak their own language, until these are all but forgotten. For some, assimilation results in the tragic loss of a distinctive racial or ethnic identity. This is true for many Native Americans, for instance, who in just a few generations have lost the ability to speak their tribal languages or have forgotten cultural practices of their not-so-distant ancestors.

Pluralism

Pluralism not only permits racial and ethnic variation within one society, it actually encourages people to embrace diversity—to exchange the traditional melting pot image for a "salad bowl." In the last few decades, the United States has seen more and more groups celebrating their racial or ethnic roots, developing a strong common consciousness, and expressing pride in their unique identity.

At the core of multiculturalism is tolerance of racial and ethnic differences. A country like Switzerland provides an interesting example. Although the Swiss are largely homogenous in terms of race, the country is made up of several major ethnic and linguistic groups, including Protestants and Catholics as well as speakers of French, German, and Italian, who live in relative harmony and equality. There is little of the prejudice and discrimination that characterize other, diverse European countries. But the Swiss were not always so tolerant of diversity; their history is rife with ethnic conflict and the threat of civil war. It was not until 1848 that a new constitution established a legal system designed to share power among different groups, making sure that each had proportional representation at all levels of government. There is also no one "official" language; rather, all three are considered the national languages. Although some have called Switzerland an exception when it comes to multiculturalism, others claim that its success is due precisely to a political system that legislates democratic pluralism and depends on minorities being continually accommodated so that none become disenfranchised (Schmid 1981).

Another example of successful multiculturalism is Canada. This country's population is even more diverse than Switzerland's, composed of not only two official linguistic groups (English and French) but also ethnic and racial minorities that include European, Chinese, and Indian immigrants as well as members of "First Nations," or Canadian native peoples. The Canadian government is committed to the ideals of multiculturalism, with a great deal of funding directed to programs aimed at improving race relations and encouraging multicultural harmony. As a sign of that commitment, the 1988 Canadian Multiculturalism Act declares that the role of government is to bring about "equal access for all Canadians in the economic, social, cultural, and political realms" (K. Mitchell 1993).

The United States is still moving toward becoming a more multicultural and egalitarian society, although in recent years there has been a backlash against the idea of pluralism. Some critics blame the educational system for allowing what they consider marginal academic areas, such as ethnic studies, women's studies, gay and lesbian studies, and the like, to be featured alongside the classic curriculum. Others question the need for bilingual education and English as a Second Language (ESL) programs, despite research showing benefits to nonnative speakers (Krashen 1996). And groups such as U.S. English and English First advocate for legislation making English the national language and setting limits on the use of other languages. Nevertheless, since the future seems sure to bring an ever greater racial and ethnic mix to the country, Americans may yet be able to incorporate multiculturalism into our sense of national identity.

Closing Comments

Constructing categories of race and ethnicity seems inevitably to lead to stratification and inequality and such destructive social processes as stereotyping, segregation, prejudice, and discrimination. Are there any positive consequences, either for society or for individuals? As it turns out, there are.

Racial and ethnic categories help create a sense of identity for members of these groups, which can lead to feelings of unity and solidarity—a sense of belonging to something that is larger than oneself, of cultural connection, and of shared history. We see this in action during ethnic festivals and holidays. When we share our own group unity with others in this way, we contribute to the diversity of our community and society. The more we understand and appreciate the diverse population of our nation, the less likely we may be to contribute to the destructive consequences of racial and ethnic categorization.

The important sociological insight here is that since categories of race and ethnicity are socially constructed, their meanings are socially constructed as well. Historically, we have constructed meanings that favor some and exploit and oppress others. Is it possible to construct meanings for racial and ethnic categories that value and celebrate them all? Over time, and with your newly acquired sociological insights, we hope you will be part of that transformation.

 Find more review materials online at
www.wwnorton.com/studyspace

CHAPTER SUMMARY

- **Defining Race and Ethnicity** Social scientists see race and ethnicity as social constructions: they are not rooted in biological differences, they change over time, and they never have firm boundaries. In America, almost everyone has ancestors from multiple racial groups, regardless of which race or ethnicity they identify with. Similarly, sociologists have found that the boundaries of "whiteness" in America have changed over the years, especially with regard to non-Protestant European immigrants.

- Both race and ethnicity are social categories, but they are not interchangeable. Race is based on real or perceived physical differences, while ethnicity is based on cultural differences, like language, religion, or history. The distinction is important, because ethnicity can be displayed or hidden, depending on individual preference, whereas racial identities are always on display and never optional. Symbolic and situational ethnicity both refer to the display of ethnicity on special occasions or when it is beneficial.

- **What Is a Minority?** Race and ethnicity are often the basis for social stratification and unequal distribution of resources. Those racial and ethnic groups that are denied access to power and resources are called minority groups, even though they may outnumber the dominant group. Membership in a minority group is often a master status that matters in almost every aspect of life.

- **Racism, Prejudice, and Discrimination** Social inequality based on race and ethnicity persists because of racism, which leads to discrimination and prejudice. Prejudice involves using a belief about a whole group to prejudge individual group members. Prejudice often leads to discrimination, actions or behaviors that deny someone opportunities or resources because of her racial or ethnic identity. Although many white Americans believe that racism is no longer a serious problem, most racial and ethnic minorities still see discrimination as commonplace.

- **Theoretical Approaches to Race in America** Sociologists have offered several theories to explain the critical role of race in our society. Functionalist theorists focus on the ways that race creates social ties and strengthens group bonds, though they also recognize that racial issues can lead to social conflict. Conflict theorists emphasize the ways that race is related to class and the economy. Early conflict theories, often focused on the American South, tried to explain race as the result of economic oppression; newer conflict theories aim to explain race in a more diverse society. Symbolic interactionists have focused on the ways that race, class, and gender intersect to produce individuals' identities. This chapter is rooted in the symbolic interactionist tradition, which sees race not as some essence that individuals possess but as an aspect of identity established through interaction.

- **Race, Ethnicity, and Life Chances** Race and ethnicity influence every part of our lives, including health, education, work, family, and interactions with the criminal justice system. In all of these areas people of color suffer wide-ranging effects as a result of racism and discrimination. Nonwhites tend to have less access than whites to education, well-paying jobs, and health care, and they tend to interact with law enforcement more often. Because we live in a racially stratified society, whites tend to take for granted privileges denied to others.

- **Race Relations** Interactions between dominant and subordinate groups can take the form of genocide, population transfer, internal colonialism, segregation, assimilation, and pluralism. The first four of these patterns are manifestations of hostility and antagonism on the part of the dominant group. Many people believe that assimilation is a positive change, but others worry that it erases distinctive and valuable elements of racial and ethnic identities. For this reason, multiculturalism has become more popular within the United States in recent years, as it emphasizes the value of preserving many different identities.

QUESTIONS FOR REVIEW

1. How do you identify yourself in terms of race or ethnicity? Are there special occasions or situations in which you are more likely to display your ethnicity or race? Do you identify with more than one racial or ethnic group or know anyone who does? What does this tell you about the origin of these categories?

2. Do you ever find yourself buying into prejudices? Can you think of examples of prejudices based on positive attitudes? What do you think is the long-term effect of such "positive" prejudices?

3. Many sociologists believe that institutional discrimination causes more harm than individual discrimination in the long run. Can you think of a social, political, or economic institution whose policies systematically benefit one racial group more than another?

4. This chapter argued that racial and ethnic identities are accomplished in interaction. Do you notice anything about the way you talk, the type of clothes you wear, your body movements, or facial expressions that project your racial identity? Have you ever changed something about yourself because you weren't comfortable with the identity it projected?

5. Robert Park, a functionalist theorist, believed that communication and exchange between racial and ethnic groups would inevitably lead to integration and the elimination of racial diversity, though it has become apparent that this theory is more applicable to some groups than to others. For whom is this kind of integration effective, and why?

6. Affirmative action in college admissions is one of the most controversial topics in America today. Why would a college want to consider race or ethnicity when making admissions decisions? What factors do you think admissions boards should consider?

7. Two metaphors are often used to describe the future of racial and ethnic relations in the United States: the "melting pot" and the "salad bowl." What are the differences between these two phrases, and which one do you think best describes the United States? What are the advantages and disadvantages of each model?

8. Although the Supreme Court ruled against antimiscegenation laws in 1967, homogamy, or assortive mating, is reinforced by social conventions. Would you date someone of a different race? Does your answer change depending on which racial or ethnic group you're thinking about?

9. This chapter described six different types of intergroup relations, ranging from genocide to multiculturalism. Choose three of these patterns and provide real-world examples not mentioned in the chapter. Do you think modern societies are trending one way or another?

SUGGESTIONS FOR FURTHER EXPLORATION

Ararat. 2002. Dir. Atom Egoyan. Miramax Films. Examines the Armenian genocide that took place in Turkey in 1915 as well as the contemporary cultural memory of the event and its lasting impact on the Turkish and Armenian peoples.

Bamboozled. 2000. Dir. Spike Lee. New Line Cinema. In this dark, biting satire of the television industry, a new minstrel show, complete with actors in blackface, becomes a surprise hit. Lee makes parallels between minstrel and contemporary hip-hop, pointing out the ways that blacks are involved in perpetuating racism.

Crash. 2005. Dir. Paul Haggis. Lion's Gate Films. This movie follows the interlocking lives of two dozen Los Angeles residents over the course of two days. In this socially and racially diverse group, people collide with one another in shocking and sometimes unsettling ways.

Darfur Is Dying (www.darfurisdying.com). This free, web-based video game about the atrocities in the Darfur region of Sudan aims to inspire social activism by connecting players to the lives of those suffering in the genocide. In the game, the player's character must try to provide for the needs of his or her fellow refugees without being captured by militiamen.

Gourevitch, Philip. 1998. *We Wish to Inform You that Tomorrow We Will Be Killed with Our Families: Stories from Rwanda.* New York: Picador. Details the modern genocide between the Tutsi and Hutu people in Rwanda. Although the book is an excellent illustration of the way that racial categories are socially constructed, Gourevitch writes for many of the same reasons that museums record the testimony of Holocaust survivors. As he puts it, "the best reason I have come up with for looking more closely into Rwanda's horror stories is that ignoring them makes me more uncomfortable about existence and my place in it."

Kingston, Maxine Hong. 1989. *The Woman Warrior: Memoirs of a Girlhood among Ghosts.* New York: Vintage. A memoir of growing up Chinese American in California, the child of immigrant parents. Like many social theorists, Kingston focuses on race as it is experienced by the individual and the ways that the meaning of race changes depending on one's social position.

Massey, Douglas, and Nancy Denton. 1993. *American Apartheid: Segregation and the Making of the Underclass.* Cambridge, MA: Harvard University Press. A sociological analysis of the way that segregation continues in America and its important consequences for race relations.

Moraga, Cherríe, and Gloria Anzaldúa, eds. 1984. *This Bridge Called My Back: Writings by Radical Women of Color.* New York: Kitchen Table/Women of Color Press. A collection of writings that approach race, class, gender, and sexuality from many different angles, always emphasizing the meaning of race as individuals experience it and the relationships between these categories.

Oliver, Melvin, and Thomas Shapiro. 1997. *Black Wealth, White Wealth: A New Perspective on Racial Inequality.* London: Routledge. A contemporary, class-based account of racial inequality; the authors argue that differences in wealth, not income, hold the key to understanding racial inequality.

Project Implicit (implicit.harvard.edu). An intriguing research project at Harvard University that is finding new ways to measure racial attitudes, assuming that any traditional survey of attitudes about race and ethnicity will be hampered because on these issues, "people don't always 'speak their minds,' and it is suspected that people don't always 'know their minds.'"

Rose, Tricia. 1994. *Black Noise: Rap Music and Black Culture in Contemporary America.* Middletown, CT: Wesleyan University Press. The fourth chapter, "Prophets of Rage: Rap Music and the Politics of Black Cultural Expression," offers a detailed analysis of the way that songs like "Illegal Search" by LL Cool J and "Who Protects Us from You" by KRS-ONE protest police harassment and brutality toward young black men.

Senna, Danzy. *Caucasia.* New York: Riverhead Trade. A moving novel about one young girl's experience of "passing." Birdie, the narrator, is the child of a racially mixed couple in Boston in the 1970s. When her parents split up, she stays with her mother and passes as white. The novel takes an unflinching look at the cost of being the child of a mixed-race couple in a racially intolerant society and the equally demanding pressures of passing as white.

CHAPTER 10

Constructing Gender and Sexuality

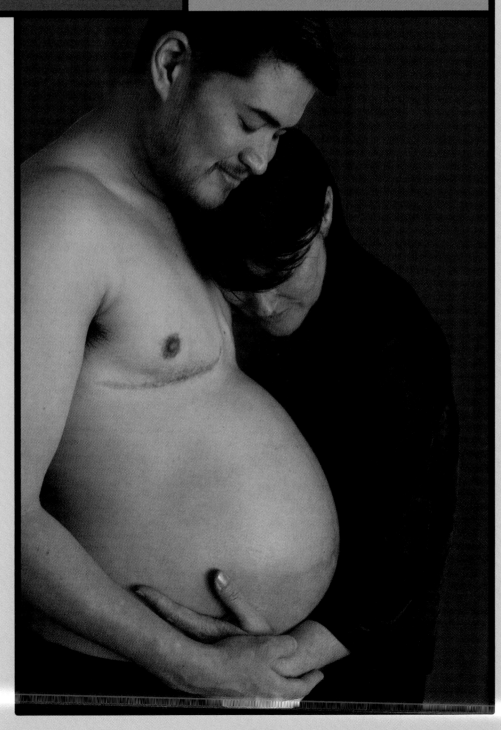

As far as their neighbors were concerned, there didn't seem to be anything particularly unusual about Thomas Beatie and his wife Nancy Roberts, a happily married couple in Bend, Oregon, with their own successful printing company. There's also nothing especially newsworthy about a healthy pregnancy, five months along, with no complications, and two happy parents-to-be. But in the case of Thomas and Nancy, reporters from all over the world were suddenly focused on their growing family. Why the interest? Because it was Thomas who was pregnant, not Nancy.

In March of 2008, *The Advocate* (a magazine devoted to a largely gay and lesbian readership) published an autobiographical piece, "Labor of Love," by Thomas Beatie, describing his decision to become pregnant. For most people the phrase "pregnant man" is an oxymoron, something that can't exist in reality. In fact, several neighbors told reporters they thought the whole thing was a hoax. Even the picture that ran in *The Advocate*, showing a clearly masculine Thomas naked from the waist up with a neatly trimmed beard and a pregnant belly, failed to convince everyone. But even the most skeptical had to admit he was really pregnant after an appearance on *Oprah*, when he let her camera crew tag along to the doctor's office for his ultrasound.

Beatie has been described as the world's first pregnant man, which isn't exactly true, but he certainly is the first one most Americans have heard of. He was born a girl, named Tracy Lagondino, but in his early 20s he decided to transition from female to male. He had a double-mastectomy and took testosterone, which helps to increase muscle mass, lower the register of the voice, and grow facial hair. Thomas, like many **transsexual** men, or "transmen," had not had his ovaries or uterus removed when he transitioned. His wife, Nancy, had a difficult pregnancy earlier in life that had left her unable to bear any children. So when they decided to start a family, Thomas stopped taking his hormones so he could carry the child. The couple used an anonymous sperm donor and did the insemination themselves at home, and Thomas conceived without the need for any fertility drugs or other treatment. On June 29, 2008, after 40 hours in labor, Thomas gave birth to a 9 pound, 5 ounce baby girl named Susan. When she arrived, her mother, Nancy, breastfed her.

Thomas and Nancy had encountered a lot of opposition to starting their family. They were rejected by nine different doctors when they first tried to get pregnant,

SocIndex

Then and Now

1960: Most American hospitals ban fathers from the delivery room

2008: Some 93–98% of expectant fathers plan to attend their child's birth

Here and There

Afghanistan: Maternal mortality rates equal 1,900 per 100,000 live births

United States: Maternal mortality rates equal 17 per 100,000 live births

This and That

Most common cause of death for women in the United States: heart disease

Most common cause of death for pregnant women in the United States: homicide

expressive roles. In your family, were the nurturing and emotional support primarily provided by women? How do these gendered expectations reinforce the traditional family structure? How do they perpetuate gender inequality?

5. From an interactional perspective, gender is not an internal essence, but something we achieve through interaction. This implies that throughout everyday life we are "doing gender." Picture the gendered differences in behaviors like sitting, walking, or conversing. Can you think of a time when you did gender "wrong" and other people reacted negatively? Why did they react this way?

6. Consider the ways you were socialized by your family. In what ways was your socialization gendered? What toys did you play with as a child? What extracurricular activities were you encouraged to pursue? What household chores did you perform?

7. The second shift refers to the housework that must be done after the day's paid labor is complete; women do a disproportionate amount of this work. Why do you think this is? What types of tasks does our society expect women to do? How do the tasks expected of men differ?

8. Do you believe that there is a "gay gene"? Why do you think so many people have strong opinions on the possibility of a genetic component of sexual orientation, even though research in this area is just beginning? What is at stake in this debate?

9. Television has played an important role in perpetuating stereotypes about homosexuals. For years, portrayals of gays and lesbians on television were quite rare—and typically negative. In recent years this has started to change, with more shows offering positive representations of homosexual characters. How have such changes affected social attitudes about gays and lesbians?

SUGGESTIONS FOR FURTHER EXPLORATION

The Aggressives. 2005. Dir. Daniel Peddle. Image Entertainment. A documentary that follows women who feel more comfortable dressing and acting as men. The film documents the women's efforts at passing—even those who interact with them closely don't always know they are women—and as the name suggests, this involves changes in demeanor as much as in clothing and hair cuts.

Amnesty International's *Stop Violence Against Women* campaign (web.amnesty.org/actforwomen/index-eng). This site provides information and resources to help fight violence against women around the world.

Bly, Robert. 2004. *Iron John*. Cambridge, MA: DaCapo Press. A touchstone of the branch of the men's movement that remains allied with feminist goals. Bly argues that men need to find ways to become more introspective about aggression and responsibility.

Butler, Judith. 2000. *Gender Trouble: Feminism and the Subversion of Identity*, 10th ed. New York: Routledge. A demanding read and one of the most influential studies of the social and political origins of the sex/gender system.

Eugenides, Jeffrey. 2003. *MiddleSex*. New York: Picador. A novel about Cal Stephanides, born Calliope Stephanides, who discovers at age 14 that genetically and chromosomally—even if not anatomically—he is male. The novel incorporates fantastical elements to explore issues surrounding the scientific study and the lived experience of gender.

Naylor, Gloria. 1985. *The Women of Brewster Place*. New York: Penguin. This novel follows a group of seven African American women living in the same apartment building who must rely on each other to survive in a world where they are disadvantaged by their race, class, and gender.

Paragraph 175. 2000. Dir. Rob Epstein and Jeffrey Friedman. Telling Pictures. A documentary about the persecution of homosexuals in Nazi Germany, named after the section of the German penal code that criminalized homosexuality. This law, written long before the Nazis came to power, stayed on the books until 1973.

Sedgewick, Eve Kosofsky. 1991. *The Epistemology of the Closet*. Berkeley: University of California Press. This highly influential work of queer theory closely examines the ways that our categories for sexual identities shape contemporary society.

Russo, Vito. 1987. *The Celluloid Closet: Homosexuality in the Movies*. New York: HarperCollins. Like the 1995 documentary of the same name, this book offers a sharp, insightful analysis of the ways that institutional homophobia has played out in the movies, in everything from *Spartacus* to *Philadelphia*.

Trembling Before G-d. 2001. Dir. Sandi Simcha Dubowski. New Yorker Films. This film documents the lives of gays and lesbians in the Orthodox Jewish community, paying close attention to the tensions that result from the strict prohibition of homosexuality within Orthodox Judaism.

PART IV

Examining Social Institutions as Sites of Everyday Life

Our everyday lives take place within the contexts of many overlapping and interdependent social institutions. A social institution is a collection of patterned social practices that are repeated continuously and regularly over time and supported by social norms. Politics, the economy, family, religion, and education are all social institutions, and you have contact with many of these (and others) on a daily basis. The patterns and structures of social institutions shape your individual experiences; at the same time, it's important to remember that social institutions are created, maintained, and changed by individual actions.

In the next four chapters, we will look at specific social institutions, such as politics, education, and religion (Chapter 11), the economy (Chapter 12), the family (Chapter 13), and recreation and leisure (Chapter 14), and their role in structuring your everyday life. You will be introduced to a variety of sociological research that focuses on how these social institutions and others work; here, we highlight a sociological researcher whose work integrates many of them. In his book *Heat Wave: A Social Autopsy of Disaster in Chicago* (2002), Eric Klinenberg examines the circumstances surrounding Chicago's catastrophic heat wave in 1995, which killed over 700 people. Klinenberg analyzes the week-long heat wave as more than a meteorological phenomenon. People died, he argues, because of a combination of disturbing demographic trends and dangerous institutional policies present at all times in all major urban areas.

For one week in mid-July of 1995, the city of Chicago suffered the worst heat wave in its history: Temperatures exceeded 100 degrees for four days in a row, and heat indices (the "real feel" air temperature) hit a high of 126 degrees. Historic buildings baked like ovens, but fear of crime left many people feeling trapped inside their apartments. Children passed out in overheated school buses. City residents blasted their air conditioning (if they had it), mobbed the tiny beaches on Lake Michigan, and broke open fire hydrants to stay cool. As a result, power outages peppered the area and water pressure dropped dangerously. Roads buckled, train tracks warped, and people suffered from heat-related illnesses in large numbers. The city's 911 emergency system overloaded, and some callers waited two hours for ambulances to arrive; more than 20 hospitals closed their emergency rooms, overwhelmed with patients. The death toll mounted, with the elderly and the poor especially vulnerable. In this single week, 739 Chicagoans died as a result of the heat. According to Klinenberg, the individual "isolation, deprivation, and vulnerability" that led to these deaths resulted from a variety of institutional structures, including poverty, racial segregation, family dislocation, and city politics. These institutional arrangements must be examined and changed in order to avoid future tragedies.

Many of those who died during the heat wave were elderly people who lived alone: sick or fragile, their mobility compromised, their neighborhoods changing around them, their families far away or neglectful, and their social networks dissolving. In many cases, the elderly victims of the heat wave were so isolated that no one ever claimed their bodies (p. 15). The story of Pauline Jankowitz, 85, who survived the heat wave, illustrates these demographic trends (pp. 50–54). Pauline lives alone on the third floor of an apartment building with no elevator. She suffers from incontinence and walks with a crutch. She recognizes her vulnerability, and leaves her apartment only once every two months. Her two children live in other states and rarely visit, so a volunteer from a charitable organization does Pauline's weekly grocery shopping. However, Pauline no longer has any connections with her immigrant neighbors and spends most of her time in her apartment listening to radio talk shows. Pauline's isolation is hardly unique. Her circumstances

illustrate the ways that the geographic mobility of the contemporary family, the changing populations of urban neighborhoods, the financial limitations of retirement incomes, and the lack of supportive social services all contribute to situations in which elderly individuals may live, face crises, and die alone.

Klinenberg argues that race and class inequality also contributed to the death toll in the Chicago heat wave. He shows that the death tolls were highest in the city's "black belt," a group of predominantly African American neighborhoods on the south and west sides of the city. (These neighborhoods also have relatively high levels of poverty and crime and relatively large populations of elderly residents.) Social ties in these neighborhoods are hard to maintain: Poverty contributes to residential transiency, so neighbors may not get to know one another before they must move to different housing elsewhere. Gang activity and crime make residents afraid to walk down the street or sit on their own front porches. And although some of the neighborhoods in question have powerful religious organizations in their midst, even the most proactive church needs significant financial resources to reach out to its members—and such resources may be hard to come by in poor neighborhoods. So, a person's risk of heat-related death during July of 1995 was partly place-based. In Chicago, as in most major cities, place, race, and class are closely connected.

In July 1995, Chicago's government services also failed in a number of ways when the city's residents needed them most. However, Klinenberg argues that the city's bureaucracies were no more ill-prepared to deal with catastrophe during that week than during any other. Long-term, macro-level changes in city politics mean that both the political will and the material resources to provide assistance to the poor were fatally absent. For example, overextended paramedics and firefighters had no centralized office with which to register their observations or complaints. As a result, many problems went unheeded by the city until emergency services were too swamped to provide timely assistance. There was little coordination between the local, state, and federal agencies that dealt with social welfare and emergency services. Finally, Klinenberg indicts city officials for "governing by public relations" (p. 143)—that is, for using the mass media to deflect attention from the city's problems, including minimizing both the scope of the heat wave and the city's accountability.

Klinenberg's "social autopsy" reveals the failure of social institutions on a massive scale—and the disturbing prospect that this disaster could happen again, anywhere, if we do not take steps to change flawed social systems. Structural and institutional arrangements—including city government, race- and class-based segregation, families, schools, religious organizations, and the media—must change in order to avoid individual tragedies. But individual actions help bring about institutional change, and *Heat Wave* reveals important ways in which all our fates intertwine, as they are shaped by the social institutions we encounter every day. How can we better manage this interdependence, for the good of all?

The Macro-Micro Link in Social Institutions

CHAPTER 11

Politics, Education, and Religion

You probably know the Pledge of Allegiance by heart and have said it countless times in elementary and high school, but you may not have thought much about its words or why you were required to say them.

> I pledge allegiance to the Flag
>
> of the United States of America,
>
> and to the Republic for which it stands:
>
> one Nation, under God, indivisible,
>
> with Liberty and Justice for all.

Reciting the pledge was just a routine part of being a student in the United States. Could it possibly be controversial? A lot of people think so. The Pledge of Allegiance brings together questions about three important social institutions in American life: politics, education, and religion, as you will see.

Dr. Michael Newdow, an emergency room physician and self-described atheist in California, is committed to preserving the separation of church and state. When his daughter's second-grade class began reciting the Pledge of Allegiance, Newdow became disturbed because it contained the phrase "one Nation, *under God*." Acting as his own attorney, Newdow filed a lawsuit, and in February 2003 the 9th Circuit Court held the pledge to be in violation of the Constitution because the reference to God violated the separation of church and state.

Many civic and political leaders—liberals as well as conservatives—denounced the decision. The Senate passed a resolution condemning it, and the attorney general announced that the Justice Department would "spare no effort to preserve the rights of all our citizens to pledge allegiance to the American flag" (H. Weinstein 2003). Almost universally lawmakers came out in defense of the pledge, agreeing with Judge Ferdinand Fernandez, who in his dissenting opinion argued that the phrase *under God* had "no tendency to establish a religion in this country or to suppress anyone's exercise, or non-exercise, of religion, except in the fevered eye of persons who most fervently would like to drive all tincture of religion out of the public life of our polity" (Egelko 2002). Ultimately, the case went all the way to the Supreme Court, which overturned the lower court's ruling on a technicality but did not address whether the language in the pledge violates the First Amendment.

The Pledge of Allegiance was originally written in 1892 and did not contain the phrase *under God*; that was added in 1954, when President Eisenhower signed a bill making the change official. The added words generated no controversy at the time. The president declared that their addition would affirm "the dedication of our nation and our people to the Almighty" and Senator Joseph McCarthy "said it was a clear indication that the United States was committed to ending the threat of 'godless' Communism" (Brinkley-Rogers 2002).

Since as early as 1943 the Supreme Court has ruled that children cannot be forced to recite the pledge. In 1943, the issue addressed was the patriotic nature of the pledge. However, a 2002 ruling by Judge Alfred Goodwin states that reciting the pledge in public schools "places students in the untenable position of choosing between participating in an exercise with religious content or protesting," an especially damaging scenario because "the coercive effect of the policy here is particularly pronounced in the school setting, given the age and impressionability of schoolchildren" (H. Weinstein 2003). After all, how many second graders will be willing to stand out from their peers in so dramatic a fashion?

Although there is a great deal of disagreement over what should be done in this case, all the participants agree, even if only implicitly, that social institutions play an important role in the lives of Americans. **Social institutions** (systems and structures that organize our group life, such as school, religion, and the government) shape and constrain our everyday lives. For example, if school starts at 8:00 A.M. and ends at 3:00 P.M., this structures the life of an entire household—it dictates what time children should go to bed and get up in the morning; when breakfast and dinner are prepared, served, and eaten; and what types of arrangements must be made for transportation, after-school activities, and child care. In turn, these same institutions are created and sustained through our everyday interaction. For example, a school exists only because of the actions of the teachers, students, parents, and administrators who are part of the surrounding community.

Social institutions represent a bit of a sociological paradox. They function at the macro level to shape our everyday interactions, but at the micro level those same everyday interactions construct social institutions. Because they are at the center of both micro- and macrosociology, social institutions give us the opportunity to examine the connection between interaction and structure, between the individual and society. In this chapter, we will focus on the social institutions of religion, education, and government as places where the micro and the macro come together, and we will show how the intersections between social institutions shape everyday life.

social institutions systems and structures within society that shape the activities of groups and individuals

HOW TO READ THIS CHAPTER

We have devoted entire chapters to other social institutions such as work and family, but here we have grouped politics, education, and religion together for a reason. These institutions intersect in distinctive and often unexamined ways in our everyday lives—the daily recitation of the Pledge of Allegiance is just one example. Local and national controversies over school vouchers or sex education are other examples of the ways in which political, educational, and religious concerns overlap. Every day we make decisions or engage in debates that address moral values, political practicalities, and educational expectations all bundled together.

When you read this chapter, we want you to be able to see the relationships among these three social institutions as well as to make the connection between micro- and macrosociology. This is a key opportunity to use the sociological theories and methods you have learned in previous chapters to find the intersections between individual experience and social structure, and the overlaps between various social institutions in everyday life. After reading this chapter, you should have a deeper understanding of how social institutions shape your individual experience and how you as an individual contribute to shaping those institutions.

What Is Politics?

Politics has concerned social thinkers since at least the time of the philosophers in ancient Greece. The word *politics* comes from the Greek *politikos* meaning citizens, civic, civil, and political. As a sociological term, **politics** pertains especially to the methods and tactics of managing a political entity such as a nation or state, as well as the administration and control of its internal and external affairs. But it can also mean the attitudes and activities of groups and individuals. To understand the relationship between citizens and their particular political environment, we must first look at the variety of different political systems and study the American system of democracy. Then we will examine elections and voting, lobbies and special interest groups, and the role of the media in the political process.

Political Systems: Government

Government is the formal, organized agency that exercises power and control in modern society. Governments are vested with the power and authority to make laws and enforce them. As you probably remember from Chapter 2, Weber defined **power** as the ability to get others to do one's bidding. When sociologists talk about **authority**, they refer to the legitimate, noncoercive exercise of power. Throughout the world and throughout history, governments have taken a variety of forms. When evaluating types of governance as sociologists, we ask certain questions about the relationship between leaders and followers: who has power and who does not, what kind of power is exerted, and how far does that power extend?

TOTAL POWER AND AUTHORITY **Authoritarianism** is a political system that denies ordinary citizens representation by and control over their own government. Thus, citizens have no say in who rules them, what laws are made, and how those laws are enforced. Generally, political power is concentrated in the hands of a few elites who control military and economic resources. A *dictatorship* is one form of authoritarian system. In most instances, a dictator does not gain power by being elected or through succession but seizes power and becomes an absolutist ruler. Dictators may gain control through a military coup, as occurred when General Augusto Pinochet came to power in Chile in 1973. In other cases, leaders may be legally elected or appointed but then become dictators once in power, abolishing any constitutional limits on their authority—such as President Charles Taylor of Liberia, who was deposed in 2003 and is currently facing international war crime charges in The Hague. Dictators are most often individuals but can also be associated with political parties or groups such as the Taliban in Afghanistan.

Totalitarianism is the most extreme and modern version of authoritarianism. The government seeks to control every aspect, public and private, of citizens' lives. Unlike older forms of authoritarianism, a totalitarian government can utilize all the contrivances of surveillance technology, systems of mass communication, and modern weapons to control its citizens (Arendt 1958). Totalitarian governments are usually headed by a dictator, whether a ruler or a single political party. Through propaganda, totalitarian regimes can further control the population by disseminating ideology aimed at shaping their thoughts, values, and attitudes.

politics methods and tactics intended to influence government policy; policy-related attitudes, and activities

government the formal, organized agency that exercises power and control in modern society, especially through the creation and enforcement of laws

power the ability to impose one's will on others

authority the legitimate, noncoercive exercise of power

authoritarianism system of government by and for a small number of elites that does not include representation of ordinary citizens

Dictators Try to Control All Aspects of Citizens' Lives Leaders such as Kim Jong Il of North Korea, Augusto Pinochet of Chile, and Charles Taylor of Liberia led some of the world's most notorious dictatorships.

An example of a modern totalitarian ruler is Kim Jong Il of North Korea, whose nation has one of the worst human rights records in the world, restricts the basic freedoms of its people, and has a stagnant, internationally isolated economy.

MONARCHIES AND THE STATE Monarchies are governments ruled by a king or queen. In a **monarchy**, sovereignty is vested in a successive line of rulers, usually within a family, such as the Tudors of England, the Ming Dynasty of China, and the Romanovs of Russia. Nobility is handed down through family lines and can include numerous family members who hold royal titles. Monarchs are not popularly elected and not usually accountable to the general citizenry, and some may rule by "divine right," the idea that they are leaders chosen by God.

Monarchies can be divided into two categories: absolute and constitutional. Absolute monarchs typically have complete authority over their subjects, much like a dictator. Constitutional monarchs are royal figures whose powers are defined by a political charter and limited by a parliament or other governing body. Most monarchies were weakened, overthrown, or otherwise made obsolete during the many social revolutions of the eighteenth, nineteenth, and twentieth centuries such as the French Revolution (1789) and the Russian Revolution (1917). In contemporary times, some Asian and European nations, such as Japan, Thailand, Great Britain, or Sweden, still enjoy their royal families as national figureheads and celebrities, though their kings, queens, princes, and princesses don't have any real power in these constitutional monarchies.

> **monarchy** a government ruled by a king or queen, with succession of rulers kept within the family
>
> **democracy** a political system in which all citizens have the right to participate

There are, however, a few remaining modern examples of more absolute monarchies in the world, among them Saudi Arabia, Brunei, and Morocco.

CITIZENS AND DEMOCRACY Democracy originated in ancient Greece and represented a radical new political system. In a **democracy** citizens share in directing the activities of their government rather than being ruled by an autocratic individual or authoritarian group. The idea is that educated citizens should participate in the election of officials who then represent their interests in law making, law enforcement, resource allocation, and international affairs. Democracy is not only a political system but also a philosophy that emphasizes the right and capacity of individuals, acting either directly or through representatives, to control through majority rule the institutions that govern them. Democracy is also associated with the values of basic human rights, civil liberties, freedom, and equality.

Democracy may seem like the ideal system of government, but remember that not all citizens are equally represented even by a democratic government. In many democratic nations, women, ethnic or racial minorities, members of certain religions, and immigrants have been excluded from citizenship or from equal participation in the political process. In the United States, women did not have the right to vote until 1920. And while the Fifteenth Amendment to the U.S. Constitution technically gave adult males of all races voting rights in 1870, barriers such as poll taxes, literacy tests, and "grandfather clauses" kept African Americans from exercising those rights for almost 100 years, until the 1965 Voting Rights Act was passed. Native Americans were legally excluded from voting in federal elections until 1924, and residents of the District of Columbia were not allowed to vote for president until 1961. As you can see, even the world's leading democracy has not always seen all citizens as equal.

The American Political System

When American colonists rebelled against British authority in 1776, they created the first modern democracy. American democracy, however, is much more complicated than "rule by the people." In the following sections, we focus on voting, theories about who governs, the power of interest groups, and the influence of the mass media on the political system.

VOTING IN THE UNITED STATES The American political system prides itself on being a democracy, a government that confers power to the people. In this form of government, power is formally exercised through the election process, which provides each person with a vote. Sociologists have long been interested in the social factors—such as age, education, religion, or ethnic background—that influence whether and how individuals vote.

By the end of the twentieth century, many had become concerned about a steady, decades-long decline in American voter turnout. For example, in the 1960 presidential election, 63 percent of the electorate cast ballots, but by 1996, that number fell to below 50 percent for the first time since 1924.

Voter turnout began improving in the 2004 presidential election, but it is important to consider how voter turnout has been measured. Prior to the 2004 election, the voter turnout rate was typically calculated by dividing the total number of votes by the "voting-age population"—*everyone* aged 18 and older residing in the United States. This figure included people who were ineligible to vote—mainly noncitizens and felons—and excluded eligible overseas voters. Since the 2004 election, voting rates have been based on the "voting-eligible population," which changes the overall voting picture and challenges the notion of decline in voter turnout. In the 2004 election, voter turnout was 55 percent for the "voting-age population" and 60 percent for the "voting-eligible population." And among eligible voters under 25, turnout rose by almost 6 percent over the 2000 election, with some 10.5 million of them going to the polls.

Voter turnout improved again in the presidential election of 2008 in which Barack Obama, the first African American president, was elected. An estimated 61.4 percent of the voting-eligible population, or 130.9 million Americans, cast their ballots. That represents an increase of 1.3 percentage points over 2004 but falls short of the record turnout of 62.5 percent in 1968. Among young voters aged 18–29, the 2008 election represented the second highest turnout in history, with approximately 22–24 million, or 49–54 percent of eligible voters, casting their ballots. The record youth voter

Barack Obama Joined by his wife Michelle, Obama takes the oath of office to become the 44th president of the United States.

turnout belongs to the election in 1972, the first year that 18-year-olds had the right to vote.

Even so, why are voter participation rates so much lower in the United States than in some comparable democratic nations? Is it simply voter apathy or cynicism? A number of social factors affect the likelihood that someone will or will not vote. Age, race, gender, sexual orientation, religion, geographic location, social class, and education are all demographic variables that influence voter participation as well as how people vote. For example, Minnesota had the highest voter turnout of any state in the 2008 presidential election—almost 78 percent of its citizens voted, whereas only 51 percent of the eligible voters from Hawaii and 50 percent from Utah turned out. What explains this difference? Turnout may be affected by factors ranging from the number of other races on the ballot to the weather. Senior citizens are much more likely to vote than young adults—compare a 72 percent turnout for those over 55 with a 47 percent turnout among 18- to 24-year-olds. But the top reason people give for not voting, according to a 2004 survey, is that they are simply too busy (Holder 2006).

In some instances, however, people do not vote because they are **disenfranchised**—barred from voting. All states except Maine and Vermont disenfranchise convicted felons while they are incarcerated. Thirty-five states disenfranchise felons on parole, thirty-one do so for felons on probation, and seven others permanently disenfranchise them (Weedon 2004). Human rights groups have long protested this policy, arguing that it is not a legitimate function of the penal

> **disenfranchised** stripped of voting rights, either temporarily or permanently

Changing the World

Patriotism and Protest

In the United States, the Constitution guarantees freedom of the press and freedom of speech. Anyone—an individual, a newspaper's editorial staff, a group, or an organization—can criticize the system, call for change, and openly express disapproval of the president, other leaders, and government policies. In some political systems, this kind of speech could get you censured, imprisoned, "disappeared," or even executed. For instance, during Argentina's "Dirty War" in the late 1970s and early 80s, the military dictatorship killed or "disappeared" about 10,000 to 30,000 citizens.

Even though freedom of speech is a legal right in the United States, when we criticize some policy or some action of the government, we may, ironically, be called unpatriotic by those who support it. This is especially true in times of war or national crisis, when many citizens believe we should pull together as a country and present a united front to the world. During the 1960s, for example, at the height of U.S. involvement in Vietnam, many Americans considered antiwar protesters "un-American" because of their vocal criticism of American intervention in Southeast Asia. After September 11, 2001, those who questioned the competence of U.S. intelligence agencies (such as journalists, elected representatives, and survivors of those killed in the attacks) were effectively silenced until more than a year later, when Congress impaneled a commission to investigate intelligence agencies' preparation for and response to the attacks. The commission's report confirmed problems within the intelligence community that contributed to the inability to foresee and forestall the attacks—corroborating the criticisms of "unpatriotic" protesters.

Numerous protests also occurred during the Iraq war, which began in 2003. For example, in 2003, the country music group The Dixie Chicks expressed their antiwar sentiments by saying that, as Texans, they were ashamed that President George W. Bush was also from their home state. This comment caused a storm of controversy, and many radio stations all over the country refused to play The Dixie Chicks' songs. The protests at the 2004 Democratic and Republican national conventions in Boston and New York City were notable for their size, their creativity, and the intense response they provoked from law enforcement. Both protesters and police used the internet and mobile phones to coordinate their actions, and in one demonstration 5,000 bicyclists clogged the streets of Manhattan for a protest ride. Using a different strategy, peace activist Cindy Sheehan, whose son was killed in Iraq, set up camp outside George W. Bush's Texas ranch in August 2005, vowing to stay there until the president came outside and spoke with her. He never did, and in July 2006 Sheehan purchased several acres of land near the Bush ranch to create a more permanent memorial to her son.

Is it unpatriotic to criticize your government or to call for change in times of national crisis? Those who do so argue that such criticism is the most patriotic act of all: that uncritical acceptance of government is not the same as patriotism and that citizens should make every effort to correct its flaws. Those on the opposite side may say, "My country, right or wrong" and believe that the decisions of our elected leaders, once made, are beyond criticism. Regardless of your views, keep in mind that those who criticize government policies are doing exactly what our democratic system calls for and protects. Dissent and its tolerance are crucial elements of an open society, and you have a constitutionally protected right to oppose, criticize, and protest. And to boycott The Dixie Chicks if you so choose!

In Relationships

Disembodied Colleagues

Ironically, all the communication technologies that increase connections between people may ultimately make them feel more alienated from other human beings. This is a common complaint of workers in the software industry. In the novel *Microserfs* by Douglas Coupland, a neurotic Microsoft employee describes the joys of e-mail:

> I'm an e-mail addict. Everybody at Microsoft is an addict. The future of e-mail usage is being pioneered right here. The cool thing with e-mail is that when you send it, there's no possibility of connecting with the person on the other end. It's better than phone answering machines, because with them, the person on the other line might actually pick up the phone and you might have to talk. (Coupland 1995)

Coupland was probably exaggerating somewhat, but there is no doubt that the business practices first adopted by cutting-edge technology companies have influenced almost every part of the economy.

Even a seemingly minor change, like the adoption of e-mail, can profoundly affect the way people experience their workplace. In his article "Workers as Cyborgs: Labor and Networked Computers," Mark Poster details the increase in alienation that can come when a workplace switches to electronic communications. For instance, "a hospital in the Midwest that introduced a software program for ordering supplies from the Internet" saw increases in efficiency but also found that the technology "furthers the alienation of the worker" (Poster 2002). Using the new software may have gotten supplies ordered more quickly and with fewer errors, but "electronic communications are void of personal nuances characteristic of face-to-face communications" (Poster 2002). In short, it gets lonely when the only person you talk to is your computer.

Telecommuters who live alone may experience alienation and loneliness because the traditional workplace is often a major source of shared experience. Even worse, many of those who had hoped telecommuting would give them more quality time with their families are finding that working from home can actually intensify the conflict between work and family. As one study of telecommuters explains, "work can take over our personal lives. . . . If you're working from the family computer in the middle of the family room, your kids see you at work and don't understand why you're physically there, but mentally you're someplace else" (AHENS 2003).

All these situations stress increased alienation as the result of the Information Age. Will your work involve you with others in face-to-face interaction, or will you "know" your coworkers, colleagues, customers, and clients only through disembodied relationships?

Businesses get increased productivity and fewer sick days when they allow employees to telecommute. Although many employers worry that allowing employees to work from home would reduce accountability, some believe that the opposite is true. In traditional office environments the only measure of employee value is the number of hours present in the office, regardless of what gets done, whereas telecommuters must demonstrate their accomplishments more concretely. Telecommuting and similar uses of information technology have also made it easier for single parents or workers with disabilities to stay employed full-time.

There is much debate around the positive and negative aspects of telecommuting and other technologies that physically and geographically separate workers. Some suggest that new information technologies will actually increase the need for face-to-face contact and tightly knit workplaces. For example, workers who write codes for computer software can do it anywhere they have a computer and instantly send the results to those who will package and market the software, but software companies are still the most geographically concentrated of any industry. Microsoft, the world's largest software company, refers to its home office as "the campus" and has gone to great lengths to make it an appealing place for employees precisely because the company still needs them at the same location in order to work. In the Information Age, more and more work requires the creative manipulation of knowledge, and for this workers need to brainstorm and share ideas in more interactive ways than the technology allows even now. The computer industry suggests that even when work can be done anywhere there will still be a real need to bring people together, at least some of the time.

The rise of new technologies may roll back many of the original effects of the Industrial Revolution. Manufacturing made it necessary for many people to work at the same location, causing the growth of cities and the decline of rural and small-town populations. However, with new technologies that let people work from anywhere, perhaps telecommuting will cause cities to shrink again as more people will be able to live without reference to the company that employs them. Small towns are now offering an attractive alternative to outsourcing. High-tech jobs are beginning to relocate to rural areas, where companies are finding it cheaper to do business and more attractive for their employees (Pinto 2005). It's possible that information technology may one day reunite the worlds of work and home that the Industrial Revolution tore asunder.

Last, it's not just knowledge workers who rely on this new information technology. The Digital Age has also changed the way industrial and service work is conducted. Even jobs traditionally considered to be in manufacturing now have a knowledge component. For example, the big three automakers in the United States have in the past hired college graduates for the assembly line because they needed employees able to identify and suggest quality improvements (Brandon 1996). In the service sector, retail outlets and grocery stores use computer databases to predict exactly how much of a product they need to keep on hand and to order new merchandise in a timely fashion, a system called "just in time inventory," drastically reducing overhead and waste. Insurance companies use instant messaging (IM) technology to connect workers in different offices or in the field, "finding IM not only improves accuracy and provides timely customer response but adds dollars to their bottom line" (Chordas 2003).

Individual and Collective Resistance Strategies: How Workers Cope

Individuals and groups cope with their working conditions in a variety of ways called **resistance strategies**. These are tactics that let workers take back a degree of control over the conditions of their labor and feel that they have some sense of autonomy even in the face of dehumanizing,

resistance strategies ways that workers express discontent with their working conditions and try to reclaim control of the conditions of their labor

alienating constraints imposed by the terms and demands of their employment.

Individual resistance can range from the fairly benign, like using work time to surf the web, to the truly dangerous, like sabotaging the assembly line. More often, individual resistance may be simply personalizing the workspace with photos or daydreaming on the job as a type of escape (Roy 1960). Collective forms of resistance that seek solutions to shared workplace problems include union organizing and membership, strikes, walk-outs, and work stoppages.

This discussion begins with an examination of individual resistance strategies within service work. We bring Weber's theory on bureaucracy into the present to see how workers today are coping with the constraints of those organizations. Last we look at collective resistance strategies—union organization both past and present.

Individual Resistance Strategies: Handling Bureaucratic Constraints

Bureaucratic organizations are found in almost every sector of the economy. In Max Weber's theory of bureaucracies, he highlighted the rational, impersonal, and coldly efficient nature of this form of social organization (refer to Chapter 6 for a review). Workers in highly bureaucratic organizations often feel the lack of autonomy in their everyday work lives. Autonomy is the ability to direct one's individual destiny—to have the power to control the conditions of one's labor—and this is generally lacking for people who work in highly structured, rule-bound, and depersonalized environments. Their daily tasks are structured by external forces: for example, the pace of the assembly line is decided for them and they cannot slow it down or speed it up if they need to take a break or want to finish work early.

In many corporate settings, employees at all levels are under various types of surveillance: electronic key cards monitor their comings and goings, cameras record their activities, computer transactions are screened, and phone calls are recorded. In retail sales, workers' interactions with customers are often scripted, so that even what they say to others is outside their control. Not only is there a lack of autonomy, but there is also a lack of individuality in the workplace. Workers are treated more like robots than people. Unlike a robot, however, human workers can resist and undermine the bureaucratic constraints that limit their autonomy in the workplace—and they do so in a wide variety of ways.

Robin Leidner's study *Fast Food, Fast Talk* provides an in-depth look at individual resistance strategies in the workplace (Leidner 1993). The study focuses on McDonald's employees and the routinized nature of their interactions

Fast Food, Fast Talk In her study of restaurant employees, Robin Leidner looks at the ways that workers subvert the scripts that McDonald's requires them to follow when interacting with customers.

with customers. Under the golden arches, every contact between the counter staff and the hungry consumer is strictly scripted, seemingly with no room for improvisation or creativity. Or is there?

McDonald's workers are trained to interact with customers using "The Six Steps": greeting, taking orders, assembling food, presenting it, receiving payment, and thanking them for their business. As monotonous as these steps are, workers don't necessarily resent routinization—it helps them do their jobs effectively. And some workers, like this woman, improvise on the steps, personalizing them in tiny but still noticeable ways:

> Just do the Six Steps, but do it in your own way. It's not like you have to say "Hi, welcome to McDonald's." You can say, "Hi, how are you doing?" or "Good morning," "Good afternoon," "Good evening," things like that. (Leidner 1993, p. 138)

Leidner observed that there were limits within which workers could

> use the script as a starting point and inject [their] own personality into the interactions. Thus, some window workers joked or chatted with customers and tried to make the exchanges enjoyable for both parties. This stance implied an assertion of equality with customers and a refusal to suppress the self completely. (Leidner 1993, p. 190)

Leidner proposes that submitting to scripted interactions all day long suppresses the real self and that this sort of tightly controlled work environment can actually be damaging to the individual.

One of the functions of McDonald's service script is to regulate the power relationship between customer and worker:

customers' demands can be delivered with all types of attitude, but workers must always serve customers with a smile. The script constrains workers' response—if they have a rude or even abusive customer, they must still stick to the script:

> You have to take their crap. [Laughs.] I'm not the type of person to say, "OK, have it your way." I mean, I have to admit, I'm tempted to backtalk a lot. That gets me in a lot of trouble. So I mean, when a customer's rude to me I just have to walk away and say, "Could you take this order please, before I say something I'm not supposed to say?" (Leidner 1993, p. 133)

If they do pervert the script or talk back to a rude customer, workers may be inviting a reprimand from their supervisor. But they are also engaging in resistance, asserting their own identities in the face of the depersonalizing routine. They are being active rather than passive, controlling the interaction rather than being controlled by it. They are asserting their own autonomy on the job, and it is apparently worth the risk.

It is difficult to think of a form of employment that would allow us to avoid these bureaucratic constraints altogether. What types of resistance strategies have you used to regain a bit of independence and power in the workplace?

Collective Resistance Strategies: Unions in the Past and Present

Although individual resistance strategies may provide a small measure of autonomy for some workers, they don't fundamentally change the working conditions or make permanent improvements to the terms of employment for all workers. That is why workers sometimes seek more lasting solutions to their problems by organizing to instigate collective resistance strategies—by forming unions.

A **union** benefits workers in various ways and serves to counterbalance the power of employers. A labor union is an association of workers who come together to improve their economic status and working conditions. The two main types of unions are craft unions, in which all the members are skilled in a certain craft (e.g., the International Brotherhood of Carpenters and Joiners), and industrial unions, in which all the members work in the same industry regardless of their particular skill (e.g., the Service Employees International Union). Some unions are local with small memberships; others are large, national organizations representing millions of workers. Unions have legal status to represent workers in contract negotiations with employers.

> **union** an association of workers who bargain collectively for increased wages and benefits and better working conditions

Lawrence, Massachusetts, 1912 During the 1912 textile mill strike, workers demanded "bread and roses," eloquently capturing their desire for something more than the wages needed to survive.

When disagreements arise between management and employees, unionized workers may threaten to or actually stage a temporary "walkout," "work stoppage," or "strike" to express their grievance and force corporate managers and owners to negotiate. Often the striking workers will try to discourage the public from patronizing the businesses implicated in the labor dispute and try to prevent other, outside replacement workers (sometimes called "scab labor") from taking their jobs while they are out on strike. Union negotiations with employers about the terms of employment and working conditions are coordinated through collective bargaining in which contract decisions between management and union representatives must be mutually agreed upon rather than imposed unilaterally.

Unions have a long history in the United States. At various times they have existed on the margins of society and been vigorously opposed by capitalists and other free-market supporters. Unions in the nineteenth and early twentieth centuries were brutally suppressed by capitalists, and union organizers were frequently arrested and jailed. Often they were charged with conspiracy because attempts to form unions were illegal for much of American history. The Typographical Union (representing print typesetters), which formed in 1852, is usually considered the "first durable national organization of workers" in the United States. By 1881 a number of smaller labor groups had banded together to form the American Federation of Labor (AFL), which eventually became the AFL-CIO (by adding the groups in the Congress of Industrial Organizations).

Unions of this era fought for a variety of workplace reforms. During the 1912 textile mill strikes in Lawrence, Massachusetts, the workers' slogan was "bread and roses," emphasizing their desire for something more than wages sufficient to survive. Unions also led campaigns to end child labor, establish an eight-hour workday and a five-day work week, and to increase workplace safety. For this reason unions are still sometimes referred to as "the people who brought you the weekend." Before the eight-hour workday was instituted, many workers literally didn't see the sun because they went to work before daybreak and left after dark. It is not surprising that many were willing to fight for unionization even in the face of extreme opposition.

In 2007 approximately 16 million American workers belonged to a union organization (Bureau of Labor Statistics 2008e). However, union membership has been in steep decline since its peak in the 1950s. In 1955 approximately 35 percent of the labor force was unionized; by 2004 fewer than 13 percent of the workforce belonged to a union. In the 1950s an average of 352 major strikes occurred each year; by the early 2000s that number had fallen to fewer than 30 (Commission for Labor Cooperation 2003).

Perhaps the first major blow to union strength came with the Taft-Hartley Act of 1947 that instituted limitations on secondary strikes and boycotts, established restrictions on picketing, and allowed the federal government to force strikers back to work during "cooling-off periods" that not only gave workers time to reconsider but also gave businesses time to gather resources to counteract a strike. After Taft-Hartley, various states passed so-called right-to-work laws that prohibited "closed shops," workplaces where all employees had to be members of the union. Supporters say that workers should be free to decide whether to join a union; opponents argue that all employees who benefit from collective bargaining should help to support the union that represents the workers.

The laws regarding union activity were one part of larger social changes that have occurred over the last 50 years and have diminished the power of unions in the United States. Between 1945 and 1973 the economy grew rapidly, and as long as wages and benefits continued to rise, the perceived need for unions waned. However, in the 1970s the economy entered a serious decline, and American corporations found it was cheaper to move production overseas to countries whose working conditions were more like those of nineteenth-century than twentieth-century America. As a result, unions have largely changed focus from fighting for better wages and working conditions to keeping jobs in this country.

Industries that leave the United States, referred to as "runaway shops," are mostly in manufacturing, where firms take advantage of cheap labor and lax environmental laws in other countries. But even Hollywood has out-of-country production sites. Many movies purporting to depict American cities like Chicago and New York are actually filmed in Toronto, where labor costs are on average 20 percent lower than in the United States (Cooper 2003). In 1998, 27 percent of U.S. film and television productions were runaway productions (285 out of 1,075)—almost triple the number from just a decade before (Monitor Report 1999). Some 81 percent of these were made in Canada with its cheaper labor and weaker unions. The direct production expenditures lost from the United States were estimated at $2.8 billion for 1998 alone.

With a shift in the U.S. economy from manufacturing to the service sector, the only unions to grow since the early 1970s have been public employees' unions. In some instances, service jobs are being moved overseas. But even when jobs remain in the United States, other problems emerge among workers.

When Wal-Mart began opening Supercenters in the late 1990s that included full grocery stores, many industry watchers became fearful that the retail behemoth's wage policies and antiunion stance would force local grocers "to push for drastically lower wages to stay competitive with the new mega-warehouse on the block" (F. Green 2002). As a consequence, union organizers made concerted efforts to organize Wal-Mart employees, only to be met with substantial opposition. Union leaders reported that Wal-Mart maintained a "hit list" of employees to be fired because they favor unionization and that in some instances they instructed employees to call the police if organizers tried to contact them. In those rare instances when Wal-Mart employees have voted to unionize, the company has resorted to even more drastic measures. In 2002, after the butchers at the Wal-Mart Supercenter in Jacksonville, Texas, voted to join the United Food and Commercial Workers (UFCW), the company decided to eliminate the meat cutters in their Texas stores and buy precut meat from their suppliers.

The 1997 strike by UPS drivers was widely hailed as the beginning of a comeback for organized labor. It was the biggest strike in more than a decade, with 185,000 workers walking picket lines for 15 days before a new contract was

Victory for All Workers? The Hollywood writers' strike of 2007–8, in which over 3,500 Writers Guild of America members "walked out" on the TV and movie industries, was successful in gaining residual or royalty pay for writers when TV shows and movies are distributed on the internet.

signed. Shortly after the settlement, Ron Carey, then president of the Teamsters labor union, declared this is "not just a Teamster victory, this is a victory for all working people" (Roberts and Bernstein 2000). The Teamsters emphasized that their first concern was the increasing number of part-time jobs without benefits, a concern that large numbers of Americans shared. However, the UPS strike was relatively unique and unlikely to be repeated by other unions. Not only does UPS offer a service that can't be moved outside the country, but its workers also have good rapport with the customers, which may help to explain why public support for the union was so high. UPS has traditionally been a labor-friendly, worker-owned corporation, with a number of top executives who started out as drivers. Additionally, UPS is the overwhelming market leader in the parcel delivery business, which decreases the pressure for top executives to cut costs. Competitors like Federal Express aren't unionized, emphasizing the extent to which the service sector has succeeded in resisting unionization.

The successful UPS strike may still encourage other workers to pursue unionization. Despite several decades of decline in union power, the recognition of workers' rights, including the right to organize, continues to be a feature of the American economic system. Shortly after the UPS strike ended, Nelson Lichtenstein, a professor of history specializing in labor issues, predicted, "Right now discussions are going on in executive offices in Wal-Mart, Kmart, Federal Express, all these labor intensive service firms, about how to rethink their labor strategy" (Greenhouse 1997). Whether such collective resistance strategies become more prevalent again in the future remains to be seen.

The Best of Corporate America

From a Weberian perspective, we can see that large bureaucracies laden with rules and procedures can deprive employees of a sense of autonomy, individuality, and control. From a Marxist perspective, we can see how large capitalist corporations sometimes exploit their workers and cause alienation and that their power hierarchies often exclude women and minorities. These criticisms are true in the aggregate—money, power, and influence converge in corporate America, and with these forms of power come opportunities for exploitation and abuse. But not all corporations are evil, and sometimes we see major corporate players transcend self-interest and act with great altruism.

Compared to the big firms like Morgan Stanley and Goldman Sachs, Sandler O'Neill and Partners is a tiny

Jimmy Dunne In the September 11, 2001, attacks on the World Trade Center, Sandler O'Neill & Partners lost 66 of its 171 employees, including two of its three founders. Jimmy Dunne, the surviving founder, consoled the company's other survivors and inspired them to rebuild the company.

investment brokerage firm. It was located on the 104th floor of the World Trade Center in New York, and on September 11, 2001, it was devastated in the terrorist attacks. Sixty-six of its 171 employees died in the towers, all of their equipment and business information was destroyed, and only one of the senior partners survived. That partner, Jimmy Dunne, immediately began what seemed like an impossible task: address overwhelming grief, rebuild the company, and take care of the families of all 66 lost employees.

Within a matter of days, Dunne had set up shop in temporary offices (donated by Bank of America). Sandler O'Neill began trading again, but without the knowledge or experience of the employees it had lost. And in what constitutes a miracle in corporate America, its competitors began to help out. Stockbrokers from other companies started calling in market information to Sandler O'Neill's inexperienced traders. A retired vice president from Goldman Sachs just showed up one day and started volunteering at the equity desk. Major investment brokerages like Merrill Lynch and J. P. Morgan Chase cut Sandler O'Neill in on their deals, just so the crippled company could earn a portion of the commission. And Sandler O'Neill needed every penny it could get its hands on: Dunne had paid out the full year's salary and benefits to the families of all the dead employees and had guaranteed year-end bonuses as well.

These powerhouse investment brokerages—ordinarily in a position to squash a tiny firm like Sandler O'Neill—suspended their rivalries to get another corporation and its devastated employees back in the game. They shared office space, information, workers, deals, and commissions with a competitor. They subverted their own bureaucratic rules and the imperatives of capitalist competition to help a struggling company survive. And it did: Sandler O'Neill was profitable again before the end of 2001 and had the necessary funds to continue supporting the families of its lost staff members. Granted, September 11 created extraordinary circumstances, and many people and organizations rose to the challenge of this national tragedy. But the case of Sandler O'Neill shows that corporate competitors can become collaborators and provide support. Corporate America is, after all, populated by human beings.

Globalization, Economics, and Work

Globalization describes the cultural and economic changes that have occurred as a result of dramatically increased international trade and exchange in the late twentieth and early twenty-first centuries. Although there has always been some global economic trade—East Asia's ancient spice and silk trade routes and the sixteenth-century English and Dutch shipping empires are early examples of this—the effects of globalization have become more highly visible since the 1970s. Globalization has been fostered through the development of international economic institutions; innovations in technology; the movement of money, information, and people; and infrastructure that supports such expansion. Today, it is possible to view the world as having one global economy, with huge corporations whose production processes span national borders, international regulatory bodies such as the World Trade Organization (WTO), and transnational trade agreements such as the North American Free Trade Agreement (NAFTA) redefining economic relationships between and among nations.

Supporters of globalization believe that "free trade" can lead to more efficient allocation of resources, lower prices, more employment, and higher output, with all countries involved in the trade benefiting. Critics believe that free trade promotes a self-interested corporate agenda and that powerful and autonomous multinational corporations can exploit workers and increasingly shape the politics of nation-states.

International Trade: Shallow and Deep Integration

To explain economic globalization, social scientists have used the terms *shallow integration* and *deep integration* (Dicken 1998). Shallow integration refers to the flow of goods and services that characterized international trade until several decades ago. In a shallow integration model, a national company would arrange with a foreign company to either import or export products but exclusively within that single nation's economy. For example, not even 30 years ago, a Japanese car would have been made almost entirely in Japan, and a pair of American jeans would have been made in the United States. Thus Japan would export cars to the United States, which would import Japanese cars. And the United States would export jeans to Japan, which would import American jeans. To protect their interests, nations would impose taxes on imports, sometimes making those imports more expensive to buy than similar products made at home.

Deep integration refers to the global flow of goods and services in today's economy. While companies still make arrangements with other companies for imports and exports, their relationships are far more complex. Most significantly, companies are no longer national; they are multinational, with major decision-making, production, and/or distribution branches of a particular company spread all over the world. When we look at the labels on our clothing, the global nature of their origin is often concealed. The label may say "Made in . . . ," but the raw materials or other parts may have originated somewhere else.

When nations make laws to protect national economic interests, they must often do so with a host of other nations in mind. NAFTA is an excellent example of this complex web of global relationships. Many major apparel companies, such as Nike or the Gap, have marketing and design headquarters in the United States but their garment factories are in Mexico, another country in NAFTA. Under NAFTA, American companies can avoid paying taxes when they export raw materials to Mexico and then import the finished products. These global trade agreements often benefit private industry much more than they do nations.

Transnational Corporations

Transnational corporations (TNCs) are another part of the global economy. These firms purposefully transcend national borders so that their products can be manufactured, distributed, marketed, and sold from many bases all over the world. We may think of companies like Coca-Cola or General Electric as quintessentially American, but they are more accurately understood as global or transnational corporations. What is distinctive about today's TNCs is the way they shape the global economy. In the past 50 years, they have experienced unprecedented growth in both numbers of firms and amount of economic impact.

> **globalization** the cultural and economic changes resulting from dramatically increased international trade and exchange in the late twentieth and early twenty-first centuries

The United Nations 2006 list of "The World's Top 100 Non-Financial TNCs" assigns firms a "transnationality index" by assessing the ratios between foreign employment and total employment, foreign investments and total investments, and foreign sales and total sales (UNCTAD 2007). In their 2006 listing, the top five "transnational" firms included four U.S. firms: General Electric (1), Exxon Mobil (5), Ford Motor Co. (6), and Wal-Mart (10). Just over half the workforce is foreign at both General Electric and Ford—with Exxon coming in at almost two-thirds and Wal-Mart at just over one-quarter. All of these firms are marketed strongly as "American" brands, yet they are clearly global institutions.

Table 12.1 shows how much economic influence TNCs exert in the global economy. Among the top 40 global economies, ranked by either Gross Domestic Product (GDP) or total sales, there are eight TNCs. Firms such as Wal-Mart and BP (British Petroleum) actually rank higher than the nations of South Africa, Argentina, and Ireland. When we consider that firms have the economic weight of nations, we can understand just how much political clout TNCs wield in terms of global governance. For instance, an American TNC can exercise powerful influence by donating huge amounts of money to lobbyists and political campaigns. Further, in international regulatory bodies, such as the WTO, TNCs are often able to influence trade law at a global level.

Another manifestation of the ever-increasing economic power of TNCs is competition in the global market. Because TNCs can take advantage of cheap pools of labor by either relocating their own factories or outsourcing, nations compete with each other for these contracts by undercutting their citizens' wages and offering incentives such as tax-free zones. Scholars, politicians, activists, and commentators have called this the "race to the bottom." These kinds of policies hurt the local populations, often depriving workers of decent wages and the potential benefits, such as schools and hospitals, that would have been derived from taxes.

Global Sweatshop Labor

One way the race to the bottom hurts workers in their own countries is by creating an environment where sweatshop labor can exist. A **sweatshop** is a workplace where workers are subjected to extreme exploitation, including below-standard wages, long hours, and poor working conditions that may pose health or safety hazards. Sweatshop workers are often intimidated with threats of physical discipline

and are prevented from forming unions or other workers' rights groups. Historically, sweatshops originated during the Industrial Revolution as a system where middlemen earned profits from the difference between what they received for delivering on a contract and the amount they paid to the workers who produced the contracted goods. The profit was said to be "sweated" from the workers, because they received minimal wages and worked excessive hours under unsanitary and dangerous conditions.

Sweatshops, however, are not a thing of the past. Unfortunately, there are many in the world today making large numbers of the goods that we unknowingly consume. Though perhaps more prevalent overseas, sweatshops exist in the United States as well. The General Accounting Office defines a sweatshop as "an employer that violates more than one federal or state labor law governing minimum wage and overtime, child labor, industrial homework, occupational safety and health, workers compensation, or industrial regulation" (Ross 1997, p.12). The Department of Labor estimated

Are Sweatshops Good or Bad? While workers sew at *maquilas*, or sweatshops, such as this one in Guatemala City, Guatemala, students like Christine Hoffmann, left, and Bradley Heinz, right, at Stanford University are calling on universities to ensure that apparel bearing their school's logo is made in factories where workers are paid a living wage.

TABLE 12.1	**Top Forty Economies Ranked by GDP and Total Sales, 2007**	

RANKING	NATION/FIRM	GDP/SALES (IN MILLIONS $US)
1	United States	13,811,200
2	Japan	4,376,705
3	Germany	3,297,233
4	China	3,280,053
5	United Kingdom	2,727,806
6	France	2,562,288
7	Italy	2,107,481
8	Spain	1,429,226
9	Canada	1,326,376
10	Brazil	1,314,170
11	Russian Federation	1,291,011
12	India	1,170,968
13	Korea, Rep.	969,795
14	Mexico	893,364
15	Australia	821,716
16	Netherlands	754,203
17	Turkey	657,091
18	Belgium	448,560
19	Sweden	444,443
20	Indonesia	432,817
21	Poland	420,321
22	Switzerland	415,516
23	Norway	381,951
24	Saudi Arabia	381,683
25	Wal-Mart Stores	378,799
26	Austria	377,028
27	Exxon Mobil	372,824
28	Greece	360,031
29	Royal Dutch Shell	355,782
30	Denmark	308,093
31	BP	291,438
32	South Africa	277,581
33	Iran	270,937
34	Argentina	262,331
35	Ireland	254,970
36	Finland	246,020
37	Thailand	245,818
38	Toyota Motor	230,201
39	Venezuela	228,071
40	Portugal	220,241

Data on GDP: World Bank 2008
Data on firms: *Fortune* 2008b

Sweatshop Labor and "Gold Farming" in China

Many people are familiar with the concept of sweatshops, where cheap labor is exploited to make clothing and goods for people in industrialized nations. While individuals are able to understand easily how labor can be exploited for the production of material goods, a more difficult concept to grasp is how labor can be exploited in the market for virtual goods. Rather than working long hours under inhuman conditions for little pay in order to produce luxury items such as Nikes and Levi's, "gold farmers" are exploited in order to create the ultimate luxury product—status in an online computer game.

The Real World is the title of your textbook and a long-running MTV reality show. In cyberspace, the term *real world* is also used to differentiate life outside the online "virtual world." Some of the most popular forms of virtual worlds are Massively Multiplayer Online Role Playing Games (MMORPGs) such as *World of Warcraft, Ultima Online*, and *Everquest*. *World of Warcraft (WoW)* is the most popular of these games, with approximately 10.9 million monthly subscribers as of 2008. As with many MMORPGs, players make an initial investment to purchase the software for the game, and they are also charged a monthly subscription fee in order to play. In *WoW*, players use a character avatar through which they explore the virtual world, complete quests, and interact with other players or nonplayer characters (NPCs). Quests are assignments given by an NPC (who is programmed into the game) that usually involve killing a monster, gathering resources, transporting an item from one location to another, or finding a difficult-to-locate object. Successful quests are rewarded with in-game money and experience points that a character can spend to buy new skills and equipment. As with most MMORPGs, there is an emphasis on character improvement. Because of the interactive nature of *WoW*, advancing in the game isn't just a matter of personal achievement but also a matter of reputation and status in the community.

"Gold farms" profit from the importance of advancement in an MMORPG. According to estimates, around 100,000 people in China are employed as "gold farmers," making $120 to $250 (U.S.) per month playing *WoW* for 12- to 18-hour shifts. These Chinese gold farmers carry out in-game actions so that they can earn virtual money to buy equipment, skills, and status. These virtual assets are sold to real (recreational) players for real world money, creating a unique intersection of virtual and real world economies. Literally, a player can spend real world money to buy status and reputation in an online game. Since many of the beginning levels of *WoW* involve spending long hours doing repetitive and dull virtual tasks, the idea of being able to bypass this tedium to start at more advanced levels appeals to many players. Creating characters requires time and effort that players who use the services of gold farmers are unable or unwilling to devote to the game. So they buy the labor of gold farmers to advance their gaming strategies.

Many of the critiques of manufacturing sweatshops can be applied to the gold farming phenomenon. Gold farmers labor for the benefit of middle-class gamers in industrialized nations. Ge Jin, a PhD student at the University of California in San Diego, documents working conditions in the gold farming "sweatshops," where he has filmed workers crowded into an airport hangar, bleary eyed, chain-smoking, and sleeping two to a single mat on the floor (Jin, forthcoming). Are bad jobs better than no jobs? Certainly it is easier to live in most of modern society with money than without. Though most people in developed nations would view $3 a day as extremely low pay, in impoverished communities "$1 or $2 a day can be a life-transforming wage" (Kristof and WuDunn 2000). While there are those who argue that playing a computer game takes less of a physical toll than subsistence farming or factory work, it is evident that there is an imbalance between the amount of money that workers are paid to produce these virtual resources and the prices that gamers pay to buy them. The sum of $200 can

that in 2001 there were over 7,000 sweatshops in U.S. cities such as New York, Los Angeles, New Orleans, Chicago, Philadelphia, and El Paso. American companies may also manufacture goods overseas using foreign sweatshop labor. Nike and the Gap, and clothing lines associated with Mary-Kate and Ashley Olsen and Sean "Diddy" Combs, have all

been charged with using sweatshop labor in Southeast Asia, Central America, and elsewhere and have been pressured to reform their practices.

Many universities purchase their logo apparel from manufacturers that use sweatshop labor. In 1999, students at the University of Michigan, University of North Carolina,

Chinese Gold Farmers How has the popularity of online games such as *World of Warcraft* led to new forms of sweatshops?

the services of gold farmers affect the virtual economy by driving up the prices of the rarest items. Traditional players then become resentful, as these price increases require them to work longer to acquire items that players with real world cash can purchase with little effort. On the other hand, does playing a game qualify as work? After all, it is "only a game."

Strategies for retaliation against players identified as gold farmers include verbal harassment inside the game. Rather than taking out their anger and frustrations on the gold farm brokers who benefit from the process, some traditional players will follow suspected gold farmers within the game and bombard them with racist comments. Gamers have put together racist videos to post on YouTube, venting their anger over the gold farming phenomenon. Gold farming then becomes a matter not just of class and economics but also of race and racism.

buy 500 pieces of online gold in *WoW*, which would take an estimated 100 hours of playing to earn.

The gaming world is up in arms about the gold farming phenomenon. While some gamers find that the opportunity to buy gold augments their playing experience, other gamers hold that buying from gold farmers confers an unfair advantage to those with expendable income. Purists argue that MMORPGs should be free of the corruption of the real world and that escapism is not possible with people buying status and reputation in the virtual world. Players who use

Are gold farms good or bad? Are bad jobs better than no jobs at all? Should the virtual world be free of the corruption of the real world? Are gamers just too invested in their games? These are all questions to ask when pondering the intersections of the virtual world and real world that collide in the gold farming sweatshops.

University of Wisconsin-Madison, Duke University, and Georgetown University staged sit-ins to pressure their respective administrators into agreeing to fully disclose factory conditions and wages paid to workers who produce university apparel. Other similar campaigns were launched at Seattle Community College in 2004 and systemwide at the University

of California in 2005 to change university purchasing policy to allow for preferences for union-made and verifiably sweatshop-free products (Greenhouse 1999). We encourage you to do your own research on whether sweatshop products have reached the stores where you shop—or even your own closet—in completing the next Data Workshop.

DATA WORKSHOP

ANALYZING EVERYDAY LIFE

Are Your Clothes Part of the Global Commodity Chain?

You probably own and consume a large number of products that originated in faraway countries, including your car, clothing, or shoes. These items have traveled widely during the process from production to consumption. Food, pharmaceuticals, and electronics are other examples of globally made products. Social scientists call these international movements of goods "global commodity chains" (Gereffi and Korzeniewicz 1994).

Global commodity chains are networks of corporations, product designers and engineers, manufacturing firms, distribution channels (such as ocean freightliners, railroads, and trucking firms), and consumer outlets (such as Wal-Mart). Global commodity chains start with a product design and brand name and end with the consumer making a purchase. But between start and finish is often a complex global process with many different people, in many different nations, all contributing to the final product.

The manufacturing of goods, from garments to electronics to automobiles, used to happen in the United States and other Western nations; today's manufacturing centers are primarily located in poorer nations, such as the Philippines, China, Indonesia, and many Latin American countries. American corporations such as Nike, the Gap, and Levi-Strauss have closed all their U.S. manufacturing plants and hired contractors and subcontractors from East Asia and Latin America to make their products at substantially lower prices. Now these companies focus large amounts of financial resources on "branding" their products (Klein 1999). Branding is the process, usually through advertising, by which companies gain consumers' attention and loyalty. Much of the money you pay for some products goes toward financing these branding campaigns, while a much smaller sum pays the workers who actually make the products.

The following three exercises will help you to understand where the things that you buy come from and the increasing disparity between product values and workers' wages.

Exercise One: The Global Closet
Pick out five to ten items of clothing from your closet. Now check the labels. Where were your clothes made? Make a list of the nations represented in your closet. How many nations are from East Asia or Latin America? Is there a difference between where an item is made and where it is assembled? Does the label indicate where the fabric originated?

Exercise Two: No Longer "Made in the U.S.A."
Ask your parents, aunts or uncles, or grandparents if you can look at the labels of their older clothes. Or go to a thrift store and look for older or vintage clothes there. Again pick out five to ten items of clothing. How many of those items were made in the United States? Compare your answers in Exercise 1 and Exercise 2. What does this tell you about the globalization of the garment manufacturing industry over the past 50 years?

Exercise Three: Are Your Favorite Brands "Sweat Free"?
List your favorite brands of clothing, shoes, or other fashion accessories. What is your brand's stance on sweatshop labor? Do workers who make your favorite products earn a living wage? You can check many corporations' ethics regarding labor conditions by doing some research on the internet. See how your brands score at the following websites:

CorpWatch: www.corpwatch.org

Global Exchange: www.globalexchange.org/campaigns/ sweatshops

Interfaith Center on Corporate Responsibility: www.iccr.org

National Labor Committee for Workers' and Human Rights: www.nlcnet.org

There are two options for completing this Data Workshop.

• *Option 1 (informal)*: Choose one of the exercises above and follow the instructions as outlined. Bring notes to class to discuss with others in small groups. Your instructor may organize groups so that all members have done the same exercise or all members have done a different exercise. In either case, compare your findings with those of other members of the group.

• *Option 2 (formal)*: Choose one or more of the exercises above (or your instructor may assign specific exercises) and follow the instructions as outlined. Write a three- to four-page essay analyzing your findings.

Outsourcing

The U.S. economy is increasingly affected by globalization, and as a result, American companies have sought out new business models to reduce costs and remain competitive.

One increasingly popular approach is outsourcing or off-shoring. **Outsourcing** involves "contracting out" or transferring to another country the labor that a company might otherwise have employed its own staff to perform. Typically a company's decision to outsource is made for financial reasons and is usually achieved by transferring employment to locations where labor is cheap. In 1992, U.S. firms employed 7 million workers in other countries (O'Reilly 1992); but with technological advances, particularly the internet, over the past decade or more, businesses have been able to increase their foreign employment pool significantly at a minimum cost.

Information technology–producing industries, such as data entry, communication services, communication equipment, computer hardware, and software and computer services, are the main jobs involved in outsourcing. Although countries such as China, the Philippines, and Eastern Europe are also key sites, India has been the primary location for outsourcing because of the shared English language and cheap employment. A company can hire an engineer in India for $10,000 a year compared to $60,000–$90,000 in the United States. In 2005, India controlled some 44 percent of the global offshore outsourcing market for software and back-office services, with revenues worth over $17 billion (Associated Press 2005).

The economic benefits of outsourcing are gained by businesses, but the drawbacks are felt by the labor pool. Between 2001 and 2004, some 403,300 information technology jobs were lost in the United States due to outsourcing (Associated Press 2004). Some companies required their employees to train their off-shore replacements, after which the American employees were fired. A 2003 study conducted by the University of California–Berkeley warned that as many as 14 million Americans held jobs at risk of being outsourced (Bardhan and Kroll 2003). This affects not only those already in the workforce but those who are about to enter. Many new college graduates with high-tech degrees are faced with large-scale lack of employment in the United States.

While outsourcing is practiced by the majority of U.S. businesses, they are often reluctant to fully disclose details. International Business Machines (IBM) is a major information technology company that manufactures and sells computer hardware, software, and services. IBM would not say exactly how many workers it had hired under outsourcing agreements, how many it laid off, or how many jobs were moved offshore, but in 2004 the vice president of human resources stated that 3,500 to 4,500 IBM jobs would be relocated from developed nations to emerging countries (Bulkeley 2004). Financial considerations are typically the reason a company decides to outsource, leaving anxious workers with a lack of job security.

Alternative Ways of Working

There are alternative ways of working, not all of which fit into typical categories of work. First we look at professional socialization, the process by which new members learn and internalize the norms and values of their group, examining case studies of workers in three unusual fields. Then we examine the contingent workforce—those who work in positions that are temporary or freelance or who work as independent contractors. Finally, there are the nonprofit corporations—private organizations whose missions go beyond the bottom-line—and volunteerism, the work of people who seek no compensation for their investment of time and energy.

Professional Socialization in Unusual Fields

Every new job requires some sort of training for the prospective employee. Anyone in a new position confronts an unfamiliar set of expectations and workplace norms that must be learned so the new person can fit into the environment. This process, called professional socialization (see Chapter 5 for a review), involves learning not only the social role but also the various details about how to do the job. Several sociological studies have explored the process of professional socialization focusing on medical students (Fox 1957; H. Becker et al. 1961; Haas and Shaffir 1977, 1982), teachers (Lortie 1968), clergy (Kleinman 1984), nurses (Stimson 1967), social workers (Loseke and Cahill 1986), and lawyers (Granfield 1992).

Spencer Cahill's study of students preparing to become funeral directors focused on the practical skills developed by mortuary science students and the emotional labor (see Hochschild 1983) involved in this occupation. Most social interaction within the mortuary science program revolved around death; as a result, students learned how to engage in the practice of "normalizing talk." "Mortuary science education requires students to adopt an occupational rhetoric and esoteric language that communicate professional authority and a calm composure towards matters

outsourcing "contracting out" or transferring to another country the labor that a company might otherwise have employed its own staff to perform; typically done for financial reasons

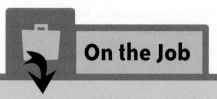

Internships and Experiential Learning

Someone mentions an internship, and you think . . . what? Bored college students making coffee for the boss? Good-looking medical students on *Grey's Anatomy*? Monica Lewinsky? In fact, internships are an increasingly important part of the college experience. According to the *New York Times* (Altschuler, 2002) more than half of the graduating seniors of 2001 had participated in some sort of experiential learning program during their college careers. At worst, the hapless intern may get really good at adding toner to the copier; at best, an internship can benefit both the intern and the company and may be useful in the long run for everyone involved.

Although most internships come with some compensation, others are unpaid; in either case, you gain valuable work experience. You may arrange an academic internship through your college or university and receive academic credit, or you may set up a nonacademic internship that leaves out the school altogether. Firms of all kinds look for college students to fill some of their employment needs. Of course, there's always the possibility that the work you're assigned as an intern will be mind numbing or pointless, so why bother with an internship?

First and most important, an internship may help you decide what you want to be—or don't want to be—when you graduate. After interning in a state's attorney's office, you may decide that being a lawyer isn't everything you thought it would be but that you would like to work with crime victims in a social service capacity. Even if you are sure about your future career path, you may want to consider branching out in the internships you apply for. You'll gain diverse skills and experience and be exposed to careers you might like just as much. Most Americans don't remain in the same job for their entire working lives, so keeping your options open during college doesn't seem like such a bad idea.

An internship on your résumé is also likely to make you an attractive job candidate. Even if your experience doesn't deal directly with the job you're applying for, having completed an internship demonstrates to potential employers your ability to work hard and manage your time. Almost two-thirds of the students from the class of 2004 who were hired after graduation had participated in an internship (McWilliams 2005). One study of recent graduates showed that those who had held internships during college were paid an average of almost 10 percent more than those without internship experience. In addition, many corporations turn first to their own interns when hiring. Results from a 2004 survey showed that employers offered full-time jobs to 57 percent of students who interned for them (Berggoetz 2005). The entire internship can, in some respects, be viewed as an extended job interview.

There will always be competition for the most prestigious positions, though interning for a big name company doesn't necessarily guarantee a good experience. But even if you decide you'd prefer not to work for that corporation or in that field, the contacts you develop may help you find another position. These are people who are already established in the profession, and a good reference is always valuable when you're in the job market.

Internships work out well for employers too. At the very least, they're getting cheap labor, but more than that, interns can be very beneficial for companies that need a highly educated or highly trained workforce. Taking on young workers can also help a company stay connected to younger consumers and may provide them with some new perspectives and ideas. Corporations also realize that providing internships can create goodwill—from the students who intern with them, from the universities through which the internships are organized, or from the general public.

that most of the lay public finds emotionally upsetting" (Cahill 1999, p. 106). In addition, students were required to control their own emotional responses to the work. "Some students told me that they found 'cases' of young children emotionally disturbing. . . . Yet these students reportedly did 'get used to it,' 'keep it down,' and deal with emotionally distressing 'cases'" (Cahill 1999, pp. 108–9). Cahill found that successful mortuary science students were those who could best deal with the emotional component of the work.

Loren Bourassa and Blake Ashforth studied how inexperienced newcomers are socialized into the work life onboard an Alaskan fishing boat. The occupation of a fisherman differs greatly from other occupations because it requires no previous experience or even a high school education, as physical strength and stamina are the primary prerequisites. Work on a fishing boat pays well for a relatively short amount of time, and this often lures a large number of workers. However, their romantic notions about life on a fishing boat are quickly dispelled. "New workers were indoctrinated collectively by their more experienced coworkers and underwent a process of divestiture. . . . Specifically newcomers were called 'new guys,' rather than by name, were subjected to constant taunts and verbal abuse, were constantly made to perform the least desirable jobs and other odd tasks, were required to obey incessant and often arbitrary instructions, and were routinely denied the privileges given to more experienced members" (Bourassa and Ashforth 1998, p. 181). This intense socialization proved effective as newcomers worked hard and came to understand the culture of the fishing boat workplace. "It became a badge of honor to survive the initiation phase" (Bourassa and Ashforth 1998, p. 189). Yet the fleeting moment of self-satisfaction and positive feelings gave way to the continuous physical demands. Even the promise of economic rewards failed to sustain them. "The money was generally held in bank accounts until the completion of a contract. Workers could not use their money or even hold their paycheck in their hands. Thus, onboard the ship, money remained an abstract and distant notion" (Bourassa and Ashforth 1998, p. 189).

Jacqueline Lewis examined the socialization of exotic dancers where the goal for those entering this field is to become competent at their job. "For exotic dancers, achieving job competence involves getting accustomed to working in a sex-related occupation, and the practice of taking their clothes off in public for money" (J. Lewis 1998, p. 1). On-the-job socialization was essential for the women who entered this line of work. "Similar to the socialization experiences of individuals in other occupations, novice dancers learn through interaction and observation while on the job. . . . Since there is no formal certification structure,

peers play an important role in this transformation process" (J. Lewis 1998, p. 5). Lewis found that several women felt the socialization process "inadequately prepared them for some of the realities of the life of an exotic dancer" (J. Lewis 1998, p. 12)—mainly the negative impact it would have on their private lives and the difficulties of having long-term heterosexual relationships with men outside the industry.

While professional socialization occurs on the job, anticipatory socialization is the process of learning the behaviors, expectations, and standards of a role or group to which one aspires but does not yet belong. One way to acquire anticipatory or early professional socialization is to do an internship while you're in college. This chapter's On the Job box describes how internships work and why they are such a valuable learning experience before entering the job market.

The Contingent Workforce: Temps, Freelancers, and Independent Contractors

Traditionally most Americans have hoped to find a job they would keep their whole lives, one that would provide 40-hour work weeks along with vacations and health and retirement benefits. Increasingly this sort of job is becoming rare. A growing percentage of Americans have less steady work arrangements that could be defined as "work that does not involve explicit or implicit contracts for long-term employment" (Bendapudi et al. 2003). These workers are referred to as the contingent workforce. It is made up of four categories: independent contractors, on-call workers, temporary help agency workers, and contract company workers—sometimes called "temps" or "freelancers." Over the last couple of decades contingent work has provided an alternative to long-term, full-time employment and has grown three times faster than traditional jobs. The Bureau of Labor Statistics reports that approximately 10 percent of the total American workforce in 2005 fell into this category and predicted that by 2010 up to 25 percent would be contingent or part-time (Whitehead 2005).

Many see this situation as a potential disaster, as inferior jobs are created by corporations seeking to slash overhead, especially those costs associated with health benefits, which are almost never available to contingent workers. Employers have a number of financial and legal responsibilities to their regular workers—overtime pay, health insurance, Social Security, disability and worker's compensation benefits—that don't apply to temps or independent contractors. Many fear businesses will increasingly turn to alternative employment arrangements solely to cut costs to the distinct disadvantage of their employees.

Changing the World

Millions of Volunteers

Have you ever donated time or money to a cause that you support? In addition to working in internships and participating in other forms of experiential learning (see "On the Job: Internships and Experiential Learning," p. 366) as a part of their academic careers, students often do community service and volunteer in a wide variety of charitable organizations and nonprofit settings. National Volunteer Week, the third week of April each year, celebrates such people and their efforts to help others.

The Bureau of Labor Statistics (2008f) reports that in 2007 an estimated 60.8 million Americans, or over 26 percent of the total population, engaged in some form of volunteer work. Volunteers spent a median of 52 hours on volunteer activities each during the same year. Women tend to volunteer in larger numbers, such that over 29 percent of all U.S. women and 23 percent of men volunteered in 2007. Men, however, spent more hours in volunteering than women, a median of 52 to 50 hours, respectively. Volunteers are represented fairly evenly from all age groups, though persons 45 to 54 years old were the most likely to volunteer. Volunteer rates were lowest among those in their early twenties (17 percent). Volunteers come from every socioeconomic level, but members of the middle and upper-middle classes are most likely to volunteer. All races and ethnicities are represented as well.

TABLE 12.2 Volunteers by Type of Organization for Which Volunteer Activities Were Performed and Selected Characteristics, 2007

	TOTAL VOLUNTEERS (THOUSANDS)	CIVIC, POLITICAL, PROFESSIONAL, OR INTERNATIONAL	EDUCATIONAL OR YOUTH SERVICE	ENVIRONMENTAL OR ANIMAL CARE
All	60,838	5.1%	26.2%	1.9%
Men	25,724	6.5	24.3	2.0
Women	35,114	4.1	27.5	1.9
16 to 24 years	7,798	3.9	30.8	2.4
25 years and over	53,040	5.3	25.5	1.9
White	52,586	5.2	26.3	2.1
African American	5,010	4.0	24.3	0.6
Asian	1,887	3.4	24.9	0.9
Hispanic	4,279	3.1	34.8	1.4
Less than High School Diploma	2,394	3.3	22.0	0.8
High School Graduates	11,379	4.2	22.3	1.4
Some College	15,468	5.4	25.3	1.7
College Graduates	23,799	6.0	27.5	2.3
Single	12,612	5.0	27.6	2.7
Married	38,876	5.0	26.8	1.7

SOURCE: U.S. Bureau of Labor Statistics 2008g

Many Americans volunteer at religious organizations to which they belong. Lawyers do "pro bono" work for those who can't afford representation. Veterinarians offer free clinics for homeless persons' animal companions. "Candy-stripers" help patients and their visitors in hospitals. Families serve in soup kitchens during holiday times such as Thanksgiving and Christmas. Every Election Day, neighborhood volunteers organize and staff local voting booths. And college students volunteer in a wide variety of organizations, from tutoring elementary school students and answering rape crisis hotlines to coaching sports teams, caring for animals at local shelters, and helping out at the Red Cross. Table 12.2 shows the types of organizations for which Americans most often volunteered in 2007.

People do volunteer work for many reasons—for social justice, social change, religious values, work experience, participation in clubs and social groups, and even out of boredom. Not only does volunteering satisfy our most altruistic ideals; it can also be a way to enhance our careers, strengthen our relationships with others, and even let us live out fantasies or dreams that are not part of our normal, everyday lives. And in so doing, volunteers help create a different world for themselves and others.

HOSPITAL OR OTHER HEALTH	PUBLIC SAFETY	RELIGIOUS	SOCIAL OR COMMUNITY SERVICE	SPORT, HOBBY, CULTURAL, OR ARTS	OTHER OR UNDETERMINED
7.8%	1.3%	35.6%	13.1%	3.5%	5.4%
5.7	2.3	35.0	13.9	4.2	6.0
9.4	0.6	36.0	12.4	3.1	5.0
8.1	1.3	29.9	13.9	2.8	6.7
7.8	1.3	36.4	13.0	3.6	5.3
8.1	1.5	34.5	13.1	3.7	5.4
5.1	0.2	47.9	11.6	0.9	5.2
7.9	0.4	38.3	12.9	4.4	6.9
6.3	0.6	35.5	10.9	2.6	4.9
5.0	0.8	48.3	13.4	2.0	4.6
6.9	1.9	41.4	13.3	3.3	5.4
8.4	1.6	36.1	13.2	3.4	4.8
8.1	0.9	33.1	12.6	4.1	5.5
9.4	1.3	27.3	15.6	4.0	7.1
6.7	1.3	39.1	11.5	3.3	4.6

"Always Low Prices," at What Cost? In October of 2003, federal agents arrested 245 illegal immigrant workers in 60 different Wal-Mart stores who were employed by the independent contractors that Wal-Mart hired to do its nightly cleaning. The subcontracted employees worked seven days a week and received no overtime pay or benefits from the contractors, who had thus violated overtime, Social Security, and workers' compensation laws.

Sometimes businesses will classify workers as "independent contractors" even though they do the same work in the same place as regular workers. In an infamous example in the late 1990s, Microsoft was forced to pay $97 million to settle a lawsuit alleging it had wrongly classified a group of employees as independent contractors, making them ineligible for benefits. These workers had been hired as freelancers to work on specific projects, but "the workers were fully integrated into Microsoft's workforce, working under nearly identical circumstances as Microsoft's regular employees . . . the same core hours at the same location and the same supervisors as regular employees" (Muhl 2002).

A different, though equally exploitative, tactic was used by the contractors hired to clean Wal-Mart stores. In October 2003, federal agents arrested 245 undocumented workers in 60 different Wal-Mart stores around the country. The workers came from 18 nations but very few of them actually worked for Wal-Mart. Instead they were employed by independent contractors hired by Wal-Mart to do its nightly cleaning (Bartels 2003). Although companies are not responsible for the actions of subcontractors they hire, they can be held responsible if it is proven they knew something illegal was going on. This is especially important when the jobs offered to the illegal aliens are abusive. When contractors hire employees who work seven days a week and receive no overtime pay or benefits, then those contractors are in violation of overtime, Social Security, and workers' compensation laws (Greenhouse 1997). Furthermore, it is much harder for legitimate contractors to win bids for contracts when their competition can offer lower prices by illegally underpaying their workers.

It is not surprising to discover a lack of job satisfaction among temporary workers, mainly clerical and manufacturing workers, and on-call workers, like substitute teachers, construction workers, nurses, and truck drivers (Cohany 1996). Many temporary workers hope they will be able to use their temp job as a springboard to a permanent one, but often this does not happen. However, the flexibility and freedom of alternative work arrangements appeal to a substantial number of workers, such as students, parents with children at home, and retirees. Though the increase in nontraditional employment has many potential negative effects, "there is as much diversity in the characteristics of jobs and workers within each type of employment arrangement, whether traditional or otherwise, as there is between different types of arrangements" (Cohany 1996).

While there is clearly a downside to being a temp or independent contractor, research indicates that there can also be great satisfaction among these freelance workers. Of the four categories tracked by the Bureau of Labor Statistics, independent contractors make up the largest group—almost two-thirds of the total. In contrast to the traditional worker, the occupational profile of the independent contractor is skewed toward several high-skilled fields including writers and artists, insurance and real estate agents, construction

TABLE 12.3	*Theory in Everyday Life*	
Perspective	**Approach to Work and the Economy**	**Case Study: Outsourcing of Work**
STRUCTURAL-FUNCTIONALISM	Different types of work (high prestige and pay to low prestige and pay) are necessary to the economy and have functions that help maintain social order.	Outsourcing is necessary to keep both national and global economies stable in the current market.
CONFLICT THEORY	A stratified labor market creates intergroup conflict—wealthier capitalists may exploit less-powerful workers.	Outsourcing exploits poor and developing nations and laid-off local workers, all while enriching corporations.
SYMBOLIC INTERACTIONISM	Work is central to our self-concept—we are intensely identified with our work, both by ourselves and by others.	Workers whose jobs are outsourced may come to see themselves as worthless and expendable because it seems that others see them that way too.

trade employees, and other technical and computer-related professions. They tend to be better paid than the average worker and prefer their employment situation for the flexibility and freedom it offers (Cohany 1996). However, even in this category, a significant minority, especially women, make less money and are less satisfied with their situation. Some also suffer from alienation, disenchantment, and burnout.

The Third Sector and Volunteerism

Not all corporations seek a profit, nor do all workers get paid a wage for their labor. Numerous organizations engage in social welfare, social justice, and/or environmental services. Typically these are churches, schools, hospitals, philanthropic foundations, art institutions, scientific research centers, and a multitude of others organizations, both permanent and temporary. They are private, rather than government, organizations and devoted to serving the general welfare, not their own financial interests. They are nonprofit organizations, designed to run as cost-effectively as possible and to direct any gains or earnings, above basic operating expenses, back into the causes they support. Together, these organizations and the workers who staff them constitute what social scientists call the **Independent** (or **Third**) **Sector** of the economy.

In 2004, over 900,000 nonprofit organizations were registered with the U.S. Treasury Department and accorded tax privileges. In addition, there may be 2 to 3 million other private nonprofit groups and associations less formal in nature. The Third Sector helps society in a number of ways. First, these organizations play a significant part in the American system of pluralism, operating alongside the first two sectors of government and business while helping to strengthen and make them work better. Although we think of nonprofits, business, and government as separate, they are really interconnected through their impact on public policy. Second, nonprofit organizations deliver a wide range of vital services

to millions of people in almost every social category. Last, they are a humanizing force in American society, allowing an important avenue of expression for altruism.

The Third Sector represents one of the most distinctive and commendable features of our society. While most nonprofits have some paid employees, they also rely on volunteers to deliver their services to the public. Volunteerism reflects a profound and important American value, that citizens in a democracy have a personal responsibility to serve those in need. Millions of Americans give their time as volunteers every year. The average value of an hour of volunteering in 2004 was estimated to be worth $17.55 (Independent Sector 2005), and the estimated total value of donated hours in 2002 was more than $256 billion.

There are many ways of working—some conventional, some alternative. Not all workers have jobs in traditional fields; not all workers have permanent or full-time jobs; and not all workers do it for a paycheck.

> **Independent** (or **Third**) **Sector** the part of the economy composed of nonprofit organizations; their workers are mission driven, rather than profit driven, and direct surplus funds to the causes they support

Closing Comments

You may never have imagined that work was such a big part of life. You might have had a job of some kind, but now you probably have a better idea of just how important work is on both a collective and an individual level. It is so important that sociologists have devoted much of their work to studying work. We can be fairly certain that work will remain a major reality in the human experience into the distant future. We hope that you have gained some insight into the structure and meaning of work in your own lives and the lives of others in society.

 Find more review materials online at
www.wwnorton.com/studyspace

CHAPTER SUMMARY

- **The Economy, Work, and Working** Through employment choices, we are linked to global economic structures. The history of work and the economy show trends of increasing efficiency and surplus because of changes in technology and technique. The Agricultural Revolution

allowed humans to gradually produce increasingly large food surpluses. This revolution happened slowly compared to the Industrial Revolution, which led to a relatively quick, radical break with the past.

The factory, the assembly line, the steam engine, and other technological developments allowed much greater quantities of goods to be produced. These technological developments also changed how people lived, encouraging immigration both internationally and from rural areas into cities. The development of the microchip in the 1970s ushered in the Information Revolution, which shifted the focus of the U.S. economy from manufacturing goods to managing information. The internet, computer networking, and all types of digital media and communications created a need for knowledge workers, who have little to do with the creation of physical goods.

- **Economic Systems: Comparing Capitalism and Socialism** In the industrial and postindustrial world, capitalism and socialism are the primary political economic systems. Pure capitalism relies on supply and demand to regulate the prices of goods and services; it is based on the private ownership of the means of production, and production for profits. A capitalist economy encourages efficiency through new technology, the expansion of markets, and cost cutting, which today means the privatization of basic human services and the tendency to move operations to other countries where labor and production costs are cheaper. Socialism is based on the collective distribution of goods and services to guarantee workers' access to basic resources. All nations' economies have both capitalist and socialist aspects. For example, the capitalist United States has some socialist economic features, including business subsidies, market regulation, and public aid programs.

- **The Nature of Industrial and Postindustrial Work** Before the Industrial Revolution, economic production took place in the household—but the birth of the factory led to the "workplace" and raised new work-related issues. Karl Marx identified the shift from household production to wage-labor and factory work as the source of modern workers' alienation. He argued that when people lose control over the conditions of production, they become alienated and view work as a means to survive rather than a rewarding activity in itself.

- In a postindustrial economy, many workers labor in service positions Some service positions are well paid, but many intensify the alienation that industrial workers felt. Service work involves direct contact with customers, as well as with a manager or supervisor who limits workers' autonomy and control. Some workers in the postindustrial economy have benefited from the Information Revolution—especially those who do knowledge work. Information technology has expanded the number of people who can work from home by allowing them to telecommute, saving time and energy, decreasing pollution, and adding flexibility to work schedules.

- **Individual and Collective Resistance Strategies: How Workers Cope** Some workers, especially in large, bureaucratic organizations, dislike their lack of autonomy on the job, and they may attempt to resist, both individually and collectively. Individual acts of resistance usually involve symbolic gestures that give an individual a sense of control over her environment. To fundamentally change the workplace, however, requires collective forms of resistance, such as unions that can bargain for all employees. Historically, unions fought for both increased wages and better working conditions. In recent years, union activity has sharply declined. After World War II, legal restrictions on strikes and work stoppages sharply limited union power, as have more recent trends toward globalization and the "runaway shop."

- **Globalization, Economics, and Work** The development of international economic institutions has fostered globalization, the cultural and economic changes caused by dramatically increased international trade and exchange. Technological innovations also support globalization by facilitating the movement of money, information, and people worldwide. Although global trade is centuries old, today's global economy is much more deeply integrated, as many companies are multinational and goods are produced in much more complicated ways. Companies constantly search for the cheapest way to produce goods, often involving global commodity chains, outsourcing, and the creation of sweatshops.

- **Alternative Ways of Working** The modern economy is characterized by the diversification of work. The increasingly specialized division of labor means that professional socialization is necessary to orient people to how to do their jobs. The contingent workforce is growing every year as more businesses rely on temps and freelancers, who often would prefer full-time employment. And in a capitalist society, we increasingly rely on a Third Sector made up of nonprofit organizations that take care of necessary but unprofitable social needs.

QUESTIONS FOR REVIEW

1. Think about the jobs you would like to get after you finish college. Do any of them involve directly participating in the production of physical goods?

2. Think about the objects you use every day. How many of them use microchips? How many of them didn't even exist 25 years ago?

3. Thinking of the United States as a capitalist nation with some socialist elements, are there any ways you directly benefit from government intervention in the economy?

4. Marx described four ways that modern wage labor is alienating. Do you think these apply to you and to the job you have or would like to have? If you have a job, would you choose to keep it even if you became independently wealthy?

5. Information technology has changed the workplace in many ways, including increasing numbers of people who telecommute. Have you experienced anything like telecommuting? How about at school? What are the advantages and disadvantages of distance learning?

6. Resistance strategies are ways that workers can assert some degree of autonomy in a workplace that increasingly exerts control and keeps workers under surveillance. What sorts of actions qualify as individual resistance strategies? Have you ever done anything like this?

7. The U.S. General Accounting Office defines a sweatshop as "an employer that violates more than one federal or state labor law governing minimum wage and overtime, child labor, industrial homework, occupational safety and health, workers' compensation, or industrial regulation." How do you think we should define sweatshops in other countries? What sort of working conditions would lead you to stop buying a product as a way to protest the treatment of the people who produced it?

8. Outsourcing involves the "contracting out" or transferring to another country tasks that used to be taken care of in-house. Have you ever noticed this sort of outsourcing? What sorts of jobs get outsourced? How does this practice affect the economy?

9. Almost every job requires some degree of professional socialization. Have you ever experienced anything like this? Did you engage in any anticipatory socialization first?

SUGGESTIONS FOR FURTHER EXPLORATION

Clerks. 1994. Dir. Kevin Smith. Miramax Films. A darkly humorous (though R-rated) take on what it means to be a service worker on the bottom rungs of the American economy and the unique challenges of dealing with customers.

The Corporation. 2003. Dir. Mark Achbar and Jennifer Abbott. Big Picture Media Corporation. A documentary arguing that because the law treats corporations as "persons," we should analyze them the same way we do real people. The film concludes that if viewed this way, corporations are psychopaths, unable to act with a conscience.

Gibson, William. 2003. *Pattern Recognition*. New York: Putnam. This novel uses a plot about a mysterious film being released little by little on the internet as a way of examining the effects of the Information Revolution. The *Economist* called it "not, strictly speaking, a business book—but probably the best exploration yet of the function and power of product branding and advertising in the age of globalization and the internet."

In Good Company. 2005. Dir. Paul Weitz. Universal Pictures. A feel-good corporate movie that gives a humorous, emotional picture of the consequences of a corporate take-over and the real human faculties that come out when the workplace lets people down.

Norma Rae. 1979. Dir. Martin Ritt. 20th Century Fox. Sally Field won an Oscar for her performance as a single mother who struggles to unionize a textile factory. Based on a true story, the movie dramatizes the challenges in convincing individuals that collective resistance can be effective and improve their lives.

Polanyi, Karl. 1944. *The Great Transformation*. Boston: Beacon Hill. In this classic account of the social changes wrought by the Industrial Revolution, Polanyi argues that the Great Depression and both World Wars can be viewed as a result of unchecked market capitalism.

Protzman, Ferdinand. 2006. *Work: The World in Photographs*. Washington, DC: National Geographic. This coffee table book celebrates the diverse ways that people in all parts of the world earn a living. The pictures, which span the last 150 years, convey wealth and poverty, pain and violence, joy and triumph, all in the workplace.

Smith, Patti. "Piss Factory." *Land (1975–2002)*. Arista Records. Inspired by her experience as a teenager working in a factory in New Jersey, Smith details in explicit terms the anger and alienation she felt toward the conditions of factory work and her desire to make a living without sacrificing her autonomy.

Von Drehle, David. 2003. *Triangle: The Fire That Changed America*. New York: Atlantic Monthly Press. A chilling description of the fire that was New York City's worst disaster until 9/11, as well as an analysis of the social, political, and economic context that gave rise to such dangerous conditions.

CHAPTER 13

Life at Home

Tom, a single doctor in his sixties, lived in the same home for 30 years with three much-loved dogs: two boxers named Blaze and Pepe, and a Boston terrier named Brownie. They were his devoted companions. When one of the dogs died, Tom would get a new dog of the same breed and keep the dog's name. Thus, if Blaze died, the new boxer would be named Blaze; if Brownie died, the new Boston terrier would also be Brownie. Tom's relationship with his dogs went on for 30 years. Are Tom and the dogs a family?

Stacie and Eric met in graduate school and married the year they received their degrees. Their job hunts, however, led them in different directions: Stacie took a job with an international policy agency in Washington, D.C., and Eric went to work for a major corporation in Miami, Florida. Living in their respective cities, they ran up huge phone bills and spent lots of money on weekend plane tickets. After about five years, Stacie became pregnant, and the baby is due in a few months. Are Stacie and Eric a family?

Jeannie and Tammy also met in graduate school—almost 20 years ago. They are both professors in Minneapolis, and together they bought and fixed up an old house. They would like to formalize their commitment to one another, but they cannot do so legally because Minnesota does not allow same-sex partners to marry. Nevertheless, they've adopted a little boy named Conor and are looking forward to celebrating his first Christmas. Are Jeannie, Tammy, and Conor a family?

For some of you, the answers may come easily, but others of you may find yourself wondering—are these groups really families? Tom loves Brownie, Blaze, and Pepe, but can you really be a family if most of your members aren't human? And is Tom's replacement policy similar to or different from the practice of remarrying when a spouse dies? What about Stacie and Eric—they're married and are having a biological child, which seems to make them easily definable as a family. Yet they don't live under the same roof. What does that make them? Even Tom and the dogs live together. And so do Jeannie and Tammy; they can own property together and designate each other as heirs in their wills—though they can't legally marry. They're raising their son Conor together, even though Tammy had to adopt Conor on her own first, and then Jeannie legally became his second parent later, since they could not adopt together like a married heterosexual couple can. Do these complications mean that they aren't a real family?

SocIndex

Then and Now

1950: Average size of a single-family home: 983 square feet

2007: Average size of a single-family home: 2,521 square feet

Here and There

United States: Average number of people per household: 2.6

Pakistan: Average number of people per household: 6.7

This and That

Average cost of a wedding in the United States: $30,000

Average cost for one year at a private university in the United States: $30,000

It all depends on how you define family. If emotional bonds and mutual support are the only criteria, then all of these groups are families. But if a marital bond is required, then only Stacie and Eric are a family. If other legal ties are included, then Tammy, Jeannie, and Conor can be a family too. If you have to be heterosexual, then Jeannie and Tammy are out, and we really don't know about Tom, do we? If the longevity of the relationships is the key, then Tom and the dogs win over both of these other potential families. But if you have to be human and irreplaceable, then all those Brownies, Blazes, and Pepes don't qualify. And if a shared residence must be part of the equation, then Tom and the dogs are in but Stacie and Eric are out. So, how do you define family?

HOW TO READ THIS CHAPTER

In this chapter, we examine society's most basic social group—the family. Yet what makes a family is subject to debate. Sociology doesn't define a family by who its members are but by what they do, how they relate to one another, and what their relationship is to the larger society. We'll look at the dynamic diversity of family forms in the contemporary United States, the functions of family for society, the hierarchies of inequality that shape family life, the work that gets done by and in families, the kinds of troubles families experience, and the political and cultural controversies that affect family life. You will learn that when it comes to family life, change is the only constant.

What Is the Family?

The U.S. Census Bureau defines family as two or more individuals related by blood, marriage, or adoption living in the same household. This definition is a good starting point, but it's too limited to encompass even the family arrangements described in the opening vignette. Contemporary sociologists use the word **family** to mean a social group whose members are bound by some type of tie—legal, biological, emotional, or a combination of all three. They may or may not share a household, but family members are interdependent and have a sense of mutual responsibility for one another's care. We don't define family by specific types of people (parents or children) or specific types of ties (marriage) because we believe the definition should be broad enough to encompass a variety of forms. However, this very variety is the source of controversy both within and outside academia. Regardless of the definition, most people recognize family as an integral social institution found in every society.

The family as an institution has always changed in response to its social, cultural, political, and economic milieu. Before the Industrial Revolution, *family* tended to mean **extended family**—a large group of **kin**, or relatives, which could include grandparents, uncles, aunts, and cousins living in one household. After the Industrial Revolution, this configuration was largely superseded by the **nuclear family**—a heterosexual couple in their own household raising children. Along the way, the family moved from a more public social institution to a private one, as many functions formerly associated with the family were transferred to other institutions. For example, work and production moved from the family to the factory, education moved from the family to the school, and government took over a variety of social welfare and medical functions formerly taken care of by the extended family.

Subsequent waves of social change, such as the women's liberation movement and the move toward individual independence and self-fulfillment, have begun to erode the dominance of the nuclear family, as increased divorce rates, working mothers, single parents, gay and lesbian families, and other alternative family arrangements become more common. Many sociologists speak of the sociology not of *the* family but rather of *families*. "Family situations in contemporary society are so varied and diverse that it simply makes no sociological sense to speak of a single ideal-type model of 'the family' at all" (Bernardes 1985 p. 209).

Even though a two-parent household with a stay-at-home mother is no longer the norm, this type of family remains the model by which new forms of the family are judged. However, there are exceptions, as commonsense definitions of the family

family a social group whose members are bound by legal, biological, or emotional ties, or a combination of all three

extended family a large group of relatives, usually including at least three generations living either in one household or in close proximity

kin relatives or relations, usually those related by common descent

nuclear family a heterosexual couple with one or more children living in a single household

reflect the changes occurring in the larger society at any given moment. Children seem to be important in our commonsense definitions, as one study found that unmarried couples, both gay and heterosexual, are more likely to be considered a family if children are present (Powell 2003). Unrelated roommates who are not romantically involved are significantly more likely to be considered family by those over the age of 65:

> I call this the *Golden Girls* effect. . . . People at retirement, on one hand, tend to be very traditional about issues of sexuality, but in terms of what they count as family, they are more likely to accept housemates as a sort of family unit. Their views may be affected by major changes in life, such as a move to a retirement home or a loss of a spouse. (Powell 2003)

Diversity in Families

Artistic representations of the traditional family generally show a mother, a father, and their two children all with the same skin tone and hair color. These pictures reflect a practice called **endogamy** that refers to marrying someone of similar race or ethnicity, class, education, religion, region, or nationality. **Exogamy** refers to marrying someone from a different social group.

As an example of how family forms and definitions change over time, marriage between people of different racial, ethnic, or national background has actually been prohibited for most of the history of the United States. From the time of slavery through the 1960s, mixed-race relationships were considered criminal and were also punished outside the law. Fears of interracial relationships led to the lynching of African American men and the creation of **antimiscegenation** laws in several U.S. states that prohibited the mixing of racial groups through marriage, cohabitation, or sexual interaction (Messerschmidt 1998). The most significant of these laws fell after the 1967 Supreme Court declared that Virginia's law banning marriage between persons of different races was unconstitutional under the Fourteenth Amendment (*Loving v. Virginia* 1967).

Though mixed-race unions are now legal, they are still uncommon but increasing. In 1960, only 0.4 percent of all couples were interracial, increasing to 2.2 percent by 1992 (U.S. Census Bureau 1994), 5.7 percent in 2000 (U.S. Census Bureau 2003), and 7 percent in 2005 (MSNBC 2007). Mixed-race couples still face discrimination; in their analysis of a white supremacist internet chat room, Glaser, Dixit, and Green (2002) found that respondents were far more threatened by interracial marriage than by persons of color moving into white neighborhoods or competing for jobs.

Monogamy, or marrying only one individual at a time, is still considered the only legal form of marriage in modern culture. **Polygamy**, or having multiple spouses, may be practiced among some subcultures around the world, but is not widely acknowledged as a legitimate form of marriage. The more commonly known form of polygamy is **polygyny**, where a man is married to multiple wives. **Polyandry**, where a woman has multiple husbands, has been documented in Tibet but is the rarer form of polygamy.

Sociological Perspectives on the Family

Among the sociological perspectives on the family, those with the structural-functionalist view see it as a cultural universal and try to identify its functions for society. Conflict theorists argue that there are inherent inequalities both within and between families. Symbolic interactionists focus on the family as the product of interactional processes. Each of these theories offers useful insights into our understanding of this unit.

Structural Functionalism

In *Suicide*, Emile Durkheim (1897/1951) argued that the Industrial Revolution and the division of labor had undermined the older social institutions that formerly regulated society, leaving some people suffering from anomie, or normlessness, that sometimes resulted in suicide. He found that marriage and family, at least for men, decreased their chances of suicide because these provide the structure and regulation that Durkheim believed people require to be happy.

The structural-functionalists who followed Durkheim argued that society's survival requires institutions that can serve its essential functions: economic production, the socialization of children, instrumental and emotional support, and sexual control. Although the family is no longer directly involved in economic production, it performs the functions

endogamy marriage to someone within one's social group

exogamy marriage to someone from a different social group

antimiscegenation the prohibition of interracial marriage, cohabitation, or sexual interaction

monogamy the practice of marrying (or being in a relationship with) one person at a time

polygamy a system of marriage that allows people to have more than one spouse at a time

polygyny a system of marriage that allows men to have multiple wives

polyandry a system of marriage that allows women to have multiple husbands

Changing the World

Who Can Marry?

Many people think of marriage as a natural right for everyone. In the United States, though, marriage is a privilege that is generally reserved for two consenting adults of opposite sexes. Historically, marriage in the United States has been restricted at times to citizens, whites, and couples of the same race. Though mixed-race unions are no longer illegal, same-sex marriages are outlawed in most states. In this box, we explore the question: who can marry?

In the United States, marriage is a contract between two people and the government. Thus, married couples enjoy legal privileges such as tax benefits, insurance protections, hospital visitation and decision making, and other legal rights denied to nonmarried couples. Even "common law" marriage (an option in some states in which a period of cohabitation is substituted for legal marriage) is recognized for heterosexual couples only.

In only a few nations in the world—the Netherlands (as of 2001), Belgium (as of 2003), Spain and Canada (as of 2004), and South Africa (as of 2006)—do same-sex couples enjoy all the rights of full legal marriage. Several other nations—including Finland, Norway, Sweden, France, Hungary, Denmark, Israel, Colombia, the Czech Republic, Germany, and Portugal—and the states of New Jersey, Washington, and Washington, DC, offer some range of legal recognition and protection of same-sex or civil unions (Legal Marriage Alliance of Washington 2007). However, these fall short of the full rights reserved for heterosexual married couples. By 2009, only six states had legally recognized same-sex marriage: Connecticut, Iowa, Maine, Massachusetts, New Hampshire, and Vermont. Gay rights activists believe that the momentum is in their favor, as at least eight other states were then poised to consider legislation that would allow gay couples to marry (Goodnough 2009). Opponents, however, have been successful in defeating some same-sex measures, and continue to launch legal and constitutional challenges to the practice.

In February 2004, San Francisco Mayor Gavin Newsom began issuing marriage licenses to gay and lesbian couples, and over 3,000 couples came from around the country and the world to avail themselves of what proved to be a narrow legal window. On August 12, 2004, the California Supreme Court nullified all those marriages and declared them to be in violation of state law. Later, in June 2008, another state Supreme Court decision legalized gay marriage again in California, but in November of that year voters narrowly approved a state constitutional amendment banning marriage between same-sex individuals.

The legal battles over this issue continue in California and other states. In October of 2008, the Connecticut Supreme Court ruled that to prohibit gay marriage was

---

that allow production to happen. Talcott Parsons (1955) argued that "the modern nuclear family was especially complementary to the requirements of an industrial economy" because it freed individuals from onerous obligations to extended family members and made possible the geographic and social mobility demanded by the modern economy (Mann et al. 1997). In the most basic sense the family is responsible for the reproduction of society as it produces and socializes children. This is what Parsons referred to as "pattern maintenance," whereby the values and norms of a society are passed on to the next generation. Family also, ideally, provides emotional support for its members and regulates sexuality by helping define with whom we can and cannot mate. These patterns, according to functionalists, help society run smoothly and maintain stability and order.

Conflict Theory

Conflict theorists realize that the family produces and socializes children to function efficiently in a capitalist economy, but they see this function as problematic. The nuclear family, a relatively recent historical invention, acts as the primary economic unit in modern capitalist society, and since conflict theorists see capitalism as oppressive, they claim that this form of family contributes to that oppression—and is often

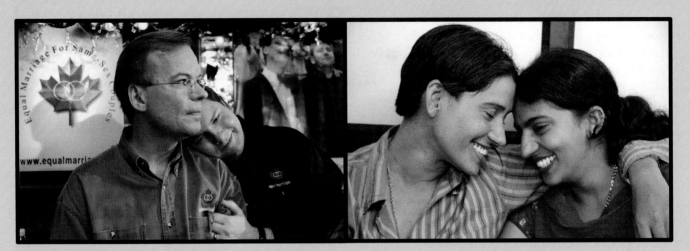

Who Gets to Marry? Kevin Bourassa and Joe Varnell (left) from Toronto are the first North American gay couple to be married. They embrace after the Supreme Court of Canada affirmed the legality of same-sex marriage in December 2004. Baljit Kaur and Raljwinder Kaur (right) from Amritsar, India, embrace after their wedding in India. Gay and lesbian couples throughout India are increasingly open about their sexuality and same-sex marriages are becoming increasingly common there.

unconstitutional. Hawaii, Alaska, Nevada, Nebraska, and Missouri have passed constitutional amendments explicitly limiting marriage to heterosexual couples. The 1996 U.S. congressional Defense of Marriage Act was also designed to reserve marriage for heterosexual couples only, and President George W. Bush was reelected in 2004 partly on his promise to amend the Constitution to prohibit gay marriage. Though some public attitudes seem to be shifting toward growing acceptance of gay marriage, not everyone is welcoming the change—including many public officials.

understood as an oppressive institution in itself. Conflict theorists believe that society revolves around conflict over scarce resources and that conflict within the family is also about the competition for resources: time, energy, and the leisure to pursue more interesting recreational activities.

In this analysis, the family can allow exploitation through a sexual rather than a class-based division of labor. Conflict perspectives overlap with feminist perspectives on the family as feminists assume that the family is a gendered social institution and that men and women experience family differently. In patriarchal societies, men wield greater power than women, both within and outside the family, and women's contributions to family and society are devalued (Thorne 1992).

Symbolic Interactionism

As Jim Holstein and Jay Gubrium point out in their book *What Is Family* (1990), the *family* does not exist, only *families*. These symbolic interactionists consider it more effective to look at how family relations are created and maintained in interaction than how they are structured. Even though the legal bond of marriage has the same technical meaning for every couple, individual marriages may have very different expectations and rules for behavior. One couple may require sexual monogamy within their marriage, while their neighbors may not; one couple may pool their finances while another husband and wife may keep separate bank accounts. This approach

Talking About Kin

In P. D. Eastman's children's book *Are You My Mother?* a newly hatched bird wanders about asking everyone—and everything—she encounters, "Are you my mother?" Sadly for the newborn, neither the construction crane, the cow, nor the cat is the parent she is searching for. On the last page of the book, however, the tiny bird is serendipitously returned to her nest and reunited with a maternal-looking chickadee.

When reading something like *Are You My Mother?* most people in the Western world would assume that the word *mother* means "female parent." However, in the Hawaiian language, *makuahine* means both "mother" and "aunt" and refers to any female relative in the generation of that person's parents (*makuakane* is the equivalent term for men) (Stanton 1995; Schwimmer 2001). In Hawaiian, then, "are you my mother?" could just as easily mean "are you my father's brother's wife?" In China, though, kinship terms are very precise. There are particular terms for a "father's brother's wife" that vary depending on whether the brother's wife is married to the older brother or a younger one (Levi-Strauss 1969)!

One reason we name our kin is to delineate the relationships and obligations we share. In some cases, we use the term **fictive kin** to refer to people who are not related to us through blood or through marriage. Such kin are created through closely knit friendships to the family. You may have a family friend you call Auntie So-and-So. In other societies fictive kin may be culturally prescribed. In Jordan it is perfectly normal for adult strangers to address one another with the Arabic equivalents of brother/sister, maternal aunt/uncle, and paternal aunt/uncle. In addition, an older Jordanian woman may affectionately refer to a child (of either gender) as "mother" (Farghal and Shakir 1994).

In China, labeling an older individual as an uncle or an older brother is a required sign of respect (Baker 1979). Sometimes fictive kin ties are formalized through ceremony,

as when a female in India ties a sacred thread around the wrist of an unrelated close male friend to indicate that she considers him a brother. In Latin America, godparents (*compadrazgo*, a word that can be translated as "coparent" rather than "godparent") are considered permanent members of their godchildren's family. Not surprisingly, the Spanish words for "daughter" and "son" are very close to the words for "goddaughter" and "godson" (Davila 1971; van den Berghe 1979).

Examining kin terms is one way to understand the diversity of families and how kin fulfill their social roles. As you can see, aunts, elder brothers, godparents, and family friends can all be important family members.

conceives of family as a fluid, adaptable set of concepts and practices that people use "for constructing the meaning of social bonds" (Holstein and Gubrium 1995b), a set of vocabularies to describe particular relationships.

Consider the number of relatives, defined by blood or marriage, most people have who play no meaningful role in their lives, who "aren't really family." When we describe people in terms of family we are making claims about the "rights, obligations, and sentiments" that exist within their relationships (Gubrium and Buckholdt 1982). Consequently we are constantly evaluating and reevaluating the attitudes and behaviors of those around us, assigning family status to new people and dismissing others from our circle of meaningful family relations. In *All Our Kin*, an ethnography of

TABLE 13.1 · *Theory in Everyday Life*

Perspective	Approach to Family	Case Study: Marriage
STRUCTURAL-FUNCTIONALISM	Family performs necessary functions, such as the socialization of children, that help society run smoothly and maintain social order.	Marriage regulates sexuality and forms the basis for family, with all its other functions.
CONFLICT THEORY	Family is a site of various forms of stratification and can produce and reproduce inequalities based on these statuses.	Marriage as a civil right is extended only to heterosexual couples in most states and nations. This is both a cause and a consequence of homophobia in society.
SYMBOLIC INTERACTIONISM	Family is a social construction; it is created, changed, and maintained in interaction.	Marriage is not made solely by completing a legal contract but is also constructed through the accretion of everyday interactions between partners over the years.

kinship relations in an urban African American community, Carol Stack found this dynamic at work in the way people talked about family—including this woman, who says,

> Most people kin to me are in this neighborhood . . . but I got people in the South, in Chicago, and in Ohio too. I couldn't tell most of their names and most of them aren't really kinfolk to me. . . . [T]ake my father, he's no father to me. I ain't got but one daddy and that's Jason. The one who raised me. My kids' daddies, that's something else, all their daddies' people really take to them—they always doing things and making a fuss about them. We help each other out and that's what kinfolks are all about. (Stack 1974)

A symbolic interactionist might say that "family members do not merely passively conform to others' expectations" but rather "actively and creatively construct and modify their roles through interactions" (Dupuis and Smale 2000)—that is, the people who help each other out, who care for each other, and who express that care are family, whether they are legally related or not.

Forming Relationships, Selecting Mates

You may think that you are attracted to certain people because of their unique individual characteristics or something intangible called "chemistry." In reality, however, Cupid's arrow is largely aimed by society. Two time-tested concepts in social science—*homogamy* and *propinquity*—tell us a lot about how the mate-selection process works.

Homogamy literally means "like marries like": we tend to choose mates who are similar to us in class, race, ethnicity, age, religion, education, and even levels of attractiveness. You can certainly find examples of people whose romantic relationships cross these category lines—interracial or inter-religious couples, or May/December romances—but these relationships are often viewed with disapproval by others in the couples' social circles. There are considerable social pressures to adhere to homogamy.

Propinquity refers to geographical proximity: we tend to choose people who live nearby. This is logical; we are likely to find possible mates among the people in our neighborhood, at work, or at school. The internet makes courtship and romance possible across much greater geographical areas, as we can now meet and converse with people in all parts of the world, so our pool of potential mates moves beyond local bounds. But even this technology may intensify homogamy by bringing together people with very specific interests and identities. Examples include internet services such as J-Date, for Jewish singles; Prime Singles, for people over 50; and EbonyConnect, for African American singles.

Courtship, romance, and intimacy are all influenced by the larger culture—and are also historically specific. While we experience courtship at an individual, interactional level, it will always be shaped by macro-structural forces in the larger society, such as racial, ethnic, or religious prejudices, and gendered role expectations. But courtship changes as other aspects of the surrounding culture change. As our society becomes less racist, sexist, and heterosexist, romantic options will expand as well. The development of intimate romantic relationships is not something "natural"; it is socially constructed to *appear* natural.

> **propinquity** the tendency to marry or have relationships with people in close geographic proximity

Doing the Work of Family

When we think of work, we usually think of activities done for a paycheck. But paid labor is not the only type of work that sociologists are interested in—especially in the study of the family. Many types of work—both paid and unpaid—are necessary to keep a family operating: child care, house-cleaning, car maintenance, cooking, bill-paying, vacation planning, and doing laundry—the list seems endless, especially when you are the one doing the work!

These tasks can be instrumental or expressive. **Instrumental tasks** generally achieve a tangible goal (washing the dishes, fixing the gutters), whereas **expressive tasks** generally achieve emotional or relational goals (remembering relatives' birthdays, playing Chutes and Ladders with the kids). In a real family, however, much of the work has both instrumental and expressive elements. The expressive work of remembering and celebrating birthdays, for example, includes all sorts of instrumental tasks such as buying presents, writing cards, and baking cakes (Di Leonardo 1987; Pleck 2000).

As a social scientist committed to making the invisible labor of family visible, Marjorie DeVault (1991) excavates all the knowledge, skills, and practices—both instrumental and expressive—we take for granted when, for example, we feed our families. Not only is the knowledge of cooking needed, but there must be appropriate shopping to keep a stocked kitchen; to make meals that account for family members' likes, dislikes, and allergies; and to create a varied and balanced menu. Producing meals that please, satisfy, and bring individuals together is just one of the ways that family is created and sustained through interactional work. We constitute family in and through meals and every other mundane activity of everyday life.

DATA WORKSHOP

ANALYZING EVERYDAY LIFE

Comparative Mealtime

Some of us carry a strong and positive image of our family gathered around the dining room table for dinner each evening. While we were growing up, dinner may have been the one time in the day when the whole family was together and shared food, stories, lessons, and news. For many of us, a great deal of socialization took place around the dinner table; we learned about manners ("sit up straight," "don't speak with your mouth full") as well as morality, politics, or anything else that seemed important to the adults raising us. Some of us, on the other hand, may have different memories of family mealtimes. Perhaps they were a time of tension and arguments, or perhaps the family rarely ate a meal together.

In this Data Workshop, you will be using participant observation as a research method (see Chapter 3 for a review) and doing ethnographic research on mealtime activity. You will compare two or more different mealtime settings and situations. You can choose from among a range of different possibilities, including the following:

- Which meal you study—breakfast, lunch, or dinner

- Where the meal takes place—in your family home; at a friend's or a relative's house; at your own apartment or dormitory dining hall; at a workplace lunch room, picnic in the park, or restaurant

- Who is eating—family members, roommates, friends, coworkers, or strangers

After you participate in and observe two mealtimes, write down answers to the following questions:

- What are the prevailing rules, rituals, norms, and values associated with the setting and situation? For example, does everyone sit down to eat at the same time? Do people leave after they finish even if others are still eating?

- What kinds of complementary roles are the various participants engaged in? Who cooks the food, sets the table, clears the table, does the dishes, and so forth?

- What other types of activities (besides eating) are taking place at mealtime? Are people watching TV, listening to music or a ball game, reading the newspaper?

- What social purposes does the setting or situation serve other than providing a mealtime environment for the participants? For example, what do the participants talk about? If children are involved, do they talk about school or their friends? Are family activities or problems discussed?

In addition to taking detailed notes, you may also wish to interview some of the participants.

There are two options for completing the assigned work in the Data Workshop.

- *Option 1 (informal)*: Make the observations described above and conduct any formal or informal interviews

instrumental tasks the practical physical tasks necessary to maintain family life

expressive tasks the emotional work necessary to support family members

What's for Dinner? Compare these two family meals. What do our mealtime practices tell us about contemporary American families?

you wish. Prepare some written notes that you can refer to during in-class discussions. Compare and contrast the analyses of the different family meals observed by participants in your group. What are the similarities and differences in your observations?

- *Option 2 (formal)*: Make the observations described above, and conduct any formal or informal interviews you wish. Write a three- to four-page essay answering the questions listed above and reflecting on your own experience in conducting this study. What do you think your observations tell us about contemporary American families and the practices of family mealtimes? Don't forget to attach your fieldnotes and interview transcripts.

Gender and Family Labor

Imagine working a labor-intensive 40 to 60 hours waiting tables, making automobile parts, typing memos, or teaching second graders. You arrive home feeling tired, hungry, and worn out, but you cannot sit down to relax. You still need to cook a meal, do some laundry and cleaning, and take care of your children or perhaps your elderly parents.

Who is more likely to come home to this scenario? Among heterosexual couples, women are more likely to have the dual workload of paid labor outside the home and unpaid labor inside the home. In this section, we will discuss the division of labor within the household.

Men and women have always performed different roles to ensure the survival of their families, but these roles were not considered unequal until after the Industrial Revolution. At that time, men began to leave their homes to earn wages working in factories. Women remained at home taking care of children and carrying out other domestic responsibilities. As men's earned wages replaced subsistence farming—in which women had always participated—these wages became the primary mechanism for providing food, clothing, and shelter for families, thus giving men economic power over women. Feminist sociologists contend that women's "second shift" is the legacy of this historic economic change.

Despite women's increasing participation in the paid workforce, they are still more likely to perform the bulk of household and caregiving labor. In a few cases, men share household chores (Coltrane 1997) but women bear the brunt of unpaid household labor. Arlie Hochschild and Machung's 1989 study of working couples and parents found that women were indeed working two jobs: paid labor outside the home, or the first shift, and unpaid labor inside the home, or the **second shift**. Hochschild and Machung found that these women tried

> **second shift** unpaid labor inside the home; often expected of women after they get home from working at paid labor outside the home

Permutations of Family Living: From Boomerang Kids to the Sandwich Generation

When people talk about the disappearance of the nuclear family, they usually are referring to the divorce rate, but, especially for the baby boom generation, families are changing in other ways as well. Traditionally, becoming middle-aged was associated with the "mid-life crisis" but also with maturity, wisdom, and increased professional skills. While this might seem like a contradiction, changes in the nature of the family make it seem more like a necessity! Increasing numbers of middle-aged people are becoming members of a "sandwich generation," adults who provide material and emotional support for both "young children and older living parents" (Lachman 2004, p. 322). This effect is magnified by the increasing number of so-called boomerang kids, who leave home at 18 to attend college but often return home for at least a short period of time afterward.

Both of these dynamics are being driven less by choice than by demographic and economic necessity. In 1970 the average age at first marriage was less than 21 for women and a little over 23 for men. Today the median age at first marriage for women is 25, and for men it's almost 27. As a result, people are having children later, increasing the chances that child rearing and elder care will overlap. Advances in life expectancy also contribute to the sandwich effect, even as many of the medical advances that allow people to live longer also increase their need for material support. While there have always been adults caring for their elderly parents, never before have there been this many elderly. According to the U.S. Census Bureau, the number of the "oldest old,"

those 85 and older, increased 274 percent between 1960 and 1994 while "the elderly population in general rose 100 percent and the entire U.S. population grew only 45 percent" (U.S. Census Bureau 1995). Meanwhile, between tuition increases, student loans, and the high price of real estate, students are leaving college more likely to need help from their parents than ever before. In 1980 fewer than 9 percent of all individuals between 25 and 34 lived with their parents. By the year 2007 this number had increased to almost 12 percent, still a small group, but one that has increased 34 percent over the last three decades.

Members of the sandwich generation have found themselves with more responsibilities than ever before. Not only are their parents living longer than before, but medical costs associated with old age are growing rapidly, and often they have children, of all ages, still dependent on them as well. Never before has there been a substantial cohort of Americans so directly burdened with such a wide range of family responsibilities. However, in some ways the more the sandwich generation adults and the boomerang kids change the family, the more they stay the same, especially in the way that gender roles manifest themselves. Even among 18- to 24-year-olds, boys are more likely to live at home than girls, and 60 percent of the boomerang kids between 25 and 34 are male. While men and women might be driven by the same financial troubles, moving back in with her parents has different consequences for a woman. She is likely to be asked to take on more domestic responsibilities, and typically she

numerous strategies to achieve balance between work and home: hiring other women to clean their houses and care for their children; relying on friends or family members for help; refusing to do certain chores, especially those considered to be generally "men's work"; lowering their expectations for cleanliness or quality of child care; or reducing

the number of hours they worked outside the home. But some women accept their dual workloads without any help to avoid conflicts with spouses and children. Hochschild and Machung called these women "Supermoms" but also found that these "Supermoms" often felt unhappy or emotionally numb.

Sandwich Generation Julie Winokur (far left) juggles taking care of her father, who is suffering from Parkinson's disease, and raising her daughter (on the far right). How typical is the Winokur family today?

feels a greater loss of independence. Gender functions in similar ways for the sandwich generation, as it is still mostly women who are called on to provide the emotional and instrumental support for elderly parents, even when those women also work. In fact, "working women who do take on caregiving tasks may reduce their work hours" (Velkoff and Lawson 1998, p. 2), finding themselves having to prioritize family over career in ways men often don't.

Despite the many costs associated with being a member of the sandwich generation, there is good news as well. Although there are challenges associated with "dual responsibilities," these are mostly experienced as "a 'squeeze' but not stress," and these relationships are also a source of happiness and well-being (Lachman 2004, p. 322). And while there is still a certain stigma associated with moving back in with your parents, the fact that so many are willing to do so suggests that today's boomerang kids may enjoy closer relationships with their parents than kids of previous generations did.

Although Hochschild and Machung's observations were groundbreaking in their analysis of post-feminist families, their concept of the "Supermom" has been applicable to working-class mothers all along. The stay-at-home parent is possible only when one salary can support the entire family. Before college-educated women were encouraged to work in the paid labor force, working-class women were there out of necessity. The strategies that middle-class women use to negotiate their second shift are available only to wealthier families. After all, a woman who cleans another family's house and takes care of their children rarely has the financial resources to hire someone to do the same for her.

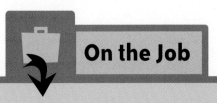

Juggling Work and Family

Since we now understand that being "on the job" can mean doing the work of family *or* the work of an employer, let's take a look at a typical day in the Brown family home in suburban Bellwood, Illinois. Deborah Brown is assistant chief of patient administration and financial services at the Veterans Administration West Side Medical Center in Chicago, and her husband, Alvin, is a data-solutions consultant for Ameritech. They have two sons: Jeffery, 9, and Jalen, 6.

5:00 A.M.: Deborah's alarm goes off. She showers and takes her daily supplements: a multivitamin for the body and 15 minutes of daily meditations for the soul.

5:30 A.M.: She packs a salad for lunch.

6:00 A.M.: Time to awaken Jeffery and nudge him toward the new week.

6:05 A.M.: She wakes up Alvin to help with the daily child-readiness project.

6:15 A.M.: Alvin awakens Jalen and helps get him dressed. "It's not easy," Alvin says. "He's a sleepyhead."

6:20 A.M.: As the rest of the family pulls together books and backpacks, Deborah makes all the beds and finishes getting dressed.

6:30 A.M.: Alvin heads out to the garage to get Deborah's car out and pull it around to the front of the house.

6:40 A.M.: Deborah and the kids head out. Alvin, who will be working from his home office, sees them off and heads back into the house to do a little cleaning.

6:55 A.M.: Arriving at the St. John's Lutheran School and Child Care in Forest Park, Deborah signs the boys in and they scamper off to the dining area. Jeffery chooses sausage and biscuits, while Jalen goes for his favorite: French toast sticks with syrup.

7:00 A.M.: Back in the car, Deborah heads to work.

7:10 A.M.: At home, Alvin tosses a load of laundry into the washer and prepares for a conference call with his sales team.

7:20 A.M.: Deborah arrives at the medical center.

7:30 A.M.: At her desk, she settles in with a bagel, milk, and her e-mail. Meanwhile, back home Alvin starts his conference call, and at school Jeffery is reading a Harry Potter book while Jalen plays during before-school care.

7:50 A.M.: Employees from the midnight shift start briefing Deborah, in preparation for a staff meeting.

8:15 A.M.: She meets with senior staff members, while at school the first bell rings and the boys head for class. At home, Alvin grabs a bagel and shower, irons his clothes and gets dressed for the day.

8:30 A.M.: At school, the students begin their daily devotional, then say the Pledge of Allegiance. Afterward, they fill in their prayer journal. Jalen later will explain that he prayed for his broken Power Rangers toy.

9:00 A.M.: Deborah begins her daily conference call with managers at remote sites, while at home, Alvin puts in another load of laundry and sits to read the newspaper. He has had the TV next to his office tuned to MSNBC since he first went downstairs. He cannot stop listening to coverage of the presidential election.

9:10 A.M.: Alvin's mother, Maryann Kirkpatrick of Calumet City, calls to say hello. "She's my best friend," Alvin says. "We talk two or three times a day."

9:20 A.M.: A coworker calls Alvin to work on quotes for a sales offer.

9:30 A.M.: Deborah starts returning calls and starts on paperwork that will carry her to lunch.

10:00 A.M.: Alvin looks through papers the boys brought home from school before the holidays.

10:40 A.M.: Still expecting a slow day of work, Alvin grabs a load of laundry from the dryer and starts folding and sorting. "I do the wash," he says. "Deborah puts it away." All the while MSNBC still can't tell him who his next president will be.

10:55 A.M.: Now the work phone won't leave Alvin alone. He has finished folding one load of laundry, but the dryer will spit out another load shortly. He is holed up in his office, in front of his computer. Though he can't watch it, the TV news remains audible.

11:15 A.M.: He leaves the office for a minute to sit in front of the TV. Still no president.

11:45 A.M.: Alvin is back in his office, going through e-mail.

12:00 P.M.: At school, the boys are having meatloaf, carrots and potatoes.

12:10 P.M.: Deborah calls Alvin to say hello, then finishes some correspondence to get to her lunch.

1:10 P.M.: Alvin grabs the last load of laundry from the dryer and starts folding, while at the hospital, Deborah is grinding out correspondence, and at school, the boys are back to their studies.

2:00 P.M.: The work phone has recaptured Alvin.

2:40 P.M.: Alvin runs upstairs to grab the mail, then heads back to his office, where he is reviewing faxes that have been trickling in all day.

3:00 P.M.: Deborah starts answering e-mails that have been mounting up. At school, class is over and the boys have gone to the after-school care program. At home, Alvin's work phone has been getting busier and busier. So much for the easy day.

4:30 P.M.: The taxi is back in business as Deborah leaves work and heads for the school.

4:40 P.M.: Alvin escapes his office and heads up to the kitchen to start getting dinner ready. He prepares potatoes for boiling and retrieves a slab of salmon from the refrigerator for broiling. He flips on the under-the-counter TV. Still no president.

5:00 P.M.: Back in his office, he is on a conference call with his boss. They have a problem and need to talk with some technicians. Upstairs, the potatoes are starting to boil.

5:05 P.M.: He runs upstairs to check the potatoes and put the fish in the broiler.

5:13 P.M.: Still waiting for someone to answer their call, Alvin races upstairs to check the food again. In a flash he's back to his phone.

5:20 P.M.: The Brown family has arrived. Alvin is still on the phone, trying to resolve the problem while Deborah rescues the salmon from the broiler and turns down the heat on the potatoes. Jeffery starts unloading his book bag, including his letter to Santa.

5:45 P.M.: Dinner is served with a prayer.

6:05 P.M.: Dinner over, Alvin and Deborah clear the table and start washing dishes.

6:45 P.M.: Jalen heads up to his room to start homework. Jeffery starts practicing on the electronic keyboard, preparing for a piano lesson the next day. Alvin returns to his office and work.

7:45 P.M.: Jalen is in the tub for a bath, and Jeffery is reading Harry Potter again but will hop into the tub once Jalen finishes.

8:00 P.M.: The boys get ready for prayers and sleep. Deborah tucks them in and gets good-night hugs.

8:15 P.M.: "Now it's time for Round 2," Deborah says. She starts gathering books and book bags and clothes for the morning routine.

8:30 P.M.: The boys are asleep, and Deborah irons the boys' clothes for tomorrow, then her own.

9:00 P.M.: Deborah packs her lunch for the next day and starts going through family mail.

9:30 P.M.: Alvin brings up a basket of the laundry he folded earlier for Deborah to put away. Then she starts getting ready for bed.

9:58 P.M.: Alvin pulls Deborah's car around and puts it in the garage, then runs to a gas station to fill his tank because he will be up early to go to work.

10:30 P.M.: Alvin is back, catches Jay Leno's monologue and starts watching the rest of the video he started the night before.

10:35 P.M.: Deborah finishes reviewing work. "It's been a long day," she says, "and it's only Monday!"

12:15 A.M.: Alvin decides to go to bed. He still hasn't been able to finish the video. And still no president. (Werland 2000)

The Browns experience the "spillover" of work and family in a number of areas: Deborah is "on the job" at home even when she's at the office, and Alvin is "on the job" from his home office even when he's folding laundry and cooking dinner. The boys' needs are attended to by both parents and are incorporated into their schedules beginning early in the morning and ending late in the evening. And the needs of extended family members (like Alvin's mother) are part of the Browns' routine, even if they don't live in the same household. This ordinary day is uncomplicated by any of the little glitches that families routinely experience—a sick child or a broken-down car—and it is still long, tiring, and complex. Spouses and parents are always "on the job" when it comes to family.

Supermom For many American women, "work" doesn't end when they leave the workplace. On returning home, many begin what Arlie Hochschild calls "the second shift," doing the unpaid work of running a household, including doing the laundry, feeding the children, and helping with homework.

Family and the Life Course

As an agent of socialization and the most basic of primary groups, the family molds everyone—young children, teenagers, adults, and senior citizens—and its influences continue throughout the life course.

When we are children, our families provide us with our first lessons in how to be members of society (see Chapter 5 on socialization). Children's experiences are shaped by family size, birth order, presence or absence of parents, socioeconomic status, and other sociological variables. Dalton Conley's 2004 work *Pecking Order* maintains that inequality between siblings and things outside the family's control such as the economy, war, illness, death, and marital discord create effects that impact each child at different stages in his or her life, resulting in different experiences for each child. Conley argues that family proves not to be the consistent influence many people view it to be.

In addition, the presence of children shapes the lives of parents. Marital satisfaction tends to decline when there are small children in the house, and couples' gendered division of labor becomes more traditional when children are born, even if it has been nontraditional up to that point. As children get older, they may exert other types of influence on their parents—for example, children can pressure their parents into quitting smoking or eating healthier food. And of course, later in life, they may be called on to care for their elderly parents as well as their own offspring—a phenomenon known as "the sandwich generation" effect.

Aging in the Family

The American population is aging—the number of Americans 65 or older is growing twice as fast as the population as a whole (Baca Zinn and Eitzen 2002). This is because of the baby boom generation (the large number of Americans born in the post–World War II era) moving into middle age and beyond, concurrent with advances in medical technology. Current average life expectancy in the United States is approximately 78 years (with women living an average of almost six years longer than men). More people are living longer, and that has an impact on families and society.

Planning for an aging population means taking into account both the basic and special needs of older individuals. Retirement income is an important part of this planning—Social Security benefits are the major source of income for about 80 percent of the elderly in the United States and the only source of income for 54 percent of America's retired population. Without other sources of income, retired citizens may find themselves with limited resources; currently, about 10 percent of the elderly live below the poverty line. Some seniors solve the problems by living with their adult children or with nonfamily members; even so, about 50 percent of women and about 20 percent of men over 65 live alone. Like other traditional functions of the family (like educating children), the care of the elderly is no longer a primary duty of family and has been taken over by other institutions: over 40 percent of senior citizens will spend time in a nursing home, being housed and cared for by people other than their family members (Baca Zinn and Eitzen 2002).

Coping with the transitions of retirement, widowhood, declining health, and death are central tasks for seniors. However, as the average life span extends, the elderly are also taking on new roles in society. Many live healthy, vibrant, active lives and are engaged with their families and communities

Marie Wilcox-Little, Age 73, Swimmer　　　　　　　　**Donald Goo, Age 73, Surfer**

in ways that are productive for both the individual and the person's groups.

Trouble in Families

While families are often a place of comfort, support, and unconditional love, some are not a "haven in a heartless world" (Lasch 1977). The family may be where we are at the greatest risk—emotionally, socially, and physically. "People are more likely to be killed, physically assaulted, sexually victimized . . . in their own homes by other family members than anywhere else, or by anyone else, in our society" (Gelles 1995, p. 450).

Because family is the site of unequal power relations and intense feelings, and because of current social norms about the privacy of family life, the circumstances for trouble and violence are ripe. The concept of private nuclear families did not occur in the United States until the early 1900s. In colonial times, child raising was a community activity in which community leaders and neighbors often overruled parental decisions about children. In the late 1800s, mothers looked to other mothers for advice about their children (Coontz 2000). Mothers' journals at the time show that the opinions of other women were often more important than the husband's in family decisions. Not until the 1900s did the isolated nuclear family become the ideal in the minds of Americans.

Domestic Violence and Abuse

Imagine that tomorrow's newspapers ran front-page headlines about a newly discovered disease epidemic that could potentially kill one-third of all American women. Between 1 million and 4 million women would be afflicted in the next year alone. What kind of public reaction would there be?

Let's reframe the scenario: in the United States, one out of every three women suffers physical violence at the hands of an intimate partner at some point in her adult life (National Domestic Violence Hotline 2003). In addition, millions of women suffer verbal, financial, and psychological abuse from those who are supposed to love them. Despite these statistics, such abuse is a silent epidemic, seldom reported.

Domestic violence is an umbrella term for the behaviors abusers use to gain and maintain control over their victims. These behaviors fall into five main categories: physical (slapping, punching, kicking, choking, shoving, restraining), verbal (insults, taunts, threats, degrading statements), financial (insisting on complete control of all household finances, including making decisions about who will work and when), sexual (rape, molestation), and psychological or emotional abuse (mind games, threats, stalking, intimidation). Although not all abusers are physically violent toward their partners, any one type of abuse increases the likelihood of the others. In an abusive relationship, it is extremely rare to find only one form of abuse.

Rates of domestic violence are about equal across racial and ethnic groups, sexual orientations, and religions (Bachman and Saltzman 1995). Women are certainly not the only demographic group to suffer from domestic abuse, but statistically, they are five to eight times

> **domestic violence** any physical, verbal, financial, sexual, or psychological behaviors abusers use to gain and maintain power over their victims

more likely than men to be victimized by an intimate partner (Greenfeld et al. 1998; National Domestic Violence Hotline 2003). According to the U.S. Department of Justice, women between the ages of 16 and 24 are victims of abuse at the hands of an intimate partner more frequently than women in any other age group (Rennison 2001). Poor women are also more likely to be abused than women with higher incomes (Bachman and Saltzman 1995). Age and economic security, however, do not make someone immune to abuse.

Contrary to popular opinion, most abusive partners are not "out of control," nor do they have "anger management problems" in the traditional sense. They often seem charming and calm to coworkers, friends, and police officers; they deliberately decide to be violent with those least likely to report the crime and over whom they maintain the most control: their family members. Domestic violence results from the abuser's desire for power over the victim, and abusers often blame their victims: I wouldn't have beaten you if dinner had been on time, or if you hadn't been "flirting" with the sales associate at the mall. One abuser is reported to have said to police officers, "Yes, I hit her five or six times but it was only to calm her down" ("Even in the Best of Homes" 2003).

A four-stage **cycle of violence** seems to occur in almost every abusive relationship. In the first stage, the abusive partner is charming, attentive, and thoughtful; disagreements are glossed over and the relationship looks stable and healthy. However, tension is building to the second stage, often described as "walking on eggshells." Here, both parties sense that something will happen no matter what the victim may do to try to avoid it. During the third stage, acute battering and violence occur, lasting for seconds, hours, or even days. Whatever happens, the abuser will invariably blame the victim for the incident. The fourth stage, often referred to as "loving contrition," is the "honeymoon" phase and is one of the reasons victims remain in violent relationships. After the violence, the abuser will apologize profusely and promise that it will never happen again. The abuser may buy the victim gifts, beg forgiveness, and talk about getting help or making a change. Most abusers, however, have no interest in changing because they don't want to give up their control over their victims. Soon the cycle starts again, with flowers and gifts giving way to tension, uneasiness, and another battering.

Victims of domestic violence stay with their abusers for many reasons. After years of abuse, victims often believe what their abusers tell them: that they can't make it on their own and are somehow responsible for the abuse. If they have not been allowed to attend school or to work, they may not have employment skills. Often children are involved, or abusers threaten to harm other family members. Many victims have been isolated from friends and family and are afraid to speak of the abuse to anyone, and they see no options but to remain where they are.

Child and Elder Abuse

Adult partners are not the only victims of domestic violence. Children and the elderly also suffer at the hands of abusive family members—and can suffer in distinctive ways that are linked to their special status in the family. Child abuse and elder abuse are likely to be underreported, partly because of the relative powerlessness of their victims and the private settings of the abuse. The best official estimates are that about 47 of every 1,000 children in the United States are abused in some way (Weise and Daro 1995) and that about 5 percent of all seniors in this country have been subject to elder abuse in some form (Wolf 2000).

In addition to physical violence and verbal, emotional, and sexual abuse, children may experience a distinctive type of abuse known as **neglect**—inadequate nutrition, insufficient clothing or shelter, and unhygienic or unsafe living conditions. Because children depend on adults for their care and well-being, they suffer when those adults abandon or pervert that responsibility. **Incest** is another form of child abuse that exploits the trust that children must place in their caregivers. Inappropriate sexual relationships between parents and children have devastating lifelong consequences for child victims, which may include self-destructive behavior (including eating disorders and substance abuse) and the inability to form trusting relationships later in life. In addition, those who were physically or sexually abused as children have a much higher likelihood of becoming abusers themselves.

Elder abuse can also take distinctive forms. As well as physical, verbal, emotional, and sexual abuse, there is financial exploitation or theft—relatives or other caregivers may steal or misuse the elder's property or financial resources. Another form is neglect and abandonment. Some elders are dependent on others to care for them. Refusal to provide food, shelter, health care, or protection can be as devastating to an elder as it is to a child. Both elder and child abuse

cycle of violence a common behavior pattern in abusive relationships; the cycle begins happily, then the relationship grows tense, and the tension explodes in abuse, followed by a period of contrition that allows the cycle to repeat

neglect a form of child abuse in which the caregiver fails to provide adequate nutrition, sufficient clothing or shelter, or hygienic and safe living conditions

incest proscribed sexual contact between family members; a form of child abuse when it occurs between a child and a caregiver

exploit the special powerlessness of victims and are difficult to monitor and control.

DATA WORKSHOP

ANALYZING MASS MEDIA AND POPULAR CULTURE

Family Troubles in Film

Family relations have long been the basis of good comedic, tragic, and dramatic films. This Data Workshop asks you to use existing sources as a research method (see Chapter 3 for a review) and to do a content analysis of a film concerning family dynamics. Choose a film to watch and then analyze its relevance to some of the family issues discussed in this chapter. Although many films feature families, this assignment asks you to focus on one or more family problems.

The following films depict a variety of family troubles such as marital problems, divorce, domestic abuse, parental neglect, disabilities and illnesses, sex and dating, pregnancy, death, delinquency, and financial difficulties. Other movies could certainly be added to this list, as long as your instructor

approves the film you would like to choose. Whatever movie you choose must be available on video or DVD so that you can view it carefully. Please be aware of the MPAA ratings for these or other movies, and watch only those titles that are appropriate for your age group and that you would feel comfortable viewing.

Affliction	*Ordinary People*
American Beauty	*Pieces of April*
Baby Boy	*Rachel Getting Married*
How to Deal	*The Royal Tennenbaums*
The Ice Storm	*Saving Face*
In America	*Spanglish*
In the Bedroom	*Stepmom*
The Joy Luck Club	*Terms of Endearment*
Kramer vs. Kramer	*Thirteen*
Mi Familia (My Family)	*We Don't Live Here Anymore*
Mrs. Doubtfire	*What's Eating Gilbert Grape?*
My Big Fat Greek Wedding	*You Can Count on Me*

Select a movie that is primarily about contemporary family relations and problems. Once you have chosen a movie, read through the rest of the workshop points and guidelines. Then watch the film closely and pay attention to the plotlines,

Family Troubles? What do films like *Saving Face* and *Mi Familia* tell us about contemporary American families?

scenes, characters, and dialogues in which family troubles are depicted. Take notes as you watch the movie; you may have to review it several times before you can do a thorough content analysis. This assignment has several parts, and you may also wish to add your own questions or comments.

Consider the following points and answer these questions:

- Give some background information on the film and why you chose it.

- Using sociological terms, describe the family troubles that are the focus of the film. How are these problems manifested in the lives of the family members? How do the various characters deal with their problems? What solutions do they propose through their actions? How effective are these solutions in addressing the family's troubles?

- Put the family's problems in a broader sociological perspective. Do you believe the family's troubles are more psychological or sociological in nature? In what ways are the individual troubles of family members linked to larger social patterns and problems? Compare the problems in the movie with their counterparts in the real world. Gather recent data relating to the family problems featured in the film, using sources such as the U.S. Census Bureau, other government or private agencies, or various news sources. How widespread are these problems? How are they being discussed and dealt with at a public level? How accurately do you think the family's troubles, and their possible solutions, were depicted in the film? What kind of a role, if any, do you think the media can play in helping to reduce family troubles or associated social problems?

There are two options for completing this Data Workshop.

- *Option 1 (informal)*: Make the observations described above and answer the preceding questions. Then prepare some written notes that you can refer to during in-class discussions. Compare and contrast the analyses of the films observed by participants in your discussion group.

- *Option 2 (formal)*: Make the observations described above and answer the preceding questions. Then write a three- to four-page essay talking about your answers and reflecting on your observations of the film. What do you think your observations tell us about contemporary

cohabitation living together as a romantically involved, unmarried couple

American families and the ways in which family troubles are portrayed on film?

Divorce and Breakups

Although many people stay in bad relationships, many couples also break up every day. In this section, we consider the changing patterns of divorce and remarriage as they affect children and adults. We also look at the resulting social problems of custody, visitation, and child support.

Changing Patterns

As of March 2002, the U.S. Census Bureau reported that more than 123 million persons were married while about 21 million were divorced. Thus, in 2002 about 55 percent of the entire U.S. population were married while just fewer than 10 percent were divorced. Figure 13.1 shows that the numbers of those who have married and the rates of divorce have increased over time. The percentage of married people who have divorced has increased more than five and a half times since 1950, indicating that about 50 percent of all first marriages now end in divorce (Kreider and Fields 2001).

Most who divorce remarry. Among parents of young children, the remarriage rate is very high. According to Cherlin and Furstenberg (1994), 75 percent of divorced men and 67 percent of divorced women ultimately remarry, and between 75 percent and 80 percent of divorced parents remarry (Weissbourd 1994). But remarriage rates in the United States are actually lower now than they were before the 1960s, a fact attributable to the increase in **cohabitation,** or living together, among unmarried couples. Census data reveal that about 5 percent of all households are occupied by unmarried heterosexual couples, which may reflect a certain caution about marriage as a result of rising rates of divorce.

In the early 1970s, the children of divorced parents were more than three times more likely to divorce than their peers from intact families. But by the mid-1990s, this figure had dropped to about one and a half times (Wolfinger 1999, 2000). According to Wolfinger (2003), the decline of intergenerational divorce and marriage rates probably has three sources. One is the growing acceptance of divorce. Children of divorced parents no longer suffer the social stigma that was

FIGURE 13.1 **U.S. Divorce Rate Over the Past Century**

SOURCE: Cherlin 2005

once the byproduct of divorce and are less likely to develop psychological problems as a result—which may have contributed to their divorces in the past. Second, the age of marriage has changed. Children of divorce are still more likely to marry as teenagers, but those not married by age 20 are more likely not to marry at all than their peers from intact families. Third, children of divorced parents are more likely to cohabit with their partners and are less likely to marry them than children of nondivorced parents. Therefore, the decline in marriage rates among children of divorced parents can be explained by both increased rates of cohabitation and an increased propensity not to marry at all.

Custody, Visitation, and Child Support

Reviewing the legal policies that address the consequences of divorce for children, sociologists are concerned with whether custody, visitation, and child support effectively replace the resources, both emotional and financial, of an intact household. Do they help children?

Custody is the physical and legal responsibility for the everyday life and routines of children. While mothers still disproportionately receive custody, there is a trend toward joint custody (Cancian and Meyer 1998). Parents who are well educated, have high socioeconomic status, live in cities, and are nonwhite are more likely than others to have joint custody of their children (Donnelly and Finkelhor 1993). A father is more likely to be awarded sole custody when his income is substantially more than the mother's (Cancian and Meyer 1998), when his children are older, or when the

oldest child is male (Fox and Kelly 1995). A mother is more likely to receive sole custody when she has a high level of education, her children are younger, and the father is unemployed (Fox and Kelly 1995).

Courts award visitation to noncustodial parents to protect parent-child relationships. Generally, parents with regular visitation patterns are better able to meet the psychological and financial needs of their children. Fathers who visit regularly are more likely to maintain strong relationships with their children and to pay child support (Seltzer, Schaeffer, and Charng 1989). Despite increased vigilance of courts and lawmakers regarding mandated child support policies, noncustodial parents often fail to make regular payments to the custodial parent. Sociologists have found that many parents make informal arrangements, or decisions without the mediation of the legal system, about child support schedules soon after the divorce (Peters et al. 1993) and the stability of payments varies substantially, even among the most reliable payers (Meyer and Bartfeld 1998).

As children are more likely to live in poverty after their parents' divorce, child support policies are important. Women are more likely to suffer downward economic mobility after divorce, especially if they retain custody of their children. Furstenberg, Hoffman, and Shrestha (1995) found that women experience on average a 25 percent decline in their economic well-being after a divorce. Accompanying this post-divorce decline in financial resources are often scholastic failure, disruptive conduct, and troubled relationships in children of divorced families (Keith and Finlay 1988;

custody the physical and legal responsibility of caring for children; assigned by a court for divorced or unmarried parents

Morrison and Cherlin 1995). Further, divorce seems to negatively affect male children more than female children as boys are more likely to act out than girls.

Stepparents and Blended Families

Most divorced people remarry, which means that one in three Americans is a member of a stepfamily (Baca Zinn and Eitzen 2002). However, statistics about stepfamilies are inconsistent and often contradictory because quantifying and defining the intricate relationships involved in a stepfamily are difficult. The 2000 U.S. Census did not account for them in its data gathering. There are historically no traditional norms or models for stepfamilies, and our firmly held notions of the "traditional" family lead many in stepfamilies to find the transition to a new family situation difficult. Stepfamilies face special challenges, for example, when there are children in different stages of the lifecycle. The needs and concerns of teenagers may be vastly different from those of their infant half-sibling, and it may take more work to adjust to the new living situation. With the added challenges of blending in-laws, finances, and households, remarriages are even more likely to end in divorce than first

The Brady Bunch America's best-known blended family.

marriages. However, in successful remarriages, partners are usually older and have learned important lessons about compatibility and relationship maintenance from the failure of their first marriages.

Trends in American Families

"There's this pervasive idea in America that puts marriage and family at the center of everyone's lives," says Bella M. DePaulo, visiting professor of psychology at the University of California at Santa Barbara, "when in fact it's becoming less and less so" (personal communication 2003). Many people live outside such arrangements. In fact, the average American now spends the majority of his or her life unmarried because people live longer, delay marriage, or choose an alternative "single" lifestyle (Kreider and Fields 2002).

Being Single

The term *single* often implies a young adult who is actively seeking a partner for a relationship or marriage. But singles also include gays and lesbians, people living alone who are in long-distance relationships, people living in communes, widows and widowers, minors in group homes, and some clergy members as well as those who are single due to divorce or deliberate choice.

Married couples were the dominant model through the 1950s, but their numbers have slipped from nearly 80 percent of households to just above 50 percent now. Married couples with children—the traditional model of family—total just 25 percent of households, and that number is projected to drop (National Opinion Research Center 1999). The remaining households are single parents, cohabiting partners, or others. A stunning 30 percent of all households are made up of people who live alone, and in 2005 unmarrieds became the new majority (U.S. Census Bureau 2005b).

Among the growing movement of activists promoting the rights of unmarried people in the United States is the nonprofit Alternatives to Marriage Project and its associated advocacy group Unmarried America (Solot and Miller 2002). They engage in research, education, and advocacy for unmarried and single adults of all types and are concerned about discrimination that is built into the American social system, especially at an economic and political level, but also in terms of culture and values. One of their efforts is to increase recognition of unmarrieds and singles as a constituency of voters, workers, taxpayers, and consumers worthy of equal rights and protection (Warner, Ihara, and Hertz 2001).

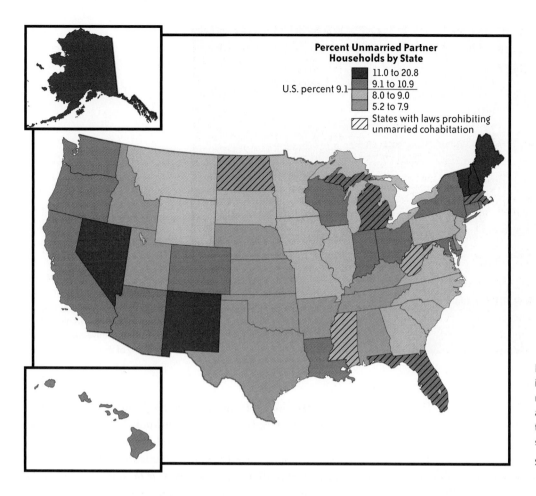

Percent Unmarried Partner Households by State

- 11.0 to 20.8
- 9.1 to 10.9
- 8.0 to 9.0
- 5.2 to 7.9

U.S. percent 9.1

States with laws prohibiting unmarried cohabitation

FIGURE 13.2 Cohabitation in the United States People are more likely to cohabit in coastal and western states, and less likely to do so in central and southern states.

SOURCE: U.S. Census Bureau 2002a

Cohabitation

Between 1960 and 2000, the number of unmarried cohabiting couples in the United States increased 1,000 percent. More than 11 million people are living with an unmarried partner, including both same-sex and different-sex couples (see Figure 13.2). In addition, marriage is no longer the prerequisite for childbearing. More than one in three unmarried-couple households have children (U.S. Census Bureau 2000a), and one-third of all first births are to unmarried parents (National Center for Health Statistics 2001). Most couples that choose to cohabit rather than marry are 25 to 34 years of age. A possible reason may be the growing economic independence of individuals today, resulting in less financial motivation for a marriage contract. Also, changing attitudes about religion have made sexual relationships outside marriage more socially acceptable.

Single Parenting

Although some people become single parents through divorce or death, others choose to have children without the support of a committed partner—through adoption, artificial insemination, or surrogacy. In the United States, only 10 percent of single parents are single fathers. Attitudes about single mothers vary greatly and are often dependent on the mother's age, education level, occupation, and income and the family's support network from friends and extended family members.

A prevailing middle-class assumption about poor single mothers is that young women in the inner city become mothers to access welfare benefits. Kathryn Edin and Maria Kefalas (2005) spent five years doing in-depth research with 162 low-income single mothers to understand their attitudes about parenthood and marriage. They dispelled the myth that these women become mothers to cash in on welfare benefits and instead found that for these young women, having a baby is a symbol of belonging and being valued. Being a good mother is an accessible role that can generate respect and admiration in the community.

Regardless of the circumstances of single parenting, raising children without the help of a partner is challenging and difficult. Financially, physically, and emotionally, single parents must perform a task that was traditionally shared by a community rather than an individual.

Intentional Communities
Members and former members of the Twin Oaks commune in Yanceyville, Virginia, celebrate the fortieth anniversary of the founding of the community.

Intentional Communities

As an increasing number of people choose to remain or become single, cohabit with others, or choose something else altogether, they are creating alternative models to organize their lives. Some join an **intentional community**, an inclusive term for a variety of different groups who form communal living arrangements that include ecovillages, cohousing, residential land trusts, communes, monasteries and ashrams, farming collectives, student co-ops, or urban housing coopera tives.

Members of an intentional community have chosen to live together with a common purpose, working cooperatively to create a lifestyle that reflects their shared core values. They may live on rural land, in a suburban home, or in an urban neighborhood, and they may share a single residence or live in a cluster of dwellings. Although quite diverse in philosophy and lifestyle, each of these groups places a high priority on fostering a sense of community—a feeling of belonging and mutual support that is increasingly hard to find in mainstream Western society (Kozeny 1995).

The Postmodern Family

intentional community any of a variety of groups who form communal living arrangements outside marriage

Families adapting to the challenges of a postmodern society may create family structures that look very different from the "traditional" family. Sociologist Judith Stacey explored some of these adaptations for her book *Brave New Families* (1990). The families and households she studied expanded and contracted over time and included members who were never part of the traditional *Leave It to Beaver* model of the nuclear family. Ex-spouses and their new partners and children, adult children and other kin, and even nonkin—friends and coworkers—populated the working-class Silicon Valley households she studied. Multiple earners and a diversity of generations, genders, and relational connections were the rule rather than the exception in her study:

> No longer is there a single culturally dominant family pattern, like the modern one, to which a majority of Americans conform and most of the rest aspire. Instead, Americans today have crafted a multiplicity of family and household arrangements that we inhabit uneasily and reconstitute frequently in response to changing personal and occupational circumstances. (Stacey 1990, p. 19)

We have entered an era of improvisation or do-it-yourself family forms; household members respond to social-structural changes in ways that fit their family's needs. These improvisational forms are not new; they are merely new to mainstream working- and middle-class families. Minorities, the poor, and gays and lesbians have always had to improvise to fit into a society that ignored or devalued their needs and activities (Stack 1974; Weston 1991; Edin and Lein 1997; Stacey 1998). These improvisational, postmodern family forms will become more and more familiar to the rest of society as we all cope with the social and cultural changes of the twenty-first century.

Closing Comments

When sociologists study the dynamics of family, they must define the subject of their interest. What exactly is family? This process sometimes leads to definitions that lie outside the traditional notions of biological or legal relations that have historically defined family. Certainly this is true if one looks outside the United States at the astonishing variety of customs and practices that define family around the world. In the early twenty-first century, the nature of the nuclear family is changing, as divorced and blended families are altering the structure and function of all families, with a tendency to decrease the amount of contact and assistance between generations. The emergence of these "brave new families" has led to a sea change in the study of families, with an increasing recognition of the diversity and plurality that characterize family arrangements.

 Find more review materials online at
www.wwnorton.com/studyspace

CHAPTER SUMMARY

- **What Is the Family?** Although the most common definition of the family involves a nuclear family living in one household, sociologists prefer a much broader definition. This chapter defines the family as any social group bound together by some type of tie—legal, biological, or emotional. This more open-ended definition takes into account the diversity among today's families, including the wide variety of ways that family units can be constituted outside marriage. The nuclear family as we know it only recently replaced an older extended family paradigm, and new models of family life are on the way. Although many kinds of bonds can constitute families, individual families tend to be made up of very similar people, as marriage in our society is highly endogamous.

- **Sociological Perspectives on the Family** Functionalist theory views the family as one of the basic institutions that keeps society running smoothly, producing and socializing children as well as providing an essential support system for the modern economy. Conflict theorists focus on the inequalities within and between families. Symbolic interactionists examine the types of social dynamics and interactions that create and sustain families, emphasizing the ways that our experiences of family bonds are socially created rather than naturally existing.

- **Family Work** Maintaining a household and a family involves a great deal of work, and recent research has focused on the ways this work is gendered. Women who don't work outside the home may have their labor devalued, while women who work for pay often find themselves taking on a second shift of housework.

- **Trouble in Families** Perhaps because the family is so important, the potential for family violence and abuse is high. Partly because of the intense emotions and power disparities between family members and the desire to keep family matters private, people are more likely to be killed or attacked by family members than by anyone else. Domestic violence between partners is by far the most common form of family violence; it is often perpetuated by the "cycle of violence" that causes victims to remain in abusive relationships. Child and elder abuse are also serious issues, particularly since children and elders are less capable of leaving an abusive relationship.

- **Divorce and Break-ups** The nature of the family is changing as rising rates of divorce and remarriage create more single-parent and blended families. Divorced parents must establish custody and visitation rights, often doing so in a court. At the same time, an increasing number of people are remaining single, raising children alone, cohabiting, or forming intentional communities beyond the parameters of marriage. These new family structures respond to the challenges of a postmodern society by including ex-spouses, new partners and children, adult children, other kin, and even nonkin such as friends and coworkers.

QUESTIONS FOR REVIEW

1. How does this chapter's definition of family differ from the one used by the U.S. Census Bureau? Make a list of everyone you consider a family member. Is there anyone on this list who wouldn't qualify according to the Census Bureau's definition?

2. What do sociologists mean when they argue that instead of the sociology of *the family* we should have a sociology of *families*? Why do we think of particular people as family members?

3. Same-sex marriage is prohibited in most of the United States. At different points in American history couples of mixed race, ethnic background, or nationality were not legally allowed to marry. What do these three groups have in common with same-sex couples? What are the advantages of a legally recognized marriage?

4. Conflict theorists believe that strife within the family is fueled by competition for resources. What is the basis for inequality within the family? In families, who tends to receive fewer resources?

5. Homogamy helps explain a lot about mate selection in contemporary society: We tend to date and marry people who are similar to us in culturally meaningful ways. What cultural factors influence your relationship choices?

6. Another important factor that helps explain mate selection is propinquity, the tendency to choose mates who live in close geographic proximity to us. Some sociologists believe that technological changes are making propinquity less important. What sorts of changes make geographic location less relevant to mate selection?

7. Throughout history there has almost always been a division of labor by gender, but before the Industrial Revolution men's and women's labor were more equally valued. What changes led to the devaluation of tasks traditionally done by women?

8. Arlie Hochschild and Anne Machung found that women who work outside the home often face a "second shift" of housework when they get home. How do men avoid doing their share of this work? Have you ever noticed someone— perhaps even yourself—adopting these tactics?

9. A popular stereotype holds that poor women have more children in order to gain welfare benefits, though researchers who have studied the issue tend to reject this idea. Why else might poor single mothers have children?

SUGGESTIONS FOR FURTHER EXPLORATION

Coontz, Stephanie. 2005. *Marriage, a History: From Obedience to Intimacy, or How Love Conquered Marriage*. New York: Penguin Books. An analysis of the "traditional" marriage associated with the nuclear family. Coontz argues that this relatively new type of marriage is in crisis today.

Hua, Cai. 2001. *A Society Without Fathers or Husbands: The Na of China*. Cambridge, MA: Zone Books. A startling counterpoint to our some of our assumptions about the family, this ethnography describes the Na people of southern China who live without marriage. In Na culture, children are raised by their mother's family, without the participation of their biological father.

Krakauer, Jon. 2003. *Under the Banner of Heaven: A Story of Violent Faith*. London: Pan Books. A compelling look at Mormon fundamentalist groups in the United States who espouse and practice polygyny. Although his book is primarily an account of a murder, Krakauer provides a wealth of background on both the history of the Mormon Church and the splinter groups who maintain some of the early church's most controversial beliefs and practices.

Number Our Days. 1976. Dir. Lynne Littman. Community Television of Southern California. This short documentary film based on the ethnographic study of elderly Jews in Venice, California, won an Oscar for its moving depiction of aging and the life course.

The OYEZ Project's site about *Loving vs. Virginia* (www.oyez.org/cases/1960-1969/1966/1966_395). A comprehensive account of the landmark case that effectively ended race-based marriage restrictions in the United States. The site includes sound files of the oral arguments and full text of the unanimous opinion written by Chief Justice Earl Warren striking down Virginia's antimiscegenation laws.

Rufus, Anneli. 2002. *Party of One: The Loners' Manifesto*. Washington, DC: Marlowe and Company. A polemic defense of the introvert and the loner, as well as a popular history of the prejudice against being alone. Rufus argues that people should be able to be single without feeling imperfect.

Three of Hearts. 2004. Dir. Susan Kaplan. Hibiscus Films. A documentary about two men in a romantic relationship who add a female partner to their home and develop a polyamorous relationship that redefines the limits of family.

Weston, Kath. 1997. *Families We Choose*. New York: Columbia University Press. A discussion of the way that members of the gay and lesbian community have reinterpreted the idea of family as a more inclusive, less kin-based institution, especially as many of them were rejected by and cut off from their birth families.

CHAPTER 14

Recreation and Leisure in Everyday Life

You're sitting in a darkened theater watching a movie unfold on the big screen. Two young lovers meet, woo, and marry. They honeymoon at a mountain resort—where, unfortunately, they are kidnapped by political rebels who break into song, swinging their rifles in unison as they dance in camouflage fatigues. After the ransom is paid, the couple return to the city, where they shop for house-wares—at a store where clerks croon and shoppers dance in the aisles. But before they are allowed to live happily ever after, their baby is switched at birth with another infant, and they must track down their child with the help of a singing police detective/spiritual adviser. The film lasts over three hours; during that time, audience members (men in one section, women and children in another) come and go, fetching delicious snacks that extend far beyond prosaic popcorn and soda. They yell, groan, sing, talk back, and even throw things at the screen—but nobody shushes them. Where are you? You're in "Bollywood."

Unless you are South Asian, have traveled to India, or are a *very* dedicated film buff, you've probably never seen a Bollywood film. This term, an obvious take-off on the American film capital, is used to describe a particular class of movies produced in Mumbai or Bombay. The Indian film industry is the most prolific in the world, and the movies it produces are very different from those Americans are used to. A typical film usually includes romance, political intrigue, and dramatic events such as kidnappings, military battles, or natural disasters—and there is always lots of singing and dancing! In other words, Indian films are a mixture of what American audiences understand to be separate genres: romance, musical, action, thriller, and so on. As a result, Americans react to Indian films as strange, exhausting, and disorganized, while Indians find American movies boring, unemotional, and too short (Srinivas 1998).

In Indian theaters, silence is not the norm; audience members respond to what's on-screen in ways that seem startling or even wrong to Americans. The only American film experience that resembles the Bollywood model is the midnight showings of *The Rocky Horror Picture Show*, where enthusiastic fans dress up, sing along, talk back, throw toast, and shoot squirt guns at the screen. In Bollywood, though, this type of behavior is the rule.

SocIndex

Then and Now

1371: The 52-playing-card deck is introduced in Europe

1998: Online card-playing is introduced on the internet

Here and There

United States: An estimated 2–3% of the population, or between 6 and 9 million adults, are addicted to gambling in 2006

Hong Kong: An estimated 5% of the population, or more than 350,000 adults, are addicted to gambling in 2008

This and That

In 2005, 57% of young men ages 14 to 22 report gambling on cards on a monthly basis.

Jeff Madsen, a 21-year-old University of California undergraduate, becomes the youngest player ever to take top prize when he wins the 2006 World Series of Poker.

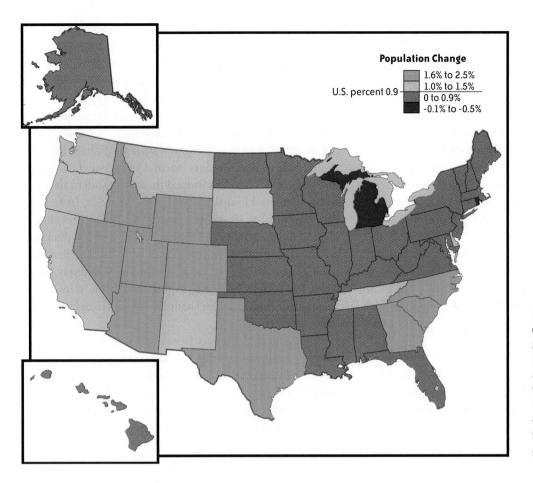

Population Change

1.6% to 2.5%
1.0% to 1.5%
U.S. percent 0.9
0 to 0.9%
-0.1% to -0.5%

FIGURE 15.4 Population Change in the United States, 2007–8 The populations of Midwest and East Coast states are holding steady or decreasing, while the populations of Inter-Mountain West, Pacific Northwest, and some Southern states are growing.

SOURCE: U.S. Census Bureau 2008*l*

in which his basic premise, the **Malthusian theorem,** stated that the population would expand at a much faster rate than agriculture; inevitably at some future point, people would far outnumber the available land and food sources. If population increases surpass the ability of the earth to provide a basic level of subsistence, then massive suffering will follow. His theory has two simple principles: that population growth is exponential or geometric (1, 2, 4, 8, 16, 32 . . .), whereas food production is additive or arithmetic (1, 2, 3, 4, 5, 6 . . .).

According to his calculations, society was headed for disaster, or what is called the **Malthusian trap**. To avoid such a catastrophe, Malthus made several rather radical policy recommendations. He may have been the first to propose that humans should collectively limit their propagation to save themselves and preserve their environments. He urged "moral restraint" in sexual reproduction to curtail overpopulation. If human beings were unable to restrain themselves (by postponing marriage or practicing abstinence), nature would exert "positive checks" on population growth through famine, war, and disease (Malthus 1997 [1798; 1803]). Malthus also advocated state assistance to the lower classes so they could more readily achieve a middle-class lifestyle

supported by decent wages and benefits and adopt the values associated with later marriage and smaller families (New School 2004).

Malthus's ideas were not always popular, though they were influential and widely read. Charles Darwin noted that Malthusian theory was an important influence on his own theory of evolution and natural selection. Malthus also influenced whole new generations of social thinkers, not just demographers but others as well, and their respective ideas on population growth.

More than 200 years later, some people, the **Neo-Malthusians**, or New Malthusians, essentially still agree with him. Among the notable modern voices looking at the problem of overpopulation are William Catton (1980), Paul and Ann Ehrlich (1990), and

Malthusian theorem the theory that exponential population growth will outpace arithmetic growth in food production and other resources

Malthusian trap Malthus's prediction that a rapidly increasing population will overuse natural resources, leading inevitably to a major public health disaster

Neo-Malthusians contemporary researchers who worry about the rapid pace of population growth and believe that Malthus's basic prediction could be true

Garrett Hardin (1993). They worry about the rapid pace of population growth and believe that Malthus's basic prediction could be true. In some respects, they claim, the problem has even gotten worse. There are a lot more people on the planet in the twenty-first century, so their continued reproduction expands even more quickly than in Malthus's time. And with continued technological advancements—such as wars that use "surgical strikes," modern standards of sanitation, and the eradication of many diseases—people are living much longer than before. When Malthus was alive there were approximately 1 billion people on the planet; it was the first time in recorded history that the population reached that number. The time required for that number to double and for each additional billion to be added has continued to shorten (Figure 15.5a). Today there are over 6 billion people on the planet—and counting. A quick look at Figure 15.5b showing how many people are added to the planet each second, minute, hour, day, week, month, and year is mind-boggling (Cohen 1995).

The New Malthusians also point to several sociological factors that influence the reproductive lives of many and promote large families. Religion still plays a role in many societies, with the Old Testament commanding, "Go forth and multiply." The Catholic Church still forbids members to practice any birth control besides the rhythm method, even though 78 percent of American Catholics said the church should allow them to use some form of artificial contraception (CNN 2005). In many poorer nations, more children mean more financial support for the family. They work various jobs in their youth to help sustain the household, and for parents, children may be the only source of support they have in old age. Some governments encourage the expansion of their population base and promote the addition of new citizens who can become taxpayers or soldiers. They may even provide incentives to parents, such as tax deductions for each child. Last, cultural influences, from "family values" to "machismo," sometimes confer more prestige on those with children; women gain status in the valued role of mother, while men gain status for their perceived virility.

At the same time, contrary arguments are proposed by the **Anti-Malthusians**. Economists such as Julian Simon (1996, 2000) and demographers such as William Peterson (2003) believe that Malthus reached faulty conclusions and that he couldn't have envisioned the many modern developments that would impact population dynamics. In fact, the Anti-Malthusians worry more about the population shrinking and the possibility of a **demographic free fall** than they do about it growing indefinitely. They don't see that happening immediately, but they forecast a very different future when the pattern of **demographic transition**, now occurring in many industrialized nations, spreads to the rest of the developing world.

The Anti-Malthusians believe that when people have a better standard of living they also prefer smaller families, as children become more of an economic liability than an asset. Better education and easier access to health care bring more reproductive choices such as methods of **family planning**. Governments in some countries are adopting policies that discourage large families. Further, the Anti-Malthusians claim that technological advancements have enabled humans to produce much larger quantities of food than ever before, thus providing for the nutritional needs of more of the world's population.

So who is right? Will the world population eventually stabilize, or will it continue to spiral out of control? We may not know the answer to those questions for many years, so in the meantime we continue to speculate. The populations of some countries continue to grow rapidly, while others remain stable or begin to decline. The **growth rate** is the number of births minus deaths plus net migration of a population, expressed as a percentage change from the beginning of the time period measured, often resulting in what is referred to as a **natural increase**. The growth rate in the United States in 2008 was 0.89 percent. It was highest in African countries such as Liberia at 4.84 percent and Burundi at 3.59 percent and lowest in Pacific Islands such as Niue at –0.03 percent and Cook Island at –1.20 percent.

What about the other elements in Malthus's theorem? Food production has grown remarkably since Malthus's time. In particular, the "Green Revolution" that began in Mexico in 1948 and spread to India and other less developed nations in the 1960s caused an explosion in food production. This was partly because of better agricultural mechanization as well as newly engineered seeds, pesticides, and artificial fertilizers. Was this a unique increase, or can it be

Anti-Malthusians contemporary researchers who believe the population boom Malthus witnessed was a temporary, historically specific phenomenon and worry instead that the worldwide population may shrink in the future

demographic free fall decrease in fertility rates among populations that have industrialized their economies as children become an economic liability rather than an asset

demographic transition a theory suggesting the possible transition over time from high birth and death rates to low birth and death rates, resulting in a stabilized population

family planning contraception, or any method of controlling family size and the birth of children

growth rate expression of changes in population size over time figured by subtracting the number of deaths from the number of births, then adding the net migration

natural increase change in population size that results from births and deaths; linked to a country's progress toward demographic transition

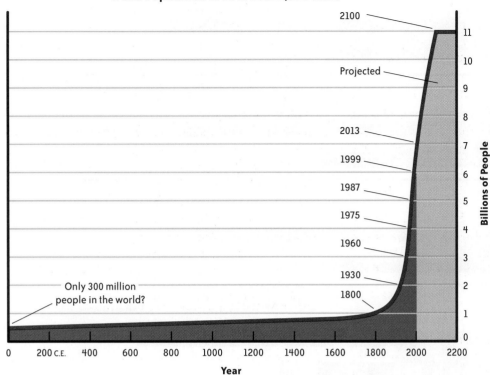

World Population Growth over 2,000 Years

Only 300 million people in the world?

1800
1930
1960
1975
1987
1999
2013
Projected
2100

Billions of People

Year

FIGURE 15.5a World Population Growth over 2,000 Years The world's population grew slowly for most of human history, then began to increase rapidly in the nineteenth century. With the world population now increasing by almost 3 people per second, as the Population Clock on the next page shows, it could reach 11 billion by 2100.

SOURCE: Population Reference Bureau 2008

expected again in the future? The United Nations Food and Agriculture Organization estimates that world agriculture will grow at a slower pace, from an annual 2.1 percent over the last two decades to 1.6 percent from 2005 to 2015 and 1.3 percent from 2015 to 2030. Growth in agriculture will continue to surpass world population growth, estimated to be 1.2 percent from 2005 to 2015 and 0.8 percent from 2015 to 2030.

Nonetheless, hunger remains widespread, not only in foreign countries but also in the United States. Worldwide, an estimated 1 billion people suffer from chronic hunger and malnutrition—a lack of adequate food plus other factors such as insufficient protein and nutrients, poor feeding habits, and unsafe water and sanitation. Some 10 million people die every year from hunger or hunger-related causes; three-fourths of them are children under the age of five (the United Nations World Food Programme 2007). In the United States, every day 11 percent of households—over 36 million people—experience hunger or food insecurity, that is, the limited or uncertain ability to acquire adequate and safe foods (U.S. Department of Agriculture 2007).

Other factors must also be considered in projecting the future of population impacts. Science constantly brings technological advancements that enhance health and prolong life, but new and deadly diseases such as AIDS claim an ever greater death toll in nations too poor to afford the medicines to treat these diseases. As the world's current occupants, we

have to live now with the consequences of our choices. Many policy and advocacy groups concerned with population matters have been established in the last few decades, including Zero Population Growth, World Overpopulation Awareness, the Population Institute, and the Population Reference Bureau. To find out more, visit their websites listed at the end of the chapter.

Urbanization

The dynamics of population growth (and sometimes shrinkage) over human history have been accompanied by the development of larger cities in which more people are now living. Cities, however, are not a modern development. They have been in existence for thousands of years. We find evidence of ancient cities in the Middle East, Africa, Asia, and South America. By comparison to today's standards, these early cities would be considered quite small. They generally had just several thousand residents and were typically agricultural centers along major trade routes. Some much larger cities, however, had hundreds of thousands of residents, such as the Mediterranean cities of Athens and Rome. One reason cities were able to thrive was the advances in agriculture that allowed surpluses of food to be readily available to support a population that was not directly involved in its production.

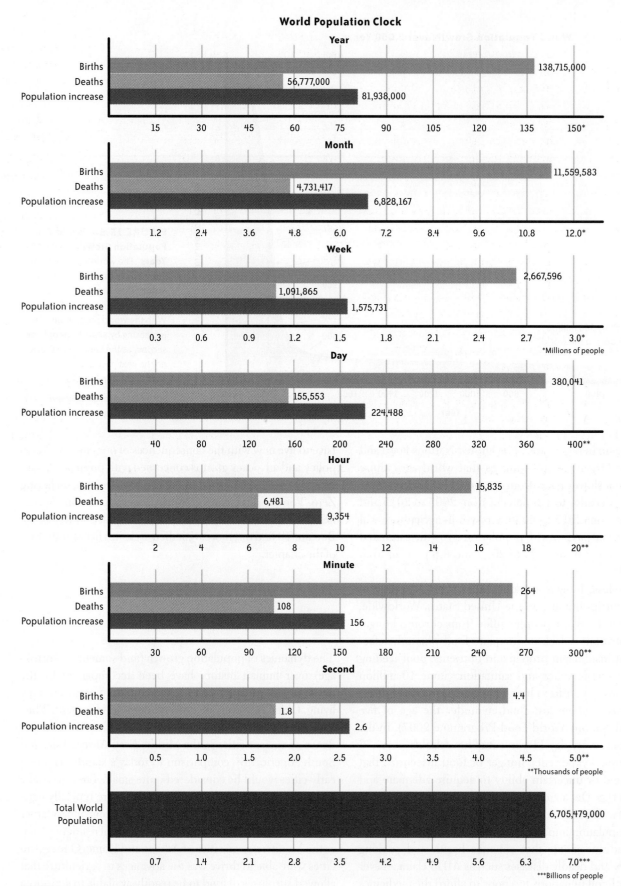

World Population Clock

Year

Births	138,715,000
Deaths	56,777,000
Population increase	81,938,000

15 30 45 60 75 90 105 120 135 150*

Month

Births	11,559,583
Deaths	4,731,417
Population increase	6,828,167

1.2 2.4 3.6 4.8 6.0 7.2 8.4 9.6 10.8 12.0*

Week

Births	2,667,596
Deaths	1,091,865
Population increase	1,575,731

0.3 0.6 0.9 1.2 1.5 1.8 2.1 2.4 2.7 3.0*

*Millions of people

Day

Births	380,041
Deaths	155,553
Population increase	224,488

40 80 120 160 200 240 280 320 360 400**

Hour

Births	15,835
Deaths	6,481
Population increase	9,354

2 4 6 8 10 12 14 16 18 20**

Minute

Births	264
Deaths	108
Population increase	156

30 60 90 120 150 180 210 240 270 300**

Second

Births	4.4
Deaths	1.8
Population increase	2.6

0.5 1.0 1.5 2.0 2.5 3.0 3.5 4.0 4.5 5.0**

**Thousands of people

Total World Population	6,705,479,000

0.7 1.4 2.1 2.8 3.5 4.2 4.9 5.6 6.3 7.0***

***Billions of people

FIGURE 15.5b World Population Clock

SOURCE: Population Reference Bureau 2008

People were thus freed to engage in other activities necessary for the functioning of the city and its residents.

Cities were not the prevalent residential areas until well into the nineteenth and twentieth centuries. Until then, the vast majority of people worldwide lived in **rural** or country areas. The wide-scale development of cities, or **urban** areas, was made possible by the significant social, economic, and political changes accompanying the Industrial Revolution, when masses of people were drawn into cities to find housing and the manufacturing jobs they needed to earn a living. Fewer families were involved in farming, as large companies, or agribusiness, began to emerge. Cities were populated not only by migrants from rural areas but also by immigrants from other countries, seeking opportunity and a better way of life. Industrialization provided the jobs and the means of communication and transportation to build the burgeoning city infrastructure that could support growing numbers of residents. This process in which growing numbers of people move from rural to urban areas is called **urbanization**.

In the early 1800s, only about 3 percent of the world's population lived in urban areas and only one city had a population greater than 1 million people: Peking, China (now called Beijing). In the early 1900s, almost 14 percent lived in urban areas, and another dozen or so cities around the world (including New York, London, Paris, Moscow, and Tokyo) had 1 million or more residents. In the early 2000s, more than 50 percent of the world's population were living in urban areas, and we now have to count as large cities those with 5 million people or more; there are more than 60 of these in the world (United Nations 2006).

A similar pattern can be seen in the United States. In the early 1800s, just 6 percent of the population lived in urban areas, whereas 94 percent lived in rural areas. In the early 1900s, the split was 40 percent urban and 60 percent in rural. In the early 2000s, 79 percent were urban and 21 percent were rural. As of 2007, nine American cities had populations over 1 million; the largest among them, New York, has over 8 million (U.S. Census Bureau 2007d).

rural relating to sparsely settled areas; in the United States, any county with a population density between 10 and 59.9 people per square mile

urban relating to cities; typically describes densely populated areas

urbanization movement of increasing numbers of people from rural areas to cities

metropolis an urban area with a large population, usually 500,000 to 1,000,000 people

Features of Urbanization

The term *city* is currently used to refer to an urban settlement with a large population, usually at least 50,000 to 100,000 people. Although a few states, including North Dakota, West Virginia, and Vermont, have no cities with populations of 100,000 people or more, California has 46 cities with more than 100,000 people, followed by Texas with 19 and Florida with 12. Urban demographers use the word **metropolis** to refer to an urban area with an even larger population—usually at least 500,000 people—that typically serves as the economic, political, and cultural center for a region. The

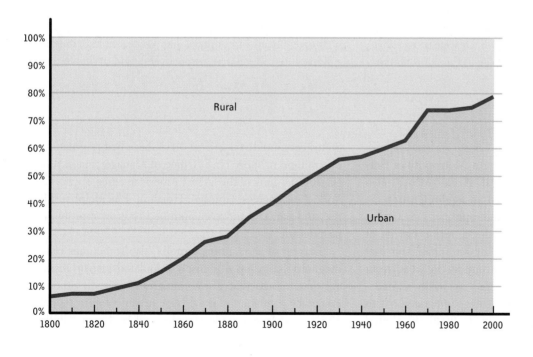

FIGURE 15.6 Rural/Urban Makeup of the U.S. Population, 1800–2000

As the U.S. population grew, so did the proportion of urban dwellers compared to rural inhabitants.

SOURCE: U.S. Census Bureau 1993 and 2000b

Global Perspective

The Asian Brown Cloud: Pollution in China and India

China and India are the two most populated countries in the world, with over a billion residents in each. In comparison, the United States, the third most populated country, has 301 million residents. According to calculations from the United Nations, no other country besides China and India will reach a population size of 1 billion. Despite the fact that the United States is the third most populated country, making up only 5 percent of the world's total population, it also consumes approximately 25 percent of its resources—in other words, we're currently the pigs of the planet. Unfortunately, though, as China and India develop into completely industrialized countries, they are following in the resource-hogging footsteps of the United States.

The "Asian Brown Cloud" is a name given to the layer of pollution that hangs over China, India, and parts of Southwest Asia. In satellite photos, the Asian Brown Cloud appears as a giant brown stain over this part of the world during the months of January through March. To the residents of China and India, the Asian Brown Cloud appears as a haze of air pollution hovering over their countries. Environmental scientists maintain that the Asian Brown Cloud consists of airborne pollutants from car and factory combustion and biomass burning that collect when there are no rains to wash it away. This atmospheric pollution has both immediate and long-term impacts on the citizens of Asia. Mumbai and Beijing report high rates of chronic respiratory problems including cancer. Air quality in large cities such as Beijing is so poor—and even dangerous—that Chinese officials have spent over 17 billion dollars in the last few years on attempts to reduce the air pollution. Despite these efforts, some Olympians refused to participate in the 2008 Summer Olympics in Beijing because of the fear that the air quality would affect their health and their performance. Projected long-term effects of this cloud of pollution include reduced crop growth leading to famine, melting glaciers creating devastating floods, and global warming affecting rainfall average, potentially leading to drought.

Much of the pollution in India and China has been a result of factory emissions, coal-burning, and garbage-burning. Now that there have been stricter regulations governing the emission produced by factories and garbage dumps, a new culprit is emerging because of the growing wealth of these Asian countries. In recent years, both China and India have registered record-breaking economic growth rates. Personal incomes have increased, and because of the constant barrage of images from the Western media, more and more Asian citizens are buying private cars rather than relying on public transportation or more traditional forms of commuting like bicycles. In Beijing alone, 1,300 new cars are registered every day. In 2008, India's Tata motors introduced the Nano, a $2,500 car that will make car ownership accessible for millions of Indians. Environmentalists fear that the Nano will flood already gridlocked roads as well as releasing millions of tons of carbon dioxide into the already polluted air.

Even with the recent increases in prices, America is still the most disproportionate consumer of fossil fuels in the world. Not only do Americans drive more cars than citizens from almost any other country, we also use many times more gas than anyone else. At 446 gallons per capita annually, we're gallons ahead of the Canadians (311 gallons), boatloads ahead of countries like Germany and Italy (130 gallons and 114 gallons, respectively), and veritable oceans

Metropolitan Statistical Area (MSA) or **agglomeration** one or more adjacent counties with at least one major city of at least 50,000 inhabitants that is surrounded by an adjacent area that is socially and economically integrated with the city

megalopolis or **megacity** a group of densely populated metropolises that grow dependent on each other and eventually combine to form a huge urban complex

U.S. Census Bureau defines the term **Metropolitan Statistical Area (MSA)**, also called an **agglomeration**, as a metropolitan area that includes a major city of at least 50,000 inhabitants that is surrounded by an adjacent area that is socially and economically integrated with the city. In 2006, the United States contained 363 MSAs; 50 of these had populations of one million or more (U.S. Office of Management and Budget 2006). Many of the largest American cities, such as New York, Los Angeles, Chicago, Houston, Philadelphia, Phoenix, and San Diego, have continued to grow rapidly in the past decade.

Largest of all is a **megalopolis**, also sometimes called a **megacity**—a group of densely populated metropolises (or agglomerations) that grow contiguous to each other and eventually combine to form a huge urban complex (Gottman 1961). One American megalopolis is referred to as "ChiPitts,"

The Asian Brown Cloud This photo from a NASA satellite shows the layer of pollution that hangs over China, India, and parts of Southwest Asia.

ahead of almost everyone else (United Nations Development Programme 2000). At the same time, developing countries like India and China are putting more and more cars on the roads. India consumed nearly 120 million tons of petroleum products in 2006–2007, according to the Petroleum Ministry, up from 113 million tons the previous year. China also saw a record high in terms of petroleum consumption in the first quarter of 2008 with a rise of 16.5 percent from the previous year. While the cars sold in China and India are not as gas-guzzling as American cars, the collective impact of the sheer number of cars owned in these densely populated countries is potentially devastating.

Rajendra Pachauri, head of the 2007 Nobel Prize–winning Intergovernmental Panel on Climate Change (IPCC), said that investing in improving urban public transportation and enforcing restrictions on industrial waste are ways that countries such as China and India could balance the need for fighting climate change with that for economic growth. However, the burden of the problem does not lie in the hands of the Chinese and Indian governments. Ultimately, the images transmitted from the United States are inspiring the world to aspire to the same excessive lifestyle and standard of living as those of Americans. People in developing countries want to achieve our level of economic development and our own trade policy benefits from their consumption rates when they buy our products. Can America lead by example? If we become more environmentally conscious, will the world follow suit? These are pressing questions that we will have to address in the very near future.

a group of metropolitan areas in the Midwest, extending from Pittsburgh to Chicago (and including Detroit, Cleveland, Columbus, Cincinnati, and Indianapolis), with a total population of more than 30 million. The ChiPitts metro areas are linked not only by geographic proximity but also by economics, transportation, and communications systems (Gottman and Harper 1990). An even larger megalopolis is "BosWash," extending from Boston to Washington, D.C., and including 22 other metropolises including New York and Philadelphia. BosWash has a total population of more than 44 million, or approximately 16 percent of the entire population of the country. Megalopolises are found worldwide, in countries including Brazil, Mexico, Indonesia, India, China, and Japan (Castells and Susser 2002). These are sometimes called **global cities** to emphasize their position in an increasingly globalized world as centers of economic, political, and social power (Sassen 1991).

Cities are often characterized by **urban density**,

global cities a term for megacities that emphasizes their global impact as centers of economic, political, and social power

urban density concentration of people in a city, measured by the total number of people per square mile

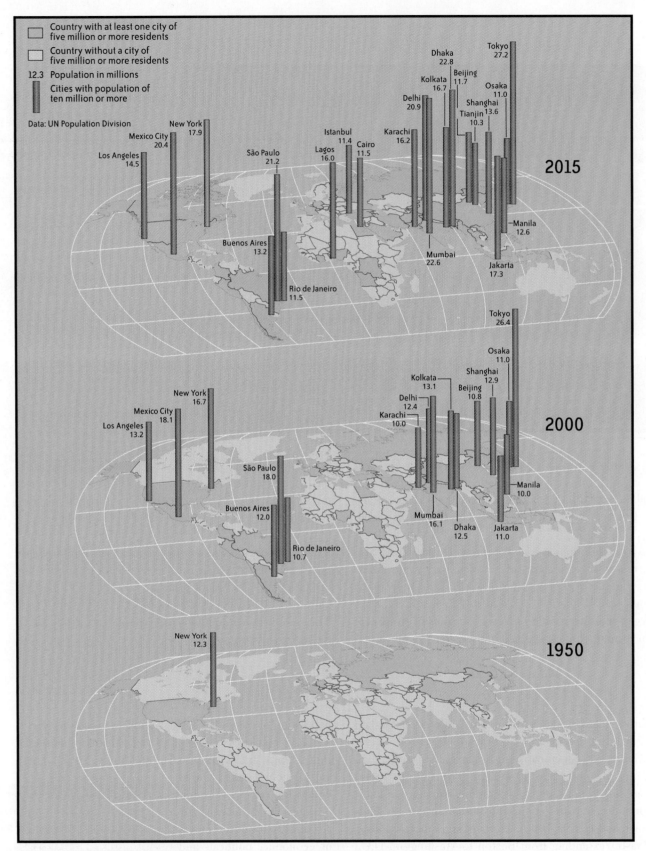

FIGURE 15.7 The Growth of Global Cities This map shows the skyrocketing growth of the world's major cities. Asia and Africa are expected to see particularly strong urban growth in the near future.

SOURCE: Zwingle 2002

measured by the total number of people per square mile. Some of the most densely populated cities in the United States include Union City, New Jersey, with 52,972 residents per square mile; New York City with 26,401; San Francisco with 16,633; and Chicago with 12,749 (U.S. Census Bureau 2005d). By contrast, rural areas are characterized by low density. Rural counties are those with populations of 10 to 59.9 people per square mile; frontier counties are those with 0.5 to 9.9 people; and remote counties are those with 0.04 people per square mile or fewer. Alaska is the most rural state in the United States, followed by Wyoming, Nevada, Utah, New Mexico, and North Dakota.

Trends in Urbanization

Along with urbanization, an important counter-trend surfaced in the years immediately following World War II. **Suburbanization** is the shift of large segments of population away from the urban core and toward the edges of cities, where larger expanses of land were available for housing developments that provided families with a chance to buy a home of their own and avoid the overcrowding of central urban life. One of the first significant suburbs in the late 1940s was called Levittown (based on the name of the builders), a community of 17,450 tract houses for 75,000 people in Hempstead, New York. The simply designed homes were mass-produced and sold at prices affordable to returning veterans and the new growing middle class (Wattel 1958). In the 1950s, the second Levittown was built near Philadelphia and in the 1960s a third in New Jersey. Herbert Gans's study *The Levittowners* (1967) found that homeownership gave suburbanites a sense of pride and more privacy and space, which they valued greatly.

Suburbanization also reflected a retreat from some of the problems associated with city living—close quarters, noise, and crime. As more families were able to afford single-family homes, large yards with the proverbial white picket fence and a two-car garage became the literal image of the "American Dream" (Fava 1956; Kelly 1993). But suburban life has its own problems: long commutes, little contact between neighbors, and de facto racial segregation in housing and schools. Some observers have also criticized the monotonous uniformity of the new suburbs, claiming that they promote listless personalities, conformity, and escapism (Riesman 1957; Whyte 1956; K. T. Jackson 1985). The decades-long shift of populations to the suburbs has accelerated and expanded throughout the nation, with more families moving farther and farther away into what's been called the "exurbs" (Frey 2003).

A problem related to suburbanization is **urban sprawl** (sometimes also called suburban sprawl). This phenomenon has to do with how cities and suburbs grow. It is often a derogatory term applied to the peripheral expansion of urban boundaries and is associated with irresponsible or poorly planned development. Critics say these areas are often unsightly, characterized by a homogenous landscape of

> **suburbanization** beginning after World War II, the shift of large segments of population away from the urban core and toward the edges of cities
>
> **urban sprawl** a derogatory term applied to the expansion of urban or suburban boundaries, associated with irresponsible or poorly planned development

Smart Growth vs. Suburban Sprawl Urban neighborhoods like this one in Brooklyn are examples of the trend toward revitalizing America's urban centers. Pedestrian-friendly neighborhoods with a mix of residential and commercial buildings are an alternative to suburban bedroom communities that have few sidewalks and many strip malls.

housing subdivisions, office parks, and corner strip-malls lacking character or green space (Kunstler 1993; Duany, Plater-Zyberk, and Speck 2001; Gutfreund 2004) and bringing problems of traffic, pollution, crowded schools, and high taxes.

While most suburbs remain "bedroom communities" or primarily residential, others have become **edge cities** with their own centers of employment and commerce (Garreau 1992). Edge cities are usually in close proximity to intersecting highways and urban areas. "Silicon Valley" is a prime example: the once-sleepy suburb of San Jose became a center of high-tech industry during the dot-com boom of the 1990s. Edge cities are one answer to the problems associated with suburbanization. **Smart growth** advocates are also promoting alternatives to suburban growth, emphasizing redevelopment of inner cities or older suburbs to create better communities. Elements of smart growth include town centers; transit- and pedestrian-friendly streets; a greater mix of housing, commercial, and retail properties; and the preservation of open space and other environmental amenities.

Many long-established cities suffered when populations began moving to the suburbs—such as Detroit, Chicago, and Philadelphia in the North and East (the rustbelt) as well as New Orleans, St. Louis, and San Francisco in the South, Midwest, and West (U.S. Census Bureau 2005d). Since the 1950s and 60s, people have left cities not only to find more space and bigger homes in the nearby suburbs but also because they were fleeing other problems endemic to the city. Largely, those escaping the cities were upper- and middle-class whites who could afford to leave—a trend often referred to as **white flight** (or sometimes suburban flight). Those remaining in cities were predominantly minorities, seniors, immigrants, working class, or poor. White flight left urban areas abandoned by businesses and financial institutions, leading to broken-down and boarded-up shops and streets and creating ghettos that further exacerbated the problems associated with inner cities (Wilson 1996).

In the 1960s and 70s, to address the problem of decaying inner cities, local city governments and private investors

Building "Green" Theressa Hamilton reads the newspaper as she eats lunch on the greenroof garden at Atlanta's City Hall. Her building is one of more than a dozen buildings in Atlanta designed to be more energy efficient.

took advantage of **urban renewal** efforts that included renovation, selective demolition, commercial development, and tax incentives aimed at revitalizing business districts and residential neighborhoods (Frieden and Sagalyn 1992). Urban renewal has been a limited success. While it did revitalize many areas, it often came at a high cost to existing communities. In many cases, it resulted in the destruction of vibrant, if rundown, neighborhoods (Mollenkopf 1983).

Urban renewal is linked to another trend that has also changed many formerly blighted cities: **gentrification**. This is the transformation of the physical, social, economic, and cultural life of formerly working-class or poor inner-city neighborhoods into more affluent middle-class communities as wealthier people return to the cities (Glass 1964). This trend, which began in the 1990s, is evident in some of the nation's largest cities, such as Boston, New York, Philadelphia, Chicago, and San Francisco (Mele 2000). Various

Real or Fake? People mingle outside Pastis restaurant in the New York City's meatpacking district. Contrast this urban scene with the City Walk in Los Angeles, which was designed to feel like an urban street.

higher-income individuals, whether they were young professionals ("yuppies"), artists, or retirees, recognized the potential for rehabilitating downtown buildings (Castells 1984). They valued the variety and excitement of urban living more than the mini-malls of sleepy suburbia (Florida 2004). The term *gentrification* carries a distinct class connotation; while converting, renovating, remodeling, and constructing new buildings beautifies old city neighborhoods, it also increases property values and tends to displace poorer residents (Zukin 1987, 1989). Gentrification, then, does not eradicate the problems of poverty; it simply forces the poor to move elsewhere.

Although urbanization (or suburbanization) is still the predominant demographic trend in the United States, an interesting reversal emerged in 1990s, called the **rural rebound** (Johnson and Beale 1994, 1995, 1998). An increase in rural populations has resulted from a combination of fewer people leaving such areas and the in-migration of urban and suburban dwellers (Long and Nucci 1998). While most rural counties continue to decline, those near urban centers or with rich scenic or amenity values are generally experiencing an upsurge in population. Gains have been greatest in the Mountain West, Upper Great Lakes, the Ozarks, parts of the South, and rural areas of the Northeast. Rural migrants include families with young children, small-scale farmers, retirees, blue-collar

> **rural rebound** population increase in rural counties that adjoin urban centers or possess rich scenic or amenity values

TABLE 15.1	*Theory in Everyday Life*	
Perspective	**Approach to the Natural Environment**	**Case Study: Urban Sprawl**
STRUCTURAL-FUNCTIONALISM	The natural world exists in order to keep the social world running smoothly. The environment provides raw materials and space for development in order to meet society's needs.	As populations increase, cities must grow in order to accommodate the growing population, so urban sprawl is functional for society.
CONFLICT THEORY	Not all groups or individuals benefit equally from society's use of the natural environment.	Urban sprawl creates largely white, upper and middle-class suburbs around cities whose residents are minorities, seniors, immigrants, working class, and/or poor. This means that suburban residents may have access to resources, like well-funded schools, which urban-dwellers may not.
SYMBOLIC INTERACTIONISM	The meanings assigned to the natural environment will determine how society sees and uses it.	Redefining open land as a scarce resource, and redefining urban areas as valuable spaces, may lead to the reduction of urban sprawl: open land could be conserved, while urban spaces could be rehabilitated and revitalized.

Operation Weed and Seed

On any given day, Ashley Enter may consult with a U.S. attorney or a local church leader, design a mental health resource directory, help set up a job training center, attend a neighborhood association meeting, or meet with landlords who want to keep their rental properties crime- and drug-free. Ashley's job as the Weed and Seed Coordinator for the city of Peoria, Illinois, means that she is in charge of a host of community-based initiatives meant to revitalize high-crime urban neighborhoods. Operation Weed and Seed is a community-based, multiagency approach to law enforcement, crime prevention, and neighborhood restoration and is sponsored by the U.S. Department of Justice. The "weeding" process involves local, state, and federal law enforcement agencies and targets violent crime and gang- and drug-related activity through programs such as community policing. But the program is not merely a crack-down on crime. The "seeding" process is equally—if not more—important.

"Seeding" involves a variety of programs designed to help transform previously unsafe neighborhoods into places where individuals, families, and community spirit can thrive. The Peoria Weed and Seed program is a good example of how many different organizations and services are necessary to effectively seed a neighborhood: a "Safe Haven" located in a local hospital provides job training, mentoring, tutoring, and computer access; Safe Havens at several area churches provide after-school services and counseling for families and individuals. Other activities include neighborhood cleanup and beautification programs, mutual assistance services (such as one program in which volunteers do chores including shoveling snow or pulling weeds for elderly or handicapped neighbors), and fun events such as block parties and cookouts.

Operation Weed and Seed's multifaceted approach is admirable in that it refuses to oversimplify the complex problems of urban living by mandating reductive remedies. It's not a panacea either, for a variety of reasons. Ashley spends a good deal of her time, for example, navigating the byzantine bureaucracies of the many local, state, and federal agencies involved in the program. Organizing and attending

Operation Weed and Seed Ascher Henrikson uses a magnifying glass to see worms and other creatures in a compost pile at the Earth Day celebrations in Peoria, Illinois.

meetings, scheduling telephone conferences, seeking committee approval for program decisions, writing and filing endless reports, and coordinating the demands of multiple funding sources are some of the challenges she faces in the office. Outside the office, the program runs up against a number of obstacles as well, not least of which is longstanding mutual suspicion between residents and police. But progress is being made.

Ashley graduated from Southern Illinois University with a bachelor's degree in public relations and a minor in community development. She joined the AmeriCorps VISTA program (Volunteers in Service to America) and built low-income housing with Habitat for Humanity. After her VISTA service was completed, she took a development job with the American Red Cross. Then she entered city government, specializing in neighborhood coordination and liaison work. She took the Weed and Seed job because she believes strongly in the values, goals, and strategies of the program, and despite the bureaucratic obstacles and funding uncertainties, she is optimistic about the program's potential to make a real difference in the city of Peoria and in the lives of the people living there.

For more information about Operation Weed and Seed, visit its website: www.ojp.usdoj.gov/ccdo/ws/welcome.html.

City of the Future In the film *The Fifth Element*, flying cars buzz between ultra-tall sky scrapers. Could this version of the future realistically occur? Would you like to live in such a future?

workers, single professionals, and disenchanted city dwellers all seeking a better way of life. They are willing to forsake the amenities of the city in exchange for a simpler, slower, more traditional rural lifestyle (K. Johnson 1999).

Another example of our contemporary ambivalence about city life is simulated cities—social spaces engineered to maximize the benefits of city life without the risks. A prime example is Universal CityWalk, a collection of shops, restaurants, and movie theaters in a suburb of Los Angeles. CityWalk mimics an urban shopping street, with sidewalk café seating and strolling street performers. However, it has no connection to a real urban street—CityWalk is bordered on one side by a theme park (Universal Studios) and on the other by a vast expanse of parking lots and freeway traffic. The parking fees to visit this street range from $7.50 to $17.50, which makes CityWalk a semiprivate attraction—distinctly unlike a real city street, which anyone can walk on without paying high fees for parking. The parking fees were instituted to minimize certain kinds of visitors found on real city streets including homeless people and hustlers of various sorts.

The urban experience provided by CityWalk is sanitized, soothing, and a model of social control through architectural planning. Says Kevin McNamara, of the University of Houston, "They omitted . . . the handbill-passers, bag ladies, streetcorner salesmen, and three-card-monte—because part of CityWalk's attraction rests on the certainty that distractions will remain pleasing, never truly surprising, let alone shocking" (McNamara 1999). CityWalk doesn't reject the grit of urban life entirely: when laying the sidewalks, developers embedded fake trash in the concrete. CityWalk and other artificial urban environments such as Celebration and Seaside, Florida, reveal our desire to experience the positive aspects of urban life without having to endure the

problems. But this kind of engineering tends to turn cities into theme parks, erasing what is authentically urban—for better and for worse.

DATA WORKSHOP
ANALYZING MASS MEDIA AND POPULAR CULTURE
Imagining the Cities of Tomorrow

People have always been interested in the future. Storytellers, inventors, scientists, politicians, and daydreamers have tried to imagine and in some instances create a vision of what will come.

Imagining the city of tomorrow is an almost constant theme in contemporary popular culture—books and comics, radio and TV, movies, and video games. Some of these represent a brighter vision of tomorrow, a **utopia** where humankind is finally freed from drudgery and disease, strife and suffering. Some represent a darker vision of tomorrow, a **dystopia** where humankind is trapped in a ruthless, apocalyptic world of machines and nature gone mad.

Although examples of the city of the future appear in many different media, this Data Workshop asks that you focus on film. You may have a favorite movie depicting the future, whether it's in the genre of science fiction, fantasy, thriller, horror, drama, or comedy. In deciding which movie to choose for your content analysis, consider

utopia literally "no place"; an ideal society in which all social ills have been overcome

dystopia opposite of a utopia—a world where social problems are magnified and the quality of life is extremely low

whether the movie proposes a serious or realistic possibility of the future and avoid anything too far out in terms of monsters, aliens, or fantasy worlds.

Below is a partial list of movies that could satisfy the assignment. This list is not exhaustive, and you may prefer to use a film not in the list.*

12 Monkeys	*Left Behind*
1984	*Mad Max*
A.I. (Artificial Intelligence)	*The Matrix*
Back to the Future	*Metropolis*
Blade Runner	*Minority Report*
Brazil	*Road Warrior*
Children of Men	*Slaughterhouse Five*
The Day after Tomorrow	*Solaris*
Demolition Man	*Strange Days*
eXistenZ	*The Terminator*
Fahrenheit 451	*Terminator 2: Judgment Day*
The Fifth Element	*Total Recall*
Gattaca	*Tron*
Idiotocracy	*The Truman Show*
Independence Day	*Videodrome*

Watch the movie while keeping in mind the concepts you have learned from this chapter, especially with regard to urbanization. Note the settings and environments in the movie. Capture key scenes or dialogue that can serve as examples of your argument. In conducting your content analysis, consider some of the following questions.

- At what point in the future does the movie take place?

- What is the major theme of the movie? What is its overall message?

- Does the movie represent a utopian or dystopian vision of the future? Does it represent positive or negative changes to society?

- What sorts of futuristic elements are included in the movie (such as time travel, virtual reality, mind control, wars between humans and machines, apocalyptic destruction)?

- How is the modern city or landscape of the future depicted? What are its structural features in both public and private realms?

* Please be aware of MPAA ratings for movies and select appropriate material for your age group.

- Compare the future with the present. How is the future the same or different? How is it better or worse?

- What are people like in the future? How are they affected by their environment? How does their environment impact their lives?

- Could this version of the future realistically occur? Would you like to live in such a future?

There are two options for completing this Data Workshop.

- *Option 1 (informal)*: Follow the instructions for viewing the movie, and reflect on the questions above. You may wish to take notes to prepare for a discussion with other students in small groups. Compare and contrast the movies you watched with others in the group. What similarities or differences are there between movies?

- *Option 2 (formal)*: Follow the instructions for viewing the movie, and write a three- to four-page essay answering the questions above.

Living in the City

Who lives in cities? What about city life continues to attract droves of people? Big cities offer residents bright lights, a fast pace, excitement, and opportunity. They differ from small rural towns and suburban neighborhoods, so a certain type of person is more likely to be found living there.

Louis Wirth, a member of the Chicago School of sociology, proposed "urbanism as a way of life" that affected the outlook, mentality, and lifestyle of those who lived in the city. He believed that cities provided personal freedom, relaxed moral restraints, relative anonymity, variety, and diversity. At the same time there was a certain social cost involved. People tended to belong to more formal organizations with more narrow goals and to engage less frequently in intimate interaction with one another. His analysis was in line with the belief that cities caused **social atomization**, that they were filled with free-floating individuals rather than members of a community (Wirth 1938).

Another sociologist, Claude Fischer, found that people create a sense of community by dividing the city into little worlds within which they feel familiar and involved. These groups allowed for informal and close relationships, giving city dwellers more intimacy and a feeling of belonging (C. Fischer 1976).

In 1962, Herbert Gans published a major ethnographic study, *Urban Villagers*, in which he identified distinct categories of **urbanites**, or people who live in urban areas. The first are called *cosmopolites*—students, intellectuals,

Encounters with Strangers

Cities are places where strangers come together. Before there were cities, there were also no strangers; those who were unknown were driven off, killed, or quickly assimilated into the clan, tribe, or group (Lofland 1973). With the advent of cities came the prospect of living life in close proximity to hundreds, thousands, or even millions of people we will never know and from whom we cannot be completely segregated. City life would seem to bring the prospect for all sorts of chaos and conflict—and yet every day, in contemporary cities, millions of people go about their business in relative harmony, brushing elbows with each other on the sidewalk or subway in encounters that are neither friendly nor unfriendly but merely orderly.

What are the interactional structures that order urban life? Public interactions with strangers can be treacherous, as we encounter people we do not know and whose reactions we cannot predict. For the most part, we are not talking about the danger of physical attack. More common than getting mugged is being "looked at funny," getting "goosed," or being the target of "wolf whistles." These are threats to self more than anything else—being treated as a nonperson, or as a piece of meat. How do we guard against these minor molestations when we walk down the street every day?

A specific way we deal with strangers in public is by doing what Erving Goffman calls **civil inattention**. This is a taken-for-granted rule of public place interaction, a basic public courtesy we extend to one another that helps guard against unpleasant interactions with strangers (Goffman 1971). About eight or ten feet away from one another, we tend to look at and then look away from the person we are

Sidewalk Etiquette Whether listening to an iPod, talking on a cell phone, or just averting their gaze, urbanites use civil inattention to order public place interaction.

approaching—all in one sweep of our gaze. We have looked, but not too intently or for too long. This allows us to navigate through urban spaces without bumping into strangers and to avoid the kinds of interactions that might lead to trouble. The practice of civil inattention is so commonplace that you may not realize you do it every day. Now, walk down the street and notice your own gazework and that of others—with full comprehension of how this simple act helps avoid conflict, enables smooth interactions between strangers, and basically makes city life possible.

artists, entertainers, and other professionals who are drawn to the city because of its cultural benefits and convenience to their lifestyles. The next group are the *singles*, unmarried people seeking jobs, entertainment, and partners with whom to settle down. Singles may include cosmopolites as well. When singles do find a marriage partner or mate, they tend to move to the suburbs, often in preparation to start a family.

Another group of city dwellers are the *ethnic villagers*, often recent immigrants to the area. They tend to settle near others with whom they share a common racial, ethnic, national, religious, or language background; these are often distant relatives or others with whom they have a connection. This is why many major cities still have Chinatowns, Little Italys, and other ethnic neighborhoods. Once here, immigrants form tightly knit ethnic enclaves that resemble the villages of their home countries. The last group of urban dwellers is the *deprived* and the *trapped*. These are the people at the bottom of the social hierarchy—the poor, homeless, disabled, elderly, and mentally ill. Without resources and means of support they cannot afford to leave the city, even if they could find jobs, services, or housing elsewhere; they are inescapably stuck where they are. This perpetuates a cycle of poverty and despair.

Alienation and Altruism: The Case of New York City

As products of the Industrial Revolution, cities are celebrated for providing unprecedented degrees of freedom for individuals. Life in rural agricultural communities was much more restrictive, with family and neighbors placing tight constraints on behavior. However, sociology has been suspicious of cities, seeing this very freedom as a source of **alienation**. Early sociologist Georg Simmel argued that while urban environments "allowed a much greater degree of individual liberty," they did so only "at the expense of treating others in objective and instrumental terms" relating to others only through a "cold and heartless calculus" (Harvey 1990). In short, except for their chosen subcultures, city dwellers fail to develop community, feel little connection with neighbors, have relationships that are largely shallow and impersonal, and fail to care about each other (Simmel 1950).

The murder of Catherine "Kitty" Genovese has come to represent all such fears about urban life. Late March 13, 1964, she was returning home from her job as a bar manager when she was attacked by a man named Winston Moseley. He first attacked Genovese after she parked her car outside the Kew Gardens apartment building where she lived. She was stabbed several times before her attacker was frightened off when lights went on in nearby apartments. Badly wounded and bleeding Genovese was later reported to have shouted, "Oh, my God, he stabbed me! Please help me! Please help me!" (Gansberg 1964). Somehow she then made her way to the back of the building, apparently trying to get to the staircase that led to her apartment. However, her assailant returned and stabbed and beat her to death, before sexually assaulting her. The entire attack, although intermittent, was reported to have lasted nearly 30 minutes.

As horrible as this was, it wouldn't be remembered today if it were just a tragic murder. What has made this case memorable was the number of bystanders who must

Kitty Genovese

have heard the crime taking place but failed to take action. A friend of Genovese made the following comments during an interview on National Public Radio in 2004, some 40 years after the crime took place.

> The police later established that 38 people either saw Kitty Genovese stabbed and raped or heard her scream for her life, but no one called the police; no one rushed down to the street to try to scare off her attacker. Her death was a small story in the next day's newspapers, but two weeks later, the *New York Times* ran a story on how shocked the Queens police had been that so many people heard Kitty Genovese being murdered and didn't lift a finger to help her. The story set off a national soul-searching. How could so many Americans, even New Yorkers, it was sometimes added, have turned away from cries for help? The murder of Kitty Genovese became a kind of modern morality tale. Her death seemed to symbolize an age in which people counseled, "Don't get involved." "Mind your own business." "Not in my back yard." (S. Simon 2004)

A. M. Rosenthal, who was the editor of the *New York Times* in 1964, later wrote a book about the incident, which focused attention on the most disturbing aspect of the case: why didn't somebody help her? For many this seemed to be the ultimate indictment of big cities in general, and New York City in particular, but much of the press coverage seemed to demonize the individuals involved. Regardless of the individual responsibility, it's important to also look at the social factors that made the situation possible.

alienation decreasing importance of social ties and community and the corresponding increase in impersonal associations and instrumental logic

Especially useful in understanding the social origins of this unfortunate incident has been the work of social psychologists John Darley and Bibb Latane (1968), who conducted several experiments on **altruism** and helping behaviors. These experiments were designed to test what came to be called the **bystander effect**, or the **diffusion of responsibility**. In one experiment, different-sized groups of test subjects heard what sounded like a woman having an accident in the next room. Darley and Latane found that the higher the number of bystanders present, the lower the chances that any of them would attempt to help. Basically, they theorized that the responsibility "diffused" throughout the crowd so that no one person felt responsible enough to do anything, most assuming that someone else would help. However, when groups were small, the chances that someone would do something increased greatly.

In a similar experiment, they placed different-sized groups of subjects in a room, under the pretense of taking a test, and gradually filled the room with smoke. Again, they found that the greater the number of subjects in a room, the lower the chances that anyone would mention the smoke. Here, along with the diffusion of responsibility, they argued that **pluralistic ignorance** was at work. When large groups of people encounter an ambiguous or unusual situation, they tend to look to each other for help in defining the situation. If no member of the group decides that it is an emergency, and therefore worthy of worry, it is likely that all members will continue to ignore the situation.

On the twentieth anniversary of the Genovese murder, Fordham University held the "Catherine Genovese Memorial Conference on Bad Samaritanism," which attempted to shed some light on what sorts of situations would produce bystanders who would help. Although no single character trait correlated with being a Good Samaritan, they largely confirmed earlier findings—that bystanders in groups were tentative about helping, especially when they were unsure of the nature of the problem.

These conclusions can also help to explain a time when New Yorkers did come to each other's aid out of a sense of belonging and **community**: in the September 11, 2001, attacks on the World Trade Center. In the hours and days after the attacks, Americans rushed to help however they could. "Tens of thousands of patriotic Americans rolled up their sleeves and gave blood," monetary donations poured in, and ordinary New Yorkers rushed to pitch in (Stapleton 2002). Some of the most heroic rescue efforts at the World Trade Center were made by ordinary people who rushed to help as soon as they heard. Two Port Authority Police Officers, Will Jimeno and John McLoughlin, were the last people to be found alive in the collapsed remains of the World Trade Center towers. They were discovered by Charles Sereika, a former paramedic, and David Karnes, "an accountant from Connecticut" who "had changed into his Marine camouflage outfit" and driven down to Manhattan as soon as he heard the news (Dwyer 2001). The movie *World Trade Center* (2006) by Oliver Stone depicts their story. And even if things have somewhat returned to normal (meaning people are less friendly now), almost everyone agrees that New Yorkers "were wonderful during the crisis, and we were tender to each other. . . . Volunteers streamed to the site" and "after only a few days there were so many, they were turned away by the hundreds. . . . Strangers spoke to each other in the street, in stores, and on the subway" (Hustvedt 2002).

So what made the difference in the two events? Many of those who heard Kitty Genovese being murdered believed that it was a bar fight or a lover's quarrel. Not knowing what was happening, they were unsure how to respond. With September 11 there was no ambiguity. Also, on September 11 many people understood where to go and what to do to help. In 1964 the "911" emergency system didn't exist, and many people were reluctant to get personally involved with the police. This largely supports the conclusions of sociologists like Lee Clarke (2001), who has studied how people respond to various kinds of disasters. His work shows that altruism, rather than panic, tends to prevail in disasters. Clarke posits that the rules for behavior in extreme situations are essentially the same as the rules of ordinary life—that when faced with danger, people help those next to them before helping themselves. This was the case in the destruction of the World Trade Center. People survived the disaster because they did not become hysterical but instead helped to facilitate a successful evacuation of the buildings (Clarke, 2001). There are many obvious reasons why the September 11 attacks would bring people together in ways that the attack on Kitty Genovese did not. September 11 was clearly and obviously a disaster; it was also an attack on the entire country, so loyalties were further cemented. Formal institutions were set up so people could easily volunteer and receive positive social sanctions in return. Kitty Genovese was just one young woman living in a building full of immigrants and elderly pensioners. However, whenever bystanders do jump in to help, it is in part because of the outrage her murder provoked.

altruism unselfish concern for the well-being of others and helping behaviors performed without self-interested motivation

bystander effect or **diffusion of responsibility** the social dynamic wherein the more people there are present in a moment of crisis, the less likely any one of them is to take action

pluralistic ignorance a process in which members of a group individually conclude that there is no need to take action because of the observation that other group members have not done so

community a group of people living in the same local area who share a sense of participation and fellowship

Urban Legends Worried about razor blades or poison in his children's Halloween candy, Ray Orozco inspects their haul after a night of trick-or-treating in Miami, Florida.

In the aftermath of the Kitty Genovese murder, the "911" emergency system was created, neighborhood watch groups were formed, Good Samaritan laws were passed to protect bystanders from liability in emergencies, and people started to get more involved.

Urban Legends

The story of Kitty Genovese's murder is true. But that cannot be said about every sensational story you hear, especially if it is passed along through informal social networks among friends or over the internet.

Did you hear the one about the missing kidneys? A businessman was attending a convention in Las Vegas, and after a hard day's work he stopped off for a drink in the hotel lounge. A prostitute approached him, and after a few drinks, she suggested they go up to his room. The next morning the business traveler woke up in a bathtub, filled with ice, and a note telling him that if he wanted to live he should call "911" immediately. The emergency dispatcher asked him to examine his lower back, where he found two neat incisions. The traveler was then told to get back in the tub and wait for help because his kidneys had been removed by black market organ thieves.

> **urban legend** modern folklore; a story that is believed (incorrectly) to be true and is widely spread because it expresses concerns, fears, and anxieties about the social world

Or maybe you're more familiar with the alligators in the New York City sewers, purchased as pets when still small but flushed down the toilet, where they grew to full size. Perhaps you've heard about apples with razor blades given to trick-or-treaters on Halloween. Or that the taco restaurant down the street has an earthworm farm that supplies their "ground beef." Or maybe you even got an e-mail from Bill Gates promising to give you a $1,000 if you forwarded an e-mail often enough, because he was testing new e-mail tracking software. If you live near Southern California or in Puerto Rico you may have even heard about the "chupacabra," a blood-sucking alien devil beast that preys on goats and the occasional stray dog.

All are examples of **urban legends**, a specific and very modern variety of folklore. The study of folklore involves "collecting, classifying, and interpreting in their full cultural context the many products of everyday human interaction that have acquired a somewhat stable underlying form" (Brunvand 1981, p. 2). Folklorists look at fairy tales, legends, folk music, jokes, and other forms of popular art because understanding the themes and ideas that commonly appear in such material can tell you a great deal about the culture that produced it. Urban legends, in particular, are defined by their believability and their contemporary setting; they are often legitimated or "authenticated" through either personal acquaintance with a supposed witness or some sort of media coverage.

An urban legend can be defined as a story that is bizarre, whimsical, 99 percent apocryphal yet believable, a story that is almost, but not quite, too good to be true (Brunvand 2001). Incredible stories exist in many forms, like ghost stories that are told around a campfire; but to work as an urban legend, people must believe that the story is true or could be true. Jan Brunvand, a noted folklorist, says that urban legends are particularly compelling because someone claims that "the story is true; it really occurred, and recently, and always to someone else who is quite close to the narrator, or at least a 'friend of a friend'" (1981, p. 4).

Urban legends are like a folk sociology, as every successful urban legend is told and retold because it expresses "in a succinct and entertaining form what narrators wish to present as a truth about contemporary life and behavior" (Boyes 1984, p. 64). Two qualities of an urban legend can contribute to its success. First, the most popular legends are repeated and spread because they speak to our concerns, fears, and anxieties about our social world. Often there is a moral expressing the "fears and anxieties of a group and serv[ing] as warnings about potentially dangerous situations, behaviors, and assumptions." In this way urban legends serve a function in society "whether of education, social control, expression of attitudes and emotions, or strengthening of social bonds" (Whatley and Henken 2000, pp. 2, 6). For instance, stories about Halloween candy with razor blades warn us not to trust strangers (Best and Horiuchi 1985). Stories about condoms or intravenous needles in soft drink cans play on fears about the purity of our food. Stories about serial killers and crime often reveal our fears of being alone or of being among strangers in the darkened world outside the security of our own home or car (Brunvand 1981).

A second quality that contributes to the success of an urban legend is its affective punch. Urban legends that circulate the most tend to inspire an emotional reaction—typically anger, fear, disgust, or amusement. One study conducted at Duke University to determine what drives urban legends took a number of familiar stories and created several variations, each inspiring varying degrees of disgust. Undergraduates in the study were then asked to retell the stories. The researchers found that while transmitting basic information was important, the students preferred to tell versions that elicited the most emotion from listeners (Lockman 2002).

The most popular urban legends may be circulated for years, and though they may traverse the nation, they are often given local details in the telling, which makes them seem more believable (Best and Horiuchi 1985). In some ways modern technology has changed the dissemination of urban legends. The internet and e-mail have vastly accelerated the speed and reach of the modern urban legend. As Brunvand recounts, "a combination of oral tradition, electronic communication and mass media exposure have sustained a wide range of modern urban legends over broad areas of space and long stretches of

time" (1981); stories that "are simply too beguiling to fade away" are now spread faster and to more people than ever before (Jensen 2000). Ironically, electronic communication may actually slow the rate of change to stories, as people may simply cut and paste or forward e-mail messages verbatim. Whether told face-to-face or through electronic media, the continued circulation of urban legends speaks to the enduring power of a few compelling themes about modern social life.

DATA WORKSHOP

ANALYZING EVERYDAY LIFE

Urban Legends

Surely you've heard an urban legend. Perhaps it was from a family member, friend, classmate, or colleague, or you might have found it on the internet. Urban legends are compelling because they reflect a near-universal fear of the unknown, of the mysterious forces that may come at us unexpectedly and at any moment. They are often a response to social strain caused by fears and anxieties of modern life. And in a world of terrorism, drive-by shootings, biological weapons, and natural disasters, such tales resonate, reflecting the very real social conditions in which we live.

The wonderful thing about looking at urban legends is the opportunity they give anyone to engage in sociological research. Content analysis of urban legends helps us come to a better understanding of our own culture. Here are the instructions for this Data Workshop.

1. Identify and select an urban legend (you may find your own sources or use those listed at www.snopes.com).

   a. Where did you find this urban legend? Is it available from a variety of sources? Had you heard it before?
   b. Can you determine how long it has been circulating and through what types of social networks?
   c. What made you choose this particular story? Why does it intrigue you?

2. Apply the following definition to make sure that the content of the urban legend you selected has the necessary elements:

   a. Believable—Can it be assumed to be true as told? Is there, or could there be, an actual event that inspired this urban legend?
   b. Contemporary—Are the settings and events part of everyday life?
   c. Legitimizing or authenticating element—Does it contain a reference to a personal acquaintance or

friend-of-a-friend who was a supposed witness? Or has it been covered in the media?

3. Why has this urban legend been repeated and spread? What makes it so appealing? Most urban legends will have most or all of the following elements:

    a. Does it play on easily shared emotions like fear, anger, disgust, amusement, greed, or shock?
    b. Could it serve as a moral or cautionary tale? Would there be some advantage to heeding the warning of the story?
    c. Does it illustrate the anxieties, fears, concerns, values, attitudes, interests, or beliefs of the cultural group telling it?

Use the preceding outline as a guide to doing a content analysis of the urban legend you selected. Explain why you think it meets the criteria described above. Consider these additional questions: In what ways is the urban legend you selected similar to or different from others? Does the story help to support the status quo, reconfirming the need for social order? Or does it somehow undermine conventional norms and values? What truths does it reveal about modern life?

There are two options for completing this Data Workshop.

- *Option 1 (informal):* Follow the instructions above for selecting and analyzing an urban legend. You will need to bring to class a copy of the story plus any informal notes regarding your analysis to discuss with other students in small groups. Compare stories among group members, looking for similarities and differences.

- *Option 2 (formal):* Follow the instructions above for analyzing the urban legend you selected. Write a three- to four-page essay answering all of the questions above. Don't forget to include an exact copy of the story in your paper.

The Environment

The final section of this chapter once again considers the connection between the social and the natural worlds. Human populations have grown tremendously, as have the cities in which most of them live. Now how do those people interact with the natural environment and what impact does the environment have on how they live? Whether we go camping, go surfing, or just take a walk through Central Park, we all go to nature to escape, to recreate, to relax. It is ironic that we now seek out nature as a retreat from the demands of society because society itself originated and evolved at least in part to protect us against the demands of nature. The cooperation and interdependence that characterize most social groups allow individuals to withstand the risks of the natural environment. The products of culture—clothing, architecture, automobiles, and many others—contribute to our ability to live in what would otherwise be inhospitable surroundings. Without her insulated house and its furnace, her layers of clothing topped with a Gore-Tex parka, and her car with a remote starter and all-weather tires, Dr. Ferris would have a hard time surviving the harsh winters in northern Illinois. And all these survival tools are supplied because she is part of a society whose other members have created what she needs to be safe and warm in the elements. Society provides all of us with a buffer against nature; without it, we wouldn't last very long in the ocean, the snowdrifts, or the desert plains.

Social Ecology

While society buffers individuals against the rigors of nature, it also allows them to impact the natural world. Trees are cut down to build homes; furnaces and automobiles burn fuels and create air pollution; and manufacturing artificial fibers creates chemical waste—just a few of the ways the collective actions of a society impact the natural world. The study of human populations and their impact on the natural world is called **social ecology**. Under this heading you might study how cities are organized, how populations migrate, or how technological developments influence the social order, to see how these social developments occur within a physical environment that shapes and responds to social trends.

Sociologists are interested in both the social and the natural worlds because those worlds interact with each other. Even the most remote corner of the Amazon rainforest is not immune from the effects of society, even if no human has ever set foot there. Global warming is slowly changing that forest's climate; jets fly above the trees, creating noise and pollution; and animals that have been squeezed out of their natural habitats elsewhere (by trends like urban sprawl) may begin moving into new territories, upsetting the balance of native creatures and plants. Society impacts nature relentlessly—and vice versa—as the rhythms, rigors, and risks of the natural world shape how society is organized.

Social Ecology Society affects nature even in the remotest places—including on the highest mountaintops and in outer space! Hikers leave garbage on Mount McKinley (left), and NASA illustrates the debris orbiting the Earth (right). The European Space Agency estimates that there are 8,500 objects larger than 3 inches wide currently circling the planet.

Studying the Environment

The environment is a recent area of interest among sociologists, coinciding with the general public's concern about environmental issues (Guber 2003). When sociologists use the term **environment**, it encompasses aspects of both the natural and the human-made environment and includes everything from the most micro level of organisms to the entire **biosphere**. Sociologists study the ways that societies are dependent on the natural world; how cultural values and beliefs shape views about and influence usage of the environment; the politics and economics of natural resources; and the social construction of conflicts, problems, and solutions that are a result of our relationship to the natural world.

Environmental sociology is a growing subfield within the larger discipline that has continued to gain scholarly interest and to impact other academics, policy makers, and society as a whole. Its emergence paralleled the modern environmental movement in the late 1970s. The contours of the subfield are still being established, as we will see in the next section.

First, we will look at the environment as a social problem. This encompasses two big areas: problems of consumption and problems of waste. Sociologists, however, must look beyond descriptions of problems and attempt to apply analytic frameworks for understanding the social complexities underlying them.

The Environment as a Social Problem

Many students first become acquainted with the subject of the environment as a social problem. Learning the "three R's" in schools has now come to mean Reduce, Reuse, Recycle. We need to help "save" the environment because it is under threat from consumption and waste.

PROBLEMS OF CONSUMPTION: RESOURCE DEPLETION

The planet Earth provides an abundance of natural resources, including air, water, land, wildlife, plants, and minerals. We have learned to exploit these resources not only for basic survival but also to build everything in material culture that is part of the modern world. Humans have long been presented with the challenge of managing their use of natural resources, but those challenges have changed in the postindustrial era.

Renewable resources are natural resources that can be regenerated—for instance, oxygen is replenished by plants and trees, water by evaporation and rain clouds, trees and plants by pollens and seeds, and animals by mating and reproduction. **Nonrenewable resources** are those that cannot be replaced (except through tens of thousands of years of geological processes)—for instance, fossil fuels like oil or minerals like coal, copper, or iron.

environment in sociology, the natural world, the human-made environment, and the interaction between the two

biosphere the parts of the earth that can support life

environmental sociology the study of the interaction between society and the natural environment, including the social causes and consequences of environmental problems

renewable resources resources that replenish at a rate comparable to the rate at which they are consumed

nonrenewable resources finite resources, including those that take so long to replenish as to be effectively finite

Threats to Biodiversity Rainforests, which play a key role in regulating the global climate and are home to almost 50 percent of the world's plant and animal species, are being destroyed at a rate of millions of acres each year.

All natural resources are susceptible to overuse or overconsumption and eventually to depletion or even exhaustion. As a result of rising demands, we have already seen rising costs or outright shortages for such commodities as seafood, timber, and gasoline.

It may be hard to imagine that we'll ever run out of some things, like air and water, but even these are threatened. We may not be aware of the connection between the things we consume in our everyday life and their sources. We're removed from the fields and the mines, the oceans and the mountains that are the origin of our goods. But we are already confronting real problems of resource depletion, and the course of such depletion may now be irreversible.

One of the world's most pressing problems is how to meet enormous and growing demands for energy. We need energy—gas, electric, or nuclear—to help us power everything from our cars and televisions to factories and airplanes. But these forms of energy are not inexhaustible. We have relied primarily on nonrenewable sources such as coal and fossil fuels to meet our needs. The current mix of fuel sources comes from 78 percent fossil, 18 percent renewables, and 4 percent nuclear. Some renewable sources besides wood and hydroelectric (water-generated) power, such as wind or solar power, are being developed, but they are not sufficient yet to provide us with the substantial quantities of energy we will need in the future.

Industrialized nations are the largest consumers of energy, using approximately 70 percent of the total energy produced in the world; of those nations, America uses nearly 25 percent, Japan uses close to 6 percent, and Germany 4 percent. Developing nations that now use the remaining 30 percent are becoming more industrialized, and their energy needs will also increase, thus closing the energy usage gap among nations over the next 25 years. In that same time, total worldwide energy consumption is projected to grow between 50 and 60 percent (Energy Information Administration 2004). Oil is a finite resource, and at some point the supply will be exhausted. We may have already hit a peak of production and are in decline. We know that limited amounts and rising costs of energy are likely to spur development of substitutes for oil.

Another critical area of consumption is the rainforests in South America, Central America, Australia, Africa, and Southeast Asia. Rainforests are ecosystems located in tropical and temperate regions that are home to diverse plant and animal life (as well as indigenous peoples). Although rainforests cover only about 6 percent of the earth's landmass, they contain close to 50 percent of all microorganisms and plant and animal species in the world (Mittermeier, Myers, and Mittermeier 2000). Previously unknown life forms are being discovered there every year, while at the same time thousands are being driven to extinction. Products derived from the rainforest include not only foods and woods, but importantly, pharmaceuticals; more than 7,000 medical compounds are derived from native plants. Rainforests also play a key role in global climate control, evaporation and rainfall, and clearing the air of carbon dioxide (Myers and Kent 2005).

In 1950, rainforests covered twice as much area as they do today, and they are disappearing at an alarming rate. Currently, there are approximately 3.5 billion acres of rainforest worldwide, down from more than 7 billion. More than 78 million acres of rainforest are lost every year—215,000 acres every day, or about 150 acres every minute! Destruction of the rainforests is of sociological import because it results from collective human behavior. The immediate cause of this destruction is to accommodate the logging, mining, and ranching industries. Although these industries benefit the peoples of those regions, they are primarily providing for the consumption demands of the more developed nations of the world (Myers and Kent 2004).

In addition to rainforests, worldwide **biodiversity** is in dangerous decline. According to a 2005 United Nations report prepared by 1,360 scientists from 95 countries, humans pose a distinct threat to thousands of other species on the planet. The report asserts that the natural rate of extinction has multiplied by as much as a thousand times within the past century. Perhaps hardest hit has been marine life, with a 90 percent decrease in the number of fish in the world's oceans. In addition, roughly 12 percent of birds, 23 percent of mammals, 25 percent of conifers, and 32 percent of amphibians are threatened with extinction. These mass die-offs are being driven by human activities, including the destruction of habitats, pollution, the introduction of nonnative species, and overuse. "We will need to make sure that we don't disrupt the biological web to the point where collapse of the whole system becomes irreversible," says Anantha Duraiappah of Canada, who cochaired the study.

PROBLEMS OF WASTE: POLLUTION Problems of consumption are linked to problems of waste, often two sides of the same coin. Consider water and air. Water is another natural resource that can be overused—we understand what happens during a drought, or when lakes, rivers, or underground aquifers are drained and then go dry. But water can also be damaged by what we put into it. And while we don't normally think of consuming air, it is an essential natural resource, and we can damage its quality and change for the worse the very atmosphere of the planet. Let's look at these examples of **pollution**.

Water is indispensable for life. Some 70 percent of the earth's surface is covered with water. Almost 97 percent of this is in oceans of saltwater, home to a vast array of sea creatures and plants. Only 1 percent of the total accounts for freshwater, found in lakes, rivers, and underground aquifers; the other 2 percent is in polar ice caps and glaciers. This is a small percentage to meet human needs—from drinking water to water for agricultural and ranching purposes. The world's water supply, both in oceans and freshwater, has been under increased threat from pollution by industrial development and population growth—mostly by allowing contaminants to enter the oceans, lakes, and rivers or to seep into underground water supplies. The sources of this pollution are many: factories dumping chemical and solid wastes, agricultural run-off of pesticides

and fertilizers, human sewage and urban run-off, and toxic chemicals falling from the skies in rain.

Access to freshwater is not equal throughout the world. Most Americans can take safe drinking water for granted. Although the **Environmental Protection Agency (EPA)** claims that the United States has one of the safest supplies of drinking water, even here more than 10 percent of water systems in the nation don't meet EPA standards (U.S. EPA 2008). In developing nations, waterborne diseases are a significant cause of disease and death. There is a definite link between water scarcity and poverty; in some African countries up to 50 percent of the population are without access to adequate water (Gleick 1998).

The atmosphere is made up of thin layers of gases surrounding the planet and making life possible. It interacts with the land, oceans, and sun to produce the earth's climate and weather. The air that we breathe is ubiquitous, so that we might not even think of it as a natural resource. But our earth's atmosphere and its ability to sustain life are at risk from pollution. Not all sources are human—for instance, volcanoes or forest fires started by lightning can emit massive clouds of smoke, ash, and debris into the atmosphere. Human activity, however, accounts for a tremendous amount of air pollution, especially emissions from factories and automobiles. The most common pollutants (carbon monoxide, lead, nitrogen dioxide, ozone, sulfur dioxide, and particulates such as soot, smoke, and dust) together are often referred to as **greenhouse gases**. These not only create ugly smog and haze but also are hazardous to the health of humans and other species.

The U.S. Congress passed the first Clean Air Act in 1963, which has been followed over the decades by numerous amendments and other legislation to help regulate industries involved in emissions. Regulations and technological advancements have helped reduce air pollution in the United States. Still, we have the highest per capita rate of any nation, emitting some 6.6 tons of greenhouse gases per person per year. It is estimated that over 100 million people, or about 40 percent of the U.S. population, live in areas reporting higher levels of ozone than are safe by national standards (U.S. EPA 2003). The problem may be even greater in developing nations that are rapidly becoming industrialized.

biodiversity the variety of species of plants and animals existing at any given time

pollution any environmental contaminant that harms living beings

Environmental Protection Agency (EPA) a government agency organized in 1969 to "create and maintain conditions in which man and nature can exist in productive harmony"

greenhouse gases any gases in the earth's atmosphere that allow sunlight to pass through but trap heat, thus affecting temperature

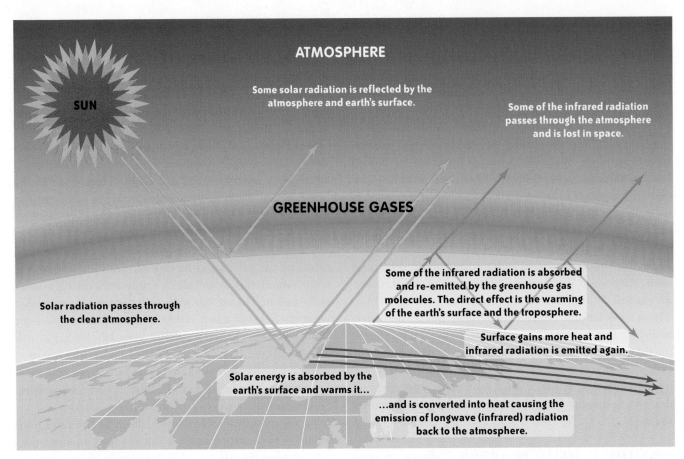

ATMOSPHERE

Some solar radiation is reflected by the atmosphere and earth's surface.

Some of the infrared radiation passes through the atmosphere and is lost in space.

GREENHOUSE GASES

Some of the infrared radiation is absorbed and re-emitted by the greenhouse gas molecules. The direct effect is the warming of the earth's surface and the troposphere.

Solar radiation passes through the clear atmosphere.

Surface gains more heat and infrared radiation is emitted again.

Solar energy is absorbed by the earth's surface and warms it...

...and is converted into heat causing the emission of longwave (infrared) radiation back to the atmosphere.

FIGURE 15.8 The Greenhouse Effect Emissions from factories and automobiles contribute to the layer of greenhouse gases that trap heat within the atmosphere.

Greenhouse gases are also contributing to a change in the makeup of the earth's atmosphere. Scientists call this the **greenhouse effect.** The earth's climate is regulated through a process in which some of the sun's heat and energy is retained within the atmosphere. Naturally occurring gases (such as water vapor or carbon dioxide) help trap some of the earth's outgoing heat, which in turn maintains a stable, livable climate. An increase in greenhouse gases from air pollution results in greater retention of heat within the earth's atmosphere, leading to **global warming**, an increase in the world's average temperature.

Scientists believe that in the past 50 to 100 years, the average temperature of the earth has risen one degree Fahrenheit. They predict that greenhouse gases will continue to increase the earth's temperature another one to five degrees over the next 50 years, and two to ten degrees in the next 100 years (U.S. EPA 2000). A climate change of a few degrees can cause catastrophic consequences for the world and its inhabitants. Even slightly higher temperatures could melt polar ice caps and increase the sea level, shrink the landmasses of islands and continents, change global weather patterns, and alter ecosystems that support life on Earth.

In addition to the greenhouse effect, pollutants in the air have also caused **global dimming** (or **solar dimming**). This newly discovered phenomenon means that the earth is becoming darker than it used to be. Because of all the particles in the atmosphere, some natural and some from human activity, less light from the sun's rays reaches the earth. Climate researchers estimate that the earth's surface is receiving 15 percent less sunlight than it did just 50 years ago (Boyd 2004). The sun has remained as bright as always, but the amount of energy or solar radiation that hits the earth has been shrinking by about 3 percent per decade. In some

greenhouse effect the process in which increased production of greenhouse gases, especially those arising from human activity (e.g., carbon dioxide, nitrous oxide, and methane) cause the earth's temperature to rise

global warming gradual increase in the earth's temperature, driven recently by an increase in greenhouse gases and other human activity

global (or **solar**) **dimming** a decline in the amount of light reaching the earth's surface because of increased air pollution, which reflects more light back into space

Opening Day of the Beijing Olympics Heavy pollution practically shrouds the Olympic stadium in Beijing in 2008.

respects, global dimming is counteracting global warming, but that only means that global warming would be worse were it not for the pollutants that are blocking the sun.

Another pollution problem is garbage—all the trash we throw out. U.S. waste production is twice that of any other nation. The average American generates four pounds of trash per day—1,460 pounds per year. The country dumps about 200 million tons of garbage a year, and less than 25 percent of it is recycled, leaving the rest for landfills and incinerators. Some of our trash even gets blasted into outer space (such as satellites and other objects that have become obsolete), where more than 600,000 pieces of litter are orbiting the planet! And have you ever thought about light pollution or noise pollution? Depending on your sensitivity to these, you may be dismayed not to see stars in the night sky because of so many street lights and neon signs, or be annoyed by the almost constant sound of traffic and other noise, both of which are part of life in big cities.

Environmental Sociology

To analyze problems of the environment, sociologists have developed "environmental sociology," a distinct subfield of sociology that describes environmental issues and examines the reciprocal interactions between the physical environment, social structure, and human behavior. Although this subfield is still developing, four major analytic frameworks within environmental sociology have emerged over the last 30 years. These concern the political economy of the environment, attitudes about the environment, environmental movements (including environmental justice), and sustainable development.

THE POLITICAL ECONOMY OF THE ENVIRONMENT The political economy of the environment is a core area of study within environmental sociology that takes a classical or neo-Marxist and Weberian approach to understanding the environment (Schnaiberg 1975). Its focus is on how economic factors influence the way organizations (typically corporations) use the environment and how this use is often supported by political systems and policies.

Contemporary industrial societies have been built on the premise of progress—on conquering nature and using natural resources to fuel production and expand profits (Schnaiberg and Gould 1994). Government policies and economic systems have frequently supported this belief. While progress has usually meant great wealth for some and goods and services for many, it has come at a price: environmental degradation and the accompanying social problems.

Environmental sociologists refer to this process as the **treadmill of production**. They assert that the drive for economic growth in capitalist societies persists, even at

> **treadmill of production** term describing the operation of modern economic systems that require constant growth, which causes increased exploitation of resources and environmental degradation

Changing the World

Julia "Butterfly" Hill

On New Year's Day, 1997, a giant mudslide destroyed seven homes in Stafford, a small town in California's Humboldt County. Heavy December rains played a role, but many were convinced that the real cause was logging that had stripped nearby slopes bare of vegetation. The Pacific Lumber Corporation owned the land and had recently clear-cut the timber from the mountain, harvesting all the significant trees from an area and using fire and herbicides to clear the area of plants that would impede the growth of "merchantable timber."

Shortly after the slide, Pacific Lumber received permission to begin clear-cutting timber on the slopes immediately around the slide. At this point Earth First!, a radical environmental group, decided to act. A reconnaissance team explored the slopes scheduled for logging and discovered that an enormous redwood known to locals as the "Stafford Giant," estimated to be between 600 and 1,000 years old, was marked to be harvested. Late one night, members of the team hiked in and built a small platform 180 feet above the ground where a volunteer protestor could sit in the tree and thus prevent it from being cut down. To commemorate the moonlight by which they worked, they named the tree "Luna."

Julia Hill, in Arkansas, had worked in a restaurant until the fall of 1996, when she was seriously injured in a car accident. Ten months later, after long and intensive therapy for her injuries, she emerged with a deep-seated conviction that her life had to be about more than just a paycheck, "that our value as people is not in our stock portfolios and bank accounts but in the legacies we leave behind" (Hill 2000,

p. 5). She resolved that as soon as she was well enough she wanted to find a sense of purpose, and on a visit to the California coast to see the redwoods, she found one.

She put her belongings in storage, moved to Humboldt County, and made her way to the Earth First! base camp; there she adopted her own "forest name," Butterfly, and got ready to help however she could. That chance came when organizers were looking for someone to sit in Luna for at least five days. No one could have guessed that Julia would eventually sit in Luna continuously for over two years.

Tree sitting is a rather radical form of activism. Almost all tree sits fail, because missing one day of sitting can allow the loggers to return and cut down the tree—if activists aren't forcibly removed before then. Pacific Lumber made the process as uncomfortable for Julia as possible. Foghorns and floodlights disturbed her sleep, and the company's helicopter sprayed her with rotor wash—the dust and wind kicked up underneath the helicopter (Garlington 1998). The company even tried to starve her down by preventing her support team from delivering fresh supplies.

Julia stayed on the platform. Although the tree sit started with little fanfare, the number of requests for interviews rose rapidly as the protest continued. Julia could contact the outside world with a solar-powered radio phone. Her supporters built an official website and set up a media office to field local, national, and international inquiries. Musicians Bonnie Raitt and Joan Baez played at a rally for Luna, and actor Woody Harrelson even stayed in the tree overnight, joining the protest (Hill 2000).

mainstream environmentalism beginning in the 1980s, the third major stage of the environmental movement; characterized by increasing organization, well-crafted promotional campaigns, sophisticated political tactics, and an increasing reliance on economic and scientific expertise

Through a series of amendments and executive orders, the EPA was given broader powers that included the means to investigate ecological crises, organize cleanups, punish offenders, establish further regulations, and research environmentally friendly technologies.

The third era of the environmental movement, referred to as **mainstream environmentalism**, began in the 1980s. It emerged, in part, as a response to the Reagan administration's anti-environmental deregulation policies. National and international environmental organizations, such as the Sierra Club or Greenpeace as well as other watchdog groups, were becoming increasingly institutionalized. They began using well-crafted promotional campaigns and sophisticated political tactics to gain the attention of legislators and secure victories in their ongoing battles. Mainstream

Eventually the group's tactics and Hill's perseverance paid off. By putting a human face on the struggle to save the forests, public pressure mounted on Pacific Lumber to reach a settlement that preserved Luna. On December 18, 1999, a little more than two years after Julia began her treetop residency, a deed of covenant was signed that protected Luna and a 200-foot buffer zone around it in perpetuity. Despite a serious attack by vandals almost a year later, the tree is still standing today.

Of course, this wasn't the end of the story for Hill. She established the Circle of Life Foundation, with the stated goal of "inspiring, supporting and networking individuals, organizations and communities to create environmental solutions with respect for the interconnectedness of all life" (Shakara 2004). Hill's second book, *One Makes the Difference: Inspiring Actions That Change Our World* (2002), claims that any individual can and should make a difference. The book opens with a quote from Bette Reese: "If you think you're too small to be effective, you have never been in bed with a mosquito."

Julia "Butterfly" Hill   The environmental activist perches near the top of Luna, a 200-foot redwood tree.

environmentalism evolved into a cluster of public interest groups, many of which had their own political action committees, or PACs, to lobby for positive legislative change. In addition to legal expertise, they developed economic and scientific expertise to support research, generate grants, and acquire land for preservation.

A link between the modern era and the mainstream era of environmentalism is **Earth Day**. The original event was conceived of by environmental activist and then-Senator Gaylord Nelson as both a "teach-in" and a protest gathering to express concerns about environmental issues. In the first Earth Day, celebrated on March 22, 1970, 20 million people participated. Earth Day is still celebrated nationally and internationally. Typically it includes a variety of groups—environmentally friendly businesses, nonprofit organizations, local government agencies, and others—teaching people about

> **Earth Day** a holiday conceived of by environmental activist and Senator Gaylord Nelson to encourage support for and increase awareness of environmental concerns; first celebrated on March 22, 1970

The 1969 Oil Spill in Santa Barbara Workers rake hay along a Southern California beach in an effort to protect the coast from more than 200,000 gallons of oil that leaked into the sea when an off-shore oil rig broke.

ways to help the environment while celebrating their relationship to it.

A fourth era of the environmental movement representing grassroots efforts emerged after criticism that although mainstream environmental organizations were serving important functions in the overall effort, they were too accommodating to industry and government. **Grassroots environmentalism** is distinguished from mainstream environmentalism by its belief in citizen participation in environmental decision making. Its focus is often regional or local, and it can include both urban and rural areas. Grassroots groups are often less formally organized than their mainstream counterparts, and in some instances this frees embers from ineffective bureaucratic structures as they fight for issues of great importance to them. Grassroots environmentalism draws on a variety of ideologies, including feminist, native, and spiritual ecologies, and cuts across ethnic, racial, and class lines.

NIMBY, which stands for "Not in My Back Yard," was originally a derogatory term applied to those who complained about any kind of undesirable activity in their neighborhoods that would threaten their own health or local environment but were not concerned if it happened to people somewhere else. Now the term *NIMBY* has been appropriated by the environmental movement for the people "somewhere else" who are fighting against environmental degradation on their home turf, often without significant resources, to protect their families and surrounding communities. Sometimes it makes sense to wage battles at the local level where the problems are readily apparent and the approaches to solving them more tangible. And of course if people everywhere were willing to fight in this way, then antienvironmental corporations would have to change their practices or be forced out of all possible locations.

Another expression of grassroots environmentalism is the **Green Party**. Established in 1984, the basic Green Party platform of ten principles includes a commitment to environmentalism, social justice, decentralization, community-based economics, feminism, and diversity. The environmental goal is a sustainable world in which nature and human society coexist in harmony. The Green Party seeks to be an alternative voice in political and policy debates that often challenges the mainstream Republican and Democratic parties and rejects corporate backing. They would like to see the political process returned to the people. Candidates from the Green Party have been elected to various political seats at the local and state levels, and Ralph Nader, a longtime

grassroots environmentalism fourth major stage of the environmental movement; distinguished by the diversity of its members and belief in citizen participation in environmental decision making

NIMBY short for "Not in My Back Yard"; originally referred to protests that aimed at shifting undesirable activities onto those with less power; now sometimes used without negative connotations to describe local environmental activists

Green Party a U.S. political party established in 1984 to bring political attention to environmentalism, social justice, diversity, and related principles

Ecoterrorism To protest logging, wild horse roundups, genetic engineering of plants, SUV sales, and the expansion of the Rocky Mountain resort town of Vail, Colorado, ecoterrorists firebombed this mountain lodge restaurant and other buildings in the Northwest.

consumer protection advocate, was its candidate in the presidential election of 2000, garnering enough votes to have perhaps changed the outcome of that election.

Ecoterrorism is an example of radical grassroots environmentalism. Ecoterrorists (or ecoextremists) use violent and often criminal methods to achieve their goals of protecting the environment. These groups operate underground, without centralized organization or known membership. Their tactics include arson, explosives, vandalism, theft, sabotage, and harassment, called by law enforcement officials "direct action" campaigns to disrupt or destroy businesses and organizations they believe are a threat to the environment. They have so far avoided targeting people, though there may be victims in the course of ecoterrorist operations. FBI counterterrorism agents recently told a Senate committee that radical environmental and animal rights activists represented the nation's top domestic terrorist threat (Heilprin 2005).

It is unclear how many ecoterrorist groups currently exist in the United States, Canada, England, and elsewhere. One visible group calls itself the Earth Liberation Front, or ELF, and claims to have originated in 1977 near Santa Cruz, California. Although it disavows any connection to illegal activity, the ELF acknowledges that some individuals have used its name to claim responsibility for their actions. The ELF says that those individuals have acted on their own without ELF's direction or endorsement. Targets are often chosen for their symbolic nature and have included logging operations, sport-utility-vehicle dealerships, recreational resorts, and new home and condominium developments.

The **environmental justice** (or "ecojustice") movement represents a significant branch of the environmental movement and is also an example of grassroots organization. It emerged as a response to environmental inequities, threats to public health, and the differential enforcement and treatment of certain communities with regard to ecological concerns. Despite significant improvements in environmental protections, millions of people in the United States live in communities threatened by ecological hazards. The poor and minorities are disproportionately at risk and bear a greater portion of the nation's environmental problems. The term **environmental racism** is applied when an environmental policy or practice negatively affects individuals, groups, or communities based on race

ecoterrorism use of violence or criminal methods to protect the environment, often in high-profile, publicity-generating ways

environmental justice a movement that aims to remedy environmental inequities such as threats to public health and the unequal treatment of certain communities with regard to ecological concerns

environmental racism any environmental policy or practice that negatively affects individuals, groups, or communities because of their race or ethnicity or color (Bullard 1993). Access to environmental equality, or living in a healthy environment, has been framed as a basic human right.

Research on environmental justice is one of the fastest growing areas of scholarship within environmental sociology. Sociologist Robert Bullard is among the leading researchers in this area, linking social justice to environmental movements. His book *Dumping in Dixie: Race, Class, and Environmental Quality* (Bullard 1990) examined the economic, social, and psychological impacts associated with locating noxious facilities (such as landfills, hazardous-waste dumps, and lead smelters) within lower-income African American communities where they have been less likely to meet with significant opposition.

Blacks have historically been underrepresented in the environmental movement. Often they were already engaged in other civil rights causes that seemed more pressing. They also lacked the experience and money to fight large corporations, and many had little hope of change, even though they strongly opposed environmental destruction, especially the kinds found in their communities. However, some groups have been moved to action.

Bullard looked at five black communities in the South that challenged public policies and industrial practices threatening their neighborhoods. After years of environmental problems, these activists began to demand environmental justice and equal protection. They grew increasingly incensed at the industries and the government regulatory agencies that allowed those industries to violate codes and continue polluting. The industries, though heavy polluters, had often gained favor in the communities by promising a better tax base and much-needed jobs. Real environmental justice, however, would mean that communities could enjoy jobs and economic development but not at the expense of their health and the environment. That is just what they achieved.

Work by Bullard and others in the field of environmental justice has had profound impacts not only on academia but also on public policy, industry practices, and community organizations. Environmental justice groups are beginning to sway administrative decisions and have won several important court victories (Bullard and Wright 1990; Kaczor 1996; Bullard, Johnson, and Wright 1997). The EPA was even convinced to create an Office on Environmental Equity. There is still much work to be done in this area. Some of the most important battles in the environmental justice movement

sustainable development economic development that aims to reconcile global economic growth with environmental protection

ecological footprint an estimation of the land and water area required to produce all the goods an individual consumes and to assimilate all the wastes he or she generates

will be fought beyond the U.S. borders, in other countries suffering from similar and even worse environmental problems.

SUSTAINABLE DEVELOPMENT The study of **sustainable development** is among the most recent areas of environmental sociology, having emerged in the 1990s, and it continues to generate some controversy (McMichael 1996). The idea of sustainable development was popularized in a United Nations World Commission on Environment and Development report entitled "Our Common Future," often referred to as the Brundtland Report (1987). Sustainable development is a broad concept that tries to reconcile global economic development with environmental protection; it is based on the premise that the development aspirations of all countries cannot be met by following the path already taken by industrialized nations because the world's ecosystems cannot support it. Yet since improving the conditions of the world's poor is an international goal, we must find ways of promoting economic growth that both respect social justice and protect the environment, not only in the present but for future generations (Humphrey, Lewis, and Buttel 2002; Agyeman, Bullard, and Evans 2003).

One way to grasp the magnitude of supporting humans on the planet is the **ecological footprint**, an estimation of how much land and water area is required to produce all the goods we consume and to assimilate all the wastes we generate. The current ecological footprint of the average American, approximately 30 acres, represents about three times her or his fair share of the earth's resources (Wackernagel and Rees 1996). Compare that to someone from the United Kingdom, whose ecological footprint is approximately 15 acres, or someone from Burundi with a little over one acre (People and the Planet 2002). Modern industrialized countries are appropriating the carrying capacity of "land vastly larger than the areas they physically occupy" (Rees and Wackernagel 1994). Projections are that we would need four additional planet Earths to support the world's population if everyone else were to adopt the consumption habits of Americans. (You can measure your own ecological footprint by following the link listed in "Suggestions for Further Exploration" at the end of this chapter.)

Working toward sustainable development is a challenge. We have to find ways to meet the needs of a growing world population—for food, shelter, health care, education, and employment—while ensuring that we sustain nature and the environment, whether that is fresh water, clean air, natural resources, nontoxic communities, or the protection of wildlife. Often these goals are posed as adversaries. It is even more important to work toward sustainable development as we become increasingly globalized and have to think about the rest of the world and far into the future (Holdren, Daily, and Ehrlich 1995).

Some solutions toward sustainable development are already being implemented. These include lifestyle modifications—engaging in voluntary simplicity, recycling, vegetarianism and veganism, buying organic foods, and using goods or services from environmentally friendly and fair trade companies. Others are modifications to our infrastructure, such as green building, ecological design, xeriscape (water-conserving) gardening, and land conservation. Technological changes can be made in the way we use energy—from hybrid or biodiesel cars to solar power. Some state and local governments are enforcing higher environmental standards and regulations than those imposed at the federal level. In 2005 more than 160 U.S. mayors signed on to an urban anti–global warming agreement that some call the "municipal Kyoto" in reference to the Kyoto Protocol, an international treaty on global climate change that the United States has declined to ratify (Caplan 2005). All these efforts help move us toward sustainable development, but much more must be done if we are to create that vision for the future.

Closing Comments

In this chapter we have crossed a huge terrain—from population through urbanization to the environment. We hope that you can now see the connection among these three seemingly disparate areas of study. Human population has grown over history, particularly in the last 200 years. The rate at which the population increases is influenced by both biological and social factors. Where all these people live has also changed over time. As more of them locate in cities, cities play a key role in how we inhabit the world and what kind of world that becomes. The billions of people inhabiting the planet are part of an ecosystem, and they continue to have an impact on it. The natural environment both affects and is affected by human activity. So population, urbanization, and the environment are intimately related. There is a mutual effect and interdependence between them, where trends and changes in one reverberate through the others. As residents of planet Earth, we all take part in the dynamic, both enjoying or suffering current realities and creating future ones.

 Find more review materials online at
www.wwnorton.com/studyspace

CHAPTER SUMMARY

- **Demography** Demographics—statistical descriptions of populations in terms of birth rate, mortality rate, and migration—are used to analyze the movements of entire populations as well as smaller groups within a population. Demographers also attempt to predict population changes and their consequences. Historically, the most important debate among demographers has involved the theories of Thomas Malthus. The Neo-Malthusians believe that population growth will eventually outpace available resources and lead to a global catastrophe, while the Anti-Malthusians believe that family planning and other changes wrought by industrialization will eventually cause population shrinkage.

- **Urbanization** One of the most important recent demographic changes is the population shift from rural areas to cities, such that 83 percent of Americans now live

in cities. The growth of cities created new problems including noise, pollution, overcrowding, alienation, and the diffusion of responsibility. In the 1950s and 60s, many who could afford to leave the cities moved to the suburbs, where urban sprawl created its own set of problems including racial segregation, conformity, and long commutes. Urban legends often capture fears and anxieties about the problems of city life.

- **Social Ecology** Sociologists are interested in social ecology, or the relationships between a social group and its physical environment, especially as environmental degradation has increasingly become a social problem. Modern, industrial societies create environmental problems as greater production and consumption deplete resources and cause pollution. Ever-increasing demands for energy have spurred use of nonrenewable resources, and this use often generates pollution. As more of the world industrializes, consumes more energy, and produces more pollution, these problems will intensify.

- **Environmental Sociology** Environmental sociology analyzes the relationships among the environment, social structure, and human behavior, focusing on four areas: the political economy of the environment, environmental attitudes, the environmental movement, and sustainable development. The political economy of the environment is concerned with how economic factors influence the exploitation of natural resources. Capitalism demands constant growth, creating a treadmill of production. Governments rely on the taxes generated by growth, and most individuals need the jobs this growth supports—but this growth can also have widespread environmental consequences.

- Some who are concerned with the relationship between humans and the natural world join the environmental movement. Its first efforts in the nineteenth century focused on conservation of wilderness areas. The modern environmental movement arose in the mid-twentieth century in response to ecological disasters that threaten public health and safety. Mainstream environmentalism grew in the 1980s as the movement consolidated, organized, and increasingly lobbied government about environmental concerns. In the movement's most recent stage, grassroots environmentalism has emerged in response to perceived blind spots in the larger mainstream groups. Grassroots organizers focused on local action and community involvement.

QUESTIONS FOR REVIEW

1. How many children would you like to have? The demographic predictions of the Neo-Malthusians and the Anti-Malthusians disagree sharply. According to the Anti-Malthusians, what changes in social structure might make people less interested in having lots of children?

2. This chapter described Americans as "pigs of the planet," in reference to the way we consume resources. Make a list of all the ways you use water other than for drinking. Do you believe that the planet can continue to support the kind of consumption and waste of the American standard of living? What do you think will happen when growing populations in developing nations want to live like Americans?

3. Do you prefer to live in a dense urban area, or a more lightly populated suburban one? What are the advantages and disadvantages of each? What sorts of social and/or environmental problems are created by the situation you prefer?

4. The chapter describes the social problems associated with the environment in terms of consumption and waste. How are these two types of social problems connected? Describe one thing you've consumed today in terms of the pollution that can be directly linked to it.

5. What is the difference between an anthropocentric point of view and the new ecological paradigm? How do these ways of understanding the relationship between human beings and the natural world relate to the social construction of environmental problems?

6. Today the environmental movement is much more diverse than when it began in the latter part of the nineteenth century. Although few would object outright to national parks, what sort of criticisms might those concerned with environmental racism have for conservationists?

7. In the past, NIMBY has been used as a derogatory term, but grassroots environmental activists have reclaimed it as a positive one. When does "not in my backyard" become a worthwhile resistance strategy?

8. Mainstream environmental activism focused on influencing government. Grassroots environmentalism often stresses the importance of direct action, like that of Julia "Butterfly" Hill, who stayed in a redwood tree for two years to keep it from being cut down. Pick a contemporary environmental problem and describe how you would attempt to remedy it if you belonged to a mainstream environmental organization. How would you approach it differently as a member of a grassroots organization?

9. How and why is it helpful to consider the environment and urbanization as related issues? Specifically, think about the issues associated with internal migration. Describe how internal migration within the United States affects three of the environmental problems described in this chapter.

SUGGESTIONS FOR FURTHER EXPLORATION

Climate Challenge (www.bbc.co.uk/sn/hottopics/climate-change/ climate_challenge). A free online video game that puts the earth's future in your hands. As the president of the European nations, you must tackle climate change while remaining popular enough with voters to stay in office.

Released in 2007, the game uses carbon dioxide emission forecasts produced by the Intergovernmental Panel on Climate Change.

Davis, Mike. 1999. *Ecology of Fear*. New York: Vintage. A case study in social ecology, examining the impact of the city of Los Angeles on the natural world and the ways that its residents have been affected by local ecology. Wildfires, mudslides, and mountain lions may seem to be purely natural, but as Davis illustrates, they are closely connected to social forces.

Ecological Footprint Quiz (www.earthday.net/footprint). This quiz allows you to estimate how much productive land and water you need to support what you use and what you discard. After answering 15 simple questions, you can compare your ecological footprint to those of others and to the planet's available resources.

Erickson, Kai. 1995. *A New Species of Trouble*. New York: W. W. Norton. A sociological investigation of disasters caused by human beings. Erickson argues that the social disruptions caused by pollution, poisoned groundwater, nuclear waste, and other troubles cause the same sort of trauma as natural disasters and should be treated as such.

Hawken, Paul, Amory Lovins, and L. Hunter Lovins. 2000. *Natural Capitalism: Creating the Next Industrial Revolution*. Boston: Back Bay Books. A controversial look at "natural capitalism," which the authors believe can be simultaneously good for business and good for the environment, primarily through closer attention to waste and energy use.

An Inconvenient Truth. 2006. Dir. Davis Guggenheim. Paramount. A documentary featuring former vice president Al Gore. This is an in-depth discussion of global warming and its potential consequences on weather, biodiversity, disease, and sea level. The film echoes the concerns of those who study the political economy of the environment.

Into the Wild. 2007. Dir. Sean Penn. Paramount Vantage. A retelling of the story of Chris McCandless based on Jon Krakauer's book of the same name. This film addresses the relationship between the social world and the natural world by chronicling McCandless's travels and his shifting allegiances to nature, himself, and his society.

Kolbert, Elizabeth. 2006. *Field Notes from a Catastrophe*. New York: Bloomsbury. An accessible overview of the linkages between human action and climate change, with chapters covering specific case studies from the melting glaciers of the arctic to conservation efforts in Burlington, Vermont.

Leopold, Aldo. 1949. *A Sand County Almanac*. New York: Oxford University Press. A classic collection of essays on nature and conservation written while the author observed the changing seasons on his Wisconsin farm. Leopold, who began his career as a forest ranger, called for the development of a "land ethic" that would not use economic growth as the sole measure of the worth of the natural world.

Lopez, Barry. 2004. *Of Wolves and Men*. New York: Scribner. A social history of the interaction between American society and *canis lupus*. Lopez demonstrates the importance of cultural values and beliefs in determining public reaction to wolves, from a history of extermination to an increasing belief in wolf conservation.

The Meatrix (www.themeatrix.com). A short online animation that describes the effects of factory farms including negative impacts on animal welfare, antibiotic-resistant bacteria, pollution, and destroyed communities.

Waldie, D. J. 2005. *Holy Land: A Suburban Memoir*. New York: W. W. Norton. An account of Lakewood, California, the world's largest suburb. Waldie combines memoir with real estate history to explore the creation of the second suburb in the United States and the social attitudes and values of the era of suburbanization.

CHAPTER 16

Social Change: Looking Toward Tomorrow

Of you haven't seen one already, ask your parents (or maybe one of your professors) to show you the scar from their smallpox vaccination. It's a dime-sized circle that was made with multiple pricks of a tiny fork-like needle that held one drop of vaccine, and it would now be almost invisible as it sits at the top of their left arm. This little scar protects your parents and professors from a disease that has killed billions of people and left billions more blind and disfigured, for which there is no effective treatment. Yet if you check your own arm, you will see that you do *not* have a similar scar; you are not protected from smallpox. Why not?

Smallpox is one of the diseases that have been effectively eliminated by the advances of medical technology. Scientific discoveries during the eighteenth and nineteenth centuries meant that by the middle of the twentieth century, a global campaign to stamp out the disease was well underway. The last natural case of smallpox in the world occurred in Somalia in 1977, and a lab accident killed a British researcher in 1978. But since then, no one has contracted the disease. The World Health Organization (WHO) declared smallpox officially eradicated in 1979, and vaccinations were discontinued worldwide by 1986.

Does the WHO declaration mean that smallpox virus no longer exists? No—two high-security research labs, one in the United States and one in Russia, hold samples of the virus, and another lab in the Netherlands houses the seed virus used to produce the vaccine. Why keep samples of a vanquished virus? If it ever reappears, if even the smallest amount somehow escapes laboratory quarantine, an epidemic is almost certain: smallpox is transmitted through face-to-face contact before individuals even know they are infected, and it can also be spread through building ventilation systems. It will thus be critical for us to have stores of the virus ready so that more vaccines can be made. The fact that large portions of the world's population—including you—are unprotected makes us vulnerable to the use of smallpox as a biological weapon. In the wake of the terrorist attacks of 9/11, U.S. health officials began considering reinstituting mass vaccination programs (although at this date they have not yet done so).

The story of smallpox is a story of social change—change in the incidence, experience, and meaning of smallpox over time. The disease was a ubiquitous killer for thousands of years, up to the 1940s; in some cultures, families waited to name babies until after they had contracted and survived smallpox. It killed peasants and royalty alike, but through deliberate human effort a defense against the disease was eventually

SocIndex

Then and Now

1983: Motorola introduces the first portable phones on the market, nicknamed "bricks" because of their size; each one weighs over a pound and costs $3,500.

2008: The Motorola RAZR2 weighs just over 4 ounces and costs nothing with a phone service contract. It features two full-color displays, long-range Bluetooth, voice-activated dialing, a digital and video camera, GPS system, high-speed wireless internet service, e-mail, text-messaging, and video games.

Here and There

United States: In July and August 2004, at the Democratic and Republican conventions, 5,459 people join text-messaging lists from TXTmob.com to coordinate protests in Boston and New York; on their cell phones they exchange 1,757 messages among 322 "mobs."

Kuwait: In March 2005, 400–600 women rally to win the right to vote. Using cell phones and text-messaging to coordinate the protest, organizers are able to attract the largest group of demonstrators in Kuwaiti history. Their efforts succeed: the following May, Kuwaiti lawmakers grant full political rights to all women.

This and That

Capitalizing on the musical ringtone fad, the mobile musical company Zed earned millions in 2008 from sales of Lil Wayne's "Lollipop" ringtone, the most commercially successful ringtone of the year.

Total sales of ringtones peaked in 2006 at $600 million, before more fans began downloading ringtones for free.

developed. Medicine, politics, culture, demography, individual and collective actions—smallpox was conquered through the synergy of all these elements. In the late 1700s, for example, English physician Edward Jenner observed a pattern of smallpox immunity in milkmaids who had previously contracted the less virulent cowpox, and he developed the first vaccine. Beginning in the 1950s, the WHO sought political and financial support for a worldwide vaccination campaign. Your grandparents obeyed the law and took your parents to be vaccinated when they were children. All of these processes contributed to change in the meaning and incidence of smallpox. And the meaning may change yet again as a result of the actions of another group: international terrorists. So perhaps no disease can ever truly be eradicated—ironically, it is our lingering fear of smallpox that means we must keep it with us in some form.

HOW TO READ THIS CHAPTER

There are a couple of reasons why we are ending this book with a chapter on social change. The first is that, to paraphrase an old cliché, change is the only constant. It is happening everywhere, all the time, in myriad variations. One of your challenges after reading this chapter will be to identify some of these social changes and to understand their patterns, causes, and consequences.

The other reason is more personal: we hope that reading this chapter will motivate you to work for social change yourself. The study of sociology can sometimes be a bit disheartening, as we learn the many ways in which our lives are constrained by social forces and institutional structures. But this chapter helps us remember that C. Wright Mills's "intersection of biography and history" is a two-way street: while society shapes the individual, the individual can shape society. You have the power to bring about social change, especially when you work together with others who share your views, values, and visions for a better world. So we want you to read this chapter with optimism; by understanding the processes of social change, you will be better qualified to make it happen yourself.

What Is Social Change?

No doubt you've heard your parents, grandparents, or other older family members reflect on "the way things were" when they were children. Hard-to-imagine times such as those before indoor plumbing or television, or during the Great Depression or World War II, undeniably made their lives very different from your own. People born even one generation apart can have different overall life experiences as a result of ongoing processes of social change. Consider how different life might be for American children growing up in the immediate aftermath of the tragedies of September 11, 2001, or for those who have never known a time without cell phones and the Internet. Our culture evolves over time, as do our social institutions—the family, work, religion, education, and political systems. Sociologists define the transformation of culture over time as **social change**.

It's easy to identify particular historical periods where major social transformation was unmistakable: the Renaissance, the French Revolution, the Civil War, the women's rights movement. But it's important to realize that social change is occurring at all times, not just at moments of obvious cultural or political upheaval. The rate at which it happens, however, varies over time, with some historical periods experiencing rapid social change and others experiencing more gradual change. For example, social scientists recognize several major "social revolutions"—periods of time during which large-scale social change took place so rapidly that the whole of human society was dramatically redefined. The Agricultural Revolution made it possible for previously nomadic peoples to settle in one place, store surplus food for future use, and sustain larger populations with the products of their farms, herds, and flocks. The Industrial Revolution altered the way people worked, produced, and consumed goods and lived together in cities. And the Information Revolution (which is ongoing in Western countries) saw the advent of computer and internet technology and a profound shift from economies based on manufacturing to economies based on information technologies (Castells 2000).

social change the transformation of a culture over time

experiments Formal tests of specific variables and effects, performed in a controlled setting where all aspects of the situation can be controlled.

expressions given Expressions that are intentional and usually verbal, such as utterances.

expressions given off Observable expressions that can be either intended or unintended and are usually non-verbal.

expressions of behavior Small actions such as an eye roll or head nod, which serve as an interactional tool to help project our definition of the situation to others.

expressive leadership Leadership concerned with maintaining emotional and relational harmony within the group.

expressive role The position of the family member who provides emotional support and nurturing.

expressive tasks The emotional work necessary to support family members.

extended family A large group of relatives, usually including at least three generations living either in one household or in close proximity.

extrinsic religiosity A person's public display of commitment to a religious faith.

fads Interests or practices followed enthusiastically for a relatively short period of time.

false consciousness A denial of the truth on the part of the oppressed when they fail to recognize the interests of the ruling class in their ideology.

family A social group whose members are bound by legal, biological, or emotional ties, or a combination of all three.

family planning Contraception, or any method of controlling family size and the birth of children.

fashion The widespread custom or style of behavior and appearance at a particular time or in a particular place.

feeling rules Socially constructed norms regarding the expression and display of emotions; expectations about the acceptable or desirable feelings in a given situation.

feminism Belief in the social, political, and economic equality of the sexes; also the social movements organized around that belief.

feminist theory A theoretical approach that looks at gender inequities in society and the way that gender structures the social world.

feminization of poverty The economic trend showing that women are more likely than men to live in poverty, caused in part by the gendered gap in wages, the higher proportion of single mothers compared to single fathers, and the increasing costs of childcare.

fertility rate A measure of population growth through reproduction; often expressed as the average number of births per 1,000 people in the total population or the average number of children a woman would be expected to have.

feudal system A system of social stratification based on a hereditary nobility who were responsible for and served by a lower stratum of forced laborers called serfs.

fictive kin People to whom we refer with kinship terms in order to describe a particularly close relationship even though they are not related by blood, marriage, or adoption.

fieldnotes Detailed notes taken by an ethnographer describing her activities and interactions, which later become the basis of the ethnographic analysis.

first wave The earliest period of feminist activism in the United States, including the period from the mid-nineteenth century until American women won the right to vote in 1920.

527 committees Organizations that have no official connection to a candidate but that raise and spend funds like a campaign does; named after the section of the tax code that authorizes their existence.

folkway A loosely enforced norm involving common customs, practices, or procedures that ensure smooth social interaction and acceptance.

Fourth Estate The media, which are considered like a fourth branch of government (after the executive, legislative, and judiciary) and thus serve as another of the checks and balances on power.

front In the dramaturgical perspective, the setting or scene of performances that helps establish the definition of the situation.

frontstage In the dramaturgical perspective, the region in which we deliver our public performances.

fundamentalism The practice of emphasizing literal interpretation of texts and a "return" to a time of greater religious purity; represented by the most conservative group within any religion.

game stage The third stage in Mead's theory of the development of self wherein children play organized games and take on the perspective of the generalized other.

gender The physical, behavioral, and personality traits that a group considers normal for its male and female members.

gender identity The roles and traits that a social group assigns to a particular gender.

gender role socialization The lifelong process of learning to be masculine or feminine, primarily through four agents of socialization: families, schools, peers, and the media.

generalized other The perspectives and expectations of a network of others (or of society in general) that a child learns and then takes into account when shaping his or her own behavior.

genocide The deliberate and systematic extermination of a racial, ethnic, national, or cultural group.

gentrification Transformation of the physical, social, economic, and cultural life of formerly working-class or poor inner-city neighborhoods into more affluent middle-class communities.

gestures The ways in which people use their bodies to communicate without words; actions that have symbolic meaning.

global cities A term for megacities or megalopolises that emphasizes their global impact as centers of economic, political, and social power.

global dimming A decline in the amount of light reaching the earth's surface because of increased air pollution, which reflects more light back into space.

global village Marshall McLuhan's term describing the way that new communication technologies override barriers of space and time, allowing people all over the globe to interact.

global warming Gradual increase in the earth's temperature, driven recently by an increase in greenhouse gases and other human activity.

globalization The cultural and economic changes resulting from dramatically increased international trade and exchange in the late twentieth and early twenty-first centuries.

government The formal, organized agency that exercises power and control in modern society, especially through the creation and enforcement of laws.

grassroots environmentalism Fourth major stage of the environmental movement; distinguished by the diversity of its members and belief in citizen participation in environmental decision making.

Green Party A U.S. political party established in 1984 to bring political attention to environmentalism, social justice, diversity, and related principles.

greenhouse effect The process in which increased production of greenhouse gases, especially those arising from human activity (e.g., carbon dioxide, nitrous oxide, and methane) cause the earth's temperature to rise.

greenhouse gases Any gases in the earth's atmosphere that allow sunlight to pass through but trap heat, thus affecting temperature.

grounded theory An inductive method of generating theory from data by creating categories in which to place data and then looking for relationships between categories.

group A collection of people who share some attribute, identify with one another, and interact with each other.

group cohesion The sense of solidarity or loyalty that individuals feel toward a group to which they belong.

group dynamics The patterns of interaction between groups and individuals.

groupthink In very cohesive groups, the tendency to enforce a high degree of conformity among members, creating a demand for unanimous agreement.

growth rate Expression of changes in population size over time figured by subtracting the number of deaths from the number of births, then adding the net migration.

Hawthorne effect A specific example of reactivity, in which the desired effect is the result not of the independent variable, but of the research itself.

hegemony Term developed by Antonio Gramsci to describe the cultural aspects of social control whereby the ideas of the dominant social group are accepted by all of society.

hermaphroditic Term to describe a person whose chromosomes or sex characteristics are neither exclusively male nor exclusively female.

heterogamy Choosing romantic partners who are dissimilar to us in terms of class, race, education, religion, and other social group membership.

hidden curriculum Values or behaviors that students learn indirectly over the course of their schooling because of the structure of the educational system and the teaching methods used.

high culture Those forms of cultural expression usually associated with the elite or dominant classes.

homeschooling The education of children by their parents, at home.

homogamy Choosing romantic partners who are similar to us in terms of class, race, education, religion, and other social group membership.

homophobia Fear of or discrimination toward homosexuals or toward individuals who display purportedly gender-inappropriate behavior.

homosexuality The tendency to feel sexual desire toward members of one's own gender.

horizontal social mobility The occupational movement of individuals or groups within a social class.

human exemptionalism The attitude that humans are exempt from natural ecological limits.

human sexual dimorphism The extent, much debated in recent years, to which inherent physical differences define the distinctions between the two sexes.

hypergamy Marrying "up" in the social class hierarchy.

hypodermic needle theory A theory that explains the effects of media as if their contents simply entered directly into the consumer, who is powerless to resist their influence. Also called the magic bullet theory.

hypogamy Marrying "down" in the social class hierarchy.

hypothesis A theoretical statement explaining the relationship between two or more phenomena.

id According to Freud, one of three interrelated parts that make up the mind; the id consists of basic inborn drives that are the source of instinctive psychic energy.

ideal culture The norms, values, and patterns of behavior that members of a society believe should be observed in principle.

identification A type of conformity stronger than compliance and weaker than internalization, caused by a desire to establish or maintain a relationship with a person or a group.

ideology A system of beliefs, attitudes, and values that directs a society and reproduces the status quo of the bourgeoisie.

idioculture The customs, practices, and values expressed in a particular place by the people who interact there.

immigration Entering one country from another to take up permanent residence.

impression management The effort to control the impressions we make on others so that they form a desired view of us and the situation; the use of self-presentation and performance tactics.

incapacitation An approach to punishment that seeks to protect society from criminals by imprisoning or executing them.

incest Proscribed sexual contact between family members; a form of child abuse when it occurs between a child and a caregiver.

Independent Sector The part of the economy composed of non-profit organizations; their workers are mission driven, rather than profit driven, and such organizations direct surplus funds to the causes they support. Also called the Third Sector.

independent variable Factor that is predicted to cause change.

individual discrimination Discrimination carried out by one person against another.

Industrial Revolution The rapid transformation of social life resulting from the technological and economic developments that began with the assembly line, steam power, and urbanization.

infant mortality Average number of infant deaths per 1,000 live births in a particular population.

influential power Power that is supported by persuasion.

Information Revolution The recent social revolution made possible by the development of the microchip in the 1970s, which brought about vast improvements in the ability to manage information.

informed consent A safeguard through which the researcher makes sure that respondents are freely participating and understand the nature of the research.

in-group A group that one identifies with and feels loyalty toward.

in-group orientation Among stigmatized individuals, an orientation away from mainstream society and toward new standards that value their group identity.

innovators Individuals who accept society's approved goals, but not society's approved means to achieve them.

institutional discrimination Discrimination carried out systematically by institutions (political, economic, educational, and other) that affect all members of a group who come into contact with them.

institutional review board A group of scholars within a university who meet regularly to review and approve the research proposals of their colleagues and make recommendations for how to protect human subjects.

instrumental leadership Leadership that is task or goal oriented.

instrumental role The position of the family member who provides the family's material support and is often an authority figure.

instrumental tasks The practical physical tasks necessary to maintain family life.

intentional community Any of a variety of groups who form communal living arrangements outside marriage.

intergenerational mobility Movement between social classes that occurs from one generation to the next.

internal colonialism The economic and political domination and subjugation of the minority group by the controlling group within a nation.

internal migration Movement of population within a country.

internalization The strongest type of conformity, occurring when an individual adopts the beliefs or actions of a group and makes them her own.

interpretive community A group of people dedicated to the consumption and interpretation of a particular cultural product and who create a collective, social meaning for the product.

interpretive strategies The ideas and frameworks that audience members bring to bear on a particular media text to understand its meaning.

intersexed Term to describe a person whose chromosomes or sex characteristics are neither exclusively male nor exclusively female.

intervening variable A third variable, sometimes overlooked, that explains the relationship between two other variables.

interviews Face-to-face, information-seeking conversation, sometimes defined as a conversation with a purpose.

intragenerational mobility The movement between social classes that occurs over the course of an individual's lifetime.

intrinsic religiosity A person's inner religious life or personal relationship to the divine.

iron cage Max Weber's pessimistic description of modern life, in which the "technical and economic conditions of machine production" control our lives through rigid rules and rationalization.

just-world hypothesis Argues that people have a deep need to see the world as orderly, predictable, and fair, which creates a tendency to view victims of social injustice as deserving of their fates.

kin Relatives or relations, usually those related by common descent.

knowledge workers Those who work primarily with information and who create value in the economy through ideas, judgments, analyses, designs, or innovations.

labeling theory Howard Becker's idea that deviance is a consequence of external judgments, or labels, which modify the individual's self-concept and change the way others respond to the labeled person.

language A system of communication using vocal sounds, gestures, or written symbols; the basis of symbolic culture and the primary means through which we communicate with one another and perpetuate our culture.

latent functions The less obvious, perhaps unintended functions of a social structure.

law A common type of formally defined norm providing an explicit statement about what is permissible and what is illegal in a given society.

leading questions Questions that predispose a respondent to answer in a certain way.

legal-rational authority Authority based in laws, rules, and procedures, not in the heredity or personality of any individual leader.

leisure A period of time that can be spent relaxing, engaging in recreation, or otherwise indulging in freely chosen activities.

liberation theology A movement within the Catholic Church to understand Christianity from the perspective of the poor and oppressed, with a focus on fighting injustice.

life expectancy Average age to which people in a particular population live.

lifestyle enclaves Groups of people drawn together by shared interests, especially those relating to hobbies, sports, and media.

Likert scale A way of organizing categories on a survey question so that the respondent can choose an answer along a continuum.

literature review A thorough search through previously published studies relevant to a particular topic.

looking-glass self The notion that the self develops through our perception of others' evaluations and appraisals of us.

lower-middle class Mostly "blue-collar" or service industry workers who are less likely to have a college degree; they constitute about 30 percent of the U.S. population.

macrosociology The level of analysis that studies large-scale social structures in order to determine how they affect the lives of groups and individuals.

magic bullet theory A theory that explains the effects of media as if their contents simply entered directly into the consumer, who is powerless to resist their influences. Also called the hypodermic needle theory.

mainstream environmentalism Beginning in the 1980s, the third major stage of the environmental movement; characterized by increasing organization, well-crafted promotional campaigns, sophisticated political tactics, and an increasing reliance on economic and scientific expertise.

male liberationism A movement that originated in the 1970s to discuss the challenges of masculinity.

Malthusian theorem The theory that exponential population growth will outpace arithmetic growth in food production and other resources.

Malthusian trap Malthus's prediction that a rapidly increasing population will overuse natural resources, leading inevitably to a major public health disaster.

manifest functions The obvious, intended functions of a social structure for the social system.

mass behavior Large groups of people engaging in similar behaviors without necessarily being in the same place.

mass society theory A theory of social movements that assumes people join social movements not because of the movements' ideals, but to satisfy a psychological need to belong to something larger than themselves.

master status A status that is always relevant and affects all others statuses we possess.

material culture The objects associated with a cultural group, such as tools, machines, utensils, buildings, and artwork; any physical object which we give social meaning.

McDonaldization George Ritzer's term describing the spread of bureaucratic rationalization and the accompanying increases in efficiency and dehumanization.

means of production Anything that can create wealth: money, property, factories, and other types of businesses, and the infrastructure necessary to run them.

mechanical solidarity Term developed by Emile Durkheim to describe the type of social bonds present in premodern, agrarian societies, in which shared tradition and beliefs created a sense of social cohesion.

megalopolis A group of densely populated metropolises that grow dependent on each other and eventually combined to form a huge urban complex; also called a megacity.

men's rights movement An offshoot of male liberationism whose members believe that feminism promotes discrimination against men.

merger The legal combination of two companies, usually in order to maximize efficiency and profits by eliminating redundant infrastructure and personnel.

meritocracy A system in which rewards are distributed based on merit.

metropolis An urban area with a large population, usually 500,000 to 1,000,000 people.

Metropolitan Statistical Area (MSA) One or more adjacent counties with at least one major city of at least 50,000 inhabitants that is surrounded by an adjacent area that is socially and economically integrated with the city.

microsociology The level of analysis that studies face-to-face and small-group interactions in order to understand how those interactions affect the larger patterns and institutions of society.

middle class Composed primarily of "white-collar" workers with a broad range of incomes; they constitute about 30 percent of the U.S. population.

migration Movement of people from one geographic area to another for the purposes of resettling.

minority group Members of a social group that is systematically denied the same access to power and resources available to society's dominant groups but who are not necessarily fewer in number than the dominant groups.

miscegenation Romantic, sexual, or marital relationships between people of different races.

modern environmental movement Beginning in the 1960s, the second major stage of the environmental movement; focused on the environmental consequences of new technologies, oil exploration, chemical production, and nuclear power plants.

modernism A paradigm that places trust in the power of science and technology to create progress, solve problems, and improve life.

monarchy A government ruled by a king or queen, with succession of rulers kept within the family.

monogamy The practice of marrying (or being in a relationship with) one person at a time.

monopoly A situation in which there is only one individual or organization, without competitors, providing a particular good or service.

monotheistic A term describing religions that worship a single divine figure.

more A norm that carries great moral significance, is closely related to the core values of a cultural group, and often involves severe repercussions for violators.

mortality rate A measure of the decrease in population due to deaths; often expressed as the number of deaths expected per 1,000 people per year in a particular population.

multiculturalism A policy that values diverse racial, ethnic, national, and linguistic backgrounds and so encourages the retention of cultural differences within society rather than assimilation.

natural increase Change in population size that results from births and deaths; linked to a country's progress toward demographic transition.

nature vs. nurture debate The ongoing discussion of the respective roles of genetics and socialization in determining individual behaviors and traits.

negative questions Survey questions that ask respondents what they don't think instead of what they do.

neglect A form of child abuse in which the caregiver fails to provide adequate nutrition, sufficient clothing or shelter, or hygienic and safe living conditions.

Neo-Malthusians Contemporary researchers who worry about the rapid pace of population growth and believe that Malthus's basic prediction could be true.

net migration Net effect of immigration and emigration on an area's population in a given time period, expressed as an increase or decrease.

new ecological paradigm A way of understanding human life as just one part of an ecosystem that includes many species' interactions with the environment; suggests that there should be ecological limits on human activity.

NIMBY Short for "not in my backyard"; originally referred to protests that aimed at shifting undesirable activities onto those with less power; now sometimes used without negative connotations to describe local environmental activists.

nonrenewable resources Finite resources, including those that take so long to replenish as to be effectively finite.

norm A rule or guideline regarding what kinds of behavior are acceptable and appropriate within a culture.

nuclear family A heterosexual couple with one or more children living in a single household.

objectivity Impartiality, the ability to allow the facts to speak for themselves.

open system A social system with ample opportunities to move from one class to another.

open-ended question A question asked of a respondent that allows the answer to take whatever form the respondent chooses.

operational definition A clear and precise definition of a variable that facilitates its measurement.

opinion leaders High-profile individuals whose interpretation of events influences the public.

organic solidarity Term developed by Emile Durkheim to describe the type of social bonds present in modern societies, based on difference, interdependence, and individual rights.

out-group Any group an individual feels opposition, rivalry, or hostility toward.

outsiders According to Howard Becker, those labeled deviant and subsequently segregated from "normal" society.

outsourcing "Contracting out" or transferring to another country the labor that a company might otherwise have employed its own staff to perform; typically done for financial reasons.

paradigm A set of assumptions, theories, and perspectives that make up a way of understanding social reality.

paradigm shift The term used to describe a change in basic assumptions of a particular scientific discipline.

participant observation A methodology associated with ethnography whereby the researcher both observes and becomes a member in a social setting.

particular or significant other The perspectives and expectations of a particular role that a child learns and internalizes.

passing Presenting yourself as a member of a different racial or ethnic group than the one you were born into.

patriarchy Literally meaning "rule of the father"; a male-dominated society.

personal front The expressive equipment we consciously or unconsciously use as we present ourselves to others, including appearance and manner, to help establish the definition of the situation.

pilot study A small study carried out to test the feasibility of a larger one.

play stage The second stage in Mead's theory of the development of self wherein children pretend to play the role of the particular or significant other.

pluralism A cultural pattern of intergroup relations that encourages racial and ethnic variation within a society.

pluralist model A system of political power in which a wide variety of individuals and groups have equal access to resources and the mechanisms of power.

pluralistic ignorance A process in which members of a group individually conclude that there is no need to take action because of the observation that other group members have not done so.

political action committee (PAC) An organization that raises money to support the interests of a select group or organization.

politics Methods and tactics intended to influence government policy; policy-related attitudes and activities.

pollution Any environmental contaminant that harms living beings.

polyandry A system of marriage that allows women to have multiple husbands.

polygamy A system of marriage that allows people to have more than one spouse at a time.

polygyny A system of marriage that allows men to have multiple wives.

polysemy Having many possible meanings or interpretations.

popular culture Usually contrasted with the high culture of elite groups; forms of cultural expression usually associated with the masses, consumer goods, and commercial products.

population transfer The forcible removal of a group of people from the territory they have occupied.

positive deviance Actions considered deviant within a given context, but which are later reinterpreted as appropriate or even heroic.

positivism The theory, developed by Auguste Comte, that sense perceptions are the only valid source of knowledge.

postmodernism A paradigm that suggests that social reality is diverse, pluralistic, and constantly in flux.

postmodernity A term encompassing the forms of social organization characteristic of postindustrial societies, including a focus on the production and management of information and skepticism of science and technology.

power The ability to control the actions of others.

power elite C. Wright Mills's term for a relatively small number of people who control the economic, political, and military institutions of a society.

pragmatism A theoretical perspective that assumes organisms (including humans) make practical adaptations to their environments. Humans do this through cognition, interpretation, and interaction.

praxis Practical action that is taken on the basis of intellectual or theoretical understanding.

prejudice An idea about the characteristics of a group that is applied to all members of that group and is unlikely to change regardless of the evidence against it.

preparatory stage The first stage in Mead's theory of the development of self wherein children mimic or imitate others.

prescriptions Behaviors approved of by a particular social group.

prestige The social honor people are given because of their membership in well-regarded social groups.

primary deviation In labeling theory, the act or attitude that causes one to be labeled deviant.

primary groups The people who are most important to our sense of self; members' relationships are typically characterized by face-to-face interaction, high levels of cooperation, and intense feelings of belonging.

probability sampling Any sampling scheme in which the probability of selecting any given unit is known.

profane The ordinary, mundane, or everyday.

pro-feminist men's movement An offshoot of male liberationism whose members support feminism and believe that sexism harms both men and women.

progressive Term describing efforts to promote forward-thinking social change.

proletariat Workers; those who have no means of production of their own and so are reduced to selling their labor power in order to live.

property crime Crimes that do not involve violence, including burglary, larceny theft, motor vehicle theft, and arson.

propinquity The tendency to marry or have relationships with people in close geographic proximity.

proscriptions Behaviors a particular social group wants its members to avoid.

psychoanalysis The therapeutic branch of psychology founded by Sigmund Freud in which free association and dream interpretation are used to explore the unconscious mind.

psychosexual stages of development Four distinct stages of the development of the self between birth and adulthood, according to Freud. Each stage is associated with a different erogenous zone.

public goods dilemma A type of social dilemma in which individuals must incur a cost to contribute to a collective resource, though they might not benefit from that resource.

qualitative A type of data that can't be converted into numbers, usually because they relate to meaning.

qualitative research Research that works with nonnumerical data such as texts, fieldnotes, interview transcripts, photographs, and tape recordings; this type of research more often tries to understand how people make sense of their world.

quantitative A type of data that can be converted into numbers, usually for statistical comparison.

quantitative research Research that translates the social world into numbers that can be treated mathematically; this type of research often tries to find cause-and-effect relationships.

queer theory A paradigm that proposes that categories of sexual identity are social constructs and that no sexual category is fundamentally either deviant or normal; this paradigm emphasizes the importance of difference and rejects as restrictive the idea of innate sexual identity.

race A socially defined category based on real or perceived biological differences between groups of people.

racial assimilation The process by which racial minority groups are absorbed into the dominant group through intermarriage.

racism A set of beliefs about the superiority of one racial or ethnic group; used to justify inequality and often rooted in the assumption that differences between groups are genetic.

rapport A positive relationship often characterized by mutual trust or sympathy.

rationalization The application of economic logic to human activity; the use of formal rules and regulations in order to maximize efficiency without consideration of subjective or individual concerns.

reactivity The tendency of people and events to react to the process of being studied.

real culture The norms, values, and patterns of behavior that actually exist within a society (which may or may not correspond to the society's ideals).

rebels Individuals who reject society's approved goals and means and instead create and work toward their own (sometimes revolutionary) goals using new means.

recreation Any satisfying, amusing, and stimulating activity that is experienced as refreshing and renewing for body, mind, and spirit.

reference group A group that provides a standard of comparison against which we evaluate ourselves.

reflexivity How the identity and activities of the researcher influence what is going on in the field setting.

region In the dramaturgical perspective, the context or setting in which the performance takes place.

regressive Term describing resistance to particular social changes, efforts to maintain the status quo, or attempts to reestablish an earlier form of social order.

rehabilitation An approach to punishment that attempts to reform criminals as part of their penalty.

reinforcement theory Theory that suggests that audiences seek messages in the media that reinforce their existing attitudes and beliefs and are thus not influenced by challenging or contradictory information.

relative deprivation A relative measure of poverty based on the standard of living in a particular society.

relative deprivation theory A theory of social movements that focuses on the actions of oppressed groups who seek rights or opportunities already enjoyed by others in the society.

reliability The consistency of a question or measurement tool, the degree to which the same questions will produce similar answers.

religion Any institutionalized system of shared beliefs and rituals that identify a relationship between the sacred and the profane.

religiosity The regular practice of religious beliefs, often measured in terms of frequency of attendance at worship services and the importance of religious beliefs to an individual.

renewable resources Resources that replenish at a rate comparable to the rate at which they are consumed.

replicability Research that can be repeated, and thus verified, by other researchers later.

representative sample A sample taken so that findings from members of the sample group can be generalized to the whole population.

representativeness The degree to which a particular studied group is similar to, or represents, any part of the larger society.

repression The process that causes unwanted or taboo desires to return via tics, dreams, slips of the tongue, and neuroses, according to Freud.

residential segregation The geographical separation of the poor from the rest of the population.

resistance strategies Ways that workers express discontent with their working conditions and try to reclaim control of the conditions of their labor.

resocialization The process of replacing previously learned norms and values with new ones as a part of a transition in life.

resource mobilization theory A theory of social movements that focuses on the practical constraints that help or hinder social movements' action.

respondent Someone from whom a researcher solicits information.

response rate The number or percentage of surveys completed by respondents and returned to researchers.

retreatists Individuals who reject both society's approved goals and the means by which to achieve them.

retribution An approach to punishment that emphasizes retaliation or revenge for the crime as the appropriate goal.

riot Continuous disorderly behavior by a group of people that disturbs the peace and is directed toward other people and/or property.

ritual A practice based on religious beliefs.

ritualists Individuals who have given up hope of achieving society's approved goals, but still operate according to society's approved means.

role The set of behaviors expected of someone because of his or her status.

role conflict Experienced when we occupy two or more roles with contradictory expectations.

role exit The process of leaving a role that we will no longer occupy.

role model An individual who serves as an example for others to strive toward and emulate.

role strain The tension experienced when there are contradictory expectations within one role.

role-taking emotions Emotions like sympathy, embarrassment, or shame that require that we assume the perspective of another person or many other people and respond from that person or group's point of view.

rural Relating to sparsely settled areas; in the United States, any county with a population density between 10 and 59.9 people per square mile.

rural rebound Population increase in rural counties that adjoin urban centers or possess rich scenic or amenity values.

sacred The holy, divine, or supernatural.

sample The part of the population that will actually be studied.

sanction Positive or negative reactions to the ways that people follow or disobey norms, including rewards for conformity and punishments for norm violations.

Sapir-Whorf hypothesis The idea that language structures thought and that ways of looking at the world are embedded in language.

school vouchers Payments from the government to parents whose children attend failing public schools; the money helps parents pay private school tuition.

scientific method A procedure for acquiring knowledge that emphasizes collecting concrete data through observation and experiment.

second shift The unpaid housework and childcare often expected of women after they complete their day's paid labor.

second wave The period of feminist activity during the 1960s and 1970s often associated with the issues of women's equal access to employment and education.

secondary deviation In labeling theory, the deviant identity or career that develops as a result of being labeled deviant.

secondary groups Larger and less intimate than primary groups; members' relationships are usually organized around a specific goal and are often temporary.

secular Nonreligious; a secular society separates church and state and does not endorse any religion.

segregation The formal and legal separation of groups by race or ethnicity.

self The individual's conscious, reflexive experience of a personal identity separate and distinct from other individuals.

self-fulfilling prophecy An inaccurate statement or belief that, by altering the situation, becomes accurate; a prediction that causes itself to come true.

service workers Those whose work involves providing a service to businesses or individual clients, customers, or consumers rather than manufacturing goods.

sex An individual's membership in one of two biologically distinct categories—male or female.

sexual orientation The inclination to feel sexual desire toward people of a particular gender or toward both genders.

sign A symbol that stands for or conveys an idea.

simple random sample A particular type of probability sample in which every member of the population has an equal chance of being selected.

simplicity movement A loosely knit movement that opposes consumerism and encourages people to work less, earn less, and spend less in accordance with nonmaterialistic values.

simulacrum An image or media representation that does not reflect reality in any meaningful way but is treated as real.

situational ethnicity An ethnic identity that can be either displayed or concealed depending on its usefulness in a given situation.

slavery The most extreme form of social stratification, based on the legal ownership of people.

smart growth Term for economic and urban planning policies that emphasize the redevelopment of inner cities or older suburbs.

social atomization A social situation that emphasizes individualism over collective or group identities.

social change The transformation of a culture over time.

social class A system of stratification based on access to resources such as wealth, property, power, and prestige.

social construction The process by which a concept or practice is created and maintained by participants who collectively agree that it exists.

social control The formal and informal mechanisms used to increase conformity to values and norms and thus increase social cohesion.

social dilemma A situation in which behavior that is rational for the individual can, when practiced by many people, lead to collective disaster.

social ecology The study of human populations and their impact on the natural world.

social identity theory A theory of group formation and maintenance that stresses the need of individual members to feel a sense of belonging.

social inequality The unequal distribution of wealth, power, or prestige among members of a society.

social influence (peer pressure) The influence of one's fellow group members on individual attitudes and behaviors.

social institutions Systems and structures within society that shape the activities of groups and individuals.

social learning The process of learning behaviors and meanings through social interaction.

social loafing The phenomenon in which as more individuals are added to a task, each individual contributes a little less; a source of inefficacy when working in teams.

social mobility The movement of individuals or groups within the hierarchal system of social classes.

social movement Any social groups with leadership, organization, and an ideological commitment to promote or resist social change.

social network The web of direct and indirect ties connecting an individual to other people who may also affect her.

social reproduction The tendency of social classes to remain relatively stable as social class status is passed down from one generation to the next.

social sciences The disciplines that use the scientific method to examine the social world; in contrast to the natural sciences, which examine the physical world.

social stratification The division of society into groups arranged in a social hierarchy.

social ties Connections between individuals.

socialism An economic system based on the collective ownership of the means of production, collective distribution of goods and services, and government regulation of the economy.

socialization The process of learning and internalizing the values, beliefs, and norms of our social group, by which we become functioning members of society.

society A group of people who shape their lives in aggregated and patterned ways that distinguish their group from other groups.

socioeconomic status (SES) A measure of an individual's place within a social class system; often used interchangeably with "class."

sociological imagination A quality of the mind that allows us to understand the relationship between our particular situation in life and what is happening at a social level.

sociology The systematic or scientific study of human society and social behavior, from large-scale institutions and mass culture to small groups and individual interactions.

solar dimming A decline in the amount of light reaching the earth's surface because of increased air pollution, which reflects more light back into space.

solidarity The degree of integration or unity within a particular society; the extent to which individuals feel connected to other members of their group.

special interest groups Organizations that raise and spend money to influence elected officials and/or public opinion.

spurious correlation The appearance of causation produced by an intervening variable.

status A position in a social hierarchy that carries a particular set of expectations.

status inconsistency A situation in which there are serious differences between the different elements of an individual's socioeconomic status.

stereotyping Judging others based on preconceived generalizations about groups or categories of people.

stigma Erving Goffman's term for any physical or social attribute that devalues a person or group's identity, and which may exclude those who are devalued from normal social interaction.

structural functionalism A paradigm that begins with the assumption that society is a unified whole that functions because of the contributions of its separate structures.

structural mobility Changes in the social status of large numbers of people due to structural changes in society.

structural strain theory Robert King Merton's argument that, in an unequal society, the tension or strain between socially approved goals and an individual's ability to meet those goals through socially approved means will lead to deviance as individuals reject either the goals or the means or both.

structure A social institution that is relatively stable over time and that meets the needs of society by performing functions necessary to maintain social order and stability.

subculture A group within society that is differentiated by its distinctive values, norms, and lifestyle.

sublimation The process in which socially unacceptable desires are healthily channeled into socially acceptable expressions, according to Freud.

suburbanization Beginning after World War II, the shift of large segments of population away from the urban core and toward the edges of cities.

suffrage movement The movement organized around gaining voting rights for women.

superego According to Freud, one of three interrelated parts that make up the mind; the superego has two components (the conscience and the ego-ideal) and represents the internalized demands of society.

surface acting Trying to "act the part" expected in a specific situation, even if that part does not match your underlying mood.

survey A method based on questionnaires that are administered to a sample of respondents selected from a target population.

sustainable development Economic development that aims to reconcile global economic growth with environmental protection.

sweatshop A workplace where workers are subject to extreme exploitation, including below-standard wages, long hours, and poor working conditions that may pose health or safety hazards.

symbolic culture The ideas associated with a cultural group, including ways of thinking (beliefs, values, and assumptions) and ways of behaving (norms, interactions, and communication).

symbolic ethnicity An ethnic identity that is only relevant on specific occasions and does not significantly impact everyday life.

symbolic interactionism A paradigm that sees interaction and meaning as central to society and assumes that meanings are not inherent but are created through interaction.

synergy A mutually beneficial interaction between parts of an organization that allows them to create something greater than the sum of their individual outputs.

synthesis The new social system created out of the conflict between thesis and antithesis in a dialectical model.

taboo A norm ingrained so deeply that even thinking about violating it evokes strong feelings of disgust, horror, or revulsion.

target population The entire group about which a researcher would like to be able to generalize.

taste cultures Areas of culture that share similar aesthetics and standards of taste.

taste publics Groups of people who share similar artistic, literary, media, recreational, and intellectual interests.

technological determinism A theory of social change that assumes changes in technology drive changes in society, rather than vice versa.

technology Material artifacts and the knowledge and techniques required to use them.

telecommuting Working from home while staying connected to the office through communications technology.

tertiary deviation In labeling theory, the rejection or transformation of the stigma of a deviant identity.

textual poaching Henry Jenkins's term describing the ways that audience members manipulate an original cultural product to create a new one; a common way for fans to exert some control over the media they consume.

Thanatos In Freudian psychology, the drive or instinct toward aggression or destruction.

theories In sociology, abstract propositions that explain the social world and make predictions about future events.

thesis The existing social arrangements in a dialectical model.

third place Any informal public place where people come together regularly for conversation and camaraderie when not at work or at home.

Third Sector The part of the economy composed of non-profit organizations; their workers are mission driven, rather than profit driven, and such organizations direct surplus funds to the causes they support. Also called the Independent Sector.

third wave The most recent period of feminist activity, focusing on issues of diversity and the variety of identities women can possess.

Thomas theorem Classic formulation of the way individuals define situations, whereby "if people define situations as real, they are real in their consequences."

total institution An institution in which individuals are cut off from the rest of society so that their lives can be controlled and regulated for the purpose of systematically stripping away previous roles and identities in order to create new ones.

tracking The placement of students in educational "tracks," or programs of study (e.g., college prep, remedial), that determine the types of classes students take.

traditional authority Authority based in custom, birthright, or divine right.

tragedy of the commons A particular type of social dilemma in which many individuals' overexploitation of a public resource depletes or degrades that resource.

transgendered Term describing an individual whose sense of gender identity is at odds with her or his physical sex but who has not necessarily sought sex-reassignment surgery.

transsexuals Individuals who identify with the opposite sex and have surgery to alter their own sex so it fits their self-image.

treadmill of production Term describing the operation of modern economic systems that require constant growth, which causes increased exploitation of resources and environmental degradation.

triad A three-person social group.

two-step flow model Theory on media effects that suggests audiences get information through opinion leaders who influence their attitudes and beliefs, rather than through direct firsthand sources.

unchurched A term describing those who consider themselves spiritual but not religious and who often adopt aspects of various religious traditions.

underclass The poorest Americans who are chronically unemployed and may depend on public or private assistance; they constitute about 5 percent of the U.S. population.

Uniform Crime Report (UCR) An official measure of crime in the United States, produced by the FBI's official tabulation of every crime reported by over 17,000 law enforcement agencies.

union An association of workers who bargain collectively for increased wages and benefits and better working conditions.

upper class A largely self-sustaining group of the wealthiest people in a class system; in the United States they constitute about 1 percent of the population and possess most of the wealth of the country.

upper-middle class Mostly professionals and managers, who enjoy considerable financial stability; they constitute about 14 percent of the U.S. population.

urban Relating to cities; typically describes densely populated areas.

urban density Concentration of people in a city, measured by the total number of people per square mile.

urban legend Modern folklore; a story that is believed (incorrectly) to be true and is widely spread because it expresses concerns, fears, and anxieties about the social world.

urban renewal Efforts to rejuvenate decaying inner cities, including renovation, selective demolition, commercial development, and tax incentives.

urban sprawl A derogatory term applied to the expansion of urban or suburban boundaries, associated with irresponsible or poorly planned development.

urbanites People who live in cities.

urbanization Movement of increasing numbers of people from rural areas to cities.

uses and gratifications paradigm Approaches to understanding media effects that focus on individuals' psychological or social needs that consumption of various media fulfills.

utopia Literally "no place"; an ideal society in which all social ills have been overcome.

validity The accuracy of a question or measurement tool; the degree to which a researcher is measuring what he thinks he is measuring.

value-free sociology An ideal whereby researchers identify facts without allowing their own personal beliefs or biases to interfere.

values Ideas about what is desirable or contemptible and right or wrong in a particular group. They articulate the essence of everything that a cultural group cherishes and honors.

variables One of two or more phenomena that a researcher believes are related and hopes to prove are related through research.

verstehen "To understand"; Weber's term to describe good social research, which tries to understand the meanings that individual social actors attach to various actions and events.

vertical social mobility The movement between different class statuses, often called either upward mobility or downward mobility.

violent crime Crimes in which violence is either the objective or the means to an end, including murder, rape, aggravated assault, and robbery.

virtual community A community of people linked by their consumption of the same electronic media. Also called electronic community.

weighting Techniques for manipulating the sampling procedure so that the sample more closely resembles the larger population.

white flight Movement of upper- and middle-class whites who could afford to leave the cities for the suburbs, especially in the 1950s and 60s.

white-collar A description characterizing workers and skilled laborers in technical and lower-management jobs.

white-collar crime Crime committed by a high-status individual in the course of her or his occupation.

working class Mostly "blue-collar" or service industry workers who are less likely to have a college degree; they constitute about 30 percent of the U.S. population.

working poor Poorly educated workers who work full-time but remain below the poverty line; they constitute about 20 percent of the U.S. population.

REFERENCES

ACLU. 2003. "Inadequate representation." American Civil Liberties Union online publication, October 8. http://www.aclu.org/capital/unequal/10390pub20031008.html

Access Clark County. 2009. "Clark County/Las Vegas Valley average population and growth rates, 1990–2008." http://www.accessclark-county.com/depts/comprehensive_planning/demographics/Pages/demographics.aspx

Adams, Damon. 1994. "Holocaust survivors face cameras; Spielberg heading project to create videotape library." *Times-Picayune,* November 24, p. D1.

Addams, Jane. 1895. *Hull-House Maps and Papers, by Residents of Hull-House, a Social Settlement, a Presentation of Nationalities and Wages in a Congested District of Chicago, Together with Comments and Essays on Problems Growing Out of the Social Conditions.* New York: Crowell.

_____. 1910. *Twenty Years at Hull-House.* New York: Macmillan. Adler, Patricia A.; and Adler, Peter. 1991. *Backboards and Blackboards: College Athletes and Role Engulfment.* New York: Columbia University Press.

_____. 2000. *Constructions of Deviance: Social Power, Context and Interaction.* Belmont, CA: Wadsworth.

Adorno, T.; and Horkheimer, M. 1979. "The culture industry: Enlightenment as mass deception." In T. Adorno and M. Horkheimer, eds., *Dialectic of Enlightenment.* London: Verso.

AFP. 2009. "*House* becomes world's most popular TV show." June 12. http://www.huffingtonpost.com/2009/06/12/house-becomes-worlds-most_h_214704.html

Aguirre, Benigno; Quarantelli, Enrico; and Mendoza, Jorge L. 1988. "The collective behavior of fads: The characteristics, effects and career of streaking." *American Sociological Review,* vol. 53, 569–589.

Agyeman, Julian; Bullard, Robert D.; and Evans, Bob; eds. 2003. *Just Sustainabilities: Development in an Unequal World.* Cambridge, MA: MIT Press.

AHENS. 2003. "Setting boundaries between work, life helps families thrive." *Ascribe Higher Education News Service,* May 8.

Alcoholics Anonymous. 2001 (orig. 1939). *Alcoholics Anonymous: The Story of How Many Thousands of Men and Women Have Recovered from Alcoholism.* 4th ed. New York: Alcoholics Anonymous World Service.

Alatas, Syed Farid; and Sinha, Vineeta. 2001. "Teaching classical sociological theory in Singapore: The context of Eurocentrism." *Teaching Sociology,* vol. 29, no. 3, 316–331.

Alexander, Jeffrey. 1988. "Parsons' 'structure' in American sociology." *Sociological Theory,* vol. 6, no. 1, 96–102.

Alexander, Jeffrey; and Smelser, Neil. 1998. *Diversity and Its Discontents: Cultural Conflict and Common Ground in Contemporary American Society.* Princeton, NJ: Princeton University Press.

Allan, G. 1989. *Friendship: Developing a Sociological Perspective.* Boulder, CO: Westview Press.

Allen L. S.; and Gorski, R. A. 1992. "Sexual orientation and the size of the anterior commissure in the human brain." Proceedings of the National Academy of Sciences, USA, vol. 89, no. 15, 7199–7202.

Allport, G.; and Ross, M. 1967. "Personal religious orientation and prejudice." *Journal of Personality and Social Psychology,* vol. 5, no. 4, 432–443.

Almaguer, Tomas. 2001. "Tomas Almaguer talks trash, too." Interview with Robert Soza. *Bad Subjects: Political Education for Everyday Life,* vol. 55 (May): 24.

_____. 2008. *Racial Fault Lines: The Historical Origins of White Supremacy in California.* Berkeley, CA: University of California Press.

Altermatt, Ellen Rydell; and Pomerantz, Eva M. 2005. "The implications of having high-achieving versus low-achieving friends: A longitudinal analysis." *Social Development,* vol. 14, no. 1, 61–81.

Altschuler, Glenn C. 2002. "College prep: A tryout for the real world." *New York Times,* April 14. http://www.nytimes.com/2002/04/14/education/college-prep-a-tryout-for-the-real-world.html?scp=5&sq=2001%20internships&st=cse, accessed 4/24/09.

American Association of Community Colleges. 2007. "First responders: Community colleges on the front line of security." http://www.aacc.nche.edu/Content/ NavigationMenu/HotIssues/Homeland_Security/AACC_1st_Responders_web.pdf

American Board of Plastic Surgery. 2008. www.aboardcertifiedplasticsurgeonresource.com

American Interactive Consumer Survey. 2006. www.workingfromanywhere.org/news/Trendlines_2006.pdf, accessed 10/27/08.

American Presidency Project. 2008. "Voter turnout in presidential elections 1824–2008." http://www.presidency.ucsb.edu/data/turnout.php, accessed 11/14/08.

American Society of Plastic Surgeons. 2008. *National Plastic Surgery Statistics 2000/2006/2007.* http://www.plasticsurgery.org/media/statistics/index.cfm

Amott, Teresa; and Matthaei, Julie. 1996. *Race, Class, Gender, and Work: A Multicultural Ethnic History of Women in the United States.* 2nd ed. Boston: South End Press.

Ananat, Elizabeth Oltmans. 2005. "The wrong side of the tracks: Estimating the causal effects of racial segregation on city outcomes." Unpublished working paper. MIT Department of Economics.

Anderson, Elijah. 1990. *Streetwise: Race, Class and Change in an Urban Community.* Chicago: University of Chicago Press.

Anderson, Steven W.; Bechara, Antoine; Damasio, Hann; Tranel, Daniel; and Damasio, Antonio R. 1999. "Impairment of social and moral behavior related to early damage in human prefrontal cortex." *Nature Neuroscience,* vol. 2, no. 11 (November): 1032–1037.

Anzaldúa, Gloria. 1987. *Borderlands/La Frontera: The New Mestiza.* San Francisco: Aunt Lute Books.

Arendt, Hannah. 1958. *The Origins of Totalitarianism.* London: Allen and Unwin Press.

Armitage, Angus. 1951. *The World of Copernicus.* New York: Mentor Books.

Asch, S. 1958. "Effects of group pressure upon the modification and distortion of judgments." In E. E. Maccoby, T. M. Newcomb, and

E. L. Hartley, eds., *Readings in Social Psychology.* New York: Holt, Rinehart, & Winston.

Associated Press. 2004. "Bush warns CIA against 'groupthink' culture." http://www.msnbc.msn.com/id/6571310/.

_____. 2005. "India controls 44 percent of outsourcing." June 12. http://www.enable24x7.com/MustRead_44percent.asp.

Atkin, C. 1973. "Instrumental utilities and information seeking." In P. Clark, ed., *New Models for Mass Communication Research.* Beverly Hills, CA: Sage.

_____. 1985. "Informational utility and selective exposure." In D. Zillmann and J. Bryant, eds., *Selective Exposure to Communication.* Hillsdale, NJ: Erlbaum.

"Avoid obsession with cars: UN to China and India." 2008. Reuters, April 14. http://www.financialexpress.com/news/avoid-obsession-with-cars-un-to-china-and-india/296597/1, accessed 12/18/08.

Babbie, Earl. 2002. *The Basics of Social Research.* Belmont, CA: Wadsworth.

Babiak, T. 2004. "Everything goes at Burning Man: Counterculture fest is everything that North America isn't." *National Post,* September 6, p. B10, accessed 9/11/04 from LexisNexis online database.

Baca Zinn, Maxine; and Eitzen, D. Stanley. 2002. *Diversity in Families.* Boston: Allyn and Bacon.

Bachman, R.; and Saltzman, L. 1995. "Violence against women: Estimates from the redesigned survey." Bureau of Justice Statistics Special Report. http://www.ojp.usdoj.gov/bjs/pub/pdf/femvied.pdf, accessed 1/14/04.

Bagdikian, Ben H. 2004. *The New Media Monopoly.* Boston: Beacon Press.

Bailey, J. M.; and Pillard, R. C. 1991. "A genetic study of male sexual orientation." *Archives of General Psychiatry,* vol. 48, 1089–1096.

Bailey, Ronald. 2002. "*Silent Spring* at 40: Rachel Carson's classic is not aging well." *Reason Online Magazine,* June 12. http://reason.com/rb/rb061202.shtml

Baker, H.D.R. 1979. *Chinese Family and Kinship.* London: Macmillan Press.

Baker, J. P.; and Crist, J. L. 1971. "Teacher expectancies: A review of the literature." In J. D. Elashoff and R. E. Snow, eds., *Pygmalion Reconsidered: A Case Study in Statistical Inference: Reconsideration of the Rosenthal-Jacobson Data on Teacher Expectancy.* Worthington, OH: Charles A. Jones.

Baldwin, Tom. 2007. "Fear and blogging on the campaign trail." *London Times,* December 29, Times Magazine: 36.

Bales, Kevin. 2000. *Disposable People: New Slavery in the Global Economy.* Berkeley, CA: University of California Press.

Bandura, A. 1965. "Influence of models' reinforcement contingencies on the acquisition of imitative response." *Journal of Personality and Social Psychology,* vol. 1, 589–595.

Bandy, Joe. 1996. "Managing the other of nature: Sustainability, spectacle, and global regimes of capital in ecotourism." *Public Culture,* vol. 8, no. 3, 539–566.

Banfield, Edward. 1970. *The Unheavenly City.* Boston: Little, Brown.

"Bar-Bat Mitzvah in Israel." 2007. www.goisrael.com, accessed 4/16/07.

Barbazoa, David. 2005. "Ogre to slay? Outsource it to Chinese." *New York Times,* December 9.

Bardhan, Ashok D.; and Kroll, Cynthia. 2003. "The new wave of outsourcing." Fisher Center for Real Estate and Urban Economics. Berkeley, CA: University of California Press.

Barner, Mark R. 1999. "Sex-role stereotyping in FCC-mandated children's educational television." *Journal of Broadcasting & Electronic Media,* vol. 43, no. 4 (fall): 551.

Barrett, David B.; and Johnson, Todd M. 2004. *International Bulletin of Missionary Research.* Center for the Study of Global Christianity,

Gordon-Conwell Theological Seminary, South Hamilton, Massachusetts, January.

Barry, Dave. 1994. *The World According to Dave Barry.* Illus. Jeff MacNelly. New York: Wings Books.

Bartels, Chuck. 2003. "Wal-Mart starting to look at all its 1.1 million U.S. workers." *Times-Picayune* (New Orleans, LA), October 25, "Money," p. 1.

Barth, Johann Christian. 1731. *The Gallant Ethic, in which it is shown how a young man should commend himself in polite society through refined acts and complaisant words. Prepared for the special advantage and pleasure of all amateurs of present-day good manners.* Dresden and Leipzig.

Basow, Susan A. 2006. "Women and their body hair." *Psychology of Women Quarterly* vol. 15, no. 1: 83–96.

Batan, Clarence M. 2004. "Of strengths and tensions: A dialogue of ideas between the classics and Philippine sociology." *UNITAS,* vol. 77, no. 2: 163–186.

Baudrillard, Jean. 1994 (orig. 1981). *Simulacra and Simulation.* Trans. Sheila Glaser. Ann Arbor, MI: University of Michigan Press.

Bauer, Martin W.; and Gaskell, George; eds. 2000. *Qualitative Researching with Text, Image and Sound.* London: Thousand Oaks; New Delhi: Sage.

Baum, S.; and Payea, K. "Education pays 2004: The benefits of higher education for individuals and society." New York: The College Board. http://eprints.ecs.org/html/Document.asp?chouseid=5664

BBC News. 2006. "CSI show 'most popular in world.'" July 31. http://news.bbc.co.uk/2/hi/entertainment/5231334.stm, accessed 8/10/06.

Beamish, Thomas. 2002. *Silent Spill: The Organization of an Industrial Crisis.* Boston: MIT Press.

Beatie, Thomas. 2008. "Labor of love." *The Advocate,* March 26. http://www.advocate.com/exclusive_detail_ektid52947.asp

Becker, A.; Burwell, R.; Herzog, D.; Hamburg, P.; and Gilman, S. 2002. "Eating behaviours and attitudes following prolonged exposure to television among ethnic Fijian adolescent girls." *British Journal of Psychiatry,* 180, 509–514. http://bjp.rcpsych.org/cgi/content/full/180/6/509, accessed 8/30/04.

Becker, Howard S. 1963. *Outsiders: Studies in the Sociology of Deviance.* Chicago: University of Chicago Press.

_____. 1982. *Art Worlds.* Berkeley, CA: University of California Press.

_____. 1986. *Doing Things Together: Selected Papers.* Evanston, IL: Northwestern University Press.

_____; Greer, Blanche; Hughes, Everett C.; and Strauss, Anselm L. 1961. *Boys in White: Student Culture in Medical School.* Chicago: University of Chicago Press.

Beeghley, Leonard. 2005. *The Structure of Social Stratification in the United States.* Boston: Allyn and Bacon.

Bell, Daniel. 1976. *The Coming of Post-Industrial Society: A Venture in Social Forecasting.* New York: Harper Colophon.

Bellah, Robert; Sullivan, William; and Tipton, Steven. 1985. *Habits of the Heart: Individualism and Commitment in American Life.* Berkeley, CA: University of California Press.

Bendapudi, Venkat; Mangum, Stephen L.; Tansky, Judith W.; and Fisher, Max M. 2003. "Nonstandard employment arrangements: A proposed typology and policy planning framework." *Human Resource Planning,* vol. 26, no. 1, 3.

Berends, M. 1995. "Educational stratification and students' social bonding to school." *British Journal of Sociology of Education,* vol. 16, no. 3, 327–351.

Berger, Bennett M., ed. 1992. *Authors of Their Own Lives: Intellectual Autobiographies of Twenty American Sociologists.* Berkeley, CA: University of California Press.

Berger, Peter. 1963. *Invitation to Sociology.* New York: Bantam Doubleday.

_____. 1977. *Facing Up to Modernity: Excursions in Society, Politics, and Religion.* New York: Basic Books.

_____; and Luckmann, Thomas. 1966. *The Social Construction of Reality: A Treatise in the Sociology of Knowledge.* Garden City, NY: Doubleday.

Berggoetz, Barb. 2005. "Internships pay off for 2005 grads: Real-world experience is dividend for job hopefuls." *Indianapolis Star,* May 8.

Bernardes, Jon. 1985. "Do we really know what the family is?" In P. Close and R. Collins, eds., *Family and Economy in Modern Society.* New York: Macmillan.

Bernstein, Jared. 2008. "Compared to 1990s, middle-class working families lose ground in the 2000s." *Economic Policy Institute Economic Snapshots Aug 27, 2008.* http://222.epi.org/content.cfm/webfeatures_snapshots_20080827

_____; McNichol, Elizabeth C.; Mishel, Lawrence; and Zahradnik, Robert. 2000. "Pulling apart: A state-by-state analysis of income trends." Economic Policy Institute Study. http://www.epi.org/content.cfm/studies_pullingapart

Berry, Sharon. 1993. "Will curbing PACs hurt black reps? Impact of new politication action committee financing rules on African American congressmen." *Black Enterprise,* September.

Best, Joel; and Horiuchi, Gerald. 1985. "The razor blade in the apple: The social construction of urban legends." *Social Problems,* vol. 32, no. 5, 488–499.

Best, Samuel J., and Brian S. Krueger. 2004. *Internet Data Collection.* Sage University Paper Series no. 141. Thousand Oaks, CA: Sage, 2004.

Billings, Andrew C.; and Eastman, Susan Tyler. 2000. "Sportscasting and sports reporting." *Journal of Sport and Social Issues,* vol. 24, no. 2, 192–213.

Blau, Judith R.; and Blau, Peter M. 1982. "The cost of inequality: Metropolitan structure and violent crime." *American Sociological Review,* vol. 47, no. 1 (February): 114–129.

_____; and Golden, Reid M. 1985. "Social inequality and the arts." *American Journal of Sociology,* vol. 91, no. 2, 309–331.

Blaunstein, Albert; and Zangrando, Robert; eds. 1970. *Civil Rights and the Black American.* New York: Washington Square Press.

Bloom, Allan. 1987. *The Closing of the American Mind.* New York: Simon and Schuster.

Blumer, Herbert. 1969. *Symbolic Interactionism: Perspective and Method.* Berkeley, CA: University of California Press.

Blumler, J. G.; and Katz, Elihu. 1974. *The Uses of Mass Communication: Current Perspectives on Gratifications Research.* Beverly Hills, CA: Sage.

Bly, Robert. 1992. *Iron John: A Book About Me.* New York: Vintage.

Bobo, Lawrence; Kluegel, James R.; and Smith, Ryan A. 1997. "Laissez-faire racism: The crystallization of a 'kinder, gentler' anti-black ideology," in Jack Martin, ed., *Racial Attitudes in the 1990s: Continuity and Change.* Westport, CT: Praeger.

Bobo, Lawrence; and Smith, Ryan A. 1998. "From Jim Crow racism to laissez-faire racism: The transformation of racial attitudes in America," in Wendy Katkin, Ned Landsman, and Andrea Tyree, eds., *Beyond Pluralism: Essays on the Conception of Groups and Group Identities in America.* Urbana, IL: University of Illinois Press.

Bogle, Kathleen. 2008. *Hooking-Up: Sex, Dating and Relationships on Campus.* New York: New York University Press.

Bohner, Gerd; Siebler, Frank; and Schmelcher, Jurgen. 2006. "Social norms and the likelihood of raping: Perceived rape myth acceptance of others affects men's rape proclivity." *Personality and Social Psychology Bulletin,* vol. 32, no. 3, 286–297.

Bonacich, Edna. 1980. *The Economic Basis of Ethnic Solidarity: Small Business in the Japanese American Community.* Berkeley, CA: University of California Press.

Bond, Rod; and Sussex, Peter B. 1996. "Culture and conformity: A meta-analysis of studies using Asch's (1952b, 1956) line judgment task." *Psychological Bulletin,* vol. 119, no. 1, 111–137.

Booth, A.; Shelley, G.; Mazur, A.; Tharp, G.; and Kittock, R. 1989. "Testosterone and winning and losing in human competition." *Hormones and Behavior,* vol. 23, 556–571.

Bornstein, Kate. 1998. "Who's on top?" *My Gender Workbook: How to Become a Real Man, a Real Woman, the Real You, or Something Else Entirely.* New York: Routledge.

Bourassa, Loren; and Ahforth, Blake E. 1998. "You are about to party *Defiant* style: Socialization and identity aboard an Alaskan fishing boat." *Journal of Contemporary Ethnography,* vol. 27 (July): 171–196.

Bourdieu, Pierre. 1973. "Cultural reproduction and social reproduction." In Richard Brown, ed., *Knowledge, Education, and Social Change: Papers in the Sociology of Education.* London: Tavistock.

_____. 1984. *Distinction: A Social Critique of the Judgement of Taste.* Cambridge, MA: Harvard University Press.

Bourdreau, Abbie, and Zamost, Scott. 2008. "Girlfriend: Shooter was taking cocktail of three drugs. CNN.com, February 20. http://www.cnn.com/2008/CRIME/02/20/shooter.girlfriend/index.html, accessed 3/12/09.

Bowles, Samuel; and Gintis, Herbert. 1977. *Schooling in Capitalist America: Educational Reform and the Contradictions of Economic Life.* New York: Basic Books.

boyd, danah. 2007. "Why youth (heart) social network sites: The role of networked publics in teenage social life." In *MacArthur Foundation Series on Digital Learning—Youth, Identity and Digital Media Volume,* ed. David Buckingham. Cambridge, MA: MIT Press.

Boyd, Robert. 2004. "World may be darkening as clouds, air pollution dim the sun's rays." Knight Ridder News Service, *Santa Barbara News-Press,* May 9.

Boyes, Georgina. 1984. "Belief and disbelief: An examination of reactions to the presentation of rumour legends," in Paul Smith, ed., *Perspectives on Contemporary Legend.* Sheffield, UK: Continuum International.

Bradley, Graham; and Wildman, Karen. 2002. "Psychosocial predictors of emerging adults' risk and reckless behaviors." *Journal of Youth and Adolescence,* vol. 31, no. 4, 253–265.

Brandon, Michael C. 1996. "From need to know to need to know." *Communication World,* vol. 13, no. 8 (October–November): 18.

Brief, Arthur P.; Buttram, Robert T.; Elliott, Jodi D.; Reizenstein, Robin M.; and McCline, Richard L. 1995. "Releasing the beast: A study of compliance with orders to use race as a selection criterion." *Journal of Social Issues,* vol. 51, no. 3 (fall): 177–193.

Brinkley-Rogers, Paul. 2002. "Pledge of allegiance reflects timeline of nation's history." *Columbus Dispatch,* June 28, p. 2A.

Brodkin, Karen. 1999. *How Jews Became White Folks and What That Says about Race in America.* New Brunswick, NJ: Rutgers University Press.

Brooks, James F. 2002. *Confounding the Color Line: The Indian-Black Experience in North America.* Lincoln, NE: University of Nebraska Press.

Brown, L.; Flavin, C.; French, H.; Abramovitz, J.; Bright, C.; Dunn, S.; Halweil, B.; Gardner, G.; Mattoon, A.; Platt McGinn, A.; O'Meara, M.; Postel, S.; Renner, M.; and Starke, L. 2000. *State of the World, 2000.* New York: Norton.

Brunvand, Jan Harold. 1981. *The Vanishing Hitchhiker.* New York: Norton.

_____. 2001. *Encyclopedia of Urban Legends.* Santa Barbara, CA: ABC-Clio.

Bulkeley, William M. 2004. "New IBM jobs can mean fewer jobs elsewhere." *Wall Street Journal,* March 8, p. B1.

Bullard, Robert. 1990. *Dumping in Dixie: Race, Class and Environmental Quality.* Boulder, CO: Westview Press.

_____. 1993. *Confronting Environmental Racism: Voices from the Grassroots.* Boston: South End Press.

_____; Johnson, Glenn S.; and Wright, Beverly H. 1997. "Confronting environmental injustice: It's the right thing to do." *Race, Gender & Class,* vol. 5, no. 1, 63–79.

Bullard, Robert; and Wright, Beverly H. 1990. "The quest for environmental equity: Mobilizing the African-American community for social change." *Society and Natural Resources,* vol. 3, 301–311.

Burchfield, Keri, and Mingus, William. 2008. "Not in my neighborhood: Assessing registered sex offenders' experiences with local social capital and social control." *Criminal Justice and Behavior* vol. 35, no. 3: 356–374.

Burkhalter, Byron. 1999. "Reading race online." In Marc Smith and Peter Kollock, eds., *Communities in Cyberspace.* London: Routledge

Burns, Stacy Lee. 2004. "Pursuing 'deep pockets': Insurance-related issues in judicial settlement work." *Journal of Contemporary Ethnography,* vol. 33, no. 2, 111–153.

Burt, Martha; and Aron, Laudan. 2000. "America's homeless II: Populations and services." *Urban Institute Report,* February 1.

Butler, Judith. 1993. *Bodies That Matter: On the Discursive Limits of "Sex."* New York: Routledge.

———. 1999. *Gender Trouble.* New York: Routledge.

Buttel, Frederick H. 1987. "New directions in environmental sociology." *Annual Review of Sociology,* iss. 13, 465–488.

Byrne, D. G. 1981. "Sex differences in the reporting of symptoms of depression in the general population." *British Journal of Clinical Psychology,* vol. 20, 83–92.

Cabot, Mary Kay. 1999. "Against opponents or cancer, Stefanie and Chris Spielman prove what devotion can do." *Cleveland Plain Dealer,* May 9.

Cahill, Spencer. 1999. "Emotional capital and professional socialization: The case of mortuary science students (and me)." *Social Psychology Quarterly,* vol. 62 (June): 101–116.

Caincross, Francis. 1995. "The death of distance." Survey Telecommunications, *The Economist,* 30 September, p. 5.

Califano, Joseph A., Jr. 1999. "What was really great about the Great Society." *Washington Monthly,* October.

Cancian, Maria; and Meyer, Daniel R. 1998. "Who gets custody?" *Demography,* vol. 35, no. 2, 147–157.

Caplan, Jeremy. 2005. "How green is my town." U.S. Snapshot, *Time,* July 18.

Carnegie, Dale. 1936. *How to Win Friends and Influence People.* New York: Simon and Schuster.

Carns, Donald. 1973. "Talking about sex: Notes on first coitus and the double standard." *Journal of Marriage and the Family,* vol. 35, no. 4 (November): 677–688.

Carroll, Andrew, ed. 2006. *Operation Homecoming: Iraq, Afghanistan, and the Home Front, in the Words of U.S. Troops and Their Families.* New York: Random House.

Carson, Rachel. 1962. *Silent Spring.* New York: Houghton Mifflin.

Castells, Manuel. 1984. "Cultural identity, sexual liberation and urban structure: The gay community in San Francisco." In *The City and the Grassroots: A Cross-Cultural Theory of Urban Social Movements.* Berkeley, CA: University of California Press.

———. 2000. *The Rise of the Network Society,* vol. 1. 2nd ed. Malden, MA: Blackwell.

———; and Susser, Ida. 2002. *The Castells Reader on Cities and Social Theory.* Malden, MA: Blackwell.

Catton, William R., Jr. 1980. *Overshoot: The Ecological Basis of Revolutionary Change.* Urbana, IL: University of Illinois Press.

———; and Dunlap, Riley E. 1978. "Environmental sociology: A new paradigm." *American Sociologist,* vol. 13, 41–49.

———. 1980. "A new ecological paradigm for post-exuberant society." *American Behavioral Scientist,* vol. 24, no. 1, 15–47.

Caughey, John L. 1984. *Imaginary Social Worlds: A Cultural Approach.* Lincoln, NE: University of Nebraska Press.

———. 1999. "Imaginary social relationships." In Joseph Harris and Jay Rosen, eds., *Media Journal: Reading and Writing about Popular Culture.* Boston: Allyn and Bacon.

Center for Responsive Politics. 2008a. "Banking on becoming president." http://www.opensecrets.org/pres08/index.php

———. 2008b. "Money wins presidency and 9 of 10 congressional races in priciest U.S. election ever." http://www.opensecrets.org/news/2008/11/money-wins-white-house-and.html

———. 2008c. "Top 20 PAC contributors to candidates, 2007–2008." http://www.opensecrets.org/pacs/toppacs.php?cycle=2008&party=A

Chambliss, William J. 1973. "The saints and the roughnecks." *Society,* November, pp. 24–31.

Champagne, Duane. 1994. *Native America: Portrait of the People.* Canton, MI: Visible Ink Press.

Charles, Camille Zubrinsky. 2001. "Processes of racial residential segregation." In Alice O'Connor, Chris Tilly, and Lawrence Bobo, eds., *Urban Inequality: Evidence from Four Cities.* New York: Russell Sage.

Chen, Katherine K. 2004. "The Burning Man organization grows up: Blending bureaucratic and alternative structures." Doctoral Dissertation. Harvard University.

Cherlin, Andrew J. 2005. "Figure 12.1 Annual divorce rate, United States, 1860–2002." *Public and Private Families: An Introduction,* 4th ed. New York: McGraw-Hill.

———; and Furstenberg, Frank F., Jr. 1994. "Stepfamilies in the United States: A reconsideration." *Annual Review of Sociology,* vol. 20, 359–381.

Chin, Tiffani; and Phillips, Meredith. 2004. "Social reproduction and child-rearing practices: Social class, children's agency, and the summer activity gap." *Sociology of Education,* vol. 77, no. 3, 185–210.

"China's oil consumption reaches record high in Q1." Xinhuanet.com. April 29, 2008. http://news.xinhuanet.com/english/2008-04/29/content_8075648.htm, accessed 12/18/08.

Chodorow, Nancy. 1978. *The Reproduction of Mothering: Psychoanalysis and the Sociology of Gender.* Berkeley, CA: University of California Press.

———. 1994. *Femininities, Masculinities, Sexualities: Freud and Beyond.* Lexington, KY: University Press of Kentucky.

Chordas, Lori. 2003. "Instant connection: Instant messaging is taking the business world by storm, and some insurers already are finding it improves productivity and reduces costs." *Best's Review,* vol. 104, no. 3 (July): 100.

Christakis, N. A. 1995. "The similarity and frequency of proposals to reform U.S. medical education: Constant concerns." *Journal of the American Medical Association,* vol. 274, 706.

Christian Science Monitor. 2007. "Gender bias in college admissions." July 24. http://www.csmonitor.com/2007/0724/p08s01-comv.html

Chuang, Tamara. 2008. "*The Sims* tops 100 million in sales worldwide." *Seattle Times,* April 21. http://seattletimes.nwsource.com/html/businesstechnology/2004362492_btsims21.html

CIA World Factbook. 2008. https://www.cia.gov/library/publications/the-world-factbook

Cialdini, Robert B. 1998. *Influence: The Psychology of Persuasion,* rev. ed. Foxboro, Canada: Perennial Currents.

———; and Trost, M. R. 1998. "Social influence: Social norms, conformity, and compliance." In D. T. Gilbert, S. E. Fiske, and G. Lindzey, eds., *Handbook of Social Psychology,* vol. 2. 4th ed. Boston: McGraw-Hill.

Cicourel, Aaron V. 1972. "Basic and normative rules in the negotiation of status and role." In D. Sudnow, ed., *Studies in Social Interaction.* New York: Free Press.

Clarke, Lee. 2001. *Mission Improbable: Using Fantasy Documents to Tame Disaster.* Chicago: University of Chicago Press.

Clawson, Dan; Neustadtl, Alan; and Scott, Denise. 1992. *Money Talks: Corporate PACs and Political Influence.* New York: Basic Books.

Clayman, Steven E. 2002. "Sequence and Solidarity." *Advances in Group Processes,* vol. 19, 229–253.

Clinton, Catherine; and Gillespie, Michelle; eds. 1997. *The Devil's Lane: Sex and Race in the Early South.* New York: Oxford University Press.

CNN. 2005. "Poll: U.S. Catholics would support changes." April 3. http://edition.cnn.com/2005/US/04/03/pope.poll/

———. 2007. "Massacre at Virginia Tech. CNN.com. http://edition.cnn.com/SPECIALS/2007/virginiatech.shootings/, accessed 3/12/09.

Codell, Esmé Raji. 1999. *Educating Esmé: Diary of a Teacher's First Year.* Chapel Hill, NC: Algonquin Books.

Cohany, Sharon. 1996. "Workers in alternative employment arrangements." *Monthly Labor Review,* vol. 119, no. 10 (October): 31.

Cohen, Jackie. 2005. "America's culture of entertainment: U.S. spending on recreation equals Canada's entire GNP." CBS Marketwatch.com, January 11. http://www.marketwatch.com/story/americans-value-entertainment-studies-show, accessed 5/1/09.

Cohen, Joel E. 1995. *How Many People Can the Earth Support?* New York: Norton.

Cohen, S. P. 2001. *India: Emerging Power.* Washington, DC: Brookings Institution Press.

Coleman, John R. 1983. "Diary of a homeless man." *New York Magazine,* February.

Collins, Patricia Hill. 2006. *From Black Power to Hip Hop: Racism, Nationalism, and Feminism.* Philadephia: Temple University Press.

Collins, Randall. 1979. *The Credential Society: An Historical Sociology of Education and Stratification.* New York: Worthington Press.

Coltrane, Scott. 1997. *Family Man: Fatherhood, Housework and Gender Equity.* New York: Oxford University Press.

Commission for Labor Cooperation. 2003. "Work stoppages in North America." Briefing Note, October. http://www.naalc.org/english/pdf/work_stoppage_eng.pdf

Common Cause. 1996. "CC pushes for action campaign reform bills." spring–summer.

Comte, Auguste. 1988 (orig. 1842). *Introduction to Positive Philosophy.* Edited, with introduction and revised translation, by Frederick Ferré. Indianapolis, IN: Hackett.

Conley, Dalton. 2002. *Wealth and Poverty in America: A Reader.* Malden, MA: Blackwell.

———. 2004. *The Pecking Order: Which Siblings Succeed and Why.* New York: Pantheon.

Connell, R. W. 1995. *Masculinities.* Berkeley, CA: University of California Press.

Contemporary Pediatrics. 2000, vol. 17, no. 10 (October): 12.

Conti, Joseph. 2003. "Trade, power, and law: Dispute settlement in the World Trade Organization, 1995–2002." Unpublished Master's Thesis. University of California, Santa Barbara.

———. 2005. "Power through process: Determinants of dispute resolution outcomes in the World Trade Organization." Unpublished Dissertation. University of California, Santa Barbara, Department of Sociology.

Cook, Noble David. 1998. *Born to Die: Disease and New World Conquest, 1492–1650.* Cambridge, UK: Cambridge University Press.

Cooley, Charles Horton. 1909. *Social Organization: A Study of the Large Mind.* New York: Scribner.

Coontz, Stephanie. 2000. *The Way We Never Were: American Families and the Nostalgia Trap.* New York: Basic Books.

Cooper, Marc. 2003. "Runaway shops." *The Nation,* vol. 270, no. 13 (April 3): 28.

Cota, A. A.; Evans, C. R.; Dion, K. L.; Kilik, L. L.; and Longman, R. S. 1995. "The structure of group cohesion." *Personality and Social Psychology Bulletin,* vol. 21, 572–580.

Coupland, Douglas. 1995. *Microserfs.* New York: HarperCollins.

Crenshaw, Kimberle; Gotanda, Neil; Peller, Garry; and Thomas, Kendall; eds. 1996. *Critical Race Theory: The Key Writings That Formed the Movement.* New York: New Press.

Cummings, Jeanne. 2008. "2008 campaign costliest in U.S. history." *Politico,* November 5. http://www.politico.com/news/stories/1108/15283.html

Dahl, Robert A. 1961. *Who Governs?* New Haven, CT: Yale University Press.

Darley, John; and Latane, Bibb. 1968. "Bystander intervention in emergencies: Diffusion of responsibility." *Journal of Personality and Social Psychology,* vol. 8.

Davila, M. 1971. "Compadrazgo: Fictive kinship in Latin America." In N. Graburn, ed., *Readings in Kinship and Social Structure.* New York: Harper and Row.

Davis, Angela Y. 2001. "Outcast mothers and surrogates: Racism and reproductive politics." In Laurel Richardson, Verta Taylor, and Nancy Whittier, eds., *Feminist Frontiers IV.* Boston: McGraw-Hill.

Davis, Kingsley. 1940. "Extreme social isolation of a child." *American Journal of Sociology,* vol. 45 (January): 554–565.

———. 1947. "Final note on a case of extreme isolation." *American Journal of Sociology,* vol. 52, no. 5, 432–437.

Davis, T. 1995. "The occupational mobility of Black males revisited—Does race matter?" *Social Science Journal,* vol. 32, no. 2, 121–135.

Dearmore, Roy F. 1997. Biblical Missions: History, Principles, Practice. Garland, TX: Rodgers Baptist Church.

de Beaumont, Gustave. 1958. *Marie.* Stanford, CA: Stanford University Press.

De Graaf, John; Waan, David; and Naylor, Thomas. 2002. *Affluenza: The All-Consuming Epidemic.* San Francisco: Berrett-Koehler.

Derrida, Jacques. 1967. *Of Grammatology (De la grammatologie).* Paris: Seuil.

de Tocqueville, Alexis. 1994. Democracy in America. 2 vols. New York: Alfred A Knopf.

DeVault, Marjorie. 1994 (orig. 1991). *Feeding the Family: The Social Organization of Caring as Gendered Work.* Chicago: University of Chicago Press.

De Villiers, M. 2000. *Water: The Fate of Our Most Precious Resource.* Boston: Houghton Mifflin.

Di Leonardo, Micaela. 1987. "The female world of cards and holidays: Women, families, and the work of kinship." *Signs,* vol. 12, no. 3, 340–350.

Diamond, Sara. 1995. *Roads to Dominion: Right Wing Movements and Political Power in the United States.* New York: Guilford Press.

Dicken, Peter. 1998. *The Global Shift: Transforming the World Economy,* 3rd ed. New York: Guilford Press.

Doherty, B. 2000. "Burning Man grows up." *Reason,* vol. 31, 24–33. http://reason.com/0002/fe.bd.burning.shtml, accessed 9/9/04.

Domhoff, G. William. 1983. *Who Rules America Now? A View from the Eighties.* Englewood Cliffs, NJ: Prentice Hall.

———. 1987. *Power Elites and Organizations.* Newbury Park, CA: Sage.

———. 1990. *The Power Elite and the State: How Policy Is Made in America.* New York: de Gruyter.

———. 2002. *Who Rules America Now? Power and Politics in the Year 2000.* 3rd ed. Mountain View, CA: Mayfield.

Donnelly, Denise; and Finkelhor, David. 1993. "Who has joint custody? Class differences in the determination of custody arrangements." *Family Relations,* vol. 42, no. 1, 57–60.

Dorsey, Malynda. 2007. "VSU expels student." *Valdosta Daily Times,* October 4. http://www.valdostadailytimes.com/local/local_story_277232726.html, accessed 8/22/08.

Draut, Tamara; and Silva, Javier. 2004. "Generation broke: The growth of debt among young Americans." A Demos Group Report, October 13.

Dresser, Norine. 2005. *Multicultural Manners: Essential Rules of Etiquette for the 21st Century.* Hoboken, NJ: Wiley.

Dretzin, Rachel (Writer); and Goodman, Barak (Director). 2001, February 27. "The Merchants of Cool." In David Fanning and Michael Sullivan (Executive Producers), *Frontline*. Boston: WGBH Educational Foundation. http://www.pbs.org/wgbh/pages/frontline/shows/cool/

Drucker, Peter. 1959. *Landmarks of Tomorrow: A Report on the New "Post-Modern" World*. New York: Harper.

_____. 2003. *The Essential Drucker: The Best of Sixty Years of Peter Drucker's Writings on Management*. New York: Collins.

Duany, Andres; Plater-Zyberk, Elizabeth; and Speck, Jeff. 2001. *Suburban Nation: The Rise of Sprawl and the Decline of the American Dream*. New York: North Point Press.

DuBois, W.E.B. 1903. "The Negro problem." *The Souls of Black Folk*. Chicago: McClurg.

_____. 1915. *The Negro*.

_____. 1924. *The Gift of Black Folk*. Boston: Stratford.

_____. 1939. *Black Folk: Then and Now*. New York: Holt.

_____. 1940. *Dusk of Dawn*. New York: Harcourt, Brace.

Duneier, Mitchell; and Carter, Ovie. 1999. *Sidewalk*. New York: Farrar, Straus and Giroux.

Dunlap, Riley, E.; and Catton, William, Jr. 1979. "Environmental sociology." *Annual Review of Sociology*, iss. 5, 243–273.

_____. 1994. "Struggling with human exemptionalism: The rise, decline, and revitalization of environmental sociology." *American Sociologist*, vol. 25, no. 1, 5–30.

Dupuis, Sherry L.; and Smale, Bryan J. A. 2000. "Bittersweet journeys: Meanings of leisure in the institution-based caregiving context." *Journal of Leisure Research*, vol. 32, no. 3 (June): 303.

Durbin, Dee-Ann. 2008. "U.S. hybrid sales up 38% in 2007; Prius leads the pack." Associated Press. *Houston Chronicle*, April 21. http://www.chron.com/disp/story.mpl/business/5716489.html, accessed 6/9/09.

Durkheim, Emile. 1951 (orig. 1897). *Suicide: A Study in Sociology*. Trans. John A. Spaulding and George Simpson. Glencoe, IL: Free Press of Glencoe.

_____. 1964 (orig. 1893). *Suicide*. New York: Free Press.

_____. 1984 (orig. 1893). *The Division of Labor in Society*. Trans. W. D. Halls. New York: Free Press.

_____. 1995 (orig. 1912). *The Elementary Forms of Religious Life*. Trans. Karen E. Fields. New York: Free Press.

Dwyer, Jim. 2001. "A nation challenged." *New York Times*, November 6, p. A1.

Dye, Thomas R. 2002. *Who's Running America? The Bush Restoration*. 7th ed. Upper Saddle River, NJ: Prentice Hall.

Early College High School Initiative. 2007. "Overview and FAQ." http://www.earlycolleges.org/overview.html#basics6

Economic Policy Institute. 2001. "Not making ends meet." Economic Policy Institute Snapshot Report, August 1. http://www.epi.org/content.cfm/webfeatures_snapshots_ archive_08012001

Edgerton, Robert B. 1992. *Sick Societies: Challenging the Myth of Primitive Harmony*. New York: Free Press.

Edin, Kathryn. 2000. "Few good men." *American Prospect*, vol. 11, no. 4 (January 3).

_____; and Kefalas, Maria. 2005. *Promises I Can Keep: Why Poor Women Put Motherhood Before Marriage*. Berkeley, CA: University of California Press.

_____; and Lein, Laura. 1997. *Making Ends Meet*. New York: Russell Sage Foundation.

Egelko, Bob. 2002. "Pledge of allegiance ruled unconstitutional; many say ruling by S.F. court hasn't a prayer after appeals." *San Francisco Chronicle*, June 27, p. A1.

Eggers, Dave. 2006. *What Is the What*. San Francisco: McSweeny's Books.

Ehrenreich, Barbara. 1990. *The Worst Years of our Lives: Irreverent Notes from a Decade of Greed*. New York: Pantheon.

_____. 2001. *Nickel and Dimed: On (Not) Getting by in America*. New York: Metropolitan Books.

_____. 2004. "All together now." *New York Times*, July 15. http://www.nytimes.com/2004/07/15/opinion/

Ehrlich, Paul R.; and Ehrlich, Anne H. 1990. *The Population Explosion*. New York: Simon and Schuster.

Eisenstein, Zillah. 1979. "Capitalist patriarchy and the case for socialist feminism." *Monthly Review*, February.

Elias, Norbert. 1978. *The History of Manners. The Civilizing Process: Volume I*. New York: Pantheon Books.

Eller, Cynthia. 2003. *Am I a Woman? A Skeptic's Guide to Gender*. Boston: Beacon Press.

Ellis, Carolyn. 1995. "Emotional and ethical quagmires in returning to the field." *Journal of Contemporary Ethnography*, vol. 24, 68–96.

_____. 1997. "Evocative autoethnography: Writing emotionally about our lives." In W. G. Tierney and Y. S. Lincoln, eds., *Representation and the Text: Re-framing the Narrative Voice*. Albany, NY: SUNY Press.

Energy Information Administration. 2004. "International energy outlook 2004: Highlights." http://www.eia.doe.gov/oiaf/ieo/highlights.html

England, Paula. 1992. *Comparable Worth: Theories and Evidence*. Edison, NJ: Aldine Transaction.

English, Bella. 2003. "Dinner and a movie? No thanks. On college campuses, the idea of dating is quite outdated. Couples have been replaced by 'friends with benefits.'" *Boston Globe*, December 11, p. B17.

Entertainment Software Association. 2008. "2008 sales, demographic, and usage data: Essential facts." http://www.theesa.com/facts/pdfs/ESA_EF_2008.pdf

Epps, Edgar. 2001. "Race, class, and educational opportunity: Trends in the sociology of education." In Bruce R. Hare, ed., *Race Odyssey: African Americans and Sociology: A Critical Analysis*. Syracuse, NY: Syracuse University Press.

Epstein, Keith. 2004. "Pain in the Rust Belt." Media General News Service. http://www.writewizard.com/rustbelt.html, accessed 4/25/04.

ESPN. 2008. "Major league baseball attendance report 2008." http://sports.espn.go.com/mlb/attendance, accessed 4/15/08

Esquith, Rafe. 2003. *There Are No Shortcuts*. New York: Pantheon Books.

Etzioni, Amitai. 1996. "The responsive community: A communitarian perspective." *American Sociological Review*, vol. 61, no. 1, 1–11.

"Even in the best of homes." 2003. http://www.vday.org/ contents/victory/success/0305051, accessed 1/16/04.

Fabes, Richard A.; Martin, Carol Lynn; and Hanish, Laura D. 2003. "Young children's play qualities in same-, other-, and mixed-sex peer groups." *Child Development*, vol. 74, no. 3 (May–June): 921.

Fairbanks, C. 1992. "Labels, literacy and enabled learning: Glenn's story." *Harvard Educational Review*, vol. 62, no. 4, 475–493.

Fairfax County Public Schools, Office of Testing and Evaluation. 1999. "Assessments: State & Fairfax County public schools passing rates." Data: Virginia Standards of Learning, 11/4/99, as cited in Bracey, Gerald. 2000. "High Stakes Testing." Center for Education Research, Analysis, and Innovation, School of Education, University of Wisconsin-Milwaukee. http://www.asu.edu/educ/epsl/EPRU/documents/cerai-00-32.htm#_ednref22.

Falconer, Renee C.; and Byrnes, Deborah A. 2003. "When good intentions are not enough: A response to increasing diversity in an early childhood setting." *Journal of Research in Childhood Education*, vol. 17, no. 2 (spring–summer): 188.

Faludi, Susan. 1999. *Stiffed: The Betrayal of the American Man*. New York: William & Morrow.

Farell, Warren. 1975. *The Liberated Man*. New York: Bantam.

Farghal, M.; and Shakir, A. 1994. "Kin terms and titles of address as relational social honorifics in Jordanian Arabic." *Anthropological Linguistics,* iss. 36, 240–253.

Fausto-Sterling, Anne. 2000. *Sexing the Body: Gender Politics and the Construction of Sexuality.* New York: Basic Books.

Fava, S. F. 1956. "Suburbanism as a way of life." *American Sociological Review,* vol. 21, 34–37.

Federal Bureau of Investigation. 2003. *Crime in the United States, 2003.* "Table 2.3. Murder victims by race and sex, 2003." Uniform Crime Reports. http://www.fbi.gov/filelink.html?file=/ucr/cius_03/xl/03tbl2-3.xls

———. 2008. "Table 1: Crime in the United States by volume and rate per 100,000 inhabitants, 1988–2007." *Crime in the United States, 2007.* http://www.fbi.gov/ucr/cius2007/data/table_01.html, accessed 4/16/09.

Federal Election Commission. 2009 "Summary campaign finance data: PAC financial summaries, 2003–04." http://www.fec.gov/finance/disclosure/ftpsum.shtml accessed 6/2/09.

Ferris, Kerry. 2001. "Through a glass, darkly: The dynamics of fan-celebrity encounters." *Symbolic Interaction,* vol. 24, no. 1 (February).

———. 2004a. "Seeing and being seen: The moral order of celebrity sightings." *Journal of Contemporary Ethnography,* vol. 33, no. 3 (June): 236–264.

———. 2004b. "Transmitting ideals: Constructing self and moral discourse on *Loveline.*" *Symbolic Interaction,* vol. 27, no. 2 (spring): 247–266.

———. 2005. "Threat management: Moral and actual entrepreneurship in the control of celebrity stalking." In Stacy Burns, ed., *Ethnographies of Law and Social Control.* Sociology of Crime, Law and Deviance Series, vol. 6. Oxford, UK: JAI/Elsevier Science Press.

Fields, Jason; and Casper, Lynne. 2001. "America's families and living arrangements: Population characteristics." *Current Population Reports No. P20-537.* Washington, DC: U.S. Government Printing Office.

Fine, Gary Alan. 1983. *Shared Fantasy: Role Playing Games as Social Worlds.* Chicago, IL: University of Chicago Press.

———. 1993. "The sad demise, mysterious disappearance, and glorious triumph of symbolic interactionism." *Annual Review of Sociology,* vol. 19, 61–87.

———. 1996. *Kitchens: The Culture of Restaurant Work.* Berkeley, CA: University of California Press.

———. 1998. *Morel Tales: The Culture of Mushrooming.* Cambridge, MA: Harvard University Press.

Finegold, Kenneth; and Wherry, Laura. 2004. "Race, ethnicity, and economic well-being." Urban Institute. http://www.urban.org/url.cfm?ID=310968

Fischer, Claude. 1976. *The Urban Experience.* New York: Harcourt Brace Jovanovich.

Fischer, Claude S. 1994. "Changes in leisure activities, 1890–1940." *Journal of Social History,* vol. 27, no. 3 (spring): 453.

Fischer, Mary J.; and Kmec, Julie A. 2004. "Neighborhood socioeconomic conditions as moderators of family resource transmission: High school completion among at-risk youth." *Sociological Perspectives,* vol. 47, no. 4 (winter): 507–527.

Fish, Stanley. 1980. *Is There a Text in This Class? The Authority of Interpretive Communities.* Cambridge, MA: Harvard University Press.

Fishman, Pamela. 1978. "Interaction: The work women do." *Social Problems,* vol. 25, 433.

Fiske, Jonathan. 1989. *Understanding Popular Culture.* London: Unwin Hyman.

FitzGerald, Frances. 1980. *America Revised: History Schoolbooks in the Twentieth Century.* New York: Vintage Books.

Flannery, Matthew. 2005. "Kiva is micromedia." *Kiva Chronicles,* December 4. Social Edge. http://www.socialedge.org/blogs/kiva-chronicles, accessed 7/28/08.

Florida, Richard. 2002. *The Rise of the Creative Class: And How It Is Transforming Work, Leisure, Community and Everyday Life.* New York: Basic Books.

———. 2004. *Cities and the Creative Class.* New York: Routledge.

Foeman, A. K.; and Nance, T. 1999. "From miscegenation to multiculturalism: Perceptions and stages of interracial relationship development." *Journal of Black Studies,* vol. 29, 540–557.

Forbes Businesswire. 2008. "North American hospitality and tourism sector: A company and industry analysis." June. http://www.forbes.com/businesswire/feeds/businesswire/2008/10/13/businesswire20081013005502r1.html

Fortune. 2008a. "Fortune 500." May 5. CNNMoney.com. http://money.cnn.com/magazines/fortune/fortune500/2008/full_list/index.html, accessed April 7, 2009.

———. 2008b. "Global 500." July 21. http://money.cnn.com/magazines/fortune/global500/2008/full_list/.

Foucault, Michel. 1980. *Power/Knowledge: Selected Interviews and Other Writings.* Ed. Collin Gorder. New York: Pantheon.

Foundation for National Progress. 2007. Dmitry Krasny/Deka Design. Figure, "And then there were eight: 25 years of media mergers," *Mother Jones,* March/April, 49.

Fox, Greer Litton; and Kelly, Robert F. 1995. "Determinants of child custody arrangements at divorce." *Journal of Marriage and the Family,* vol. 57, no. 3, 693–708.

Fox, John. 1997. *Applied Regression Analysis, Linear Models, and Related Methods.* Thousand Oaks, CA: Sage.

Fox, Renee. 1957. "Training for uncertainty." In Robert Merton, ed., *The Student Physician.* Cambridge, MA: Harvard University Press.

Frerking, Beth. 2007. "For achievers, a new destination." *New York Times.* Education Life special section. April 27, pp. 23–25.

Freud, Sigmund. 1955 (orig. 1900). *The Interpretation of Dreams.* London: Hogarth.

———. 1905. *Three Essays on the Theory of Sexuality.* New York: Avon Books.

———. 1930. *Civilization and Its Discontents.* [in German].

Frey, William H. 2003. "The new migration equation." *Orlando Sentinel,* November 9.

Freyre, Gilberto. 1970. *The Masters and the Slaves.* New York: Alfred A. Knopf.

Friedan, Betty. 2001 (orig. 1963). *The Feminine Mystique.* New York: Norton.

Frieden, Bernard; and Sagalyn, Lynne B. 1992. *Downtown, Inc.: How America Rebuilds Cities.* Cambridge, MA: MIT Press.

Friedkin, Noah E. 2004. "Social cohesion." *Annual Review of Sociology,* vol. 30 (August): 409–425.

———; and Cook, Karen S. 1990. "Peer group influence." *Sociological Methods and Research,* vol. 19, no. 1, 122–143.

———; and Granovetter, Mark, eds. 1998. *A Structural Theory of Social Influence.* Structural Analysis in the Social Sciences. Cambridge, UK: Cambridge University Press.

Friedman, Ina R. 1995. *The Other Victims: First-Person Stories of Non-Jews Persecuted by the Nazis.* New York: Houghton Mifflin.

Fuller, Robert C. 2002. *Spiritual but Not Religious: Understanding Unchurched America.* New York: Oxford University Press.

Furstenburg, Frank; Hoffman, Saul; and Shrestha, Laura. 1995. "The effect of divorce on intergenerational transfers: New evidence." *Demography,* vol. 32, no. 3: 319–333.

Fussell, Paul. 1983. *Class: A Guide Through the American Status System.* New York: Touchstone.

Gallup Organization. 2006 (orig. 1996). *Religion in America.* Princeton, NJ: Princeton Religion Research Center.

Gamson, Joshua. 1999. *Freaks Talk Back: Tabloid Talk Shows and Sexual Nonconformity*. Chicago: University of Chicago Press.

Gans, Herbert J. 1962. *The Urban Villagers: Group and Class in the Life of Italian-Americans*. New York: MacMillan.

———. 1967. *The Levittowners: Ways of Life and Politics in a New Suburban Community*. New York: Columbia University Press.

———. 1971. "The uses of poverty: The poor pay all." *Social Policy*, July–August, 20–24.

Gans, Herbert J. 1999. *Popular Culture and High Culture: An Analysis and Evaluation of Taste*. New York: Basic Books.

Gansberg, Martin. 1964. "37 who saw murder didn't call the police: Apathy at stabbing of Queens woman shocks inspector." *New York Times*, March 27.

Garber, Marjorie. 1997. *Vested Interests: Cross Dressing and Cultural Anxiety*. London: Routledge.

———. 1998. *The Symptoms of Culture*. New York: Routledge.

Garfinkel, Harold. 1984 (orig. 1967). *Studies in Ethnomethodology*. Englewood Cliffs, NJ: Prentice Hall.

Garlington, Phil. 1998. "Protester lives in Redwoods 7 months; California environmentalists take a stand." *Pittsburgh Post-Gazette*, September 13, p. A13.

Garr, Emily. 2008. "The unemployment trend by state." Economic Policy Institute Economic Snapshots. www.epi.org/content.cfm/ webfeatures_snapshots_20080924

Garreau, Joel. 1992. *Edge City: Life on the New Frontier*. New York: Anchor Books.

Garrity, Brian. 2008. "Ringtone sales fizzling out." *New York Post*, March 28. http://www.nypost.com/seven/03282008/business/ringtone_ sales_fizzling_out_103910.htm

Garry, Patrick M.; and Spurlin, Candice J. 2007. "The effectiveness of media rating systems in preventing children's exposure to violent and sexually explicit media content: An empirical study." *Oklahoma City University Law Review*, vol. 32, no. 2. http://ssrn.com/ abstract=1139167

Geertz, Clifford. 1973. "Deep play: Notes on the Balinese cockfight." *The Interpretation of Cultures*. New York: Basic Books.

Gelles, Richard J. 1995. *Contemporary Families: A Sociological View*. Thousand Oaks, CA: Sage.

Gerbner, George; and Gross, L. 1976. "Living with television: The Violence Profile." *Journal of Communication* (spring).

———; Morgan, M.; and Signorielli, N. 1980. "The mainstreaming of America: Violence Profile No. 11." *Journal of Communication*, vol. 30, 10–29.

Gereffi, Gary; and Korzeniewicz, Miguel; eds. 1994. *Commodity Chains and Global Capitalism*. Westport, CT: Praeger.

Gergen, Kenneth. 1991. *The Saturated Self*. New York: Basic Books.

g42. 2006. "Facebook: Who is watching you?" *New Media & Community*, November 26. http://www.mysocialnetwork.net/blog/410/g42/, accessed 8/22/08.

Gibson, Campbell; and Lennon, Emily. 2001. "Historical census statistics on the foreign-born population of the United States: 1850–1990." U.S. Bureau of the Census, Population Division. http://www.census.gov/ population/www/ documentation/twps0029.html

Gilbert, Derrick I. M. 1998. *Catch the Fire!!! A Cross-Generation Anthology of Contemporary African-American Poetry*. New York: Riverhead Books.

Gilligan, Carol. 1982. *In a Different Voice: Psychological Theory and Women's Development*. Cambridge, MA: Harvard University Press.

Gilstrap, Peter. 2007. "Perez Hilton blog having problems." *Variety*, June 20.

Glaser, Jack; Dixit, Jay; and Green, Donald P. 2002. "Studying hate crime with the Internet: What makes racists advocate racial violence?" *Journal of Social Issues*, vol. 58, no. 1, 177–193.

Glaser, Mark. 2007. MediaShift. PBS. "Your guide to the digital divide." January 17. http://www.pbs.org/mediashift/2007/01/digging_deepery-our_guide_to_th.html

Glass, Ruth. 1964. "Aspects of change." In Centre for Urban Studies, ed., *London: Aspects of Change*. London: MacGibbon and Kee.

Gleick, P. H. 1998. "The world's water 1998–1999." Washington, DC: Island Press. Companion website: http://www.worldwater.org/table7. html, accessed 5/17/04.

Glenn, Norvell; and Marquard, Elizabeth. 2001. "Hooking up, hanging out and hoping for Mr. Right: College women on mating and dating." American Values Institute Report to the Independent Women's Forum. http://www.americanvalues.org/html/r-hooking_up.html

Glionna, John M. 2004. "TV ad contest targets president; Moveon.Org will run the winners nationally, a sign of interest groups' new election-year clout." *Los Angeles Times*, January 11, p. A27.

Global Gambling Guidance Group. 2008. "Higher risk of gambling addiction as more casinos open up in Asia." *G4Newsletter*, August. http:// www.gx4.com/newsletters/newsletter_september_08/.

Goffman, Erving. 1956. *Presentation of Self in Everyday Life*. Garden City, NY: Anchor Books.

———. 1961. *Asylums: Essays on the Social Situation of Mental Patients and Other Inmates*. Garden City, NY: Anchor Books.

———. 1962. *Stigma: Notes on the Management of Spoiled Identity*. Upper Saddle River, NJ: Prentice Hall.

———. 1971. *Relations in Public: Microstudies of the Public Order*. New York: Basic Books.

Goldberg, Herb. 1976. *The Hazards of Being Male*. New York: Nash.

González, Eduardo. 2007. "Migrant farm workers: Our nation's invisible population." National Extension Diversity Center. http://www.ediver-sitycenter.net/migrantfarmers.php

Goodacre, Daniel M. 1953. "Group characteristics of good and poor performing combat units." *Sociometry*, vol. 16, no. 2 (May): 168–179.

Goode, Erich. 1997. *Deviant Behavior*. 5th ed. Upper Saddle River, NJ: Prentice Hall.

Goode, William J. 1982. *The Family*. Englewood Cliffs, NJ: Prentice Hall.

Goodman, Ellen. 2002. "College gender gap stirs old bias." *Boston Globe*, August 4.

Goodnough, Abby. 2009. "Gay rights groups celebrate victories in marriage push." *New York Times*, April 7. http://www.nytimes. com/2009/04/08/us/08vermont.html, accessed 5/1/09.

Goodstein, Laurie. 2004. "Personal and political, Bush's faith blurs lines." *New York Times*, October 26, p. A21.

Gottdiener, Mark; Collins, Claudia C.; and Dickens, David R. 1999. *Las Vegas: The Social Production of an All-American City*. Malden, MA: Blackwell.

Gottman, Jean. 1961. *Megalopolis: The Urbanized Northeastern Seaboard of the United States*. New York: Twentieth Century Fund.

———; and Robert Harper. 1990. *Since Megalopolis: The Urban Writings of Jean Gottman*. Baltimore, MD: Johns Hopkins University Press.

Gottschalk, Simon. 1993. "Uncomfortably numb: Countercultural impulses in the postmodern era." *Symbolic Interaction*, vol. 16, no. 4, 357–378.

Goyette, Kimberly; and Xie, Yu. 1999. "Educational expectations of Asian-American youth: Determinants and ethnic differences." *Sociology of Education*, vol. 71, 24–38.

Gozzi, Raymond, Jr. 1996. "Will the media create a global village?" *ETC: A Review of General Semantics*, vol. 53, 65–68.

GPO Access. 2008. "Budget of the United States government: Browse fiscal year 2008." January 28. http://www.gpoaccess.gov/usbudget/fy08/ browse.html, accessed 3/12/09.

Graham, Lawrence Otis. 1996. *A Member of the Club: Reflections on Life in a Racially Polarized World*. New York: Harper Perennial.

Gramsci, Antonio. 1985. *Selections from Cultural Writings*. Cambridge, MA: Harvard University Press.

———. 1988. *An Antonio Gramsci Reader*. Ed. David Forgacs. Boston: Schocken.

Grandey, A. 2003. "When 'the show must go on': Surface and deep acting as determinants of emotional exhaustion and peer-rated service delivery." *Academy of Management Journal,* vol. 46, no. 1, 86–96.

Granfield, Robert. 1992. *Making Elite Lawyers.* New York: Routledge.

Granovetter, Mark. 1973. "The strength of weak ties." *American Journal of Sociology,* vol. 78, no. 6, 1360–1380.

Grealy, Lucy. 1994. *Autobiography of a Face.* Boston: Houghton Mifflin.

Green, Frank. 2002. "Food fight: County's 11,000 unionized grocery workers fear pay will plummet when Wal-Mart enters the market." *San Diego Union Tribune,* August 18, p. H1.

Green, John C. 2004. "Fourth national survey of religion and politics." In *The American Religious Landscape and Politics, 2004.* Pew Forum on Religion and Public Life, Washington, DC. http://www.pewforum.org/publications/surveys/green.pdf

Greenfeld, L., et al. 1998. "Violence by intimates: Analysis of data on crimes by current or former spouses, boyfriends, and girlfriends." *Bureau of Justice Statistics Factbook.* http://www.ojp.usdoj.gov/bjs/pub/pdf/vi.pdf, accessed 1/14/04.

Greenhouse, Steven. 1997. "Concluding the UPS strike." *New York Times,* August 20, p. A1.

———. 1999. "Activism surges at campuses nationwide, and labor is at issue." *New York Times,* March 29. http://www.sweatshopwatch.org/swatch/headlines/1999/nyt_mar.html

Guber, Deborah Lynn. 2003. *The Grassroots of a Green Revolution: Polling America on the Environment.* Cambridge, MA: MIT Press.

Gubrium, Jaber; and Buckholdt, D. R. 1982. "Fictive family: Everyday usage, analytic, and human service considerations." *American Anthropologist,* vol. 84, no. 4, 878.

Gubrium, Jaber; and Holstein, James. 1990. *What Is Family?* New York, NY: Mayfield Publishing.

Gutfreund, Owen. 2004. *Twentieth Century Sprawl: Highways and the Reshaping of the American Landscape.* New York: Oxford University Press.

Haas, Jack; and Shaffir, William. 1977. "The professionalization of medical students: Development competence and a cloak of competence." *Symbolic Interaction,* vol. 1, 71–88.

———. 1982. "Taking on the role of doctor: A dramaturgical analysis of professionalization." *Symbolic Interaction,* vol. 5, 187–203.

Habermas, Jürgen. 1984. *The Theory of Communicative Action, Vol. 1: Reason and the Rationalization of Society.* Trans. Thomas McCarthy. Boston: Beacon Press.

———. 1987. *The Theory of Communicative Action, Vol. 2: Lifeworld and System: A Critique of Functionalist Reason.* Trans. Thomas McCarthy. Boston: Beacon Press.

Hagberg, Richard; and Heifetz, Julie. 2002. "How to tell the CEO his baby is ugly." http://w3.hcgnet.com/research_uglybaby.html

Haizlip, Shirlee Taylor. 1994. *The Sweeter the Juice: A Family Memoir in Black and White.* New York: Simon and Schuster.

Hakim, Danny. 2001. "Fidelity picks a president of funds unit." *New York Times,* May 22, p. C1.

Haley, A. J.; and Johnston, B. S. 1998. "Menaces to management: A developmental view of British soccer hooligans, 1961–1986." *Sport Journal,* vol. 1. http://www.thesportjournal.org/1998journal/vol1-no1/menaces.asp, accessed 2/2/04.

Hall, Stuart. 1980. "Encoding/decoding." In S. Hall, D. Hobson, A. Lowe, and P. Willis, eds., *Culture, Media, Language.* London: Hutchinson.

Halle, David. 1993. *Inside Culture: Art and Class in the American Home.* Chicago, IL: University of Chicago Press.

Hamer D. H.; Hu, S.; Magnuson, V. L.; Hu, N.; and Pattatucci, A. M. 1993. "A linkage between DNA markers on the X chromosome and male sexual orientation." Science, vol. 261, no. 5119, 321–327.

Hao, Lingxin; and Cherlin, Andrew J. 2004. "Welfare reform and teenage pregnancy, childbirth, and school dropout." *Journal of Marriage and Family,* vol. 66, 179–194.

Hardin, Garrett. 1968. "The tragedy of the commons." *Science,* vol. 162, 1243–1248.

———. 1993. *Living within Limits.* New York: Oxford University Press.

Hartley, Heather; and Drew, Tricia. 2001. "Gendered messages in sex ed films: Trends and implications for female sexual problems." *Women & Therapy,* vol. 24, nos. 1–2, 133–146.

Harvard Magazine. 2008. "Race in a genetic world." May–June: 62–65.

Harvey, David. 1989. *The Condition of Postmodernity: An Enquiry into the Origins of Cultural Change.* Cambridge, MA: Blackwell.

Havitz, Mark E.; and Dimanche, Frederic. 1999. "Leisure involvement revisited: Drive properties and paradoxes." *Journal of Leisure Research,* vol. 31, no. 2 (spring): 122.

Hawley, Amos H. 1950. *Human Ecology: A Theory of Community Structure.* New York: Ronald Press.

Hays, Sharon. 2003. *Flat Broke with Children: Women in the Age of Welfare Reform.* New York: Oxford University Press.

Heeks, Richard. 2008. "Real world production in developing countries for the virtual economies of online games." Developmental Informatics Group IDPM, SED, University of Manchester, UK. http://www.sed.manchester.ac.uk/idpm/research/publications/wp/di/documents/di_wp32.pdf, accessed 10/22/08.

Heilprin, John. 2005. "FBI: Radical-activist groups are major threat." *Seattle Times,* May 19, 2005. http://seattletimes.nwsource.com/html/nationworld/2002280292_ecoterror19.html

Herek, G. M. 1990. "The context of anti-gay violence: Notes on cultural and psychological heterosexism." *Journal of Interpersonal Violence,* vol. 5, 316–333.

Hertz, Marci Feldman, and David-Ferdon, Corrine. 2008. "Electronic media and youth violence: A CDC issue brief for educators and caregivers." Atlanta, GA: Centers for Disease Control.

Hewitt, John. P. 2000. *Self and Society: A Symbolic Interactionist Social Pyschology.* Boston: Allyn and Bacon.

Hill, Jason. 2008. "Game girls." *Sydney Morning Herald,* May 8. http://www.smh.com.au/news/articles/game-girls/2008/05/07/1209839660016.html.

Hill, Julia. 2000. *The Legacy of Luna: The Story of a Tree, a Woman and the Story to Save the Redwoods.* San Fancisco: HarperCollins.

———. 2002. *One Makes the Difference: Inspiring Actions That Change Our World.* San Francisco: HarperCollins.

Hill, Peter; and Wood, Ralph. 1999. *Measures of Religiosity.* Birmingham, AL: Religious Education Press.

Hizer, Cynthia. 1997. "Versatile vegetarian; Diet based on plants has saving graces." *Atlanta Journal-Constitution,* June 5, p. H3.

Hobbs, Frank; and Damon, Bonnie. 1999. "Sixty-five plus in the United States." *Current Population Reports,* Special Studies, no. P23-190. Washington, DC: U.S. Dept. of Commerce, Bureau of the Census.

Hochschild, Arlie Russel. 1975. "The sociology of feeling and emotion." In Marcia Millman and Rosabeth Moss Kanter, eds., *Another Voice.* Garden City, NJ: Doubleday.

———. 1985 (orig. 1983). *The Managed Heart: The Commercialization of Human Feeling.* Berkeley, CA: University of California Press.

———; and Machung, Anne. 1989. *The Second Shift: Working Parents and the Revolution at Home.* New York: Viking.

Hochschild, Jennifer L. 1996. *Facing Up to the American Dream: Race, Class, and the Soul of the Nation.* Princeton, NJ: Princeton University Press.

Hodge, Robert; and Tripp, David. 1986. *Children and Television: A Semiotic Approach.* Cambridge, UK: Polity Press.

Hoffman, Matt; and Torres, Lisa. 2002. "It's not only 'who you know' that matters: Gender, personal contacts, and job lead quality." *Gender and Society,* vol. 16, no. 6, 793–813.

Hogan, Jackie. 2003. "Staging the nation: Gendered and ethnicized discourses of national identity in Olympic opening ceremonies." *Journal of Sport and Social Issues,* vol. 27, no. 2, 100–123.

Holder, Kelly. 2006. "Voting and registration in the election of November 2004." U.S. Census Bureau Report, March.

Holdren, John P.; Daily, Gretchen; and Ehrlich, Paul R. 1995. "The meaning of sustainability: Biogeophysical aspects." In M. Munasinghe and W. Shearer, eds., *Defining and Measuring Sustainability: The Biogeophysical Foundations.* Washington, DC: World Bank.

Holstein, James; and Gubrium, Jaber. 1995a. *The Active Interview.* Thousand Oaks, CA: Sage.

———. 1995b. "Deprivatization and the construction of domestic life." *Journal of Marriage and the Family,* vol. 57, no. 4 (November): 894.

———. 2000. *The Self We Live By: Narrative Identity in a Postmodern World.* New York: Oxford University Press.

Homans, George. 1951. *The Human Group.* New York: Harcourt Brace Jovanovich.

hooks, bell. 1990. *Yearning: Race, Gender and Cultural Politics.* Boston: South End Press.

———. 2003. *We Real Cool: Black Men and Masculinity.* London: Routledge.

Hughes, Jonathon; and Cain, Louis. 1994. *American Economic History.* 4th ed. New York: HarperCollins College Publishers.

Hughes, Z. 2003. "Why some brothers only date whites and 'others.'" *Ebony,* vol. 58, 70–74.

Hull, Elizabeth. 2002. "Florida's former felons: You can't vote here." *Commonwealth,* vol. 129, no. 12 (June 14): 16.

Human Rights Watch. 2007, July. *Forced Apart: Families Separated and Immigrants Harmed by United States Deportation Policy.* New York: Human Rights Watch. http://www.hrw.org/reports/2007/us0707/

Humphrey, Craig R.; Lewis, Tammy L.; and Buttel, Frederick H. 2002. *Environment, Energy, and Society: A New Synthesis.* Belmont, CA: Wadsworth.

Hunt, G.; and Satterlee, S. 1986. "Cohesion and division: Drinking in an English village." *Man* (New Series), vol. 21, no. 3, 521–537.

Hustvedt, Siri. 2002. "9/11 six months on." *The Observer,* March 10, Special Supplement, p. 6.

Ignatiev, Noel. 1996. *How the Irish Became White.* London: Routledge.

INC.com. 1999. "Employee theft still costing business." http://www.inc.com/articles/1999/05/13731.html

Independent Sector. 2005. "Value of volunteer time." http://www.independentsector.org/programs/research/ volunteer_time.html

Independent Women's Forum. 2001. "Hooking up, hanging out, and hoping for Mr. Right: College women on dating and mating today." Foundation report.

Insurance Institute for Highway Safety. 2006. "Fatality facts 2006: Teenagers." http://www.iihs.org/research/fatality_facts_2006/teenagers.html

International Business Times. 2008. "Which U.S. cities rank highest in foreclosure rates?" October 23. http://www.ibtimes.com/articles/20081023/which-cities-rank-highest-foreclosure-rates.htm

International Game Developers Online Games Quarterly. 2005. "The demographics issue: Understanding the casual gamer." Vol. 1, no. 2 (Spring). http://www.igda.org/online/quarterly/1_2/casual.php

Isikoff, Michael. 2004. "The dots never existed." *Newsweek,* July 19.

Jackson, Edgar L. 1999. "Leisure and the Internet." *Journal of Physical Education, Recreation & Dance,* vol. 70, no. 9 (November): 18.

Jackson, K. T. 1985. *Crabgrass Frontier: The Suburbanization of the United States.* New York: Oxford University Press.

Jackson, Phillip. 1968. *Life in Classrooms.* New York: Holt, Rinehart, and Winston.

Jackson-Jacobs, Curtis. 2004. "Taking a beating: The narrative gratifications of fighting as an underdog." In Hayward et al., eds., *Cultural Criminology Unleashed.* London: Glasshouse.

Jahnke, A. 2001. "Can free trade save the world?" *Darwin Magazine,* April 23. http://www.darwinmag.com/connect.opinion/column.html?ArticleID-97

Janofsky, Michael; and Lee, Jennifer Lee. 2003. "Net group tries to click Democrats to power." *New York Times,* National Desk, November 18, p. A22.

Janus, Irving L. 1971. "Groupthink." *Psychology Today,* November.

———. 1982. *Groupthink.* 2nd ed. Boston: Houghton-Mifflin.

Jenkins, Henry. 1992. *Textual Poachers: Television Fans and Participatory Culture.* London. Routledge.

Jensen, Joyce. 2000. "Old urban legends never die (but they don't get any truer)." *New York Times,* April 8, p. B9.

Jin, Ge. Forthcoming. "Chinese gold farmers." http://www.we-make-money-not-art.com/archives/2006/03/ge-jin-a-phd-st.php.

Johnson, Cathryn. 1994. "Gender, legitimate authority, and leader-subordinate conversations." *American Sociological Review,* vol. 59, no. 1 (February): 122–135.

Johnson, Kenneth M. 1999. "The rural rebound." *Population Reference Bureau Reports on America,* vol. 1, no. 3 (August).

Johnson, Kenneth M.; and Beale, Calvin L. 1994. "The recent revival of widespread population growth in nonmetropolitan America." *Rural Sociology,* vol. 59, no. 4, 655–667.

———. 1995. "The rural rebound revisited." *American Demographics,* July.

———. 1998. "The revival of rural America." *Wilson Quarterly,* vol. 22, no. 2, 16–27.

Jones, Steve. 1997. *Virtual Culture: Identity and Communication in Cybersociety.* Thousand Oaks, CA: Sage.

———; and Philip Howard, eds. 2003. *Society Online: The Internet in Context.* Thousand Oaks, CA: Sage.

Juergensmeyer, Mark. 2003. *Terror in the Mind of God: The Global Rise of Religious Violence.* Berkeley, CA: University of California Press.

Kaczor, Bill. 1996. " Neighborhood blames years of woe on 'Mount Dioxin.'" *Charleston Gazette,* March 11.

Kaiser Commission. 2006. "The uninsured: A primer: Key facts about Americans without health insurance." http://www.kff.org/uninsured/upload/7451-021.pdf

Kalmijn M. 1998. "Intermarriages and homogamy—Causes, patterns, trends." *Annual Review of Sociology,* vol. 24, 395–421.

Kao, Grace; and Joyner, Kara. 2005. "Interracial relationships and the transition to adulthood." *American Sociological Review,* vol. 70, no. 4, 563–582.

Karau, S. J.; and Williams, K. D. 1993. "Social loafing: A meta-analytic review and theoretical integration." *Journal of Personality and Social Psychology,* vol. 65, 681–706.

Kass, Leon R. 1997. "The end of courtship." *Public Interest,* vol. 126 (winter): 39.

Katz, Elihu. 1959. "Mass communication research and the study of popular culture." *Studies in Public Communication,* 2.

———; and Lazarsfeld, Paul F. 1955. *Personal Influence: The Part Played by People in the Flow of Mass Communications.* New York: Macmillan Free Press.

Katz, Jack. 1988. *Seductions of Crime: Moral and Sensual Attractions of Doing Evil.* New York: Basic Books.

———. 1997. "Ethnography's warrants." *Sociological Methods & Research,* vol. 25, no. 4, 391–423.

———. 1999. *How Emotions Work.* Chicago: University of Chicago Press.

Katz, Jack, and Robert Garot. 2003. "Provocative looks: Gang appearance and dress codes in an inner-city alternative school." *Ethnography* vol. 4, no. 3: 421–454.

Katznelson, Ira. 2005. *When Affirmative Action Was White: An Untold History of Racial Inequality in Twentieth Century America.* New York: Norton.

Kaufman, Jason. 2008. Harvard University, Department of Sociology home page. http://www.wjh.harvard.edu/soc/faculty/kaufman/, accessed 7/29/08.

Keith, Verna M.; and Finlay, Barbara. 1988. "The impact of parental divorce on children's educational attainment, marital timing, and likelihood of divorce." *Journal of Marriage and the Family,* vol. 50, no. 3, 797–809.

Kellner, Douglas. 2001. "Globalization, technopolitics and revolution." *Theoria,* iss. 98, 14–34.

Kellner, Douglas. 2005. *Media Spectacle and the Crisis of Democracy: Terrorism, War and Election Battles.* Boulder, CO: Paradigm.

Kelly, Barbara. 1993. *Expanding the American Dream: Building and Rebuilding Levittown.* Albany, NY: State University of New York Press.

Kennedy, R. 2001. "Interracial marriages should be encouraged" in M. Williams, ed., *Interracial America: Opposing Viewpoints.* San Diego: Greenhaven Press.

Kephart, William. 2000. *Extraordinary Groups: An Examination of Unconventional Lifestyles.* New York: W. H. Freeman.

Kerbo, Harold R.; and Gonzalez, Juan J. 2003. "Class and non-voting in comparative perspective: Possible causes and consequences in the United States." *Research in Political Sociology,* vol. 12, 175–196.

Kessler, R. C. 2003. "Epidemiology of women and depression." *Journal of Affective Disorders,* vol. 74, no. 1, 5–13.

Kilbourne, Jean. 1999. *Killing Us Softly 3.* Dir. Sut Jhally. Center for Media Literacy.

Kilmartin, Christopher. 2004. *The Masculine Self.* New York: Macmillan.

Kimmel, Michael. 1987. *Changing Men: New Directions in Research on Men and Masculinity.* Thousand Oaks, CA: Sage.

King, A. 1995. Outline of a practical theory of football violence." *Sociology,* vol. 24, 635–652.

Kinsey, Alfred C.; Pomeroy, Wardell B.; and Martin, Clyde E. 1998 (orig. 1948). *Sexual Behavior in the Human Male.* Bloomington, IN: Indiana University Press.

———; and Gebhard, Paul H. 1998 (orig. 1953). *Sexual Behavior in the Human Female.* Bloomington, IN: Indiana University Press.

Kinsley, Michael. 2002. "Deliver us from evil." *Slate,* September 19. http://www.slate.com/id/2071148

Kitsuse, John I. 980. "Coming out all over: Deviants and the politics of social problems." *Social Problems,* vol. 28, 1–13.

Kitzinger, C. 1987. *The Social Construction of Lesbianism.* London: Sage.

Kiva. "Press center: Facts and statistics." http://www.kiva.org/about/facts, accessed 6/28/08.

Klapper, J. 1960. *The Effects of Mass Communication.* New York: Free Press.

Klein, Naomi. 2000. *No Logo: Taking Aim at the Brand Bullies.* New York: Picador.

Kleinenberg, Eric. 2002. *Heat Wave: A Social Autopsy of a Disaster in Chicago.* Chicago: University of Chicago Press.

———. 2007. "Breaking the news." *Mother Jones,* March/April. http://www.motherjones.com/news/feature/2007/03/breaking_the_news.html

Kleinman, Sherryl. 1984. *Equals Before God: Seminarians as Humanistic Professionals.* Chicago: University of Chicago Press.

Kolbe, Richard H.; Langefeld, Carl D. 1993. "Appraising gender role portrayals in TV commercials." *Sex Roles,* vol. 28, no. 7, 393–417.

Kollock, Peter. 1998. "Social dilemmas: The anatomy of cooperation." *Annual Review of Sociology,* vol. 24, 183–214.

———; Blumstein, Phillip; and Schwartz, Pepper. 1985. "Sex and power in interaction: conversational privileges and duties." *American Sociological Review,* vol. 50, no. 1. (February): 34–46.

Kosmin, Barry A.; Mayer, Egon; and Keysar, Ariela. 2001. American Religious Identification Survey. The Graduate Center of the City University of New York. http://www.gc.cuny.edu/faculty/research_briefs/aris/aris_index.htm

Koteskey, Ronald L. 2003. *What Missionaries Ought to Know: A Handbook for Life and Service.* Wilmore, KY: New Hope International Ministries.

Kouri, Jim. 2008. "MoveOn.org gave $88 million for Obama victory." November 7. http://www.intellectualconservative.com/2008/11/07/moveonorg-gave-88-million-for-obama-victory/

Kozeny, Geoff. 1995. "Intentional communities: Lifestyle based on ideals." http://www.ic.org/pnp/cdir/1995/01kozeny.html

Kozol, J. 1991. *Savage Inequalities: Children in America's Schools.* New York: Crown Publishing.

Krakauer, Jon. 1997. *Into the Wild.* New York: Anchor Books.

Krashen, S. D. 1996. *Under Attack: The Case against Bilingual Education.* Culver City, CA: Language Education Associates.

Kraus, Richard G. 1995. "Play's new identity: Big business." *Journal of Physical Education, Recreation & Dance,* vol. 66, no. 8 (October): 36.

Krausz, Tibor. 2007. "In exile, a former gang member finds a reason to dance." *Christian Science Monitor,* October 23, 20.

Kreider, Rose M.; and Fields, Jason M. 2001. "Number, timing, and duration of marriages and divorces: Fall 1996." In U.S. Bureau of the Census, *Current Population Reports,* P70-80. Washington, DC: U.S. Government Printing Office.

———. 2002. "Number, timing, and duration of marriages and divorces: 1996," in U.S. Bureau of the Census, *Current Population Reports.* Washington, DC: U.S. Government Printing Office.

Kristof, N.; and WuDunn, S. 2000. "Two cheers for sweatshops." *New York Times Magazine,* September 24. http://www.nytimes.com/library/magazine/home/20000924mag-sweatshops.html

Krueger, Alan B. 2002. "The apple falls close to the tree, even in the land of opportunity." *New York Times,* November 14, p. C2.

Krugman, Paul. 1997. "In praise of cheap labor: Bad jobs at bad wages are better than no jobs at all." *Slate,* March 21. http://slate.msn.com/id/1918

Krupat, K 1997. "From war zone to free trade zone." In A. Ross, ed., *No sweat: Fashion, free trade, and the rights of garment workers.* New York: Verso.

Kuhn, Manfred; and McPartland, T. S. 1954. "An empirical investigation of self-attitude." *American Sociological Review,* vol. 19, 68–79.

Kuhn, Thomas S. 1957. *The Copernican Revolution: Planetary Astronomy in the Development of Western Thought.* Cambridge, MA: Harvard University Press.

———. 1970 (orig. 1962). *The Structure of Scientific Revolutions.* Chicago, IL: University of Chicago Press.

Kunstler, J. H. 1993. *The Geography of Nowhere: The Rise and Decline of America's Man-Made Landscape.* New York: Simon and Schuster.

Kurzweil, Ray. 1990. *The Age of Intelligent Machines.* Cambridge, MA: MIT Press.

Lachman, Margie. 2004. "Development in midlife." *Annual Review of Psychology,* vol. 55: 305–31.

Lakshmanan, Indira. 2006. "Gangs roil Central America; troubles linked to US deportees." *Boston Globe,* April 17, A1.

Lane, J. Mark; and Tabak, Ronald J. 1991. "Judicial activism and legislative 'reform' of federal habeas corpus: A critical analysis of recent developments and current proposals." *Albany Law Review,* vol. 55, no. 1, 1–95.

Lareau, Annette. 2003. *Unequal Childhoods: Class, Race and Family Life.* Berkeley, CA: University of California Press.

Larson, R. W.; and Richards, M. H. 1991. "Daily companionship in late childhood and early adolescence: Changing developmental contexts." *Child Development,* vol. 62, 284–300.

Lasch, Christopher. 1977. *Haven in a Heartless World: The Family Besieged.* New York: Basic Books.

Lazarsfeld, Paul; and Katz, Elihu. 1955. *Personal Influence.* New York: Free Press.

Le, C. N. 2001. "Interracial dating and marriage." *Asian-Nation: The Landscape of Asian America.* http://www.asian-nation.org/issues3. html, accessed 2/28/03.

Le Bon, Gustave. 1896. *The Crowd: A Study of the Popular Mind.* New York: Viking Press.

Legal Marriage Alliance of Washington. 2007. "FAQs—quick answers about the freedom to marry." http://www.lmaw.org/faqs.htm#a5 and http://www.lmaw.org/faqs.htm#a6, accessed 3/12/07.

Leidner, Robin. 1993. *Fast Food, Fast Talk.* Berkeley, CA: University of California Press.

Lemert, Edwin M. 1951. *Social Pathology: A Systematic Approach to the Theory of Sociopathic Behavior.* New York: McGraw-Hill.

Lepowsky, Maria Alexandra. 1993. *Gender and Power from Fruit of the Motherland.* New York: Columbia University Press.

Lerner, Melvin. 1965. "Evaluation of performance as a function of performer's reward and attractiveness." *Journal of Personality and Social Psychology,* vol.1, no. 4.

———. 1980. *The Belief in a Just World: A Fundamental Delusion.* New York: Plenum Press.

LeVay, Simon. 1991. "A difference in hypothalamic structure between heterosexual and homosexual men." *Science,* vol. 253, 1034–1037.

———. 1993. *The Sexual Brain.* Cambridge, MA: MIT Press.

Levinson, David. 2002. *Encyclopedia of Crime and Punishment.* Thousand Oaks, CA: Sage.

Levi-Strauss, C. 1969 (orig. 1949). *The Elementary Structures of Kinship.* Rev. ed. Ed. R. Needham. Trans. J. Bell and J. von Sturmer. Boston: Beacon Press.

Lewis, Christopher Alan; Shelvin, Mark; McGuckin, Conor; and Navratil, Marek. 2001. "The Santa Clara Strength of Religious Faith Questionnaire: Confirmatory factor analysis." *Pastoral Psychology,* vol. 49, no. 5. http://www.infm.ulst.ac.uk/~chris/64.pdf

Lewis, Jacqueline. 1998. "Learning to strip: The socialization experiences of exotic dancers." *Canadian Journal of Human Sexuality,* vol. 7, 1–16.

Lewis, Oscar. 1959. *Five Families: Mexican Case Studies in the Culture of Poverty.* New York: Basic Books.

Li, J.; and Singelmann, J. 1998. "Gender differences in class mobility: A comparative study of the United States, Sweden, and West Germany." *Acta Sociologica,* vol. 41, no. 4, 315–333.

Liazos, Alexander. 1972. "The poverty of the sociology of deviance: Nuts, sluts and perverts." *Social Problems,* vol. 20, 103–120.

Lockman, Darcy. 2002. "What fuels urban legends? (emotional selection)." *Psychology Today,* vol. 35, no. 2 (March–April): 21.

Lofland, Lyn. 1973. *A World of Strangers: Order and Action in Urban Public Space.* New York: Basic Books.

Long, L.; and Nucci, A. 1998. "Accounting for two population turnarounds in nonmetropolitan America." *Research in Rural Sociology and Development,* iss. 7, 47–70.

Longley, Robert. 2005. "Number of 'majority-minority' states grows: Texas' minority population hits 50.2 percent." About.com. http:// usgovinfo.about.com/od/censusandstatistics/a/minmajpop.htm.

Lortie, Dan. 1968. "Shared ordeal and induction to work." In Howard Becker, Blancher Greer, David Reisman, and Robert Weiss, eds., *Institutions and the Person.* Chicago: Aldine.

Loseke, Donileen; and Cahill, Spencer. 1986. "Actors in search of a character: Student social workers' quest for professional identity." *Symbolic Interaction,* vol. 9, 245–258.

Loving v. Virginia. 1967. 388, U.S. 1. June 12.

Lumpkin, Angela; and Williams, Linda D. 1991. "An analysis of *Sports Illustrated* feature articles, 1954–1987." *Sociology of Sport Journal,* vol. 8, no. 1, 16–32.

Lynd, Robert S.; and Lynd, Helen Merrell. 1937. *Middletown in Transition: A Study in Cultural Conflicts.* New York: Harcourt Brace.

———. 1959 (orig. 1929). *Middletown: A Study in Modern American Culture.* San Diego, CA: Harvest Books/Harcourt Brace.

Maag, Christopher. 2007. "A hoax turned fatal draws anger but no charges." *New York Times,* November 28, A23. http://www.nytimes. com/2007/11/28/us/28hoax.html

Maccoby, E. E.; and Jacklin, C. N. 1987. "Sex segregation in childhood." In H. W. Reese, ed., *Advances in Child Development and Behavior.* Orlando, FL: Academic Press.

Macfarquhar, Neil. 2001. "As anger smolders in the streets, Arab governments temper remarks, or say nothing." *New York Times,* October 9, p. B8.

MacKinnon, Catharine A. 2005. *Women's Lives, Men's Laws.* Cambridge, MA: Belknap Press.

Madison, Amber. 2006. *Hooking Up: A Girl's All-Out Guide to Sex and Sexuality.* Amherst, NY: Prometheus Books.

"Madonna has still got it." 2008, July 28. *What Would Tyler Durden Do?* http://www.wwtdd.com/index.phtml?t=madonna&start=36, accessed 3/11/09.

Magleby, David B., ed. 2000. *Outside Money: Soft Money and Issue Advocacy in the 1998 Congressional Elections.* Lanham, MD: Rowman & Littlefield.

Malamuth, Neil; and Donnerstein, Edward; eds. 1984. *Pornography and Sexual Aggression.* New York: Academic Press.

Malthus, Thomas. 1997 (orig. 1798). *An Essay on the Principle of Population: An Essay on the Principle of Population, as it Affects the Future Improvement of Society with Remarks on the Speculations of Mr. Godwin, M. Condorcet, and Other Writers.* London: printed for J. Johnson, St. Paul's Churchyard. Rendered into HTML format by Ed Stephan, 8/10/97. www.ac.wwu.edu/~stephan/malthus/ malthus.0.html, accessed 5/19/04.

Mann, Susan A.; Grimes, Michael D.; Kemp, Alice Abel; and Jenkins, Pamela J. 1997. "Paradigm shifts in family sociology? Evidence from three decades of family textbooks." *Journal of Family Issues,* vol. 18, no. 3 (May): 315.

Marcelo, Karlo Barrios; Lopez, Mark Hugo; and Kirby, Emily Hoban. 2007. "Civic engagement among minority youth." College Park. MD: Center for Information and Research on Civic Learning and Engagement (CIRCLE). January 1. Based on the 2006 Civic and Political Health of the Nation Survey. http://www.civicyouth.org/PopUps/ FactSheets/FS_07_minority_ce.pdf

Marcuse, Herbert. 1991 (orig. 1964). *One-Dimensional Man: Studies in the Ideology of Advanced Industrial Society.* Boston: Beacon Press.

Marklein, Mary Beth. 2008. "Community colleges at a turning point." *USA Today,* August 1. http://www.usatoday.com/news/ education/2008-07-22-comcol-main_N.htm

Martin, Laura. 1986. "Eskimo words for snow: A case study in the genesis and decay of an anthropological example." *American Anthropologist,* vol. 88, no. 2, 418–423.

Martineau, Harriet. 1837. *Society in America.* London: Saunders and Otley.

———. 1838. *Retrospect of Western Travel.* London: Saunders and Otley.

———. 1853. *The Positive Philosophy of Auguste Comte.* London: Chapman

Marx, Karl. 1982 (orig. 1848). *The Communist Manifesto.* New York: International.

———. 2001. *Selected Writings.* Ed. David McLellan. Oxford: Oxford University Press.

———. 2006 (orig. 1890). *Das Kapital.* Miami, FL: Synergy International of the Americas, Ltd.

Marx, Karl; and Engels, Friedrich. 1962. *Selected Works.* 2 vols. Moscow: Foreign Language Publishing House.

Massey, D. S.; and Denton N. A. 1993. *American Apartheid: Segregation and the Making of the Underclass.* Cambridge, MA: Harvard University Press.

Matsuda, Mari J.: Lawrence, C. R.; Delgado, Richard; and Crenshaw, Kimberle. 1993. *Words That Wound: Critical Race Theory, Assaultive Speech and the First Amendment.* Boulder, CO: Westview Press.

Matza, David. 1969. *Becoming Deviant.* Englewood Cliffs, NJ: Prentice Hall.

Mauss, Armand L. 1975. *Social Problems as Social Movements.* Philadelphia, PA: J. B. Lippincott.

Mayer, Susan. 1997. *What Money Can't Buy: Family Income and Children's Life Chances.* Cambridge, MA: Harvard University Press.

McCaa, Robert. 1994. "Child marriage and complex families among the Nahuas of ancient Mexico." *Latin American Population History Bulletin,* 26, 2–11.

McCall, L. 2001. "Sources of racial wage inequality in metropolitan labor markets: Racial, ethnic, and gender differences." *American Sociological Review,* vol. 66, no. 4 (August): 520–541.

McChesney, Robert. 1997. *Corporate Media and the Threat to Democracy.* Open Media Pamphlet Series. New York: Seven Stories Press.

_____. 2000. *Rich Media, Poor Democracy: Communication Politics in Dubious Times.* New York: New Press.

_____. 2004. *The Problem of the Media: U.S. Communication Politics in the Twenty-First Century.* New York: Monthly Review Press.

McCloskey, Deirdre. 1999. *Crossing: A Memoir.* Chicago, IL: University of Chicago Press.

McCombs, Maxwell; and Shaw, Donald. 1972. "The agenda-setting function of mass media." *Public Opinion Quarterly,* vol. 36, no. 2 (Summer): 176–187.

_____. 1977. "The agenda-setting function of the press." In D. Shaw and M. McCombs, eds., *The Emergence of American Political Issues: The Agenda-Setting Function of the Press* (pp. 89-105). St. Paul, MN: West Publishing.

McDonald, Michael. 2008. United States Election Project. "2008 preliminary voter turnout." http://elections.gmu.edu/preliminary_vote_2008.html, accessed 11/14/08.

McGhee, Paul E.; and Frueh, Terry. 1980. "Television viewing and the learning of sex-role stereotypes." *Sex Roles,* vol. 6, no. 2, 179.

McGinn, Daniel. 2006. "Marriage by the numbers." *Newsweek,* June 5.

McGrane, Bernard. 1994. *The Un-TV and the 10 mph Car: Experiments in Personal Freedom and Everyday Life.* New York: Small Press.

McIntyre, Shelby; Moberg, Dennis J.; and Posner, Barry Z. 1980. "Preferential treatment in preselection decisions according to sex and race." *Academy of Management Journal,* vol. 23, no. 4 (December): 738–749.

McLuhan, Marshall. 1964. *Understanding Media: The Extensions of Man.* New York: McGraw Hill.

McMichael, Philip. 1996. *Development and Social Change: A Global Perspective.* Thousand Oaks, CA: Pine Forge Press.

McNamara, Kevin. 1999. "CityWalk: Los(t) Angeles in the shape of a mall." In Ghent Urban Studies Team, ed., *The Urban Condition.* Rotterdam: 010 pub.

McPhail, Clark. 1991. *The Myth of the Madding Crowd.* New York: de Gruyter.

McWilliams, James. 2005. "Internships pay off in opportunity." *The State,* August 5. http://www.thestate.com/mld/thestate/business/12307544.htm

Mead, George Herbert. 1934. *Mind, Self and Society.* Ed. Charles Morris. Chicago: University of Chicago Press.

Mele, Christopher. 2000. *Selling the Lower East Side: Culture, Real Estate, and Resistance in New York City.* Minneapolis, MN: University of Minnesota Press.

Menzel, Peter; and Mann, Charles. 1994. *Material World: A Global Family Portrait.* San Francisco: Sierra Club Books.

Merrow, John. 2007. "Dream catchers." *New York Times.* Education Life special section. April 27, sec. 4A, pp. 18–22.

Merton, Robert K. 1948. "The self-fulfilling prophecy." *Antioch Review,* vol. 8, no. 2 (June): 193–210.

_____. 1967. *On Theoretical Sociology: Five Essays, Old and New.* New York: Free Press.

_____. 1968. *Social Theory and Social Structure.* 2nd rev. ed. New York: Free Press.

Messerschmidt, James W. 1993. *Masculinities and Crime: Critique and Reconceptualization of Theory.* Totowa, NJ: Rowman and Littlefield.

_____. 1998. "Men victimizing men: The case of lynching: 1865–1900." In Lee H. Bowker, ed., *Masculinities and Violence.* Thousand Oaks, CA: Sage.

Messner, M. A. 2007. *Out of Play: Critical Essays on Gender and Sport.* Albany, New York: State University of New York Press.

_____; Duncan, M. C.; and Willms, N. 2005, July. "Gender in televised sports: News and highlights shows, 1989–2004." Amateur Athletic Foundation of Los Angeles. http://www.la84foundation.org/9arr/ResearchReports/tv2004.pdf

Meyer, D. 2000. "Social movements: Creating communities of change." In R. Teske and M. Tetreault, eds., *Conscious Acts and the Politics of Social Change.* Columbia, SC: University of South Carolina Press.

Meyer, Daniel R.; and Bartfeld, Judi. 1998. "Patterns of child support compliance in Wisconsin." *Journal of Marriage and the Family,* vol. 60, no. 2, 309–318.

Meyerson, Harold. 2003. "Democrats' online appeal." *Washington Post,* June 18, p. A25.

Meyrowitz, Joshua. 1985. *No Sense of Place: The Impact of Electronic Media on Social Behavior.* New York: Oxford University Press.

Mid-Atlantic Equity Consortium and the NETWORK. 1993. "Beyond Title IX: Gender equity issues in schools." September. http://www.maec.org/pdf/beyondIX.pdf

Milgram, Stanley. 1963. "Behavioral Study of Obedience." *Journal of Abnormal Social Psychology,* vol. 67, 371–378.

_____. 1974. *Obedience to Authority; An Experimental View.* New York: Harper & Row.

Military Prison Service Dog Training Program. 2009. http://www.carolinacanines.org/militaryprogram.html

Miller, Alice. 1990. *For Your Own Good: Hidden Cruelty in Child-Rearing and the Roots of Violence.* New York: Noonday Press.

Miller, Donald E.; and Miller, Lorna Touryan. 1999. *Survivors: An Oral History of the Armenian Genocide.* Berkeley, CA: University of California Press.

Miller, Laura. 1997. "Women in the military." *Social Psychology Quarterly,* vol. 60, no. 10 (March).

Miller, L. L. 1997. "Not just weapons of the weak: Gender harassment as a form of protest for Army men." *Social Psychology Quarterly,* vol. 60, no. 1, 32–51.

Mills, C. Wright. 1959. "The promise." *The Sociological Imagination.* New York: Oxford University Press.

_____. 1970 (orig. 1956). *The Power Elite.* New York: Oxford University Press.

Miner, Horace. 1956. "Body ritual among the Nacirema." *American Anthropologist,* vol. 58, no. 3 (June).

Miringoff, Marc; and Miringoff, Marque-Luisa. 1999. *The Social Health of the Nation: How America Is Really Doing.* New York: Oxford University Press.

Mishel, Lawrence; Bernstein, Jared; and Alegretto, Sylvia. 2007. Tables 3.18 and Table 3.19 in *The State of Working America 2006/2007.* Ithaca, NY: Cornell University Press.

Mitchell, Katharyne. 1993. "Multiculturalism, or the united colors of capitalism?" *Antipode,* vol. 25, no. 4, 263–294.

Mitchell, Richard. 2001. *Dancing at Armageddon: Survivalism and Chaos in Modern Times.* Chicago: University of Chicago Press.

Mitchell, Richard; and Charmaz, Kathy. 1996. "The myth of silent authorship: Self, substance and style in ethnographic writing." *Symbolic Interaction,* vol. 19, no. 4 (winter): 285–302.

Mittermeier, Russell A.; Myers, Norman; and Mittermeier, Cristina Goettsch. 2000. *Hotspots: Earth's Biologically Richest and Most Endangered Terrestrial Ecoregions.* Arlington, VA: Conservation International.

Mollenkopf, John. 1983. *The Contested City.* Princeton, NJ: Princeton University Press.

Molotch, Harvey. 1970. "Oil in Santa Barbara and power in America." *Sociological Inquiry,* vol. 40, 131–144.

Monitor Report. 1999. "U.S. runaway film and television production study report." http://www.dga.org/thedga/leg_rp_runaway.pdf

Montagu, A. 1998. *Man's Most Dangerous Myth: The Fallacy of Race.* 6th ed. Thousand Oaks, CA: Altamira Press.

Morgenstern, Claire. 2008. "Election 2008: Second-largest youth voter turnout in American history." *The Tartan,* November 10. http://thetartan.org/2008/11/10/news/elections

Morrison, Donna Ruane; and Cherlin, Andrew J. 1995. "The divorce process and young children's well-being: A prospective analysis." *Journal of Marriage and the Family,* vol. 57, no. 3, 800–812.

MSNBC. 2007. "After 40 years, interracial marriage flourishing." MSNBC.com, April 15. http://www.msnbc.msn.com/id/18090277/.

Muhl, Charles J. 2002. "What is an employee? The answer depends on the federal law; in a legal context, the classification of a worker as either an employee or an independent contractor can have significant consequences." *Monthly Labor Review,* vol. 125, no. 1 (January).

Muldoon, Bob. 2002. "White collar man in a blue collar world." *Newsweek,* February 4.

Mullins, N. 1973. *Theories and Theory Groups in Contemporary American Sociology.* New York: Harper and Row.

Mydans, Seth. 2008. "U.S. deportee brings street dance to street boys of Cambodia." *New York Times,* November 30, A6.

Myers, Norman; and Kent, Jennifer. 2004. *The New Consumers: The Influence of Affluence on the Environment.* Washington, DC: Island Press.

———, eds. 2005. *The New Atlas of Planet Management.* Berkeley, CA: University of California Press.

Myerson, A. R. 1997. "In principle, a case for more 'sweatshops.'" *New York Times,* June 22, p. E5.

Narang, Sonia. 2006. "Web-based microfinancing." *New York Times,* December 10, Section 6.

National Center for Health Statistics. 2001. "Number and percent of office visits with corresponding standard errors, by the 20 principal reasons for visit most frequently mentioned by patients according to patient's sex: United States, 1999."

———. 2002. "Increases in reported light to moderate physical activity by demographics." April.

———. 2007a. *National Vital Statistics Reports.* "United States life tables, 2004." Elizabeth Arias. http://www.cdc.gov/nchs/data/nvsr/nvsr56/nvsr56_09.pdf

National Center for Heath Statistics. 2007b. "Birth data." http://www.cdc.gov/nchs/births.htm.

National Domestic Violence Hotline. 2003. "What is domestic violence?" http://www.ndvh.org/dvInfo.html, accessed 3/25/03.

National Education Association. 2003. "National Education Association to challenge provisions of No Child Left Behind Act: Litigation to focus on the impact of unfunded mandates." Press Release, July 2. http://www.nea.org/newsreleases/2003/nr030702.html

National Indian Gaming Commission. 2008. "NIGC announces 2007 Indian gaming revenues." June 18. http://www.nigc.gov/ReadingRoom/PressReleases/PressReleasesMain/PR93062008/tabid/841/Default.aspx

National Opinion Research Center, University of Chicago. 1999. "The emerging 21st century American family." GSS Social Change Report No. 42.

———. 2001. *General Social Surveys 1972-2000: Cumulative Codebook.* Storrs, CT: Roper Center for Public Opinion Research. http://www.webuse.umd.edu/handouts/gss/GSS_2000_Codebook.pdf

National Public Radio. 2003. "Interracial marriage." *Odyssey.* WBEZ, Chicago. February 28.

———, Kaiser Family Foundation, and Harvard University Kennedy School of Government. 2001. National Survey on Poverty in America: Summary of Findings. http://www.kff.org/kaiserpolls/3118-index.cfm

NationMaster.com. 2009. "Motor vehicle statistics: Countries compared." http://www.nationmaster.com/graph/tra_mot_veh-transportation-motor-vehicles, accessed 6/9/09.

Nattras, Nicoli; and Seekings, Jeremy. 2001. "Two nations? Race and economic inequality in South Africa today." *Daedalus,* vol. 139 (winter): 45–70.

New School. 2004. "Thomas Robert Malthus, 1766–1834." Economics Department, New School. The History of Economic Thought web site. http://cepa.newschool.edu/het/profiles/malthus.htm, accessed 5/19/04.

New York City Department of Homeless Services. 2008. "Hope 2008: The NYC street survey." http://www.nyc.gov/html/dhs/downloads/pdf/hope08_results.pdf

Newman, David M. 2000. *Sociology: Exploring the Architecture of Everyday Life.* 3rd ed. Thousand Oaks, CA: Pine Forge Press.

Newton, Michael. 2004. *Savage Girls and Wild Boys: A History of Feral Children.* New York: Picador.

Noah, Timothy. 2004. "Something nice about Bush." *Slate,* November 4. http://slate.msn.com/id/2109228/, accessed 1/9/05.

Nobel Foundation. 2006. "The Nobel Peace Prize for 2006." Nobelprize.org, October 13. http://nobelprize.org/nobel_prizes/peace/laureates/2006/press.html, accessed 7/16/06.

Nogaki, Sylvia Weiland. 1993. "Judge oks Nordstrom lawsuit settlement." *Seattle Times,* April 13.

Norris, Pippa. 2001. *Digital Divide: Civic Engagement, Information Poverty, and the Internet Worldwide.* Cambridge: Cambridge University Press.

Norton, Eleanor Holmes. 2006. "Where's school voucher 'success' in Washington, D.C.?" *USA Today,* August 23.

Nuwer, Hank. 1999. *Wrongs of Passage: Fraternities, Sororities, Hazing and Binge Drinking.* Bloomington, IN: Indiana University Press.

Oakes, Jeannie. 1985. *Keeping Track: How Schools Structure Inequality.* New Haven, CT: Yale University Press.

O'Brien, Jodi; and Kollock, Peter. 1997. *The Production of Reality: Essays and Readings on Social Interaction.* Thousand Oaks, CA: Pine Forge Press.

Ochs, Elinor. 1986. "Introduction." In Bambi B. Schieffelin and Elinor Ochs, eds., *Language and Socialization Across Cultures.* New York: Cambridge University Press.

Office of the Secretary of the Defense. 2000. Selected manpower statistics, FY99.

———. 2002. Selected manpower statistics, FY2001.

Ogburn, William. 1964. *On Cultural and Social Change: Selected Papers.* Chicago: University of Chicago Press.

Oldenburg, Ray. 1999. *The Great Good Place.* New York: Marlowe and Company.

Omi, Michael; and Winant, Howard. 1989. *Racial Formation in the United States: From the 1960s to the 1980s.* New York: Routledge.

O'Reilly, Brian. 1992. "Looking ahead: Jobs are fast moving abroad." *Fortune,* December 14, pp. 52–66.

Orfield, Gary. 2001. "Schools more separate: Consequences of a decade of resegregation." Civil Rights Project Report. Harvard University. http://www.civilrightsproject.harvard.edu/research/deseg/separate_schools01.php

Osborne, Lawrence. 2002. "Consuming rituals of the suburban tribe." *New York Times Magazine,* January 13.

Oser, Kris. 2004. "Madison+Vine: Friendster uses imaginary pals to lure real ones." *Advertising Age,* vol. 75, no. 29, 3.

Papper, Robert; Michael Holmes, Mark Popovich and Mike Bloxham. 2005. "Media Day." Report of the Ball State University Center for Media Design. June 1.

Park, Robert Ezra. 1961. "Human ecology." Reprinted in G. A. Theodorson, ed., *Studies in Human Ecology.* New York: Row, Peterson & Company.

Parker, Lonnae O'Neal. 1998. "Brand identities." *Washington Post,* May 11.

Parsons, Talcott. 1955. "The American family: Its relation to personality and social structure." In Talcott Parsons and R. Bales, eds., *Family Socialization and Interaction Process.* New York: Free Press.

_____; and Bales, R.; eds. 1955. *Family, Socialization and Interaction Process.* New York: Free Press.

Patchett, Ann. 2001. *Bel Canto.* New York: Harper Perennial.

_____. 2004. *Truth & Beauty: A Friendship.* New York: Harper-Collins.

Pathways to Hope Prison Dog Project. 2009. http://www.pathwaystohope.org/prison.htm.

Patterson, Margot. 2004. "The rise of global fundamentalism." *National Catholic Reporter,* May 7.

Peavy, Linda; and Smith, Ursula. 1998. *Pioneer Women: The Lives of Women on the Frontier.* Norman, OK: University of Oklahoma Press.

People and the Planet. 2002. "Two more Earths needed by 2050." http://www.peopleandplanet.net/doc.php?id+ 1685&section=17, accessed 4/14/04.

"Perez Hilton." Wikipedia entry. http://en.wikipedia.org/wiki/Perez_Hilton, accessed 7/28/08.

Perls T. T.; and Fretts, R. 1998. "Why women live longer than men." *Scientific American Presents: Women's Health: A Lifelong Guide,* vol. 9, no. 4, 100–104.

Perrin, S.; and Spencer, C. P. 1980. "The Asch effect: A child of its time." *Bulletin of the British Psychological Society,* vol. 32, 405–406.

_____. 1981. "Independence or conformity in the Asch experiment as a reflection of cultural and situational factors." *British Journal of Social Psychology,* vol. 20, 215–210.

Perry, J.; and Pugh, M. 1978. *Collective Behavior: Response to Social Stress.* St. Paul, MN: West Publishing Company.

Peters, H. Elizabeth; Argys, Laura M.; Maccoby, Eleanor E.; and Mnookin, Robert H. 1993. "Enforcing divorce settlements: Evidence from child support compliance and award modifications." *Demography,* vol. 30, no. 4, 719–735.

Peterson, Julie. 2003. "U.S. Supreme Court rules on University of Michigan cases." http://www.umich.edu/news/Releases/2003/Jun03/supremecourt.html

Peterson, William. 2003. *From Persons to People: Further Studies in the Politics of Population.* Edison, NJ: Transaction.

Pettit, Becky; and Western, Bruce. 2004. "Mass imprisonment and the life course: Race and class inequality in U.S. incarceration." *American Sociological Review,* vol. 69, 151–169.

Pew Forum on Religion and Public Life. 2008. U.S. Religious Landscape Survey. http://religions.pewforum.org

Pew Internet and American Life Project. 2009. "Who's online." Updated January 6. http://www.pewinternet.org/trends.asp.

Pew Research Center. 2004. "Cable and Internet loom large in fragmented political news universe." Report. January 11. http://www.pewinternet.org/~/media/Files/Reports/2004/PIP_Political_Info_Jan04.pdf.pdf

_____. 2008a. "Growing doubts about McCain's judgment, age and campaign conduct." Section 2: Candidate Traits. Survey Report, October 21. http://people-press.org/report/462/obamas-lead-widens

_____. 2008b. "Internet's broader role in campaign 2008." January 11. http://people-press.org/report/384/internets-broader-role-in-campaign-2008

Pinto, Barbara. 2005. "Small town USA may offer solution to outsourcing: Company redeploys workers to rural towns instead of sending jobs overseas." *ABC World News Tonight,* television broadcast, August 25.

Pleck, Elizabeth H. 2000. *Celebrating the Family: Ethnicity, Consumer Culture, and Family Ritual.* Cambridge. MA: Harvard University Press.

Pleis, J.R.; and Lethbridge-Çejku, M. 2007. "Summary health statistics for U.S. adults: National Health Interview Survey, 2006." National Center for Health Statistics. Vital Health Stat 10(235). http://www.cdc.gov/nchs/data/series/sr_10/sr10_235.pdf.

Politics1.com. 2008. *U.S. Presidency 2008.* http://www.politics1.com/p2008.htm

Pollack, Andres. 1999. "Aerospace gets Japan's message: Without military largess, industry takes the lean path." *New York Times,* March 9, p. C1.

Pollner, Melvin; and Stein, Jill. 1996. "Narrative mapping of social worlds: The voice of experience in Alcoholics Anonymous." *Journal of Symbolic Interaction,* vol. 19, no. 3, 203–223.

_____. 2001. "Doubled-over in laughter: Humor and the construction of selves in Alcoholics Anonymous." In Jaber Gubrium and James Holstein, eds., *Institutional Selves: Personal Troubles in Organizational Context.* New York: Oxford University Press.

Pool, Robert. 1997. *Beyond Engineering: How Society Shapes Technology.* Oxford, UK: Oxford University Press.

Poor, T. 1994. "Singapore caning brings outpouring of agreement here." *St. Louis Post-Dispatch,* April 10, p. 1A.

Population Reference Bureau. 2008. "2008 world population data sheet." Carl Haub and Mary Mederios Kent. http://www.prb.org/pdf08/08WPDS_Eng.pdf [World Population Clock, 2008 based on data available at http://www.prb.org/Articles/2008/worldpopulation-clock2008.aspx]

Poster, Mark. 2002. "Workers as cyborgs: Labor and networked computers." *Journal of Labor Research,* vol. 23, no. 3 (summer): 339.

Postman, Neil. 1987. *Amusing Ourselves to Death: Public Discourse in the Age of Show Business.* New York: Methuen.

Powell, Brian. 2003. Unpublished survey results. Indiana University, Department of Sociology, Center for Survey Research, Bloomington.

Price, Jammie. 1999. *Navigating differences: Friendships between gay and straight men.* New York: Harrington Park Press.

Pullum, Geoffrey K. 1991. *The Great Eskimo Vocabulary Hoax and Other Irreverent Essays on the Study of Language.* Chicago: University of Chicago Press.

Putnam, Robert D. 1995. "Tuning in, tuning out: The strange disappearance of social capital in America." *Political Science & Politics,* vol. 28, no. 4 (December): 664.

_____. 2000. *Bowling Alone: The Collapse and Revival of American Community.* New York: Simon and Schuster.

Quist-Arcton, Ofeibea. 2002. "Ghana seeks African American dollars, skills." National Public Radio, March 14.

Rabinowitz, Gavin. 2008. "India's Tata Motors unveils $2,500 car, bringing car ownership within reach of millions." Associated Press, February 11. http://climate.weather.com/articles/cheapcar011108.html

Rabow, Jerome; and Stein, Jill. 1996. "Charisma and its varieties in the lives of students: The impact of popular music." *Journal of Culture and Society,* vol. 96, no. 2, 1–24.

_____; and Conley, Terri. 1999. "Teaching social justice and encountering society: The pink triangle experiment." *Youth and Society,* vol. 30, no. 4, 483–514.

_____. 2001. "Teaching students about stigmatization through first-hand experience: The gay pride pin experiment." In Howard J. Ehrlich, ed., *Teaching about Ethnoviolence and Hate Crimes.* Washington, DC: American Sociological Association.

Radway, A. Janice. 1991. *Reading the Romance: Women, Patriarchy, and Popular Literature.* Chapel Hill, NC: University of North Carolina Press.

Ramanathan, Veerabhadran. 2007. "Warming trends in Asia amplified by brown cloud solar absorption." *Nature* 448 (August 2): 575–578.

Ramshaw, Emily. 2007. "Is race keeping exec out of club?" *Dallas Morning News*, February 1.

RAND Education. 2003. *Charter School Operation and Performance: Evidence from California*. Santa Monica, CA: The Rand Corporation. http://www.rand.org/pubs/monograph_reports/MR1700

Rashad, Ahmad. 1988. *Rashad: Vikes, Mikes and Something on the Backside*. New York: Viking.

Ray, Brian. 1997. "Strengths of their own—home schoolers across America: Academic achievement, family characteristics, and longitudinal traits." Salem, OR: National Home Education Research Institute.

———. 2008. "Research facts on homeschooling." National Home Education Research Institute. http://www.nheri.org/Research-Facts-on-Homeschooling.html

Rees, W.; and Wackernagel, M. 1994. "Ecological footprints and appropriated carrying capacity: Measuring the natural capital requirements of the human economy." In A-M. Jansson, M. Hammer, C. Folke, and R. Costanza, eds., *Investing in Natural Capital: The Ecological Economics Approach to Sustainability*. Washington, DC: Island Press.

Rennison, Callie Marie. 2001. "Intimate partner violence and age of victim, 1993–1999." Bureau of Justice Statistics Special Report. Washington, DC: U.S. Department of Justice. NCJ #187635.

Reuters. 2008. "Visa study shows Canada and Mexico are top destinations for Americans traveling abroad." July 24. http://www.reuters.com/article/pressRelease/idUS135782+24-Jul-2008+BW20080724

Riesman, D. 1957. "The suburban dislocation." *Annals of the American Academy of Political and Social Science,* vol. 314, 123.

Ritzer, George. 1996. *The McDonaldization of Society*. Thousand Oaks, CA: Pine Forge Press.

Robbins, John. 1987. *Diet for a New America: How Your Food Choices Affect Your Health, Happiness and the Future of Life on Earth*. Walpole, NH: H. J. Kramer.

Roberts, D.; and Bernstein, A. 2000. "A life of fines and beating." *Business Week,* October 2, pp. 122–128.

Robson, D. 2001. "Women and minorities in economics textbooks: Are they being adequately represented?" *Journal of Economic Education*, vol. 32, no. 2 (Spring), 186–191.

Rojek, Chris. 1985. *Capitalism and Leisure Theory*. London: Tavistock.

———. 1995. *Decentering Leisure: Rethinking Leisure Theory*. London: Sage.

———. 1997. "Leisure theory: Retrospect and prospect." *Loisir et Société/Society and Leisure*, vol. 20, no. 2, 383–400.

———. 2000. "Leisure and the rich today: Veblen's thesis after a century." *Leisure Studies*, vol. 19, no. 1, 1–15.

Roscoe, W. 2000. "How to become a berdache: Toward a unified analysis of gender." In G. Herdt, ed., *Third Sex, Third Gender: Beyond Sexual Dimorphism in Culture and History*. New York: Zone Books.

Rosen, Karen. 2007. "Women still lag in college sports." Cox News Service, June 6.

Rosenbloom, Stephanie. 2007. "On Facebook, scholars link up with data." *New York Times*, December 17. http://www.nytimes.com/2007/12/17/style/17facebook.html?ex=1355720400&en=33ca15953318a6f5&ei=5124&partner=permalink&exprod=permalink, accessed 7/31/08.

Rosenfeld, Dana. 2003. *The Changing of the Guard: Lesbian and Gay Elders, Identity, and Social Change*. Philadelphia: Temple University Press.

Rosenhan, David. 1973. "On being sane in insane places." *Science*, vol. 179 (January): 250–258.

Rosenthal, R.; and Jacobson, L. 1968. *Pygmalion in the Classroom: Teacher Expectation and Pupils' Intellectual Development*. New York: Rinehart and Winston.

Ross, Andrew. 1997. "Introduction." In Andrew Ross, ed., *No Sweat: Fashion, Free Trade and the Rights of Garment Workers*. New York: Verso.

Roth, Andrew L. 2002. "Social epistemology in broadcast news interviews." *Language in Society,* vol. 31, no. 3, 355–381.

Roth, Benita. 2003. *Separate Roads to Feminism: Black, Chicana and White Feminist Movements in America's Second Wave*. Cambridge, UK: Cambridge University Press.

Rothblum, Esther. 1996. *Preventing Heterosexism and Homophobia*. Thousand Oaks, CA: Sage.

Rothkop, David. 1997. "In praise of cultural imperialism? Effects of globalization on culture." *Foreign Policy,* June 22.

Roy, Donald. 1960. "'Banana time': Job satisfaction and informal interaction." *Human Organization*, vol. 18, 158–168.

Rubel, Paula; and Rosman, Abraham. 2001. "The collecting passion in America." *Zeitschrift fur Ethnologie* (English), vol. 126, no. 2, 313–330.

Rubin, Zick; and Peplau, Letitia Anne. 1975. "Who believes in a just world?" *Journal of Social Issues*, vol. 31, no. 3, 65–89.

Rupp, Leila; and Taylor, Verta. 2003. *Drag Queens of the 801 Cabaret*. Chicago: University of Chicago Press.

Ryan, George. 2003. "The death penalty: Arbitrary and capricious." Salon.com, accessed 1/14/03.

Sadker, Myra; and Sadker, David. 1995. *Failing at Fairness: How Our Schools Cheat Girls*. New York: Scribner.

Sampson, Robert J.; and Wilson, William Julius. 2005. "Toward a theory of race, crime and urban inequality." In Shaun L. Gabbidon and Helen Taylor Greene, eds., *Race, Crime and Justice: A Reader*. New York: Routledge.

Sanchez-Jankowski, Martin. 1991. *Islands in the Street: Gangs and American Urban Society*. Berkeley, CA: University of California Press.

Sapir, Edward. 1949. *Selected Writings in Language, Culture, and Personality*. Ed. David G. Mandelbaum. Berkeley, CA: University of California Press.

Sapolsky, Robert. 1997. *Trouble with Testosterone and Other Essays on the Biology of Human Nature*. New York: Scribner.

Sassen, Saskia. 1991. *The Global City: New York, London, Tokyo*. Princeton, NJ: Princeton University Press.

Sayer, Liana C.; and Mattingly, Maribeth. 2006. "Under pressure: Gender differences in the relationship between free time and feeling rushed." *Journal of Marriage and Family,* vol. 68, no. 1 (February): 205–221.

Schegloff, Emanuel. 1986. "The routine as achievement." *Human Studies*, vol. 9, nos. 2–3, 111–151.

———. 1999. "What next? Language and social interaction study at the century's turn." *Research on Language and Social Interaction*, vol. 32, nos.1–2, 141–148.

Schein, Edgar H. 1997. *Organizational Culture and Leadership*. San Francisco: Jossey-Bass.

Schell, Orville. 2002. "Gross national happiness." *Red Herring*, January 15. http://www.pbs.org/frontlineworld/stories/bhutan/gnh.html

Scheyvens, Regina. 2000. "Promoting women's empowerment through involvement in ecotourism: Experiences from the Third World." *Journal of Sustainable Tourism*, vol. 8, no. 3, 232–249.

Schiller, Herbert I. 1976. *Communication and Cultural Domination*. White Plains, NY: International Arts and Sciences Press.

———. 1992. *Mass Communications and American Empire*. 2nd ed. Boulder, CO: Westview Press.

———. 1995. "The global information highway: Project for an ungovernable world." In J. Brook and I. A. Boal, eds., *Resisting the Virtual Life: The Culture and Politics of Information*. San Francisco: City Lights Books.

———. 1996. *Information Inequality*. New York: Routledge.

———; Schlenker, Jennifer A.; Caron, Sandra L.; and Halteman, William A. 1998. "A feminist analysis of *Seventeen* magazine: Content analysis from 1945 to 1995." *Sex Roles: A Journal of Research*, vol. 38, no. 1–2, 135.

Schiller, Herbert I; Schlosser, Eric. 2002. *Fast Food Nation: The Dark Side of the All-American Meal*. New York: Perennial.

_____. 2003. *Reefer Madness: Sex, Drugs and Cheap Labor in the American Black Market.* Boston: Houghton Mifflin.

Schmid, C. L. 1981. *Conflict and Consensus in Switzerland.* Berkeley, CA: University of California Press.

Schnaiberg, Allan. 1975. "Social synthesis of the societal-environmental dialectic: The role of distributional impacts." *Social Science Quarterly,* vol. 56, 5–20.

_____; and Gould, Kenneth Alan. 1994. *Environment and Society: The Enduring Conflict.* New York: St. Martin's Press.

Schofield, Jack. 2004. "Social network software; software to help you network." *Computer Weekly,* March 16, p. 32.

Schor, Juliet B. 1999. *The Overspent American: Why We Want What We Don't Need.* New York: HarperCollins.

Schudson, Michael. 2003. *The Sociology of News.* New York: Norton.

Schutz, Alfred P. 1962. "The stranger: An essay in social psychology." In A. Brodersen, ed, *Collected Papers II: Studies in Social Theory.* Dordrecht, The Netherlands: Martinus Nijhoff.

Schwellenbach, Nick. 2008. "Finance: A good time to be a white-collar criminal?" Center for Public Integrity, December 18. http://www.publicintegrity.org/blog/entry/1096

Schwimmer, B. 2001. "Figure 43. Hawaiian kin terms (actual usage)." http://www.umanitoba.ca/faculties/arts/ anthropology/tutor/image_list/43.html, accessed 12/4/03.

Sedgwick, Eve Kosofsky. 1993. *Tendencies.* Durham, NC: Duke University Press

Seekings, Jeremy; and Nattras, Nicoli. 2005. *Class, Race and Inequality in South Africa.* New Haven, CT: Yale University Press.

Seidman, Steven. 2003. *The Social Construction of Sexuality.* New York: Norton.

Segal, Lynne. 1990. *Slow Motion: Changing Masculinities, Changing Men.* New Brunswick, NJ: Rutgers University Press.

Seltzer, Judith A.; Schaeffer, Nora Cate; and Charng, Hong-Wen. 1989. "Family ties after divorce: The relationship between visiting and paying child support." *Journal of Marriage and the Family,* vol. 51, no. 4, 1013–1031.

Sennett, Richard. 1977. *The Fall of Public Man.* New York: Norton.

Sessions Stepp, Laura. 2001. "A lesson in cruelty: Anti-gay slurs common at school; Some say insults increase as gays' visibility rises." *Washington Post,* June 19.

Severin, W. J.; and Tankard, J. W. 1997. *Communication Theories: Origins, Methods, and Uses in the Mass Media.* 4th ed. New York: Longman.

Shah, Anup. 2007. "Media conglomerates, mergers, concentration of ownership." *Global Issues,* April 29 http://www.globalissues.org/article/159/media-conglomerates-mergers-concentration-of-ownership

Shakara, Aaron. 2004. "More than a tree sitter." *Oregon Daily Emerald,* April 29.

Sherman, Alexa; and Tocantins, Nicole. 2004. *The Happy Hook-Up: A Single Girl's Guide to Casual Sex.* BErkeley, CA: Ten Speed Press.

Sherwood, Steven J. 2006. "Seeker of the sacred: A late-Durkheimian theory of the artist." In Ron Eyerman and Lisa McCormick, eds., *Myth, Meaning and Performance: Toward a Cultural Sociology of the Arts.* New York: Paradigm Press.

Shiach, Morag. 1999. *Feminism and Cultural Studies.* New York: Oxford University Press.

Shipler, D. K. 1997. *A Country of Strangers: Blacks and Whites in America.* New York: Alfred A. Knopf.

Shippers, Mimi. 2002. *Rockin' Out of the Box: Gender Maneuvering in Alternative Hard Rock.* New Brunswick, NJ: Rutgers University Press.

Simmel, Georg. 1950. *The Sociology of George Simmel.* Ed. Kurt Wolff. New York: Free Press.

Simon, Julian. 1996. *The Ultimate Resource 2.* Princeton, NJ: Princeton University Press

_____. 2000. *The Great Breakthrough and Its Cause.* Ann Arbor, MI: University of Michigan Press.

Simon, Scott. 2004. "Friend of Kitty Genovese discusses her memories of Kitty and her murder." *National Public Radio,* "Weekend Edition Saturday," March 13.

Singh, Gopal K.; and Siahpush, Mohammad. 2006. "Widening socioeconomic inequalities in U.S. life expectancy, 1980–2000." *International Journal of Epidemiology,* online journal, May 9. http://ije.oxfordjournals.org/cgi/reprint/dyl083v1.pdf

Skarzynska, Krystyna. 2004. "Politicians in television: The big five in impression formation." *Journal of Political Marketing,* vol. 3, no. 2, 31–45.

Skocpol, Theda. 1979. *States and Social Revolutions: A Comparative Analysis of France, Russia and China.* Cambridge, UK: Cambridge University Press.

Sloan Consortium. 2006. "Making the grade: Online education in the United States, 2006." I. Elaine Allen and Jeff Seaman. Needham, MA: Sloan-C. http://www.sloan-c.org/publications/survey/survey06.asp

_____. 2007. "Online nation: Five years of growth in online learning." I. Elaine Allen and Jeff Seaman. Needham, MA: Sloan-C. http://www.sloan-c.org/publications/survey/online_nation

Smelser, Neil. 1985. "Evaluating the model of structural differentiation in relation to educational change in the nineteenth century." In Jeffrey C. Alexander, ed., *Neofunctionalism.* Beverly Hills, CA: Sage Publications.

Smith, Dorothy. 1999. "Schooling for inequality." *Signs: Journal for Women in Culture and Society,* vol. 5, no. 4, 1147–1151.

Smith, Gerry. 2008. "Support your local farmer." *Chicago Tribune,* July 6, p. 1.

Smith, Herbert L. 1990. "Specification problems in experimental and non-experimental social research." *Sociological Methodology,* vol. 20, 59–91.

Smith, Kara. 2005. "Gender talk: A case study in prenatal socialization." *Women and Languages,* March 22.

Smith, Marc; and Kollock, Peter. 1998. *Communities in Cyberspace.* London: Routledge.

Smith-Lovin, Lynn; and Brody, Charles. 1989. "Interruptions in group discussions: The effects of gender and group composition." *American Sociological Review,* vol. 54, no. 3 (June): 424–435.

Sniezek, Tamara. 2005. "Is it our day or the bride's day? The division of wedding labor and its meaning for couples." *Qualitative Sociology,* vol. 28, no. 3, 215–234.

Solot, Dorian; and Miller, Marshall. 2002. *Unmarried to Each Other: The Essential Guide to Living Together as an Unmarried Couple.* New York: Marlowe and Co.

Sonner, Scott. 2002. "Burning Man gives fodder for questing sociologists." Associated Press, August 28. http://www.religionnewsblog.com/641-Scientists_find_Burning_Man_a_research_bonanza.html

Sorauf, Frank J. 1988. *Money in American Elections.* Boston: Scott, Foresman and Company.

Sozou, Peter; and Seymour, Robert. 2005. "Costly but worthless gifts facilitate courtship." Proceedings of the Royal Society B: *Biological Sciences,* 272.

Spector, Robert; and McCarthy, Patrick D. 1996. *The Nordstrom Way: The Inside Story of America's #1 Customer Service Company.* Hoboken, NJ: John Wiley & Sons.

Spellings, Margaret. 2006. "Opportunity for all children." *USA Today,* August 13.

Spencer, Herbert. 1862. *First Principles.* London: Williams and Norgate.

_____. 1873. *The Study of Sociology.* London: King.

_____. 1897. *The Principles of Sociology.* 3 vols. New York: Appleton.

Spielberg, E. 1997. "The myth of nimble fingers." In A. Ross, ed., *No Sweat: Fashion, Free Trade, and the Rights of Garment Workers.* New York: Verso.

Sprecher, Susan; McKinney, Kathleen; and Orbuch, Terri. 1987. "Has the double standard disappeared? An experimental test." *Social Psychology Quarterly,* vol. 50, no. 1 (March): 24–31.

Srinivas, Lakshmi. 1998. "Active viewing: An ethnography of the Indian film audience." *Visual Anthropology,* vol. 11, no. 4.

Stacey, Judith. 1990. *Brave New Families: Stories of Domestic Upheaval in Late Twentieth-Century America.* New York: Basic Books.

———. 1998. "Gay and lesbian families: Queer like us." In Mary Ann Mason, Arlene Skolnick, and Stephen D. Sugarman, eds., *All Our Families: New Policies for a New Century.* New York: Oxford University Press.

Stack, Carol. 1974. *All Our Kin.* New York: Harper & Row.

Stamou, Anastasia G.; and Paraskevopoulos, Stephanos. 2003. "Ecotourism experiences in visitors' books of a Greek reserve: A critical discourse analysis perspective." *Sociologia Ruralis,* vol. 43, no. 1, 34–55.

Stannard, David E. 1993. *American Holocaust: The Conquest of the New World.* New York: Oxford University Press.

Stanton, M. E. 1995. "Patterns of kinship and residence." In B. Ingoldsby and S. Smith, eds., *Families in Multicultural Perspective.* New York: Guilford Press.

Stapleton, Christine. 2002. "Donated blood sold off overseas after 9/11." *Atlanta Journal-Constitution,* September 8, p. 19A.

Stein, Jill. 1997. "Rock musician careers: The culture of the long-term professional." Unpublished Doctoral Dissertation. University of California, Los Angeles.

———; Rabow, Jerome; and El Mouchi, Darryl. 1994. "Popular music and the opening of the American mind: Allan Bloom . . . meet the Beatles." *Journal of Culture and Society,* vol. 94, no. 2, 1–32.

Steiner, I. D. 1972. *Group Process and Productivity.* New York: Academic Press.

Stimson, Ida H. 1967. "Patterns of socialization into professions: The case of student nurses." *Sociological Inquiry,* vol. 37, 47–54.

Strauss, Neil. 2003. "The pop life: Apple finds a route for online music sales." *New York Times,* May 29, E5.

Stripling, Sherry. 1998. "The pet projects of Sister Pauline: A maverick nun builds her esteem while aiding others." *Seattle Times,* March 22, L1.

Sudnow, David. 1972. "Temporal parameters of interpersonal observation." In D. Sudnow, ed., *Studies in Social Interaction.* New York: Free Press.

Sue, Valerie M., and Lois A. Ritter. 2007. *Conducting Online Surveys.* Thousand Oaks, CA: Sage.

Sumner, William Graham. 1906. *Folkways: A Study of the Sociological Importance of Usages, Manners, Customs, Mores, and Morals.* Boston: Ginn and Co.

Sutherland, Edwin. 1939. *Principles of Criminology.* 3rd ed. Philadelphia: J.B. Lipincott.

———; Cressey, Donald R.; and Luckenbill, David F. 1992. *Principles of Criminology.* 11th ed. Dix Hills, NY: General Hall.

Sutton, Robert. 2001. *Weird Ideas That Work: 11½ Practices for Promoting, Managing and Sustaining Innovation.* New York: Free Press.

Svazlian, Verjine. 2000. *The Armenian Genocide: Testimonies of the Eye-Witness Survivors.* Yerevan, Armenia: Gitutiun Publishing House of the NAS RA. (In Armenian, with English, French and Russian summaries.)

Sweatshop Watch. 1999. "Code of conduct for university trademark licensees." http://www.sweatshopwatch.org/swatch/codes/code.html

Swim, Dannell. 2008. "On dads in the delivery room." May 5. http://www.truebirth.com/2008/05/fairlady-on-dads-in-delivery-room/

Tahmincioglu, Eve. 2008. "Facebook friends as job references?" MSNBC, August 18. http://www.msnbc.msn.com/id/26223330/, accessed 8/22/08.

Tannen, Deborah. 2001. *You Just Don't Understand: Men and Women in Conversation.* New York: Perennial Currents.

Tapscott, Don. 1997. *Growing Up Digital: The Rise of the Net Generation.* New York: McGraw-Hill.

Taylor, R. 2000. "The empire strikes back: Soccer violence continues to be England's ugliest export." *Time International,* vol. 155 (July 19): 36.

Telles, Edward. 2004. *Race in Another America: The Significance of Color in Brazil.* Princeton, NJ: Princeton University Press.

Texas Department of Public Safety. 2008. "Annual report of 2007 UCR data collection: Crime in Texas 2007 overview." May 6. http://www.txdps.state.tx.us/director_staff/public_information/2007CIT.pdf, accessed 4/20/09.

Thomas, W. I.; and Thomas, D. S. 1928. *The Child in America.* New York: Alfred A. Knopf.

Thorne, Barrie. 1992. "Feminism and the family: Two decades of thought." In Barrie Thorne and Marilyn Yalom, eds., *Rethinking the Family: Some Feminist Questions.* Boston: Northeastern University Press.

———. 1993. *Gender Play: Girls and Boys in School.* New Brunswick, NJ: Rutgers University Press.

Thornton, Stephen J. 2003. "Silence on gays and lesbians in social studies curriculum." *Social Education,* vol. 67, no. 4 (May–June), 226.

Thye, Shane R.; and Lawler, Edward J., eds. 2002. *Advances in Group Processes: Group Cohesion, Trust and Solidarity,* vol. 19. Oxford, UK: Elsevier Science.

Tomlinson, John. 1991. *Cultural Imperialism.* Baltimore, MD: John Hopkins University Press.

Toor, Rachel. 2001. *Admissions Confidential: An Insider's Account of the Elite College Selection Process.* New York: St. Martin's Press.

"Tracing your ancestry." 2007. www.discoverireland.com, accessed 4/16/07.

Trebay, Guy. 2008. "He's pregnant, you're speechless." *New York Times.* Style section, June 22, 1.

Trexler, R. C. 2002. "Making the American berdache: Choice or constraint." *Journal of Social History,* vol. 35, 613–636.

Turkle, Sherry. 1997. *Life on the Screen: Identity in the Age of the Internet.* New York: Touchstone Books.

———. 2005. *The Second Self: Computers and the Human Spirit* Cambridge, MA: MIT Press.

Turner, J. C.; with Hogg, M. A.; Oakes, P. J.; Reicher, S. D.; and Wetherell, M. S. 1987. *Rediscovering the Social Group: A Self Categorization Theory.* Blackwell, UK: Oxford University Press.

Turner, Ralph. 1972. "Deviance avowal as neutralization of commitment." *Social Problems,* vol. 19, no. 3, 308–321.

———. 1976. "The real self: From institution to impulse." *American Journal of Sociology,* vol. 81, 989–1016.

———. 1978. "The role and the person." *American Journal of Sociology,* vol. 84, no. 1, 1–3.

———; and Killian, Lewis M. 1987. *Collective Behavior.* 3rd ed. Englewood Cliffs, NJ: Prentice Hall. 2006 Civic and Political Health of the Nation Survey (CIRCLE) Civic Engagement Among Minority Youth. By Karlo Barrios Marcelo, Mark Hugo Lopez, and Emily Hoban Kirby, January 1, 2007.

Uggen, Christopher; and Manza, Jeff. 2002. "Democratic contraction? Political consequences of felon disenfranchisement in the United States." *American Sociological Review,* vol. 67, iss. 6, 777–803.

Ulbrich, Chris. 2004. "Blogs pump bucks into campaigns." *Wired,* February 18.

Ulrichs, Karl H. 1994. *The Riddle of Man-Manly Love: The Pioneering Work on Male Homosexuality.* Amherst, NY: Prometheus Books.

United Nations. 2006. "World population prospects, 2006 revision." http://www.un.org/esa/population/publications/wpp2006/WPP2006_Highlights_rev.pdf, accessed 12/18/2008.

United Nations Conference on Trade and Development (UNCTAD). 2007. "The world's top 100 non-financial TNCs, ranked by foreign assets, 2006." http://www.unctad.org/sections/dite_dir/docs/wir2008top100_en.pdf

United Nations Department of Economic and Social Affairs Population Division. 1999. "India becomes a billionaire." http://www.un.org/esa/population/pubsarchive/india/india.htm

United Nations Development Programme. 2006. World Population Prospects, 2006 revision. http://www.un.org/esa/population/publications/wpp2006/WPP2006_Highlights_rev.pdf, accessed 12/18/08.

United Nations Development Programme, The United Nations Environment Programme, The World Bank, and World Resources Institute. 2000. *World Resources 2000–2001*. Washington, DC: World Resources Institute.

United Nations Environment Programme. 2005. "Ecosystems and human well being: The biodiversity synthesis report." May 2005. http://www.unep.org/Documents.Multilingual/Default.asp?DocumentID=433&ArticleID=4801&l=en

United Nations Millennium Project. 2001. http://www.unmillenniumproject.org

United Nations World Commission on Environment and Development. 1987. *Our Common Future*. Oxford, UK: Oxford University Press.

United Nations World Food Programme. 2007. World hunger series: 2007. http://www.wfp.org/policies/introduction/other/documents/pdf/WHS_leaflet_English_2007.pdf, accessed 12/18/08.

United Students Against Sweatshops (USAS). 2003. "History of USAS." http://www.people.fas.harvard.edu/~fragola/usas/history.html

Unofficial RPG Site. "The ethics of gold farming." October 7. http://pc.rpgsite.net/editorials/1/78.html, accessed 10/27/08.

Urry, John. 1990. *The Tourist Gaze*. London: Sage.

———. 1992. "The tourist gaze and the 'environment.'" *Theory, Culture & Society*, vol. 9, no. 3, 1–26.

———. 2002. *The Tourist Gaze*. 2nd ed. London: Sage.

Useem, E. L. 1990. "You're good but you're not good enough: Tracking students out of advanced mathematics." *American Educator*, vol. 14, no. 3, 24–27, 43–46.

U.S. Bureau of Justice Statistics. 2005. National Crime Victimization Survey. "Criminal victimization, 2005." http://www.rainn.org/docs/statistics/ncvs_2005.pdf

———. 2008. "Prison inmates at midyear 2007." William J. Sabol and Heather Couture. http://www.ojp.usdoj.gov/bjs/pub/pdf/pim07.pdf

U.S. Bureau of Labor Statistics. 2008a. Economic News Release Table 5. "Employment status of the population by sex, marital status, and presences and age of own children under 18, 2006–07 annual averages." http://www.bls.gov/news.release/famee.t05.htm

———. 2008b. "Employed persons by detailed occupation, sex, race, and Hispanic or Latino ethnicity 2007." http://www.bls.gov/cps/cpsaat11.pdf

———. 2008c. "News: Employment characteristics of families in 2007." http://www.bls.gov/news.release/pdf/famee.pdf, accessed 10/27/08.

———. 2008d. Employment Situation Report, October. http://www.bls.gov/news.release/empsit.to1.htm

———. 2008e. Union Membership Data. http://www.bls.gov/news.release/unionz.nr0.htm

———. 2008f. Volunteer Data. http://www.bls.gov/news.release/volun.t04.htm

———. 2008g. Volunteering in the United States. "Table 4. Volunteers by type of main organization for which volunteer activities were performed and selected characteristics, September 2007." http://www.bls.gov/news.release/volun.t04.htm

U.S. Census Bureau. 1993. 1990 Census Tabulations, *Population and Housing Unit Counts*. "Table 4. Population: 1790 to 1990" http://www.census.gov/population/censusdata/table-4.pdf

———. 1994. "Table 1. Race of wife by race of husband: 1960, 1970, 1980, 1991, and 1992." *Interracial Tables*. Washington, DC: U.S. Government Printing Office. www.census.gov, accessed 11/7/03.

———. 1995, May. Statistical Brief. "Sixty-five plus in the United States." http://www.census.gov/population/socdemo/statbriefs/agebrief.html, accessed 5/1/09.

———. 2000a. "Marital status of women 15 to 44 years old at first birth by selected characteristics: 1990–94." Statistical Abstract of the United States: 2000. Washington, DC: U.S. Government Printing Office.

———. 2000b. "GCT-P1. Urban/Rural and Metropolitan/Nonmetropolitan Population: 2000." Data from Census 2000 Summary File 1. http://factfinder.census.gov

———. 2001. "Table MS1: Marital status of the population 15 years old and over, by sex and race: 1950 to present." http://www.census.gov/population/www/socdemo/hh-fam.html

———. 2002a. "Children's living arrangements and characteristics: March 2002, Table A1. Marital status of people 15 years and over, by age, sex, personal earnings, race, and Hispanic origin." http://www.census.gov/population/www/socdemo/hh-fam/cps2002.html

———. 2002b. "No. 32. Annual averages: Unemployed persons by occupation, industry, and duration of unemployment." ftp://ftp.bls.gov/pub/special.requests/lf/aat32.txt. 2004. "Figure 1. Family groups with children by type of family group: 1970 to 2003" and "Table 4. Single parents by sex and selected characteristics: 2003." *America's Families and Living Arrangements: 2003*. Current Population Report (November). http://www.census.gov/prod/2004pubs/p20-553.pdf

———. 2003. "Married couple and unmarried partner households: 2000." Census 2000 Special Report. February. http://www.census.gov/prod/2003pubs/censr-5.pdf

———. 2005a. *2005 American Community Survey*. "S1101. Households and families." http://factfinder.census.gov/servlet/DatasetMainPageServlet?_program=ACS&_submenuId=datasets_2&_lang=en

———. 2005b. *2005 American Community Survey*. "S1201. Marital status." http://factfinder.census.gov/servlet/DatasetMainPageServlet?_program=ACS&_submenuId=datasets_2&_lang=en

———. 2005c. "Income stable, poverty rate increases, percentage of Americans without health insurance unchanged." Press Release, August 30. http://www.census.gov/Press Release/www/releases/archives/income_wealth/005647.html

———. 2005d. "Interim projections: Ranking of Census 2000 and projected 2030 state population and change: 2000 to 2030." April. http://www.census.gov/Press-Release/www/2005/stateproj7.xls

———. 2006. "Child support, 2005: Detailed tables." http://www.census.gov/hhes/www/childsupport/chldsu05.pdf.

———. 2007a. "Custodial mothers and fathers and their child support: 2005." Timothy S. Grail. http://www.census.gov/prod/2007pubs/p60-234.pdf

———. 2007b. Statistical Abstract of the United States: 2007 (126th Edition) Washington, DC. "No. 73. Self-described religious identification of adult population: 1990 and 2001." http://www.census.gov/compendia/statab/population/eligion

———. 2007c. Table 604. "Unemployed workers—summary: 1980 to 2006." http://www.census.gov/compendia/statab/tables/08s0604.pdf

———. 2007d. "Table 1: Annual estimates of the population for incorporated places over 100,000, ranked by July 1, 2007 Population: April 1, 2000 to July 1, 2007." 2007 Population Estimates. July 10. http://www.census.gov/popest/cities/tables/SUB-EST2007-01.csv

———. 2008a. "America's families and living arrangements." http://www.census.gov/population/www/socdemo/hh-fam/cps2007.html

———. 2008b. "Educational attainment of the population 18 years and over, by age, sex, race, and Hispanic origin: 2007." http://www.census.gov/population/www/socdemo/education/cps2007.html

———. 2008c. "Income, poverty, and health insurance coverage in the United States: 2007." Carmen DeNavas-Walt, Bernadette D. Proctor, and Jessica C. Smith. http://www.census.gov/prod/2008pubs/p60-235.pdf

———. 2008d. *Public Education Finances: 2006*. http://www.census.gov/Press-Release/www/releases/archives/education/011747.html

———. 2008e. Table A1. "Marital status of people 15 years and over, by age, sex, personal earnings, race, and Hispanic origin/1, 2007." http://www.census.gov/population/socdemo/hh-fam/cps2007/tabA1-all.xls

————. 2008f. Table 2. "Poverty status, by family relationship, race, and Hispanic origin." http://www.census.gov/hhes/www/poverty/histpov/hstpov2.xls

————. 2008g. Table 3. "Poverty status, by age, race and Hispanic origin." http://www.census.gov/hhes/www/poverty/histpov/hstpov3.xls

————. 2008h. Table 98. "Expectation of life at birth, 1970 to 2004, and projections, 2010 and 2015." http://www.census.gov/compendia/statab/tables/08s0098.pdf

————. 2008i. Table 1000, *Statistical Abstract of the United States: 2008.* http://www.census.gov/compendia/statab/tables/08s1000.xls

————. 2008j. Table 1099, *Statistical Abstract of the United States: 2008.* http://www.census.gov/compendia/statab/tables/08s1099.xls

————. 2008k. 2007 Report on Housing Characteristics. http://www.census.gov/const/www/highanncharac2007.html

————. 2008l. "Table 3. Estimates of resident population change for the United States, regions, states, and Puerto Rico and region and state rankings: July 1, 2007 to July 1, 2008." Population Division. Released December 22. http://www.census.gov/popest/states/tables/NST-EST2008-03.xls

————. 2009. "Educational attainment in the United States: 2007" *U.S. Census Current Population Reports.* Sarah R. Crissey. http://www.census.gov/prod/2009pubs/p20-560.pdf

U.S. Charter Schools. "State profiles: State by state numbers." http://www.uscharterschools.org/cs/sp/query/q/1595, accessed 3/27/09.

U.S. Department of Agriculture. 2007. "2007 briefing on food security status of U.S. households." http://www.ers.usda.gov/Briefing/FoodSecurity/stats_graphs.htm, accessed 12/18/08.

U.S. Department of Agriculture, Economic Research Service. 2004a. "Household food security in the United States: Conditions and trends, 2003." Food Assistance and Nutrition Research Report No. 42 (FAN-RR 42), October. http://www.ers.usda.gov/Publications/FANRR42

————. 2004b. "Food stamp participation up in 2003." *Amber Waves,* April issue. http://www.ers.usda.gov/Amberwaves/April04/Findings/FoodStamp.htm

————. 2007. Briefing on Food Security Status of U.S. Households. http://www.ers.usda.gov/Briefing/FoodSecurity/stats_graphs.htm, accessed 12/18/08.

U.S. Department of Commerce and U.S. Census Bureau. 2002. "Poverty in the United States: 2001 consumer income." *Current Population Reports.* September.

U.S. Department of Defense. 2006. Defense Manpower Data Center. September 30. http://www.infoplease.com/ipa/A0004600.html, accessed 6/4/09.

U.S. Department of Education. 2007. "Education options in the states: State programs that provide financial assistance for attendance at private elementary or secondary schools." http://www.ed.gov/parents/schools/choice/educationoptions/index.html

U.S. Department of Education, National Center for Education Statistics. 1998. "Pursuing excellence: A study of U.S. twelfth-grade mathematics and science achievement in international context." http://nces.ed.gov/pubs98/twelfth

————. 2005. High School and Beyond Longitudinal Study of 1980 Sophomores (HS &B-So:80/82), "First Follow-up, Student Survey, 1982, Data Analysis System"; National Education Longitudinal Study of 1988 (NELS:88/92), "Second Follow-up, Student Survey, 1992"; and Education Longitudinal Study of 2002 (ELS:02/04), "First Follow-up, Student Survey, 2004"; previously unpublished tabulations (October 2005).

————. 2008. "Outcomes of education." http://nces.ed.gov/pubs2008/2008022_5.pdf

————. 2009. "Numbers and types of public elementary and secondary schools from the common core of data: School year 2006-2007." http://nces.ed.gov/pubs2009/2009304.pdf

U.S. Department of Health and Human Services. 2006. "The 2006 HHS poverty guidelines: One version of the [U.S.] federal poverty measure." http://aspe.hhs.gov/poverty/06poverty.shtml

————. 2008. "2008 HHS poverty guidelines." http://aspe.hhs.gov/poverty/08Poverty.shtml.

U.S. Department of Health and Human Services, Administration for Children and Families. 2005. *TANF Seventh Annual Report to Congress.* Ch. 1. http://www.acf.hhs.gov/programs/ofa/annualreport7/chapter01/chap01.html

U.S. Department of Justice. 2001. *Intimate Partner Violence, 1993-2001.* Bureau of Justice Statistics Crime Data Brief, February. http://www.ojp.usdoj.gov/bjs/pub/pdf/ipv01.pdf

————. 2005. NCJ 207846, *Bureau of Justice Statistics, Family Violence Statistics: Including Statistics on Strangers and Acquaintances, at 31-32 (2005).* Matthew R. Durose et al. http://www.ojp.usdoj.gov/bjs/pub/pdf/fvs.pdf

————. 2006. *Bureau of Justice Statistics Bulletin: Prisoners in 2005.* "Table 10. Number of sentenced prisoners under state or federal jurisdiction, by gender, race, Hispanic origin, and age, yearend 2005." http://www.ojp.usdoj.gov/bjs/pub/pdf/p05.pdf

————. 2007a. Crime in the United States. Table 35. "Five-year arrest trends by sex, 2003–2007." http://www.fbi.gov/ucr/cius2007/data/table_35.html.

————. 2007b. "2006 hate crime statistics." http://www.fbi.gov/ucr/hc2006/incidents.html.

U.S. Department of Labor, Bureau of Labor Statistics. 2004. "Female-to-male earnings ratio and median earnings of full-time, year-round workers 15 years and older by sex: 1960–2004." *Income, Poverty, and Health Insurance Coverage: 2004,* p. 10. http://www.census.gov/Press-Release/www/releases/archives/2004iphi_cps.pdf

————. 2005. "Table 11. Employed persons by detailed occupation and sex, 2004 annual averages." http://www.bls.gov/cps/wlf-table11-2005.pdf

U.S. Environmental Protection Agency (EPA). 2000. "Climate—global warming." http://yosemite.epa.gov/oar/globalwarming.nsf/content/climate.html, accessed 5/17/04.

————. 2003. "The Ozone Report: Measuring progress through 2003." Office of Air Quality Planning and Standards Emissions, Monitoring, and Analysis Division. Triangle Park, NC. EPA Publication No. EPA 454/K-04-001. http://www.epa.gov/air/airtrends/pdfs/2003ozonereport.pdf#page=8, accessed 5/17/04.

————. 2008, November. "Factoids: Drinking water and ground water statistics for 2008." http://www.epa.gov/safewater/databases/pdfs/data_factoids_2008.pdf, accessed 4/24/09.

U.S. Office of Management and Budget. 2005a. *Budget of the United States Government, Fiscal Year 2004.* http://www.whitehouse.gov/omb/budget/fy2004/db.html

————. 2005b (orig. 2003). "New definitions to metropolitan areas." June 2003 (revised February 2005). http://www.policom.com/metrodef.htm

————. 2006. "Update of statistical area definitions and guidance on their uses." OMB Bulletin No. 07-01, December 18. http://www.whitehouse.gov/omb/bulletins/fy2007/b07-01.pdf

U. S. Sentencing Commission. 2000. USFY00 Datafile, as cited in "Table 3. Demographic characteristics of federal cocaine offenders." *Cocaine and Federal Sentencing Policy,* p. 63. http://www.ussc.gov/r_congress/02crack/2002crackrpt.htm

Van Cleve, Thomas Curtis. 1972. *The Emperor Frederick of Hohenstaufen, Immutator Mundi.* Oxford, UK: Clarendon Press.

van den Berghe, P. L. 1979. *Human Family Systems: An Evolutionary View.* New York: Elsevier/North-Holland.

Van Goozen, S.; Frijda, N.; and Van DePoll, N. 1994. "Anger and aggression in women: Influence of sports choice and testosterone administration." *Aggressive Behavior,* vol. 20, 213–222.

Van Leuven, Linda. 1998. "'I need a screw': Workplace sexualization as an interactional accomplishment." In Jodi O'Brien and Judith A. Howard, eds., *Everyday Inequalities: Critical Inquiries.* Malden, MA: Blackwell.

———. 2001. "What does the service include?" In Jodi O'Brien and Peter Kollock, eds., *The Production of Reality,* 254–264. Thousand Oaks, CA: Pine Forge Press.

Van Maanen, John. 1973. "Observations on the making of policemen." *Human Organizations,* vol. 32, 407–418.

———. 1983. *Qualitative Methodology.* Thousand Oaks, CA: Sage.

———. 1988. *Tales of the Field: On Writing Ethnography.* Chicago: University of Chicago Press.

Vaughan, Diane. 1996. *The Challenger Launch Decisions: Risky Technology, Culture and Deviance at NASA.* Chicago: University of Chicago Press.

Veblen, Thorstein. 2004 (orig. 1921). *Engineers and the Price System.* Whitefish, MT: Kessinger Publishing.

Velkoff, Victoria; and Lawson, Valerie. 1998. "Caregiving." *Gender and Aging* December: 1–7.

Wackernagel, Mathis; and Rees, William. 1996. *Our Ecological Footprint: Reducing Human Impact on the Earth.* Philadelphia: New Society.

Waldron, T.; Roberts, B.; and Reamer, A. 2004. "Working hard, falling short: America's working families and the pursuit of economic security." A national report by the Working Poor Families Project. Baltimore, MD: Annie E. Casey Foundation.

Walker, Karen. 1994. "Men, women and friendship: What they say, what they do." *Gender and Society,* vol. 8, no. 2 (June).

Walker, Samuel. 1997. *Popular Justice: A History of American Criminal Justice.* New York: Oxford University Press.

Walker, Sarah. 2005. "Fisher College expels student over website entries." *Boston Globe,* October 6. http://www.boston.com/news/local/articles/2005/10/06/fisher_college_expels_student_over_website_entries/, accessed 8/22/08.

Walker, Susan C. 2004. "U.S. consumer credit card debt may crash economy." FoxNews.com, December 31.

Wallerstein, Immanuel. 1997 (orig. 1974). *The Modern World System: Capitalist Agriculture and the Origins of the European World Economy in the Sixteenth Century.* New York: Academic Press.

Walsh, J. 1994. "The whipping boy." *Time,* vol. 14, 80. [PerAbs No. 01944977]

Warner, Ralph; Ihara, Toni; and Frederick Hertz. 2001. *Living Together: A Legal Guide for Unmarried Couples.* Berkeley, CA: Nolo.

Waters, Mary. 1990. *Ethnic Options: Choosing Identities in America.* Berkeley, CA: University of California Press.

Wattel, Harold. 1958. "Levittown: A suburban community." In William M. Dobriner, ed., *The Suburban Community.* New York: Putnam.

Watts, Duncan. 2003. *Six Degrees: The Science of a Connected Age.* New York: Norton.

Wearing, Stephen; and Wearing, Michael. 1999. "Decommodifying ecotourism: Rethinking global-local interactions with host communities." *Loisir et Société/Society and Leisure,* vol. 22, no. 1, 39–70.

Weber, Max. 1930 (orig. 1904). *The Protestant Ethic and the Spirit of Capitalism.* Trans.Talcott Parsons. New York: Scribner's.

———. 1962 (orig. 1913). *Basic Concepts of Sociology.* Westport, CT: Greenwood Publishing.

———. 1946 (orig. 1925). "Science as a vocation." In Hans Gerth and C. Wright Mills, ed. and trans., *From Max Weber: Essays in Sociology.* New York: Oxford University Press.

———. 1968 (orig. 1921). *Economy and Society.* Ed. and trans. Guenther Roth and Claus Wittich. New York: Bedminster Press.

Weedon, Joey R. 2004. "Voting rights restored." *Corrections Today,* vol. 66, iss. 6, 16.

Weinberg, Adam; Bellows, Story; and Ekster, Dara. 2002. "Sustaining ecotourism: Insights and implications from two successful case studies." *Society and Natural Resources,* vol. 15, no. 4, 371–380.

Weinberg, George. 1972. *Society and the Healthy Homosexual.* New York: St. Martin's Press.

Weinstein, Deena. 1991. *Heavy Metal: A Cultural Sociology.* New York: Macmillan/Lexington.

———. 2000. *Heavy Metal: The Music and Its Culture.* New York: DaCapo.

Weinstein, Harvey. 2003. "Controversial ruling on pledge reaffirmed." *Los Angeles Times,* Metro Desk, March 1, p. 1:1.

Weise, D.; and Daro, D. 1995. *Current Trends in Child Abuse Reporting and Fatalities.* Chicago: National Committee to Prevent Child Abuse.

Weiss, Kenneth R. 2001. "Minority applications to UC rise." *Los Angeles Times,* January 31.

Weissbourd, Richard. 1994. "Divided families, whole children." *American Prospect,* vol. 18 (summer): 66–72.

Wellman, Barry. 2004. "Connecting community: On- and off-line." *Contexts* vol. 3, no. 4 (Fall): 22–28.

Werland, Ross. 2000. "Busy schedule has this family bushed." *Chicago Tribune,* December 10, sec. 13, p. 7.

Weston, Kath. 1991. *Families We Choose.* New York: Columbia University Press.

Wharton, Amy S.; and Blair-Loy, Mary. 2002. "Employees' use of work-family policies and the workplace social context." Social Forces, vol. 80, no. 3, 813–845.

Whatley, Marianne H.; and Henken, Elissa R. 2000. *Did You Hear About the Girl Who . . . ? Contemporary Legends, Folklore, and Human Sexuality.* New York: New York University Press.

White, Glen. 1989. "Groupthink reconsidered." *Academy of Management Review,* vol. 14.

Whitehead, Jay. 2005. "Outsourcing pioneers another niche." *Human Resources Outsourcing Today Magazine,* June.

Whorf, Benjamin. 1956. *Language, Thought and Reality: Selected Writings of Benjamin Lee Whorf.* Ed. John B. Carroll. Cambridge, MA: MIT Press.

Whyte, W. H. 1956. *The Organization Man.* New York: Simon and Schuster.

Williams, Christine L. 1995. *Still a Man's World: Men Who Do Women's Work.* Berkeley, CA: University of California Press.

Williams, Patricia J. 1997. "Of race and risk." *The Nation,* December 29, p. 10.

Williams, Robin. 1965. *American Society: A Sociological Interpretation.* 2nd ed. New York: Knopf.

Willyand, Cassandra. 2008. "China's Olympic race for cleaner air." Geotimes, May. http://www.geotimes.org/may08/article.html?id=nn_china.html

Wilson, William Julius. 1980. *The Declining Significance of Race.* Chicago: University of Chicago Press.

———. 1996. *When Work Disappears: The World of the New Urban Poor.* New York: Knopf.

Winkleby, Marilyn; Cubbin, Catherine; and Ahn, David. 2006. "Effect of cross-level interaction between individual and neighborhood socio-economic status on adult mortality rates." *American Journal of Public Health,* vol. 96, no. 12, 2145–2153.

Wirth, Louis. 1938. "Urbanism as a way of life." *American Journal of Sociology,* vol. 44, 3–24.

———. 1945. "The problem of minority groups." In Ralph Litton, ed., *The Science of Man in the World Crisis.* New York: Columbia University Press.

Wiseman, Rosalind. 2002. *Queen Bees and Wannabes.* New York: Three Rivers Press.

Wolf, Rosalie S. 2000. "The nature and scope of elder abuse." *Generations,* vol. 24 (summer): 6–12.

Wolff, Edward. 2002. *Top Heavy: The Increasing Inequality of Wealth in America and What Can Be Done About It.* New York: New Press.

———. 2004. "Changes in household wealth in the 1980s and 1990s in the U.S." Working paper no. 407. Levy Economics Institute of Bard College. April.

Wolfinger, Nicholas H. 1999. "Trends in the intergenerational transmission of divorce." *Demography,* vol. 36, no. 3, 415–420.

———. 2000. "Beyond the intergenerational transmission of divorce: Do people replicate the patterns of marital instability they grew up with?" *Journal of Family Issues,* vol. 21, 1061–1086.

———. 2003. "Parental divorce and offspring marriage: Early or late?" *Social Forces,* vol. 82, no. 1, 337–353.

Wolfson, Andrew. 2005. "A hoax most cruel." [Louisville, KY] *Courier-Journal.* October 9. http://www.courier-journal.com/apps/pbcs.dll/article?AID=/20051009/NEWS01/510090392, accessed 4/17/09.

Wood, Megan Epler. 2002. *Ecotourism: Principles, Practices and Policies for Sustainability.* Burlington, VT: International Ecotourism Society.

World Bank. 2004. "Total GDP 2004." http://www.worldbank.org/data/databytopic/GDP.pdf

World Bank. 2008. World Development Indicators database, revised September 10. http://siteresources.worldbank.org/DATASTATISTICS/Resources/GNIPC.pdf

World Food Programme/Food and Agriculture Organization of the United Nations/United Nations High Commission for Refugees (WFP/FAO/UNHCR). 2006. "Joint needs assessment. Burundi, Rwanda and Tanzania." March 18 to 8 April 8. http://www.fao.org/giews/english/shortnews/joint_needs.pdf

World Resources Institute. 2003. "Forests, grasslands and drylands: Country profiles." http://earthtrends.wri.org/country_profiles/index.php?theme=9

Wright, Erik Olin. 1997. *Class Counts: Comparative Studies in Class Analysis.* Cambridge, UK: Cambridge University Press.

Wright, Erik Olin; Costello, Cynthia; Hachen, David; and Spragues, Joey. 1982. "The American class structure." *American Sociological Review,* vol. 47, no. 6, 709–726.

Yin, Sandra. 2003. "The art of staying at home." *American Demographics,* vol. 25, no. 9 (November 1).

Zellner, William W. 1995. *Countercultures: A Sociological Analysis.* New York: St. Martin's Press.

Zemke, Ron; and Schaaf, Dick. 1990. *The Service Edge: 101 Companies That Profit from Customer Care.* New York: Plume.

Zerubavel, Eviatar. 2003. *Time Maps: Collective Memory and the Social Shape of the Past.* Chicago: University of Chicago Press.

Zimbardo, Philip G. 1971. "The power and pathology of imprisonment." *Congressional Record.* (Serial No. 15, October 25, 1971). Hearings before Subcommittee No. 3, of the Committee on the Judiciary, House of Representatives, 92nd Congress, *First Session on Corrections, Part II, Prisons, Prison Reform and Prisoner's Rights: California.* Washington, DC: U.S. Government Printing Office.

Zirakzadeh, C. 1997. *Social Movements in Politics: A Comparative Study.* London: Longman.

Zolli, Andrew. 2004. "Socialize this!" *American Demographics,* vol. 26, no. 7.

Zukin, S. 1987. "Gentrification: Culture and capital in the urban core." *American Review of Sociology,* vol. 13, 139–147.

———. 1989. *Loft Living: Culture and Capital in Urban Change.* New Brunswick, NJ: Rutgers University Press.

———. 2004. *Point of Purchase: How Shopping Changed American Culture.* London: Routledge.

Zurcher, Louis. 1977. *The Mutable Self.* Beverly Hills, CA: Sage.

Zwingle, Erla. 2002. "Map of megacities." In "Cites: Challenges for humanity," *National Geographic*, November. Ng Maps/National Geographic Image Collection.

CREDITS

Text and Figures

Page 118: "Moore Thoughts and Girl Interrupted" by James Sosnicky, copyright © 2006 by James Sosnicky, "Introduction and Headnotes" by Andrew Carroll, copyright © 2006 by Andrew Carroll, "One Small Village" by Jared Jones, copyright © 2006 by Jared Jones, from *Operation Homecoming*, edited by Andrew Carroll, copyright © 2006 by Southern Arts Federation. Used by permission of Random House, Inc.

Pages 386-7: "Busy Schedule Has This Family Bushed" by Ross Werland, from *The Chicago Tribune*, Dec. 10, 2000. Reprinted with permission of the Chicago Tribune; copyright Chicago Tribune, all rights reserved.

Figure 8.3: Jared Bernstein, Graph: Real median income for working-age households, 1989–2007, from "Compared to 1990s, Middle-Class Working Families Lose Ground in the 2000s," 8/27/08. Reprinted by permission of Economic Policy Institute.

Figure 13.1: Figure 12.1, "Annual Divorce Rate, United States, 1860–2002," Public and Private Families: An Introduction, 4th Edition by Andrew J. Cherlin, p. 406. © 2005. Reprinted by permission of The McGraw-Hill Companies, Inc.

Figure 14.1: Dmitry Krasny/Deka Design, Figure "And Then There Were Eight: 25 Years of Media Mergers," *Mother Jones*, March/April 2007, p. 49. © 2007, Foundation for National Progress. Reprinted by permission.

Figure 15.8: Erla Zwingle, "Map of Megacities" from "Cities: Challenges for Humanity", *National Geographic*, November 2002. Ng Maps/National Geographic Image Collection. Reprinted with permission.

Photographs

Page ii (top): © MTV/Courtesy: Everett Collection; **p. ii (bottom left):** Andrew Holbrooke/Corbis, **(bottom right):** AFP/Getty Images; **p. iii (top):** AFP/Getty Images, **(bottom right):** Design Pics Inc./Alamy; **p. vii (top):** © MTV/Courtesy: Everett Collection, **(bottom):** AFP/Getty Images; **p. viii:** Photograph by for the U.S. Census Bureau, Public Information Office; **p. ix:** AFP/Getty Images; **p. x (top):** AP Photos, **(bottom):** AFP/Getty Images; **p. xi:** Design Pics Inc./Alamy; **p. xii (top):** Andrew Holbrooke/Corbis, **(bottom):** Reuters/Danny Moloshok; **p. xiii:** Kristian Dowling/Getty Images for Beatie; **p. xiv:** AFP/Getty Images; **p. xv:** NBC/Photofest; **p. xvi (top):** Alan S. Weiner/*The New York Times*/Redux, **(bottom):** The Kobal Collection; **p. xvii:** © Chris Jordan; **p. xviii:** Kacper Pemple/Reuters/Landov.

CHAPTER 1 **Page 2 (top):** Time & Life Pictures/Getty Images. Reprinted through the courtesy of the editors of *Time* magazine © 2009; **(bottom):** AP Photos; **p. 3:** Courtesy Pepper Schwartz; **p. 4:** © MTV/Courtesy: Everett Collection; **p. 8 (left):** Getty Images, **(right):** Najlah Feanny/Corbis; **p. 9:** Abbot Genser/HBO/Everett Collection; **p. 11 (left):** Bettmann/Corbis, **(center):** AP Photos, **(right):** AP Photos; **p. 12 (left):** AP Photos, **(right):** AP Photos; **p. 14:** AP Photos; **p. 15:** Jolanda Cats & Hans Withoos/zefa/Corbis; **p. 16:** Time & Life Pictures/Getty Images; **p. 17:** Reuters/Corbis; **p. 19:** Manuel Acevedo; **p. 20:** © ABC/Courtesy: Everett Collection; **p. 21:** James Leynse/Corbis; **p. 23:** Mary Evans Picture Library/Alamy; **p. 24 (top):** Getty Images, **(bottom):** Jon Hicks/Corbis; **p. 25 (left):** AP Photos, **(right):** Getty Images; **p. 27 (left):** Dynamic Graphics Group/Creatas/Alamy, **(right):** WorldFoto/Alamy; **p. 28 (left):** Bernd Obermann/Corbis, **(right):** Sean AdairReuters/Corbis; **p. 29 (right):** Roberto Schmidt/AFP/Getty Images, **(left):** James Colburn/Lincoln Star Journal/Polaris.

CHAPTER 2 **Page 32:** AFP/Getty Images; **p. 34:** Jason Hunt, artist; **p. 36 (top):** Bettmann/Corbis, **(bottom):** Hulton-Deutsch Collection/Corbis; **p. 38:** Trip/Alamy; **p. 39 (top left):** Bridgeman Art Library, **(top right):** Richard Milner/Handout/epa/Corbis, **(center right):** Bettmann/Corbis; **p. 40:** Bettmann/Corbis; **p. 42 (top):** Getty Images, **(bottom):** Bettmann/Corbis; **p. 45:** Simon Marcus/Corbis; **p. 46 (both):** Courtesy American Sociological Association; **p. 48:** Warder Collection; **p. 49:** Everett Collection; **p. 51:** Granger Collection; **p. 52:** Library of Congress; **p. 53 (both):** Hmong Cultural Center; **p. 55:** Shirlaine Forrest/Getty Images; **p. 56:** Rob Kim/Landov; **p. 57:** Najlah Feanny/Corbis; **p. 59 (left and center):** Steve Pyke/Getty Images, **(right):** STF/AFP/Getty Images.

CHAPTER 3 **Page 64:** U.S. Census Bureau, Public Information Office; **p. 66:** Ovie Carter; **p. 67:** Bandura, Ross and Ross, from "Social Learning of Aggression through Imitation of Film-Mediated Aggressive Models," *Journal of Abnormal and Social Psychology* 66 (1963), 3–11; **p. 69:** Warner Brothers/Photofest; **p. 70:** Courtesy Judith Stacey; **p. 71:** AP Photos; **p. 73:** Brooke Fasini/Corbis; **p. 77:** Bettmann/Corbis; **p. 79:** Rick Friedman/*The New York Times*/Redux; **p. 81:** Michael Dunning/Getty Images; **p. 83:** AP Photo; **p. 85:** Bettmann/Corbis; **p. 86:** Corbis.

CHAPTER 4 **Pages 92-3:** Courtesy of Verta Taylor and Leila Rupp; **p. 94:** AFP/Getty Images; **p. 96 (left):** AP Photos, **(right):** Getty Images; **p. 98:** Getty Images; **p. 99 (top):** Robert Nickelsberg/Getty Images, **(center and bottom):** AP Photo; **p. 101:** Carl & Ann Purcell/Corbis; **p. 102:** www.ulturwerk118.ch/guestbook; **p. 102 (clockwise from top left):** Peter A. Smith/Boston Herald/Polaris, Alessandro Digaetano/Polaris, Getty Images, AP Photo, AP Photo, Jupiter Images/AP Photo; **p. 103 (left):** Everett Collection, **(right):** *Mean Girls*, 2004. Paramount Pictures; **p. 105 (left):** AP Photos, **(right):** Eric Grigorian/Polaris; **p. 107 (left):** Bettmann/Corbis, **(right):** AFP/Getty Images; **p. 108 (top):** Everett Collection, **(bottom):** George A. Hirliman Productions Inc./Photofest; **p. 109 (left):** AP Photos, **(right):** AP Photos; **p. 110 (left):** Tom Strickland/ABC/American Broadcasting Companies, Inc., **(right):** Conrad Mulcahy © Comedy Central/Courtesy: Everett Collection; **p. 111:** AFP/Getty Images; **p. 112 (top):** Bridgeman Art Library, **(bottom):** The Last Supper, 1986. Founding Collection, The Andy Warhol Museum, Pittsburgh. © Andy Warhol Foundation for the Visual Arts/ARS, New York; **p. 114:** Getty Images; **p. 116:** AP Photos; **p. 119:** Howard Davies/Corbis.

CHAPTER 5 **Page 124:** AP Photos; **p. 127:** © Walt Disney Pictures/Courtesy: Everett Collection; **p. 128:** © 2008 The Jacob and Gwendolyn Lawrence

Foundation, Seattle/Artists Rights Society (ARS), New York. Smithsonian American Art Museum/Art Resource, NY; Smithsonian American Art Museum, Washington, DC/Art Resource, NY; **p. 130 (left):** Jupiter Images/AP Photos, **(right):** Getty Images; **p. 132 (left):** AP Photos, **(right):** A&E/The Kobal Collection; **p. 134:** © 20th Century Fox/Photofest; **p. 136:** Giovanni Rufino/© The CW/Courtesy Everett Collection; **p. 140 (left):** AP Photos, **(right):** AP Photos; **p. 139 (both):** Courtesy Sister Pauline Quinn; **p. 141:** Time Life Pictures/Getty Images; **p. 143 (top):** AP Photos, **(center):** Alan Chin/Corbis Sygma, **(bottom):** AP Photos; **p. 146:** Getty Images; **p. 145 (both):** AP Photos.

CHAPTER 6 Page 150: AFP/Getty Images; **p. 153:** AP Photos; **p. 154:** Image via OurChart.com; **p. 155 (left):** Bettmann/Corbis, **(right):** Getty Images; **p. 157:** AP Photos; **p. 161:** AP Photos; **p. 162:** Reuters/Corbis; **p. 163:** AP Photos; **p. 165:** Courtesy of Alexandra Milgram; **p. 166:** PGZimbardo Inc.; **p. 167 (top):** Tim de Waele/Corbis, **(bottom):** Jeff Mitchell/Reuters/Corbis; **p. 168:** Wally McNamee/Corbis; **p. 169:** © 2006 Scott Adams, Inc. Dist. by UFS, Inc.; **p. 171 (top):** Kapoor Baldev/Sygma/Corbis, **(center):** Andy Rain/epa/Corbis, **(bottom):** Reuters/Corbis; **p. 172:** Bettmann/Corbis; **p. 173 (left):** PBS/Photofest, **(right):** Everett Collection; **p. 174:** AP Photos.

CHAPTER 7 Page 178: Design Pics Inc./Alamy; **p. 182 (top left):** Gavriel Jecan/Corbis, **(top right):** Remi Benali/Corbis, **(bottom pair):** AP Photos; **p. 183:** AP Photos; **p. 184:** Illustration by Diane DiMassa; **p. 186:** © 20th Century Fox Film Corp./Everett Collection; **p. 187:** Mark Seliger/SHOWTIME/Everett Collection; **p. 189:** Stuart Isett/Polaris; **p. 191:** Everett Collection; **p. 192:** © Marion Ettlinger; **p. 193:** Gilles Mingasson/Liaison/Getty Images; **p. 194:** Reuters/Corbis; **p. 195:** AP Photos; **p. 196 (left):** Scott Gries/© A&E/Courtesy: Everett Collection, **(right):** Comedy Central/Courtesy: Everett Collection; **p. 201:** AP Photos.

CHAPTER 8 Pages 206–7 (all): © Ovie Carter; **p. 208:** Andrew Holbrooke/Corbis; **p. 210 (clockwise from top left):** © Peter Menzel www.menzelphoto.com, Photo by p. Luis Psihoyos Science Faction, © Peter Menzel www.menzelphoto.com, © Peter Menzel www.menzelphoto.com, photo by Peter Ginter/Science Faction, © Peter Menzel www.menzelphoto.com; **p. 215 (left):** Time & Life Pictures/Getty Images. Reprinted through the courtesy of the editors of *Time* magazine © 2009; **(right):** Mike Blake/Reuters/Corbis; **p. 216:** Wolfgang Kaehler/Corbis; **p. 217:** AFP/Getty Images; **p. 218:** *The Chess Game*, film directed by Erik Olin Wright, produced at the Carpenter Center for the Visual Arts, Harvard University, 1968; **p. 221 (top):** Andreas von Einsiedel, Elizabeth Whiting & Associates/Corbis, **(bottom):** Robert Spencer/Retna Ltd.; **p. 227:** Everett Collection; **p. 228:** Najlah Feanny/Corbis; **p. 234:** Robert Maass/Corbis; **p. 235:** AFP/Getty Images; **p. 236:** © Warner Bros./Courtesy Everett Collection; **p. 237:** AP Photo.

CHAPTER 9 Page 242: Reuters/Danny Moloshok; **p. 245:** Library of Congress; **p. 246 (left):** AP Photo, **(right):** Nik Wheeler/Corbis; **p. 249:** © Lions Gate/Courtesy Everett Collection; **p. 252:** Photo by Roger Erickson; Courtesy Faith Childs; **p. 253:** AP Photo; **p. 254:** Time Life Pictures/Getty Images; **p. 255:** Focus Films/courtesy Everett Collection; **p. 257:** Roger Ressmeyer/Corbis; **p. 261 (left):** Ziv Koren/Polaris, **(right):** Getty Images.

CHAPTER 10 Page 266: Kristian Dowling/Getty Images for Beatie; **p. 271 (left):** National Anthropological Archives/Smithsonian Institution, **(right):** Karan Kapoor/Corbis; **p. 272:** Courtesy Everett Collection; **p. 274:** Mel Svenson/Getty Images; **p. 275:** Jeff Greenberg/The Image Works; **p. 276:** Jeff Greenberg/Photo Edit; **p. 285:** © Columbia Pictures/courtesy Everett Collection; **p. 286:** Bettmann/Corbis; **p. 287:** JP Laffont/Sygma/Corbis; **p. 289 (top):** Mark Peterson/Redux, **(bottom):** The Kobal Collection; **p. 290:** AP Photo; **p. 293:** Jeff Christensen/Reuters/Landov; **p. 295:** © NBC/Courtesy: Everett Collection.

CHAPTER 11 Page 300 (top): Maury Tannen/Polaris Images, **(bottom):** Getty Images; **p. 301:** AP Photo; **p. 302:** AFP/Getty Images; **p. 306 (all):** AFP/Getty Images; **p. 307:** AP Photo; **p. 309 (top, bottom left):** AP Photo, **(bottom right):** Getty Images; **p. 311:** Lawrence Berkeley National Lab; **p. 314 (top right):** Sean Adair Reuters/Corbis, **(top left):** Bettmann/Corbis, **(bottom):** Vincent Laforet/epa/Corbis; **p. 317:** AP Photo; **p. 318 (both):** Everett Collection; **p. 319:** Granger Collection; **p. 321 (left):** AP Photo, **(right):** Getty Images; **p. 324 (left):** Photo by Ellen Domke; courtesy Algonquin Books, **(right):** Courtesy Lavin Agency; **p. 326:** AP Photo; **p. 327:** Najlah Feanny/Corbis; **p. 330 (left):** Leif Skoogfors/Corbis, **(right):** J. L. Atlan/Corbis Sygma; **p. 332 (top):** Jehad Nga/Corbis, **(bottom):** AP Photo; **p. 334:** Jason Reed/Reuters/Landov; **p. 335 (left):** AP Photo, **(right):** Corbis Sygma.

CHAPTER 12 Page 340: NBC/Photofest; **p. 342 (all):** Courtesy Kerry Ferris; **p. 343:** Schomburg Center in Black Culture, New York Public Library; **p. 344:** Granger Collection; **p. 346:** Kimberly White/Corbis; **p. 347 (both):** ABC/Photofest; **p. 349:** Reuters; **p. 350:** Jeff Greenberg/Photo Edit; **p. 351:** David Bacon/The Image Works; **p. 352:** William Perlman/Star Ledger/Corbis; **p. 355:** Bill Aron/Photo Edit; **p. 356:** Granger Collection; **p. 357:** Matthew Simmons/WireImage/Getty Images; **p. 358:** Ruth Fremson/*The New York Times*/Redux; **p. 360 (both):** AP Photo; **p. 363:** Ge Jin, © 2008; **p. 370:** James Leynse/Corbis.

CHAPTER 13 Page 374: Alan S. Weiner/*The New York Times*/Redux; **p. 379 (left):** AP Photo, **(right):** AFP/Getty Images; **p. 380:** Random House; **p. 383 (left):** Charles Gullung/zefa/Corbis, **(right):** Pixland/Corbis; **p. 385:** Ed Kashi/Corbis; **p. 388:** Getty Images; **p. 389 (both):** Etta Clark Photography; **p. 391 (left):** Photofest, **(right):** The Kobal Collection; **p. 394:** Photofest; **p. 396:** AP Photo.

CHAPTER 14 Page 400: The Kobal Collection; **p. 403:** Advertising Archives; **p. 404:** Alamy; **p. 407 (left):** Robb D. Cohen/Retna Ltd., **(right):** Retna Ltd.; **p. 410:** David Pearson/Alamy; **p. 411:** Eric Fowke/Photo Edit; **p. 413:** Everett Collection; **p. 414:** Landov; **p. 415:** Susan Van Etten/Photo Edit; **p. 418:** Getty Images; **p. 419:** Reuters/Corbis; **p. 420:** Nik Wheeler/Corbis; **p. 421 (top):** Monty Brinton/© CBS/Courtesy Everett Collection, **(bottom):** Robert Voets/Showtime/Courtesy Everett Collection.

CHAPTER 15 Page 426: AP Photo; **p. 427 (left):** Bob Krist/Corbis, **(right):** Lindsay Hebberd/Corbis; **p. 428:** © Chris Jordan; **p. 439:** NASA/Goddard Space Flight Center, The SeaWiFS Project and GeoEye, Scientific Visualization Studio; **p. 441 (left):** Mark Peterson/Redux, **(right):** Joshua Lutz/Redux; **p. 442:** AP Photo; **p. 443 (left):** Richard Levine/Alamy, **(right):** Larry Brownstein/Ambient Images; **p. 444:** AP Photo; **p. 445:** © Columbia/Tristar Pictures/Courtesy Everett Collection; **p. 447:** Richard Perry/*The New York Times*/Redux; **p. 448:** *New York Daily News*; **p. 450:** Joe Raedle/Getty Images. **p. 453 (left):** Galen Rowell/Corbis, **(right):** NASA/Getty Images; **p. 454 (left):** Julio Etchart/Alamy, **(right):** Rickey Rogers/Reuters/Corbis; **p. 457:** Stephen Shaver/UPI/Landov; **p. 459:** Library of Congress; **p. 461:** AP Photo; **p. 462:** Bettmann/Corbis; **p. 463:** AP Photo.

CHAPTER 16 Page 468: Kacper Pemple/Reuters/Landov; **p. 471:** Ian Waldie/Getty Images; **p. 472:** David Butow/Corbis Saba; **p. 474:** Giovanni Rufino/© The CW/Courtesy Everett Collection; **p. 475:** AP Photos; **p. 476:** Phil Schermeister/Corbis; **p. 477:** AP Photos; **p. 479:** AP Photos; **p. 481 (top):** Spencer Grant/Photo Editm, **(bottom):** Mario Villafuerte/Getty Images; **p. 482:** FPG/Hulton Archive/Getty Images; **p. 483:** AP Photos; **p. 485:** Fox Broadcasting/Photofest; **p. 487:** Ana Cecila Gonzalez-Vigil/*The New York Times*/Redux; **p. 489:** Alamy.

INDEX

Note: Page numbers in **boldface** refer to definitions of key words.

authority, 168–69, **168, 305**
    conversation patterns and, 285–86
*Authors of Their Own Lives:
    Intellectual Autobiographies of
    Twenty American Sociologists*
    (Berger), 2, 3
Autobiography of a Face (Grealy), 192
autoethnographic research, 84
autoethnography, **133**
autonomy, 354
Babbie, Earl, 85
baby boom generation, 384, 388, 471
backstage (in dramaturgical perspective),
    132
Baez, Joan, 460
Bailey, J. M., 289
"Bailout Bill," 349
Bakke, Alan, 257
Baldwin, Alec, 415
Balkans, genocide in, 260
Ballmer, Steve, 218
Bandura, Albert, 67
Baptists, 329, 461
Barkley, Charles, 416
Barnes, Hayden, 156
Barry, Dave, 65–66
baseball, 404
basic research, **82**
Baskin, Bert, 476
Batan, Clarence, 38
Bateson, Gregory, 97
Baudrillard, Jean, 23–24, 59, 317
Beatie, Thomas, 267–68, 273
Beaumont, Gustave de, 23
Becker, Howard, 9, 114, 186, 191
Beckham, David, 418
beginner's mind, 20–21, **20**
Beijing Olympics (2008), pollution and,
    438, 457
beliefs, **328**
Bellah, Robert, 417
Bellow, Saul, 10, 11
berdaches, 270–71
Berger, Bennett, 2, 3
Berger, Peter, 17
Bernard, Jessie, 2, 3
Berry, Halle, 243
Bhutan and Gross National Happiness,
    488–89
Bhutan Broadcasting System, 489
bias, research, **72,** 75, 82, 85
Biko, Steve, 213
bin Laden, Osama, 179
biocentrism, 458
biodiversity, 454, 455, **455**
biosphere, **453**
birth control, 434

bisexuals, 290, **291**
Bizel, Loic, 83
Black Folk: Then and Now (DuBois), 48
Black Panther Party, 107
blacks, *see* African Americans
Black Student Union, 49
Blader, Joan, 479
blended families, 394
"Blind Man and the Elephant, The,"
    33–34
blogs, bloggers, 55, 196, 411
blue collar workers, 214–15, **214**
Blumer, Herbert, 50, 51–54
Bly, Robert, 289
body language, 102
    see also gestures
body modification, 181–82
"Body Ritual Among the Nacirema,"
    97–98
Bogle, Kathleen, 285
Bohemian Grove, 311
Bold and the Beautiful, The, 486
Bonacich, Edna, 250
Bono, Sonny, 315
"boomerang kids," 384–85
Bornstein, Kate, 184
Bourassa, Loren, 367
Bourdieu, Pierre, 220
bourgeoisie, **41,** 47, 218
Bowles, Samuel, 321
*Bowling Alone: The Collapse and Revival
    of American Community*
    (Putnam), 155
Boyd, Wes, 479
Bradley, Bill, 315
Bradley, Graham, 136
Bradley University Student Handbook,
    106
Brady Bunch, 394
Branch Davidians, 107, 328
branding, 181, 364
*Brave New Families: Stories of
    Domestic Upheaval in Late
    Twentieth-Century America*
    (Stacey), 70, 396
Brazil, social stratification in, 216–17
breast augmentation, 181
British Empire, imperialism and, 117, 260
British Petroleum, 360
Brothers & Sisters, 294
Brown, Jerry, 169
Brown v. Board of Education, 85
Brundtland Report, 464
Brunvand, Jan, 451
Buddhism, 328, 334, 335
Buffy the Vampire Slayer, 294
Bullard, Robert, 464

bullies, internet, 195–96
bureaucracies, **42,** 169–75, **169**
    resistance strategies in the workplace,
        354–55
    responding to constraints of, 171–75
    stages in social movements, 482
Bureau of Labor Statistics, 367, 368, 370
Burgess, Robert, 151
Burkhalter, Byron, 252
Burnham, Gracia and Martin, 486
Burning Man festival, 173–74
Burns, Stacy, 56
Bush, George W., 179, 332
    Iraq war and, 308, 309
    religion and, 332, 335
    same-sex marriage and, 290, 379
Bustad, Leo, 138
Butler, Judith, 58
bystander effect, **449**
Cahill, Spencer, 365
California:
    environmentalism in, 460–61
    ethnic groups in, 248
    history of race relations in, 250
    net population change, 432
    same-sex marriage in, 378
    Santa Barbara oil spill of 1969, 459,
        462
    "three strikes" law, 200
Calley, Lieutenant William, 201
Cambodia, 188–89
Campaign Reform Act of 2002, 313
Canada, multiculturalism and, 262
Canadian Multiculturalism Act (1988),
    262
caning, 162
capitalism, **39,** 41, 50, 117, 321, **348,**
        350–51
    patriarchy and, 273
    U.S. as capitalist society with some
        socialist attributes, 349–50
capital punishment, **200,** 226
Capone, Al, 480
careers, *see* work and workplace
Carey, Ron, 358
Carnegie Corporation, 325
Carson, Rachel, 459
"cash register honesty," 199
caste system, **212**
    apartheid in South Africa, 212–13
Castro, Fidel, 55
Catholic Church, birth control and, 434
Catholicism, 328
Catholic Worker, The, 172
Catholic Worker Movement, 172
Catton, William, 433, 458
Caughey, John, 333, 414